EUROPEAN MIGR

EUROPEAN MIGRATION LAW

Pieter BOELES
Maarten DEN HEIJER
Gerrie LODDER
Kees WOUTERS

2nd edition

intersentia

Cambridge – Antwerp – Portland

Intersentia Ltd.
Sheraton House | Castle Park
Cambridge | CB3 0AX | United Kingdom
Tel.: +44 1223 370 170 | Email: mail@intersentia.co.uk

Distribution for the UK:
NBN International
Airport Business Centre, 10 Thornbury Road
Plymouth, PL6 7 PP
United Kingdom
Tel.: +44 1752 202 301 | Fax: +44 1752 202 331
Email: orders@nbninternational.com

Distribution for the USA and Canada:
International Specialized Book Services
920 NE 58th Ave. Suite 300
Portland, OR 97213
USA
Tel.: +1 800 944 6190 (toll free)
Email: info@isbs.com

Distribution for Austria:
Neuer Wissenschaftlicher Verlag
Argentinierstraße 42/6
1040 Wien
Austria
Tel.: +43 1 535 61 03 24
Email: office@nwv.at

Distribution for other countries:
Intersentia Publishing nv
Groenstraat 31
2640 Mortsel
Belgium
Tel.: +32 3 680 15 50
Email: mail@intersentia.be

European Migration Law. 2nd edition
Pieter Boeles, Maarten den Heijer, Gerrie Lodder and Kees Wouters

© 2014 Intersentia
Cambridge – Antwerp – Portland
www.intersentia.com | www.intersentia.co.uk

Artwork on front cover: Titian, 'Ecce Homo' © Kunsthistorisches Museum, Vienna; Artwork on back cover: Titian, 'The rape of Europe', © Isabella Stuart Gardner Museum, Boston.

ISBN 978-1-78068-155-9 (hardcover)
ISBN 978-1-78068-253-2 (paperback)
D/2014/7849/121
NUR 820

British Library Cataloguing in Publication Data. A catalogue record for this book is available from the British Library.

SERIES PREFACE

The role of European law is becoming more and more central in comparative law, in the law of the other Member States and as an outstanding model for legal policy. Insiders have known for a long time that in almost all core areas of law, the important spurs to reform have been coming from Europe and that European law increasingly dominates the cornerstones of our legal systems. Therefore, a discussion of European law involves addressing the main problems and guiding principles but, in practical terms, it also increasingly entails raising questions that are threatening to revolutionise national legal traditions and render entire libraries obsolete.

Since 2002, the year marking the introduction of the Euro, a new law of obligations has been in place in Germany, with the old codifications in France and Austria following to a lesser extent. The next years were characterised by unrestricted cross-border mobility of court decisions; re-writing of core areas of company law such as accounting, cross-border mobility, but as well the promulgation of supranational types of company, with some of the largest German enterprises becoming 'European Companies' (SE); and also cross-border crediting of contributions to social security systems becoming a reality. The law on competition and subsidies has been primarily European for a long time and its mighty implementing mechanisms – overriding Heads of State – fill title pages. The same applies to intellectual property law, foreign exchange law, banking and insurance law and environmental law. These have become genuinely European subjects. Then, in the last years, the cross-border arrest warrant fundamentally changed European Criminal Law; anti-discrimination law is all encompassing; there is now a proposal for a European Optional Contract Law (Code); the Lisbon Treaty – though formally not a constitution – installed a new institutional setting strengthening democratic legitimacy and powers of the European Union; and the financial and state debt crises, not even ten years after the introduction of the Euro, triggered measures which considerably strengthened and broadened financial stability schemes at the EU level, from banking law to capital market law and collaboration with respect to systemic risk. The near future will show whether Europe is to have an institutionalised economic collaboration for its political economy ('true economic government') in some way, reflecting the now global importance of the Euro and the responsibility attached to it!

European law – in all legal areas – has long since assumed dimensions that make it absolutely necessary to refer to more than a single book. This series, now beginning its second edition, is structured so as to provide the relevant European complement to a traditional legal area. It offers the internal market package organised in this way, with those areas being chosen for users that have a significant internal market dimension. In comparison with a multi-volume looseleaf work, it has advantages not only in terms of price, but also in that it puts a greater emphasis on classification and limits the material to the essential, which is important in an overflowing area such as European law, of which only very few people manage to preserve an overview.

The dynamic nature of European law is impressive, as its development hurtles along, gathering momentum. There is a need for direction. A serious application of law can no longer focus solely on national transposition. The original, the European guideline, which *de facto* almost always has to be directly applied (even in national legal processes), must be considered. Such direction can best be provided by presenting the contents of European law in context and in the necessary detail – in the present case, up to twelve individual volumes. Some of the volumes have already had considerable success in one national market and are now presented to a pan-European public.

The volumes cover the most important topics in the 'Europeanisation' of law. For practitioners – solicitors and barristers, corporate lawyers, judges or lawyers in state authorities or ministries – who do not wish to turn a blind eye to European law, these volumes provide a reliable treatment of the important problems, with sufficiently detailed references. They provide practitioners with all they need on the EU level, and moreover give comparative law and legal policy insight. As a series, they give an overview of those areas most affected by European law. Likewise, they provide advanced students with material for excellent examination results. Students must study European law seriously as part of their main subject if they really wish to specialise in this in the future and do more than pass their examination with an average result. Works with comparative law and interdisciplinary aspects also prepare students for a possible period of study abroad, help them to analyse law in terms of function and also support studies in related subjects. Thus, IUS COMMUNITATIS makes European substantive law accessible in the form of the classic systematic textbook and specialist work.

All volumes on the applicable law of the Union begin by presenting the necessary tools: in each case, the EC/EU law and the instruments whereby this law enters into the national legal systems are introduced. In all volumes, a thorough description of the EC/EU law rules forms the core of the discussion. However, economic or other interdisciplinary references of significance to the legislation in question are also explained, i.e. what the rules are intended to achieve and, where there are lacunae, the various models that exist and are discussed throughout Europe. European law is, indeed, a law in the making. Each legal area is presented in a logical order, as an organic whole; this implies that the approximated or harmonised law forms only the skeleton or hard nucleus and is supplemented by comparative law explanations where harmonisation is not advanced. In this way, the relationship to national law becomes clearer and the ability of readers to deal with European law will improve, as they are given a coherent picture rather than the fragmentary one often complained of. These are to be textbooks, discussion books and, above all, practical books – sufficiently condensed to contain all the necessary details and yet clear in their outlines. This was the objective we strive for and the challenge. The authors and the editor (Stefan.Grundmann@rewi.hu-berlin.de) thank those who have criticised and inspired us and who may do so in the future.

The entire IUS COMMUNITATIS series owes much to the Thyssen Foundation, which considered the European aspect and in particular the connection with comparative law so important that it generously supported a good number of the volumes. As the editor, I should like to express my deepest thanks.

Berlin, Spring 2014   Stefan Grundmann

PREFACE TO THE SECOND EDITION

Since the launch of the first edition, EU migration law has gradually matured into a comprehensive system covering all basic topics of migration. This result was not yet evident when the first edition came out. At that time, the building of EU migration law was still under construction and we deemed it an adequate approach to describe European Migration Law as a multilayered assembly of different legal spheres placed adjacent to each other. Nowadays, this format seems to be less appropriate.

The Treaty of Lisbon entered into force. The Charter of Fundamental Rights of the European Union became the binding body of fundamental rights applicable within the scope of Union law. The law of the EU concerning migration now offers a comprehensive structure both at the concrete level of specific provisions and at the abstract level of principles and fundamental rights. In the context of Union law, important human rights treaties such as the European Convention of Human Rights, the UN Refugee Convention and the UN Convention on the Rights of the Child, must be understood not on their own merits but as the primary sources of inspiration for the interpretation of the Charter of Fundamental Rights.

In view of this, we felt that a new approach was necessary. In this second edition, therefore, the legal sphere of EU law is consequently put on the foreground. One consequence is that, as much as possible, relevant aspects of human rights law are no longer discussed separately, but are integrated in the framework of Union law. The book still recognises however, the impact for migration law of human rights regimes outside the EU context such as the case law of the European Court of Human Rights on the right to respect for private and family life (discussed in chapter 5), and the Refugee Convention as primary source of EU refugee status (discussed in chapter 7).

The structure of the book has been simplified as much as possible. We hope that this will add to the readability.

The division of tasks between the authors remained more or less the same. Chapter 4 was written by Gerrie Lodder, the greater part of chapter 7 was written by Kees Wouters, chapters 6 and 8 and a part of chapter 7 were written by Maarten den Heijer. The remaining chapters were written by Pieter Boeles, who also did most of the editing.

CONTENTS – SUMMARY

CONTENTS

PART III.   FORCED MIGRATION

6.   THE COMMON EU ASYLUM SYSTEM 243

PART IV.   ENFORCEMENT AND PROCEDURAL PROTECTION

9.   EXTERNAL BORDER CONTROLS, VISAS AND EXPULSION MEASURES. 375

PART I
INTRODUCTION

1. INTRODUCTION

1.1. GENERAL REMARKS

1.1.1. OUTLINE

This book will provide an overview of the present state of migration law in Europe. Although the notion of migration covers both immigration and emigration, this book will concentrate on immigration. European migration law as dealt with in this book focuses on the immigration regime in Europe, which encompasses rules on (1) immigration from third countries into Europe and (2) intra-European migration. As will be explained in section 1.3, relevant law is divided over different levels: national legislation (which will not be dealt with in this book), EU law, regional and worldwide international law. At all these levels, the development of European migration law is in an ongoing process, each level having its own pace, its own legal parameters, its own tradition. In this book we will take EU law as the primary source to be dealt with. Thus, Union law will provide a leading structure against the background of which the other levels will be described. Further, we make a global distinction between voluntary and forced migration because of the characteristic differences in approach between the two.

1.1.2. VOLUNTARY AND FORCED MIGRATION

The law on forced migration (asylum) tends to develop along other lines than the law on voluntary migration. Forced migration is the movement of persons compelled to flee a bad situation in their home country and seeking protection in a new country. Voluntary migration (sometimes referred to as 'legal migration' as opposed to asylum, wrongly implying that forced migration would not be legal) covers a wide range of migration purposes. Roughly sketched, the main purposes for voluntary migration are economic activity, knowledge-related activity, the receipt of (medical) services and family reunion. It should be borne in mind that the movement of persons of these categories is not always purely 'voluntary', as people may be urged to migrate for more or less compelling economic or humanitarian reasons. Though the distinction is not as sharp as it might seem at first glance, it appears to be sufficiently useful for our goal of delineating the various subjects to be described.

1.1.3. STRUCTURE OF THE BOOK

The book is divided into four parts. *The first part*, which you are reading now, consists of six introductory chapters deemed necessary to understand the context in which European migration law is shaped. Chapter 1.2 contains an exposé on the basic concepts of migration law, as they are defined in international law. Chapter 1.3 explains the multi-level structure of European Migration Law. Chapter 1.4 gives a brief historic survey of migration in Europe, and Chapter 1.5 describes the historic development of movement of persons in EU law. A survey of the system of entry, residence and return of third country nationals under Union Law is provided in Chapter 1.6. Finally, Chapter 1.7 explains the elementary significance of the Charter of Fundamental Rights of the EU and its relation to the European Convention of Human Rights.

The second part, called '*Voluntary Migration*', consists of four chapters (2, 3, 4 and 5). Chapter 2 deals with 'Free movement of persons under EU Law'. Chapter 3 describes the rights of Turkish citizens in the EU, which are comparable with the classical free movement rights of EU citizens. Chapter 4 discusses the EU Directives on family reunification, labour and science migration and a Directive securing special rights for long-term residents. Chapter 5 elaborates on the case law of the ECtHR regarding the way in which Article 8 ECHR entails both the right to join one's family and the right to be protected against arbitrary expulsion.

The third part is called '*Forced Migration*'. It consists of three chapters (6, 7 and 8). Chapter 6 discusses the 'Common European asylum system' formed by the Directives and Regulations dealing with the criteria for eligibility of asylum protection, minimum standards for asylum procedures, reception conditions, the responsibility of one particular Member State for processing asylum applications, and temporary protection. Chapter 7 describes the refugee status, as provided for in the Common European Asylum System, in accordance with the law on international refugee protection under the Refugee Convention. In Chapter 9 the status of subsidiary protection is analysed, often referring to important case law of the European Court of Human Rights on the prohibition of torture, inhuman or degrading treatment or punishment.

In the fourth part, on *Enforcement and Procedural Protection*, attention is paid to measures controlling migration and to guarantees for procedural protection of the individuals concerned. In Chapter 9 a survey is given of EU legislation on external border controls, expulsion measures and visas. Chapter 10 provides an overview of the various ways in which procedural protection is offered in relevant EU law. Here, reference is also made to case law of the European Court of Human Rights.

1.2. BASIC CONCEPTS OF MIGRATION LAW

1.2.1. WHAT IS MIGRATION?

The concept of migration refers to the international movement of persons. In principle, anyone who can afford the transport or who is prepared to walk long distances has the possibility of moving around the world. The liberty to do so is, however, restricted by the fact that the world is divided into states. States normally have territories delimited by borders. States normally have an exclusive bond with a group of persons, normally identified by their nationality. Persons possessing the nationality of a state are in principle entitled to enter the territory of that state and to reside there as long as they wish. In principle, all others do not have those rights. In relation to that state, they are foreign persons, aliens. For them, that state is a foreign state.

Often, the concept of migration is associated with the purpose of establishing a new residence elsewhere. In this book, a wider concept of the term is used, which includes all types of international movement of persons, both for short term and long term purposes. Arguably, it would be artificial to exclude the short-term movement of persons from the definition, as it would result in the necessity to invent a new term for this particular type of movement, and it may not, moreover, always be easy to distinguish between migration and short-term movement. Often, migration law is also referred to as the law on aliens or the law on (free) movement. Because this book deals predominantly with rights relating to entry and residence, migration law appears to be the most appropriate term.

Where migration is at stake, states and persons have different, sometimes opposite, interests. Characteristic problems for persons wishing to migrate are:

- how to get access to the territory of a state?
- how to obtain permission to stay within the territory of a state?
- how to obtain protection against expulsion from a state?

Characteristic problems for states *vis-à-vis* migrating persons are:

- how to control the borders?
- how to formulate norms for permitting access and residence?
- how to organise effective implementation of those norms, including the removal of persons who are not entitled to stay within the territory?

These questions form some of the essential elements of the study of migration law. Migration law is a field of law dealing with the cross-border movement of persons, establishing rights and obligations for both states and persons. For an adequate assessment of states, persons and their mutual relationship in the context of migration, the clarification of a number of legal concepts is necessary. Hereunder, a succinct description will be given of some key concepts that play a prominent role in migration law: the concepts of state, territory, borders, nationality and citizenship. Furthermore, several doctrines of international law are addressed, which are of special importance to issues of migration: state sovereignty and immigration control; the position of individuals under international law; and the principle of non-discrimination in relation to immigration.

1.2.2. STATE, TERRITORY AND BORDERS

1.2.2.1. *What is a State?*

When assessing whether an entity is a state, most commentators refer to three criteria: a defined territory, a permanent population and an effective government.[1] Often reference is made to the Montevideo Convention of 1933, adding as a fourth element the capacity to conduct relations with other states.[2] Not all commentators deem all four elements decisive for statehood. Conversely, other commentators refer to more than four characteristics.[3] Often sovereignty or independence is mentioned as an essential element.[4]

Globalisation has gradually changed states into regional entities functioning within an interdependent world. According to some authors, this trend is so well developed, that the reality is that state, civil society and market are inextricably intertwined and that all three are drawn further and further by the very process of transnationalisation into a 'structured field of action'. By this, we suggest a fluid pattern of fragmentation and integration deriving from the deepening, and at times, contradictory, interconnections between world polity, world economy and global society.[5] However influential this tendency may be, it certainly does

---

[1]   E.g. A. Nollkaemper, *Kern van het International Publiekrecht,* Den Haag: Boom Juridische uitgevers 2011, Chapter 3; M.N. Shaw, *International Law,* USA: Cambridge University Press 2008, p. 198–199; A. Kaczorowska, *Public International Law,* London: Routledge Chapman & Hall 2010.

[2]   Montevideo Convention on Rights and Duties of States, 26-12-1933, League of Nations Treaties Series Bd. CLXV, 25.

[3]   See Ian Brownlie, *Principles of Public International Law,* Oxford University Press, 1990, p. 72; J.G. Starke, *Introduction to International Law,* Butterworths, London, 1984, p. 91; Alfred Verdross, Bruno Simma, *Universelles Völkerrecht,* Duncker & Humblot, Berlin, 1984, p. 225.

[4]   N. Q. Dinh, P. Daillier, A. Pellet, *Droit international public,* L.G.D.J. Paris, 1980, p. 352; E.R.C. van Bogaert, *Volkenrecht,* Kluwer, Antwerpen, 1982, p. 64; Knut Ipsen, *Völkerrecht,* Beck, München, 1990, p. 56; Ian Brownlie, *The Rule of Law in International Affairs, International Law and the Fifth Anniversary of the United Nations,* Martinus Nijhoff Publishers, The Hague, London, Boston, 1998, p. 37.

[5]   E.g. Joseph A. Camilleri, Antony P. Jarvis, Albert J. Paolini (ed.), *The State in transition, Reimagining Political Space,* Lynne Rienner Publishers, Boulder London, 1995, p. 223.

not mean that independent and sovereign states have ceased to exist. It hardly requires emphasis that the traditional model of territorial order based on the principle of state sovereignty stands firm.[6] This is especially so when migration is at issue. Migration law is precisely about the right of sovereign states to control entry and residence of non-nationals with regard to their territories.

From these brief remarks it may be clear that the question, what is a state, will not always be answered unequivocally. Who decides, in case of doubt, if a certain area is a state? According to international law, existing states must decide whether and when they recognise a new state.[7] For the purposes of this book, the following definition seems to be sufficiently tenable:

> A state is a state in relation to another state recognising it as such. A state is characterised by a defined territory, a permanent population, a government and the capacity to conduct international relations with other states.

1.2.2.2. Territory and Borders

One of the cornerstones of international law is the principle of sovereign equality of states.[8] From this principle stems another principle: states have exclusive jurisdiction over their own territory.[9] In order for states to be able to exert exclusive jurisdiction over their territories, a demarcation is indispensable. Historically, state territories have been delineated by special geographical features providing some means of defence.[10] Legally, the question of what the exact demarcation is should ultimately be decided by the states involved. The legal form of an agreement on boundaries is not decisive.[11] Territorial jurisdiction can also be exerted on water and air. In the 1958 Convention on the Territorial Sea and the Contiguous Zone and the 1982 Convention on the Law of the Sea, sea zones adjacent to a state's coast are recognised, extending the exercise of sovereign control to parts of the sea.[12] The 1944 Chicago Convention

---

[6]   E.g. Surya P. Sharma, *Territorial Acquisition, Disputes and International Law*, Martinus Nijhoff Publishers, The Hague, Boston, London, 1997, p. 327.

[7]   H.G. Schermers, *Internationaal publiekrecht voor de rechtspraktijk*, Kluwer, 1982, p. 145; Otto Kimminich, *Einführing in das Völkerrecht*, Saur, München, 1983, p. 135.

[8]   See Article 2(1) Charter of the United Nations.

[9]   Ibid, Articles 2(1) and (7).

[10]   Thomas R. van Dervort, *International Law and Organization*, SAGE publications, Thousand Oaks, London, New Delhi, 1998, p. 355.

[11]   ICJ 3 February 1994, *Territorial Dispute (Libyun Aruh Jamuhiriyu v. Chad)* (judgment), ICJ Reports 1994, p. 23, §45; M.N. Shaw, *International Law*, USA: Cambridge University Press 2008, p. 488–492; A. Aust, *Handbook of International Law*, USA: Cambridge University Press 2005.

[12]   Convention on the Territorial Sea and the Contiguous Zone, 29 April 1958, Articles 1 and 24; UN Convention on the Law of the Sea, 10 December 1982, 1833 UNTS 3,397, Article 2; A. Nollkaemper, *Kern van het Internationaal Publiekrecht*, Den Haag: Boom Juridische uitgevers 2011; M. N. Shaw, *International Law*, USA: Cambridge University Press 2008; G. Boas, *Public International Law: Contemporary Principles and Perspectives*, UK: Edward Elgar Publishing Limited 2012, p. 169–174.

on International Civil Aviation[13] recognises that every state has complete and exclusive sovereignty over the airspace above his territory. This zone includes the land areas and territorial waters adjacent thereto under the sovereignty of such state.

In migration law, the demarcation of frontiers may be relevant for establishing whether a person has entered a country or not. However, the geographical delineation of the borders must be distinguished from the legal question as to whether a person has been granted access to the territory. From a legal point of view, it is perfectly conceivable that a person having geographically entered the territory remains in the legal position that he is denied entry. In many countries this legal construction is used. It plays a topical role at airports.

In most cases, aeroplanes cross the national boundaries before landing. Thus, persons getting off the plane at the airport are *de facto* within the territory. Can they still meaningfully be denied access to the country? In Article 2 of the Schengen Borders Code, 'External borders' are defined as the land and sea borders and their airports, river ports, sea ports and lake ports, provided that they are not internal borders.[14] So, according to the Schengen Borders Code, a person arriving at an airport situated within the territory of a Member State is considered not to have passed the external borders. Should we now categorically conclude that, as long as a person does not pass the border post at the airport, he is still outside the territory of the state? This issue arose when asylum seekers who were refused entry were kept in the transit zone (or 'international zone') of a European airport. In the *Amuur v. France* judgment,[15] the European Court of Human Rights considered that, despite its name, the international zone does not have extraterritorial status. Even though the applicants were not in France within the meaning of the applicable French legislation, holding them in the international zone of Paris-Orly airport made them subject to French jurisdiction.

1.2.3. NATIONALITY

Nationality legally binds an individual to a state. In the *Nottebohm* case, the International Court of Justice described this legal bond as follows:

> According to the practice of States, to arbitral and judicial decisions and to the opinions of writers, nationality is a legal bond having as its basis a social fact of attachment, a genuine connection of existence, interests and sentiments, together with the existence of reciprocal rights and duties. It may be said to constitute the juridical expression of the fact that the individual upon whom it is conferred, either

---

[13]   Convention on Civil Aviation, 7 December 1944, 84 UNTS 389.
[14]   Regulation EC No. 562/2006 of 15 March 2006, see further chapter 9.
[15]   ECtHR 25 June 1996, *Amuur v. France,* No. 19776/92, para. 52.

directly by the law or as a result of an act of the authorities, it is in fact more closely connected with the population of the State conferring nationality than with any other State.[16]

1.2.3.1. Acquiring Nationality

Although the Universal Declaration of Human Rights boldly pronounces that everyone has the right to a nationality,[17] the state is competent to decide who its nationals are.[18] In conferring nationality, states normally operate on two underlying principles. The first is known as *jus soli*, which is an inherently territorial means of conferring nationality. The fact of birth within a specific territory, regardless of the parents' nationality, determines the nationality of the newborn. Employing the *jus soli* principle can easily lead to the conferral of nationality to persons without a solid bond or genuine link with the state of which they acquire nationality, such as children born to tourists or other short-term visitors. Therefore, this principle rarely operates in unmodified form. Within Europe, Ireland operated a particular unrestrained *jus soli* regime prior to 2004, which was challenged as inciting exploitation by immigrants. The new Irish Citizen Act now requires that the non-Irish parent of a child born in Ireland has been lawfully residing in the state for three years for the child to acquire Irish citizenship. Of the other EU Members, France still operates a nationality regime mainly based on *jus soli*, although with a number of alleviating elements.

The other principle of conferring nationality is known as *jus sanguinis*. This principle is the preferred means of passing on nationality in the majority of European countries. *Sanguis* is Latin for 'blood', and according to the regime of *jus sanguinis*, newborns automatically acquire the nationality of their parents, regardless of the territory in which they are born. Again, this principle is not without disadvantages, the main one being that descendants of immigrants will not be able to acquire the nationality of the country with which they may have

---

[16] ICJ 6 April 1955, *Nottebohm Case (Liechtenstein v. Guatemala)* (judgment), ICJ Reports 1955, p. 23.

[17] Article 15 Universal Declaration of Human Rights. Article 24(3) ICCPR and Article 7(1) Convention on the Rights of the Child recognise the right of children to acquire a nationality. These provisions do not stipulate, however, which state must grant its nationality to children. Although it can be derived from these provisions that states should adopt appropriate measures to ensure that every child has a nationality when he is born, states are not necessarily under an obligation to give their nationality to every child born in their territory. See also Human Rights Committee, General Comment No. 17: Rights of the Child, 1989, §8.

[18] According to the Convention on Certain Questions relating to the Conflict of Nationality Laws (The Hague 12 April 1930, Article 1): 'It is for each State to determine under its own law who are its nationals. This law shall be recognised by other States in so far as it is consistent with international conventions, international custom, and the principles of law generally recognised with regard to nationality.' This provision is restated in Article 3 of the 1997 European Convention on Nationality.

the closest bond. Another complication connected to the *jus sanguinis* principle is that children of parents with different nationalities will acquire multiple nationalities at birth. For a long time, this latter complication was circumvented by legislation providing that the nationality of the father would be decisive in passing on nationality. Partly due to the adoption in 1979 of the Convention on the Elimination of All Forms of Discrimination against Women (CEDAW), this discriminatory legislation has been gradually abolished.[19]

All European countries now have some mixture of *jus sanguinis* and *jus soli*, with specific provisions on acquiring nationality for second and later generation immigrants. Germany's new nationality law (as of 1 January 2000), for example, provides that children born in Germany to foreign parents acquire German nationality at birth when one of the parents has resided lawfully in Germany for at least eight years, and is entitled to further legal residence for at least three years. If the child also acquires one of its parents' nationalities (as provided by that country's nationality legislation), the child will, upon reaching the age of 18, have to choose between its German and other nationality. Under this regime, the 'risk' of retaining dual nationality is minimised, although the German legislation does provide for an exception if renouncement of the other nationality is not possible (due to legislation in the parent's country of nationality).

Apart from acquiring nationality by birth, states commonly provide for the possibility of obtaining nationality by naturalisation, a process in which a non-national, by fulfilling a number of conditions, may apply for another nationality. Such conditions may include a minimum period of legal residence; knowledge or familiarity with a state's language, culture and society; and the willingness to renounce the other nationality.

It may be noted that although states have the sovereign right to provide for rules on conferring nationality, not all grants of nationality are internationally effective. In the *Nottebohm* case mentioned above, the ICJ was asked whether the state of Liechtenstein was entitled to assert diplomatic protection over Mr. Nottebohm, who had renounced his German nationality for that of Liechtenstein, and had been deported from Guatemala, where he had been living as businessman for more than thirty years. Liechtenstein had claimed restitution of property and compensation from Guatemala on the ground that Guatemala had acted contrary to international law. The ICJ considered, however, that, whereas Nottebohm's connections with Guatemala were considerably stronger than his ties with Liechtenstein (to which he had only once paid a visit), Guatemala was under no obligation to recognise the diplomatic protection asserted by Liechtenstein.

It has sometimes been inferred from the *Nottebohm* case that a genuine and close link between the individual and the state conferring nationality is

---

[19] Article 9(2) CEDAW provides: 'States Parties shall grant women equal rights with men with respect to the nationality of their children.'

necessary for the conferral of nationality to have international effect, *i.e.* for other states to be obliged to treat that individual as the former state's national. This is not what the Court said, however. The ICJ was concerned with the particular question of whether a state has a right to diplomatic protection over a naturalised citizen with whom it has no real links *vis-à-vis* a state which does have real links with that person. The ICJ did not contest the legality of the conferral of nationality as such.[20]

1.2.3.2. Nationality and Citizenship

Nationality can be distinguished from citizenship. While nationality is best described as a legal bond confirming the close ties of the individual with a state, citizenship implies the possibility for an individual to politically participate in the life of the community. Often, nationality and citizenship coincide, but not all persons having the nationality of a state have full citizenship rights. Minors will normally have the nationality of a state, but will not be able to exercise rights of political participation. Conversely, persons without the nationality of the state in which they reside, may still be granted limited citizenship rights, such as the right to vote and to stand as a candidate at municipal elections.

As O'Leary has observed, discussion of the meaning and content of nationality is often obscured by the fact that jurists tend not to differentiate between the terms 'national' and 'citizen'.[21] In migration law, 'nationality' is generally the predominant concept. 'Aliens' are those who do not possess the nationality of a particular state and the accompanying right of abode in that state. In essence, they have no right to enter or remain in the state, and may be susceptible to deportation. States can agree to mutually grant rights of access and residence to each other's nationals. In defining the legal position of a person under migration law, the first question will normally concern his or her nationality.

Under European Union law, the concept of 'citizen of the Union' has emerged as a primary source of the right to move and reside freely within the territory of the Member States. In defining this concept, Article 20 of the Treaty on the Functioning of the European Union exclusively links the citizenship of the Union to the nationality of a Member State. Hence, citizenship of the Union does not replace national citizenship, but is supplementary to national citizenship and conditional upon holding the nationality of a Member State. The European Union is not a state comprising a federation of Member States, and, consequently, the citizenship of the Union is not a nationality of that Union.[22]

---

[20]   G.-R. de Groot, *Staatsangehörigkeit im Wandel*, Carl Heymans Verlag KG Köln, 1989, pp. 21–22.

[21]   Siofra O'Leary, *The evolving Concept of Community Citizenship, From the Free Movement of Persons to Union Citizenship*, Kluwer Law International, The Hague, London, Boston, 1996, p. 9.

[22]   'Under international law, it is for each Member State, having due regard to Community law, to lay down the conditions for the acquisition and loss of nationality'; see, in particular, ECJ

1.2.4. STATELESSNESS

1.2.4.1. *Nationality and Statelessness*

Nationality comes with rights. Apart from rights at the domestic level, such as rights of political participation, the concept of nationality has a number of functions in international relations. The first of these is the right invoked by Liechtenstein in the *Nottebohm* case to protect its nationals from wrongdoing by other states. This is termed *diplomatic protection*, and embodies the right of a state, derived from customary international law,[23] to intervene on behalf of its own nationals, if their rights are violated by another state, in order to obtain redress. Another important international function of nationality is the right of individuals not to be expelled from the country of nationality and the right to enter one's own country. These rights will be discussed in the next section.

It is without question that it is important for individuals to have a nationality. The legal position of persons without a nationality, also called stateless persons, is precarious, since they may not be able to claim a right of residence in any country in the world, may not be able to invoke protection by a state, and do not have citizenship rights. Some commentators refer to stateless persons as persons without a legal identity, as *res nullius* or anomalies: beings who, from the point of view of international law, are without legal existence.[24] It is widely accepted that, to avoid the detrimental consequences of being without a nationality, statelessness should be reduced as much as possible. As a consequence, several international instruments have been devised specifically targeted at eliminating statelessness.

The 1954 Convention relating to the Status of Stateless Persons defines stateless persons as persons who are not considered as a national by any state.[25] This definition implies that domestic rules for acquiring nationality are particularly significant in rendering persons stateless. For example, a child born on the territory of a state employing the *jus sanguinis* principle in conferring

---

7 July 1992, *Micheletti and Others*, Case C-369/90, para. 10, and ECJ 20 February 2001, *Kaur*, Case C-192/99, para. 19. However, in ECJ 2 March 2010, *Rottmann*, Case C-135/08, it was decided that Member States are not completely free to withdraw their nationality once it has been given.

23   The rules on diplomatic protection have recently been codified in the *International Law Commission's* Draft articles on Diplomatic Protection. See *Official Records of the General Assembly, Sixty-first Session, Supplement No.10* (A/61/10).

24   P. Weis, *Nationality and Statelessness in International Law*, 2nd Ed., Alphen a/d Rijn: Sijthoff & Noordhoff International Publishers, 1979, p. 162; P. Weis, 'The United Nations Convention on the Reduction of Statelessness, 1961', *International and Comparative Law Quarterly*, Vol. 11, 1962, p. 1073.

25   Article 1 Convention relating to the Status of Stateless Persons, New York, 1954. EU Member States party to the 1954 Convention include: Belgium, Denmark, Finland, France, Germany, Greece, Ireland, Italy, Latvia, Luxembourg, Netherlands, Slovakia, Slovenia, Spain, Sweden, United Kingdom.

nationality, while both his parents are nationals of states employing the principle of *jus soli*, will be rendered legally stateless. Apart from becoming stateless at birth, persons may also become stateless subsequent to birth by losing their nationality. Some countries provide for legislation that deprives persons of their nationality when they, for example, enter the civil or military service of another state, or when they sojourn abroad for a certain number of years. A major cause for statelessness, furthermore, is state succession, in particular when a state dissolves in a number of its constituent parts. Although normally arrangements will be made for acquiring the nationality of one successor state or another, the legal position of former nationals of one successor state living in another successor state has turned out to be specifically problematic, due to the practice of putting up requirements on the part of the successor state for a former national to prove his or her relationship or 'genuine link' to the successor state. A majority of the stateless persons presently living in Europe, including many people of Roma origin, became stateless as a result of the dissolution of the Soviet Union and Yugoslavia.

1.2.4.2. *International Treaties on Statelessness*

International treaties on statelessness generally cover two issues: the protection of stateless persons and the avoidance of statelessness. Rights of stateless persons are set out in the 1954 Convention relating to the Status of Stateless Persons. Apart from laying down a definition of the term stateless person, this Convention grants a number of civil, economic, social and cultural rights to stateless persons living in the contracting states. The Convention does not however, oblige state parties to grant a right of residence to stateless persons. The 1951 Refugee Convention extends protection to stateless refugees. Denationalisation on discriminatory grounds amounts to persecution under the Refugee Convention.[26] The regime applicable to refugees in general, including stateless refugees, will be set out in Chapter 6 of this book.

The primary international instrument aimed at preventing statelessness is the 1961 Convention on the Reduction of Statelessness. It obliges contracting states to grant their nationalities to persons born in their territories who would otherwise be stateless; and not to deprive a person of his nationality if such deprivation would render him stateless.[27] The latter obligation allows for exceptions, however, and only 26 states have ratified the Convention.[28] Prompted

---

[26]   See Article 9 Convention on the reduction of Statelessness, and Article 8 CRC. See also report United Nations Sub-Commission's Special Rapporteur on the right to leave any country, including his own, and to return to his own country, UN doc. E/CN.4/Sub.2/1988/35, para. 107.

[27]   Articles 1 and 8(1) Convention on the Reduction of Statelessness, New York, 1961.

[28]   Including 10 EU Member States: Austria, Czech Republic, Denmark, Germany, Ireland, Latvia, Netherlands, Slovakia, Sweden, United Kingdom.

by the experiences of state succession in Eastern Europe in the 1990s, the United Nations General Assembly requested the International Law Commission to draft a code on the question of nationality of persons in relation to the succession of states. This code was adopted by the General Assembly as the UN Declaration on the Nationality of Natural Persons in Relation to the Succession of States in the year 2000.[29] This Declaration, which is not legally binding, pronounces in its first Article the right of every individual who had the nationality of the predecessor state, to have the right to the nationality of at least one of the successor states. The declaration, furthermore, calls upon states to take all measures necessary to prevent persons from becoming stateless as a result of state succession, and lays down the presumption that persons having their habitual residence in a successor state acquire the nationality of that state.[30]

As may be evident from the fact that according to estimates of the UNHCR, there are currently approximately 10 million stateless persons around the world, the current array of international instruments relating to nationality and statelessness may be important tools for reducing statelessness, but must not be seen as effectively eliminating the root causes of statelessness.[31] Thus, notwithstanding the bold pronouncement in the Universal Declaration on Human Rights that 'everyone has the right to a nationality',[32] discrepancies between domestic nationality laws, ethnic tensions relating to state succession and the reluctance on the side of states to give up prerogatives in the sphere of granting nationality and citizenship, remain substantial hurdles for individuals to obtain a nationality.

1.2.5. STATE SOVEREIGNTY AND IMMIGRATION CONTROL

1.2.5.1. The Right to Leave and the Right to Enter

International law presents us with two opposing principles on migration. On the one hand, international human rights treaties guarantee the freedom to leave any country. According to Article 13 of the Universal Declaration of Human Rights everyone has the right to leave any country, including his own. This right has been confirmed in Article 12 of the ICCPR and Article 2 Fourth Protocol to the ECHR. Although the right to leave any country may be subject to restrictions

---

[29] GA Res 55/153, 12 December 2000. The ILC draft was published in *Official Records of the General Assembly, Fifty-fourth Session, Supplement No. 10* (A/54/10).

[30] Ibid, Articles 1, 4 and 5.

[31] UNHCR identified 5.8 million stateless persons in 2006; the real total was believed to be nearer to 15 million. UNHCR Report 2007–2008, 'Protecting Refugees & the Role of UNHCR', Geneva, September 2007, p. 31.

[32] Article 15(1) Universal Declaration of Human Rights.

in order to prevent, for example, criminals from escaping justice, these restrictions may not nullify the principle of liberty of movement.[33] According to the Human Rights Committee, every person is allowed to leave a country to travel abroad for whatever reason, including permanent emigration or asylum. And since international travel will normally require a person to be in possession of a passport, this may also mean that a state is obliged to issue a passport to its nationals.[34]

On the other hand, international law does not provide for a right to enter another country. The ICCPR and ECHR only provide that persons who possess the nationality of a state have to right to enter that state (see Article 12(4) ICCPR and Article 2(3) Fourth Protocol to the ECHR). The right of states to deny entry to foreigners stems from the principle that states are exclusively competent with respect to their internal affairs. Already in 1892, the US Supreme Court found that:

> It is an accepted maxim of international law that every sovereign nation has the power, as inherent in sovereignty, and essential to self-preservation, to forbid the entrance of foreigners within its dominions, or to admit them only in such cases and upon such conditions as it may see fit to prescribe.[35]

This is also the view taken by the European Court of Human Rights, albeit in a somewhat less strict manner. In the *Abdulaziz, Cabales and Balkandi* cases the Court said that 'as a matter of well-established international law and subject to its treaty obligations, a state has the right to control the entry of non-nationals into its territory.'[36]

It is important to note that, although states have the right to control entry of non-nationals, this does not mean that states are always free to deny entry to foreigners. In the *Abdulaziz* judgment, the Court added that the right of states to control entry is subject to its *treaty obligations*. This means that bilateral or multilateral treaties concluded by the Contracting state may oblige that state to allow entry to a foreigner. An obvious example is the Treaty on the Functioning of the EU, under which EU citizens are entitled to move to another Member State. Further, immigration control may not go so far as to unjustifiably interfere with human rights of the immigrant concerned. Human rights treaties may

---

[33] See Article 12(3) ICCPR and Article 2(3) Fourth Protocol of the ECHR. On the conditions under which restrictions may be imposed, see especially Human Rights Committee, General Comment No. 27, 2 November 1999, UN Doc. CCPR/C/21/Rev.1/Add.9, para 2.

[34] Human Rights Committee, General Comment No. 27, 2 November 1999, UN Doc. CCPR/C/21/Rev.1/Add.9, para. 9. See also, Human Rights Committee, *Vidal Martins v. Uruguay*, Communication No. 57/1979, 23 March 1982.

[35] U.S. Supreme Court 18 January 1892, *Nishimura Ekiu v. United States et al.*, 142 U.S. 651, p. 142.

[36] ECtHR 28 May 1985, *Abdulaziz, Cabales and Balkandali*, Nos. 9214/80, 9473/81, 9474/81, para. 67.

imply that states are under an obligation to allow entry to a foreigner in order to guarantee his human rights. As we will see in Chapter 5, this is the case, for example, if entry to that country is the only possible way for the immigrant to be able to live with his family.

1.2.5.2. *The Right not to be Expelled*

The right to return to one's own country carries with it a prohibition of expulsion from one's own country, otherwise termed the right of sojourn or to remain. The prohibition of expulsion of nationals is laid down in Article 3(1) of the Fourth Protocol to the ECHR. In the ICCPR, this prohibition is not expressly provided for, but it follows indirectly from the right to enter.

Foreigners cannot benefit from a general prohibition of expulsion, although it is generally accepted that the collective expulsion of aliens is prohibited. This prohibition is to be found in Article 4 of the Fourth Protocol to the ECHR.[37] The absence of a right not be expelled does not mean that states may expel foreigners at will. Firstly, both the ICCPR and the ECHR contain a number of procedural safeguards with regard to the expulsion of aliens. These provide, among others, that aliens who have been lawfully residing in a country, may only be expelled if such expulsion is provided for in national legislation; that the expelling state must submit reasons for the expulsion; and that the alien has the right to have his case reviewed (see Article 13 ICCPR and Article 1 Seventh Protocol to the ECHR). Moreover, the expulsion of an alien may not jeopardise treaty obligations entered into by the expelling state, which again implies that human rights of the immigrant may prevent removal. In this regard, one could firstly think of the Refugee Convention, which prohibits removal to a state where a person would risk persecution. Secondly, one can think of general human rights, such as the right to respect for family life, which protects persons against the break-up of a family as a result of expulsion.

1.2.6. THE POSITION OF INDIVIDUALS UNDER INTERNATIONAL LAW

According to the classical 19th and 20th century view, only states can be the 'subjects' of public international law, that is to say, bearers of rights and obligations under international law. Individuals can, according to this doctrine, only be 'objects' of international law, which means that they cannot bring international claims, cannot conclude treaties and cannot be held accountable

---

[37] See also the (non-binding) Declaration on the Human Rights of Individuals Who are not Nationals of the Country in which They Live, Adopted by General Assembly resolution 40/144 of 13 December 1985, Article 7.

for international wrongdoings. According to the classical doctrine, individuals can only be associated with public international law *via* the medium of the state. The nationality of an individual indicates which state must protect him *vis-à-vis* other states. A number of developments in the 20th century are hard to reconcile with this strict classical doctrine. These include the formation of international organisations such as the United Nations and the European Union, the international recognition of human rights, the vastly increased mobility of persons and the increased 'voice' of citizens towards their own authorities in a number of countries. The individual right of complaint, such as laid down in, *inter alia*, the ECHR and in the Optional Protocol to the ICCPR, gives individuals, regardless of their nationality, a legal position *versus* states before an international forum. In the legal order of the European Community, which is applied directly within the legal spheres of the Member States, individuals may invoke rights granted by Community law before the national courts.

The question arises as to whether we should now acknowledge that individuals can also be subjects of international law. A wide variety of opinions is to be found on this issue.[38] The differences in the answers given seem greater than they actually are. The distinction seems to come down to a question of definition. If one finds that it is sufficient, in order to be a 'subject of law', that the party in question is a bearer of rights and duties, then the question of whether individuals are subjects of international law will be answered affirmatively. Conversely, if it is deemed necessary that in order to be a 'subject of law' the party in question is able to participate independently in the creation of norms and to create rights and duties, the answer will be negative. Whatever definition of 'subject' may be used, it would be incorrect to view the individual purely as an object of international law. The Permanent Court of International Justice considered as far back as 1928:

> It cannot be disputed that the very object of an international agreement, according to the intention of the contracting Parties, may be the adoption by the Parties of some definite rules creating individual rights and obligations and enforceable by the national courts.[39]

In the 1949 *Reparations for Injuries* Opinion, the International Court of Justice (ICJ) accepted that the United Nations, not being a state, has international legal

---

[38] Marek St. Korowicz, *Introduction to International Law*, Nijhoff, Den Haag, 1964, p. 325 *et seq.*, gives an overview of opinions up to 1964. See also H. Lauterpacht, *International Law and Human Rights*, Archon, 1968, p. 27 *et seq.*; Verdross-Simma, *Universelles Völkerrecht*, Duncker & Humblot, Berlin, 1984, p. 255 *et seq.*; J.G. Starke, *Introduction to international law*, Butterworths, London, 1989, p. 56 *et seq.*; and for an analysis of this question in relation to the ECHR: H. Walter, *Die Europäische Menschenrechtsordnung*, Heymans, Keulen, 1970.

[39] PCIJ 3 March 1928, *Jurisdiction of the Courts of Danzig (Pecuniary Claims of Danzig Railway Officials who have Passed into the Polish Service, against the Polish Railways Administration)* (Advisory Opinion), Series B – No. 15, pp. 17–18.

personality and can possess international rights and duties. In the opinion of the ICJ, the issue of being a 'subject' of international law is not a matter of all or nothing:

> The subjects of law in any legal system are not necessarily identical in their nature or in the extent of their rights, and their nature depends upon the needs of the community. Throughout its history, the development of international law has been influenced by the requirements of international life, and the progressive increase in the collective activities of States has already given rise to instances of action upon the international plane by certain entities which are not States.[40]

In the classical way of thinking, reduced here to its simplified pattern in which only states are subjects of international law, the nationality of an individual is of prime importance for the international legal protection to which he is entitled. Under customary international law, the state has a right (but no obligation which can be enforced by individuals) in relation to other states to protect its nationals outside its territory. This implies that individuals would only become involved in international proceedings if they are nationals of a state other than that in whose territory they are situated.[41] This traditional understanding has since long been abandoned. Fundamental changes began after the Second World War, with the drafting of the Charter of the United Nations and the Universal Declaration of Human Rights, the European Convention for the Protection of Human Rights and Fundamental Freedoms of 1950 and the International Covenant on Civil and Political Rights in 1966. In these instruments, rights are formulated for 'everyone', regardless of their nationality. Minimum standards for the treatment of persons are now set out in treaties that enjoy a broad degree of support. People can take the initiative themselves in having states' behaviour reviewed against those standards by international tribunals or independent bodies. It is no longer nationality that determines the group of individuals for whom the minimum standards apply. Of course, this does not mean that all distinctions based on nationality have become irrelevant in international law. But it does mean that an individual's nationality is no longer the sole basis for affording him/her certain minimum standards of treatment.

---

[40] ICJ 11 April 1949, *Reparation for Injuries Suffered in the Service of the United Nations* (Advisory Opinion), ICJ Reports 1949, p. 178.

[41] H.F. van Panhuys, *The role of nationality in international law*, Nijhoff, Dordrecht, 1959, pp. 64–73, gives the following, non-exhaustive, list of exceptions to the requirement of the possession of nationality in order to be eligible for the protection of a state: a. persons belonging to 'protected' or 'administered' territories; b. diplomatic protection on behalf of a foreign state; c. exceptions pursuant to treaties; d. (alleged) exception on behalf of stateless persons; e. intervention on humanitarian grounds.

1.2.7. DISCRIMINATION AND DISTINCTION ACCORDING TO NATIONALITY IN MIGRATION LAW

1.2.7.1. *Can Migration Law Amount to Discrimination?*

It is beyond dispute that the distinction between nationals and non-nationals is a fundament of migration law. It appears therefore hardly conceivable that such a distinction could ever amount to discrimination. However, to state the opposite – that distinctions on the grounds of nationality in immigration matters are automatically justified – would be an over-simplification. Discrimination is normally defined as an unjustified distinction between comparable cases. A distinction is deemed to be justified if it serves a legitimate purpose in an adequate and proportionate manner. If we apply this definition of discrimination to distinguishing individuals according to nationality, such distinction would only be justified in so far as it adequately and proportionately serves a legitimate purpose.

Immigration control of non-nationals is, in itself, a legitimate aim according to the leading legal perception. The European Court of Human Rights has repeatedly accepted that policies of immigration control can serve the legitimate purposes of the prevention of disorder, the protection of rights and freedoms of others, or the economic well-being of the country.[42] But even in exerting immigration control, states are not allowed to distinguish between nationals and non-nationals if the distinction does not adequately and proportionately serve the purpose of immigration control. For instance, if the frontier authorities of a certain state were instructed, in quite normal circumstances, to shoot at any non-national approaching the border, this would be neither functional nor proportionate to the aim, and thus would not be justified.[43] The distinction between nationals and non-nationals may not go so far as to determine the difference in being allowed to live or not, because it is unnecessary for the purposes of border control to kill all non-nationals seeking to cross the border. This is, of course, quite a crude example. It is mentioned in order to convince the reader that it is possible to find clear cases in which distinction between nationals and non-nationals is not always legitimate just because it serves the legitimate aim of border control. If the reader is convinced so far, he or she may be ready to look at less clear cases, where more subtle scrutiny is needed to draw the line between justified and unjustified distinctions. Is it, for example, justifiable to take fingerprints of all non-nationals crossing the borders of a state? And, if only some non-nationals are affected, such as those who are found to have crossed the borders without consent of the state, would this be justified? Or, is it justifiable to

---

[42]   E.g. ECtHR 21 June 1988, *Berrehab v. The Netherlands*, Appl. 10730/84, §25–26.
[43]   *Cf.* ECtHR 22 March 2001, *Streletz, Kessler and Krenz v. Germany*, Nos. 34044/96, 35532/97 and 44801/98, para. 100, concerning the GDR border-policing regime.

demand that non-nationals prove their identity by producing evidence that they are known not to have at their disposal?

As we see in these examples, measures of immigration control may affect non-nationals in their enjoyment of more or less fundamental rights. In the example of the shooting instruction, their right to life is affected. In the fingerprint example, their privacy is at issue. Denying a would-be immigrant entry into the country does not, *per se*, appear to involve the denial of any right (since there is no right to enter any country other than one's own). However, if we examine the reasons an immigrant seeks to enter the country, a right may well be at issue. For instance, if an immigrant seeks protection from torture or serious illness in his country of origin, or if his closest family members live in the country he seeks to enter, he invokes the right not to be tortured and the right to respect family live. Thus, his interest is weightier then if entering the country were merely a matter of pleasure or convenience. In such cases, it seems self-explanatory that, if a state wishes to avoid the reproach of discrimination, it will have to advance a more substantial justification for immigration measures differentiating between nationals and non-nationals.

It is possible, and arguably even illuminating, to look at migration law as a problem of non-discrimination on grounds of nationality. Presumably, all questions relating to the legitimacy of immigration legislation or immigration measures can – on a theoretical level – be reduced to questioning the legitimacy of a distinction between nationals and non-nationals. If this proposition were to be accepted, we might also accept that distinctions between nationals and non-nationals should *only* be allowed provided that they serve a legitimate aim, and if so, provided that they are functional for that goal and proportionate in relation to the interests involved. If these conditions are not met, a provision of immigration law or an immigration measure would constitute discrimination. For example, while immigration detention is not discriminatory *per se*, since it facilitates a decision about entry or removal, detention of an immigrant for many years would be disproportionate and, hence, discriminatory in relation to nationals of the expelling country. Similarly, if an immigrant has resided in a country for five or ten years while being engaged in regular employment, it is hard to find a legitimate aim served by denying this person a position similar to nationals of the host country, for instance, in the form of a permanent residence permit. One could argue that such a denial would therefore amount to discrimination.

This mode of thinking, translating a problem of migration law into a problem of discrimination, is as yet mainly important from a theoretical point of view, and not very familiar to the European Courts. The Court of Justice EU has indeed attached huge value to the prohibition of discrimination on grounds of nationality, as it is now laid down in Article 18 TFEU, but only as far as mutual differences between Union citizens are concerned. In the *Vatsouras and*

Koupatantze judgment,[44] the Court of Justice said that the prohibition of discrimination on grounds of nationality concerns situations falling within the scope of EU law in which a national of one Member State suffers discriminatory treatment in relation to nationals of another Member State, solely on the basis of his nationality. According to the Court, this prohibition is not, however, intended to apply to cases of a possible difference in treatment between nationals of Member States and nationals of non-member countries (see section 2.3.7).

Arguably, the Court failed to acknowledge that situations of both Union citizens and third-country nationals may fall within the scope of EU law nowadays, and that Article 18 TFEU, prohibiting discrimination on grounds of nationality within the scope of Union law, is unavoidably applicable to both categories. Third-country nationals, too, have a right not to be discriminated against on the sole ground of nationality. Article 18 TFEU does not, admittedly, oblige the Union and the Member States to give third-country nationals the same privileged position as Union citizens occupy, but it does, in principle, impose an obligation to apply the proportionality principle to differential treatment of those categories.

Under Article 14 of the European Convention of Human Rights, the prohibition to discriminate on 'any ground' in securing the enjoyment of rights and freedoms set forth in the Convention includes a prohibition to discriminate on grounds of nationality. In several judgments, the Court has held that very weighty reasons would have to be put forward before it could regard a difference of treatment based exclusively on the ground of nationality as compatible with the Convention.[45] However, this notion has not been applied as yet to cases of migration law proper (see, further, section 5.13).

1.3. THE MULTI-LEVEL STRUCTURE OF EUROPEAN MIGRATION LAW

1.3.1. SOURCES OF EUROPEAN MIGRATION LAW

In this book, we will concentrate on EU legislation concerning Migration Law. However, it must be noted that the EU is not the only legal sphere providing for binding rules relating to Migration Law applicable in the region of Europe. There are at least five legal spheres where relevant and binding rules can be found:

1. the national legislation of European states;
2. European Union legislation on the movement of European Union citizens and the movement of third-country nationals;

---

[44] ECJ 4 June 2009, *Vatsouras and Koupatantze*, Cases C-22/08 and C-23/08, para 52.
[45] ECHR 16 September 1996, *Gaygusuz*, no. 17371/90 para 42; ECHR 30 September 200, *Koua Poirrez*, no. 40892/98, para 46; ECHR 18 February 2009, *Andrejeva*, no. 55707/00 para 87.

3. treaties concluded within the Council of Europe, like the European Convention for the Protection of Human Rights and Fundamental Freedoms (ECHR);
4. treaties concluded within the framework of the United Nations, like the Geneva Convention relating to the Status of Refugees (Refugee Convention), the International Covenant of Civil and Political Rights (ICCPR), the Convention against Torture (CAT), and the Convention on the Rights of the Child (CRC);
5. bilateral and multilateral treaties concluded between Member States of the European Union and third states.

This book only deals with three of those five legal spheres. We will not elaborate on national legislation or on bilateral or multilateral treaties between Member States and third states. We will deal with European Union law, Council of Europe law and United Nations law. In discussing these legal spheres, we will always take Union law as the explicit point of departure.

But first, it is necessary to set out the parallels and the differences between the various legal spheres.

1.3.2. THE RELATIONSHIP BETWEEN NATIONAL LAW AND HUMAN RIGHTS TREATIES

Both Council of Europe and United Nations human rights treaties secure rights to everybody on the territory or subject to the jurisdiction of a contracting state. The difference is that the Council of Europe has only a regional dimension, whereas the United Nations involves all states in the world. For our purpose, describing the state of the law in the European region, this difference is not terribly important, because the jurisdiction of the EU is overlapped by jurisdictions of both the Council of Europe[46] and the United Nations.

The effect human rights treaties have in the domestic law of a State Party is determined by domestic law. Under a monist system, like that of Belgium, France and The Netherlands, national law must yield to international law in the case of conflicting provisions. International law can be invoked directly before national courts. Under a dualist system, as employed by Germany, Italy and the United Kingdom, international law must first be incorporated into national law before the courts may take it into account. National courts in dualist countries only apply rules of international law in their capacity as national law. Provisions of human rights treaties may only have direct effect in a Contracting State in as far as the law of that state provides for this possibility.

---

[46] All EU Member States are members of the Council of Europe.

The difference between monistic and dualistic systems is somewhat mitigated by the individual right to complain that some human rights treaties offer. The admissibility of such a complaint is not subordinated to any condition relating to the question of whether the country against which the complaint is directed has monistic or dualistic system. Complaints under the European Convention for the Protection of Human Rights and Fundamental Freedoms (ECHR) are dealt with by the European Court of Human Rights (ECtHR) in Strasbourg. Under the International Covenant on Civil and Political Rights (ICCPR), the Human Rights Committee (HRC) in Geneva is competent to deal with individual complaints. For the Convention against Torture and Other Cruel, Inhuman or Degrading Treatment or Punishment (CAT), there is the Committee against Torture (ComAT).[47] Under the UN Convention on the Rights of the Child, the Third Protocol provides for an individual right of complaint. This Optional Protocol will enter into force when ten states have ratified it. Before these treaty-monitoring bodies, individuals can directly invoke provisions of Human Rights treaties, regardless of whether they invoke these rights against a country employing a monist or dualist system. Contrary to the judgments of the European Court of Human Rights, the decisions of the Human Rights Committee and the Committee against Torture are not legally binding, and are normally referred to as 'views' rather than judgments.

1.3.3.   THE RELATIONSHIP BETWEEN NATIONAL LAW AND EU LAW

The distinction between monist and dualist approaches is irrelevant under the EU Treaties and secondary legislation adopted under it. Under Union law, a substantially new relationship between treaty law and national law of States Parties has been established. Because the Union has its own legal order,[48] which, on the entry into force of the EEC Treaty, became an integral part of the legal systems of the Member States, and which their courts are bound to apply,[49] there is no discretion left for national law as to the manner in which Union law affects national law. Union law is equally binding in monist and in dualist Member States.

---

[47]   Since the entry into force of Protocol 11 to the ECHR in 1998, the right to individual complaint under the ECHR has been expressly guaranteed. Under the ICCPR, Contracting States must first confer the right to individual complaint by ratifying the First Optional Protocol to the ICCPR. Under the CAT, States must have recognised this right by making a declaration in accordance with Article 22 CAT.

[48]   *Van Gend & Loos*, ECJ 5 February 1963, Case 26/62 ECR 1963, 1.

[49]   *Costa Enel*, ECJ 15 July 1964, Case 6/64, ECR 1964, 585.

1.3.4. THE RELATIONSHIP BETWEEN THE ECHR AND THE EU

The difference between EU law and the law of the ECHR can, in simplified terms, be characterised as follows.

a. Union law has its own legal order. It is binding on the Member States and prevails over national legislation. Individuals can invoke Union law before the national courts. The national courts must apply Union law. If a national court hesitates about the correct interpretation of Union law, preliminary questions can be asked to the Court of Justice of the EU (Luxembourg), which will provide a binding interpretation. In some cases, the European Commission and other institutions of the Union may address the Court. The Court of Justice is not a court of higher appeal and cannot quash national judgments, but its case law is authoritative and binding.

b. The ECHR is a treaty, binding on the Contracting States under relevant rules of international law. Individuals within the jurisdiction of a Contracting State have the right to complain with the European Court of Human Rights (Strasbourg) about alleged violations by this state of the rights secured in the Convention. The European Court of Human Rights is not a supranational court of higher appeal, though its case law has, to a certain extent, the same effect as judgments of a supreme court. A complaint can only be lodged after the available local remedies have been exhausted.

From the perspective of a private person, the ECtHR has the advantage that it can be addressed in individual cases when the national remedies fail to protect his human rights. He cannot address the European Court of Justice in a particular case. Only the national courts may decide to ask preliminary questions.

The ECHR is ratified by all EU Member States. As yet, the European Union itself is no party to any of these treaties, but the Treaty of Lisbon has added a protocol to the EU Treaty, according to which, the EU will accede to the ECHR.[50] On 5 April 2013, a draft Agreement on the Accession of the European Union to the ECHR was finalised by an *ad hoc* negotiating group of the Steering Committee for Human Rights (Council of Europe) and the European Commission.[51] According to the representative of the EU on this Committee, an opinion of the Court of Justice EU will be sought on the compatibility of the draft agreement with the EU Treaties. Consecutively, the Council will have to

---

[50] Protocol No. 8 relating to Article 6(2) of the Treaty on European Union on the accession of the Union to the European Convention on the Protection of Human Rights and Fundamental Freedoms.

[51] Final Report to the CDDH, 47+1(2013)008.

adopt unanimously the decision authorising the signature of the Accession Agreement. According to the Draft Agreement, accession to the Convention and the Protocols thereto shall impose on the European Union obligations with regard only to acts, measures or omissions of its institutions, bodies, offices or agencies, or of persons acting on their behalf.

Member States will remain responsible in the same manner as they were before the accession: an act, measure or omission of organs of a Member State of the European Union or of persons acting on its behalf shall be attributed to that State, even if such act, measure or omission occurs when the State implements the law of the European Union, including decisions taken under the TEU and the TFEU. This shall not preclude the European Union from being responsible as a co-respondent for a violation resulting from such an act, measure or omission.

1.4. EUROPEAN MIGRATION: A BRIEF HISTORIC SURVEY

1.4.1. A CONCISE HISTORY OF EUROPEAN MIGRATION

Roughly sketched, the current legal regime on migration in Europe can be characterised as the result of two concurrent historical developments. The first is the process of European integration – an ever-deepening harmonisation of various policy areas and gradual geographical expansion of the European Community through which a single European living space has come into existence, with a distinct and supranational legal order. The second development is that of the transformation of Europe from a continent of emigration into a continent of immigration, which has forced governments across Europe to fundamentally rethink, unilaterally and jointly, their policies regarding entry and residence of persons coming from outside Europe. This chapter will briefly describe these historical developments, with a focus on how they have influenced migration policies in Europe.

Born out of rationales of reconciliation, reconstruction and security, the European integration process, started in the aftermath of the Second World War, has greatly facilitated intra-European migration. As part of the organisation of a single internal market – which was seen to foster economic growth and intertwine the European economies – the free movement of persons developed into one of the four core European economic freedoms, together with services, goods and capital. The first step was made with the 1951 treaty establishing the European Coal and Steel Community (ECSC), which provided for a right to free movement for workers in the coal and steel industries. The Treaty of Rome of 1957 establishing the European Economic Community provided for the free movement of all workers within the European Economic Community. This encompassed the right to accept offers of employment in another Member State, to move about freely for that purpose within the territories of the Member States, and to live in the territory of a Member State after having been employed there.

Ever since, the European integration process has facilitated the abolishment of all sorts of bureaucratic barriers for entry and residence of European workers; the extension of free movement rights to other categories than workers; and the creation of rights of equal treatment of European citizens with nationals of the Member State in which they reside. Important developments were the Schengen Conventions of 1985 and 1990, by which internal border controls were abolished and the introduction of European citizenship by the 1992 Maastricht Treaty. Parallel to the process of increasing opportunities of free movement, this common European living space was substantially widened geographically through the successive enlargements of the European Union, culminating in the accession of most of the former Eastern bloc countries in 2004, 2007 and 2013.

Whereas the process of European integration may be seen as a linear development facilitating possibilities of intra-European free movement as a consequence of clearly stated policy aims, Europe's relationship with immigration from non-EU countries has only in part been the consequence of conscious policy decisions. To a considerable extent, immigration patterns to and from Europe reflect Europe's changing role in the world order, whereby European governments have adopted reactive rather than proactive measures.

Similar to the European integration process, World War II could, in several respects, be regarded as a turning point for Europe's relationship with immigration from other continents. For centuries, global trade and politics had been dominated by European expansion, resulting in the setting up of trading posts and permanent settlements in parts of the Americas, Africa and the Far East. Although devastation, the readjustment of borders and the birth of the State of Israel gave rise to a new wave of emigration from Europe after the Second World War, the late 1940s and 1950s also marked the beginning of the influx of large groups of non-Europeans into Europe. A first development was the process of decolonisation, which not only caused many Europeans to return to their motherlands, but also resulted in many natives from the former colonies coming to Europe. They were either economic migrants who were allowed entry and citizenship, or refugees who fled from violent struggles for independence. This process was soon followed by another influx of foreigners, which resulted from the post-war economic boom in Europe and the accompanying shortage of labour. Countries like Austria, Germany and the Netherlands operated recruitment systems for guest workers, who initially came from Spain, Portugal, Italy and Greece, and were followed by workers from the Maghreb countries and Turkey. Like the natives in the former colonies, a significant part of labour migrants not only migrated for economic reasons, but often fled from persecution stemming from dictatorial regimes, such as in Spain (up to 1975) and Greece (1967–1974). Liberal labour migration regimes often enabled these escapees to avoid an explicit application for asylum.

The official recruitment of workers came to an abrupt end as a result of the recession caused by the 1973 oil crisis. At that time, around 11 million migrant workers, both from within Europe and from abroad, were already living in Europe. While a majority of Southern European guest workers returned home due to improved political and social conditions in their countries of origin, workers from North Africa and Turkey often stayed, which resulted in a new form of immigration into Europe: the phenomenon of family reunification. During the 1970s and 1980s, immigrant communities in north-western Europe continued to grow as a consequence of wives, children and other relatives accompanying the guest workers. Ever since, family migration has been a major source of immigration into Europe, which is also due to the fact that second generation immigrants often chose to marry a partner from the parents' country of origin. Currently, family migration is the predominant source of immigration in most northern and western European countries. In Sweden and France, family migration accounts for more than 50% of the total of residence permits granted.

As a consequence of higher levels of unemployment and stagnating economic growth rates, the gates of entry for general labour migrants were closed by many European states in the 1970s. European governments employed stricter requirements for the issuing of work permits, and increasingly focused on mechanisms which would only allow entry for high-skilled workers or workers for specific economic sectors. With the restriction of possibilities for labour migration, persons fleeing to Europe from violent conflicts could no longer avoid revealing their asylum purposes. They were forced to apply for residence as refugees, or to try to illegally cross the borders and settle as illegal residents. At the same time, migration as a means of evading poverty became more apparent, and also led to an increase in asylum applications and persons trying to obtain entry in Europe by irregular means.

The influx of refugees into Europe has steadily increased since the 1940s and 1950s. In the first post-war decades most refugees coming to Western Europe came from Communist countries. Increased availability of means of transportation and communication stimulated larger groups from the Third World to make their way to Europe. In the beginning of the 1970s there were only around 5 million displaced persons globally, the vast majority of whom found safer places in their regions of origin. Only occasionally did European countries provide shelter for large numbers, e.g. the Vietnamese boatpeople in the 1970s. By the turn of the 21st century, the number of refugees had risen to approximately 20 million, with increasing numbers trying to find shelter on the European continent. A peak of refugees into European countries was reached in the mid-1990s, although this was mainly caused by a European affair: the civil war in Yugoslavia. Since then, the numbers of asylum applications in the EU have gradually dropped. According to Eurostat, some 424,000 applications were received in 2001, compared to approximately 193,000 in 2006. However, the wars in Afghanistan and Iraq have contributed to an increase of this figure in the years 2007 and 2008.

The number of people migrating to Europe outside the official channels has substantially grown. Stricter conditions for entry in the field of work, but also on asylum and family reunification have pushed potential migrants into irregular forms of migration, often heading for jobs in informal parts of the economy or illegal residence with family members or compatriots. Some of these irregular migrants cross Europe's borders illegally; others may have legally gained entry, but overstayed their visas or residence permits or chose to stay after their request for asylum had been denied. Southern countries like Greece, Italy and Spain have become especially attractive for irregular labour migrants, in part due to the abundant availability of job opportunities in the informal economy. Although there are hardly reliable statistics on the number of illegally residing immigrants, estimates vary between 5 and 10% of the legally resident immigrants.

A majority of European countries have become countries of immigration, a fact that some governments have indeed found hard to accept. Not only do governments sometimes perceive immigration as a potential threat to national economies and social security systems, but the increased ethnic and religious diversity of communities is also seen as potentially undermining social cohesion. Present migration policies are sometimes described as having resulted in the establishment of 'Fortress Europe', in which European citizens can freely move, and to which third-country nationals can barely gain access. This metaphor is only partly apposite. European governments are very aware that their national economies are in continuous need of immigrant labour from outside Europe, which is not least due to the ageing population in virtually all European countries. Moreover, there is wide agreement that migration policies should in part be based on humanitarian considerations, which has lead to the invention of various forms of residence permits apart from refugee status, such as temporary protection permits, permits on general humanitarian grounds, or permits for medical reasons.

1.4.2. THE FORMATION OF EUROPEAN MIGRATION LAW

Against the background of facilitating the free movement of nationals from the EU Member States on the one hand, and finding ways to better control migration from non-EU countries on the other, European migration law has gradually emerged as a distinct field of law. Arguably, the most striking feature of European migration law is the regime on free movement of persons under Union law, of which the foundations were laid with the 1957 Treaty on the European Economic Community (EEC). The free movement of EU nationals has turned out to be a key pillar of the European integration process. Immigration from third countries, on the other hand, only came to the fore as an area of competence of the European Union in more recent decades. The 1992 Maastricht Treaty recognised immigration and asylum to be matters of common interest, and the 1997 Amsterdam Treaty inserted a new title IV into the EC Treaty, which provided for the adoption of measures in the areas of visas, asylum and immigration. Since the Amsterdam Treaty, a range of specific Regulations and Directives on migration have been adopted, such as the Directive on family reunification and various legal measures on the protection of asylum seekers. In order to better deal with phenomena as illegal migration, human smuggling and trafficking, the European Commission has presented a series of further initiatives for Member State cooperation. Also, the entry to and (forced) return from the common territory is regulated. With the Treaty of Lisbon, the legal basis for these Regulations and Directives has found a place in Title V of the Treaty on the Functioning of the EU (TFEU).

Although the European Union currently has fairly wide competences regarding both the movement of Member State nationals within Europe and immigration from third countries, it would go too far to conclude that the European Union has now become the sole source for migration law in Europe. In the first place, migration law in Europe is not fully harmonised. Not only do some areas of migration law remain (largely) uncovered by EU law, such as the field of integration of immigrants and labour immigration of unskilled third-country nationals, much of the adopted measures at the EU level, moreover, leave discretionary powers to Member States. As a result, the domestic immigration regimes of the Member States remain divergent. Secondly, treaties concluded outside the framework of the European Union have notable bearing on the legal position of immigrants in Europe. These could be treaties targeted specifically at the issue of migration, such as the Refugee Convention, or treaties of a general nature, such as the European Convention on Human Rights.

Still, it can be said that the present EU legislation on migration covers all aspects of the migration process, from entry to exit, regarding both voluntary and forced migration. An overview of the system of entry, residence and return under Union Law is given in section 1.6.

1.5. EU CITIZENS AND THIRD-COUNTRY NATIONALS: THE DEVELOPMENT OF MOVEMENT OF PERSONS IN THE EU

1.5.1. MOVEMENT OF PERSONS IN THE EU: AN ONGOING DEVELOPMENT WITH UPS AND DOWNS

Because it has developed and still develops in stages, a historical approach is probably most fruitful for explaining the concept of movement of persons under EU law. The development of EU migration legislation, case law and political views goes steadily, though not smoothly, rather faltering, often wavering, and sometimes caught in a sudden process of acceleration. Generally, it can be said that the law on the movement of EU citizens is the oldest and therefore much more complete than the law on the movement of what we call 'third-country nationals'. A citizen of a Member State has, to a great extent, the right to move and reside freely within the territory of the Member States. This right is guaranteed by Article 21(1) of the Treaty on the Functioning of the EU (TFEU). Thus, a EU citizen has a certain legal relationship with other Member States deriving from his nationality. When we refer to an EU citizen in relation to *other* Member States than his own as a 'second-country national' (a label we never use), it might become clear why non-EU citizens are commonly referred to as 'third-country nationals': they are nationals not of the host state, not of another EU Member State, but of a third state. For issues of free movement, the concept of 'third-country national' normally includes stateless persons.[52] Further, nationals of countries that have established close ties with the EU, like Switzerland, Liechtenstein, Norway and Iceland fall outside the definition of third-country nationals for the purposes of border control.[53]

1.5.2. FREE MOVEMENT OF THE MARKET CITIZEN

Free movement of nationals of the Member States has been a key goal of European integration since the establishment of the European Economic Community in 1957. Originally, only the movement of economically active persons was stimulated as a tool for creating a 'common market'. Workers (now: Articles 45 – 48 TFEU) and self-employed persons wishing to settle in another Member State (now: Articles 49 – 55 TFEU), or simply to provide cross-border services (now: Articles 56 – 62 TFEU), were granted the right to leave their own country, to enter other Member States and to reside there. These rights were,

---

[52] See, for instance, the definition in Article 2 Directive 2003/86 (Family reunification).
[53] See section 4.1, below.

however, made subject to exception clauses connected with the public policy, public security or public health in the receiving Member State (see now Articles 45(3), 52(1) and 62 TFEU).

Like any other foreign worker, Europeans who intended to work in another Member State were for some time still covered by national immigration laws, and had to request a work and residence permit. The adoption of secondary legislation gradually harmonised the conditions under which the substantial Treaty rights could be exerted. Some of this legislation provided corollary rights of residence, such as the right of workers to remain in the territory of a Member State after having been employed in that State and the right of temporary residence for jobseekers. Other Directives were targeted at removing administrative formalities for taking up employment, such as on the mutual recognition of diplomas, certificates and other evidence of formal qualifications. Of major importance was the adoption of Regulation 1612/68/EC in 1968, which prohibited all discrimination between workers based on nationality regarding conditions of work, remuneration, dismissal, taxes and the enjoyment of various benefits. As we will see in Chapter 2.1, another factor responsible for the development of free movement rights has been the European Court of Justice (ECJ), which, through its judgments, has clarified and expanded the scope of the right to freedom of movement.

For a long time, the rules on free movement of persons could only be invoked by the economically active (or 'market citizens'). In 1990, three Directives were adopted, granting the right to residence also to nationals of EC Member States who are not economically active, but who are able to financially support themselves. These Directives concerned students, pensioners and a general category of persons who are financially self-supporting.[54] All three Directives provided that beneficiaries may not become a burden on the social assistance system of the host Member State, and must be covered by sickness insurance. Thus, whereas the right to freely move was extended beyond the market citizen, the principle was upheld that EU citizens may not become a burden on the social assistance systems of the host Member State.

At the beginning of the 1990s, the goal of the free movement of citizens of the EC had, to a great extent, been achieved. Two further developments should be noted here. Firstly, the introduction of *Citizenship of the European Union* by the Treaty of Maastricht in 1992. In the present Articles 20–24 TFEU the definition of a citizen of the EU and his/her rights are laid down. This turned out to be more than mere cosmetic upgrading of the concept of the 'nationality of a Member State'. The Court of Justice has ruled that citizenship of the EU is a fundamental status of nationals of the Member States. Every citizen of the Union 'shall have the right to move and reside freely within the territory of the Member

---

[54] See Directives 90/364 (financially self-supporting); 90/365 (pensioners); and 90/366 (students). The 1990 directive on students was, in 1993, replaced by Directive 93/96.

States, subject to the limitations and conditions laid down in this Treaty and by the measures adopted to give it effect.' Though this provision could be read as having no particular meaning by itself, the Court, in 2002, designated the provision now known as Article 21(1) TFEU as the primary legal source of the right of nationals of EU Member States to travel and to reside in the territories of the Member States.[55]

A second development has been the adoption in April 2004 of Directive 2004/38 ('Citizens' Directive'), in which the total *acquis* of the free movement of EU citizens is summed-up, reshaped and laid down in one all-embracing legal text. In Chapter 2, the rules governing free movement of EU citizens and their families will be examined.

Under certain conditions, third country nationals are also involved in these free movement rights, as a corollary of the freedom of movement of a national of a Member State, mostly when they belong to his or her family. But the migration of third-country nationals under their own steam was, for a long time, excluded from the scope of Community law. This phenomenon became the subject of European interest in the last 15 years of the 20th century, as will be described in the next section.

1.5.3. INTERGOVERNMENTAL COOPERATION RELATING TO IMMIGRANTS FROM THIRD COUNTRIES: SCHENGEN AND DUBLIN

In the 1980s, Member States were increasingly confronted with immigration from third countries. Governments of the Member States were worried by growing numbers of asylum seekers, family migrants and illegally residing persons. Awareness arose that cooperation and coordination might be necessary for a more effective policy of immigration control. But at the same time, steps were made to abolish internal border controls in Europe. In the Single European Act of February 1986, which entered into force on 1 July 1987, the progressive establishment of the 'internal market' before 31 December 1992 was proclaimed. One of the characteristics of the internal market, distinguishing it from the older concept of the 'common market', was that it would comprise *an area without internal frontiers in which free movement of persons is ensured.*[56] The prospect of an area of common territories without internal border controls aroused a sense of urgency to create 'compensatory measures' at the external borders in order to restrict free flows of asylum seekers and illegal entrants on the one hand, and criminals, on the other. For this purpose, a number of intergovernmental groups of consultation came into being, like the Trevi group, the *ad hoc* group on

---

[55] See section 2.4, below.
[56] See the present Article 14 TEC.

immigration; the European Political Cooperation Group and others. Thus, two conflicting goals, lifting immigration controls on European citizens on the one hand, and intensifying immigration controls on third-country nationals, on the other, dominated the debate. A further conflict of goals lay in the fact that Member States genuinely wished to cooperate in immigration measures, but still showed great reluctance to give up national sovereignty in favour of Community competence. This reluctance was the main cause of the phenomenon of 'intergovernmental cooperation', i.e. cooperation between EC Member States outside the scope of the European Community.

Two movements came into being: intergovernmental cooperation between five pioneering EC Member States and intergovernmental cooperation between all – then twelve – Member States. In 1985, the first movement led to the Agreement of Schengen concluded between France, the Federal Republic of Germany and the three Benelux countries. Schengen is a town in Luxemburg where the Agreement was signed. Five years later, the same states concluded the Convention implementing the Agreement of Schengen (19 June 1990). This treaty is normally referred to as the Schengen Implementing Convention (SIC). The SIC regulated a broad range of subjects. The key provision was Article 2, according to which internal borders might be crossed at any point without any checks on persons being carried out. All the other 141 provisions of the SIC contained 'compensating measures', predominantly in the field of police cooperation in criminal matters, but also, partly, in the field of border controls, visas and asylum. A common Schengen visa for short-term stays was introduced, and a system was put into place countering the phenomenon of 'asylum shopping', based on the principle, according to which, an asylum application could only be filed in one of the Member States. Further, the Schengen Information System (SIS) was created, enabling the contracting states to prevent undesired aliens from entering their common territories by putting an alert onto a common database.

Within the second intergovernmental movement the twelve Member States undertook to draft two Conventions partly covering the same subject matter. One draft treaty, dealing with external border controls, never came into being, as the United Kingdom and Ireland opposed abolishing border controls between these two islands and the continent, and because of a conflict between the United Kingdom and Spain about the borders of Gibraltar. But another treaty was signed indeed. On 15 June 1990, in Dublin, the twelve Member States concluded a treaty on the attribution of responsibility for dealing with asylum requests, on the same footing as the relevant paragraph of the SIC. This treaty was referred to as the 'Dublin Convention'. This Convention did not have the disadvantage of the Schengen Implementing Convention of being concluded by only a small group of Contracting States, but it was far less elaborate. When the Dublin Convention entered into force on 1 September 1997, the concurring provisions on inter-state attribution of responsibility for the processing of asylum applications in the SIC were abolished.[57] Mainly due to the consistent refusal of the UK and Ireland to lift internal border controls, the then twelve Member States did not reach a consensus on the abolition of internal border controls. In the case of the UK, this was because of its geographic position as an island, coupled with fear about relinquishing sovereignty. For Ireland, this was because it wished to maintain its Common Travel Area with the UK. The signing of the Dublin Convention was not followed by the signature of other 12-state-treaties, but the pioneering approach of the five Schengen states proved to be successful: in time, all EC Member States, except for the UK and Ireland, acceded to the Schengen Implementing Convention. Norway and Iceland – not belonging to the Community – also joined, and Switzerland implemented the Schengen Agreement in 2008.

1.5.4.   THE TREATIES OF MAASTRICHT, AMSTERDAM AND LISBON

The period since 1990 may be characterised as one in which intergovernmental activity in the area of immigration and asylum was gradually absorbed into European Community law. First, in 1992, the Treaty on European Union (TEU) was signed in Maastricht. The existing Treaty on the European Community (TEC)[58] was incorporated into the new TEU. In Title VI of the TEU (Justice and Home Affairs) issues of immigration and asylum were designated as matters of common interest. Cooperation between the Member States in this area was thus brought within the ambit of the EU. In 1997, the Treaty of Amsterdam finished the absorption process by bringing immigration and asylum under the aegis of the European Community. This was done by moving them from the third (EU) pillar to the first (EC) pillar. In the process, the TEC got a new Title IV on visas, asylum, immigration and other fields connected with free movement of persons. Title IV laid down a legislative programme with a time schedule (5 years) within which the Council had to adopt a range of measures.

A further result of the Treaty of Amsterdam was that the most important product of intergovernmental cooperation, 'Schengen', was incorporated into the TEU. It was decided that many of the Schengen provisions, dealing with matters of cooperation in criminal matters, would have their new legal basis in the sixth Title of the TEU (Justice and Home Affairs). The first part of the Schengen Implementing Convention, dealing with matters of entry and visas, was allocated to the new Title IV TEC. The Dublin Convention initially retained its separate

---

[57]   Protocol of 26 April 1994, Bonn.
[58]   In Maastricht the European Economic Community was renamed European Community.

status as an intergovernmental treaty, but was replaced by a Community regulation under Title IV TEC in 2003.[59]

Despite these legislative activities, the absorption of intergovernmental functions in the Community framework was not entirely complete. Firstly, the UK and Ireland, joined by Denmark, wished to remain free to abstain from the harmonisation of immigration and asylum law under Title IV TEC. Secondly, the incorporation of the Schengen *acquis* led to an extremely ambiguous legal construction: for Norway, Iceland and Denmark, the Schengen Implementing Convention had kept its character of a Treaty, but for the Member States united under Title IV TEC, the Convention had partly changed into something equivalent to an EC Regulation, and partly remained a Convention under Article 34(2)(d) TEU.

In the period from 1999 to 2005, the European Community displayed intense legislative activity implementing the programme laid down in Title IV TEC. For most of the core issues on immigration and asylum law, Regulations and Directives have been adopted and implemented. In Chapter 6 of this book, the EU legislation on asylum will be dealt with more extensively. Directives on family reunification, long-term residents, workers, students and researchers, are described in Chapter 4.

The Treaty of Lisbon entered into force on 1 December 2009, with some delay caused by the Irish 'no' vote in June 2008. The Treaty brought a fundamental overhaul of the then existing EU and EC Treaties. It amended both the Treaty on European Union (TEU) and the European Community (EC) Treaty, and renamed the latter Treaty on the functioning of the European Union (TFEU). The Lisbon Treaty renumbered the articles in the TEU and TFEU. Provisions on Police and Judicial Cooperation are now brought together under a new Title with the existing provisions on migration, visa and border control. The Lisbon Treaty also foresees the accession of the European Union to the European Convention on Human Rights (new Article 6(2) TEU), and explicitly endows the Charter of Fundamental Rights with legally binding character (new Article 6(1) TEU).[60]

Although renumbered, the core provisions on the free movement of persons (EU citizens) remained virtually unaltered. The TFEU does provide a broadening of the legal basis for adopting legislation on asylum and immigration issues, as a consequence of which we may expect further European harmonisation efforts in these areas. The most disappointing feature of the new Title V on the Area of Freedom, Security and Justice is perhaps that it does not abolish the existing fragmented structure under which Denmark, Ireland and the United Kingdom retain the possibility of abstaining from further cooperation. According to

---

[59] Regulation EC 343/2003.
[60] Regarding the Charter, a Protocol introduces specific measures for the United Kingdom and Poland concerning exceptions to the justiciability of the Charter before national courts; see Protocol No. 30 on the application of the Charter of Fundamental Rights of the European Union to Poland and the United Kingdom.

protocols annexed to the Lisbon Treaty, the United Kingdom and Ireland will continue to have a full right to opt out from all AFSJ measures; and Denmark will also maintain its special position.[61]

1.5.5. EU CITIZENS AND THIRD-COUNTRY NATIONALS: REFINING THE DISTINCTION

The above-described dichotomy of EU citizens and third-country nationals is in some respects too simple. Some EU citizens may not (yet) benefit from the full range of free movement rights. Conversely, some categories of third-country nationals do benefit from free movement rights equal to EU citizens. Four categories of 'exceptions' to the simple dichotomy can be distinguished.

First, there are third-country nationals who have the same rights to free movement as citizens of the EU Member States on the basis of treaties that their countries concluded with the European Community (now: EU). The Treaty on the European Economic Area (EEA, 2 May 1992) grants free movement to nationals of Norway, Iceland and Liechtenstein on an equal footing with EU citizens. The Treaty between the EU and Switzerland on free movement of persons (21 June 1999) has the same effect for Swiss citizens.

Secondly, citizens of Croatia, which joined the EU on 1 July 2013, do not yet have the full right of free movement in some of the 'old' Member States. According to the Accession Treaty, Member States may, during a period of transition, suspend the right to free movement of workers from Croatia. Though, strictly speaking, states acceding to the EU are no longer third countries, their nationals may, during a transitional period, be treated in some respects like third-country nationals or – if you wish – like temporary second-rate EU citizens.

Thirdly, third-country nationals may fall within the remit of the free movement of Union citizens when they are family members of an EU citizen or employees of an EU company providing cross-border services within the European Union.

Finally, the EU has concluded a number of association and cooperation treaties with third countries that give preferential treatment in various spheres to nationals from these third countries. Such preferences may include the freedom of movement to the EU for workers and members of their family. The most prominent example, the Association Treaty concluded with Turkey, is described in Chapter 3.

---

[61]   See Protocol No. 21 on the position of the United Kingdom and Ireland in respect of the Area of Freedom, Security and Justice; and Protocol No. 22 on the Position of Denmark.

It follows from the above that third-country nationals may fall within the remit of Union law in one of three ways:

(a) under Article 21 and Title IV TFEU, when they are family members of an EU citizen or employees of an EU company providing cross-border services within the European Union (see Chapter 2);
(b) as nationals of a third state which concluded an association or accession treaty with the European Community (see Chapter 3);
(c) under Title V TFEU (see Chapter 4).

Although in ordinary discourse the term 'third-country national' remains in use to depict any person not having the nationality of one of the Member States, from a legal perspective the designation of 'third-country national' is insufficiently precise to describe a person's legal position as regards rights of entry and residence in the European Union. This has also been recognised in more recent legal instruments adopted by the Brussels legislature. In Article 3 Returns Directive (Directive 2008/115/EC) and Article 2(6) Schengen Borders Code (Regulation EC 562/2006), a 'third-country national' is defined as any person who is not: (i) a Union citizen; (ii) a third-country national family member of a Union citizen exercising his or her right to free movement; or (iii) a third-country national who, under agreements between the Community and third countries, enjoys rights of free movement equivalent to those of Union citizens.

1.6. THE SYSTEM OF ENTRY, RESIDENCE AND RETURN UNDER UNION LAW

1.6.1. INTRODUCTION

Today's Union law contains a comprehensive and almost all-encompassing migration law system. It covers both voluntary and forced migration. It controls entry, residence and return. It covers both Union citizens and third-country nationals. Though there are fields not affected by Union law and left to the Member States, the overall picture drawn by the existing EU instruments is fairly complete. Still, its application may be complex for a number of reasons. As we saw in section 1.5.5, a strict division between Union citizens and others would be too simple. There are various categories of non-EU citizens who are treated equally to Union citizens, or, at least, in a more favourable way than the average third-country national. Further, the sources of EU migration law are scattered. EU Migration law is laid down in the Treaties and in a series of secondary law instruments – instruments that are not always fully consistent with each other, as they have been drafted at different stages in different political situations.

And the meaning and scope of EU migration law provisions are not uncontested. While it is an absolutely normal phenomenon that any provision of law will be interpreted in different ways, this phenomenon gets an extra dimension here as there is often, in the background, a dispute ongoing about distribution of powers between the Member States and the Union. Finally, the territorial applicability is not univocal. Parts of the common migration law system are not applicable in every EU Member State. On the other hand, parts of EU migration law are also applicable in a number of non-Member States. In this section we confine ourselves to depicting the general framework in order to give an overall impression of the migration law system of the Union.

1.6.2. ENTRY INTO THE SCHENGEN AREA

As we saw in para 1.5.3, the Schengen area does not fully overlap with the common territory of the European Union. Ireland and the UK do not join the system. On the other hand, three non-EU Member States (Norway, Iceland and Switzerland), do. All in all, it is a huge territory spreading from Cyprus to Norway and from Spain to Finland.

Within this area, control at the internal borders has been abolished. Controlling external borders is a common matter, regulated in the Schengen Borders Code (Reg. (EC)562/2006). The conditions for entry of Union citizens and third-country nationals are harmonised. For third-country nationals, there is a uniform EU visa valid for a period of less than three months (per six months), regulated in the Visa Code (Reg. (EC)810/2009). After lawful entrance, third-country nationals have a right to circulate within the Schengen area during, at most, three months. See, more extensively, sections 9.2 and 9.3, below.

Visas for periods longer than three months are still within the exclusive power of the Member States.

1.6.3. RESIDENCE RIGHTS

Residence rights granted under Union law are only defined in relation to the territory of one Member State. There is no right to a residence permit covering the total area of the EU territory. This is true for both Union Citizens and third-country nationals, even where it is possible that persons, for instance, frontier workers, may have a right to stay in more than one Member State. The right to free movement of Union Citizens gives them the possibility to cross all internal borders of the common territory of the EU Member States. In that respect, it can be said that Union citizens have access to the whole territory of the EU, but it is for the individual Member States to secure these rights. For third-country nationals, there is a right to circulate within the Schengen Area during a short term of, at most, three months after legal entry. This right, directly granted to third-country nationals by Union law, is valid within the Schengen area.

In respect to residence rights, distinction must be made between Union citizens and third-country nationals.

Union citizens are free to enter any Member State and to stay there for three months. After that period they have a right to further lawful residence for the purposes of economic activity or study. They are also allowed to reside there for any other purpose, provided that they have sufficient resources and sickness insurance coverage not to become a burden on the social security system of the receiving state. After five years they are entitled to a permanent residence right. All these rights are automatically derived from Union law and not subject to approval of national authorities. These rights also extend to the members of their families, regardless of their nationality. Under the EEA treaty and a treaty between the EU and Switzerland, a treatment similar to that of Union citizens is given to nationals of those countries. In this paragraph, these nationalities will be presumed to be included in the term 'Union citizens'.

Third-country nationals have no self-evident right, like Union citizens, to enter or reside in EU Member States for purposes of economic activities. For them, Union law provides no freedom of movement of workers, no freedom of establishment or provision of services. Union citizens have prioritised access to the labour market in the Member States. In contrast, third-country nationals may only do work for which no Union citizen is available. For access to the EU labour market of highly qualified third-country nationals, the Blue Card Directive 2009/50 formulates relatively lenient conditions. Pertaining to third-country nationals with a lesser degree of education, Union law provides, in the Single Application Procedure Directive 2011/98, for nothing more than procedural rules facilitating and coordinating applications by employers and employees. As it becomes clear from the Blue Card Directive, knowledge is welcome to the EU. This can also be seen from Directive 2004/114 and Directive 2005/71, admitting third-country nationals for the purposes of study and scientific research.

A qualified right to family reunification for third-country nationals is laid down in the Family Reunification Directive 2003/86. Members of the core family are allowed to stay with third-country nationals who have already obtained a right to reside in a Member State if they comply with the conditions posed by the Directive.

After five years of lawful residence, third-country nationals can apply for a Long-term Residence Permit under the conditions laid down in Directive 2003/109, a status which no longer needs to be renewed and offers stronger protection against removal. Holders of the long-term resident status have, in principle, a right to move their residence to other Member States, but in that respect, Directive 2003/109 offers predominantly symbolic possibilities.

Thus far, we have described the EU structure for *voluntary migration*. For *forced migration*, a different system is shaped. Asylum in the EU is a matter that does not normally concern Union citizens, although it is of course not inconceivable that a national of a Member State would wish to seek protection in another Member State. Most Union citizens have so many possibilities to obtain lawful residence in foreign Member States for economic and other purposes that they will rarely need to beg for asylum. This may not, however, be self-evident for minorities or vulnerable groups like Roma, fleeing Member States where they claim to be discriminated against. Nevertheless, EU law formally excludes, almost categorically, the possibility that Member States may be unsafe for their own citizens. Protocol No. 24 on asylum for nationals of Member States of the European Union (the so-called Aznar protocol),[62] provides that Member States 'shall be regarded as constituting safe countries of origin in respect of each other for all legal and practical purposes in relation to asylum matters.' Accordingly, any application for asylum made by a national of a Member State may be taken into consideration or declared admissible for processing by another Member State only in exceptional cases.

For third-country nationals, a Common European Asylum System is laid down in a number of Regulations and Directives. Asylum seekers arriving at the external border may apply for protection according to procedures for which minimum standards are laid down in Directive 2005/85 (Asylum Procedures Directive), recast as Directive 2013/32. Under Regulation 343/2003 (Dublin Regulation), recast as Regulation 604/2013, there is only one Member State responsible for the examination of the application. The basic rule is, that the Member State where the asylum seeker first arrived is responsible. Minimum conditions for the reception of these asylum seekers in the Member State are formulated in Directive 2003/9 (Reception Conditions Directive), recast as Directive 2013/33.

According to the Qualification Directive (2004/83, recast as 2011/95), asylum seekers may be granted two types of statuses: (a) refugee status or (b) subsidiary protection. The refugee status means that the person concerned is recognised as a refugee as defined in the Refugee Convention, according to the interpretation of that Convention, which is laid down in the Directive. Subsidiary protection is given to a third-country national or a stateless person who does not qualify as a refugee, but in respect of whom substantial grounds have been shown for believing that the person concerned, if returned to his or her country of origin, or in the case of a stateless person, to his or her country of former habitual residence, would face a real risk of suffering serious harm as defined in the

---

[62]   OJ C 326, 26.10.2012, p. 205–306.

Directive, and is unable, or, owing to such risk, unwilling to avail himself or herself of the protection of that country.

Further, there is a Directive 2001/55, on temporary protection in cases of mass influx, which has never been applied as yet, and is not very likely to be applied in the near future, as it requires a prior decision by a qualified majority of the Council assessing that the Directive will be applied to a particular group of persons, and leads to fairly extensive obligations for the Member States.

1.6.4. BORDER CONTROL AND INTERNAL CONTROL MECHANISMS

A range of organisational and technical instruments has been developed under Union law, in order to secure an effective surveillance of the external borders and the regions neighbouring these borders. The basic rules for entry control are laid down in the Schengen Borders Code (Regulation 562/2006). A supportive instrument is provided by the Schengen Information System (SIS II Regulation 1987/2006), containing data on persons to be refused entry to the Schengen Area. Another supportive instrument is the Visa Information System (VIS, Regulation 767/2008), containing information on entry and the (late) return of holders of Schengen visas. An instrument primarily developed to support the implementation of the Dublin regulation is the Eurodac Regulation 2725/2000, containing fingerprints and other data about asylum applicants in the EU. Sophisticated systems of operational support in border and pre-border control are organised on the basis of the Frontex regulation 2007/2004 (see more extensively, sections 9.6–9.8, below).

1.6.5. INDIVIDUAL CONTROL MEASURES: EXPULSION, DETENTION, ENTRY BANS

Elementary rules on measures against the unlawful stay of third-country nationals on the territory are laid down in the Returns Directive 2008/115.

Third-country nationals who are found to be illegally on the territory must be issued a so-called 'return decision', unless they are issued any residence permit or other legal status. A return decision implies an obligation to leave the territory of the EU. If the person concerned does not leave the territory in time, he or she may be detained in order to prepare the return and/or carry out the removal process, but only if less coercive measures cannot be applied effectively. Further, an entry ban, prohibiting entry into, and stay on, the territory of the Member States for a specified period, may be imposed (see more extensively, section 9.4, below).

1.7. THE ELEMENTARY SIGNIFICANCE OF THE EU CHARTER OF FUNDAMENTAL RIGHTS

1.7.1. THE CHARTER AND ITS SCOPE OF APPLICATION

The entering into force of the Lisbon Treaty on 1 December 2009 involved an essential enrichment of the fundamental rights paradigms of the Union. From that moment on the Charter of Fundamental Rights of the EU has been the primary binding source on rights, freedoms and principles for all situations within the scope of application of EU law, together with the unwritten principles of Union law. According to Article 6(1) TEU, the Union recognises the rights, freedoms and principles set out in the Charter, which shall have the same legal value as the Treaties.

The Charter is only applicable to situations falling within the realm of Union law. According to Article 51(2), the Charter does not extend the field of application of European Union law beyond the powers of the Union, and it does not establish any new power or task for the Union, or modify powers and tasks as defined in the Treaties.

The Charter addresses both the institutions of the Union and the Member States. Article 51(1) of the Charter says that the provisions of this Charter are addressed to the institutions and bodies of the Union with due regard for the principle of subsidiarity and to the Member States only 'when they are implementing Union law.' These words, which are decisive for the extent to which Member States are bound by the Charter, leave room for different interpretations. Is 'implementing' meant in the restrictive sense of transposing EU law into national legislation? Or does it refer to all situations of application of Union law?

The question of the extent to which Member States are bound by the Charter was at issue in the case of *Åkerberg Fransson*. Before the Grand Chamber of the Court of Justice, several Member States and the European Commission had advocated a narrow interpretation. It was a case about the application of the *ne bis in idem* principle in tax offences.[63] The said Member States and the Commission disputed the admissibility of the posed preliminary questions, stating that the Court of Justice would have jurisdiction to answer the questions only if the subject matter of the main proceedings arose from the implementation of European Union law into national legislation. The Court rejected this restrictive interpretation of Article 51(1) of the Charter in a principled and extensively reasoned judgment. The Court considered that Article 51(1) Charter confirms the Court's case law relating to the extent to which actions of the Member States must comply with the requirements flowing from the

---

[63]   ECJ 26 February 2013 (Grand chamber), *Åkerberg Fransson*, Case C-617/10.

fundamental rights guaranteed in the legal order of the European Union. In paras. 19–22, the Court said:

> The Court's settled case law indeed states, in essence, that the fundamental rights guaranteed in the legal order of the European Union are applicable in all situations governed by European Union law, but not outside such situations. In this respect the Court has already observed that it has no power to examine the compatibility with the Charter of national legislation lying outside the scope of European Union law. On the other hand, if such legislation falls within the scope of European Union law, the Court, when requested to give a preliminary ruling, must provide all the guidance as to interpretation needed in order for the national court to determine whether that legislation is compatible with the fundamental rights the observance of which the Court ensures (…).

> That definition of the field of application of the fundamental rights of the European Union is borne out by the explanations relating to Article 51 of the Charter, which, in accordance with the third subparagraph of Article 6(1) TEU and Article 52(7) of the Charter, have to be taken into consideration for the purpose of interpreting it (…). According to those explanations, 'the requirement to respect fundamental rights defined in the context of the Union is only binding on the Member States when they act in the scope of Union law'.

> Since the fundamental rights guaranteed by the Charter must therefore be complied with where national legislation falls within the scope of European Union law, situations cannot exist which are covered in that way by European Union law without those fundamental rights being applicable. The applicability of European Union law entails applicability of the fundamental rights guaranteed by the Charter.
> Where, on the other hand, a legal situation does not come within the scope of European Union law, the Court does not have jurisdiction to rule on it and any provisions of the Charter relied upon cannot, of themselves, form the basis for such jurisdiction (…).

So, the criterion for applicability of the Charter with regard to the obligations of Member States is in itself very simple: whenever a situation falls within the scope of application of Union law, the Charter is applicable and must be abided with by the Member States.

The Court could have gone a step further by reasoning that already the Charter itself, being a primary source of Union law, governs the question of whether Union law is applicable. In that line of thought, the mere fact that the Charter was invoked would automatically have brought the issue within the scope of Union law. In the *Dereci* judgment, the Court barred this reasoning. Simply invoking the EU Charter is not sufficient to bring a situation under the remit of Union law when the situation in itself is not governed by Union law.[64]

---

64   ECJ 15 November 2011, *Dereci and others*, Case C-265/11, paras. 69–72.

In this book, we will deal with European Migration law primarily by describing the relevant EU legislation. Consequently, the subject matter of this book is normally within the scope of application of Union law, which makes the Charter applicable. If questions arise as to the compatibility of such legislation with fundamental rights, the test is always and solely about compliance with the rights, freedoms and principles set out in the EU Charter. In investigating such issues, it may be very important to take into account the meaning and content of comparable norms under the ECHR and other relevant Conventions, but only as supporting evidence of the meaning of the Charter.

However, there are situations in migration law practice where it is necessary to apply the ECHR on its own merits. The next section discusses when the Charter and when the ECHR should be applied.

1.7.2. CHOOSING BETWEEN ECHR AND CHARTER

Migrants may pursue two avenues when it comes to invoking fundamental rights in an individual case: they may state that a situation falls within the ambit of Union law and should therefore be judged under the Charter, or they may claim that a State, as a contracting State of the ECHR, violates its obligations under that Convention, and should therefore be judged under the ECHR. These are separate avenues with their own legal arguments. Even when both approaches are applied in one and the same case, they remain fundamentally different. The Court of Justice EU does not explain the ECHR, nor does the European Court of Human Rights explain the law of the EU.

From a tactical point of view, it may be important for the migrant to always put his eggs in both baskets where this is possible, but one must remain aware of the difference between the two approaches. Further, there may be situations in which only the ECHR can be invoked. In the *Dereci* judgment, the Court recalled that national judges can apply human rights Conventions like the ECHR, to situations under national law which are not covered by Union law and the Charter:

> (...) if the referring court considers, in the light of the circumstances of the disputes in the main proceedings, that the situation of the applicants in the main proceedings is covered by European Union law, it must examine whether the refusal of their right of residence undermines the right to respect for private and family life provided for in Article 7 of the Charter. On the other hand, if it takes the view that that situation is not covered by European Union law, it must undertake that examination in the light of Article 8(1) of the ECHR.[65]

---

[65]   Ibid, para 72.

It should be emphasised here that the ECHR is not legally binding within the ambit of EU law. That may seem strange as this Convention contains important and binding obligations for the Member States who ratified it. But the European Union is – as yet – not a party to the ECHR or other human rights treaties.

The relevance of the ECHR for EU law goes under the guise of background to general principles of Union law. The Court of Justice ensures the observance of fundamental rights as they form an integral part of the general principles of law. For that purpose, the Court draws inspiration from the constitutional traditions common to the Member States and from the guidelines supplied by international instruments for the protection of human rights on which the Member States have collaborated or to which they are signatories.[66] In that sense, the ECHR and other Conventions have constantly had an important impact on Union law in their role of sources of inspiration for principles of Union law.

As of 1 December 2009, these Conventions are also important in their role of source of inspiration of the Charter. According to Article 53(3) Charter, the meaning and scope of rights in the Charter that correspond to rights guaranteed by the ECHR, shall be the same as those laid down by the ECHR. Union law is not, however, prevented from providing more extensive protection.

This book is written from the perspective of Union law. As we are primarily describing the legislation of the EU, it is self-explanatory that we find ourselves within the scope of application of Union law. It follows, that the Charter will be the frame of reference in this book when fundamental rights are concerned. When relevant, the case law of the ECtHR will be described, but mostly in its function of source of inspiration for the interpretation of the Charter.

However, there are some exceptions to this rule. Chapter 5 deals with the case law of the ECtHR on Article 8 ECHR, securing respect for family life on its own merits, and not in relation to the Charter. The reason therefore is, as explained in section 5.1, that there are still many situations in which family reunification is not covered by Union law. Further, in Chapter 8 on subsidiary (asylum) protection, a substantive part of the text is dedicated to the case law of the European Court of Human Rights on the prohibition of torture and inhuman or degrading treatment or punishment, laid down in Article 3 ECHR. In asylum cases, still, many complaints with the ECtHR are lodged, and the judgments of this court are of great importance.

A special position, in this regard, is occupied by the Refugee Convention, as the Qualification Directive is based on a full and inclusive application of the Refugee Convention.[67] Therefore, Chapter 7 describes the refugee protection regime as it is based on the Refugee Convention and as it is regulated in and developed under the Qualification Directive.

---

[66] See, for instance, ECJ 27 June 2006, *Parliament v. Council*, Case C-540/03, para. 35.
[67] Qualification Directive, recital 3.

PART II
VOLUNTARY MIGRATION

2. FREE MOVEMENT OF EU CITIZENS AND MEMBERS OF THEIR FAMILY

2.1. INTRODUCTION

2.1.1. THREE LEVELS

This chapter examines the scope of free movement rights of EU citizens and their family members as laid down in the TFEU and secondary legislation. There are three levels on which free movement is provided:

- the *general* Treaty level of the principal provision creating Union citizenship in Article 21 TFEU;
- the *specific* Treaty level of the provisions on the freedoms of movement of workers, establishment and services in Articles 45–62 TFEU; and
- the level of *secondary legislation* in the Citizens' Directive 2004/38.

2.1.1.1. General Level

The citizenship of the European Union is intended to be the fundamental status of nationals of the Member States.[68] Article 20(1) TFEU says that every person holding the nationality of a Member State shall be a citizen of the Union. It thus remains up to the Member States to decide who will be an EU citizen. The sovereign power of Member States to grant, deny or withdraw nationality is principally not affected by the Treaty.[69]

Normally, nationality of a Member State is mainly important for the holder in relation to the *Member State* concerned. The impact of that nationality in relation to the *Union* has a supplementary character. According to the last sentence of the first paragraph of Article 20(1) TFEU, citizenship of the Union shall be additional to, and not replace, national citizenship. Especially relevant for this chapter is the right of Union citizens to move and reside freely within the territory of the Member States, laid down in Articles 20(2) and 21 TFEU. The concept of Union citizenship was introduced in the Treaty on European Union

---

[68] Case C-184/99 *Grzelczyk* [2001] ECR I-6193, para 31; Case C-413/99 *Baumbast and R* [2002] ECR I-7091, para. 82; *Garcia Avello*, para. 22; *Zhu and Chen*, paragraph 25; and *Rottmann*, para. 43; ECJ 8 March 2011, *Ruiz Zambrano*, Case C-34/09, para. 41.
[69] See hereunder, section 2.4.2.

of Maastricht of 1992. As will emerge from this chapter, some tension can be observed between the EU dimension of citizenship and the national dimension of nationality.

2.1.1.2. Specific Level

At a more specific level, the freedoms of movement of workers, establishment and services are pronounced in Articles 45–48, 49–55 and 56–62 TFEU. These provisions are older than the general Union citizen provisions and originate from the Treaty establishing the European Economic Community (TEEC) of 1957. Initially, the freedom of movement was limited to movement for economic purposes. These purposes are still highly relevant. Any Union citizen is free to enter other Member States and reside there in order to be employed or self-employed or to provide or receive services. The Court of Justice sees these provisions as giving specific expression to the general rule of Article 21 TFEU.[70]

2.1.1.3. Secondary Legislation Level

In Directive 2004/38 ('Citizens' Directive'), the right to free movement is regulated in more detail for Union citizens and their family members for economic and non-economic activities. Both Article 21 TFEU and Articles 45, 49 and 56 TFEU form a legal basis of this Directive. The Directive substitutes a number of older instruments and codifies the jurisprudence of the Court of Justice. Further, there are more instruments of secondary legislation, like Regulation 492/2011, containing specific rules on the freedom of movement for workers within the Union, and the Services Directive 2006/123.

It may make a difference to which of these three levels one refers. For instance, a person enjoying a right derived from Article 21 TFEU does not necessarily enjoy all the rights mentioned in the Citizens' Directive. This will be set out in more detail below. In the following sections, each of these three levels will be dealt with.

The Treaty on the Functioning of the EU itself does not indicate in any of its provisions to what extent *family members*, regardless of their nationality, benefit from the rights to free movement of the Union citizen. Their position is laid down in secondary legislation, namely the Citizens' Directive and in Article 10 Regulation 492/2011.

---

[70] See, for instance, ECJ 16 December 2010, *Josemans*, C-137/09, para. 53.

2.1.2. REVERSE ORDER OF DESCIPTION

From a purely systematic point of view it would only be logical to start describing the general meaning of Union citizenship in Articles 20 and 21 TFEU, then to deal with the more specific provisions on free movement in Articles 45–62 TFEU, and finally to elaborate on the details of secondary legislation, especially the Citizens' Directive. However, for the sake of understandability it appears to be better to operate precisely the other way around. In particular, the case law of the Court of Justice on Union citizenship, often showing the additional value of Union citizenship as compared to the rights granted in secondary legislation, is easier to understand with prior knowledge of the content of the Citizens' Directive.

For that reason, this chapter starts with a rather factual description of the free movement rights given to Union citizens and the members of their family in the text of the Citizens' Directive. Consecutively, the underlying jurisprudence of the Court of Justice on the freedom of movement of workers, freedom of establishment and services, is explained. This may elucidate the historic developments preceding the drafting of the Citizens' Directive and give insight into the rights-based approach of the Court of free movement issues. Finally, the principles of Union citizenship stemming from Articles 20 and 21 TFEU are illustrated by discussing the relevant case law of the Court.

2.2. THE CITIZENS' DIRECTIVE

2.2.1. RIGHT OF RESIDENCE

Provided that they satisfy certain conditions, Union citizens and their family members are endowed by the Citizens' Directive with three respective rights of residence: the right of residence for up to three months (Article 6), the right of residence for more than three months (Article 7), and the right of permanent residence (Articles 16–18). All Union citizens have the right of residence on the territory of another Member State for a period of up to three months without any conditions or any formalities other than the requirement to hold a valid identity card or passport.[71] Under the same conditions, Union citizens have the right to leave and enter the territory of a Member State.[72] No visa or equivalent formality may be imposed on them.[73] Although this right is broadly formulated indeed, Article 14(1) of the Directive holds that persons enjoy this short-term right to

---

[71] Article 6(1) Citizens' Directive.
[72] Articles 4, 5 Citizens' Directive.
[73] Article 4(2) Citizens' Directive.

residence only as long as they do not become an unreasonable burden on the social assistance system of the host Member State, although workers and jobseekers are exempted from this requirement.[74]

The right of residence for a period longer than three months is subject to a more specific set of conditions. Three categories of Union citizens enjoy this right:[75]

(a) Union citizens who are economically active as workers or self-employed persons in the host Member State;
(b) Union citizens who have sufficient resources for themselves and their family members not to become a burden on the social assistance system of the host Member State during their period of residence and have comprehensive sickness insurance cover;
(c) Union citizens who are students and have comprehensive sickness insurance cover and who can give the assurance of sufficient resources not to become a burden on the social assistance system of the host Member State.

After five continuous years of legal residence in the host Member State, Union citizens obtain a right of permanent residence that is no longer subject to any of the above-mentioned conditions.[76] For workers or self-employed persons, who become pensioners or who stop working due to permanent incapacity, a period of less than five years is sufficient for obtaining the right of permanent residence.[77] The same applies to workers and self-employed persons who, after three years of continuous employment and residence in the host Member State, work in an employed or self-employed capacity in another Member State, while retaining their place of residence in the host Member State, to which they return, as a rule, each day, or at least once a week.[78]

2.2.2. FAMILY MEMBERS

All these rights also extend to the family members, irrespective of their nationality, provided that they belong to the family circle as defined in Article 2(2).[79] Special provisions for family members on the consequences of death or departure of the Union citizen, or divorce, annulment of marriage or termination of registered partnership are laid down in Articles 12 and 13 of the

---

[74]   Article 14(4) Citizens' Directive.
[75]   Article 7(1) Citizens' Directive.
[76]   Article 16 Citizens' Directive.
[77]   Article 17(1)(a)(b) Citizens' Directive.
[78]   Article 17(1)(c) Citizens' Directive.
[79]   See Articles 3, 4(1), 5(2), 6(2), 7(1d)(2)(4), 9, 17(3)(4) Citizens' Directive.

Directive. The circle of family members is laid down in Article 2(2). It defines family members as:

(a) the spouse;
(b) the registered partner, but only if the legislation of the Member State treats registered partnerships as equivalent to marriage;
(c) the direct descendants who are under the age of 21 or are dependants and those of the spouse or partner;
(d) the dependent direct relatives in the ascending line and those of the spouse or partner.

Although this enumeration is in itself consistent, it raises two problems. First, the definition of spouse is not the same in all Member States. This may lead to complications touching on fundamental differences between the Member States. In a growing number of Member States a marriage for same-sex spouses is considered valid, in other countries, it is not. Should those other countries just recognise same-sex marriages and confer a right of residence to the migrating partner, which would be an approach based on the primacy of free movement? Alternatively, should they rely on rules of private international law, which may enable a state to apply the private law of the host state to such unions and, accordingly, refuse to recognise same-sex marriages?

The second problem is that unmarried partners, who have not been registered as such, are not within the definition of family members. The position of those unmarried partners is only partly secured by Article 3(2)(b) of the Directive, which only obliges Member States to 'facilitate' entry and residence of other family members than defined in Article 2, including 'the partner with whom the Union citizen has a durable relationship, duly attested', the conditions of which must be laid down in national legislation. The same obligation to 'facilitate' goes for 'any other family members, irrespective of their nationality, not falling under the definition in point 2 of Article 2 who, in the country from which they have come, are dependants or members of the household of the Union citizen having the primary right of residence, or where serious health grounds strictly require the personal care of the family member by the Union citizen.'

In the *Rahman* judgment,[80] the Court of Justice analysed the impact of the word 'facilitate'. The Member States are not required to grant every application for entry or residence submitted by family members of a Union citizen who do not fall under the definition in Article 2(2) of that Directive, even if they show that they fall within the scope of Article 3(2). It is, however, incumbent upon the Member States to ensure that their legislation contains criteria that enable those persons to obtain a decision on their application for entry and residence that is founded on an extensive examination of their personal circumstances, and, in

---

[80]   ECJ 5 September 2012, *Rahman*, Case C-83/11.

the event of refusal, is justified by reasons. The Member States have a wide discretion when selecting those criteria, but the criteria must be consistent with the normal meaning of the term 'facilitate' and of the words used in Article 3(2), and must not deprive that provision of its effectiveness.

When unmarried partners are at issue, it should be borne in mind that the *Reed* judgment of the ECJ is still valid.[81] In *Reed*, the Court held the principle of equal treatment[82] to require that a Member State that permits the unmarried companions of its nationals, who are not themselves nationals of that Member State, to reside in its territory, cannot refuse to grant the same benefit to migrant workers who are nationals of other Member States. This means that for each Member State whose nationals have the right to have non-national unmarried partners with them, Union citizens should be treated the same way – but only to the extent to which national law of that State offers a residence right to unmarried partners. Family members, irrespective of their nationality, who are allowed to reside in a Member State on the basis of the Directive have, apart from the right to equal treatment, the right to take up employment or self-employment there.[83]

The question of whether a family member is dependant of the Union citizen with whom he or she wishes to reside must be assessed according to the situation in the state of origin. Dependency means, according to the *Jia* judgment, the need for material support of that Union citizen or his or her spouse in order to meet the essential needs in the state of origin.[84] The proof of the need for material support may be adduced by any appropriate means. The mere fact that the Union citizen undertakes to support the family member concerned need not be regarded as establishing the existence of the family members' situation of real dependence. According to the *Reyes* judgment,[85] the mere fact that a relative – due to personal circumstances such as age, education and health – is deemed to be well-placed to obtain employment in the Member State, and in addition, intends to start to work there, does not affect the interpretation of the requirement in that provision that he be a 'dependant'. On the other hand, a Member State cannot require a direct descendant, who is 21 years old or older, to prove that he tried unsuccessfully to obtain employment or to obtain subsistence support from the authorities of his country of origin.

The rights of family members are not in every aspect the same as those of the Union citizen with whom they reside. Family members who have the nationality of a third country are, according to Article 16(2) Citizens' Directive, entitled to a

---

81 ECJ 17 April 1986, *Reed*, Case 59/85.
82 The Court referred to Article 7 of the EEC Treaty (now Article 18 TFEU), in conjunction with Article 48 of the Treaty (now Article 45 TFEU) and Article 7(2) of Regulation 1612/68 (now Article 7(2) of Regulation 492/2011).
83 Article 23 Citizens' Directive.
84 ECJ 9 January 2007, *Jia*, Case C-1/05.
85 ECJ 16 January 2014, *Reyes*, Case C-423/12.

permanent residence status, if they have legally resided with the Union citizen in the host Member State for a 'continuous period' of five years. However, if they have been in prison during their stay in the Member State, the continuity of residence is interrupted. In the *Onuekwere* judgment,[86] the Court considered that the imposition of a prison sentence by a national court is such as to show the non-compliance by the person concerned with the values expressed by the society of the host Member State in its criminal law. The taking into consideration of periods of imprisonment for the purposes of the acquisition of the right of permanent residence by third-country family members of a Union citizen would 'clearly be contrary' to the aim pursued by Article 16(2) Citizens' Directive. Thus, the periods of imprisonment in the host Member State of a third-country national, who is a family member of a Union citizen who has acquired the right of permanent residence in that Member State during those periods, cannot be taken into consideration of the context of the acquisition by that national of the right of permanent residence for the purposes of Article 16(2) Citizens' Directive.

2.2.3. ADMINISTRATIVE FORMALITIES

The residence rights of Union citizens are not embodied in a residence permit. Union citizens derive these rights directly from Union law. However, after three months of residence, Member States *may* require Union citizens to register with the 'relevant authorities', whereupon a registration certificate is issued to them.[87] This requirement must be seen as corresponding to the practice in most Member States whereby citizens have the duty to have themselves entered on the population register, such as for the purpose of the right to vote.

When Union citizens have acquired the right of permanent residence, they are entitled to a document certifying this right.[88] This document is meant as proof that the EU citizen is entitled to important additional rights, such as access to social welfare or immunity from expulsion. For family members who do not possess the nationality of a Member State, the proof of the right of residence is somewhat differently shaped. After three months they must be given a 'residence card'.[89] When they obtain the right of permanent residence, a 'permanent residence card' must be issued to them.[90] The 'residence card' serves as evidence of the residence right of the family members, but it has a limited validity for five

---

[86]   ECJ 16 January 2014, *Onuekwere*, Case C-378/12.
[87]   Article 8 Citizens' Directive.
[88]   Article 19 Citizens' Directive.
[89]   Articles 9 and 10 Citizens' Directive.
[90]   Article 29 Citizens' Directive.

years or for the envisaged period of residence of the Union citizen if that period is less than five years.[91]

It is not clear from the wording of Article 11 taken alone whether the residence right is supposed to end after expiry of the period of validity of the residence card. The arrangement in Article 11(2) on the effect of temporary absences on the validity of the card could be taken to suggest that there is a link between the card and the right. However, in Article 14 of the Directive, which lays down more explicit rules on the validity and expiry of the right of residence, this link is notably absent. According to the latter provision, Union citizens and their family members have the short-term right of residence as long as they do not become an unreasonable burden on the social assistance system of the host Member State; and they have the right of residence for a longer period as long as they meet the conditions set out in Articles 7, 12 and 13. Since no reference in these provisions is made to a residence card, the existence of the residence right is apparently not dependent on the possession of a card. This is confirmed by Article 25, which categorically states that neither the possession of a certificate or card, nor the completion of an administrative formality may be made a precondition for the right, since residence rights may be attested by any other means of proof.[92]

2.2.4. TERMINATION OF RESIDENCE

The system of expiry of a right to residence is not always explicitly regulated in the Citizens' Directive. However, the following can be inferred: (a) the right to stay for three months would automatically have to end after three months, except for persons seeking work;[93] (b) the right to stay for a longer period expires, when the conditions are no longer met;[94] and (c) the right to permanent residence expires through absence from the host Member State for a period exceeding two consecutive years.[95]

The expiry of a residence right after the three-month period has no effect if the person concerned has – in the meantime – acquired a residence right on the basis of Article 7. A complication hereby is that it is also possible to acquire a right of residence on the basis of other provisions of Union law. Union citizens

---

[91]   Articles 10(1) and 11 Citizens' Directive.
[92]   This corresponds with the view of the ECJ, which in the case of *Royer*, held that: '[T]he right of nationals of one Member State to enter the territory of another Member State and to reside there is conferred directly, on any person falling within the scope of Community law, by the Treaty, especially Articles 48, 52 and 59, or, as the case may be, by its implementing provisions independently of any residence permit issued by the host State.' ECJ 8 April 1976, *Royer*, Case 48/75, para. 50.
[93]   Articles 6 and 14(1)(4) Citizens' Directive.
[94]   Article 14(2) Citizens' Directive.
[95]   Article 16(4) Citizens' Directive.

may – under circumstances – derive a residence right from Article 21 TFEU (see section 2.4). Another example is the right to reside of service recipients, who cannot be designated as workers or self-employed persons – and fall, therefore, outside the scope of Article 7 Citizens' Directive – but who have the right to freely receive services in another Member State in accordance with Article 56 TFEU. As the Treaty prevails, the Directive cannot exclude that recipients of services, like tourists or people receiving medical treatment, who may possibly overstay the three month period, derive a residence right directly from the Treaty (see further section 2.3.5).

Apart from expiry of the right to residence, there are two other ways through which residence rights may be terminated. The first is provided by Article 35 of the Directive, which authorises the Member States to refuse, terminate or withdraw any right in cases of abuse of rights or fraud. The issue of abuse of rights will be dealt with in section 2.2.9. A second way through which residence rights may be terminated is through expulsion and/or exclusion.

2.2.5. EXPULSION

Expulsion of Union citizens and their family members is only allowed by the Directive on two grounds: (a) if the residence right has expired;[96] or (b) if the right to entry and residence is legitimately restricted by the host Member State on grounds of public policy, public security or public health.[97] Expulsion on the ground that the residence right has expired is, however, limited by two further restrictions. An expulsion measure cannot be the automatic consequence of a Union citizen's or his or her family member's recourse to the social assistance system of the host Member State.[98] Secondly, an expulsion measure for expiry reasons may in no case be adopted against Union citizens who are workers or self-employed persons, or who have entered the host state to seek employment, including their family members.[99]

The restrictions on grounds of public policy, public security or public health are extensively dealt with in Chapter VI of the Citizens' Directive. The general principles concerning *public policy* and *public security* are laid down in Article 27. This provision codifies the extensive case law of the Court of Justice on the permissibility of invoking these Treaty exceptions. Public policy

---

[96]   Article 14(3)(4) Citizens' Directive.

[97]   Articles 27–33 Citizens' Directive.

[98]   Article 14(3) Citizens' Directive. This provision corresponds with the ECJ judgment in *Grzelczyk*, see paragraph 4.3.

[99]   Article 14(4) Citizens' Directive. If the Union citizens are seeking employment, they and their family members may not be expelled for as long as the Union citizens can provide evidence that they are continuing to seek employment and that they have a genuine chance of being engaged.

exceptions and public security exceptions cannot be invoked to serve economic ends; measures taken on these grounds have to comply with the principle of proportionality and must be based exclusively on the personal conduct of the individual concerned; previous criminal convictions cannot *per se* constitute grounds for taking such measures; and the personal conduct of the person must represent a genuine, present and sufficiently serious threat affecting one of the fundamental interests of society. Further, justifications for invoking the exceptions which are isolated from the particulars of the case, or that rely on considerations of general prevention, are not acceptable.[100] Before taking an expulsion decision on grounds of public policy or public security, the host Member State must, moreover, take account of considerations such as, how long the individual concerned has resided on its territory, his or her age, state of health, family and economic situation, social and cultural integration in the host Member State, and the extent of his or her links with the country of origin.[101]

For holders of a right of permanent residence, the criteria are even stricter than those to be applied to holders of the 'short-term' residence rights. An expulsion measure cannot be taken against these persons except on '*serious* grounds of public policy or public security'.[102] Thus, the danger emanating from these persons must be of a more severe nature and the ground of public health cannot serve to justify expulsion.

An even higher threshold applies to Union citizens who are minors or who have resided in the host Member State for the previous ten years. Article 28(3)a does not require that the residence has been *lawful*. However, the 10-year period of residence referred to in that provision must, in principle, be continuous and must be calculated by counting back from the date of the decision ordering the expulsion of the person concerned.[103] In order to determine whether a Union citizen has resided in the host Member State for the 10 years preceding the expulsion decision, all the relevant factors must be taken into account in each individual case, in particular, the duration of each period of absence from the host Member State, the cumulative duration and the frequency of those absences, and the reasons why the person concerned left the host Member State – reasons which may establish whether those absences involve the transfer to another State of the centre of the personal, family or occupational interests of the person concerned.[104]

The persons meant in Article 28(3) Citizens' Directive can only be expelled on '*imperative* grounds of *public security*', hence excluding the somewhat more amorphous and frequently invoked public policy exception. The Court of Justice has given some guidance on the meaning of this enhanced protection against

---

[100] Article 27(2) Citizens' Directive.
[101] Article 28(1) Citizens' Directive.
[102] Article 28(2) Citizens' Directive.
[103] ECJ 16 January 2014, *M.G.*, Case 400/12.
[104] ECJ 27 November 2010, *Tsakouridis*, Case C-145/09.

expulsion on grounds of public policy, in particular, by describing types of crimes falling within the ambit of 'serious grounds of public policy or public security' or 'imperative grounds of public security'. Namely: dealing in narcotics as part of an organised group[105] and the sexual exploitation of children.[106] The Court left open whether there is a relevant difference between 'serious grounds' and 'imperative' grounds of public security. From the case of *Tsakouridis*,[107] one may get the impression that there is no such difference. The Court interpreted Article 28(3) as meaning that the fight against crime in connection with dealing in narcotics as part of an organised group is capable of being covered by the concept of 'imperative grounds of public security', which may justify a measure expelling a Union citizen who has resided in the host Member State for the preceding 10 years. Also, Article 28(2) must be interpreted as meaning that the fight against crime in connection with dealing in narcotics as part of an organised group is covered by the concept of 'serious grounds of public policy or public security'.

In the case of *P.I.*,[108] the Court said that Article 28(3)(a) must be interpreted as meaning that it is open to the Member States to regard the sexual exploitation of children as constituting a particularly serious threat to one of the fundamental interests of society, which might pose a direct threat to the calm and physical security of the population, and thus be covered by the concept of 'imperative grounds of public security', capable of justifying an expulsion measure under Article 28(3), as long as the manner in which such offences were committed discloses particularly serious characteristics, which is a matter for the referring court to determine on the basis of an individual examination of the specific case before it.

Even if such serious crimes are at issue, the justification of any expulsion measure is conditional on the requirement that the personal conduct of the individual concerned must represent a genuine, present threat affecting one of the fundamental interests of society or of the host Member State, which implies, in general, the existence in the individual concerned of a propensity to act in the same way in the future. Before taking an expulsion decision, the host Member State must take account of considerations such as how long the individual concerned has resided on its territory, his/her age, state of health, family and economic situation, social and cultural integration into that State, and the extent of his/her links with the country of origin. Periods during which a Union citizen stayed in prison may have a negative impact in two ways.

According to the *M.G.* judgment,[109] a period of imprisonment is, in principle, capable both of interrupting the continuity of the period of residence for the purposes of Article 28(3)a and of affecting the decision regarding the grant of the

---

[105] ECJ 27 November 2010, *Tsakouridis*, Case C-145/09.
[106] ECJ 22 May 2012, *P.I.*, Case C-348/09.
[107] ECJ 27 November 2010, *Tsakouridis*, Case C-145/09.
[108] ECJ 22 May 2012, *P.I.*, Case C-348/09.
[109] ECJ 16 January 2014, *M.G.*, Case 400/12.

enhanced protection provided for thereunder, even where the person concerned resided in the host Member State for the 10 years prior to imprisonment. However, the fact that that person resided in the host Member State for the 10 years prior to imprisonment may be taken into consideration as part of the overall assessment required in order to determine whether the integrating links previously forged with the host Member State have been broken.

The *public health* exception is carefully delimited and leaves little room for manoeuvre by the Member States. It can only serve as a ground for restricting freedom of movement in the case of (1) diseases with epidemic potential, as defined by the relevant instruments of the World Health Organisation; and (2) other infectious diseases or contagious parasitic diseases, if they are the subject of protection provisions applying to nationals of the host Member State. In other words, the diseases must have been nationally or internationally recognised as endangering public health. Moreover, diseases occurring after a three-month period from the date of arrival can no longer constitute grounds for expulsion.[110]

2.2.6. PROHIBITION TO LEAVE

The right to leave the territory of a Member State and to a passport or identity card is secured in Article 4 Citizens' Directive. This right is part and parcel of the general right to free movement of Union citizens given in Article 21 TFEU. In some Member States, legislation exists enabling the authorities to restrict the right of their nationals to leave the territory. In Romania, such legislation was applied to a Romanian man, *Georghe Jipa*, who had been expelled from Belgium for illegal presence on the territory in the period before Romania's accession to the EU. In its judgment this case, the Court stated that Article 18 of the Treaty establishing the European Community (now: Article 21 TFEU) and the Citizens' Directive do not preclude national legislation that allows the right of a national of a Member State to travel to another Member State to be restricted on the ground that he has previously been repatriated from the latter Member State on account of his 'illegal residence' there, provided that the personal conduct of that national constitutes a genuine, present and sufficiently serious threat to one of the fundamental interests of society and that the restrictive measure envisaged is appropriate to ensure the achievement of the objective it pursues and does not go beyond what is necessary to attain it. While in principle allowing such restrictions, the Court confined the room for applying them by posing strict conditions.

A prohibition to leave the Member State for reasons of criminal conduct will, under circumstances, be permitted. In the case of *Gaydarov*,[111] the Court stated

---

[110]   Article 29(1)(2) Citizens' Directive.
[111]   ECJ 17 November 2011, *Gaydarov*, Case C-430/10. See also ECJ 10 July 2008, *Jipa*, Case C-33/07.

that Article 21 TFEU and Article 27 of the Citizens' Directive do not preclude national legislation that permits the restriction of the right of a national of a Member State to travel to another Member State, in particular, on the ground that he has been convicted of a criminal offence of narcotic drug trafficking in another State, provided that (i) the personal conduct of that national constitutes a genuine, present and sufficiently serious threat affecting one of the fundamental interests of society, (ii) the restrictive measure envisaged is appropriate to ensure the achievement of the objective it pursues and does not go beyond what is necessary to attain it, and (iii) that measure is subject to effective judicial review permitting a determination of its legality as regards matters of fact and law in the light of the requirements of European Union law.

Less room is there for legislation barring exit from a Member State for reasons of safeguarding the collection of taxes. In the *Aladzhov* case,[112] the Court added to the criteria mentioned in the *Gaydarov* judgment, that a restriction to travel, based on tax purposes, must also comply with the condition that the objective thus pursued does not solely serve economic ends. Further, the Court made clear that such a restriction could only in exceptional cases be allowed. A travel restriction on the ground that a tax liability of a company of which the EU citizen is one of the managers has not been settled is precluded if it is founded solely on the existence of the tax liability of the company of which he is one of the joint managers, and on the basis of that status alone.

2.2.7. EXCLUSION

Apart from being expelled, a person may also be excluded from the territory of a Member State. An exclusion order is a prohibition to return to or to be present on the territory for a limited or unlimited period of time. According to Article 32 Citizens' Directive, exclusion orders are not, as such, precluded. Member States may even exclude an individual from the territory pending the redress procedure against an expulsion measure, but they may not prevent the individual from submitting his or her defence in person, except when his or her appearance would jeopardise public policy or public security, or when the appeal or judicial review concerns a denial of entry to the territory.[113] Persons excluded on grounds of public policy or public security are entitled to submit an application to have the exclusion order lifted after a reasonable period, depending on the circumstances, and in any event, after three years from enforcement of the final exclusion order, by putting forward arguments to establish that there has been a material change in the circumstances from those that justified the decision

---

[112] ECJ 17 November 2011, *Aladzhov*, Case C-434/10.
[113] Article 31(4) Citizens' Directive.

ordering their exclusion.[114] Member States must decide upon such a request within 6 months. The persons concerned have no right of entry to the territory of the Member State while their application is being considered.[115]

In the Returns Directive, which is not applicable to Union citizens and members of their families,[116] the term 'entry ban' is used. According to Article 3 of that Directive, an entry ban is an administrative or judicial decision prohibiting entry into, and stay in, the territory of the Member States for a specified period, accompanying a return decision. It is uncertain whether – and if so to what extent – the concepts of an 'exclusion order' and 'entry ban' overlap each other, but it is reasonable to assume that the concepts are identical.

2.2.8. PROCEDURAL SAFEGUARDS

Procedural safeguards with regard to restrictions on the freedom of movement and residence are laid down in Articles 30 and 31 of the Directive. The person subject to a restriction must be notified in writing of the decision, in such a way that he/she is able to understand its content and implications. The person must be informed, precisely and in full, of the grounds on which the decision is based, unless this is contrary to the interests of state security. The notification must specify the court or administrative authority with which the person concerned may lodge an appeal, the time limit for the appeal and, where applicable, the time allowed for the person to leave the territory of the Member State. Save in duly substantiated cases of urgency, the time allowed to leave the territory should not be less than one month from the date of notification.[117]

The person concerned should have access to a judicial redress procedure in the host Member State to appeal against or seek review of any decision taken on the grounds of public policy, public security or public health.[118] Where the application for appeal or judicial review of an expulsion decision is accompanied by an application for an interim order to suspend enforcement of expulsion, actual removal from the territory cannot take place until such time as the decision on the interim order has been taken, except in three cases: (a) where the expulsion decision is based on a previous judicial decision; (b) where the person concerned has had previous access to judicial review; or (c) where the expulsion decision is based on imperative grounds of public security.[119]

The redress procedures must allow for examination of the legality of the decision, as well as of the facts and circumstances on which the proposed

---

[114]   Article 32(1) Citizens' Directive.
[115]   Article 32(2) Citizens' Directive.
[116]   Article 2(3) Returns Directive in connection with Article 2 point 5 Schengen Borders Code.
[117]   Article 30 Citizens' Directive.
[118]   Article 31(1) Citizens' Directive.
[119]   Article 31(2) Citizens' Directive.

measure is based. It should ensure that the decision is not disproportionate. The person's personal circumstances, the length of time he or she has resided in the host state and, in the case of a minor, the best interests of the child, should thereby be taken into account.[120] According to the *Z.Z.* judgment,[121] appropriate procedural guarantees must be offered when a decision to expel an EU citizen or to refuse (re-)entry for reasons of state security, is based on secret information. If, in exceptional cases, a national authority opposes precise and full disclosure to the person concerned of the grounds which constitute the basis of a decision taken under Article 27 of the Citizens' Directive, by invoking reasons of State security, the court with jurisdiction in the Member State concerned must have at its disposal and apply techniques and rules of procedural law which accommodate, on the one hand, legitimate State security considerations regarding the nature and sources of the information taken into account in the adoption of such a decision, and, on the other hand, the need to ensure sufficient compliance with the person's procedural rights, such as the right to be heard and the adversarial principle. To that end, the Member States are required, first, to provide for effective judicial review both of the existence and validity of the reasons invoked by the national authority with regard to State security and of the legality of the decision, and, second, to prescribe techniques and rules relating to that review. The competent national authority has the task of proving, in accordance with the national procedural rules, that State security would, in fact, be compromised by precise and full disclosure to the person concerned of the grounds that constitute the basis of the decision and of the related evidence. There is no presumption that the reasons invoked by a national authority exist and are valid.

2.2.9. ABUSE OF RIGHTS

Member States may adopt all necessary measures to refuse, terminate or withdraw any right conferred by the Directive in the case of abuse of rights or fraud, such as marriages of convenience. Any such measure must be proportionate and subject to the procedural safeguards provided for in Articles 30 and 31, discussed above.[122]

The Court of Justice has, on a number of occasions, given its opinion on the issue of abuse of rights. In the *Surinder Singh* judgment, the Court recalled that 'the facilities created by the Treaty cannot have the effect of allowing the persons who benefit from them to evade the application of national legislation and of prohibiting Member States from taking the measures necessary to prevent such

---

[120] Articles 31(3) and 28 Citizens' Directive.
[121] ECJ 4 June 2013, *Z.Z.*, Case C-300/11.
[122] Article 35 Citizens' Directive.

abuse.'[123] In *Akrich*, the Court explained however, that to make use of Union law to gain a privileged status regarding the right to be accompanied by family members must not be automatically labelled as abuse:

> [I]t should be mentioned that the motives which may have prompted a worker of a Member State to seek employment in another Member State are of no account as regards his right to enter and reside in the territory of the latter State provided that he there pursues or wishes to pursue an effective and genuine activity (...).
>
> Nor are such motives relevant in assessing the legal situation of the couple at the time of their return to the Member State of which the worker is a national. Such conduct cannot constitute an abuse within the meaning of paragraph 24 of the *Singh* judgment even if the spouse did not, at the time when the couple installed itself in another Member State, have a right to remain in the Member State of which the worker is a national.
>
> Conversely, there would be an abuse if the facilities afforded by Community law in favour of migrant workers and their spouses were invoked in the context of marriages of convenience entered into in order to circumvent the provisions relating to entry and residence of nationals of non-Member States.[124]

In the *Chen* case the Court confirmed that the mere making use of legal facilities provided by Union law should not be labelled as 'abuse'. In that case, a Chinese mother, who had previously resided in Britain, gave birth to her child on the soil of Northern Ireland, to the effect that her baby acquired Irish nationality. When the child and the mother returned to mainland United Kingdom, the issue was whether the baby might have a residence right under Union law. The British government argued before the Court that Mrs. Chen's move to Northern Ireland, with the aim of having her child acquire the nationality of another Member State, constituted an attempt improperly to exploit the provisions of Union law. The Court rejected this argument. It was true, according to the Court, that the purpose of Mrs. Chen's stay in Northern Ireland was to create a situation in which the child she was expecting would be able to acquire the nationality of another Member State, in order thereafter to secure for her child and for herself a long-term right to reside in the United Kingdom. The Court continued:

> 'Nevertheless, under international law, it is for each Member State, having due regard to Community law, to lay down the conditions for the acquisition and loss of nationality (...). None of the parties that submitted observations to the Court questioned either the legality, or the fact of the child's acquisition of Irish nationality. Moreover, it is not permissible for a Member State to restrict the effects of the grant of the nationality of another Member State by imposing an additional condition for

---

[123]   ECJ 7 July 1992, *Surinder Singh*, Case C-370/90, para. 24.
[124]   ECJ 23 September 2003, *Akrich*, Case C-60/00, paras. 55, 56, 57.

recognition of that nationality with a view to the exercise of the fundamental freedoms provided for in the Treaty (…).'[125]

Accordingly, baby Chen (having appropriate sickness assurance and being in the care of a parent having sufficient resources) could invoke her EU right to reside in the United Kingdom. And since refusal to allow Mrs. Chen to reside with her child 'would deprive the child's right of residence of any useful effect', a right of residence should also be granted to the mother, even though Mrs. Chen could not claim to be a 'dependent' relative of the child in the ascending line.[126]

Concluding, it may be inferred from these judgments, that only marriages of convenience have as yet been recognised as constituting 'abuse'.

2.3. TREATY FREEDOMS

2.3.1. FREE MOVEMENT RIGHTS IN THE CASE LAW OF THE COURT OF JUSTICE

The Citizens' Directive described above is meant to be a compilation of the law governing the free movement of Union citizens and their families as it has developed since 1957. To a considerable extent, the case law of the Court of Justice on the free movement of persons has been incorporated into the Directive. For a number of reasons, it remains important to study the case law of the Court on former Directives and treaty provisions relating to the free movement of persons. In the first place, case law interpreting former legislation is relevant for the interpretation of the new Directive as well, because a number of provisions in the new Directive are copied from Directives that have now been repealed. Secondly, interpretations of primordial provisions of the Treaty obviously remain binding and have not all found expression in the Citizens' Directive. For example, the Directive does not explicitly deal with freedom of services laid down in Article 56 TFEU. Service providers do not need to establish themselves in another Member State in order to fall within the scope of application of Article 56 TFEU, and fall beyond the scope of application of the Citizens' Directive if they stay in their home country. Further, the Citizens' Directive does not regulate the residence right of a recipient of services who does move to another Member State, for instance, to receive medical treatment. In principle, this period is not longer than the term during which the service is provided, but this criterion may be difficult to apply especially for recipients of a range of short-term services like tourists. Thirdly, the Court of Justice has often

---

[125]   ECJ 19 October 2004, *Chen*, Case C-200/02, paras. 37–39.
[126]   *Ibid*, paras. 44–46.

opened up new horizons through its case law. It is useful, therefore, to gain insight into the approach of the Court.

In the following sections, the case law on the free movement of workers (Article 45 TFEU), the freedom of establishment (Article 49 TFEU) and the freedom to provide services (Article 56 TFEU), is examined. Further, the relationship between free movement rights and the prohibition of discrimination on grounds of nationality (Article 18) and the fundamental provision on European citizenship (Article 21(1)) is explored. But first, some typical features of the Court's case law on free movement are presented. In quotes from the Court, the term 'Community law' will often be used. Community law refers to the law under the Treaty establishing the European Community, which ceased to exist when the Treaty of Lisbon entered into force. Translated into the present situation, the term may be understood as referring to Union law.

2.3.2. GENERAL APPROACH OF THE COURT

One of the characteristic elements in the case law of the Court of Justice is the expansive interpretation of provisions on fundamental treaty rights and, conversely, the restrictive interpretation of exceptions allowed under these rights. In doing so, the Court has removed obstacles to the effective exertion of freedom of movement. For instance, in the *Reyners* judgment, the Court held:

> Having regard to the fundamental character of freedom of establishment and the rule of equal treatment with nationals in the system of the Treaty, the *exceptions* allowed by the first paragraph of Article 55 [current Article 49 TFEU] *cannot be given a scope which would exceed the objective* for which this exemption clause was inserted.[127]

The Court added that any restriction on the freedom of establishment:

> must (...) take into account *the Community character of the limits* imposed by Article 55 on the exceptions permitted to the freedom of establishment in order *to avoid the effectiveness of the Treaty being defeated by unilateral provisions of Member States.*[128]

Accordingly, the Court made clear that the exception to freedom of establishment for activities connected with the exercise of official authority, as currently provided for by Article 49 TFEU, must be restrictively interpreted. It found that a lawyer's profession does not involve a direct and specific connection with the exercise of official authority, and cannot, therefore, be brought under

---

[127] ECJ 21 June 1974, *Reyners*, Case 2/74, para. 43, emphasis added.
[128] *Ibid*, para. 50, emphasis added.

this exception. Since *Reyners*, it has been established as a general rule that all restrictions on the freedom of movement must be restrictively interpreted.[129]

Another characteristic approach of the Court of Justice is that terms which are closely connected with fundamental freedoms may not be interpreted by the Member States with reference to national legislation. In the *Levin* judgment, for instance, the Court confirmed that the term 'worker' has a community meaning (in terms of today: a Union law meaning):

> '[T]he terms 'worker' and 'activity as an employed person' may not be defined by reference to the national laws of the Member States but have a community meaning. If that were not the case, the community rules on freedom of movement for workers would be frustrated, as the meaning of those terms could be fixed and modified unilaterally, without any control by the Community institutions, by national laws which would thus be able to exclude at will certain categories of persons from the benefit of the treaty.'[130]

2.3.3. FREE MOVEMENT OF WORKERS

Article 45 TFEU articulates that 'Freedom of movement for workers shall be secured within the Union'. This leaves no doubt that the free movement of workers is a paramount objective of the Union's common market. Article 45 provides not only for a right of residence but also for equal treatment in working conditions. As a result of the case law of the Court of Justice, the existence of the right to legal residence in the host Member State is directly linked to qualifying as a 'worker'. Effective and genuine economic activity on the part of an EU citizen creates a right to enter and to reside, directly originating from Union law. In the Citizens' Directive, the right of residence for workers is laid down in Article 7(1)(a).[131] This right must be interpreted in the light of case law of the ECJ on the term 'worker' and on Article 45 TFEU in general.

The right to free movement of workers is subject to limitations justified on grounds of public policy, public security and public health (see section 2.2.5). Further, the provisions of Article 45 shall, according to its fourth paragraph, not apply to employment in the public service. The Court of Justice has ruled that this exception to the freedom of workers and the freedom of establishment must be restricted to those activities which in themselves involve a direct and specific connection with the exercise of official authority.[132] Employment in the public service, within the meaning of this Article, must be connected with the specific

---

[129]   See also e.g. ECJ 4 December 1974, *Van Duyn*, Case 41/74, para. 18; and ECJ 12 February 1974, *Sotgiu*, Case 152/73, para. 5.
[130]   ECJ 23 March 1982, Case 53/81, para. 11.
[131]   See also Articles 14(1) and 24(2) Citizens' Directive.
[132]   ECJ 21 June 1974, *Reyners*, Case 2/74.

activities of the public service in so far as it is entrusted with the exercise of powers conferred by public law and with responsibility for safeguarding the general interests of the state, including the specific interests of local authorities such as municipalities.[133] The mere fact that a person is employed by the government is not decisive.

Much of the case law on Article 45 concerns the personal scope of the provision: who, exactly, is a worker, and thus entitled to the rights granted by this Article? According to the Court, workers are natural persons engaged in an employment relationship. The essential feature of an employment relationship is that for a certain period of time a person performs services for and under the direction of another person, in return for which he receives remuneration.[134] It follows that the nature of the legal relationship between the worker and the employer is not decisive for the purposes of determining whether a person is a worker within the meaning of Union law.[135] Among others, the Court has ruled that part-time workers, on-call workers and trainees may all derive rights from Article 39.[136]

Jobseekers can, under certain conditions, also invoke Article 45. In *Antonissen* the Court found it:

> not contrary to the provisions of Community law governing the free movement of workers for the legislation of a Member State to provide that a national of another Member State who entered the first State in order to seek employment may be required to leave the territory of that State (subject to appeal) if he has not found employment there after six months, unless the person concerned provides evidence that he is continuing to seek employment and that he has genuine chances of being engaged.[137]

This rule has now been laid down in Article 14(4) Citizens' Directive. Although an EU citizen looking for a job in another Member State cannot be expelled, his right to residence is less strong than if he had found work. In the *Collins* judgment, the Court made clear that the right to seek employment and consequently to move within the Community, does not entail a right to a residence card, and that the Union citizen seeking work has, in principle, no right to social assistance.[138] This runs parallel with Article 24(2) Citizens' Directive.

Similar considerations were made by the Court with regard to Union citizens who are in prison. The fact that prisoners are temporarily unavailable to the

---

133 ECJ 26 May 1982, *Commission v. Belgium*, Case 149/79.
134 *E.g.* ECJ 3 July 1986, *Lawrie-Blum*, Case 66/85, paras. 16 and 17.
135 The quote is from *Birden*, ECJ 26 November 1998, C-1/97, para. 25.
136 *E.g.* ECJ 23 March 1982, *Levin*, Case C-53/81; ECJ 26 February 1992, *Raulin*, Case C-357/89; ECJ 3 July 1986, *Lawrie-Blum*, Case 66/85.
137 ECJ 26 February 1991, *Antonissen*, Case C-292/89, para. 22.
138 ECJ 23 March 2004, *Collins*, Case C-138/02.

employment market does not automatically mean that they can no longer benefit from Article 45, provided that the person resumes working within a reasonable time after his release.[139]

To qualify as a worker, it is not imperative that one earns the local minimum income. In the *Levin* case,[140] the Court held that the provisions of Union law relating to the freedom of movement for workers also cover a national of a Member State who pursues, within the territory of another Member State, an activity as an employed person which yields an income lower than that which, in the latter state, is considered as the minimum required for subsistence. This is the case whether that person supplements the income from his activity as an employed person with other income so as to arrive to that minimum, or is satisfied with means of support lower than the said minimum, provided that he pursues an activity as an employed person that is effective and genuine. Later, in the *Kempf* case, the Court specified that the status of 'worker' is not lost when the worker enjoys supplementary income from social benefits.[141]

Although the right to free movement entitles the worker to a residence permit, the right to reside is not dependent on the issuing of this permit. The Court has made clear that a right of residence is conferred directly by the Treaty and exists independently of the issue of a residence permit.[142] In the case of *Sagulo and others* the Court ruled that issuing an EEC residence card has a merely declaratory character.[143] In *Pieck*, the Court held that:

> the right of Community workers to enter the territory of a Member State which Community law confers may not be made subject to the issue of a clearance to this effect by the authorities of that Member State.[144]

The principle that free movement rights are acquired independently from residence permits or other entry clearances is laid down in Article 25 Citizens' Directive.

2.3.4. FREEDOM OF ESTABLISHMENT

Within the framework of Articles 49–55 TFEU, restrictions on the freedom of establishment of nationals of a Member State in the territory of another Member State shall be prohibited. Such prohibition shall also apply to restrictions on the

---

[139]   ECJ 10 February 2000, *Nazli*, Case C-340/97, para. 40–41.
[140]   ECJ 23 March 1982, *Levin*, Case C-53/81.
[141]   ECJ 3 June 1986, *Kempf*, Case 139/85.
[142]   ECJ 8 April 1976, *Royer*, Case 48/75, paras. 31–33.
[143]   ECJ 14 July 1977, *Sagulo and others*, Case 8/77.
[144]   ECJ 3 July 1980, *Pieck*, Case C-157/79, para. 8.

setting-up of branches or subsidiaries by nationals of any Member State established in the territory of another Member State.

Whereas the term 'worker' refers to natural persons engaged in an employment relationship under the direction of another person, 'freedom of establishment' applies to self-employed persons. 'Establishment' is defined by the Court of Justice as 'participating, on a stable and continuous basis, in the economic life of a Member State other than his state of origin and to profit thereof, in the sphere of activities as self-employed persons.'[145] The definition of a self-employed person is, as it were, the opposite of the definition of a worker. All economic activity that is not employed activity is self-employed activity. In Article 7(1)(a) Citizens' Directive self-employed persons are granted the same residence right as workers. This is in accordance with Article 49 TFEU. It should be borne in mind that the right to establishment laid down in the TFEU extends to legal persons (companies and firms) as well. Legal persons are not covered by the Citizens' Directive, which only applies to EU citizens and their family members. Case law on the right to establishment often relates to questions about the right of companies to transfer the seat of the company to another Member State, to set up branches or subsidiaries, or with diplomas and requirements for starting a business in a Member State. These issues fall outside the scope of this book.

2.3.5. FREEDOM TO PROVIDE AND RECEIVE SERVICES

Article 56 TFEU prohibits restrictions on the freedom to provide services within the Union in respect of nationals of Member States who are established in a state of the EU other than that of the person for whom the services are intended. Providers of services are self-employed persons, who are not covered by Article 49 TFEU. The difference between persons making use of the freedom of establishment and service providers is that the latter do not establish themselves in another Member State, but temporarily provide cross-border services to a person established in the other Member State.

The scope of the freedom to provide services has been substantially widened by the Court of Justice. It is now understood to apply to four different situations: the situation in which the service provider travels to another Member State;[146] the

---

[145] ECJ 30 November 1995, *Gebhard*, case C-55/94, para. 25; ECJ 12 December 1996, *Broede*, case C-3/95, para. 20. Note that the Services Directive provides a slightly different definition: 'establishment' means the actual pursuit of an economic activity, as referred to in Article 43 of the Treaty, by the provider for an indefinite period and through a stable infrastructure from where the business of providing services is actually carried out.' Article 4(5) Directive 2006/123/EC.

[146] ECJ 3 December 1974, *Van Binsbergen*, Case 33/74.

situation in which the service recipient travels to another Member State;[147] the situation in which both the service provider and the service recipient travel to a third Member State;[148] and the situation in which the service itself moves.[149] The last situation was also relevant in the *Carpenter* case,[150] in which the Court ruled that a businessman who provided services to advertisers established in other Member States, availed himself of the right to freely provide services guaranteed by the TFEU, despite the fact that he did not leave the Member State in which he was established.

Although the TFEU only speaks of the provision of services, the Court made clear that *service recipients* are also covered by Article 56.[151] Tourists, persons receiving medical treatment and persons travelling for the purpose of education may all be regarded as recipients of services.[152] Decisive is whether the service received is provided for remuneration and is not covered by any of the other freedoms such as capital or goods (see Article 57). In Article 7(1)(a) of the Citizens' Directive, no distinction is made between self-employed persons who are providers of services and self-employed persons using their right of establishment. Strikingly, the right to the free movement of recipients of services is not mentioned in the Citizens' Directive. However, according to the *Oulane* judgment, the rights of recipients of services laid down in Articles 4(2) and 6 of Directive 73/148 (which is repealed as of 30 April 2006) have not been altered by the new Directive, as they apparently derive the rights of service recipients directly from Article 56 TFEU.[153] As we will see below, the Services Directive, which was adopted in 2006, does explicitly mention the right to free movement of service recipients.

The criterion that employment must be 'effective and genuine' for an employee to qualify as a 'worker' in the sense of the Treaty (laid down in the *Levin* judgment) is, *mutatis mutandis*, also applicable to self-employed persons. This is clear from the *Carpenter* judgment, in which the Court deemed it relevant that providing cross-border services was 'a significant proportion' of Mr. Carpenter's business.[154]

Persons who continuously provide services in another Member State will normally be covered by Article 56, if it can be established that they perform self-employed activities on a stable and continuous basis. The question might be asked whether continuously *receiving* services in another Member State will also lead to a continuous residence right. In the *Zhu and Chen* judgment already

---

147 ECJ 31 January 1984, *Luisi and Carbone*, Joined Cases 286/82 and 26/83.
148 ECJ 26 February 1991, *Commission v. France (tourist guides)*, Case C-154/89.
149 ECJ 26 April 1988, *Bond van Adverteerders*, Case 352/85.
150 See *Carpenter*, ECJ 11 July 2002, Case C-60/00.
151 This was first established in ECJ 31 January 1984, *Luisi and Carbone*, Case 286/82.
152 *Ibid*. See also ECJ 2 February 1989, *Cowan*, Case 186/87, para. 15.
153 ECJ 17 February 2005, *Oulane*, Case C-215/03.
154 ECJ 11 July 2002, *Carpenter*, Case C-60/00.

discussed above, the Court gave reasons why this is highly unlikely to happen. The question was whether baby Catherine could derive a residence right from receiving childcare services. The Court considered:

> According to the case law of the Court, the provisions on freedom to provide services do not cover the situation of a national of a Member State who establishes his principal residence in the territory of another Member State with a view to receiving services there for an indefinite period (...). The childcare services to which the national court refers fall precisely within that case.
>
> As regards the medical services that Catherine is receiving on a temporary basis, it must be observed that, under the first subparagraph of Article 4(2) of Directive 73/148, the right of residence of persons receiving services by virtue of the freedom to provide services is co-terminous with the duration of the period for which they are provided. Consequently, that Directive cannot in any event serve as a basis for a right of residence of indefinite duration of the kind with which the main proceedings are concerned.[155]

2.3.6. POSTING OF WORKERS DIRECTIVE AND SERVICES DIRECTIVE

The right to provide services implies, for companies, a certain right to bring employees to another Member State. In the *Vander Elst* case[156] the Court concluded from what are now Articles 56 and 57 TFEU, that no work permit may be required for third-country nationals who are employed on a regular basis by a company providing services (with those employees) in another Member State. The aspect of posting of workers in another Member State is not dealt with in the Citizens' Directive, but in the Posting of Workers Directive (Directive 96/71/EC). This Directive facilitates the provision of services by posting workers in another Member State, by providing that short-term social protection such as minimum wages and conditions on health and safety at work are governed by the rules of the Member State where the services are provided, while long-term benefits, such as pension and unemployment contributions, remain governed by the law of the home Member State.

Specific provisions on the freedom to provide services, including the right of free access to another Member State, are, furthermore, laid down in Directive 2006/123/EC on services in the internal market, better known as the Services Directive. The Directive lays down a definition of what services are, and provides specific provisions on the right of access to another Member State for both service providers and service recipients.[157] Most of the Directive's provisions are

---

[155]   ECJ 19 October 2004, *Zhu and Chen*, Case C-200/02, paras. 22, 23.
[156]   ECJ 9 August 1994, *Vander Elst*, Case C-43/93.
[157]   See, especially, Articles 16 and 19 Directive 2006/123/EC.

devoted to the abolishment of legal or administrative barriers regarding cross-border services, the categories of services that are excluded from the freedom to provide services, and the harmonisation of quality standards of services.

2.3.7. PROHIBITION OF DISCRIMINATION ON GROUNDS OF NATIONALITY

Within the scope of application of the Treaties, and without prejudice to any special provisions contained therein, Article 18 TFEU prohibits any discrimination on grounds of nationality. The prohibition of discrimination on grounds of nationality has a wide impact on Union law. Although the prohibition contains no limitation as to the nationalities covered, the Court of Justice has, as yet, only taken the nationalities of the Member States into consideration in the application of Article 18. In the *Vatsouras and Koupatantze* judgment,[158] the Court considered that Article 18 TFEU concerns situations falling within the scope of Union law, in which a national of one Member State suffers discriminatory treatment in relation to nationals of another Member State solely on the basis of his nationality, and is not intended to apply to cases of a possible difference in treatment between nationals of Member States and nationals of non-member countries who are resident in the host Member State. Accordingly, the standard for measuring discrimination is the treatment of the nationals of a host Member State.

For the right of free movement of EU citizens, the importance of Article 18 is shown in a vast array of judgments of the Court of Justice. It follows from these judgments that the prohibition of discrimination on grounds of nationality can be directly invoked and may even lead to a right of residence. In the *Reyners* judgment, the Court held:

> The rule on equal treatment with nationals is one of the fundamental legal provisions of the Community. As a reference to a set of legislative provisions effectively applied by the country of establishment to its own nationals, the rule is, by its essence, capable of being directly invoked by nationals of all the other Member States.[159]

Non-discrimination was also the decisive principle in the *Reed* judgment.[160] A Member State offering its nationals the possibility of obtaining permission for their unmarried partner to reside on its territory, cannot refuse that same benefit to migrating workers who have the nationality of another Member State. Here, the potential impact was shown of a non-discrimination norm creating an

---

[158] ECJ 4 June 2009, *Vatsouras and Koupatantze,* Cases C/22–08 and C/23–08, para. 52.
[159] ECJ 21 June 1974, *Reyners*, Case 2–74, paras. 24, 25.
[160] ECJ 17 April 1986, *Reed*, Case 59/85.

obligation for Member States to offer a right to residence to EU citizens on similar terms as granted to nationals. In the *Raulin* judgment, the Court went one step further, by deriving directly from the prohibition of discrimination on grounds of nationality a right of residence for a student residing in another Member State, as this right was conditional on being able to have access to vocational training on equal footing as nationals. The Court considered that:

> [T]he right of residence of a student who is a national of a Member State is merely a corollary to the right of non-discriminatory access to vocational training and that right of residence is therefore confined to what is necessary to allow the person concerned to pursue vocational training.[161]

This meant that Ms. *Raulin*, of French nationality, who had worked as a waitress in the Netherlands and was subsequently admitted to a full-time study in visual arts in Amsterdam, had a right to reside in the Netherlands for the duration of that study. In a later judgment, the Court confirmed its findings in *Raulin*, and ruled that Article 12 TEC (now Article 18 TFEU) should be considered the legal basis for the Directive on the right to residence of students.[162]

2.3.8. RIGHTS OF FAMILY MEMBERS

As we have seen, the rights of EU citizens to enter and stay in other Member States extend to their family members, regardless of their nationalities. The case law of the Court of Justice on the rights of family members did as yet only relate to *third-country nationals* claiming a right of residence as a family member of a Union citizen. The position of family members who had EU nationality themselves has never been questioned before the Court of Justice. That is not surprising, whereas family members who themselves possess the nationality of a Member State already have strong residence rights of their own and rarely need to rely on rules protecting their position as relatives.

The right of a Union citizen to be accompanied by his relatives is not expressly laid down in the TFEU. In the *Carpenter* judgment, the Court characterised the protection of family life as a means of eliminating obstacles to the exercise of the free movement rights of Union citizens:

> [T]he Community legislature has recognised the importance of ensuring the protection of the family life of nationals of the Member States in order to eliminate obstacles to the exercise of the fundamental freedoms guaranteed by the Treaty, as is

---

[161]   ECJ 26 February 1992, *Raulin*, Case C-357/89, para. 39.
[162]   ECJ 7 July 1992, *Parliament v. Council*, Case C-295/90. Due to the wrong choice of legal basis, Directive 90/366/EEC was annulled and replaced by Directive 93/96 (now repealed by Citizens' Directive).

particularly apparent from the provisions of the Council regulations and directives on the freedom of movement of employed and self-employed workers within the Community.[163]

The obvious reasoning is that persons who would like to make use of their free movement rights could be inclined not to do so when their family members are not allowed to follow them. The rights for family members are presently laid down in Article 3, read together with Article 2(2) of the Citizens' Directive. However, this Directive is only applicable where a Union citizen exercises his right of freedom of movement by becoming established in a Member State other than the Member State of which he is a national. The Citizens' Directive does not confer a derived right of residence on third-country nationals who are family members of a Union citizen in the Member State of which that citizen is a national.[164]

The right to family reunification for Union citizens has always been dealt with by the Court as self-explanatory, a right that rather has to be facilitated than restricted. In the *MRAX* judgment, the Court ruled that the rights of spouses are not dependent on being in the possession of valid travel documents or visa, provided that they can prove their identity and marital status:

> [A] Member State may not send back at the border a third-country national who is married to a national of a Member State and attempts to enter its territory without being in possession of a valid identity card or passport or, if necessary, a visa, where he is able to prove his identity and the conjugal ties and there is no evidence to establish that he represents a risk to the requirements of public policy, public security or public health within the meaning of [applicable provisions of Community law].[165]

Member States are not, further, according to the *MRAX* judgment, permitted to refuse a residence permit and to issue an expulsion order against a third-country national who is able to furnish proof of his identity and of his marriage to a national of a Member State, on the sole ground that he has entered the territory of the Member State concerned unlawfully.[166] Moreover, a Member State may neither refuse a residence permit nor issue an expulsion order on the sole ground that the visa expired before the third-country national applied for a residence permit.[167]

Though the rights of family members were primarily perceived as a corollary of the rights of the Union citizens they accompany, the Court of Justice has also developed a doctrine of the principle of respect for family life. While this

---

[163] ECJ 11 July 2002, *Carpenter*, Case C-60/00, para. 38.
[164] ECJ 12 March 2014, *S. and G.*, Case C-457/12, para. 34.
[165] ECJ 25 July 2002, *MRAX*, Case C-459/99, para. 62.
[166] Ibid, para. 80.
[167] Ibid, para. 91.

principle is inspired by Article 8 ECHR, it is of a different nature. In contrast
with the ECHR, which was – at the time – only binding on the Member States
and not on the Union, EU principles belong to Union law. In the *Carpenter*
judgment, referred to above, the Court was asked whether a British national who
provided cross-border services without leaving his country, had the right to have
his Filipino wife living with him. The Court decided that Mr. Carpenter was
availing himself of the right freely to provide services guaranteed by (presently)
Article 56 TFEU. However, the difficulty was that the scope of then applicable
Directive 73/148 was limited to family members of EU nationals crossing the
borders. In this case, no borders were crossed as the wife remained with Mr.
Carpenter in the UK. The Court considered:

> Since the Directive does not govern the right of residence of members of the family of
> a provider of services in his Member State of origin, the answer to the question
> referred to the Court therefore depends on whether, in circumstances such as those
> in the main proceedings, a right of residence in favour of the spouse may be inferred
> from the principles or other rules of Community law.[168]

Subsequently, the Court reasoned that the separation of the spouses would be
detrimental to their family life and, therefore, to the conditions under which Mr.
Carpenter exercised a fundamental freedom. That freedom would not be fully
effective if Mr. Carpenter were to be deterred from exercising it by obstacles
raised in his country of origin against the stay of his wife. The deportation
decision of Mrs. Carpenter was an interference with Mr. Carpenter's exercise of
the right to respect for family life within the meaning of Article 8 ECHR. In the
circumstances of the case, a decision to deport Mrs. Carpenter did not, according
to the Court, strike a fair balance between the competing interests of the right of
Mr. Carpenter to respect for his family life *versus* the maintenance of public
order in the United Kingdom. The marriage of the Carpenters was genuine, and
the infringement of immigration laws of the UK by Mrs. Carpenter was not a
sufficient ground for interference in his family life. Accordingly, the Court
concluded that the right to provide services, *read in the light of the fundamental
right to respect for family life*, must be interpreted as prohibiting the refusal to
grant Mrs. Carpenter a right of residence.[169]

A similar situation, but now with regard to the freedom of workers, was
brought before the Court in the case of *S. and G.* (2014).[170] Ms. S. was a Ukrainian
national claiming to be entitled, under Union law, to a right of residence with her
son-in-law, a Netherlands national. Her son-in-law resided in the Netherlands
and worked for an employer established in the Netherlands, but he travelled to

---

[168] ECJ 11 July 2002, *Carpenter*, Case C-60/00, para. 36.
[169] *Ibid*, para. 46. Emphasis added.
[170] ECJ 12 March 2014, *S. and G.*, Case C-457/12.

Belgium at least once a week. Ms. G., a Peruvian national, married a Netherlands national. The couple lived in the Netherlands, but the Dutch spouse worked for an undertaking established in Belgium. He travelled daily between the Netherlands and Belgium for his work. The Court made clear that the Citizens' Directive does not apply to such situations, as the Union citizens did not settle in the other Member State (Belgium). However, the Union citizens in these situations did fall within the scope of Article 45 TFEU, securing the right to the free movement of workers. According to the Court, Article 45 TFEU does indeed confer a derived right of residence to third-country family members of Union citizens in their Member State of origin, if the refusal to grant such a right of residence discourages the worker from effectively exercising his rights under Article 45 TFEU. However, it is not automatically assumed that this is always the case. It is for the national court to determine whether refusing a residence right to the family members would discourage the Union citizen from using his right to work.

> In that regard, the fact (...) that the third-country national in question takes care of the Union citizens' child may, as is apparent from the judgment in *Carpenter*, be a relevant factor to be taken into account by the referring court when examining whether the refusal to grant a right of residence to that third-country national may discourage the Union citizen from effectively exercising his rights under Article 45 TFEU. However, it must be noted that, although in the judgment in *Carpenter* the fact that the child in question was being taken care of by the third-country national who is a family member of a Union citizen was considered to be decisive, that child was, in that case, taken care of by the Union citizen's spouse. The mere fact that it might appear desirable that the child be cared for by the third-country national who is the direct relative in the ascending line of the Union citizen's spouse is not therefore sufficient in itself to constitute such a dissuasive effect.[171]

In this recent *S. and G.* judgment, a more cautious approach is noticeable than in the Carpenter judgment from 2002. Apparently, the Court does not wish to encourage an excessively easy applicability of Union law for the purpose of facilitating legal stay of third-country family members who would otherwise not be allowed legal residence under applicable national law. See, for a similar sign of a more restraint approach, the *O. and B.* judgment from the same date, discussed in section 2.3.9.[172] Still, the principle is upheld, that refusing legal stay to family members may undermine the freedom of movement.

A case in which the fundamental principle inspired by Article 8 ECHR was invoked by the Court in order to substantiate a judgment that could not solely be based on the text of applicable law, was the *Baumbast* case. Mr. Baumbast, a German national, had initially been residing in the United Kingdom as a worker,

---

[171] ECJ 12 March 2014, *S. and G.*, Case C-457/12, para. 43.
[172] ECJ 12 March 2014, *O. and B.* Case C-456/12, para 61.

together with his Colombian wife and two minor daughters, but was subsequently employed by German companies in China and Lesotho, and left his family behind in the United Kingdom. One of the questions referred to the Court was whether the fact that the two children were entitled under Community law to continued legal residence in order to receive education in the United Kingdom, should also give rise to a right to residence on the part of the mother. The Court considered that:

> ... in accordance with the case law of the Court, Regulation No 1612/68 must be interpreted in the light of the requirement of respect for family life laid down in Article 8 of the European Convention. That requirement is one of the fundamental rights, which, according to settled case law, are recognised by Community law (...).[173]

Although the Court explicitly referred to Article 8 ECHR, respect for family life was not the predominant reason for the Court to rule that Ms. Baumbast was entitled to stay with her daughters. Decisive was the effectiveness of the right of the children to remain in England:

> The right conferred by Article 12 of Regulation No 1612/68 on the child of a migrant worker to pursue, under the best possible conditions, his education in the host Member State necessarily implies that that child has the right to be accompanied by the person who is his primary carer and, accordingly, that that person is able to reside with him in that Member State during his studies. To refuse to grant permission to remain to a parent who is the primary carer of the child exercising his right to pursue his studies in the host Member State infringes that right.[174]

This right of the parent to remain with the child who has an education right under Article 12 Regulation 1612/68 (currently Article 10 Regulation 492/2011) may extend to a period after the child reaches the age of majority. According to the *Alarape and Tijani* judgment,[175] the parent may continue to have a derived right of residence if the child remains in need of the presence and care of that parent in order to be able to continue and to complete his or her education. On the other hand, this residence right cannot be placed on a par with the residence rights granted by the Citizens' Directive, and may not be taken into consideration for the purposes of acquisition by those family members of a right of permanent residence under that Directive.

In these cases, the right of the third-country national to stay with a Union citizen, as a primary carer, was perceived as a corollary of the right of the child, having an EU nationality, to reside in the UK. Similarly, the Chinese mother,

---

[173] ECJ 17 September 2002, Case C-413/99, para. 72.
[174] Ibid, para. 73.
[175] ECJ 8 May 2013, *Alarape and Tijani*, Case C-529/11.

Chen, of baby *Zhu*, who was Irish by birth in Belfast, was considered to have a residence right with her child in her quality of primary carer.[176]

> a refusal to allow the parent, whether a national of a Member State or a national of a non-member country, who is the carer of a child to whom Article 18 EC and Directive 90/364 grant a right of residence, to reside with that child in the host Member State, would deprive the child's right of residence of any useful effect. It is clear that enjoyment by a young child of a right of residence necessarily implies that the child is entitled to be accompanied by the person who is his or her primary carer, and accordingly, that the carer must be in a position to reside with the child in the host Member State for the duration of such residence

These judgments date from before the Treaty of Lisbon turning the Charter of Fundamental Rights of the EU into a binding instrument. The general principle of respect for family life is now embodied in Article 7 of the Charter. Like the fundamental principles developed by the Court, the Charter is only applicable after it has been assessed that a situation is covered by Union law.[177]

The self-evidence of the right of a minor child to be cared for by its parent(s) in the country where he has the right to reside was put to the test when the Court applied it to the situation of children who lived in the Member State of their nationality in the *Ruiz Zambrano* judgment.[178] The judgment, which will be discussed hereunder in section 2.4.5, raised many critical comments, amongst other reasons, because the Court had applied Union law to what had as yet been considered to be a strictly internal situation. What a strictly internal situation means is explained in the next section.

2.3.9. STRICTLY INTERNAL SITUATIONS

Normally, the right to free movement cannot be invoked in situations not involving a cross-border economic activity. Union law on free movement does not apply in strictly internal situations. However, there are circumstances under which Union law is applicable also to a national of a Member State who resides in his own country. It was concluded already that a service provider who stays in his country of origin but provides cross-border services is able to successfully invoke Union law.[179]

An example of the rule of non-applicability of Union law in internal situations was the *Morson and Jhanjan* case. A Dutch national of Surinam origin

---

[176] ECJ 19 October 2004, *Zhu and Chen*, Case C-200/02.
[177] ECJ 15 November 2011, *Dereci and others*, Case C-265/11, paras. 69–72. See also section 1.7.2 above.
[178] ECJ 8 March 2011, *Ruiz Zambrano*, Case C-34/09.
[179] ECJ 11 July 2002, *Carpenter*, Case C-60/00.

tried to invoke the right to have his dependent Surinam parents with him in the Netherlands, basing this on the fact that he was employed as a worker in the Netherlands.[180] The Court unequivocally stated that since he was a Dutch national who had never been employed in another Member State, his situation was strictly internal and not governed by Union law. Therefore, he could not claim a right to have his family with him on the right to free movement, nor on the prohibition of discrimination on grounds of nationality.[181]

Later, in the *Surinder Singh* judgment, the Court thought differently of a situation in which a British woman had travelled with her Indian husband to Germany, where she worked for two years before returning to the UK. The woman established herself in the UK as a self-employed person. The fact that she had used her right to free movement was decisive for her spouse to be permitted residence in the United Kingdom. The Court held:

> A national of a Member State might be deterred from leaving his country of origin in order to pursue an activity as an employed or self-employed person as envisaged by the Treaty in the territory of another Member State if, on returning to the Member State of which he is a national in order to pursue an activity there as an employed or self-employed person, the conditions of his entry and residence were not at least equivalent to those which he would enjoy under the Treaty or secondary law in the territory of another Member State. He would in particular be deterred from so doing if his spouse and children were not also permitted to enter and reside in the territory of his Member State of origin under conditions at least equivalent to those granted them by Community law in the territory of another Member State.[182]

In the *Eind* judgment, the Court explicitly considered that the right of a Union worker to return to the Member State of which he is a national cannot be considered to be a purely internal matter:

> [T]he right of the migrant worker to return and reside in the Member State of which he is a national, after being gainfully employed in another Member State, is conferred by Community law, to the extent necessary to ensure the useful effect of the right to free movement for workers under Article 39 EC and the provisions adopted to give effect to that right, such as those laid down in Regulation No 1612/68.[183]

After the *Surinder Singh* judgment, it appeared likely that third-country national spouses who, under national immigration legislation, were not allowed legal residence in a Member State with a national of that Member State, could use a 'U-turn' construction in order to create an entitlement to residence in that

---

[180] At that time provided for by Article 10 Reg. 1612/68; currently Article 2(2)(d), in conjunction with Article 7(1)(d) Citizens' Directive.
[181] ECJ 27 October 1982, *Morson and Jhanjan*, Cases 35/82 and 36/82, paras. 11–18.
[182] ECJ 7 July 1992, *Surinder Singh*, Case C-370/90, paras. 19–20.
[183] ECJ 11 December 2007, *Eind*, Case C-291/05, para. 32.

Member State under Union law. This construction would entail the movement of the EU citizen to another Member State, where he would exercise his right to free movement, and accordingly, would be entitled to be accompanied by his family members, and subsequently to return to the Member State of origin, stating that the third-country national spouse had a right of residence according to Union law. However, in the *Akrich* judgment the ECJ restricted this potential use of EU law by ruling that previous unlawful stay of a spouse in the country of the nationality of an EU citizen could not be 'repaired' when the EU citizen uses his right to move to another Member State.[184] The ECJ noted that, to be able to benefit from Union law in such a situation, the third-country national spouse must be lawfully resident in a Member State before he moves to another Member State to which the EU citizen is migrating. In 2008, this *Akrich* doctrine was, nonetheless, 'reconsidered' by the Court in its ruling in the case of *Metock*.[185] In that judgment, the Court unequivocally held that the Citizens' Directive *precludes* legislation of a Member State which requires a national of a non-member country who is the spouse of a Union citizen residing in that Member State, but not possessing its nationality, to have previously been lawfully resident in another Member State before arriving in the host Member State, in order to benefit from the provisions of that Directive:

> Article 3(1) of Directive 2004/38 must be interpreted as meaning that a national of a non-member country who is the spouse of a Union citizen residing in a Member State whose nationality he does not possess and who accompanies or joins that Union citizen benefits from the provisions of that directive, irrespective of when and where their marriage took place and of how the national of a non-member country entered the host Member State.[186]

In *O. and B.* (2014), the Court of Justice clarified a number of issues concerning the 'U-turn'. From a doctrinal point of view, it is important to realise that the Citizens' Directive is not applicable to the situation of a third-country family member of a Union citizen who returns to his own Member State after having resided in another Member State. The residence rights of such a family member are derived from Article 21 TFEU (see, for an extensive discussion of this provision, section 2.4). The Citizens' Directive is applied by analogy.[187] Further, the Court put beyond doubt that such rights are only merited by a family member who joined the Union Citizen when he or she made use of the right to free movement to another Member State. It is necessary, in that respect, that the family member resided, at least during part of his residence, in the other Member

---

[184] ECJ 23 September 2003, *Akrich*, Case C-109/01, see, especially, paras. 52–54.
[185] ECJ 25 July 2008, *Metock*, Case 127/08.
[186] *Ibid*, para. 99.
[187] ECJ 12 March 2014, *O. and B.* Case C-456/12, para 61.

State with the Union citizen 'pursuant to and in conformity with the conditions' for legal residence set out in the Citizens' Directive:

> Accordingly, it is genuine residence in the host Member State of the Union citizen and of the family member who is a third-country national, pursuant to, and in conformity with, the conditions set out in Article 7(1) and (2) and Article 16(1) and (2) of Directive 2004/38 respectively, which creates, on the Union citizen's return to his Member State of origin, a derived right of residence, on the basis of Article 21(1) TFEU, for the third-country national with whom that citizen lived as a family in the host Member State.[188]

The cumulative effect of various short periods of residence in the host Member State does not create a derived residence right in the Member State of origin. So, using the right to free movement during the first 3 months means Article 6 Citizens' Directive is not sufficient. Only if the Union citizen and his family member(s) genuinely intend to settle in the host Member State in a way which would be such as to create or strengthen family life in that Member State, may the 'U-turn' have effect. It is for the national court to determine whether the family settled and, therefore, genuinely resided in the host Member State.

Thus, the boundaries within which a strictly internal situation can be spoken of have been narrowed and specified by the case law of the Court of Justice. A further narrowing took place in the *Ruiz Zambrano* judgment, discussed in section 2.4.5. This judgment was one in a row of judgments in which the concept of the fundamental status of Union citizenship was worked out. This status is the subject of the next section.

2.4. UNION CITIZENSHIP

2.4.1. THE FUNDAMENTAL STATUS OF UNION CITIZENSHIP

Article 21(1) TFEU stipulates: 'Every citizen of the Union shall have the right to move and reside freely within the territory of the Member States, subject to the limitations laid down in the Treaty and by the measures adopted to give it effect.' An innocent reader of these words would probably not immediately recognise their primary importance. It would not be peculiar to interpret the provision as a solemn declaration, a mere reiteration of existing provisions on free movement of persons. The Court has ruled otherwise, using principled and promising wordings. In the *Baumbast* judgment, the Court stated that Article 21(1) TFEU is a 'clear and precise provision', which directly confers the right to reside within

---

[188]   *Ibid*, para. 56.

the territory of the Member States on every citizen of the EU.[189] A Union citizen has the right to rely on the citizenship provision of Article 18 EC Treaty (now Article 21(1) TFEU) 'purely as a national of a Member State, and consequently a citizen of the Union'. Still, the extent to which the Union citizenship can be invoked in practice is a rich object of study and debate.

Up to now, the Court of Justice has shown the relevance of Articles 20 and 21(1) in four different situations, which have little in common, other than that they turned out to be affected by the notion of Union citizenship in a rather surprising way. Surprising, because citizenship was sometimes able to shake premises that were perceived as stable and beyond discussion. The following issues arose:

a. Are there limits to the discretion of Member States to deprive their own citizens of their nationality?
b. Does the *general provision* of Article 21(1) TFEU grant additional residence rights in relation to the *specific rules* of Articles 45–62 TFEU and the Citizens' Directive?
c. Do Union citizens have a right to social security in another Member State than their own, on an equal footing with the citizens of that Member State?
d. Does Article 21(1) TFEU apply to the situation of Union citizens of minor age wishing to live in their own countries together with their parents, who are third-country nationals?

These four issues are dealt with hereunder.

2.4.2. UNION CITIZENSHIP AND THE DEPRIVATION OF NATIONALITY

As it turns out, the fundamental character of Union citizenship can be invoked with some effect in situations that used to be under the exclusive control of the Member States. An example of the competence transgressing potential of the concept is the *Rottmann* judgment.[190] In order to demonstrate the exceptional impact of this judgment, it is necessary, first, to explain the normal state of affairs.

It is for each Member State to lay down the conditions for the acquisition and loss of nationality.[191] Member States must recognise each other's nationality decisions if there is no reason to challenge the legality of such decisions. It is not

---

[189] ECJ 17 September 2002, *Baumbast and R.*, Case C-413/99.
[190] ECJ 2 March 2010, *Rottmann*, Case C-135/08.
[191] Case 369/90, *Micheletti and Others* [1992], para.10; Case C-179/98 *Mesbah* [1999] ECR I-7955, para.29; Case C-192/99, *Kaur*, [2001], ECR I-01237, para. 19; Case C-200/02 *Zhu and Chen* [2004] ECR I-9925, para. 37). See also Declaration No 2 on nationality of a Member State,

permissible for a Member State to restrict the effects of the grant of the nationality of another Member State by imposing an additional condition for recognition of that nationality with a view to the exercise of the fundamental freedoms provided for in the Treaty. In the *Micheletti* case,[192] the Court had to deal with a person of dual Argentine and Italian nationality, who asked for a residence card in Spain in order to set up as a dentist. The card was refused, disregarding the Italian nationality, because Mr. *Micheletti* had his earlier habitual residence in Argentina, not in Italy. However, according to the Court, the recognition of the status of Community national (nowadays: Union citizen) could not be made subject to any additional condition, such as the habitual residence of the person.

Nevertheless, the Court has consistently ruled that the Member States must, when exercising their powers in the sphere of nationality, have due regard to European Union law. Accordingly, the Court considered itself competent to rule on questions that concern the conditions under which a citizen of the Union may, because he loses his nationality, lose his status of citizen of the Union, and thereby be deprived of the rights attaching to that fundamental status. In the *Rottmann* case,[193] the Court stated that it is not contrary to European Union law, in particular, to Article 17 EC (currently Article 20 TFEU), for a Member State to withdraw from a citizen of the Union the nationality of that State acquired by naturalisation, when that nationality has been obtained by deception, on condition that the decision to withdraw observes the principle of proportionality.

By posing the condition of a proportionality test, the Court limited the discretion of Member States to withdraw the nationality of their own nationals, even in cases of fraud. The fundamental character of the status of EU citizens turned out to be able to affect what had previously been an unfettered competence of the Member States.

2.4.3. UNION CITIZENSHIP AND RESIDENCE RIGHTS IN OTHER MEMBER STATES

In contrast to the Treaty basis for residence rights of Union citizens pursuing an economic activity which can be found both in Article 21(1) TFEU and in the specific provisions of Articles 45–62 TFEU, the legal basis for residence rights for economically non-active citizens can solely be located in the general Article 21(1) TFEU. The jurisprudence of the Court of Justice on Union citizenship can be seen as confirming this legal basis, and shifting the attention from the textual

---

annexed by the Member States to the final act of the Treaty on European Union (OJ 1992 C 191, p. 98).

[192] Case 369/90, *Micheletti and Others* [1992], para. 10.

[193] ECJ 2 March 2010, *Rottmann*, Case C-135/08.

interpretation of secondary legislation to an interpretation according to the purpose of this basic provision in the Treaty.

The first opportunity for the Court to do so was given in the case of the German, Mr. *Baumbast*, who almost complied with the conditions for legal stay as an economically non-active EU citizen, according to the rules currently formulated in Article 7(1)b Citizens' Directive, except for the requirement that his sickness insurance should also cover emergency treatment. Although he could not derive a residence from the applicable rules, he could successfully invoke the fact that he was a Union citizen, deriving the right to move and reside freely within the territory of the Member States directly from (presently) Article 21(1) TFEU. The Court acknowledged that the right conferred by Article 21(1) TFEU is not unconditional, and that it is subject to the limitations and conditions laid down by the Treaty and secondary legislation. But that does not mean that a simple referral to applicable legislation will do. According to the Court, these limitations and conditions are based on the *general* idea that the exercise of the right of residence of citizens of the Union can be subordinated to the legitimate interests of the Member States.[194] With regard to the right of residence, this legitimate interest is, in particular, that beneficiaries of that right must not become an unreasonable burden on the public finances of the host Member State. In order to meet this legitimate aim, the limitations and conditions:

> must be applied in compliance with the limits imposed by Community law and in accordance with the general principles of that law, in particular, the principle of proportionality. That means that national measures adopted on that subject must be necessary and appropriate to attain the objective pursued.[195]

The Court considered:

> Under those circumstances, to refuse to allow Mr. Baumbast to exercise the right of residence which is conferred on him by Article 18(1) EC[196] by virtue of the application of the provisions of Directive 90/364 on the ground that his sickness insurance does not cover the emergency treatment given in the host Member State would amount to a disproportionate interference with the exercise of that right.[197]

The limits of the residence right derived from Article 21(1) TFEU became visible in the judgment in *Trojani*. The Court was confronted with the situation in which a French national, working in Belgium for about 30 hours a week for the Salvation Army in a socio-occupational reintegration programme for a certain

---

[194]   *Ibid*, para. 90.
[195]   *Ibid*, para. 91.
[196]   Article 18(1) EC was the predecessor of the present Article 21(1) TFEU.
[197]   *Ibid*, para. 93, emphasis added.

remuneration, had asked for supplementary social assistance from the Belgian authorities. The question arose as to whether Mr. Trojani would enjoy a right of residence, simply by virtue of being a citizen of the EU. The Court found that Mr. Trojani could not derive that right from the Treaty provision on Union citizenship:

> Contrary to the case of Baumbast and R (…), there is no indication that, in a situation such as at issue in the main proceedings, the failure to recognise that right would go beyond what is necessary to achieve the objective pursued by that Directive.[198]

In the case of *Baumbast*, there had only been a relatively small deficiency in respect of the conditions to be fulfilled: his sickness insurance did not cover emergency treatment in the UK, whereas he did have comprehensive sickness insurance in another Member State. Mr. *Trojani*, on the other hand, clearly failed to show he had sufficient resources, and had in fact applied for social benefits.

It is not necessary that the Union citizen himself is the owner of the income enabling him not to become a burden of the social security system of the host Member State. In the case of *Zhu and Chen*,[199] some Member States contended that the condition concerning the availability of sufficient resources means that the person concerned must possess those resources personally, and may not use for that purpose those of an accompanying family member. The Court rejected this interpretation, as this would entail an additional requirement regarding the origin of the resources which, not being necessary for the attainment of the objective pursued, namely the protection of the public finances of the Member States, would constitute a disproportionate interference with the exercise of the fundamental right of freedom of movement and of residence upheld by Article 18 EC (currently Article 21 TFEU).

Hence, the right granted by Article 21(1) TEC governs the rights that are expressly regulated in the Citizens' Directive. All restrictions imposed on the freedom of movement, as guaranteed by Article 21(1) TFEU, must be in compliance with general principles of Union law, in particular, with the principle of proportionality.

The right to lawful residence in another Member State for a Union citizen under the condition that he does not constitute an unreasonable burden of the social security system of the host Member State, may be at risk once he takes the decision to apply for social security. The next section deals with the question how the Court deals with this dilemma.

---

[198] ECJ 7 September 2004, *Trojani*, Case C-456/02, para. 36.
[199] ECJ 19 October 2004, *Zhu and Chen*, Case C-200/02.

2.4.4.   UNION CITIZENSHIP AND A RIGHT TO EQUAL TREATMENT CONCERNING SOCIAL ASSISTANCE IN OTHER MEMBER STATES

It follows from the case law of the Court of Justice that all discriminatory measures which may, directly or indirectly, have a negative impact on a person's right to freely move and reside, are prohibited.[200] This not only includes rules or measures governing the conditions for the exercise of treaty freedoms, such as rules regulating access and conditions of employment, but also rules which may indirectly affect a person in the exercise of treaty rights, such as access to social welfare and state benefits. This implies that the right of equal treatment is also applicable to discriminatory measures taken in the context of fields of law that are not, or not fully, harmonised under EU law, such as criminal law or social security law. Accordingly, in the case of *Cowan*, the Court held that a British tourist, making use of his right to free movement by visiting France, and who was violently assaulted after exiting the metro in Paris, was entitled to state compensation for physical injury because that compensation was also available for French nationals:

> When Community law guarantees a natural person the freedom to go to another Member State, the protection of that person from harm in the Member State in question, on the same basis as that of nationals and persons residing there, is a corollary of that freedom of movement. It follows that the prohibition of discrimination is applicable to recipients of services within the meaning of the Treaty as regards protection against the risk of assault and the right to obtain financial compensation provided for by national law when that risk materialises.[201]

Later, the central question arose of under which circumstances an EU citizen may invoke a right to social assistance or social security in a host Member State. The Court has adjudicated a number of cases in which a national of a Member State was lawfully residing in another Member State and claimed social security benefits on an equal footing with nationals of the host country. The *Martínez Sala* case concerned a Spanish woman who had lived in Germany for more than 20 years and had applied for a child-raising allowance. Although Mrs. Martínez Sala was allowed to reside in Germany, she was at some time refused a permit certifying this right, which was a precondition to obtaining child-raising allowance. The Court found that a national of a Member State who is lawfully residing in another Member State, falls under the scope of the Treaty in his or her quality of an EU citizen, and may therefore invoke the prohibition of discrimination on grounds of nationality.[202] This meant that Germany was

---

[200]   *E.g.* ECJ 12 February 1974, *Sotgiu*, Case 152/73, para. 11.
[201]   ECJ 2 February 1992, *Cowan*, Case 186/87, para. 17.
[202]   ECJ 12 May 1998, *Martínez Sala*, Case C-85/96, paras. 61–62.

precluded from requiring a formal residence permit from Martínez Sala in order to receive a child-raising allowance, since German nationals only had to show they were permanently or ordinarily resident in Germany.[203]

The case of *Grzelczyk* concerned a student whose lawful residence was based on the then-existing Students Directive 93/96. Grzelczyk was a French national who studied in the Belgian city of Louvain-la-Neuve, and who applied, in his final year of study, for a social benefit called the 'minimex'. Although being in possession of sufficient means of subsistence is precisely one of the conditions for the right to residence, according to the Students Directive,[204] Grzelczyk was entitled, in his quality as EU citizen making use of his free movement right under Article 21(1) TFEU, to receive temporary social assistance on equal footing with Belgian nationals:

> The fact that a Union citizen pursues university studies in a Member State other than the State of which he is a national cannot, of itself, deprive him of the possibility of relying on the prohibition of all discrimination on grounds of nationality laid down in Article 6 of the Treaty [currently Article 18 TFEU].[205]

The Court admitted that having recourse to social assistance could jeopardise Grzelczyk's residence right as it was granted by the Directive, and considered that Member States are not prevented from taking the view that a student who has recourse to social assistance no longer fulfils the conditions of his right of residence or from taking measures, within the limits imposed by Union law, either to withdraw his residence permit or not to renew it.[206] Nevertheless, said the Court, 'in no case may such measures become the automatic consequence of a student who is a national of another Member State having recourse to the host Member State's social assistance system.'[207] In this regard, the Court took note of the difficult financial position students may find themselves in, and observed that Grzelczyk's recourse to social assistance would only be temporary. He could therefore hardly be labelled as becoming an 'unreasonable burden'. In the light of these circumstances, the Court concluded that Grzelczyk had not forfeited his right of residence, and could rely on the right not be treated differently from Belgian students.

The right to equal treatment relating to social security, as recognised by the Court in the judgments on *Martínez Sala* and *Grczelczyk*, has been codified since then in Article 24 of the Citizens' Directive. All EU citizens, including family members who are EU citizens, *and* family members who are third-country nationals, who are allowed to reside in another Member State on the basis of the

---

[203] *Ibid*, para. 64–65.
[204] Presently: Article 7(1)(c) Citizens' Directive.
[205] ECJ 20 September 2001, *Grzelczyk*, Case C-184/99, paras. 35–36.
[206] Ibid, para. 42.
[207] Ibid, para. 43.

Directive, are entitled to equal treatment 'within the scope of the Treaty' (Article 24(1)). In the second paragraph of Article 24, two derogations to the principle of equal treatment are formulated. The host Member State is not obliged, in the first place, to confer entitlement to social assistance during the first three months of residence or to jobseekers who continue to stay after that three-month period. Secondly, a Member State is neither obliged to grant maintenance aid for studies to persons other than workers, self-employed persons and the members of their families, prior to the acquisition of the right of permanent residence.

The Court of Justice however, put the latter derogation in perspective, even before the transposition period for the Citizens' Directive expired (30 April 2006). Mr. *Bidar*, a French national who was lawfully resident in the United Kingdom, where he had received a substantial part of his secondary education, was refused a student loan on the ground that he was not settled in the United Kingdom. In principle, this would have been consistent with Article 24(2) Citizens' Directive. However, the UK legislation had precluded any possibility of a national of another Member State obtaining settled status as a student, which would mean that Mr. Bidar would never qualify for social assistance. The Court considered that to prevent a person who has established a genuine link with the society of a Member State, from being able to pursue his studies under the same conditions as a student who is a national of that state and is in the same situation, amounts to prohibited discrimination under Article 18 TFEU.[208] In the *Förster* judgment,[209] the Court specified that Article 18(1) TFEU does not preclude the application to nationals of other Member States of a requirement of five years' prior residence.

The equal treatment of students also extends to transport fares. In the *Commission v. Austria* judgment,[210] the Court said that making the reduced transport fares subject to the grant of Austrian family allowances, as provided for by certain *Länder*, gives rise to unequal treatment between Austrian students pursuing their studies in Austria and students from other Member States pursuing their studies there as well, since such a condition is more easily fulfilled by Austrian students because their parents, as a rule, receive those allowances.

The central criterion, that a Union citizen applying for social security or social assistance may not become an 'unreasonable burden' on the social security system of the host Member State, was further worked out in the judgment in *Brey*.[211] It was about a German couple living in Austria on an invalidity pension and a care allowance. Mr. Brey applied for a compensatory supplement that was refused because Mr. Brey did not have sufficient resources to establish his lawful

---

[208]   ECJ 15 March 2005, *Bidar*, Case C-209/03, para. 62.
[209]   ECJ 18 November 2008, *Förster*, Case C-158/07.
[210]   ECJ 4 October 2012, *Commission v. Austria*, Case C-75/11.
[211]   ECJ 19 September 2013, *Brey*, Case C-140/12.

residence in Austria. In other words, he was considered not to comply with the conditions for lawful residence under Article 7(1)b Citizens' Directive. The Court said that the fact that a national of another Member State who is not economically active may be eligible, in light of his low pension, to receive a benefit, could be an indication that that national does not have sufficient resources to avoid becoming an unreasonable burden on the social assistance system of the host Member State for the purposes of Article 7(1)(b) of Directive 2004/38. However, the competent national authorities cannot draw such conclusions without first carrying out an overall assessment of the specific burden which granting that benefit would place on the national social assistance system as a whole, by reference to the personal circumstances characterising the individual situation of the person concerned. For this purpose, the Court developed a quite extensive test, stating that:

> it is important that the competent authorities of the host Member State are able, when examining the application of a Union citizen who is not economically active, and is in Mr. Brey's position, to take into account, *inter alia*, the following: the amount and the regularity of the income which he receives; the fact that those factors have led those authorities to issue him with a certificate of residence; and the period during which the benefit applied for is likely to be granted to him. In addition, in order to ascertain more precisely the extent of the burden which that grant would place on the national social assistance system, it may be relevant, as the Commission argued at the hearing, to determine the proportion of the beneficiaries of that benefit who are Union citizens in receipt of a retirement pension in another Member State.

Thus, the Court sails between *Scylla* and *Charibdis*, upholding on one hand the right for economically non-active Union citizens to stay in another Member State as long as they do not become an unreasonable burden on the social assistance system, and on the other hand, the right to equal treatment as citizens of the host Member State in applying for such social assistance.

2.4.5. UNION CITIZENSHIP AND NATIONAL MIGRATION LAW OF THE MEMBER STATES

The *Ruiz Zambrano* judgment[212] illustrates how difficult it is for the EU Court to follow a consistent path developing the concepts of Union law in view of the far-reaching consequences that may be entailed. The case was about the scope of the right of residence for third-country nationals who were the parents of an infant Union citizen who had not, as yet, left the Member State of his birth. A father of Colombian nationality wished to stay in Belgium with his minor children, who

---

[212]   ECJ 8 March 2011, *Ruiz Zambrano*, Case C-34/09.

2. Free Movement of EU Citizens and Members of Their Family

had obtained Belgian nationality under a provision of Belgian nationality law. He and his wife had applied in vain for lawful residence in Belgium. The case fell beyond the scope of applicability of the Citizens' Directive for two reasons: (1) the Directive does not regulate the stay of parents with minor children; and (2) the Directive is only applicable to border crossing situations and not to Union citizens, like the children of Ruiz Zambrano, who always remained in their own country and never used their right to free movement between Member States. Situations like these have always been considered as strictly internal within the Member State, having no factor linking them with Union law (see section 2.3.9). It has been standing case law of the Court of Justice that it does not have jurisdiction in strictly internal situations,[213] and in 2003, the Court repeated that citizenship of the Union is not intended to also extend the scope *ratione materiae* of the Treaty to internal situations which have no link with Union law.[214] Nevertheless, the Belgian court asked the Court of Justice whether the children, in their quality of Union citizens, were entitled to have their parents living with them in Belgium.

In her interesting and evocative opinion for this case, Advocate General Sharpston wrote that the Court would have a number of difficult and important choices to make.

> What precisely does Union citizenship entail? Do the circumstances giving rise to the national proceedings constitute a situation that is 'purely internal' to the Member State concerned, in which European Union ('EU') law has no role to play? Or does full recognition of the rights (including the future rights) that necessarily flow from Union citizenship mean that an infant EU citizen has a right, based on EU law rather than national law, to reside anywhere within the territory of the Union (including in the Member State of his nationality)? If so, ensuring that he can exercise that right effectively may entail granting residence to his third-country national parent if there would otherwise be a substantial breach of 'fundamental rights'.
>
> At a more conceptual level, is the exercise of rights as a Union citizen dependent – like the exercise of the classic economic 'freedoms' – on some trans-frontier free movement (however accidental, peripheral or remote) having taken place before the claim is advanced? Or does Union citizenship look forward to the future, rather than back to the past, to define the rights and obligations that it confers? To put the same question from a slightly different angle: is Union citizenship merely the non-economic version of the same generic kind of free movement rights as have long existed for the economically active and for persons of independent means? Or does it mean something more radical: true citizenship, carrying with it a uniform set of rights and obligations, in a Union under the rule of law in which respect for fundamental rights must necessarily play an integral part?

---

213   ECJ 27 October 1982, *Morson and Jhanjan*, Joined cases 35 and 36/82.
214   ECJ 2 October 2003, *Garcia Avello*, Case C-148/02, para. 26. See also joined Cases C-64/96 and C-65/96 *Uecker and Jacquet* [1997] ECR I-3171, para. 23.

Inspired by this opinion or not, the Court of Justice considered itself competent and gave a surprising judgment granting the parents a residence right to remain with their children in Belgium. The Court repeated that citizenship of the Union is intended to be the fundamental status of nationals of the Member States. Article 20 TFEU precludes national measures that have the effect of depriving citizens of the Union of the genuine enjoyment of the substance of the rights conferred by virtue of their status as citizens of the Union. According to the Court of Justice, a refusal to grant a right of residence to a third-country national with dependent minor children in the Member State where those children are nationals and reside, and also a refusal to grant such a person a work permit, has such an effect. The Court assumed that such a refusal would lead to a situation where those children, citizens of the Union, would have to leave the territory of the Union in order to accompany their parents. Similarly, if a work permit were not granted to such a person, he would risk not having sufficient resources to provide for himself and his family, which would also result in the children, citizens of the Union, having to leave the territory of the Union. In those circumstances, those citizens of the Union would, in fact, be unable to exercise the substance of the rights conferred on them by virtue of their status as citizens of the Union. Deportation of the father (and the mother) would force these young Union citizens to leave *the territory of the European Union as a whole.* This constituted the link with Union law that made the Court competent to judge the situation, which would otherwise have been a strictly internal affair of the Member State concerned. The relevant considerations were extremely short in relation to their potential impact:

> 42. In those circumstances, Article 20 TFEU precludes national measures that have the effect of depriving citizens of the Union of the genuine enjoyment of the substance of the rights conferred by virtue of their status as citizens of the Union (see, to that effect, *Rottmann*, paragraph 42).
>
> 43. A refusal to grant a right of residence to a third-country national with dependent minor children in the Member State where those children are nationals and reside, and also a refusal to grant such a person a work permit, has such an effect.
>
> 44. It must be assumed that such a refusal would lead to a situation where those children, citizens of the Union, would have to leave the territory of the Union in order to accompany their parents. Similarly, if a work permit were not granted to such a person, he would risk not having sufficient resources to provide for himself and his family, which would also result in the children, citizens of the Union, having to leave the territory of the Union. In those circumstances, those citizens of the Union would, in fact, be unable to exercise the substance of the rights conferred on them by virtue of their status as citizens of the Union.

The judgment raised many comments – both praising and critical. On one hand, the judgment was seen as an encroachment upon the liberty of the Member States to draft their own migration law concerning family reunification with their own citizens. The *Ruiz Zambrano* case would arguably open the door to various claims of nationals *vis-à-vis* their own governments that the substance of their rights of Union citizens had been infringed. On the other hand, it was acclaimed that children were recognised to have a natural right to live in their own countries together with their parents, regardless of the nationality of those parents. The most intriguing question was, what more could be considered a deprivation of 'the substance of the rights conferred on them by virtue of their status as citizens of the Union'? Would violation of one of the fundamental rights granted by the Charter also constitute a deprivation of the substance of the rights of Union citizens? For instance, if the right to family life were at stake?

Soon, the Court put an end to such speculations. In the *Dereci* judgment[215] the Court clarified that extensive interpretation of the criterion relating to the denial of 'the genuine enjoyment of the substance of the rights' is not an issue. The criterion (solely) refers to situations in which the Union citizen has, in fact, to leave not only the territory of the Member State of which he is a national, but also the territory of the Union as a whole. In paragraph 67 of the judgment, the Court stressed the narrow scope of application of the criterion:

> That criterion is specific in character inasmuch as it relates to situations in which, although subordinate legislation on the right of residence of third-country nationals is not applicable, a right of residence may not, exceptionally, be refused to a third-country national, who is a family member of a Member State national, as the effectiveness of Union citizenship enjoyed by that national would otherwise be undermined.

The fundamental character of the right to family life was played down. The possibility that violating this right laid down in the EU Charter might on its own merits entail the substance of the right of a Union citizen was not considered. In view of the question whether the Union citizen would be forced to leave the Union territory, the issue of family unity was framed, in paragraph 68, in terms of 'desirability':

> Consequently, the mere fact that it might appear desirable to a national of a Member State, for economic reasons or in order to keep his family together in the territory of the Union, for the members of his family who do not have the nationality of a Member State to be able to reside with him in the territory of the Union, is not sufficient in itself to support the view that the Union citizen will be forced to leave Union territory if such a right is not granted.

It is, in particular, the relationship of dependency between the Union citizen who is a minor and the third-country national who is refused a right of residence that must be assessed. This was confirmed by the Court in the *O, S and L*

---

[215]   ECJ 15 November 2011, *Dereci*, Case C-256/11.

judgment.[216] For it is that dependency that would lead to the Union citizen being obliged, in fact, to leave the territory of the European Union as a whole, as a consequence of refusal of legal residence to the third-country national. The national court, confronted with a claim under the *Ruiz Zambrano* criterion, must examine all the circumstances of the case in order to determine whether, in fact, the decisions refusing residence permits at issue in the main proceedings are liable to undermine the effectiveness of the Union citizenship enjoyed by the Union citizens concerned. In the *O, S and L* judgment, the Court of Justice elaborated on the elements that must be taken into account in that assessment. Whether the person for whom a right of residence is sought on the basis of family reunification lives together with the sponsor and the other family members, is not decisive. Neither are the principles stated in the *Ruiz Zambrano* judgment confined to situations in which there is a blood relationship between the third-country national concerned and the Union citizen who is a minor.

In the end, not much was realised of the wide prospects sketched in the opinion of Advocate General Sharpston. Instead of introducing 'true citizenship, carrying with it a uniform set of rights and obligations, in a Union under the rule of law in which respect for fundamental rights must necessarily play an integral part', the *Ruiz Zambrano* judgment turned out to produce a rare curiosity, a criterion which only applies in exceptional circumstances. There is no clear right of an infant Union citizen to have his primary carer with him in his own country. On the contrary, the right to unity of the family was now described in terms of 'desirability'. That may be a huge step backwards. Until the *Dereci* judgment, the dependency of the child of his primary carer had always been presupposed by the Court. In the judgments on *Baumbast*, *Zhu and Chen*, *Alarape and Tijani*, the Court took it as self-explanatory that the effectiveness of the residence right of the child, possibly even after reaching the age of majority, would be deprived of its useful effect if the primary carer were to be expelled (see section 2.3.8 above). But for cases in which the minor Union citizen did not use his right to free movement to other Member States, this point of departure has been abandoned. The *Ruiz Zambrano* criterion cannot lead to a residence right for the parent, having the nationality of a third country, without a prior assessment that expulsion of the parent would force the child to leave the territory of the Union. Unfortunately, this assessment is, in itself, not covered by Union law – that is, not at the moment of writing. Thus, Member States have the discretion to restrict the scope of applicability of the dependency criterion to cases of extreme hardship.

The strange situation happens now, that Member States decide whether Union law is applicable or not, by making a factual assessment. Once it is established that the infant Union citizen would be forced to leave the EU territory in the case of expulsion of his parent, Union law is applicable and the

---

[216]   ECJ 6 December 2012, *O, S and L*, Case C-356/22.

parent consequently obtains a residence right, but the question of whether this assessment is right or wrong appears to fall beyond the scope of Union law, and, therefore, beyond the scope of the Charter of the Fundamental Rights of the EU.[217]

2.5.   FINAL REMARKS

The scope of free movement of Member State nationals has significantly expanded since the EEC Treaty entered into force on 1 January 1958. The Court of Justice has interpreted the Treaty freedoms expansively and, conversely, asserted a strict scrutiny on the permissibility of invoking Treaty exceptions. The steadily evolving case law of the Court of Justice and the gradual adoption of various Regulations and Directives have resulted in the extension of free movement rights to a range of persons who initially fell outside the ambit of the European integration process. Family members, pensioners, students, financially independents and even prisoners can, to a considerable extent, all derive residence rights from Union law. The adoption of the Citizens' Directive can be seen as an important beacon in the integration process of free movement of persons, marking the progressive achievements in this field of law. The introduction of EU citizenship turned out to be another important development, in particular, due to the scope accorded to Article 20 TFEU by the Court of Justice.

Nonetheless, the freedom of EU citizens to freely move within the Member States is far from absolute. Apart from the narrowly defined exceptions of public policy, public security and public health, the general premise delimiting the scope of free movement is that this freedom may not lead to EU citizens becoming an unreasonable burden on the public finances of the host state. It is only after five years of legal residence in another Member State that Union citizens obtain a residence right that is no longer dependent on considerations of having an income or being financially self-supporting. On the other hand, it has also been accepted that freedom of movement may imply a certain level of financial or social solidarity between nationals of one Member State and those of another.[218] Workers may become unemployed and students may suddenly find themselves running out of pocket money. When, exactly, a person transgresses

---

[217]   ECJ 15 November 2011, *Dereci*, Case C-256/11, para. 71, 72, 73.
[218]   See, in particular, ECJ 20 September 2001, *Grzelczyk*, Case C-184/99, para. 44: 'Whilst Article 4 of Directive 93/96 does indeed provide that the right of residence is to exist for as long as beneficiaries of that right fulfil the conditions laid down in Article 1, the sixth recital in the Directive's preamble envisages that beneficiaries of the right of residence must not become an unreasonable burden on the public finances of the host Member State. Directive 93/96, like Directives 90/364 and 90/365, thus accepts a certain degree of financial solidarity between nationals of a host Member State and nationals of other Member States, particularly if the difficulties which a beneficiary of the right of residence encounters are temporary.'

the boundaries of free movement law by becoming an 'unreasonable burden', remains, to a considerable extent, undefined as a question. This boundary has, moreover, turned out not to be static but subject to progressive interpretation.

FURTHER READING

Steve Peers, Elspeth Guild, Jonathan Tomkin, *Commentary on the EU Citizenship Directive*, Oxford University Press (2014).

Roel Fernhout, Kees Groenendijk, Helen Oosterom-Staples, & Paul Minderhoud, *Report on the Free Movement of Workers in the Netherlands in 2012–2013.* Nijmegen: Centre for Migration Law (2013).

Michael Johns, *Post-Accession Polish Migrants in Britain and Ireland: Challenges and Obstacles for Integration in the European Union*, EJML 2013, p. 29–45.

3. RESIDENCE RIGHTS OF TURKISH NATIONALS UNDER THE ASSOCIATION AGREEMENT

3.1. ASSOCIATION AND COOPERATION TREATIES

3.1.1. INTRODUCTION

Paradoxically, the remarkable situation that Turkey has been waiting for more than 50 years to be admitted as a member of the European Union has created the opportunity for the Court of Justice to develop an impressive series of judgments through which the residence rights of Turkish nationals in the Member States of the European Union have been gradually enhanced. Starting in 1987, the ECJ has interpreted the EEC-Turkey Association Treaty of 1963 and subsequent Agreements under that Association as providing for clear and directly applicable residence rights of Turkish workers and their family members, which form an integral part of the EU legal order.[219] Association law has, accordingly, become of major importance for the legal position of Turkish nationals residing in one of the EU Member States.

This chapter will mainly be devoted to an overview of the extensive system of residence rights of Turkish citizens, which was thus built by the Court of Justice. But first, in sections 3.1.2–3.1.5 a short account will be given of the migration-related rights in other association and cooperation treaties between the EU and third states.

3.1.2. MIGRATION ASPECTS OF ASSOCIATION AND COOPERATION TREATIES

The European Union, formerly the European Community, has concluded many treaties with third countries. From the perspective of migration, the Association and Cooperation Treaties deserve special attention. Association Agreements are commonly concluded in exchange for commitments in the political or economic sphere, such as on trade or human rights reform. The purpose of an Association

---

[219] ECJ 30 September 1987, *Demirel*, Case 12/86.

Treaty may also be to anticipate the planned accession of a new Member State to the Union. In such a treaty, first steps may be taken to develop a regime of the free movement of persons between the EU and the associated country. Most of the treaties anticipating accession have become obsolete due to the accession of the former associated country to the Union. The so-called Europe Agreements concluded in 1994 with Eastern and Middle European countries, which became members of the EU in 2004 and 2007, are nowadays only interesting because of a number of judgments delivered by the Court of Justice having an impact beyond the mere interpretation of foregone provisions.

There are other categories of treaties, the purpose of which has a more permanent character. For instance, the Agreement on the European Economic Area (EEA) with Norway, Iceland and Liechtenstein and the association treaties between the EU and Switzerland are meant to establish a durable relationship between those countries and the Union, and provide, amongst others, for full free movement of persons.[220] Further, the Euro-Mediterranean Association Agreements also have a permanent character and provide for cooperation in many aspects. Hereunder, each of the categories mentioned will be briefly addressed.

3.1.3. THE EUROPEAN ECONOMIC AREA AND THE ASSOCIATION WITH SWITZERLAND

Under both the EEA and the treaties with Switzerland, the associated countries undertake to accept the Union *acquis* in the field of free movement, which has effectively resulted in full freedom of movement of persons between the EU, the EEA and Switzerland, in accordance with the conditions laid down in Union legislation. Under both Association Agreements, a Joint Committee has been established, the primary task of which is to ensure incorporation of Union legislation into the Agreements. Although the EEA Treaty initially did not cover the right to stay as economically non-active persons, and Switzerland retained the right to set annual quota for granting residence permits, these derogations have subsequently been abolished. In daily practice, nationals from Norway, Iceland, Liechtenstein and Switzerland are hardly considered 'third-country nationals' anymore. But according to the simple definition of the term (everybody who does not have the nationality of an EU Member

---

[220] The association between the EU and Switzerland has been moulded in several bilateral treaties, one of which exclusively deals with the free movement of persons (the EC-Switzerland Agreement on Free Movement of Persons), which came into force on 1 June 2002. As a result of the EU enlargement on 1 May 2004, this Agreement has been supplemented by an Additional Protocol containing provisions for the gradual introduction of the free movement of persons regime extending to the new EU Member States. This Protocol came into force on 1 April 2006.

State), they are. See, however, Article 3 Returns Directive (Directive 2008/115/EC), defining third-country nationals – with reference to Article 2(5) Schengen Borders Code – as not being either a: (i) EU citizen; (ii) third-country national family member of an EU citizen exercising his or her right to free movement; or (iii) third-country national who, under agreements between the Community and third countries, enjoys rights of free movement equivalent to those of Union citizens.

3.1.4. COOPERATION WITH MEDITERRANEAN COUNTRIES

In the 1970s, Cooperation Agreements were concluded with several Maghreb countries. Unlike the Association Agreement with Turkey, these agreements do not have a far-reaching impact on immigration issues, but they are not without importance. In the *Kziber* judgment[221] the Court attributed direct effect to a provision (Article 41(1)) in the Cooperation Agreement between the EEC and Morocco, according to which workers of Moroccan nationality and the members of their families residing with them enjoy freedom from discrimination on grounds of nationality in the field of social security. This provision was deemed irreconcilable with the refusal by a Member State to grant an unemployment allowance to a member of the family of a Moroccan worker on the sole ground that he had Moroccan nationality. In another judgment however, the Court added that if the dependent children of a Moroccan worker do not reside in the Community, with regard to study finance, neither the Moroccan worker concerned, nor his children, can rely on the principle of prohibition of discrimination on the basis of nationality laid down in that provision.[222] Moreover, dual nationals do not seem to be covered by the prohibition of discrimination on grounds of nationality laid down in the Cooperation Agreement. In the case of *Mesbah*, who obtained Belgian nationality in addition to his Moroccan nationality before a member of his family took up residence in Belgium, the Court found Article 41(1) of the Agreement not to apply to that family member.[223]

The Cooperation Agreements concluded in the 1970s have been replaced by Euro-Mediterranean Association Agreements.[224] In the Euro-Mediterranean

---

[221] ECJ 31 January 1991, *Kziber*, Case C-18/90.
[222] ECJ 20 March 201, *Fahmi*, Case C-33/99.
[223] ECJ 11 November 1999, *Mesbah*, Case C-179/98.
[224] Since 2008, Mediterranean Association Agreements have been concluded with Tunisia, Israel, Morocco, Jordan, Egypt, Algeria and Lebanon. Further, an Agreement has been concluded on an interim basis with the Palestinian Authority and an Agreement was signed with Syria in 2004. For the Agreements in force, see: Decision 2005/690/EC, Decision 2004/635/EC, Decision 2002/357/EC, Decision 2000/384/EC, Decision 2000/204/EC, Decision 98/238/EC, concerning the conclusion of a Euro-Mediterranean Agreement establishing an association

Agreement of 26 February 1996 establishing an association between the EC and Morocco[225] a similar provision on non-discrimination on grounds of nationality is included (Article 64).

3.1.5. EUROPE AGREEMENTS

In the 1990s, Association Agreements were concluded with Middle and Eastern European Countries as an overture to their accession to the European Union.[226] All these states have subsequently acceded to the EU. The ECJ has produced some noteworthy judgments on the Europe Agreements, which may remain of value for the interpretation of current provisions laid down in Community law. It is evident from these judgments that the Court applies its consistent approach regarding issues of free movement to treaties concluded with third countries, without neglecting specific characteristics distinguishing these treaties from general community law.

The main issue under the Europe Agreements was the scope to be accorded to a provision common to all Europe Agreements, which provided that nationals and companies of the associating countries were to be treated no less favourably than companies and nationals of the host Member State with respect to establishment. According to the Court in the cases of *Barkoci and Malik*,[227] this provision had direct effect and provided nationals of the associating states with a right of entry and residence for the purpose of establishment. However, this was not an absolute right, because the Association Agreements also contained a provision stating that the Contracting Parties were not prevented from applying their laws and regulations regarding entry and stay, work, labour conditions and the establishment of natural persons and supply of services, provided that they did not apply them in a manner as to nullify or impair the benefits accruing to any Party under the terms of a specific provision of the Agreement. In the *Barkoci and Malik* judgment, the Court sought to balance the two conflicting requirements, by stating that Member States are allowed to have a system of prior national control before an entry clearance is given, but that it may not be made impossible or very difficult for a person from an association country arriving at the border without an entry clearance, to be able to benefit from his right to enter and to reside.

---

between the European Communities and their Member States, of the one part, and, respectively, the People's Democratic Republic of Algeria, the Arab Republic of Egypt, the Hashemite Kingdom of Jordan, the State of Israel, the Kingdom of Morocco and the Republic of Tunisia.

[225] OJ L 70, 18 March 2000, p. 2–204.

[226] See, for instance, Europe Agreement EC-Romania, OJ L 357, 31/12/1994, p. 0002–0189; Europe Agreement EC-Bulgaria, OJ L 358, 31/12/1994, p. 0003–0222.

[227] ECJ 27 September 2001, *Barkoci and Malik*, Case C-257/99.

In the *Panayotova* judgment,[228] the Court considered that the scheme applicable to the issuing of an entry clearance must be based on procedures that are easily accessible and capable of ensuring that the persons concerned will have their applications dealt with objectively and within a reasonable time. Refusals to grant an entry clearance must, furthermore, be capable of being challenged in judicial or quasi-judicial proceedings. As the Court based these requirements not on the text of the agreements but on the Community law principle of effective judicial protection, the requirements laid down in the *Panayotova* judgment may also be relevant for other entry procedures, like visa procedures under the Visa Code.

3.2. THE ASSOCIATION TREATY WITH TURKEY

The oldest Association Treaty still in force is the Association Agreement between the European Economic Community and Turkey of 1963, modified by an Additional Protocol in 1970.[229] An Association Council was established under this Agreement, which has made a number of implementing decisions. The Association Agreement envisaged the gradual strengthening of cooperation between Turkey and the EEC in economic and trade matters, which would eventually have to result in the establishment of a customs union. This customs union was established in 1995 by Decision No. 1/95 of the Association Council. A similar Agreement with Greece signed in 1961 led to Greece's entry into the Community in 1981. Turkey remains in the Union's waiting room, and the issue of its membership of the EU, for which negotiations began in 2005, is still subject to controversy.

For a long time, the Association Agreement and the decisions of the Association Council were considered to be of little practical importance for Turkish citizens residing in the EU. This perception began to change in 1987, when the ECJ decided that it is competent to give preliminary rulings on the Association Agreement, by reasoning that the provisions of the Agreement form an integral part of the community legal system.[230] In 1990, the ECJ confirmed that this competence extends to decisions made by the Association Council.[231] It ruled, among other things, that a number of provisions of Decision 1/80 of the Association Council, providing for the gradual strengthening of the position of

---

[228] ECJ 16 November 2004, *Panayotova*, Case C-327/02.
[229] Agreement establishing an Association between the European Economic Community and Turkey, signed 12 September 1963; Additional Protocol and Financial Protocol, signed 23 November 1970, annexed to the Agreement establishing the Association between the European Economic Community and Turkey and on measures to be taken for their entry into force. Both instruments have been published in OJ 1977 L361/2.
[230] ECJ 30 September 1987, *Demirel*, Case 12/86.
[231] ECJ 20 September 1990, *Sevince*, Case C-192/89.

Turkish workers within the EU, have direct effect and can be invoked by Turkish citizens before national authorities of the Member States. In ensuing case law, the ECJ has developed an elaborate set of directly effective rights for Turkish workers, their family members and the second generation. Moreover, self-employed persons can also derive rights from the Association Treaty and the Additional Protocol.

Similar to the Cooperation and Europe Agreements, the Court of Justice applies its characteristic Union law approach to the Association Treaty as far as possible. In section 2.3.2, above, some characteristic elements of the Court's case law were mentioned: fundamental rights are interpreted expansively, limitations to those rights are interpreted restrictively, key terms cannot be interpreted by the Member States as they wish, because they are Community concepts. In its case law on the Association Treaty, the Court applies the same principles.[232]

The Association Agreement itself does not contain many provisions that are of immediate relevance to the freedom of movement of Turks in EU countries. Two provisions apparently referring to general principles contained in Community law should be mentioned. Article 7 Association Agreement is broadly similar to Article 4(3) TEU, laying down the principle of sincere cooperation, and obliges the Contracting Parties to take all appropriate measures, whether of general or particular nature, to ensure fulfilment of the obligations arising out of the Agreement. They shall abstain from any measure that could jeopardise the attainment of the objective of the Agreement. Article 9 Association Agreement is very much alike to Article 18 TFEU, and prohibits discrimination on grounds of nationality, within the scope of application of the Agreement and without prejudice to any special provisions contained therein.

The Additional Protocol is more explicit on issues of migration. Article 36 Additional Protocol states that the free movement of workers between the EEC and Turkey will gradually be established according to the principles of the Association Agreement within 12 to 23 years after the entry into force of the Protocol. As the Protocol entered into force in 1973, the latest date for implementing Article 36 would have been 1996. Full implementation of this provision has never taken place, however, although the Association Council did issue two Decisions on the rights of Turkish workers, one in 1976, and a renewed version in 1980, Decision 1/80.[233] Since the latter Decision, no further initiatives concerning free movement of Turkish citizens have been undertaken. The

---

[232] ECJ 6 June 1995, *Bozkurt*, Case C-434/93, paras. 14, 19, 20; ECJ 23 January 1997, *Tetik*, Case C-171/95, paras. 20, 28; ECJ 30 September 1997, *Günaydin*, Case C-36/96, para. 21; ECJ 30 September 1997, *Ertanir*, Case C-98/96, para. 21, ECJ 26 November 1998, *Birden*, Case C-1/97, para. 23.
[233] Decision No 1/80 of the Association Council on the development of the Association, 19 September 1980.

freedom of establishment and the freedom of services are mentioned in Chapter 11 of the Protocol. The first provision of this chapter, Article 41(1), contains a standstill clause: the Contracting Parties refrain from introducing, between themselves, any new restrictions on the freedom of establishment and the freedom to provide services. According to the *Savas* judgment, this provision has direct effect.[234] The provision is not capable of conferring a right to establishment to Turkish nationals, but it does prohibit the introduction of new national restrictions on the freedom of establishment and the freedom to provide services as from the date on which the Protocol entered into force (1 January 1973).

Decision 1/80 of the Association Council has proven to encompass the most important body of provisions governing the rights of Turkish workers and their families. Relevant are Articles 6 to 16 (Chapter II, section 1) of the Decision, of which the core provisions are Article 6(1), granting a gradually increasing right of access to the labour market of a Member State to Turkish workers; and Article 7, which extends the gradually increasing right of access to the labour market to family members of workers duly registered as belonging to the labour force of a Member State. Under both provisions, the ECJ decided that a right of access to the labour market must be interpreted as implying a right to lawful residence.[235] As a result of the interpretation of Article 7 Decision 1/80 in particular, the residence rights of second-generation Turks are so strong that they amount to a permanent right to stay, unless they leave the Member States for a significant length of time or for reasons of public policy, public security or public health. Both provisions will be explained more extensively in the following sections.

Article 14 Decision 1/80 states that the provisions of Chapter II, section 1 of Decision 1/80 shall be applied subject to limitations justified on grounds of public policy, public security or public health. This provision has been explained as referring to the EU standards developed in the regime on free movement of EU citizens.

Article 13 Decision 1/80 contains a standstill clause, according to which, the Member States of the Community and Turkey may not introduce new restrictions on the conditions of access to employment applicable to workers and members of their family who are legally resident and employed in their respective territories. The meaning of this clause is elaborately explained in section 3.5.3.

---

[234]   ECJ 11 September 2000, *Savas*, Case C-37/98.
[235]   ECJ 16 March 2000, *Ergat*, Case C-329/97, paras. 41, 56, 58.

3.3. WORKERS

3.3.1. GRADUAL ACCESS OF TURKISH WORKERS TO THE LABOUR MARKET

The basic principle of Decision 1/80 is that Member States are free to control first access to their countries by Turkish nationals, and to determine the conditions of their legal residence. In other words, Turkish workers do not have the right of free movement into the European Union. But as we will see below, once a Turkish national is admitted under national immigration law of a Member State to work on its territory, a legal position under Decision 1/80 starts to build up.

According to Article 6(1) Decision 1/80, a Turkish worker, duly registered as belonging to the labour force of a Member State, shall be entitled, after one year of legal employment, to the renewal of his permit to work for the same employer, if a job is available. After three years of legal employment, the worker shall be entitled to respond to another offer of employment, with an employer of his choice, for the same occupation. But this right is subject to the priority Member States may give to EU workers. After four years of legal employment the Turkish worker shall enjoy free access to any paid employment of his choice in the receiving Member State, no longer subject to any priority considerations. Although Article 6 only speaks of a right of access to the labour market, the far-reaching impact of Article 6 became visible when the ECJ interpreted the right of access to the labour market as necessarily implying a right to legal residence.[236] To rule otherwise, the Court said, would deprive workers of the right of access to the labour market and the right to work as employed persons, of all effect. Further, it became settled case law that the rights conferred on Turkish workers by Article 6(1) Decision 1/80 are accorded, irrespective of whether or not the authorities of the host Member State have issued a specific administrative document, such as a work permit or a residence permit.

A number of concepts used in Article 6(1) Decision 1/80 should be clarified. What is a 'worker'? What does it mean to be 'duly registered as belonging to the labour force'? What is 'legal employment'?

3.3.2. 'WORKER'

The concept of a 'worker' in Decision 1/80 must be interpreted according to EU law.[237] As became clear in the previous chapter, this implies that the concept has

---

[236] ECJ 20 September 1990, *Sevince*, Case C-192/89, para. 29; ECJ 6 June 1995, *Bozkurt*, Case C-434/93, paras. 29, 30; ECJ 30 September 1997, *Günaydin*, Case C-36/96, para. 49; ECJ 30 September 1997, *Ertanir*, Case C-98/96, para. 55; ECJ 26 November 1998, *Birden*, Case C-1/97, para. 65.

[237] ECJ 26 November 1998, *Birden*, Case C-1/97, para. 24.

a specific Union law meaning, must not be interpreted narrowly, and must be defined in accordance with objective criteria. In order to be treated as a worker, a person must pursue an activity that is effective and genuine, to the exclusion of activities on such a small scale as to be regarded as purely marginal and ancillary.[238]

The essential feature of an employment relationship is that for a certain period of time a person performs services for, and under the direction of, another person, in return for which he receives remuneration. In the case of *Birden*, who was employed under a publicly subsidised scheme meant to enable him to improve his chance of finding other work, the Court held that the *sui generis* nature of the employment relationship and the level of productivity of a person cannot have any consequence in regard to whether or not the person is to be regarded as a worker. *Günaydin* complied with the condition of legal employment when he was legally working during his studies with a restriction in respect of the region where he was allowed to work.[239] *Kurz* also complied with this condition when he was working as an apprentice in a vocational training as a plumber.[240]

3.3.3. 'BEING DULY REGISTERED AS BELONGING TO THE LABOUR FORCE'

The concept of 'being duly registered as belonging to the labour force' must be regarded as applying to all workers who have complied with the requirements laid down by legislation in the Member State concerned, and are thus entitled to pursue an occupation in its territory. It cannot be interpreted as applying only to the labour market in general, as opposed to a specific market with a social objective supported by the public authorities.[241]

In the case of a truck driver, *Bozkurt*, who was employed by a Dutch company as an international lorry driver on routes between Turkey and the Netherlands, the question arose as to whether he could be said to belong to the Dutch labour force. According to the Court, a worker is duly registered as belonging to the labour force when the legal relationship of employment of the person can be located within the territory of a Member State, or when he retains a sufficiently close link with that territory, taking into account, in particular, the place where the Turkish national was hired, the territory on or from which the paid activity is pursued, and the applicable national legislation in the field of employment and

---

[238] See also ECJ 4 February 2010, *Genc*, Case C-14/09.
[239] ECJ 30 September 1997, *Günaydin*, Case C-36/96.
[240] ECJ 19 November 2002, *Kurz*, Case C-188/00.
[241] ECJ 26 November 1998, *Birden*, Case C-1/97, para. 51.

social security law.[242] On the basis of these criteria, it was confirmed that Bozkurt belonged to the Dutch labour force.[243]

3.3.4. 'LEGAL EMPLOYMENT'

The concept of legal employment presupposes a stable and secure situation as a member of the labour force of a Member State, and, by virtue of this, implies the existence of an undisputed right of residence.[244] *Sevince*, who was awaiting a decision appealing against a refusal of a right of residence while his expulsion was suspended during the appeal, was not considered to be in a stable and secure situation.[245] Neither was *Kuş*, who was only allowed to await the decision on an application for a residence permit.[246] The Court stated that periods during which a person is employed cannot be regarded as legal employment for the purposes of Article 6(1) Decision 1/80, so long as it is not definitively established that, during those periods, the worker had a legal right of residence. Otherwise, a judicial decision finally refusing him that right would be rendered nugatory and would enable him to acquire the rights provided in that Article during a period when he does not fulfil the conditions.[247] In the case of *Kol*, the Court held that periods of employment under a residence permit obtained only by means of fraudulent conduct, which in the case of *Kol*, led to a conviction, cannot be regarded as based on a stable and secure situation.[248] In the *Altun* judgment,[249] the Court stated that such fraudulent conduct by that worker was capable of having effects as regards legal rights of his family members. Those effects must, however, be determined with regard to the date on which the national authorities of the host Member State adopted a decision to withdraw the residence permit of the worker. If, on the date on which the residence permit of a Turkish worker is withdrawn, the rights of his family members are inchoate in so far as the condition relating to the period of actual cohabitation with the worker laid down by the first paragraph of Article 7 of Decision No 1/80 has not yet been fulfilled, the Member States are entitled to draw the appropriate conclusions from the fraudulent conduct of that worker with respect to his family members. However, if the latter

---

[242] ECJ 6 June 1995, *Bozkurt*, Case C-434/93, paras. 22, 23; ECJ 30 September 1997, *Günaydin*, Case C-36/96, para. 29; ECJ 30 September 1997, *Ertanir*, Case C-98/96, para. 39, ECJ 26 November 1998, *Birden*, Case C-1/97, para. 32.

[243] Afdeling bestuursrechtspraak Raad van State 19 March 1996, No. R.02.91.2947 *Rechtspraak Vreemdelingenrecht* 1996, 95.

[244] ECJ 20 September 1990, *Sevince*, Case C-192/89, para. 30; ECJ 6 June 1995, *Bozkurt*, Case C-434/93, para. 26; ECJ 16 December 1992, *Kuş*, Case C-237/91, paras. 12, 22.

[245] ECJ 20 September 1990, *Sevince*, Case C-192/89, para. 31.

[246] ECJ 16 December 1992, *Kuş*, Case C-237/91, para. 13.

[247] *Ibid*, para. 16.

[248] ECJ 5 July 1997, *Kol*, Case C-285/95, para. 27.

[249] ECJ 18 December 2008, *Altun*, Case C-337/07.

have acquired an autonomous right of access to the employment market of the host Member State, and, as a corollary, a right of residence there, those rights may no longer be called into question on account of irregularities which, in the past, affected the Turkish worker's right of residence.

The date of withdrawal being crucial, important consequences are connected with the question of whether a residence permit granted on grounds of family reunification of a Turkish worker, who ceased cohabiting with his spouse, may be withdrawn with retroactive effect to the date of the separation. In the judgments on *Unal* and *Gülbahce*, the Court ruled that the first indent of Article 6(1) Decision 1/80 precludes the competent national authorities from withdrawing the residence permit of a Turkish worker with retroactive effect from the point in time at which there was no longer compliance with the ground on the basis of which his residence permit had been issued under national law if there is no question of fraudulent conduct on the part of that worker and that withdrawal occurs after the completion of the period of one year of legal employment.[250]

In *Altun*, it was also made clear that Decision 1/80 does not differentiate between whether the legal residence was acquired under voluntary or forced migration. A refusal to apply Decision 1/80 on account of the status of political refugee enjoyed by Mr. Ali Altun, when his permission to enter and to stay in Germany was issued, would impair the rights that he and the members of his family derived from that decision.

From the text of Article 6(1) Decision 1/80, it is not completely clear, whether the first year of legal employment must be with one employer, or that it is sufficient that there was, in total, one year of legal employment, regardless of the number of employments. However, according to the Court in the *Sedef* case, the first year of legal employment of the first indent of Article 6(1), may not be built up by different consecutive contracts with different employers:

> (…) a Turkish migrant worker cannot, as a general rule, rely on entitlement under the third indent of Article 6(1) of Decision 1/80 merely on account of having been in legal employment in the host Member State for more than four years if he has not initially worked for more than one year for the same employer, and subsequently worked for him for two further years.[251]

A Turkish worker can only rely on the rights conferred on him by the first and second indents of Article 6(2) Decision 1/80, where his paid employment with a second employer complies with the conditions laid down by law in the host Member State governing entry into its territory and employment.[252] If he does

---

[250]   ECJ 29 September 2011, *Unal*, Case C-187/10; ECJ 8 November 2012, *Gülbahce*, Case C-268/11.
[251]   ECJ 10 January 2006, *Sedef*, Case C-230/03.
[252]   ECJ 26 October 2006, *Güzeli*, Case C-4/05.

not yet enjoy the right to free access to any paid employment of his choice under the third indent, he must be in legal employment without interruption in the host Member State, unless he can rely on a legitimate reason of the type laid down in Article 6(2) to justify his temporary absence from the labour force.

Another question is, whether legal employment on the basis of a temporary contract is sufficient for complying with the condition of Article 6(1) first indent. The temporary nature of the contract is not relevant, according to the Court. Nor is it relevant that a residence permit is issued only for a fixed period.[253] In *Ertanir*, a Turkish national had a residence permit to work as a chef specialising in Turkish cuisine for a limited period, and was supposed to return to Turkey after that period.[254] This could not prevent him from successfully invoking Article 6(1). Likewise, the reason for the issuing of the residence permit is not of any relevance.

Often, the residence permit enabling the Turkish national to work lawfully is not explicitly granted for reasons of work, but on other grounds, like family reunification. In the case of *Birden*, the Court considered that the fact that work and residence permits were granted to the worker only after his marriage to a German national did not affect his rights under Article 6(1), even though the marriage was subsequently dissolved.[255] A Turkish worker may rely on the right to free movement, which he derives from the Association Agreement, even if the purpose for which he entered the host Member State no longer exists. Where such a worker satisfies the conditions set out in Article 6(1) Decision 1/80, his right of residence in the host Member State cannot be made subject to additional conditions with regard to the existence of interests capable of justifying residence or the nature of the employment.[256]

3.3.5. TERMINATION OF THE RESIDENCE RIGHT OF A WORKER

Article 6 Decision 1/80 covers the situation of Turkish workers who are actually working. The second sentence of Article 6 holds that annual holidays and absences for reasons of maternity or an accident at work, or short periods of sickness, shall be treated as periods of legal employment. Periods of involuntary unemployment duly certified by the relevant authorities and long absences on account of sickness shall not be treated as periods of legal employment, but shall not affect rights acquired as the result of the preceding period of employment. This second sentence aims to ensure that periods of interruption of legal

---

[253]   ECJ 26 November 1998, *Birden*, Case C-1/97, para. 64.
[254]   ECJ 30 September 1997, *Ertanir*, Case C-98/96.
[255]   ECJ 26 November 1998, *Birden*, Case C-1/97, para. 66.
[256]   ECJ 4 February 2010, *Genc*, Case C-14/09.

employment on account of involuntary unemployment and long-term sickness do not affect the rights that the Turkish worker has already acquired owing to preceding periods of employment, the length of which is fixed in each of the three indents of Article 6(1) respectively.[257]

How long does the right to legal residence under Decision 1/80 last? Under what conditions can it be terminated? There are two grounds terminating the employment rights and the concomitant right of residence under Article 6(1) Decision 1/80:

- first, the right ceases to exist, according to the Court, when the Turkish worker definitively ceases to belong to the legitimate labour force of the host Member State:[258] and
- second, the residence right may be terminated by a Member State on grounds of public policy, public security or public health (Article 14 Decision 1/80).

These two termination grounds are discussed in the following sections.

3.3.6. CEASING TO BELONG TO THE LABOUR FORCE

The circumstances under which a Turkish worker is considered to have ceased to belong to the labour force have been spelled out by the Court in various judgments. According to the Court in the *Bozkurt* case,[259] Article 6 Decision 1/80 does not cover the situation of a Turkish worker who has reached the age of retirement, or becomes totally and permanently incapacitated for work, even if the incapacitation is the result of an accident at work. From the judgment in the case of *Tetik*,[260] in connection to Article 6(2) Decision 1/80, it can be concluded that lengthy and voluntary unemployment has the effect that a worker ceases to belong to the labour force. In *Doğan*, the Court added that the rights conferred on a Turkish worker by Article 6(1) may only be limited on account of the fact that he has failed to find paid employment within a reasonable time.[261]

By contrast, according to Article 6(2), a worker does not cease to belong to the labour force when his unemployment is involuntary. According to the *Altun* judgment,[262] this also has an effect on the rights of family members. Under certain conditions, voluntary unemployment may also be excused, as in the case of *Tetik*, who had free access to the labour market under the third indent of Article 6(1),

---

[257] ECJ 26 October 2006, *Güzeli*, Case C-4/05.
[258] ECJ 7 July 2005, *Doğan*, Case C-383/03.
[259] ECJ 6 June 1995, *Bozkurt*, Case C-434/93, para. 39.
[260] ECJ 23 January 1997, *Tetik*, Case C-171/95.
[261] ECJ 7 July 2005, *Doğan*, Case C-383/03.
[262] ECJ 18 December 2008, *Altun*, Case C-337/07, paras. 38, 39.

had quit his job on board a German ship, and was looking for work on land. The Court held that:

> a Turkish worker who has been legally employed for more than four years in a Member State, who decides voluntarily to leave his employment in order to seek new work in the same Member State, and is unable immediately to enter into a new employment relationship, enjoys in that State, for a reasonable period, a right of residence for the purpose of seeking new paid employment there, provided that he continues to be duly registered as belonging to the labour force of the Member State concerned, complying, where appropriate, with the requirements of the legislation in force in that State, for instance, by registering as a person seeking employment and making himself available to the employment authorities.[263]

Furthermore, when a Turkish national is late in applying for the extension of his residence permit, this does not affect his position as belonging to the labour force.[264]

If a Turkish worker is unable to work due to detention during criminal proceedings, must his situation then be labelled as involuntary unemployment because he obviously does not want to be detained, or as voluntary unemployment, because it was arguably his own fault that he ended up in that situation? The Court has avoided this discussion, and simply stated that detention is not a relevant interruption for establishing whether a person belongs to the labour force. For a Turkish national enjoying the right of free access to any paid employment under the third indent of Article 6(1) Decision 1/80, the mere fact that he is detained is of no influence on his belonging to the labour force, even if the detention is lengthy, and even if it is followed by long-term drug treatment.[265] It is, however, important that the absence from the labour market is only temporary. In the case of *Nazli*, the Court attached weight to the fact that he had found a job again within a reasonable period after his release.[266]

The approach of the *Nazli* judgment of 2000 seems to be different from the approach of the Court, in 2014, in the case of *Onuekwere*, which was not about EEC-Turkey Association law, but about the rights of third-country family members under the Citizens' Directive (see section 2.2.2).[267] There, the Court said that periods of imprisonment in the host Member State of a third-country national, who is a family member of a Union citizen who has acquired the right of permanent residence in that Member State during those periods, cannot be taken into consideration in the context of the acquisition by that national of the

263 ECJ 23 January 1997, *Tetik*, Case C-171/95.
264 ECJ 16 March 2000, *Ergat*, Case C-329/97, paras. 51–67.
265 ECJ 7 July 2005, *Doğan*, Case C-383/03; ECJ 7 July 2005, *Aydinli*, Case C-373/03.
266 ECJ 10 February 2000, *Nazli*, Case C-340/97, para. 49.
267 ECJ 16 January 2014, *Onuekwere*, Case 378/12.

right of permanent residence, and that continuity of residence is interrupted by such periods of imprisonment.

3.3.7. EXCEPTIONS OF PUBLIC POLICY, PUBLIC SECURITY AND PUBLIC HEALTH

Although detention does not deprive a Turkish worker of his residence rights, the severity of the committed criminal act as such may indeed influence the Turkish worker's right to legal residence. The conditions under which a worker may be subjected to an expulsion measure based on grounds of public policy, public security or public health, are set out in the *Nazli* judgment.[268]

Nazli, who lived in Germany and had worked for various employers, was convicted by a regional court to a term of imprisonment of 21 months, suspended in full, for being an accomplice to the trafficking of 1500 grams of heroin. The criminal court justified the suspension of the entire sentence on the basis of its firm belief that the lapse was an isolated one, and that Mr. Nazli, who was feeling genuine remorse and dismay at what he had done, would learn the necessary lessons. In addition, Mr. Nazli was well-integrated socially, had found work immediately after his release, and had played only a minor role in the commission of the offence. After the conviction, Nazli's application for extension of his residence permit was refused. The regional administrative court dealing with Nazli's appeal asked the ECJ whether expulsion on general preventive grounds, as a deterrent to other aliens, is compatible with Decision 1/80.

The Court answered that Article 14(1) Decision 1/80 precludes the expulsion of a Turkish national who enjoys a right granted directly by that Decision without the personal conduct of the person concerned giving reason to consider that he will commit other serious offences prejudicial to the requirements of public policy in the host Member State. The Court referred to the principles developed in its earlier judgments in *Bouchereau*,[269] *Calfa*,[270] and *Bonsignore*.[271] There must be a genuine and sufficiently serious threat to one of the fundamental interests of society, and there must be evidence of personal conduct constituting a present threat to the requirements of public policy. The Court underlined that the principles developed in its case law on the free movement of EU citizens are equally applicable, as far as possible, to the terms of the Association Agreement:

> The Court has consistently inferred from the wording of Article 12 of the Association Agreement and Article 36 of the Additional Protocol, as well as from the objective of Decision No 1/80, that the principles enshrined in Articles 48, 49 and 50 of the Treaty

---

[268] ECJ 10 February 2000, *Nazli*, Case C-340/97, para. 49.
[269] ECJ 27 October 1977, *Boucherau*, Case 30/77, para. 35.
[270] ECJ 19 January 1999, *Calfa*, Case C-348/96, paras. 22, 23, 24.
[271] ECJ 26 February 1975, *Bonsignore*, Case 67/74, para. 7.

must be extended, so far as possible, to Turkish nationals who enjoy the rights conferred by Decision No 1/80 (…).[272]

In the *Cetinkaya* judgment, the Court affirmed, further, that Article 14 Decision 1/80 precludes national courts, when reviewing the lawfulness of the expulsion of a Turkish national, from not taking into consideration factual matters, which occurred after the final decision of the competent authorities, which may indicate that a limitation of the rights of the person concerned is no longer justified.[273]

Turkish citizens whose rights under Decision 1/80 are terminated have the same procedural guarantees as EU citizens. In the *Dörr and Ünal* judgment,[274] the Court considered that the procedural guarantees applicable to expulsion decisions of EU citizens and their families, as laid down in Articles 8 and 9 of Directive 64/221, also apply to Turkish nationals whose legal status is defined by Articles 6 or 7 Decision 1/80. These procedural guarantees are now laid down in Article 31 of Citizens' Directive.

However, the extra strong protection for Union citizens having stayed in the host Member State longer than 10 years, provided for in Article 28(3)a Citizens' Directive, is not applicable to Turkish citizens who stayed in a Member State longer than 10 years, on the basis of Article 7 Decision 1/80. In the *Ziebell* judgment, the Court said that protection against expulsion conferred by Article 14(1) decision 1/80 on Turkish nationals does not have the same scope as that conferred on citizens of the Union under Article 28(3)(a) Citizens' Directive, with the result that the scheme of protection against expulsion enjoyed by the latter cannot be applied *mutatis mutandis* to Turkish nationals for the purpose of determining the meaning and scope of Article 14(1) of Decision No 1/80.[275]

3.4. FAMILY MEMBERS

3.4.1. RIGHTS OF FAMILY MEMBERS

In line with the underlying premise that Member States are free to control the first access of Turkish citizens to their countries, Decision 1/80 does not provide for a right to family reunification. Member States remain free to decide under what conditions family members are eligible for joining a Turkish worker

---

[272]   ECJ 10 February 2000, *Nazli*, Case C-340/97, para. 55. See also ECJ 6 June 1995, *Bozkurt*, Case C-434/93, para. 14, 19, 20; ECJ 23 January 1997, *Tetik*, Case C-171/95, paras. 20, 28; ECJ 26 November 1998, *Birden*, Case C-1/97, para. 23; ECJ 30 September 1997, *Günaydin*, Case C-36/96, para. 21; ECJ 30 September 1997, *Ertanir*, Case C-98/96, para. 21.
[273]   ECJ 11 November 2004, *Cetinkaya*, Case C-467/02.
[274]   ECJ 2 June 2005, *Dörr and Ünal*, Case C-126/03.
[275]   ECJ 18 December 2012, *Ziebell,* Case C-371/08.

resident on its territory. It should be noted, however, that Turkish nationals may derive rights from the Directive on Family Reunification adopted in 2003, which provides a (conditional) right to family reunification for third-country nationals residing in one of the Member States. The Family Reunification Directive will be discussed in Chapter 2.3 of this book. Although family reunification is not dealt with by Decision 1/80, the Decision does grant strong residence rights to family members once they have been authorised to stay with the Turkish worker.

3.4.2. INDEPENDENT RIGHTS TO RESIDENCE FOR FAMILY MEMBERS

Article 7(1) of Decision 1/80 provides that the members of the family of a Turkish worker duly registered as belonging to the labour force of a Member State, who have been authorised to join him, enjoy a gradually increasing right of access to the labour market. According to the *Dülger* judgment, these rights are also given to family members who do not have Turkish nationality, but the nationality of a third country other than Turkey.[276] Similar to Turkish workers under Article 6(1), the Court has established that a right of access to the labour market granted to family members necessarily implies a right to legal residence.[277] If family members have been resident for at least three years in a Member State, they are entitled to respond to any offer of employment, subject to the priority given to workers of the Community. After five years of legal residence, they are completely free to respond to any offer of employment. Further, under Article 7(2), children of Turkish workers who have completed a course of vocational training in the host country may respond to any offer of employment there, irrespective of the length of time they have been resident in that Member State, provided that one of their parents has been legally employed in the Member State concerned for at least three years.

This implies that *children* of Turkish workers have two grounds for obtaining a right to legal residence in the host Member State:

(a) a period of legal residence with the Turkish worker; or
(b) the completion of vocational training, subject to the proviso that the parent has been legally employed for at least three years.

Other members of the family can only invoke the ground mentioned under (a). The meaning of the concept of 'family' has not been worked out by the Court in

---

[276] ECJ 19 July 2012, *Dülger*, Case C-451/11.
[277] ECJ 5 October 1994, *Eroğlu*, Case C-355/93, paras. 20, 23.

detail.[278] The Court has predominantly been occupied with the rights of children of Turkish workers. In the *Cetinkaya* judgment, the Court extended the effect of the first paragraph of Article 7 to children who were born and have always resided in the host Member State.[279] As many Turkish nationals presently living in EU Member States belong to the second or third generation, Article 7 Decision 1/80 is nowadays of prevailing importance.

3.4.3. PERIOD OF LEGAL RESIDENCE WITH A TURKISH WORKER

How long must family members remain with the Turkish worker to acquire the residence right under Article 7(1) Decision 1/80? According to the Court in the case of *Kadiman*,[280] Member States may require the family member to live with the worker during the first three years, but there may be exceptional cases, to be established by the national courts, in which a shorter period should be deemed sufficient. Apparently, the Court is of the opinion that a residence right comes into being already after the period of three years mentioned in Article 7(1), even though the freedom of access to the labour market is, at that time still, conditional upon priority given to EU workers.

In the *Altun* judgment,[281] the Court decided that the child of a Turkish worker could enjoy rights arising by virtue of that provision, where, during the three-year period when the child was co-habiting with that worker, the latter was working for two and a half years before being involuntarily unemployed for the following six months.

In the *Ergat* judgment, the Court went so far as to stipulate that Member States are no longer entitled to attach conditions to the residence of a member of a Turkish worker's family after that three-year period.[282] This implies that the residence right is for an unlimited period. Once the right to residence is acquired, it does not cease to exist when the child attains the age of majority and/or lives independently from his parent, nor when the parent ceases to belong to the labour force of the host state, for example, when he exercises his retirement rights.[283] Further, the Court is of the opinion that a marriage, entered into by the

---

[278] In the case of *Mesbah*, ECJ 11 November 1999, Case C-179/98, the Court considered that the concept of '*membres de la famille*' in Article 41(1) of the Cooperation Agreement between the EEC and Morocco, includes the ascendants of the worker and his spouse, who live with him in the host Member State.

[279] ECJ 11 November 2004, *Cetinkaya*, Case C-467/02, para. 26.

[280] ECJ 17 April 1997, *Kadiman*, Case C-135/95.

[281] ECJ 18 December 2008, *Altun*, Case C-337/07.

[282] ECJ 16 March 2000, *Ergat*, Case C-329/97, para. 38.

[283] ECJ 7 July 2005, *Aydinli*, Case C-373/03; ECJ 11 November 2004, *Cetinkaya*, Case C-467/02, paras. 32, 34.

member of the family of a Turkish worker, before expiry of the three-year period provided for under the first paragraph of Article 7 of Decision No 1/80, is irrelevant with regard to the retention of the right of residence enjoyed by the holder of that right, in so far as, during the whole of that period, that person actually lived under the same roof as the worker.[284]

A divorce which took place after the rights were acquired as a result of residing for at least five years with a Turkish spouse is of no effect with regard to the existence of those rights, even if the person concerned committed a serious offence against his spouse, which gave rise to a criminal conviction. This does not, however, preclude a measure ordering the expulsion of a Turkish national who has been convicted of criminal offences, provided that his personal conduct constitutes a present, genuine and sufficiently serious threat to a fundamental interest of society.[285]

3.4.4. VOCATIONAL TRAINING

Under the second paragraph of Article 7, children of Turkish workers are entitled to respond to any offer of employment in the host Member State after having completed a course of vocational training there, and consequently to be issued with a residence permit, when one of the parents has, in the past, been legally employed in that State for at least three years. It is not required that the parent in question still works, or is resident, in the Member State at the time when his child wishes to gain access to the employment market.[286] Unlike the first paragraph, the second paragraph of Article 7 is not designed to create conditions conducive to family unity in the host Member State. This residence right does not cease to exist when the child attains the age of majority, when he is no longer dependent on his parents and when he lives independently in the Member State concerned.[287] The child of a Turkish worker who was previously legally employed in the host Member State for more than three years, may rely in that Member State, after completing his or her vocational training course there, on the right of access to the employment market, and the corresponding right of residence, even though, after travelling back with the parents to their State of origin, he or she returned on his or her own to that Member State in order to start that training course there.[288]

---

[284] ECJ 16 June 2011, *Pehlivan*, Case C-484/10.
[285] ECJ 22 December 2012, *Metin Bozkurt*, Case C-303/08.
[286] ECJ 19 November 1998, *Akman*, Case C-210/97.
[287] ECJ 18 July 2007, *Derin*, Case C-325/05, paras. 53, 55.
[288] ECJ 21 January 2010, *Bekleyen*, C-462/08.

3.4.5. TERMINATION OF RESIDENCE RIGHTS OF FAMILY MEMBERS

Perhaps paradoxically, as a result of the Court's interpretation of Article 7 Decision 1/80, the legal position of family members regarding residence rights is stronger than that of Turkish workers themselves. Different from those of workers, the residence rights of children and other family members do not depend on the requirement of belonging to the labour force of the host Member State. Hence, for obtaining and preserving a right of residence, it is irrelevant whether the family members work or not. This means that the residence rights of family members approximate a permanent right of residence. Once they have obtained the right of access to the labour market – without necessarily making use of this right – family members can only forfeit their residence right if: (a) they pose a threat to public policy, public security or public health (Article 14(1) Decision 1/80); or (b) they leave the territory of the host Member State for a significant length of time without legitimate reason.[289]

At first sight, it may surprise that the legal position of family members surpasses that of the workers upon whom they are dependent. The Court has explained this difference from the aim and logic of Decision 1/80. In the *Derin* judgment, the Court held:

> A different interpretation of the first paragraph of Article 7 of Decision No. 1/80 would not be consistent with the aim and broad logic of Decision No. 1/80, which is intended to promote the gradual integration in the host Member State of Turkish nationals who satisfy the conditions laid down in one of the provisions of that Decision, and thus enjoy the rights conferred on them by the Decision (…).
>
> Given that Decision No. 1/80 draws a clear distinction between the situation of Turkish workers who have been legally employed in the host Member State for a specified period (Article 6 of the decision), and that of members of the families of such workers legally resident in the territory of the host Member State (Article 7 of the decision), and that, within the scheme of the Decision, Article 7 constitutes a *lex specialis* in relation to the rights laid down in the three indents of Article 6(1), which are gradually extended according to the period of legal paid employment (…), the rights conferred by Article 7 of Decision No. 1/80 cannot be limited in the same situations as those granted by Article 6 of the decision (…).[290]

It is remarkable, further, that in several respects, the rights of family members of Turkish workers appear to be even stronger than comparable rights of family members of EU citizens. While the residence rights of children of Turkish workers do not cease to exist when they attain the age of majority, children of

---

[289]   ECJ 18 July 2007, *Derin*, Case C-325/05; ECJ 16 February 2006, *Torun*, Case C-502/04.
[290]   ECJ 18 July 2007, *Derin*, Case C-325/05.

EU citizens lose their residence right after having reached the age of 21, and can no longer be considered dependant. In the *Derin* case, the Court was asked, among other things, to examine whether the rights of family members of Turkish workers were compatible with Article 59 Additional Protocol, stating that 'Turkey shall not receive more favourable treatment than that which Member States grant to one another pursuant to the Treaty establishing the Community'. The ECJ found that the two situations cannot be usefully compared. The Court underlined that Turkish family members do not have, as do the family members of an EU citizen, a right to join a worker to live as a family; their ability to join a worker depends rather on a decision of the national authorities taken solely on the basis of the law of the Member State concerned:

> Second, pursuant to Article 11 of Regulation No. 1612/68, the children who have the right to install themselves with the worker who is a national of one Member State and is employed in the territory of another Member State, enjoy, by virtue of that fact alone, the right to take up any activity as an employed person in the host Member State, whereas the right of the children of a migrant Turkish worker to be employed is specifically regulated by the first paragraph of Article 7 of Decision No. 1/80, a provision which lays down conditions which vary according to the length of legal residence with the migrant worker from whom they derive rights. Thus, during the first three years of residence, no right of that kind is accorded to Turkish nationals, whereas, after three years of legal residence with their family, they have the right to respond to an offer of employment, subject to the priority to be given to workers from the Member States. It is only after five years of legal residence that they enjoy free access to any paid employment of their choice.
>
> Finally, the Court has repeatedly held that, unlike workers from the Member States, Turkish nationals are not entitled to freedom of movement within the Community but can rely only on certain rights in the territory of the host Member State alone (…). Moreover, the case law of the Court relating to the conditions under which rights derived from Article 7 of Decision No. 1/80 can be restricted lays down, in addition to the exception based on public policy, public security and public health, which is applicable in the same way to Turkish nationals and to Community nationals (…), a second ground of loss of those rights which is applicable only to Turkish migrants, namely if they leave the territory of the host Member State for a significant length of time without legitimate reason (see paragraphs 54 and 57 of this judgment). In such a case, the authorities of the Member State concerned are entitled to require that, should the person concerned subsequently wish to resettle in that State, he must make a fresh application, either for authorisation to join the Turkish worker if he is still dependent on that worker, or to be admitted with a view to being employed there on the basis of Article 6 of that Decision (…).
>
> Accordingly, the situation of a child of a migrant Turkish worker cannot usefully be compared to that of a descendant of a national of a Member State, having regard to the significant differences between their respective legal situations. The more

favourable situation enjoyed by Member State nationals results, moreover, from the very wording of the applicable legislation.[291]

The right for a family member to invoke Article 7 Decision 1/80 does not terminate when the migrant Turkish worker with whom he or she reunites obtains the nationality of the Member State of residence but retains the Turkish nationality.[292] The case law on expulsion of Turkish workers for public policy reasons discussed above is equally applicable to family members.

3.5. STANDSTILL CLAUSES

3.5.1. IMPACT OF THE STANDSTILL CLAUSES

Since the *Savas* judgment,[293] growing attention has been paid to the meaning and the effect of standstill clauses. Such clauses depart from the situation as it is at the moment of their creation. They prohibit the partners in the Agreement from taking steps worsening that situation in relation to the purpose of the Agreement.

Two standstill clauses are relevant here:

Article 41(1) Additional Protocol:
The Contracting Parties shall refrain from introducing between themselves any new restrictions on the freedom of establishment and the freedom to provide services.

Article 13 Decision 1/80:
The Member States of the Community and Turkey may not introduce new restrictions on the conditions of access to employment applicable to workers and members of their families legally resident and employed in their respective territories.

Both provisions prohibit, generally, the introduction of new national restrictions to the right of establishment and the freedom to provide services and freedom of movement for workers from the date of the entry into force in the host Member State of the legal measure of which those Articles form part. According to the *Abatay and Sahin* judgment,[294] both provisions have direct effect in the Member States, so that Turkish nationals to whom they apply are entitled to rely on them before the national courts to prevent the application of inconsistent rules of national law.

---

[291] *Ibid*, paras. 65–68.
[292] ECJ 29 March 2012, *Kahveci and Inan,* Cases C-7/10 and C-9/10.
[293] ECJ 11 September 2000, *Savas*, Case C-37/98.
[294] ECJ 21 October 2003, *Abatay and Sahin*, Joint Cases C-317/01 and C-369/01.

In *Commission v. the Netherlands*,[295] the Court compared the two clauses, and came to the conclusion that both of them prohibit new restrictions in respect of the entry to the Member States of Turkish nationals intending to make use of the economic freedoms envisaged in the standstill clauses:

> With regard to Article 41(1), the Court held, in accordance with the judgments in *Tum and Dari* and *Soysal and Savatli*, that that provision prohibits the introduction, as from the date of entry into force of the legal act of which that provision forms part in the host Member State, of any new restrictions on the exercise of freedom of establishment or freedom to provide services, including those relating to the substantive and/or procedural conditions governing the first admission to the territory of that Member State of Turkish nationals intending to make use of those economic freedoms (*Sahin*, paragraph 64).

> The Court ruled that, as the standstill clause in Article 13 of Decision No 1/80 is of the same kind as that contained in Article 41(1) of the Additional Protocol, and as the objective pursued by those two clauses is identical, the interpretation of Article 41(1) must be equally valid as regards the standstill obligation which is the basis of Article 13 in relation to freedom of movement for workers (*Sahin*, paragraph 65).

> It follows that Article 13 of Decision No. 1/80 precludes the introduction into Netherlands legislation, as from the date on which Decision No. 1/80 entered into force in the Netherlands, of any new restrictions on the exercise of the free movement of workers, including those relating to the substantive and/or procedural conditions governing the first admission to the territory of that Member State of Turkish nationals intending to exercise that freedom.

The question of what must be understood to be 'new restrictions', is common to both provisions. However, although these two provisions have the same meaning, each of them has been given a very specific scope, which means that they cannot be applied concurrently. In the *Dereci* judgment,[296] the Court was asked to answer a question that did not distinguish between the two. However, the Court gave its opinion only with regard to the specific standstill clause which was applicable to the case concerned, that was, Article 41(1) Additional Protocol. The question concerned the meaning of a standstill clause in situations where a more liberal regime had been installed since the standstill clause had entered into force, and a Member State wished to curb the exercise of a freedom back to the same level existing in the beginning. The Court said:

> Article 41(1) of the Additional Protocol must be interpreted as meaning that the enactment of new legislation more restrictive than the previous legislation, which, for its part, relaxed earlier legislation concerning the conditions for the exercise of the

---

[295] ECJ 29 April 2010, *Commission v. the Netherlands*, Case 92/07, paras. 47–49.
[296] ECJ 15 November 2011, *Dereci*, Case C-256/11.

freedom of establishment of Turkish nationals at the time of the entry into force of that Protocol in the Member State concerned must be considered to be a 'new restriction' within the meaning of that provision.

Earlier, in *Toprak and Oguz*,[297] a similar answer was given as regards Article 13 Decision 1/80:

Article 13 of Decision No. 1/80 must be interpreted as meaning that a tightening of a provision introduced after 1 December 1980, which provided for a relaxation of the provision applicable on 1 December 1980, constitutes a 'new restriction' within the meaning of that Article, even where that tightening does not make the conditions governing the acquisition of that permit more stringent than those which resulted from the provision in force on 1 December 1980, this being a matter for the national court to determine.

By these interpretative opinions the Court gave a relatively wide scope to the standstill clauses, as will be seen in the following sections.

3.5.2. THE STANDSTILL CLAUSE OF ARTICLE 41(1) ADDITIONAL PROTOCOL AND THE RIGHTS OF SELF-EMPLOYED TURKISH NATIONALS

Although no right to establishment is granted under EEC-Turkey Association law, the standstill clause of Article 41(1) Additional Protocol has a certain impact on the conditions under which self-employed Turkish nationals are allowed to work in EU Member States. Article 41(1) Additional Protocol prohibits the introduction of new national restrictions on the freedom of establishment and the freedom to provide services as from the date on which the Protocol entered into force (1 January 1973). In the *Savas* judgment, the Court stated that this provision has direct effect.[298]

In principle, this means that an application for a residence permit for a Turkish national starting a business should be dealt with according to the national immigration legislation of a Member State as it stood in 1973. It is often very difficult, if not impossible, to retrace the legal regime in force in a country some 35 years ago. But sometimes it can be clearly established that a new measure was introduced.

In the *Tum and Dari* judgment, the Court had to decide on the applicability of the standstill clause to Turkish nationals, staying illegally on UK territory after failed asylum requests, who started a business and wished to have legal residence as self-employed persons. The issue was whether they should previously

---

[297] ECJ 9 December 2010, *Toprak and Oguz*, Case C-303/08.
[298] ECJ 11 September 2000, *Savas*, Case C-37/98.

have applied for an entry clearance. In 1973 such a clearance was not required. The referring court asked whether Article 41(1) should be interpreted as prohibiting a Member State from introducing new restrictions, as from the date on which that Protocol entered into force in that Member State, on the conditions of, and procedure for, entry to its territory. The Court stated:

> Article 41(1) of the Additional Protocol does not, therefore, have the effect of conferring on Turkish nationals a right of entry into the territory of a Member State, since no such positive right can be inferred from the Community rules currently applicable but, on the contrary, remains governed by national law.
>
> It follows that a 'standstill' clause, such as that in Article 41(1) of the Additional Protocol, does not operate in the same way as a substantive rule by rendering inapplicable the relevant substantive law it replaces, but as a quasi-procedural rule which stipulates, *ratione temporis*, which are the provisions of a Member State's legislation that must be referred to for the purposes of assessing the position of a Turkish national who wishes to exercise freedom of establishment in a Member State. (…)
>
> The Court cannot accept the interpretation of the United Kingdom government to the effect that it is apparent from *Savas* that a Turkish national can rely on the 'standstill' clause only if he has entered a Member State lawfully, as it is irrelevant whether or not he is legally resident in the host Member State at the time of his application to establish himself, while, conversely, that clause does not apply to the conditions governing a Turkish national's first admission to the territory of a Member State.
>
> It is important to point out, in that respect, that Article 41(1) of the Additional Protocol refers, in a general way, to new restrictions, *inter alia*, 'on the freedom of establishment', and that it does not limit its sphere of application by excluding, as does Article 13 of Decision No. 1/80, certain specific aspects from the sphere of protection afforded on the basis of the first of those two provisions.[299]

The Court found that the standstill clause was applicable to the case of failed asylum seekers like Mrs. Tum and Dari. The fact that they had, prior to their applications for clearance to enter the United Kingdom for the purpose of exercising freedom of establishment, made applications for asylum that had been refused by the competent authorities of that Member State, cannot be regarded, in itself, as constituting abuse or fraud. An entry clearance is a sort of visa, which is required for long-term stay. Though the Court did not say it expressly, it follows from the *Tum and Dari* judgment that imposing the obligation of prior application for an entry clearance is prohibited if this obligation did not exist in 1973. A similar opinion was given, under the standstill clause of Article 13 Decision 1/80, in the *Demir* judgment.[300]

---

[299] ECJ 20 September 2007, *Tum and Dari*, Case C-16/05, paras. 54–55, 59–60.
[300] ECJ 7 November 2013, *Demir*, Case C-225/12, paras. 37–40.

In the *Soysal* judgment,[301] the Court stated that Article 41(1) of the Additional Protocol precludes the introduction, as from the entry into force of that Protocol, of a requirement that Turkish nationals must have a visa to enter the territory of a Member State in order to provide services there on behalf of an undertaking established in Turkey, if, on that date, such a visa was not required. Commentators argued that this would imply, for those countries where a visa was not required in 1973, an exemption of visa requirements, not only for providers, but also for recipients of services.[302] As any tourist will unavoidably receive a series of services during his travel, this could, in practice, have meant a complete exemption of a visa requirement for Turkish travellers. However, in the *Demirkan* judgment, the Court ruled that the notion of 'freedom to provide services' in Article 41(1) of the Additional Protocol must be interpreted as not encompassing freedom for Turkish nationals who are the recipients of services to visit a Member State in order to obtain services.[303] So, the practical consequences of the *Soysal* judgment remain rather limited. In the meantime, the EU and Turkey have convened to initiate a visa liberalisation dialogue.[304]

The standstill clause of Article 41(1) Additional Protocol may also be invoked by an employee of a Turkish enterprise. In the *Abatay and Sahin* judgment the Court held that the standstill clause can be relied upon not only by an undertaking established in Turkey which performs services in a Member State, but also by the employees of such an undertaking who have been subjected to a new restriction on the freedom to provide services.[305] Article 41(1) precludes the introduction into the national legislation of a Member State, of the requirement of a work permit in order for an undertaking established in Turkey to provide services in the territory of that State, if such a permit was not already required at the time of the entry into force of the Additional Protocol.

It is not relevant whether the self-employed worker has permission to engage in business. In the judgment on *Tural Oguz*, the Court said that Article 41(1) of the Additional Protocol may be relied on by a Turkish national who, having leave to remain in a Member State on condition that he does not engage in any business or profession, nevertheless enters into self-employment in breach of that condition, and later applies to the national authorities for further leave to remain on the basis of the business which he has meanwhile established.[306]

---

[301] ECJ 19 February 2009, *Soysal,* Case C-228/06.
[302] For instance, Volker Westphal, *Informationsbrief Ausländerrecht* 4/2009, p. 133; Kees Groenendijk in his comments under the judgment in *Jurisprudentie Vreemdelingenrecht* 2009 no 144.
[303] ECJ 24 September 2013, *Demirkan,* Case C-221/11.
[304] Roadmap towards a visa-free regime with Turkey, http://ec.europa.eu/dgs/home-affairs/what-is-new/news/news/docs/20131216-roadmap_towards_the_visa-free_regime_with_turkey_en.pdf.
[305] ECJ 21 October 2003, *Abatay and Sahin,* Joint Cases C-317/01 and C-369/01.
[306] ECJ 21 July 2011, *Tural Oguz,* Case C-186/10.

3.5.3. THE STANDSTILL CLAUSE OF ARTICLE 13 DECISION 1/80

There is a restriction in Article 13 Decision 1/80 as to its scope of application. It is applicable to workers and families 'legally resident and employed' in the territory of the Member State. In the *Abatay* judgment, the Court concluded that this clause can benefit a Turkish national only if he has complied with the rules of the host Member State on entry, residence, and, where appropriate, employment, and if, therefore, he is legally resident in the territory of that state. The competent authorities remain entitled, even after the entry into force of Decision 1/80, to introduce more stringent measures to deal with Turkish nationals whose position is not lawful.[307]

Thus, the requirement of lawful stay could seriously limit the effect of the standstill clause. For instance, in the *Sahin* case, a Turkish worker had refused to pay an administrative fee to the Dutch authorities for the extension of his residence permit, which he considered excessive. Consequently, at the time of the judgment it could be questioned whether he was still lawfully in the Netherlands.[308] However, the Court saw no obstacle to judge the case. The Court emphasised that it was not disputed that Mr. Sahin would have obtained an extension of his residence permit if he had paid the administrative charges attaching to his application at the right time. Further, the Court reiterated that residence permit issued by the national authorities has only declaratory and probative value. Although Member States do indeed have the right to require that foreigners on their territory hold a valid residence permit and apply for its extension in good time, and although, in principle, they retain the power to impose penalties for breach of such obligations, nevertheless, Member States are not entitled to adopt, in that regard, measures which are disproportionate as compared with comparable domestic cases.

Accordingly, the Court assumed that the condition of legality was satisfied in the present case, and gave its opinion on the question, whether member States are allowed to require the payment of administrative charges for a residence document. The Court considered that Article 13 of Decision No. 1/80 precludes the introduction of national legislation which makes the granting of a residence permit or an extension of the period of validity of such a permit conditional on payment of administrative charges, where the amount of those charges payable by Turkish nationals is disproportionate, as compared with the amount required from EU nationals. Subsequently, in the case of the *Commission v. the Netherlands*, the Court decided that the administrative charges which Turkish nationals had to pay in the Netherlands were disproportionate indeed.[309]

---

[307] ECJ 21 October 2003, *Abatay and Sahin*, Joint Cases C-317/01 and C-369/01, paras. 84–85.
[308] ECJ 17 September 2009, *Sahin*, Case C-242/06.
[309] ECJ 29 April 2010, *Commission v. the Netherlands*, Case C-92/07, para. 49.

Another example of a case, where the applicant was not lawfully resident and the Court nevertheless answered the preliminary questions, was the *Demir* judgment.[310] Mr. Demir had applied for a residence permit in view of paid employment, without first having applied in Turkey for a long-term visa (a so-called temporary residence permit) for the same purpose. Mr. Demir claimed that the requirement of prior obtainment of such a visa was contrary to the standstill clause of Article 13 Decision 1/80, as it was introduced after 1980. The Dutch authorities stated that Article 13 Decision 1/80 was not applicable because his stay was illegal. Further, they contended that they were free, according to the *Abatay* judgment, to introduce more stringent measures to deal with Turkish nationals whose position is not lawful. The Court of Justice, however, considered:

> The referring court asks whether the mere fact that the purpose of a substantive and/ or procedural condition relating to first admission into the territory of a Member State is, *inter alia*, to prevent, before an application for a residence permit is made, unlawful entry and residence, may preclude the application of the 'standstill' clause set out in Article 13 of the Decision on the ground that it constitutes a measure that can be made more stringent, within the meaning of the case law cited in the preceding paragraph.

> (…) the adoption of such measures presupposes that the position of the Turkish nationals to whom they apply is not lawful, so that, whilst those measures may apply to the effects of such unlawfulness without falling outside the scope of the 'standstill' clause set out in Article 13 of Decision No. 1/80, they must not seek to define the unlawfulness itself.

> Where a measure taken by a host Member State, after that Decision, seeks to define the criteria for the lawfulness of the Turkish nationals' situation, by adopting or amending the substantive and/or procedural conditions relating to entry, residence, and, where applicable, employment, of those nationals in its territory, and where those conditions constitute a new restriction of the exercise of the freedom of movement of Turkish workers, within the meaning of the 'standstill' clause referred to in Article 13, the mere fact that the purpose of the measure is to prevent, before an application for a residence permit is made, unlawful entry and residence, does not preclude the application of that clause.

> Such a restriction, whose purpose or effect is to make the exercise by a Turkish national of the freedom of movement of workers in national territory subject to conditions more restrictive than those applicable at the date of entry into force of Decision No. 1/80, is prohibited, unless it falls within the restrictions referred to in Article 14 of that Decision, or in so far as it is justified by an overriding reason in the public interest, is suitable to achieve the legitimate objective pursued and does not go beyond what is necessary in order to attain it.

---

[310] ECJ 7 November 2013, *Demir*, Case C-225/12, paras. 37–40.

From this judgment it can be inferred that the introduction of an obligation to apply for a long-term visa prior to entering the Netherlands was prohibited by the standstill clause of Article 13 Decision 1/80.

As discussed in section 3.5.1, the Court had already widened the ambit of Article 13 Decision 1/80 in the *Commission v. the Netherlands* judgment, stating that the standstill clause is applicable to any new restrictions on the exercise of the free movement of workers, including those relating to the substantive and/or procedural conditions governing the *first admission* to the territory of that Member State of Turkish nationals intending to exercise that freedom. From the judgments in the cases of *Sahin* and *Demir* it can be inferred that an unlawful residence situation of the Turkish person who started proceedings in the Member State concerned, is not an obstacle, as such, to the Court investigating whether a Member State complies with its obligations under the standstill clause of Article 13 Decision 1/80. Rather than looking at the actual lawfulness of the stay of the individual Turkish citizen, the Court investigates whether the national legislation under scrutiny forms an obstacle for obtaining a position as legal resident, and whether this obstacle is new since Decision 1/80.

3.6. FINAL REMARKS

Clearly, the meaning and impact of the Association Treaty, the Additional Protocol and Decision 1/80 would not have developed so extensively if Turkey were to have acceded to the European Community according to the scheme foreseen in the Agreement. At any rate, the case law of the Court of Justice on the Association with Turkey shows how influential the interpretative function of a court can be. Owing to the jurisprudential efforts of the ECJ, Turkish nationals have clearly defined rights in the Member States of the European Union. Turkish workers have a residence right developing in three stages connected to their belonging to the legal labour force of a Member State.

The second generation of Turkish migrants may derive a permanent residence right from Article 7 Decision 1/80, which cannot be limited except for strong reasons of public policy, public security and public health, or when they leave the territory of the host Member State for a significant length of time without legitimate reason. Thus, the second generation has a right comparable with the right to permanent residence of EU citizens. As discussed in sections 3.3.7 and 3.4.5 however, the legal positions regarding residence of Turkish citizens and EU citizens differ in many respects, and are not always susceptible to useful comparison. Whereas residence rights of EU citizens and their family members stem from the overarching principle of freedom of movement, the residence rights of Turkish workers have developed mainly as a corollary to the right of access to the labour market, and are built up only after initial residence has been granted.[311] This could also be seen in the *Ziebell* case.[312]

FURTHER READING

Alexander Hoogenboom, *Turkish Nationals and the Right to Study in the European Union*, EJML 2013, pp. 387–412.

C.A. Groenendijk, H. Hoffman & M. Luiten, *Das Assoziationsrecht EWG/Türkei. Rechte türkischer Staatsangehöriger in der EuGH-Rechtsprechung.* Baden Baden: Nomos, (2013).

C.A. Groenendijk & E. Guild, *Visa policy of Member States and the EU towards Turkish nationals after Soysal*, (Economic Development Foundation Publications 249). Istanbul: Economic Development Foundation, (2011).

---

[311] ECJ 18 July 2007, *Derin*, Case C-325/05.
[312] ECJ 18 December 2012, *Ziebell*, Case C-371/08.

4. MOVEMENT AND RESIDENCE RIGHTS OF THIRD-COUNTRY NATIONALS

4.1. INTRODUCTION, SCOPE

This chapter is about entry and residence rights of third-country nationals as they relate to (a) family reunification, (b) work related immigration, and (c) knowledge-related immigration in the European Union. Further, the right to long-term residence is discussed. The field of immigration policy concerning third-country nationals was brought within the competence of the European Community by the Treaty of Amsterdam. Since the entry in to force of the Treaty of Lisbon, the legal basis for a common European immigration policy can be found in Article 79 TFEU. According to Article 79(1), a common immigration policy should be 'aimed at ensuring, at all stages, the efficient management of migration flows, fair treatment of third-country nationals residing legally in Member States, and the prevention of, and enhanced measures to combat, illegal immigration and trafficking in human beings.'

Article 79(1) TFEU calls upon the European Parliament and the Council to adopt measures in the following areas:

(a) the conditions of entry and residence, and standards on the issue by Member States of long-term visas and residence permits, including those for the purpose of family reunification;
(b) the definition of the rights of third-country nationals residing legally in a Member State, including the conditions governing freedom of movement and of residence in other Member States;
(c) illegal immigration and unauthorised residence, including the removal and repatriation of persons residing without authorisation; and
(d) combating trafficking in persons, in particular, women and children.

This chapter examines the variety of measures in the field of immigration policy of third-country nationals that have been adopted since the entry into force of the Amsterdam Treaty. At its special meeting in Tampere on 15 and 16 October 1999, the European Council stated that the European Union should not only ensure fair treatment of third-country nationals residing lawfully on the territory of the Member States, but also that a more vigorous integration policy should aim at granting them rights and obligations comparable to those of citizens of the European Union. In the discussion of the various measures adopted, it will be seen whether this aim of a more comparable treatment of third-country nationals with citizens of the European Union has been achieved.

European Union law provides for explicit rights of third-country nationals to enter and to remain in Member States. At first sight, almost the whole area of voluntary migration seems to be covered by Union Regulations and Directives. Access to the Union territory, rights to short-term stay, circulation rights within the European Union, (long-term) residence rights, and the return of migrants to their home countries, are regulated by EU Law. However, a closer look reveals that due to limitations in personal or material scope, Member States still have competence to make their own national policy in certain areas.

The first limitation of scope regards nationality. It follows from Article 79 TFEU that all the measures based on that provision apply only to third-country nationals. This limitation of the personal scope can also be deduced from the definitions and purposes listed in several instruments.

Often, a 'third-country national' is defined as: 'any person who is not a Union Citizen within the meaning of article 20 TFEU'. However, according to Article 2(6) of the Schengen Border Code, a third-country national is defined as 'any person who is not a Union citizen within the meaning of Article 17(1) of the Treaty (now article 20 TFEU) and who is not covered by point 5 of this Article.' Point 5 refers to persons enjoying the EU rights of free movement. This category includes: (a) Union citizens and their third-country national family members who are exercising their right to free movement based on the Citizens' Directive; and (b) third-country nationals and their family members with whatever nationality who enjoy rights of free movement equivalent to those of Union Citizens based on agreements between the European Union and those third countries. This second category refers to the agreement between the EU and Switzerland and the EEA Treaty.

In fact, a third-country national is thus defined as a non-EU citizen who does not enjoy the extensive free movement rights granted to Union Citizens, and to some categories of privileged non-EU citizens. In the Returns Directive, the same definition is used.[313]

The second limitation in personal scope that can be found in all the Directives in the field of voluntary migration is the exclusion of third-country nationals who have applied for a form of international protection (asylum), as defined in the Qualification Directive; temporary protection; or a national form

---

[313]   Article 3(1) Returns Directive: 'any person who is not a citizen of the Union within the meaning of Article 17(1) of the Treaty and who is not a person enjoying the Community rights of Freedom, as defined in Article 2(5) of the Schengen Border Code.

of protection. For third-country nationals who already enjoy some form of asylum, the regimes differ in the various Directives. Persons enjoying temporary protection are excluded from the scope of all Directives discussed here. If they are given a *national* form of protection, they are excluded from the scope of the Long-Term Residence Directive,[314] the Blue Card Directive,[315] and the Single Application Procedure Directive.[316] If they are granted *international* protection, as meant by the Qualification Directive, they are excluded from the scope of the Blue Card Directive[317] and the Single Application Procedure Directive.[318]

Since the amendment of the Long-Term Residence Directive in 2011, third-country nationals who reside in a Member State on the basis of international protection are no longer excluded from its scope of application. The Family Reunification Directive does apply to third-country nationals who enjoy a refugee status, but excludes persons who reside on the basis of subsidiary protection.[319] The Blue Card Directive excludes all third-country nationals who are beneficiaries of international protection under the Qualification Directive, or who are beneficiaries of protection under national law international obligations or state practice.[320]

Thirdly, the territorial scope of all the Directives discussed in this chapter is limited to the continental part of the EU, with the exception of Denmark, due to the non-participation of the United Kingdom, Ireland and Denmark.

4.2. FAMILY REUNIFICATION

4.2.1. INTRODUCTION

In contrast to the European Convention of Human Rights, Union law provides for a right to family reunification. A right to family reunification is laid down in the Family Reunification Directive 2003/86/EC, adopted on 22 September 2003. The Family Reunification Directive determines the conditions under which family reunification is granted to third-country nationals residing lawfully in the territory of one of the Member States, regardless of whether the family relationship arose before or after the resident's entry. A right to family reunification under more favourable conditions is given in the Blue Card Directive 2009/50/EC. Furthermore, the Long-term Residence Directive

---

[314] Directive 2005/71/EC, Article 3 (2)a.
[315] Directive 2009/50/EC, Article 3(2) b,c.
[316] Directive 2011/98/EU, Article 3(2)h.
[317] Directive 2009/50/EC, Article 3(2)b.
[318] Directive 2011/98/EU, Article 3(2)g.
[319] Directive 2003/86/EC, Article3(2).
[320] Directive 2009/50/EC, Article 3(2) b,c.

2003/109/EC contains rules pertaining to the right to family reunification in a second Member State.

This section gives an overview of the rights to family reunification, as laid down in the Family Reunification Directive. Where one of the other Directives mentioned above provides for a more favourable family reunification regime, this is discussed here.

As will be set forth in more detail below, the Court of Justice, fairly soon after the entry into force of the Directive, delivered an important judgment, explaining how the Directive should be interpreted and applied.[321] The Court said that the Directive imposes precise positive obligations on the Member States – with corresponding clearly defined individual rights – since it requires them, in the circumstances defined in the Directive, to authorise the family reunification of certain members of a sponsor's family, without being left a margin of appreciation.

4.2.2. HISTORY

The initial proposal for a Directive, published by the Commission on 1 December 1999, attempted to place third-country nationals in a position comparable to that of EU citizens.[322] However, as there were still many differences between the Member States' national regimes on family reunification, the Commission's proposal was heavily debated and amended several times. During the negotiations, Member States tried to preserve their national rules regarding family reunification, which obstructed the achievement of a Directive setting truly common standards. When looking at the final text of the Directive, one sees that the right to family reunification of third-country nationals residing lawfully in the territory of the Member States is restricted in several ways compared to the free movement rights of EU citizens, as described in Chapter 2.

Already during the final stage of negotiations on the Directive, the Council was criticised for restricting the right to family reunification to such an extent, that the outcome would not be in conformity with the protection of family life of migrants, as developed in the case law of the European Court of Human Rights under Article 8 ECHR. In an effort to ensure that the standard of protection would be at least equivalent to the standard set by Article 8 ECHR, the European Parliament proposed a number of amendments during the advisory procedure, which were not, however, adopted by the Council. Further, a standstill clause, which had been introduced in the amended proposal[323] to ensure that Member States would not use the derogations if their legislation at the time of adoption of

---

[321] ECJ 27 June 2006, *Parliament v. Council*, Case C-540/03.
[322] COM(1999) 638 final.
[323] COM(2002) 225 final.

the Directive did not already provide for them, was removed from the final version of the Directive.

After the adoption of the Directive in September 2003, the European Parliament decided to bring an action against the Council before the Court of Justice of the EU.[324] The European Parliament claimed that the Court should annul the last subparagraphs of Article 4(1), Article 4(6) and Article 8 of the Directive, because these provisions allowed for derogations from the right to family reunification, which were deemed to go beyond the permitted restrictions on the right to respect for family life under Article 8 ECHR. In its judgment, the Court of Justice considered the contested provisions not to be in breach with Article 8 ECHR, and accordingly dismissed the action of the European Parliament. In doing so, however, the Court took the opportunity to place the Directive within the context of fundamental rights, as protected by Union law.[325] The Court stressed the importance of fundamental rights as an integral part of the general principles of Union Law, which are observed by the Court. One of these general principles is the respect for family life, which is also laid down in Article 7 of the Charter of Fundamental Rights. The Court said that the Directive does not allow Member States to use the discretion left by the Directive in such a way that fundamental rights are not respected.

As prescribed in Article 19 Family Reunification Directive, the European Commission issued, in October 2008, a report on the application of the Directive in the Member States.[326] The Commission report revealed a number of issues of incorrect transposition or misapplication of the Directive. The Commission mentioned, for example, the provisions on visa facilitation, the granting of autonomous residence permits, the way in which the best interests of the child are taken into account, the granting of legal redress, and the application of more favourable provisions for the family reunification of refugees. Furthermore, the Commission concluded that the harmonising effect of the Directive was limited. It stated that 'the low-level binding character of the Directive leaves Member States much discretion (…).'[327] A Green Paper, already announced in the report on the application, appeared in November 2011.[328] As was apparent from the contributions of the Member States and other stakeholders, no consensus existed regarding a revision of the Directive. As a result, the Commission did not undertake any action to amend the Directive.[329]

---

[324] See, for the complaint, OJ C 47 21-2-2004, p. 21 (Case C-540/03).
[325] ECJ 27 June 2006, Case 540/03, paras. 85–89.
[326] COM(2008) 610 final.
[327] COM(2008) 610 final p. 14.
[328] COM(2011) 735 final.
[329] See the 'public consultations' page of the home page of the European Commission: http://ec.europa.eu/dgs/home-affairs/what-is-new/public-consultation/2012/consulting_0023_en.htm.

4.2.3. SCOPE AND DEFINITIONS

The Directive defines *family reunification* as:

> The entry into, and residence in, a Member State by family members of a third-country national residing lawfully in that Member State in order to preserve the family unit, whether the family relationship arose before or after the resident's entry.[330]

According to Article 3(2), the Family Reunification Directive does not apply where the person who desires family reunification has applied for refugee status or has applied for a form of subsidiary or temporary protection, and is awaiting a final decision.[331] The reason behind this limitation is the uncertainty of the prospects for residence. The Directive is also not applicable where the person who desires reunification is authorised to reside on the basis of temporary protection,[332] but then there are rules on family reunification in the Temporary Protection Directive (see Chapter 6).[333]

Once a refugee is recognised by the Member States, the Directive is applicable, according to Article 9. The conditions for family reunification of sponsors who are refugees are laid down in a special regime (Chapter V. of the Directive), which offers somewhat more favourable conditions. This regime is dealt with in section 4.2.17.

The third-country national who is authorised to reside in a Member State on the basis of a subsidiary form of protection, in accordance with international obligations, national legislation or the practice of the Member States, is excluded from the scope. The legal status of third-country nationals who apply for subsidiary protection is dealt with in the Qualification Directive (see Chapter 8).[334] However, that Directive, which is applicable both for the determination of refugee status and subsidiary protection status, contains hardly any provisions concerning the right to family reunification. Article 23(1) of that Directive only states, in general terms, that Member States shall ensure that family unity can be maintained. According to Article 23(2) Qualification Directive, it is left to the

---

[330] Article 2(d).
[331] Article 3(2)(a).
[332] Article 3(2)(b).
[333] Article 15 Directive 2001/55/EC of 20 July 2001 on minimum standards for giving temporary protection in the event of a mass influx of displaced persons, and on measures promoting a balance of efforts between Member States in receiving such persons, and bearing the consequences thereof.
[334] Directive 2011/95/EU of 13 December 2011 on standards for the qualification of third-country nationals or stateless persons as beneficiaries of international protection, for a uniform status for refugees, or for persons eligible for subsidiary protection, and for the content of the protection granted (recast).

discretion of the Member States to define the conditions for the exercise of the right to family reunification.

The Family Reunification Directive is an instrument of minimum harmonisation. While the text of Article 79 (1)(a) of the TFEU and the penultimate sentence of that provision are not clear as to whether the Directive should contain minimum rules or may go further than that, the Directive itself explains its minimum character in Article 3(5), by providing that Member States may adopt or maintain more favourable provisions, which means that they may employ less strict conditions for family reunification.

The Directive is without prejudice to more favourable provisions of bilateral and multilateral agreements between the EU or the EU and its Member States, on the one hand, and third countries, on the other,[335] or of the European Social Charter and the European Convention on the Legal Status of Migrant Workers.[336]

4.2.4. THE SPONSOR

One of the key figures of the Family Reunification Directive is the *sponsor*. A sponsor is defined in Article 2(c) as a third-country national residing lawfully in a Member State who applies for reunification with family members residing outside that Member State. In order to be granted the right to family reunification, the sponsor must meet certain conditions. Article 3 of the Directive states:

> The Directive shall apply where the sponsor is holding a residence permit issued by a Member State for a period of validity of one year or more who has reasonable prospects of obtaining the right of permanent residence.

This provision restricts the right of a sponsor to be granted family reunification in two ways. First, his residence permit must have a validity of at least one year. This restriction is meant to exclude temporary workers or persons with a residence permit confined to seasonal employment from the right to family reunification.[337] Second, the scope of the Directive is limited by the requirement that the sponsor must have reasonable prospects of obtaining the right of permanent residence. The original proposal did not contain this additional

---

[335] Article 3(4)(a). This proviso concerns the following multilateral agreements: the European Economic Area (1992), the Association Agreement with Turkey (1962), The Europe Agreements with countries applying for accession in central and Eastern Europe, and the Euro-Mediterranean Association Agreement with Morocco and Tunisia.
[336] Article 3(4)(b).
[337] Explanatory memorandum to the Proposal for a Council Directive on the right to family reunification, p. 13, COM(1999) 638 final.

requirement.[338] During negotiations it appeared that delegations of some countries were of the opinion that not only the duration of the residence should be taken into account, but more importantly, that the durability and the objective of residence should be considered. The scope of the Directive was accordingly restricted.

The choice of the word 'permanent' may potentially exclude third-country nationals who reside legally in the territory of a Member State for several years but who do not qualify for a permanent residence permit, for example, because their residence permit depends on being engaged in short-term employment or because the objective of their residence excludes them under national law from obtaining a permanent residence permit, like students or *au pairs*. In the Green Paper the Commission acknowledged this second condition as being eligible, as a sponsor leaves Member States a margin of appreciation that could lead to legal insecurity and potentially excludes large groups of third-country nationals from the scope of the Directive.

Sponsors holding a Blue Card are exempted from the condition of reasonable prospects of obtaining the right of permanent residence (see section 4.3.5, below).

4.2.5. OPTIONAL CONDITIONS RELATING TO THE SPONSOR

On top of the conditions listed above, Member States have some discretion to impose additional requirements on the sponsor. In order to ensure better integration and to prevent forced marriages, Member States may require the sponsor to be of a *minimum age*, which is at most, 21 years, before the spouse is able to join him/her.[339] According to the Report on the application of the Family Reunification Directive, most Member States apply this optional condition, and at least five Member States apply the highest possible minimum age of 21.[340] The claim that setting a minimum age at 21 helps to prevent forced marriages has not been substantiated to date. This led the House of Lords to consider a comparable condition in British legislation a violation of Article 8 ECHR.[341] The European Commission, too, seems to hesitate about the legality of this age requirement, especially if the age requirement differs from the age of majority.[342] Furthermore,

---

[338] COM(1999) 638 final.
[339] Article 4(5). This limitation has been incorporated at the request of the Dutch delegation.
[340] COM(2008) 610 final, p. 5.
[341] House of Lords, *R (on the application of Quila and another) (FC) (Respondents) v Secretary of State for the Home Department (Appellant)*; and *R (on the application of Bibi and another) (FC) (Respondents) v Secretary of State for the Home Department (Appellant)*, [2011] UKSC 45 (12 October 2011).
[342] COM(2011) 735 final, p. 3.

the Commission poses questions about figures and evidence of the existence of forced marriages and about the alleged relationship between these figures and an age requirement. An Austrian Court filed preliminary questions to the Court of Justice about the interpretation of Article 4(5). It wanted to know if this condition must be interpreted as precluding a provision under which spouses and registered partners must already have reached the age of 21 years at the time of submitting the application.[343]

Article 8 Family Reunification Directive provides that Member States are also free to install a *waiting period* before family reunification can be granted. Blue Card holders are exempted from this requirement (see section 4.3.5, below). Member States may require the sponsor to have stayed lawfully in their territory for a period not exceeding two years, before having his/her family members join him/her. Further, in the special situation that the legislation of a Member State relating to family reunification in force on the date of adoption of the Directive takes into account its reception capacity, the Member State may provide for a waiting period of no more than three years between the submission of the application for family reunification and the issue of a residence permit to the family members. This provision was inserted as a concession to Austria and is only relevant for that country.[344]

In its procedure against the Council discussed in section 4.2.2, the European Parliament had argued that a waiting period could not be installed as a general rule, since this would not be in conformity with the obligation to properly weigh up all relevant interests, as required by Article 8 ECHR. The Court of Justice considered that Article 8 of the Directive cannot be regarded as running counter to the fundamental right to respect for family life or to the obligation to have regard to the best interests of children, either in itself or in that it expressly or impliedly authorises the Member States to act in such a way.[345] This seems to imply that Member States are not allowed to install the rule of a waiting period without reserving the option to deviate from this rule in individual cases. This view is subscribed by the Commission in its Green paper.[346]

Both the Blue Card Directive and the Researchers Directive contain a more favourable provision in this regard. Family reunification may not be made dependent on having a minimum period of residence of the sponsor.[347]

---

[343] Case C-338/13, 20 June 2013.
[344] In Austria immigration for the purpose of family reunification is subject to annual quotas. The waiting periods due to the quota system differ from federal to federal province. If the government sets the annual quotas in such a way that waiting periods decrease, the system can be in compliance with this provision: J. Niessen and Y. Schibel, *EU and US approaches to the management of immigration. Comparative perspectives*, Brussels: MPG, 2003, p. 38.
[345] ECJ 27 June 2006, *Parliament v. Council*, Case C-540/03, para. 103.
[346] COM(2011) 735 final, p. 5.
[347] See Directive 2009/50/EC, Art. 15(2) and Directive 2005/71/EC, Art.9(2).

4.2.6. FAMILY MEMBERS ELIGIBLE FOR FAMILY REUNIFICATION

The Directive distinguishes between the family members whose entry and residence a Member State *shall authorise* and family members whose entry and residence a Member State *may authorise*. Article 4(1) lists the categories of persons who, provided that certain conditions are met, must be granted entry and residence; Article 4(2) lists the persons who may be granted family reunification. In contrast with the conditions imposed on sponsors, the immigration status of the persons who are eligible for family reunification is of no relevance. In other words, they may reside in the same Member State for another reason than family reunification, reside outside the Member State, be an asylum seeker, be covered by measures in the field of temporary protection, *etc.*[348]

According to Article 4(1), the right to family reunification should, as a common minimum standard, apply in any case to members of the nuclear family, that is to say, the spouse and the minor children: if all the other conditions are fulfilled, the Member States *shall authorise* the entry and residence of:

(a) the sponsor's spouse;
(b) the minor children of the sponsor and of his or her spouse, including adopted children;
(c) the minor children, including adopted children of just one of them, on the condition that the spouse or partner applying for reunification has custody and the children are dependent on him or her.

The Directive narrows the category of spouses who must be granted entry and residence in a number of ways. In the event of a polygamous marriage, where the sponsor already has a spouse living with him in the territory of a Member State, the Member State concerned *shall not* authorise the family reunification of a further spouse (Article 4(4)). Polygamous marriages are considered not to be compatible with the fundamental principles of the Member States' legal orders. But where such marriages have been lawfully contracted in a non-member country, account should be taken of certain of their effects.[349] Therefore, the reunification of one spouse (and her or his children) is accepted.

---

[348] It must be noted here that according to Article 5.3, the application must be submitted and examined while the family members are residing outside the Member State where the sponsor resides. A Member State may, in appropriate circumstances, accept an application submitted when the family members are already in the territory.
[349] Explanatory memorandum to the Proposal for a Council Directive on the right to family reunification, COM(1999) 638 final, p. 16.

Another restriction concerns the discretionary power of Member States to impose an age requirement of a maximum of 21 years on the spouse, just as on the sponsor as discussed above. The children referred to must be below the age of majority, as established by the law of the Member State concerned,[350] and must not be married. There is no differentiation in the treatment of children born out of wedlock, born out of earlier marriages or legally adopted children. Member States *may* authorise the reunification of children of whom custody is shared, provided the other party sharing custody has given his or her consent. The purpose of this rule is to ensure that reunification does not have the effect of defeating the other parent's rights to custody. In the case of a polygamous marriage, Member States *may* limit the family reunification of minor children of a further spouse and the sponsor.

4.2.7. OPTIONAL DEROGATIONS RELATING TO CHILDREN

With regard to the children eligible for family reunification, Member States may opt to apply two types of derogations. In the first place, where a child is aged over 12 years and arrives independently of the rest of his/her family, the Member State may, before authorising entry and residence under the Directive, verify whether he or she meets a criterion for integration provided for by its existing legislation on the date of implementation of the Directive.[351] According to the Court of Justice, in its judgment of 2006 on the Directive, this provision does not authorise Member States making use of this derogation to infringe on the fundamental right of respect for family life, or not to take into account the best interests of the child or the factors mentioned in Article 17 of the Directive.[352] In other words, Member States may not make use of this derogation without making an individual assessment allowing for a proper weighing of all relevant interests. Since the entering into force of the Lisbon Treaty, the rights laid down in the Charter of the fundamental rights must be respected in any decision that falls within the scope of EU law. The right to family life and the best interests of the child principle are enshrined in the Charter.

---

[350]   This may also refer to the law of third countries. Belgium, for example, has concluded bilateral agreements with Algeria, Morocco and Turkey, according to which, the age of majority is set by the national law of the country of origin of the child who wishes to be admitted on the ground of family reunification.

[351]   This restriction was formulated under the pressure from the German and Austrian delegations. At the time, the proposed new Aliens Act in Germany provided for this derogation. However, in the final text of the German 'Zuwanderungsgesetz', the age limit for an integration test became 16 instead of 12. Member States may introduce an integration test from the age of 12 in their national rules or legislation until the date of implementation, but not later than 3 October 2005 (Article 20).

[352]   ECJ 27 June 2006, *Parliament v. Council*, Case C-540/03.

Secondly, Member States may also request that the applications concerning the family reunification of minor children have to be submitted before the child reaches the age of 15, again subject to a standstill clause.[353] If the application is submitted after a child has reached the age of 15, the Member States that make use of this derogation shall authorise the entry and residence of such children on grounds other than family reunification (Article 4(6)). The Directive does not clarify on what grounds these children in such cases will be admitted and what the conditions will be for admission. As for this provision, the Court said in its judgment in *Parliament v. Council*, that although Article 4(6) of the Directive has the effect of authorising a Member State not to apply the general conditions of Article 4(1) of the Directive to applications submitted by minor children over 15 years of age, it does not prohibit a Member State which applies the derogation from authorising the entry and residence of a child in order to enable the child to join his or her parents. On the contrary, the Member State is still obliged to examine the application by taking into account the best interests of the child, and with a view to promoting family life, which may well mean that the Member State remains under the obligation to authorise entry and residence, although this may be granted on other grounds than family reunification, as understood in the context of the Directive.[354]

4.2.8. OPTIONAL CATEGORIES OF ELIGIBLE FAMILY MEMBERS

The second and third paragraphs of Article 4 list the family members whose entry and residence the Member States *may authorise*. These are:

(a) first-degree relatives in the direct ascending line of the sponsor or his or her spouse, where they are dependent on them and do not enjoy proper family support in the country of origin (Article 4(2)(a));

(b) the adult unmarried children of the sponsor or his or her spouse, where they are objectively unable to provide for their own needs on account of their state of health (Article 4(2)(b)).

(c) the unmarried partner, being a third-country national, with whom the sponsor is in a duly attested stable long-term relationship, or the unmarried partner of a third-country national who is bound to the sponsor by a registered partnership, including the minor or adult dependent children of either one of them (Article 4(3)).[355]

---

[353] Article 4(2)(6). The Austrian legislation contains this restriction: J. Niessen and Y. Schibel, *EU and US approaches to the management of immigration. Comparative perspectives*, Brussel: MPG, 2003, p. 37.

[354] ECJ 27 June 2006, *Parliament v. Council*, Case C-540/03, paras. 86–88.

[355] Article 4(3).

With regard to the category of unmarried partners, the Directive does not say anything explicit about same-sex relationships. The Preamble, however, states that Member States should give effect to the provisions of this Directive without discrimination on the basis of sex (...) or sexual orientation.[356] This can only imply that when Member States decide to authorise family reunification for unmarried partners, according to the option of Article 4(3), they must extend this authorisation to same-sex relationships.

Article 4(3) Family Reunification Directive mentions both registered and unregistered partnerships. Apparently, the purpose of this provision is that Member States may apply the Directive and the requirements laid down in Chapter IV to both categories of partnerships, which would arguably create a situation of equal treatment with spouses in enjoying family reunification. Therefore, it is difficult to appreciate the value of the last sentence of Article 4(3) Family Reunification Directive, holding that Member States *may decide* that registered partners are to be treated equally as spouses with respect to family reunification.

As far as the children of an unmarried couple are concerned, the Directive merely states that 'the Member State may authorise the entry and residence of the unmarried minor children, including adopted children, as well as the adult unmarried children who are objectively unable to provide for their own needs on account of their state of health.' As the provision does not contain any specification as to whether this must be a child of both of them or whether it can also be a child of just one of them, it seems appropriate to assume that the more elaborate provisions of Article 4(1)(b)(c)(d) can be applied analogously.

Both paragraphs 2 and 3 of Article 4, providing for a wider application of the Directive, start with the same formula:

> The Member States may, by law or regulation, authorise the entry and residence, pursuant to this Directive and subject to compliance with the conditions laid down in Chapter IV (...).

Apparently, this means that Member States applying these options relocate the subject matter concerned from the realm of their discretion under national law into the binding scope of application of the Directive. Once they decide to make use of this option, Member States are bound to the provisions of Article 4(2) and (3), and can arguably not choose to apply a lower standard of guarantees. They are, further, bound to apply the requirements for the exercise of the right to family life, as provided in Articles 6 to 8; and arguably also the other provisions containing material requirements, especially Article 16; and procedural

---

[356]   Recital 5.

conditions, especially Article 5. The Commission formulates it as follows in the report on the application of the Family Reunification Directive:

> Once Member States decide to grant this possibility, the standard conditions laid down by the Directive apply.[357]

This contrasts with the situation under which Member States use their right under Article 3(5) of the Directive to adopt or maintain more favourable provisions.[358] In relying on this provision, Member States exclusively operate within the area of their national jurisdiction.

4.2.9. CONDITIONS FOR THE EXERCISE OF THE RIGHT TO FAMILY REUNIFICATION

Although Chapter IV of the Directive is called 'requirements for the exercise of the right to family reunification', the provisions of this Chapter are by far not the only ones containing conditions for family reunification. It has already been shown that several clear conditions regarding the sponsor and the circle of eligible family members are laid down in Articles 3 and 4. Further, procedural requirements for submission of an application are to be found in Article 5. Also important is Article 16, formulating a series of additional reasons for which an application may be rejected. Moreover, Articles 6 and 7 Family Reunification Directive contain facultative conditions for the exercise of the right to family reunification, which the Member States may choose to apply.

However, the Member States are not free to apply additional requirements that are not mentioned in the Directive. This follows from the binding character of the Directive and its character of set minimum standards laid down in Article 3(5), leaving the Member States free to adopt or maintain more, but not less, favourable provisions.

4.2.10. PUBLIC POLICY, PUBLIC SECURITY AND PUBLIC HEALTH

According to Article 6 Family Reunification Directive, an application for entry and residence of family members may be rejected on grounds of public policy, public security or public health.[359] Member States may also withdraw or refuse the renewal of a family member's residence permit on these grounds.[360] When

---

[357] COM(2008) 610 final, p. 6.
[358] Except in case of a polygamous marriage; see Article 4(4).
[359] Article 6(1).
[360] Article 6(2).

taking the relevant decision, the Member State shall consider the severity or type of offence against public policy or public security committed by the family member, or the potential dangers that emanate from such person.

The formulation of this provision is different from that of the comparable provision on public policy and public security in the Citizens' Directive regarding the free movement of EU citizens, codifying the 'clear and present danger' test, as employed by the Court of Justice (see Chapter 2.2.5).[361] Article 27 Citizens' Directive states that a measure of public order:

> shall comply with the principle of proportionality and shall be based exclusively on the personal conduct of the person concerned. Previous criminal convictions shall not in themselves constitute grounds for taking such measures.

Whether this criterion likewise applies to cases of family reunification of third-country nationals has yet to be clarified, but the legislative history of Article 6 Family Reunification Directive gives reason for doubt. The original draft, which provided a clear reference to the 'clear and present danger' test, was amended. The public order test of the Family Reunification Directive, as laid down in the second paragraph of Article 6, however, is very much alike the formulation of the possibility of refusing a long-term residence status based on Article 6(1) of Directive 2003/109/EC. According to this provision, when refusing a long-term residence status on grounds of public policy or public security, Member States shall take into account the severity of type of offence or the danger that emanates from the person, while also having regard to the duration of residence, and to the existence of links with the country of residence. Article 6(2) Family Reunification Directive categorically obliges the Member States to apply Article 17 of the Directive, according to which, they must take due account of the nature and solidity of the person's family relationships, the duration of his residence in the Member State, and of the existence of family, cultural and social ties with his/her country of origin. This implies that every decision under Article 6 Family Reunification Directive must be the result of a balancing act between public order considerations and the interests of the family members concerned, analogous to the approach of the European Court of Human Rights under Article 8 ECHR.

The notion of public policy may cover a conviction for committing a serious crime. This applies for all the Directives regarding entry and residence rights for third-country nationals. The preamble of the Directive expressly states that the notions of public policy and public security also cover cases in which a third-country national belongs to an association that supports terrorism, supports such an association, or has extremist aspirations.[362]

---

[361] See, especially, ECJ 27 October 1977, *Bouchereau*, Case 30/77.
[362] Preamble, recital 14.

Regarding public health, the Directive merely states that renewal of the residence permit may not be withheld, and that the competent authority of the Member State concerned may not order removal from the territory on the sole ground of illness or disability suffered after the issue of the residence permit.

4.2.11. HOUSING, HEALTH INSURANCE, MEANS OF SUBSISTENCE

Article 7(1) Family Reunification Directive contains a number of material conditions that Member States *may* impose on the sponsor, securing that family members will not become a burden on the social security system, and will enjoy a certain standard of living. Member States remain free to impose less or lower conditions, but they may not impose additional or more stringent conditions. When an application for family reunification is submitted, the Member State concerned may require evidence that the sponsor has:

(a) accommodation regarded as normal for a comparable family in the same region and which meets the general health and safety standards in force in the Member State concerned;
(b) sickness insurance in respect of all risks normally covered for its own nationals in the Member State concerned for himself/herself and the members of his/her family;
(c) stable and regular resources which are sufficient to maintain himself/herself and the members of his/her family, without recourse to the social assistance system of the Member State concerned. Member States shall evaluate these resources by reference to their nature and regularity and may take into account the level of minimum national wages and pensions as well as the number of family members.

All Member States apply one or more of these material conditions.[363] The Court of Justice made clear in the *Chakroun* case that the authorisation to impose such conditions is not unfettered.[364] The Court first sketched the outlines within which decisions on family reunification must be taken. These outlines are shaped by international obligations, the Charter and the purpose of the Family Reunification Directive, which is, in the view of the Court, 'to promote family reunification'.[365]

---

[363] See, for example, COM(2008) 610 final p. 6–7 or Groenendijk et al. (2007) p. 25–28.
[364] ECJ 4 March 2010, *Chakroun*, C-578/08.
[365] ECJ 4 March 2010, *Chakroun*, C-578/08, para. 43. The Court recalled this view and further elaborates on it in ECJ 6 December 2012, *O.S. and L, v. Finland*, Case-356/11 and C-357/11, paras. 69–80.

Since authorisation of family reunification is the general rule, the faculty provided for in Article 7(1)(c) of the Directive must be interpreted strictly. Furthermore, the margin for manoeuvre which the Member States are recognised as having must not be used by them in a manner which would undermine the objective of the Directive, which is to promote family reunification, and the effectiveness thereof.

For the application of an income criteria, this means that 'the Member States may indicate a certain sum as a reference amount,' but they may not 'impose a minimum income level below which all family reunifications will be refused, irrespective of an actual examination of the situation of each applicant.' This interpretation is supported by Article 17 of the Directive, which requires individual examination of applications for family reunification, according to the Court. This reasoning of the Court will likewise be valid for the other conditions whose imposition the Directive authorises.

From the formulation of Article 7, it follows that it is only the sponsor who must have accommodation, sickness insurance and resources for himself/herself and the members of his/her family. However, a Member State may alleviate the financial burden on the sponsor by also taking into account the earnings of other members of the family. In France, for example, the resources of both the sponsor and the spouse are taken into consideration.[366] While a Member State is not allowed to *impose* income obligations on family members other than the sponsor, the Directive leaves Member States free to take a given income of those other family members into account. When a granted residence permit is renewed, Article 16(1)(a) *obliges* the Member States to take into account the contributions of the family members to the household income.

4.2.12. INTEGRATION MEASURES

According to Article 7(2) Family Reunification Directive, Member States may require third-country nationals to comply with integration measures, in accordance with national law. While in a number of Member States third-country nationals are only subject to integration measures *after* a residence permit has been issued, the formulation of this provision implies that it is in principle permissible to impose integration measures *before* family reunification is granted.[367] This can be concluded from the second sentence of this paragraph, according to which integration measures with regard to the refugees and/or family members of refugees may only be applied once the persons concerned

---

[366] Article 29 I(1) Ordonnance No. 45–2658 of 2 November 1945.
[367] This provision was formulated this way at the behest of the Dutch delegation. In the Netherlands, new legislation entered into force in March 2006, according to which some categories of newcomers are obliged to do an integration test before they are authorised to enter.

have been granted family reunification.[368] The conclusion is also supported by Article 15 of the Blue Card Directive, according to which, the integration conditions and measures may only be applied with regard to Blue Card holders and their family members, *after* the persons concerned have been granted family reunification.

Article 7(2) Family Reunification Directive is reminiscent of the comparable condition laid down in Article 4(1) that was contested by the European Parliament before the Court. Where a child is over 12 years of age and arrives independently from the rest of the family, the Member State may, before authorising entry and residence, verify whether the child meets a condition of integration (see sections 4.2.5 and 4.2.7, above). The impact of that particular provision is restricted because the Directive requires that the criterion for integration should be provided for by existing legislation of the Member State concerned on the date of implementation of the Directive. However, what the Court said in *Parliament v. Council* about Article 4(1) may be of interest for the interpretation of the more general referral to integration measures laid down in Article 7(2).

It was disputed in Court whether imposing preconditions relating to integration is reconcilable with the right to respect for family life. The Parliament contended that the Union legislature confused the concepts 'condition for integration' and 'objective of integration'. Since one of the most important means of successfully integrating a minor child is reunification with his or her family, the Parliament found it incongruous to impose a condition for integration before the child would be allowed to join the sponsor. This could render family reunification unachievable, and accordingly, negate this right. The Court did not agree, for a number of reasons, one of which was the very specific argument that Article 4(1) limited its scope to integration provisions that were in existence already on the date that the Directive entered into force. But the other considerations of the Court were of a more general nature. According to the Court, the fact that the concept of integration is not defined cannot be interpreted as authorising the Member States to employ that concept in a manner contrary to general principles of EU law, in particular, to fundamental rights:

> As regards conditions for integration, it does not appear that such a condition is, in itself, contrary to the right to respect for family life set out in Article 8 of the ECHR. As has been noted, this right is not to be interpreted as necessarily obliging a Member State to authorise family reunification in its territory, and the final subparagraph of Article 4(1) of the Directive merely preserves the margin of appreciation of the Member States, while restricting that freedom, to be exercised by them in observance, in particular, of the principles set out in Articles 5(5) and 17 of the Directive, to examination of a condition defined by national legislation. In any event, the necessity

---

[368] Article 7(2).

for integration may fall within a number of the legitimate objectives referred to in Article 8(2) of the ECHR.[369]

Thus, integration measures, as meant in Article 7(2), must be formulated in such a way that it remains possible for the authorities of a Member State to take the particular interests of the family members into account in deciding on their application. Three Member States apply integration measures that entail the obligation to pass an integration exam abroad before permission for family reunification is granted.[370] In two Member States, failing this exam means, in principle, a refusal of the application. These measures have been heavily debated.[371] Critics claim that the imposition of an obligation to pass an exam successfully is falling beyond the realm of the word 'measure'. Others maintain that integration programmes and tests are not, in themselves, a violation of the Directive, but that the discretion of Member States is limited by Articles 5(5) and 17, which prescribe an individual assessment of all the interests in every individual application.[372] Preliminary questions regarding the admissibility of pre-entry tests were asked by a Dutch Court. However, The Court of Justice did not end up answering these questions because the Dutch authorities granted the required visa just before the hearing.[373] The same occurred in respect of questions asked by a German Court.[374] Identical questions were asked by the Court of Berlin.[375] Furthermore, on 31 May 2013 the Commission gave a formal notice to Germany, as a first step of an infringement procedure, regarding the implementation of Article 7(2) of the Directive in German legislation.[376] At the moment of writing, the outcome of this procedure is unknown.

4.2.13. GROUNDS FOR REFUSAL, NON-EXTENSION AND WITHDRAWAL

The conditions laid down in Article 4 presuppose that the applicants enjoy a genuine and real family relationship, which logically implies that fraud, misleading information and sham marriages are prohibited. Further, like the provision of Article 4(4) on polygamy already suggests, the Directive is based on

---

[369] ECJ 27 June 2006, *Parliament v. Council*, Case C-540/03, para. 66.
[370] These countries are France, Germany and the Netherlands. COM(2011) 735 final, p. 4.
[371] See, for example, Groenendijk, C.A., 'Pre-departure Integration Strategies in the European Union: Integration or Immigration Policy?' *European Journal of Migration and Law* 2011, p. 1–30.
[372] De Vries K.M., 'Integration at the Border', Hart Publishing: Oxford, 2013.
[373] ECJ 10 June 2011, *Bibi Mohammed Imran v. the Netherlands*, Case-155/11 PPU.
[374] Verwaltungsgericht Berlin, VG 29 K 138.12V, ECJ, *Ayallti v. Germany*, C-513/12.
[375] Verwaltungsgericht Berlin, VG 23 K 91.12 V, ECJ, *Dogan v. Germany*, C-138/13.
[376] http://ec.europa.eu/dgs/home-affairs/what-is-new/eu-law-and-monitoring/infringements_by_country_germany_en.htm.

the perception of an exclusive marital relationship or partnership. Accordingly, Article 16 Family Reunification Directive provides a summing-up of motives for rejecting an application, or withdrawing or refusing to renew a residence permit. Apart from the rather obvious reason that the conditions of the Directive are not, or no longer, satisfied, Article 16 mentions a number of other grounds:

- where the sponsor and his/her family member(s) do not, or no longer, live in a real marital or family relationship;
- where it is found that the sponsor or the unmarried partner is married or is in a stable long-term relationship with another person;
- in the case of false or misleading information, false or falsified documents, fraud, or other unlawful means;
- in cases where the marriage, partnership or adoption was contracted for the sole purpose of enabling the person concerned to enter or reside in a Member State, especially if the marriage, partnership or adoption was contracted after the sponsor had been issued his/her residence permit;
- when the sponsor's residence comes to an end and the family member does not yet enjoy an autonomous right of residence under Article 15.

Member States may conduct specific checks and inspections, where there is reason to suspect that there is fraud, or a marriage, partnership or adoption of convenience. Specific checks may also be undertaken at the time of the renewal of family members' residence permits.

When a Member State makes use of the option of refusal or withdrawal, Article 17 obliges the Member State to take due account of the nature and solidity of the person's family relationships, the duration of his residence in the Member State, and of the existence of family, cultural and social ties with his/her country of origin. This provision can be seen as referring to Article 8 of the ECHR. In its judgment of 27 June 2006 on the action brought by the European Parliament, the Court of Justice stressed the importance of this provision, together with Article 5(5), the provision referring to the best interests of minor children.[377]

In any event, where an application is rejected, or a residence permit is either not renewed, is withdrawn, or when a removal is ordered, the Member States shall ensure that the sponsor and/or the members of his/her family have access to the judicial redress procedures to contest the decisions.[378] The Directive does not contain detailed rules in respect of the arrangements for redress procedures. The procedure, and the competence according to which the right referred to in the first subparagraph is exercised, are to be established by the Member States.

---

[377]   ECJ 27 June 2006, *Parliament v. Council*, Case C-540/03.
[378]   Article 18.

4.2.14 SUBMISSION AND EXAMINATION OF THE APPLICATION

Article 5 Family Reunification Directive lays down a number of formalities and procedural requirements to be observed during the process of submitting and examining the application. In the original proposal it was determined that it should be the sponsor who has to submit the application, because he is the right-holder, and it would, moreover, be easier for him to handle the administrative formalities.[379] However, it emerged during the drafting process that some countries have a system whereby it is the family member wishing to join the sponsor who has to submit the application. According to the final text, Member States are free to determine whether the application must be submitted by the sponsor or by his or her family member(s).

The application must be accompanied by documentary evidence of the family relationship, as well as certified copies of family members' travel documents. If appropriate, and in order to obtain evidence that a family relationship exists, Member States may carry out interviews with the sponsor and his/her family members, and conduct other investigations that are found to be necessary.

When examining an application concerning the unmarried partner of the sponsor, Member States need to take into account, as evidence of the family relationship, factors such as a common child, previous cohabitation, registration of the partnership, and any other reliable means of proof. The Directive does not specify which documents are accepted as evidence, and whether legalisation and verification of the documents may, or shall, be prescribed. It is possible that 'the other investigations' might include verification of the facts, as presented in the documents.

Article 5(3) of the Directive provides that the family member must await the decision on the application while residing outside the territory of the Member State in which the sponsor resides.[380] This provision does not specify that the family member must await the decision in his country of origin, but merely holds that he must be outside the territory of the state in which the sponsor resides. By way of derogation, a Member State may, in appropriate circumstances, accept an application submitted when the family member is already in its territory. It is left to the Member State's discretion to decide what it considers to be 'appropriate circumstances'.

The application bears on 'entry and residence', according to Article 5(1). That implies that a sharp distinction is not made between a visa authorising entry and a permit authorising residence. In some Member States it is current practice that family members who want to join a sponsor must first apply for a visa.[381] However,

---

[379] COM(1999) 638 final, Explanatory memorandum to the proposal, p. 17.
[380] Article 5(3).
[381] This is the case, for example, in Belgium, the Netherlands and the United Kingdom.

if this does not include a double check on fulfilling the conditions – first on the occasion of assessing the visa application, and again when an application for a residence permit is considered – the visa application avenue does not violate the Directive in a material way.[382]

Member States must decide on an application 'as soon as possible', and in any event, no later than nine months from the date on which the application was lodged. The decision must be given in writing, and a rejection of the application must be motivated. The period of nine months starts with the date of application, and not on the date that the file is complete. In exceptional circumstances linked to the complexity of the examination of the application, the nine-month time limit may be extended. Exceptional circumstances exist, in particular, in the absence of proof of the family relationship that necessitates further inquiries.[383] In contrast, the residence permit for family members of Blue Card holders must be granted when the conditions are fulfilled, at the latest within six months from the date on which the application was lodged (see section 4.3.5, below).

It can be observed that the Directive does not link any legal consequences to a failure to take a decision before the end of the period provided for in Paragraph 4. This can only mean that the consequences are left to the national legislation of the Member State concerned. This leaves room for Member States not to provide for sanctions in national law, thus reducing the protective value of the time limit, which is, in itself, already rather long.

Article 5(5) ends with the statement that when examining an application, the Member States shall have due regard to the best interests of minor children. This provision is almost equal to Article 3(1) of the Convention on the Rights of the Child and Article 24(2) of the Charter of Fundamental Rights of the EU. In its judgment of 27 June 2006 on the action brought by the European Parliament, the Court of Justice underlined the importance of this provision for every decision within the scope of application of the Directive.[384]

As soon as the application for family reunification has been accepted, the Member State concerned shall authorise the entry of the family member or members.[385] If a visa is needed, the Member State concerned shall 'grant such persons every facility for obtaining the requisite visas'. According to the original proposal, Member States should refrain from charging for visas, but it appeared, during negotiations, that several Member States were not prepared to accept the principle of issuing visas free of charge. The current Directive leaves payment of

---

[382] In the Netherlands, there was a double procedure with a double check, as mentioned in the Commission's report (COM(2008) 610 final, p. 12, but this procedure was changed on 1 June 2013.
[383] Explanatory memorandum to the amended proposal, COM(2002) 225 final, p. 8.
[384] ECJ 27 June 2006, *Parliament v. Council*, Case C-540/03, paras. 63, 73 and 87.
[385] Article 13(1).

visa fees up to national law.[386] However, a judgment of the Court of Justice in relation to fees levied by the Netherlands for the acquisition of a long-term residence status made clear that the level of the charges must not have either the object, or the effect, of creating an obstacle to the obtaining of the rights conferred by the Directive, because otherwise, the objective, as well as the spirit, of the Directive, will be undermined.[387] The same reasoning will apply to fees levied in the context of an application based on the Family Reunification Directive.

Coupled with the authorisation of entry, the Member State concerned shall grant the family members a first residence permit of at least one year's duration.[388] This residence permit must be renewable.[389] The Member States are free to provide a residence permit with a duration of more than one year, but the duration of the residence permit shall not, in principle, extend beyond the date of expiry of the residence permit held by the sponsor.[390] Although this provision is formulated as an obligation, the Member States do have some discretion because of the wording 'in principle'. It is not clear in what kind of situations the Member States can use this exception. In conjunction with the 'principle' that the duration of the permit shall not extend beyond the duration of residence of the sponsor, Article 16 states that Member States may withdraw or refuse to renew the residence permit of a family member, where the sponsor's residence comes to an end and the family member does not yet enjoy an autonomous right of residence.

4.2.15. ACCESS TO WORK AND EDUCATION

When family reunification is granted, the sponsor's family members shall be entitled, in the same way as the sponsor, to access education, employment and self-employed activity, and to vocational guidance and training.[391] These rights of access are optional for relatives in the ascending line and adult children.[392] In derogation from Article 14(1), Member States may restrict access to employment and self-employed activity for a maximum of 12 months, by way of establishing certain conditions under which family members are allowed to exercise an

---

[386] See Explanatory memorandum to the proposal, COM(1999) 638 final, p. 20; and Explanatory memorandum to the amended proposal for a Council Directive on the right to family reunification, COM(2002) 225 final.
[387] ECJ 26 April 2012, *Commission v. Netherlands*, Case-508/10, par. 69.
[388] For family members of Blue Card holders, the duration of the residence permit must be the same as that of the residence permit of the Blue Card holder, in so far as the period of validity of their travel documents allows it (Article 15(5) Blue Card Directive).
[389] Article 13(2).
[390] Article 13(3).
[391] Article 14(1).
[392] Article 14(3).

employed or self-employed activity. This restriction is not allowed in respect of family members of Blue Card holders (Article 15(6) Blue Card Directive).

This is one of the provisions of secondary EU law in which a clear right to access work and education is granted to third-country nationals. As will be more extensively described in section 4.3.1, Member States experienced difficulties in reaching a consensus on conditions for allowing third-country nationals access to their labour markets. However, a right of access to work is provided in the context of a number of instruments regulating the rights of specific categories of third-country nationals, including the Family Reunification Directive, the Long-Term Residence Directive, the Qualification Directive, the Reception Conditions Directive, and the Citizens' Directive.[393]

4.2.16. AUTONOMOUS RIGHT OF RESIDENCE

The residence right granted to family members is, from the outset, a dependent one: it is related to the fate of the sponsor. After a period of time, however, family members should be considered to have established their own bonds with the host country, and thus, to be entitled to a residence right, regardless of the relationship with the sponsor. The Directive entitles family members to an autonomous residence right indeed, but does so in a rather ambiguous way, leaving considerable margin for manoeuvre on the part of the Member States.

Article 15 provides that an autonomous residence permit must be granted – upon application – to the spouse or unmarried partner and a child who has reached majority; not later than after five years of residence.[394] The first paragraph of Article 15 only holds that these family members shall be entitled to an autonomous residence permit, leaving provisions on the granting and duration of the autonomous residence permit to national law.

The Directive does not contain an obligation to issue an autonomous residence permit to adult children and to relatives in the direct ascending line who have been admitted under the optional category of Article 4(2) of the Directive. The Directive merely states that the Member States *may* issue an autonomous residence permit to these family members, without even specifying a period of residence. With regard to these persons, Member States appear to enjoy wide discretionary powers.

Another ground for obtaining an autonomous residence permit is the breakdown of the family relationship for various reasons.[395] In the event of widowhood, divorce, separation, or death of first-degree relatives in the direct

---

[393] Article 14 Family Reunification Directive; Article 21 Long Term Residence Directive; Article 26 Qualification Directive; Article 15 Reception Conditions Directive; Article 23 Citizens' Directive.
[394] Article 15(1).
[395] Article 15(3).

ascending or descending line, an autonomous residence permit may be issued to family members. Apart from this discretionary power, Member States *must* ensure the granting of an autonomous residence permit in the event of particularly difficult circumstances. Again, the Directive does not specify what these 'difficult circumstances' are. From the explanatory memorandum, one can conclude that the circumstances described in the first sentence of the third paragraph (widowhood, divorce, separation, or death) are not, in themselves, 'particularly difficult circumstances'.[396]

According to the explanatory memorandum, the 'difficult circumstances' provision was added, amongst other things, to protect women who decide to leave home because of domestic violence, or for women who are widowed, divorced or repudiated, *and* who would be in particularly difficult circumstances if they were obliged to return to their countries of origin.[397] So, in the case of widowhood, divorce, separation, or death, the Member States *may* issue an autonomous residence permit, but when the situation involved in one of these events is even worse (particularly difficult), the Member States must issue an autonomous residence permit. The exact conditions are left to national legislation.

4.2.17. FAMILY REUNIFICATION OF REFUGEES

Chapter V of the Directive contains a special regime applicable to family reunification of refugees.[398] In derogation of the general principle of the Directive not to make a distinction between family reunion and family formation, Member States may confine the application of the specific provisions of Chapter V to refugees whose family relationships predate their entry. According to the explanatory memorandum, this exclusionary path was chosen on the ground that the situation of already-existing families warrants a more favourable treatment by way of priority.[399] The European Court of Human Rights judged, in the case of *Hode and Abdi*, that making a distinction in the family reunification regime on whether the family relationship arose before or after the sponsor's entry, is an unequal treatment of comparable cases. Under Article 14 of the ECHR, states must give a reasonable justification for this difference in treatment. In this case, the reason given by the United Kingdom, that it was honouring its international obligations, did not convince the Court.[400]

---

[396] Explanatory memorandum to the proposal, COM(1999) 638 final, p. 21.
[397] *Ibid.*
[398] Article 9(1).
[399] Explanatory memorandum to the amended proposal, COM(2002) 225 final, p. 8.
[400] ECtHR 6 November 2012, *Hode & Abdi v. United Kingdom*, No. 22341/09.

Persons who enjoy a subsidiary form of protection are excluded from the scope of the Directive (Article 3(2)(c)). It is questionable whether this exclusion is fair. From the angle of a legitimate need to restore family life, persons enjoying subsidiary protection are not in an essentially different position than persons enjoying refugee status. Analogous to the reasoning of the ECtHR in the *Hode and Abdi* judgment, it could be argued that the EU should provide convincing reasons for making this distinction. There are clear signs, however, that the EU is recognising that refugee and subsidiary protection should be treated as equal statuses. The revised Procedures Directive and Reception Conditions Directive no longer distinguish between applicants for refugee status and subsidiary protection status. The Stockholm Programme refers to one protection status with equal rights as one of the objectives of a common European asylum status. This objective is underlined in the Preamble of the recast of the Qualification Directive (recital 39). In the Green Paper on the Family Reunification Directive, the Commission phrases this thought by asking two questions: firstly, whether beneficiaries of subsidiary protection should be included in the scope, and, secondly, whether they should enjoy the same more favourable treatment as refugees.[401]

The specific provisions for refugees are more favourable. A first distinction is presented in Article 10(1), which holds that, by way of derogation from Article 4(1), Member States may not impose an integration test for refugee children over the age of 12. It is notable that the two other optional conditions of Article 4 concerning the status of family members are not excluded. These are the possibility to require that both the sponsor and the spouse be of a minimum age, and at most, 21 years of age; and the optional condition (however, only allowed when relevant national legislation already existed on 3 October 2005) that an application concerning family reunification of minor children has to be submitted before the age of 15.[402]

A second distinction concerns the *obligation* on the part of the Member State to grant a refugee's first-degree relatives in the direct ascending line, family reunification, whereas under the normal regime, Member States have a discretionary power to grant these persons access. Moreover, the specific conditions concerning first-degree relatives in the direct ascending line of Article 4(2)(a) do not apply in the case of refugees (these are the requirements of dependency and not enjoying proper family support).[403]

Thirdly, and perhaps most noteworthy, refugees may not be made subject to the material conditions of having at their disposal suitable housing, healthcare insurance and stable resources, as laid down in Article 7.[404] However, Member States may limit the scope of these specific rules in several ways: first, they may

---

[401]   COM(2011) 735 final, p. 6.
[402]   Articles 4(5) and (6).
[403]   Article 10(3).
[404]   Article 12(1).

confine this exception to the nuclear family, and second, if family reunification is possible in a third country with which the sponsor and/or his family has special links, Member States may require that the material conditions are fulfilled. This is also the case if the application for family reunification is not submitted within a period of three months after the granting of a refugee status. The Commission wonders whether these limitations take sufficiently into account the particular difficulties refugees may encounter.[405]

Another important deviation is that the application of a waiting period is excluded in all cases, which means that refugees do not have to reside in a Member State for a certain period of time before a successful application for family reunification can be lodged.[406] A fifth and final deviation from the ordinary regime is provided by Article 11(2), which holds that when a refugee cannot produce all the official documentary evidence of the family relationship, the Member States must examine all other forms of evidence, and may not solely reject an application on the basis that official documents are lacking. This provision takes account of the difficulties refugees may have in providing or obtaining documentation from their countries of origin.

4.2.18. FAMILY REUNIFICATION: FINAL REMARKS

The establishment of a right to family reunification for third-country nationals is a significant step forward in the process of creating a common European migration legislation for third-country nationals. The scope of persons being able to rely on a right to family reunification is no longer confined to workers or EU citizens, or to exceptional circumstances which give rise to positive obligations under Article 8 ECHR, but has now been extended to all third-country nationals residing in the EU – provided they meet certain conditions.

This being said, the Directive leaves some major issues unsolved. First of all, it remains to be seen to what extent this Directive will truly harmonise national regimes on family reunification for third-country nationals. Not only does the Directive leave broad discretion to the Member States by using many optional formulas, but it also uses concepts of which the substance is at best, vague. What can be considered 'stable and regular resources'? When can a third-country national be considered 'a threat to public policy or public security'? And what does 'integration' mean? A further question is whether the Directive applies to dual nationality sponsors who also have the nationality of the host Member State.[407]

---

[405]   COM(2011) 735, final p. 6.
[406]   Article 12(2).
[407]   According to the Dutch State Council (*Raad van State*), Article 3(3) of the Directive implies that the answer should be negative. See ABRvS 29 March 2006, *JV* 2006/172, with critical comments of C.A Groenendijk.

Secondly, the legal position of third-country nationals regarding family reunification is still limited in comparison with that of EU citizens. The fact that applications under the Family Reunification Directive must be made from abroad, the many extra conditions compared to those required of family members of EU nationals and the ambiguities in the securing of rights, are all differences which raise issues of equal treatment.

Lastly, the Directive leaves the right to family reunification of two main groups of persons unsettled. By excluding EU citizens who do not make use of their right of free movement from the scope of the Directive, the possibility of reverse discrimination by a state of its own nationals in comparison with EU citizens, as, for example, is the case in Belgium and in the Netherlands, remains possible. Also, the exclusion from the scope of the Directive of persons who enjoy subsidiary protection, compared to the favourable position of refugees, is difficult to justify.

4.3. WORKERS, STUDENTS AND RESEARCHERS FROM THIRD COUNTRIES

4.3.1. INTRODUCTION

Where the rules for family reunification, as discussed in the previous section, are, for an important part, inspired by the goal of integrating third-country nationals and fundamental rights like respect for family life and the best interest of the child, the rules on getting access to the territory of the European Union for work or study are, rather, inspired by economic interests of the EU and its Member States. The Hague Programme of November 2004 recognised that 'legal migration will play an important role in enhancing the knowledge-based economy in Europe, in advancing economic development, and thus contributing to the implementation of the Lisbon strategy.' The Lisbon strategy is a development and action plan for the European Union, originally set out at the European Council in March 2000, and launched again in March 2005. It formulates as a strategic goal for the EU: 'to become the most competitive and dynamic knowledge-based economy in the world capable of sustainable economic growth with more and better jobs and greater social cohesion.' The Commission was asked to present a policy plan on legal migration 'including admission procedures, capable of responding promptly to fluctuating demands for migrant labour in the labour market.'[408]

---

[408]   European Council, The Hague Programme: Strengthening Freedom, Security and Justice in the European Union, 2005/C53/01, OJ C53/4.

In December 2005 the Commission presented a Policy Plan on Legal Migration.[409] This plan provided for the introduction of five legislative proposals on labour migration, between 2007 and 2009. The Stockholm Programme, adopted on 10–11 December 2009, reiterated the economic importance of a labour migration policy for the EU.[410] Labour migration can contribute to increased competitiveness and economic vitality. Furthermore, as a result of demographic developments that will face the EU, there will be an increased demand for labour. The Stockholm Programme concluded that 'flexible migration policies will make an important contribution to the Union's economic development and performance in the longer term.'[411]

Migration for study purposes is, likewise, regarded as an interest of the EU. According to Recital 6 of the Preamble of the Students Directive, '[o]ne of the objectives of Community action in the field of education is to promote Europe as a whole as a world centre of excellence for studies and vocational training. Promoting the mobility of third-country nationals to the Community for the purpose of studies is a key factor in that strategy.'[412]

Labour migration is perceived as one of the major incentives for the movement of persons. At the same time, protecting the national labour market surely is one of the major incentives for governments to control migration.

For EU citizens, the right to migrate to other Member States for reasons of work has, since the creation of the European Economic Community, been promoted as one of the fundamental freedoms that form the basis of the common market.

For third-country nationals, such a fundamental freedom has not come into being, and neither was it envisaged. From the law-making process on labour migration under Title IV EC Treaty (currently Article 79 TFEU) since the late 1990s, it has become obvious that Member States are reluctant to harmonise rules on access of third-country nationals to their labour markets, precisely because of their insistence on keeping this fundamental area of migration law within their sovereign discretion.

On 11 July 2001, the Commission presented a draft Directive on the conditions of entry and residence of third-country nationals for the purpose of paid employment and self-employed economic activities.[413] This draft envisaged a 'one-stop shop procedure' by proposing common admission criteria and a uniform application procedure resulting in a single permit valid both for residence and work. When it became clear that the draft Directive did not enjoy sufficient support, the Commission launched its Policy Plan on Legal Migration

---

[409]   COM(2005)669.
[410]   European Council, The Stockholm Programme – an open and secure Europe serving and protecting citizens, 2010/C115/01, OJ C115/1.
[411]   Stockholm Programme, OJ 4 May 2010 C115/ 27.
[412]   Students Directive, Recital 6.
[413]   COM(2001) 386 final, 11 July 2001.

in 2005, placing more emphasis on the necessity to fight illegal immigration and employment:

> An effective migration policy cannot be limited to instruments for the admission of immigrants. Other equally important legislative and operational measures are necessary, as immigration represents a complex phenomenon that needs to be addressed coherently across all its dimensions. Admission of economic immigrants is as inseparable from measures on integration on the one hand, as it is from the fight against illegal immigration and employment, including trafficking, on the other. It is in this context therefore that the EU must intensify its efforts to reduce the informal economy, a clear 'pull factor' for illegal immigration, as well as a catalyst for exploitation.[414]

In the process, the ambition of a broad harmonisation scheme for labour migration from third countries was dropped. The Commission decided to formally withdraw the proposal for a draft Directive on general admissibility criteria in 2005.[415] In the Policy Plan of 2005, the Commission instead announced a package of a general framework Directive and four instruments:

(1) a Directive on the conditions of entry and residence of highly skilled workers;
(2) a Directive on the conditions of entry and residence of seasonal workers;
(3) a Directive on the procedures regulating the entry, the temporary stay and residence of intra-corporate transferees; and
(4) a Directive on the conditions of entry and residence of remunerated trainees.[416]

The main purpose of the general framework Directive is, apart from laying down common rules for the application of a joint permit for residence and work, to guarantee a common framework of rights to all third-country nationals in legal employment, already admitted into a Member State, who do not fall within the scope of the Long-Term Residence Directive. The European Commission, since then, has tabled several proposals for Directives on labour migration, of which, at the time of writing of the second edition of this book, three have been adopted: the Blue Card Directive, the Directive on Employers' Sanctions, and the Single Application Procedure Directive.[417] The Seasonal Employment Directive has

---

[414] COM(2005) 669 final, 21 December 2005, para. 2.
[415] COM(2005) 462 final, 27 September 2005.
[416] Ibid. para. 2.
[417] Directive 2009/50/EC on the conditions of entry and residence of third-country nationals for the purposes of highly qualified employment; Directive 2009/52/EC providing for minimum standards on sanctions and measures against employers of illegally staying third-country nationals; Directive 2011/98/EU on a single application procedure for a single permit for third-country nationals to reside and work in the territory of a Member State and on a common set of rights for third-country workers legally residing in a Member State.

been formally adopted but is, at the time of writing this book, not yet formally published.[418] The proposal for an Intercompany Transferee Directive is still under negotiation.[419]

Earlier, the Council had adopted two further Directives, dealing with admission to Member States for purposes of study and research – issues that proved to be less controversial.[420] In its proposal to recast the Students Directive and the Researchers Directive, the Commission proposed to broaden their scope to remunerated trainees and au pairs, and to make mandatory provisions on unremunerated trainees that are currently discretionary.[421]

This section will provide an examination of the contents of the Blue Card Directive, the Single Application Procedure Directive, the Researchers Directive and the Students Directive. The Directive on Employers' Sanctions is discussed in Chapter 9.

This chapter may illustrate that the European Union is keen on the promotion of immigration of workers from third countries. The Member States have displayed considerably more reluctance in harmonising general immigration rules for workers from third countries. The adoption of various Directives on labour migration shows, nonetheless, that the strategy of the European Commission to replace the original plan for an all-encompassing directive on labour migration with a package of multiple Directives targeted at specific subject matters has been successful in propelling harmonisation efforts in this area. Although the rights of entry and employment created by these Directives remain fairly modest, they have the potential to simplify and converge procedures for admission in the various Member States, and may, moreover, serve as a basis for further harmonisation attempts. In the implementation reports[422] of the Researchers Directive and the Students Directive, the Commission put its finger on a number of weaknesses of these two instruments, regarding, amongst others, admission procedures and intra-EU mobility. To improve the current rules, the Commission proposed a recast of the Directives, with quicker admission procedures, extended possibilities to work for students, and enhanced intra-EU mobility rights.

---

[418] Directive on the conditions of entry and residence of third-country nationals for the purposes of seasonal employment COM(2010) 379 final, 2010/0210 (COD). The Council adopted this Directive on 17 February 2014. At the moment of finishing the text of this book, the Directive is not officially published. The Directive must be transposed in national legislation within two years of its publication in the Official Journal.

[419] Draft Directive on conditions of entry and residence of third-country nationals in the framework of an intra-corporate transfer, COM(2010) 378 final, 2010/0209 (COD).

[420] On 25 March 2013 the Commission launched a proposal for a Directive, recasting the current Directives on researchers and students. COM(2013)0151.

[421] See COM(2013) 151 final.

[422] COM(2011) 901 final; COM(2011) 587 final.

4.3.2. THE BLUE CARD DIRECTIVE

The Blue Card Directive[423] establishes a fast-track procedure for the admission of highly qualified third-country workers, based on a common definition and common criteria. Workers admitted will be issued a residence permit allowing them to work ('the EU Blue Card'). This permit will endow on them and their families a series of rights, including favourable conditions for family reunification, and the possibility to move for work to a second Member State. Importantly, the Directive does not provide for a right of admission. The issuing of the Blue Card remains subject to a 'positive decision' of the Member States. In making that decision, the Member States must not only take account of the criteria set out in the Directive, but may, further, apply national quotas and carry out a labour market test. The term 'Blue Card' was inspired by the United States' Green Card, and makes reference to the European flag, which is blue with twelve golden stars. However, the Green Card refers not only to a skills and employment related residence status, but is a permanent residence status to work and live in the US, which can be acquired on four different grounds: (1) family reunification with Green Card holders or US nationals, (2) possession of skills or employment, (3) based on a diversity policy, and (4) humanitarian interests (asylum seekers).[424]

The Directive grants a number of privileges to highly skilled third-country nationals applying for a residence permit in a Member State. After two years of lawful employment in accordance with the conditions of the Directive, Member States may decide to treat such a worker as equal to a national with regard to access to highly qualified employment. Further, a right to free movement for the purpose of highly qualified employment in other Member States is granted after 18 months of legal residence in a Member State as a Blue Card holder.

The purpose of this Directive is, according to Article 1, twofold. The first purpose is two lay down conditions for the entry and residence of third-country nationals and their family members for more than three months for highly qualified employment in the first Member State. Secondly, it is to lay down conditions for the entry and residence of Blue Card holders and their family members in a second Member State. In this sense, by also regulating the conditions for entry and residence in a second Member State, the purpose of the Blue Card Directive is comparable to the Long-Term Residence Directive.[425] According to Article 3(1), the Directive is applicable to third-country nationals

---

[423]   Directive 2009/50/EC on the conditions of entry and residence of third-country nationals for the purposes of highly qualified employment.

[424]   See also: J. Niessen and Y. Schnibel, Immigration as a labour market strategy – European and North American Perspectives, Migration Policy Group, Brussels 2005.

[425]   See section 4.7.

who apply for admission to the territory of a Member State for the purpose of highly qualified employment. However, the scope is limited by the exclusion of a range of categories of persons listed in the second paragraph of Article 3. According to Article 3(2)(a), (b) and (c), the Blue Card Directive is not applicable to third-country nationals who applied for, or reside on the basis of, some form of temporary, international or national protection. Secondly, third-country nationals who apply for, or reside on the basis of, some other Directives, are excluded from the scope. These are researchers,[426] family members of Union Citizens who reside on the basis of the Citizens' Directive, holders of long-term residence status who reside in a second Member State to be employed in an economic activity, and posted workers who are covered by the Posted Workers Directive.[427] Finally, persons who enter a Member State on the basis of international agreements facilitating the short-term stay of certain categories of trade and investment-related persons, seasonal workers, and persons whose expulsion has been extended, are excluded from the scope. In addition, the Directive does not apply to third-country nationals and their family members, whatever their nationality, who, under agreements between the EU and its Member States and those third countries, enjoy rights of free movement equivalent to those of Union citizens.

Grasping the rationale behind these excluded categories is not always straightforward. While the unfavourable treatment of asylum seekers and holders of an asylum status also features in other Directives,[428] it may be hard to think of convincing justifications for not permitting highly qualified asylum seekers or asylum status holders to apply for a Blue Card. A similar question may be posed as regards the exclusion of family members of EU citizens, Turkish workers and their family members, and the exclusion of highly qualified holders of a long-term resident status working in a second Member State.

Member States remain free to issue residence permits other than a Blue Card, however, for any cause of employment (Article 3(4)). These residence permits may not confer the right of residence in the other Member States as provided for in the Blue Card Directive. This provision articulates that the Blue Card Directive does not replace or preclude specific national arrangements regarding the entry and residence of highly skilled – and other – workers.

In principle, the Directive does not allow for more favourable provisions, except for provisions of EU legislation and bilateral and multilateral agreements between the Member States and third countries. According to the explanatory

---

[426]   Researchers Directive (Article 3(2), d).
[427]   Directive 96/71 concerning the posting of workers in the framework of the provision of services.
[428]   See section 4.1, above.

memorandum of the proposal for a Blue Card Directive, this would undermine the effect of the Directive.[429]

In the original proposal, Member States could adopt or retain more favourable provisions concerning conditions of entry and residence, except for entry into the first Member State.[430] In the final Directive, this principle is retained in a restricted version. More favourable treatment is allowed regarding procedural safeguards (Article 11), labour market access (Article 12(1), 12(2)) temporary unemployment (Article 13), equal treatment (Article 14), family reunification (Article 15) and absence from the territory of the Community with regard to long-term resident status (Article 16(4)).[431] Furthermore, more favourable provisions can be set with regard to salary requirements, as laid down in Article 5(3) in relation to movement to another Member States, based on Article 18 of the Directive.[432]

Further, the Directive pays heed to the notion of 'ethical recruitment' in order to avoid the phenomenon of brain drain. The Directive is, according to Article 3(3), without prejudice to any agreement between the Community and/or its Member States and third countries, that lists the professions which should not fall under the Blue Card Directive in order to ensure ethical recruitment, in sectors suffering from a lack of personnel, by protecting human resources in the developing countries. In addition, Article 8 gives Member States the possibility to refuse a Blue Card in order to ensure ethical recruitment in sectors suffering from a lack of qualified workers in the countries of origin.

Article 6 guarantees that the Directive does not affect the right of a Member State to determine the volume of admission of third-country nationals entering its territory for the purposes of highly qualified employment.

4.3.3. CONDITIONS, PROCEDURE FOR BLUE CARD APPLICANTS

It is left to the Member States to determine whether applications for an EU Blue Card are to be made by the third-country national and/or by his employer (Article 10). In principle, the application must be considered and examined either when the third-country national concerned is residing outside the territory of the Member State to which he wishes to be admitted, or when he is already residing in that Member State as holder of a valid residence permit or national long-stay visa. However, some derogations are formulated in paragraphs 3 and 4, allowing for a stricter, or more lenient, approach.

---

[429] COM(2007) 637 final, p. 9.
[430] COM(2007) 637 final, Article 4(2) p. 20.
[431] Article 4(2)(b).
[432] Article 4(2)(a).

In order to qualify for a Blue Card, the applicant must show that he is eligible for 'highly qualified employment'. In Article 2 sub b, highly qualified employment is defined as the employment of a person who:

–   in the Member State concerned, is protected as an employee under national employment law and/or in accordance with national practice, irrespective of the legal relationship, for the purpose of exercising genuine and effective work for, or under the direction of, someone else;
–   is paid; and
–   has the required adequate and specific competence, as proven by higher professional qualifications;

An applicant for the Blue Card must, according to Article 5, present evidence that he meets the criteria. This evidence concerns a valid work contract or binding job offer for a highly qualified employment for at least one year. In the case of a regulated profession, a document attesting to the fulfilment of the specific conditions for this profession; and in case of an unregulated profession, documents attesting to the relevant higher professional qualifications in the occupation or sector. Furthermore, he must present a valid travel document, evidence of having sickness assurance, or of having applied for this. Finally, he may not be considered to pose a threat to public policy, public safety or public health.

Further, Member States may require the applicant to provide his address in the territory. In addition to these conditions, the gross annual salary resulting from the monthly or annual salary specified in the work contract or binding job offer shall not be inferior to a relevant salary threshold defined and published for that purpose by the Member States, which shall be at least 1.5 times the average gross annual salary in the Member State concerned.[433] Member States may require that all conditions in the applicable laws, collective agreements or practices in the relevant occupational branches for highly qualified employment, are met.

During the first two years, priority may be given to nationals or EU workforce, third-country nationals lawfully resident in that Member State and already forming part of its labour market by virtue of EU or national law, or long-term residents falling under the Long-Term Residence Directive wishing to move to that Member State for highly qualified employment (Article 8(2)).

The Member States *shall* reject an application for a EU Blue Card, according to Article 8, whenever the applicant does not meet the conditions set out in

---

[433]   By way of derogation, and for employment in professions which are in particular need of third-country national workers and which belong to the major groups 1 and 2 of ISCO, the salary threshold may be at least 1.2 times the average gross annual salary in the Member State concerned. In this case, the Member State concerned shall communicate each year to the Commission the list of the professions for which a derogation has been decided.

Article 5, or whenever the documents presented have been fraudulently acquired, or falsified or tampered with.

After the issuing, a Blue card *shall*, under Article 9, be withdrawn or renewal shall be refused:

- when it has been fraudulently acquired, or has been falsified or tampered with;
- wherever it appears that the holder did not meet, or no longer meets, the conditions for entry and residence laid down in the Directive, or is residing for purposes other than that for which the holder was authorised to reside; or
- when the holder has not respected the limited labour market access during the first two years of Article 12 ((1) and (2)), (a) regarding the conditions laid down in Article 5 (salary requirements), and (b) concerning change of employer, and did not respect obligations in relation to temporary unemployment set out in Article 13.[434]

Further, Member States *may* withdraw or refuse to renew an EU Blue Card:
- for reasons of public policy, public security or public health;
- wherever the EU Blue Card holder does not have sufficient resources to maintain himself and, where applicable, the members of his family, without having recourse to the social assistance system of the Member State concerned;
- if the person concerned has not communicated his address; or
- when the EU Blue Card holder applies for social assistance, provided that the appropriate written information has been provided to him in advance by the Member State concerned.

An application for a Blue Card may also be considered as inadmissible because the volume of admission is exceeded (Article 6). Member States may further reject an application for a Blue Card in order to ensure ethical recruitment in sectors suffering from a lack of qualified workers in the countries of origin. Finally, Member States may reject an application for an EU Blue Card if the employer has been sanctioned in conformity with national law for undeclared work and/or illegal employment (see section 9.5. below).

4.3.4. RIGHTS OF BLUE CARD HOLDERS

A third-country national who fulfils the requirements set out in Article 5, and for whom the competent authorities have taken a positive decision, is issued with an EU Blue Card, according to the format as laid down in the Regulation

---

[434] The lack of communication with regard to changes in employer (Article 12(2)), and unemployment (Article 13(4)) shall not, according to Article 9(2), be considered to be a sufficient reason for withdrawing or not renewing the EU Blue Card, if the holder can prove that the communication did not reach the competent authorities for a reason independent of the holder's will.

regarding a uniform format for residence permits for third-country nationals (Article 7).[435] It can be seen here that fulfilment of the criteria does not create an entitlement to be issued the Blue Card, but that the issue remains subject to a decision of the national authorities.

After having granted the Blue Card, the Member State concerned must grant the third-country national every opportunity to obtain the requisite visas. The determination of the standard period of validity of the EU Blue Card is left to the Member States, but this period must be between one and four years. If the duration of the work contract is shorter than this period, the Blue Card shall be issued or renewed for the duration of the work contract plus three months. During the period of its validity, the Blue Card shall entitle its holder to enter, re-enter and stay in the territory of the Member State issuing the Blue Card, and to the rights recognised in the Directive.

For the first two years of legal employment as a Blue Card holder, access to the labour market for the person concerned is restricted to the exercise of paid employment activities that meet the conditions for admission set out in Article 5 Blue Card Directive. For these first two years, changes in employer shall be subject to the prior authorisation in writing of the competent authorities of the Member State of residence. Modifications that affect the conditions for admission are subject to prior communication, or, if provided for by national law, prior authorisation.

After these first two years, Member States may grant the persons concerned equal treatment with nationals in respect of access to highly qualified employment. If the Member State does not make use of this possibility, the person concerned must communicate changes that affect the conditions of Article 5 to the competent authorities of the Member State of residence.

Member States may retain restrictions on access to employment if the activities are reserved to nationals, Union or EEA citizens, according to national or Union Law (Article 12 (4)); or if the activities are reserved for nationals, and concern occasional involvement in the exercise of public authority and the responsibility for safeguarding the general interest of the state (Article 12 (3)).

Unemployment does not constitute a reason for withdrawing an EU Blue Card, unless the period of unemployment exceeds three consecutive months, or it occurs more than once during the period of validity of an EU Blue Card (Article 13). During this period of three months, the Blue Card holder is allowed to seek and take up employment under the conditions set out in Article 12.

---

[435] Council Regulation (EC) No 1030/2002 of 13 June 2002 laying down a uniform format for residence permits for third country nationals, OJ L 157/1.

4.3.4.1. Equal Treatment

Blue Card holders enjoy, according to Article 14(1) Blue Card Directive, equal treatment with nationals of the Member State issuing the Blue Card, as regards:

(a) working conditions, including pay and dismissal, as well as health and safety requirements in the workplace;
(b) freedom of association and affiliation and membership of an organisation representing workers or employers, or of any organisation whose members are engaged in a specific occupation, including the benefits conferred by such organisations, without prejudice to the national provisions on public policy and public security;
(c) education and vocational training;
(d) recognition of diplomas, certificates and other professional qualifications in accordance with the relevant national procedures;
(e) provisions in national law regarding the branches of social security, as defined in Regulation (EEC) No. 1408/71;[436]
(f) without prejudice to existing bilateral agreements, payment of income-related acquired statutory pensions in respect of old age, at the rate applied by virtue of the law of the debtor Member State(s), when moving to a third country;
(g) access to goods and services and the supply of goods and services made available to the public, including procedures for obtaining housing, as well as information and counselling services afforded by employment offices; and
(h) free access to the entire territory of the Member State concerned, within the limits provided for by national law.

With respect to points (c) and (g), the Member State concerned may restrict equal treatment as regards study and maintenance grants and loans or other grants and loans regarding secondary and higher education and vocational training, and procedures for obtaining housing.

With respect to point (c), access to university and post-secondary education may be subject to specific prerequisites in accordance with national law, and the Member State concerned may restrict equal treatment to cases where the registered or usual place of residence of the Blue Card holder, or that of the family member for whom benefits are claimed, lies within its territory.

---

[436] The special provisions in the Annex to Council Regulation (EC) No. 859/2003 of 14 May 2003 extending the provisions of Regulation (EEC) No 1408/71 and Regulation (EEC) No. 574/72 to nationals of third countries who are not already covered by those provisions solely on the basis of their nationality shall apply accordingly.

4.3.4.2.   *Mobility Rights*

A special regime for free movement of Blue Card holders is set out in Article 18 Blue Card Directive. After 18 months of legal residence in the first Member State as a Blue Card holder, the person concerned and his family members may move to another Member State for the purpose of highly qualified employment.

This right to free movement after 18 months stands apart from the rights of Blue Card holders under the Long-Term Residence Directive. Blue Card holders who fulfil the conditions for the acquisition of the EC long-term resident status receive a residence permit, with the remark 'Former EU Blue Card holder'. Here, the Blue Card Directive provides for some special arrangements in order to enable the Blue Card holder to accumulate periods of stay in different Member States (Article 16). The Blue Card holder, having made use of the possibility provided for in Article 18, is allowed to accumulate periods of residence in different Member States in order to fulfil the requirement concerning the duration of residence, if the following conditions are met:

(a) five years of legal and continuous residence within the territory of the European Union as an EU Blue Card holder;[437] and
(b) legal and continuous residence as an EU Blue Card holder for two years immediately prior to the submission of the long-term resident's permit application within the territory of the Member State where this application is lodged. Some derogations to this principle are allowed in Article 16(3)(4)(5) Blue Card Directive.

4.3.5.   FAMILY MEMBERS OF BLUE CARD HOLDERS

With regard to family members, special rules apply. According to Article 15, the Family Reunification Directive applies to the admission of family members of Blue Card holders, but with a number of derogations. Firstly, family reunification may not be made dependent on the requirement of the Blue Card holder having reasonable prospects of obtaining the right of permanent residence and having a minimum period of residence. Secondly, the integration conditions and measures referred to in the Family Reunification Directive may only be applied after the persons concerned have been granted family reunification. Thirdly, a shorter maximum term for issuing a residence permit to family members is prescribed: at the latest within six months of the date on which the application was lodged. Fourthly, the duration of validity of the residence permits of family

---

[437]   Periods of absence from the territory of the EU do not interrupt this period if they are shorter than 12 consecutive months, and do not exceed, in total, 18 months within this period of five years.

members shall not be one year, but the same as that of the residence permits issued to the Blue Card holder insofar as the period of validity of their travel documents allows it. Finally, Member States shall not apply any time limit in respect of access to the labour market.

When the Blue Card holder moves to a second Member State in accordance with Article 18, and when the family was already constituted in the first Member State, the members of his family must be authorised to accompany or join him (Article 19 Blue Card Directive). The derogations from the Family Reunification Directive listed in Article 15 of the Blue Card Directive (see above) shall apply *mutatis mutandis*. Where the family was not already constituted in the first Member State, the Family Reunification Directive with the derogations of Article 15 Blue Card Directive, applies.

4.4.   THE RESEARCHERS DIRECTIVE

According to its Preamble, the aim of the Researchers Directive[438] is to contribute to making the Community more attractive to researchers from around the world and to boost its position as an international centre for research.[439]

Under the Directive, researchers with the nationality of a third country, complying with a number of conditions, mentioned in Article 7, are granted a right to residence for the purpose of research. The system of the Directive is that an approved research organisation makes a hosting agreement with the researcher. The researcher undertakes to complete the research project and the organisation undertakes to host the researcher for that purpose. On the basis of such an agreement, a third-country national may apply for a residence permit.

For that purpose, the third-country national must present a valid travel document, a hosting agreement, and (if appropriate) a statement of financial responsibility issued by the research organisation. Further, the applicant must not be considered to pose a threat to public policy, public security or public health.[440] The Directive obliges Member States to admit the researcher to carry out the hosting agreement if they have concluded that all the conditions are met.[441] Member States must issue a residence permit for a period of at least one year, and

---

[438]   Council Directive 2005/71/EC of 12 October 2005 on a specific procedure for admitting third-country nationals for the purposes of scientific research, OJ L 289/15.

[439]   The Commission tabled a proposal to recast the Directive on 25 March 2013, 'Proposal for a Directive of the European Parliament and of the Council on the conditions of entry and residence of third-country nationals for the purposes of research, studies, pupil exchange, remunerated and unremunerated training, voluntary service and au pairing', COM(2013) 151 final.

[440]   Article 7(1).

[441]   Article 7(3).

must renew it if the conditions are still met. If the research project is scheduled to last less than one year, the residence permit must be issued for the duration of the project.[442]

Member States may withdraw or refuse to renew a residence permit issued on the basis of this Directive when it has been fraudulently acquired, or wherever it appears that the holder did not meet, or no longer meets, the conditions for entry and residence, or is residing for purposes other than that for which he was authorised to reside. Member States may also withdraw or refuse to renew a residence permit for reasons of public policy, public security or public health.[443]

The Directive does not grant a specific right to family reunification, but if a Member State decides to grant a residence permit to the family members of a researcher, the duration of validity of their residence permit shall, according to Article 9, be the same as that of the residence permit issued to the researcher insofar as the period of validity of their travel documents allows it. In duly justified cases, the duration of the residence permit of the family member of the researcher may be shortened. The issue of the residence permit to the family members of the researcher admitted to a Member State may not be made dependent on the requirement of a minimum period of residence of the researcher.

In general terms, the Directive applies to third-country nationals who apply to be admitted to the territory of a Member State for the purpose of carrying out a research project. The scope of the Researches' Directive does not include third-country nationals staying in a Member State as applicants for international protection or under temporary protection schemes, or third country-nationals whose expulsion has been suspended for reasons of fact or law.[444] Further, the Directive does not apply to third-country nationals applying to reside in a Member State as students within the meaning of the Students Directive 2004/114/EC in order to carry out research leading to a doctoral degree, and researchers seconded by a research organisation to another research organisation in another Member State.[445]

The Directive does not affect the right of Member States to adopt or retain more favourable provisions for persons to whom it applies.[446] Further, the Directive is without prejudice to more favourable provisions of (a) bilateral or multilateral agreements concluded between the EU, or between the EU and its Member States on the one hand, and one or more third countries on the other; and (b) bilateral or multilateral agreements concluded between one or more Member States and one or more third countries.[447]

---

[442]   Article 8.
[443]   Article 10.
[444]   Article 3(2)(a)(c).
[445]   Article 3(2)(b)(d).
[446]   Article 4(2).
[447]   Article 4(1).

4.4.1. MOBILITY BETWEEN MEMBER STATES

With regard to the mobility of researchers *between* the Member States, Article 13 of the Directive provides for a system that does not add much to the possibilities of intra-EU mobility. A third-country national who has been admitted as a researcher under the Directive shall be allowed to carry out part of his/her research in another Member State, but only under the conditions as set out in that provision. If the researcher stays in another Member State for a period of up to three months, the research may be carried out on the basis of the hosting agreement concluded in the first Member State, provided that he has sufficient resources in the other Member State and is not considered as a threat to public policy, public security or public health in the second Member State. If the researcher stays in another Member State for more than three months, Member States may require a new hosting agreement to carry out the research in that Member State.

In any event, the conditions set out in Articles 6 and 7 must be met in relation to the second Member State. Where the relevant legislation provides for the requirement of a visa or a residence permit, for exercising mobility, such a visa or permit shall be granted in a timely manner within a period that does not hamper the pursuit of the research, whilst leaving the competent authorities sufficient time to process the applications. Member States may not require the researcher to leave their territory in order to submit applications for the visas or residence permits. The intra-EU mobility is not really improved by this Directive. The possibility for residence in another Member State for up to a period of three months already existed based on Article 21 of the Schengen Implementation Convention (see Section X), and for longer periods a new hosting agreement may be required by the second Member State. In the proposal for a recast of the Students and Researchers Directives, intra-EU mobility is facilitated and simplified.[448] The period for which researchers are allowed to move to a second Member State on the basis of the hosting agreement concluded in the first Member State has, in the proposal, been extended from 3 to 6 months.[449] Furthermore, researchers' family members can move between Member States, together with the researcher.[450]

4.4.2. ADDITIONAL RIGHTS

The Directive lays down important additional rights relating to, *inter alia*, diplomas, working conditions and tax benefits. Researchers admitted under the

---

448 COM(2013) 151 final, p. 7.
449 Ibid. Article 26.
450 Ibid. Article 28.

Directive may teach in accordance with national legislation, although Member States may set a maximum number of hours or days for the activity of teaching.[451] Holders of a residence permit must, further, be entitled to equal treatment with nationals as regards:[452]

(a) the recognition of diplomas, certificates and other professional qualifications in accordance with the relevant national procedures;
(b) working conditions, including pay and dismissal;
(c) branches of social security;[453]
(d) tax benefits; and
(e) access to goods and services and the supply of goods and services made available to the public.

4.5. THE STUDENTS DIRECTIVE

Promoting the mobility of students is a key element in the strategy of the European Union. According to Recital 6 of the Preamble of the Students Directive,[454] 'one of the objectives of Community action in the field of education is to promote Europe as a whole as a world centre of excellence for studies and vocational training.' The approximation of the Member States' national legislation on conditions of entry and residence is one of the avenues through which this goal is pursued. Member States should not be afraid of students, Recital 7 explains:

> Migration for the purposes set out in this Directive, which is, by definition, temporary, and does not depend on the labour-market situation in the host country, constitutes a form of mutual enrichment for the migrants concerned, their country of origin and the host Member State, and helps to promote better familiarity among cultures.

For EU citizens, the right to reside in another Member State for the purposes of study is laid down in Article 7(1)(c) of the Citizens Directive (see section 2.2.1).

---

[451] Article 11.
[452] Article 12.
[453] These branches are the same – and subject to the same conditions – as those in which EU citizens moving within the Community enjoy equal treatment, and are defined in Council Regulation (EEC) No. 1408/71 of 14 June 1971 on the application of social security schemes to employed persons, to self-employed persons and to members of their families moving within the Community; the special provisions in the Annex to Council Regulation (EC) No. 859/2003 of 14 May 2003 extending the provisions of Regulation (EEC) No. 1408/71; and Implementing Regulation (EEC) No. 574/72.
[454] Council Directive 2004/114/EC of 13 December 2004 on the conditions of admission of third country nationals for purpose of studies, pupil exchange, unremunerated training or voluntary service, OJ L375/12.

For third-country nationals, a more specific and detailed regime is laid down in the Students Directive.

Under the system of the Students Directive, a residence permit must be granted to four categories of third-country nationals: students, school pupils, unremunerated trainees and volunteers, provided that they comply with several conditions. Any third-country national who applies to be admitted for these purposes must present a valid travel document; parental authorisation for the planned stay (in the case of minors, as defined under the national legislation of the host Member State); sickness insurance in respect of all risks normally covered for its own nationals in the Member State concerned; and proof, if the Member State so requests, that the fee for processing the application has been paid. Further, the applicant may not be regarded as a threat to public policy, public security or public health.[455]

Apart from these general conditions, specific conditions are set out for each of the categories. Applicants for a residence permit for the purpose of *study* must, according to Article 7 of the Directive, have been accepted by an establishment of higher education to follow a course of study. Further, they must provide the evidence requested by a Member State that they will have sufficient resources to cover their subsistence, study and return travel costs. Member States must make public the minimum monthly resources required for the purpose of this provision, without prejudice to individual examination of each case. If the Member State so requires, the student must provide evidence of sufficient knowledge of the language for the course to be followed, and evidence that the fees charged by the establishment are paid.

School pupils must not, according to Article 9, be below the minimum age, nor above the maximum age set by the Member State concerned. They must provide evidence of acceptance by a secondary education establishment, and evidence of participation in a recognised pupil exchange scheme programme operated by an organisation recognised for that purpose by the Member State concerned in accordance with its national legislation or administrative practice. The pupil exchange organisation must accept responsibility for the pupil throughout the period of presence in the territory of the Member State concerned, in particular as regards subsistence, study, healthcare, and return travel costs. Further, the pupil must be accommodated throughout the stay by a family meeting the conditions set by the Member State concerned, and selected in accordance with the rules of the pupil exchange scheme in which the pupil is participating. Member States may confine the admission of school pupils participating in an exchange scheme to nationals of third countries that offer the same opportunities to their own nationals.

Unremunerated trainees must, according to Article 10, have signed a training agreement, approved, if need be, by the relevant authority in the host Member

---

[455] Article 6(1).

State, for an unremunerated placement with a public sector enterprise, private sector enterprise or vocational training establishment recognised by the Member State. They must provide the evidence requested by a Member State that they will have sufficient resources during their stay to cover their subsistence, training and return travel costs. Finally, they may be required by the host Member State to receive basic language training so as to acquire the knowledge needed for the purposes of the placement.

Volunteers, according to Article 11, may not be below the minimum age, nor above the maximum age set by the host Member State. They must produce an agreement with the organisation responsible in the host Member State for the voluntary service scheme in which they are participating, giving a description of tasks, the conditions under which they are supervised in the performance of those tasks, their working hours, the resources available to cover travel, subsistence, accommodation costs and pocket money throughout their stay, and, if appropriate, the training they will receive to help them perform their services. Further, they must provide evidence that the organisation responsible for the voluntary service scheme in which they are participating has taken out a third-party insurance policy, and accepts full responsibility for them throughout their stay, in particular, as regards subsistence, healthcare and return travel costs. If the host Member State specifically requires it, they must receive a basic introduction to the language, history and political and social structures of that Member State.

Students receive a residence permit for a period of at least one year and it is renewable if the holder continues to meet the conditions. Where the duration of the course of study is less than one year, the permit will be valid for the duration of the course. Renewal of a residence permit may be refused or the permit may be withdrawn if the student does not respect the limits imposed on access to economic activities or does not make acceptable progress in his/her studies in accordance with national legislation or administrative practice.[456]*School pupils* receive a residence permit for a period of no more than one year.[457] The period of validity of a residence permit issued to *unremunerated trainees* must correspond to the duration of the placement, or shall be for a maximum of one year. In exceptional cases, it may be renewed, only once, and exclusively for such time as is needed to acquire a vocational qualification.[458]A residence permit issued to *volunteers* shall be issued for a period of no more than one year. In exceptional cases, if the duration of the relevant programme is longer than one year, the duration of the validity of the residence permit may correspond to the period concerned.[459]

---

[456] Article 12.
[457] Article 13.
[458] Article 14.
[459] Article 15.

Member States may withdraw or refuse to renew a residence permit issued on the basis of this Directive when it has been fraudulently acquired, or wherever it appears that the holder did not meet, or no longer meets, the conditions for entry and residence. Further, Member States may withdraw or refuse to renew a residence permit on grounds of public policy, public security or public health.[460]

4.5.1. MOBILITY BETWEEN MEMBER STATES

The Students Directive provides a certain degree of freedom of movement between EU Member States to students, which goes beyond that provided to researchers in the Researchers Directive. A third-country national who has already been admitted as a student may apply to undertake, in another Member State, part of the studies already commenced, or to complement them with a related course of study in another Member State. The student shall, according to Article 8, be admitted by the latter Member State within a period that does not hamper the pursuit of the relevant studies, whilst leaving the competent authorities sufficient time to process the application.

Students wishing to use this right to mobility must meet the relevant conditions under the Directive in relation to the second Member State. They must send, with the application for admission, full documentary evidence of their academic record and evidence that the course they wish to follow genuinely complements the one already completed. Normally, it is required that they participate in an EU or bilateral exchange programme. or have been admitted as a student in a Member State for no less than two years. These requirements do not apply in the case where the student, in the framework of the programme of studies, is obliged to complete a part of the courses in an establishment of another Member State.

Article 17 of the Directive entitles students to be employed and to exercise self-employed economic activity, outside their study time, and subject to the rules and conditions applicable to the relevant activity in the host Member State. The situation of the labour market in the host Member State may be taken into account. Where necessary, Member States must grant students and/or employers prior authorisation in accordance with national legislation. Each Member State shall determine the maximum number of hours per week or days or months per year allowed for such an activity, which shall not be less than 10 hours per week, or the equivalent in days or months per year. Access to economic activities for the first year of residence may be restricted by the host Member State. Member States may require students to report, in advance or otherwise, to an authority designated by the Member State concerned, that they are engaging in an economic activity. Their employers may also be subject to a reporting obligation, in advance or otherwise.

---

[460] Article 16.

4.6. THE SINGLE APPLICATION PROCEDURES DIRECTIVE

As the official long name of this Directive reveals, the Single Application Procedures Directive provides for: a) a single application procedure, b) a single permit, and c) a set of rights for third-country national workers legally admitted to the territory of the Member States.[461] However, the rights offered by this Directive to third-country nationals are severely limited by declaring the conditions for entry for third-country nationals solely as a matter of discretion of the Member States. Article 1(2) of the Directive states that 'this Directive is without prejudice to the Member States' powers concerning the admission of third-country nationals to their labour markets.' This Directive does not create material rights of entry for third-country national workers, but does create procedural rights, rights to equal treatment, and brings them under the scope of Union law.

The Directive formulates a very broad definition of a third-country national worker. According to Article 2(b), 'third-country worker' means:

> a third-country national who has been admitted to the territory of a Member State and who is legally residing and is allowed to work in the context of a paid relationship in that Member State in accordance with national law or practice.

It is important to note that not only third-country nationals who have applied for or have been admitted for reasons of work fall within the scope (Article 3(1) (a) and (c)), but also third-country nationals who have been admitted for other reasons, who have a residence permit and are permitted to work (Article 3(1)(b)). However, the scope of application of the Directive for third-country workers is limited by a list of derogations in Article 3(2). The Directive does not apply to third-country national family members of EU citizens making use of their right of free movement. The same holds for persons and their family members who enjoy equivalent rights of free movement as EU citizens and their family members. As already mentioned in section 4.1, third-country nationals who are applying for, or who are beneficiaries of, some sort of temporary, international or national protection, are all excluded from the scope of the Directive.

Furthermore, third-country nationals who have applied for, or are residing as, intra-corporate transferees, seasonal workers or au pairs, or who are posted in the Member State, are excluded. Finally, self-employed third-country nationals, long-term resident third-country nationals and workers on a boat sailing under the flag of an EU Member State, do not fall within the scope of this

---

[461]   Directive 2011/98/EU of the European Parliament and of the council of 13 December 2011 on a single application procedure for a single permit for third-country nationals to reside and work in the territory of a Member State and on a common set of rights for third-country workers legally residing in a Member State.

Directive. The rationale behind the exclusion of intra-corporate transferees, seasonal workers and au pairs lies in the temporary nature of their residence. As is explained in the memorandum to the proposal for a Directive for intra-corporate transferees, due to the temporary nature of the status of an intra-corporate transferee, equal treatment in several of the areas listed in the Single Application Procedure Directive is considered irrelevant. One can think, for example, of equal treatment in the field of education or vocational training.

Specific provisions as regards equal treatment for intra-corporate transferees, seasonal workers and posted workers are provided in the proposal for a Directive on intra-corporate transferees,[462] the proposal for a Directive on seasonal workers,[463] and Directive 96/71/EC on the Position of Posted Workers.[464] The provisions in these instruments contain a more limited set of equal rights for these categories of workers, due to the temporary nature of the stay, according to the explanatory memorandum of the proposal for a Directive on intra-corporate transferees.[465]

4.6.1. SINGLE APPLICATION PROCEDURE, PERMIT

The single application procedure regulates the issuing, amending or renewal of a single permit. The material requirements for issuing a permit are not regulated in this Directive, and can be partly found in the Blue Card Directive or in national law. Article 6(1) indicates that Member States shall issue a single permit using the uniform format for residence permits for third-country nationals.[466] This single permit implies that no additional permits as proof of the authorisation to work are needed or allowed (Article 6(2)). When issuing a residence permit to a third-country national in accordance with the Regulation for a Uniform Format[467] for other purposes than work, the permit should also contain information about permission to work. Also, for these permits no additional work permits are authorised, according to Article 7(2).

Member States may clarify, in their national legislation, that the application for a single permit for residence and work is made by the third-country national or the employer, or either of them (Article 4(1)). In case the application is submitted by the third-country national, the Member State shall allow the application to be introduced from a third country, or, if provided for by national law, in the territory of the Member State in which the third-country national is legally present (Article 4(1)). This formulation seems to imply that an application can also be

---

462   COM(2010) 378 final, Article 14.
463   COM(2010), 379 final, Article 16.
464   Article 3 Directive 96/71/EC.
465   COM(2010) 378 final, p. 11.
466   Regulation (EC) No. 1030/2002.
467   Ibid.

submitted from the territory of the Member State concerned. This follows also from Article 4 (4), which provides for the issuing of a single permit to third-country nationals already admitted at the territory, and who apply to renew or modify their residence permit after the entry into force of the national implementing provisions of this Directive. According to Article 4(2), a decision to issue, amend or renew the single permit shall constitute a single administrative act combining a residence permit and a work permit. The single application procedure does not affect the possibility of Member States retaining a visa requirement.

The Directive contains a very limited set of procedural guarantees. The competent authority, designated by the Member State, shall take a combined decision within four months of the application being lodged. This time limit may be extended in exceptional circumstances due to the complexity of the examination. The Directive does not provide for a maximum duration in the case of an extended time limit in exceptional circumstances. The normal time limit for deciding on an application is shorter than the time limits given in the Family Reunification Directive (nine months) and the Long-Term Residence Directive (six months). However, the Blue Card Directive provides for a shorter decision time limit of 90 days. The proposals for the Directives on seasonal workers and intra-corporate transferees contain even shorter time limits of 30 days, with the possibility of extension of the time limit for the intra-corporate transferees by a further 60 days. As the Researchers Directive does not contain a time limit for taking a decision, and researchers are not excluded from the scope of the Single Application Procedure Directive (see Article 3(2)), it can be assumed that the time limit to take a decision on the single application procedure is also valid for the application for a permit based on the Researchers Directive.[468] The consequences of exceeding the time limit provided for in Article 5(2) have to be defined by national law.

4.6.2. EQUAL RIGHTS

Third-country workers who fall within the scope of the Single Application Procedure Directive enjoy equal rights with nationals of the Member State in several areas. However, the Directive provides for a range of exemptions.

The fields in which third-country national workers enjoy, in principle, equal rights with nationals are (Article 12):

(a) working conditions, including pay and dismissal, as well as health and safety at the workplace;
(b) freedom of association and affiliation and membership of an organisation representing workers or employers, or of any organisation whose members

---

[468]   In the proposal for a recast of the Students and Researchers Directive, a time limit of 60 days in which to take a decision, is introduced. See COM(2013) 151 final, p. 13 and Article 29.

are engaged in a specific occupation, including the benefits conferred by such organisations;

(c) education and vocational training;

(d) recognition of diplomas, certificates and other professional qualifications, in accordance with the relevant national procedures;

(e) branches of social security, as defined in the EC Regulation on the coordination of social security systems;[469]

(f) tax benefits, in so far as the worker is deemed to be resident for tax purposes in the Member State concerned;

(g) access to goods and services and the supply of goods and services made available to the public, including procedures for obtaining housing, as provided by national law; and

(h) advice services afforded by employment offices.

Exemptions are possible from the rights listed under (c), (e), (f) and (g). Equal treatment in the field of education and vocational training can be limited by the exclusion of equal treatment regarding the granting of maintenance and study grants and loans, the exclusion of students who are admitted under the Students Directive and the exclusion of third-country nationals, who are permitted to work, but who are not working and who are not registered as unemployed. Furthermore, Member States may lay down specific prerequisites like a language condition or the payment of tuition fees.

4.7. LONG-TERM RESIDENCE

4.7.1. INTRODUCTION

In section 4.2 it was described how the Family Reunification Directive provides a clearly defined right to stay and remain for family members of a third-country national, which is reinforced by their entitlement, after at most, five years, to obtain an autonomous residence right. The right to stay and remain is also laid down in the various work and knowledge related Directives discussed in the previous section. However, these Directives do not provide for a right to remain in the Member State for another purpose than those set out in the applicable Directive. The notion that integrated migrants must be granted a strengthened legal position after a period of lawful residence is

---

[469] Regulation (EC) No. 883/2004 of the European Parliament and of the Council of 29 April 2004 on the coordination of social security systems, OJ 166/1.

embodied in the Long-Term Residence Directive,[470] which is the subject of this section.

The purpose of the Long-Term Residence Directive is twofold: it creates a *long-term resident status* providing a right to permanent residence based on EU law to be acquired after five years of legal residence in a Member State, which encompasses (i) strengthened protection from expulsion, and (ii) a – rather modest – right to settle in another Member State.

Differently from the Family Reunification Directive, the Long-Term Residence Directive does not contain many provisions lending themselves to direct application. This is especially so with regard to the acquisition of the status of long-term resident. In the *Iida* judgment, the Court confirmed that this status may not be obtained by mere force of Union law, without intervention of the national authorities. In order to acquire long-term resident status, the third-country national concerned must lodge an application with the competent authorities of the Member State in which he resides.[471]

4.7.2. HISTORY

The goal of creating a set of uniform rights for third-country nationals, who reside legally on the territory of the Member States, comparable to rights enjoyed by EU citizens, was first articulated when the heads of EU governments gathered in 1999 in order to set the goals for the legislative implementation programme of the Treaty of Amsterdam. The Preamble of the Directive, Recital 28, explicitly refers to this occasion:

> The European Council, at its special meeting in Tampere on 15 and 16 October 1999, stated that the legal status of third-country nationals should be approximated to that of Member States' nationals, and that a person who has resided legally in a Member State for a period of time to be determined, and who holds a long-term residence permit, should be granted, in that Member State, a set of uniform rights which are as near as possible to those enjoyed by citizens of the European Union.

The legal basis for the Directive is provided by both Article 63(3) TEC, authorising the adoption of measures on conditions of entry and residence (currently Article 79(1) TFEU); and Article 63(4) TEC, calling for measures defining the conditions under which third-country nationals residing in one Member State may reside in another Member State (currently Article 79(2)(b) TFEU). However, these provisions do not expressly oblige for the

---

[470] Council Directive 2003/109/EC of 25 November 2003 concerning the status of third-country nationals who are long-term residents, OJ L 16/44.
[471] ECJ 8 November 2012, *Iida v. Germany*, C-40/11, para. 47.

approximation of the rights of third-country nationals to the rights of EU citizens.

During the negotiations on the Directive the latter goal turned out to be too ambitious. In particular, the rights to free movement to other Member States granted in the Directive are not overwhelmingly strong. Yet, the Directive can be regarded as an important improvement in the rights of long-term residents. Even if the main result of the negotiations was the solidification of the residence status of settled migrants, its impact must not be underestimated. Many cases of expulsion on grounds of criminal behaviour would not be expected to have been brought before the European Court of Human Rights if the Long-Term Residence Directive were applicable.

This section first describes the provisions relating to the acquisition of long-term resident status in the first Member State (sections 4.7.3 – 4.7.7), and consecutively, with the position of the long-term resident when he moves to a second Member State (sections 4.7.8 – 4.7.11).

4.7.3. SCOPE

The Directive applies to third-country nationals residing legally in the territory of a Member State.[472] It does not apply to third-country nationals residing in, or wishing to move into, the United Kingdom, Ireland and Denmark, as these Member States do not to take part in the Directive (see section 1.5.4). The main condition for being able to obtain long-term resident status is that the third-country national has to be 'legally residing' in a Member State (see, more elaborately, section 4.7.4, hereunder).

The Directive explicitly excludes from its scope the third-country national who:

- resides in order to pursue studies or vocational training;
- has applied for authorisation to reside in a Member State on the basis of temporary or subsidiary protection or as a refugee, or is authorised to reside on the basis of temporary protection;[473]
- resides solely on temporary grounds, for example as an *au pair* or seasonal worker; or
- enjoys a legal status governed by the Vienna Conventions on Diplomatic or Consular Relations, or other treaties governing the status of members of special missions and special representatives.[474]

---

[472] Article 3(1) Long-Term Residence Directive.

[473] See Chapter 3.3 for the meaning of the terms temporary protection, subsidiary protection and refugee.

[474] The other conventions listed are the Convention of 1969 on Special Missions and the Vienna Convention on the Representation of States in their Relations with International Organisations of a Universal Character of 1975.

The initial exclusion from the scope of the Directive of third-country nationals authorised to stay as refugees or on the basis of subsidiary protection was, in 2011, repaired with the adoption of a Directive amending the Long-Term Residence Directive.[475] By virtue of this amendment, these asylum beneficiaries now receive, in some respects, an even more favourable treatment than other third-country nationals. This is because the period during which asylum seekers were awaiting a decision on their application for international protection must be partly taken into account in assessing the duration of legal stay that qualifies them for obtaining a long-term resident status (see section 4.7.4, below). Further, they enjoy an enhanced protection against expulsion (see section 4.7.6).

The exclusion from the scope of the Directive of immigrants staying on the basis of temporary protection, on temporary grounds, or for studies and vocational training, is not incomprehensible. From a point of view of consistency it makes sense – at least in principle – to deny a right of permanent settlement to persons who have been admitted for temporary purposes only. However, it may not always be straightforward to distinguish between forms of temporary and non-temporary stay. This is, in particular, the case with study and vocational training. It is very well conceivable that students whose initial intention was to stay in a country only for education purposes, develop, over the course of time, an interest to continue their legal stay in order to work in the field of their specialisation. The drafters of the Directive did not want to preclude this possibility, and included a provision which allows for the period of residence as a student to be partly counted in determining the required duration of lawful residence necessary to obtain the long-term residents status (see section 4.7.4, below).

The vague wording of the last part of Article 3(2)(e) has led to a preliminary ruling of the Court of Justice, interpreting the concept of a 'residence permit which is formally limited'.[476] *Mr. Mangat Singh* had a residence permit in the Netherlands as a religious leader. This kind of residence permit was labelled as being temporary in nature, although it could be extended every year for, in principle, an indefinite period. Because the permit was labelled as 'temporary', persons possessing this type of resident permit could never obtain a long-term residence permit. The Court considered that Article 3(2)(e):

> must be interpreted as precluding legislation of a Member State, such as that in question in the main proceedings, which excludes from the benefit of the status of long-term resident third-country nationals who hold a residence permit which is formally limited to the exercise of an activity or a profession which, by its very nature

---

[475] Directive 2011/51/EU of 11 May 2011 amending Council Directive 2003/109/EC to extend its scope to beneficiaries of international protection Text with EEA relevance, OJ L 132, 19/05/2011 p. 1–4.

[476] ECJ 15 May 2012, *Mangat Singh*, Case C-502/10, para. 71.

or because of the renewal and/or the extension of that permit, entails a legal and long-term stay in the territory of that Member State.

As regards the exclusion of holders of a diplomatic status, its rationale must be sought in the circumstance that host states have no discretion to refuse entry and residence to such persons, as these derive their rights directly from the pertinent treaties. It is arguable that a host state must not be compelled by the Directive to grant a permanent resident status to a person, who never would have been admitted otherwise, but whose lawful residence the host state was forced to recognise merely because of the diplomatic status. On the other hand, a disadvantage of total exclusion of this category is that Union law offers no possibilities for 'nice and decent' diplomats to obtain a settled position in a Member State after their stay as a diplomat comes to an end. Of course, national migration legislation may provide for such possibilities.

Member States may, according to Article 13 Long-Term Residence Directive, issue residence permits of permanent or unlimited validity on terms that are more favourable than those laid down in this Directive. However, such residence permits shall not confer the right of residence in other Member States as provided by this Directive. This means that the more favourable treatment granted by a Member State cannot result in a status conferring rights of free movement to other Member States. Whether this should also mean that third-country nationals receiving a permanent status based on domestic provisions are excluded from the more robust protection against expulsion offered in the Directive, is not entirely clear. Article 13 does not stipulate that more favourable treatment granted by a Member State automatically implies that the position of such beneficiaries falls outside the scope of the Directive.

The Directive applies without prejudice to more favourable provisions of several categories of treaties mentioned in Article 3(3): bilateral and multilateral agreements between the EU or the EU and its Member States with third countries; bilateral agreements already concluded between a Member State and a third country before the entry into force of the Directive; and the European Convention on Establishment, the European Social Charter, and the European Convention on the Legal Status of Migrant Workers.

Special rules for Blue Card holders are laid down in the Blue Card Directive. As they have a certain right to free movement to other Member States after 18 months, the requirements for acquiring long-term residence status are not strictly linked to legal residence in one Member State. They may accumulate legal residence in more than one Member State under certain conditions (see section 4.3.4, above)

4.7.4. REQUIREMENTS FOR LONG-TERM RESIDENCE STATUS IN THE FIRST MEMBER STATE

A third-country national will have to meet several conditions, laid down in Articles 4 to 7 Long-Term Residence Directive, before he can obtain the status of long-term resident. The key condition is laid down in Article 4(1):

> Member States shall grant long-term resident status to third-country nationals who have resided legally and continuously within its territory for five years immediately prior to the submission of the relevant application.

What is meant by 'legal residence' is not specified. Obviously, third-country nationals holding a residence permit issued by a Member State will qualify as being legally resident, but being legally resident does not necessarily depend on having a residence permit. One can firstly think of third-country national family members who accompany an EU citizen making use of his right to free movement and who enjoy a right of residence, regardless of having a permit or residence card.[477] Normally, these family members will be eligible for permanent residence under the Citizens Directive, but it may happen that the family bond with an EU citizen breaks down after some years and that the family member consecutively obtains a right of residence on other grounds. Must the previous period of legal residence – without a residence permit – in that situation also be counted? Since the lawful character of the residence cannot be denied as it stems directly from EU law, there is no reason why not. The same reasoning applies to third-country nationals who derive residence rights from the Association Treaty concluded with Turkey and citizens of Switzerland and the three EEA countries, Norway, Iceland and Liechtenstein, who can reside legally in a Member State without having a residence permit.

Another issue that has come to the fore is whether illegal residents who have been granted a residence permit as a consequence of a general regularisation programme should be entitled to long-term resident status. As they are not expressly excluded by Article 3, there is no reason why this group cannot obtain the right to a long-term resident status five years after the date of regularisation.

Less easy to answer is the question of whether the period of lawfully awaiting a decision for a residence permit – in an administrative or judicial procedure – in the territory of a Member State, must be considered as constituting legal residence within the meaning of the Directive. The text of the Directive itself does not provide any clarification. However, Directive 2011/51/ EU amending the Long-Term Residence Directive may shed light on this question. Article 4(2) creates a special regime for persons to whom international protection has been

---

[477]   Article 25 of Directive 2004/38 lays down the principle that the residence right exists independently from the acquisition of a residence permit (see Chapter 2.1).

granted. For these third-country nationals, at least half the period between the date of lodging an application for international protection and the granting of international protection counts towards legal residence. If this period exceeds 18 months, the whole period shall be taken into account. From the fact that this is a special regime for persons residing on the basis of international protection, it may be deduced that this period will probably not be taken into account for other third-country nationals. Another argument in favour of this reasoning can be derived from the case law of the Court of Justice on the EEC-Turkey Association Treaty, in which the necessity of the existence of an undisputed right of residence is stressed (see Chapter 3).[478]

In calculating the period of legal residence, not all forms of legal residence may be taken into account. According to Article 4(2), periods of prior residence on temporary grounds or as a diplomat shall not be taken into account. Prior residence as a student may only count for 50 percent. Conversely, periods of absence up to six months shall not interrupt the five-year period, and shall be taken into account if they do not exceed, in total, a period of 10 months within the period of five years. In cases of specific or exceptional reasons of a temporary nature, the Directive further allows Member States, in accordance with their national law, to accept a longer period of absence under the conditions formulated in the second subparagraph of Article 4(3), which may not, however, be taken into account in the calculation of the five-year period. By way of derogation from this latter rule, periods of absence relating to secondment for employment purposes (such as cross-border services) may be taken into account in the calculation of the five-year period.

According to Article 5(1)(a) of the Directive, the third-country national must meet an income requirement to be eligible for long-term resident status. This means that his resources must be stable, regular and sufficient to maintain him and his family. The wording of this provision gives Member States some leeway in assessing whether the income requirement is met. In determining whether the income is sufficient, Member States may 'evaluate the resources by reference to their nature and regularity and may take into account the level of minimum wages and pensions.' Further, Article 5(1)(b) requires that the third-country national has sickness insurance for himself and his dependent family members.

Additionally (and due to the explicit demand of several Member States), Article 5(2) *allows* Member States to require that a third-country national fulfils

---

[478] See, especially, ECJ 20 September 1990, *Sevince*, Case C-192/89, para. 30; ECJ 6 June 1995, *Bozkurt*, Case C-434/93, para. 26; ECJ 16 December 1992, *Kuş*, Case C-237/91, paras. 12, 22. In the context of the EC Association with Turkey, the ECJ reasoned that otherwise, a judicial decision finally refusing a disputed residence right would be rendered nugatory, and would enable the third-country national to acquire the rights provided during a period when he does not fulfil the conditions. It could, nonetheless, be argued that as applications for LTR status will normally take place after the waiting period has resulted in a favourable decision, there is nothing to be rendered nugatory when this period is counted as 'legal residence'.

certain integration conditions. Contrary to the income and health insurance requirements, putting up integration requirements is not obligatory. Since 'integration' is a fairly ambiguous term, it is possible that a range of requirements can be brought under this clause.[479]

Article 6 Long-Term Residence Directive allows for refusing the status of long-term resident on grounds of public policy or public security. When refusing the status on these grounds, the Member State must not only take into account the severity or type of offence or the danger that emanates from the person concerned, but also the duration of residence and the existence of links with the country of residence. According to the Preamble, the notion of public policy may cover a conviction for committing a serious crime.[480]

Apart from these substantive requirements, Article 7, dealing with the procedure for the acquisition of long-term resident status, introduces the possibility of imposing several administrative requirements. According to Article 7(1), the application shall be accompanied by documentary evidence regarding the conditions set out in Articles 4 and 5, as well as – and these may be seen as supplementary requirements – if the Member State so requires, a valid travel document or its certified copy, and documentation with regard to appropriate accommodation. It may be questioned whether a lack of compliance with the requirements of Article 7 may justify refusal of the long-term resident status when the substantive conditions set forth in Articles 4 and 5 are met. The wording of the third paragraph of Article 7 appears to suggest that these extra formalities cannot, in themselves, be a reason for refusing long-term resident status.

In a judgment in an infringement procedure against the Netherlands, the Court of Justice ruled that charging fees for the acquisition of a long-term residence status is not regulated in the Directive, and as such, is left to the discretion of the Member States. However, fees may not be so high as to undermine the objectives pursued by the Directive and to deprive the exercise of the rights under the Long-Term Residence Directive of their effectiveness.[481]

4.7.5. EQUAL TREATMENT IN THE FIRST MEMBER STATE

As could be seen in the previous sections, several of the work-related Directives contain provisions that provide for equal treatment of third-country nationals as

---

[479] See, however, the judgement ECJ 27 June 2006, *Parliament v. Council*, Case C-540/03 on the term 'integration': 'The fact that the concept of integration is not defined cannot be interpreted as authorising the Member States to employ that concept in a manner contrary to general principles of Community law, in particular to fundamental rights', para. 70 (see also section 4.2.12, above).

[480] Recital No. 8, Preamble.

[481] ECJ 26 April 2012, *Commission v. the Netherlands*, Case C-508/10. para. 73.

EU nationals. The areas for which equal treatment is granted in these Directives are limited to work-related issues. The Long-Term Residence Directive provides for equal treatment in the same areas, but, as is shown in more detail below, formulates equal treatment rights in a more general way. This applies especially to equal rights in the fields of social security and social assistance.

The existence of a provision on equal treatment in the Directive might presuppose that without it, long-term residents would not be entitled to equal treatment. This presumption is not necessarily valid. According to Article 18 TFEU, non-discrimination on grounds of nationality is, 'within the scope of application of the Treaty, and without prejudice to any special provisions contained therein', prohibited. The prohibition of discrimination is also laid down in Article 21 Charter, which stipulates that any discrimination based on any ground is prohibited, and it constitutes a general principle of Union law, according to which similar cases must be treated equally, and differential treatment is allowed only if it serves a legitimate aim and is proportionate to the aim pursued.[482]

This raises the question the extent to which, irrespective of Article 11 Long-Term Residence Directive, settled immigrants may be treated differently from nationals at all. What is the fundamental difference between the two categories, apart from their nationality? What legitimate goal is to be served by differentiating? Posing these questions is obviously easier than answering them, but it is important to realise that these questions may underlie all forms of differentiated treatment between nationals and third-country nationals.

The Court of Justice has refrained from applying the principle of non-discrimination on grounds of nationality to differences between Union citizens and third-country nationals,[483] and chose for a more *ad hoc* approach to the issue of equal treatment of third-country nationals. In the *Kamberaj* judgment,[484] the Court was asked to explain Article 11(1)(d) Long-Term Residence Directive. According to this provision, holders of the status enjoy equal treatment with nationals as regards social security, social assistance and social protection, 'as defined by national law'. In contrast with the *Brey* judgment,[485] where the Court gave a Union law definition of the concept 'social assistance system', as laid down in Article 7(1)(b) Citizens Directive, the Court

---

[482]   Note that, according to its Article 3(2), the Council Directive 2000/43/EC of 29 June 2000 implementing the principle of equal treatment between persons, irrespective of racial or ethnic origin, does not cover difference of treatment based on nationality, and is without prejudice to provisions and conditions relating to the entry into, and residence of, third-country nationals and stateless persons, on the territory of Member States, and to any treatment which arises from the legal status of the third-country nationals and stateless persons concerned.

[483]   ECJ 4 June 2009, *Vatsouras and Koupatantze*, Cases C-22/08, 23/08, para. 52.

[484]   ECJ 24 April 2012, *Kamberaj*, Case C-571/10, para. 77, 78.

[485]   ECJ 19 September 2013, *Brey*, Case C-140/12, para. 61.

abstained from doing the same with regard to Article 11(1)(d) of the Long-Term Residence Directive:

> when the European Union legislature has made an express reference to national law, as in Article 11(1)(d) of Directive 2003/109, it is not for the Court to give the terms concerned an autonomous and uniform definition under European Union law (...). Such a reference means that the European Union legislature wished to respect the differences between the Member States concerning the meaning and exact scope of the concepts in question.

But this does not leave Member States free to such a degree that they might undermine the effectiveness of the principle of equal treatment laid down in Article 11(1)(d) of the Directive:

> However, the absence of such an autonomous and uniform definition under European Union law of the concepts of social security, social assistance and social protection and the reference to national law in Article 11(1)(d) of Directive 2003/109 concerning those concepts do not mean that the Member States may undermine the effectiveness of Directive 2003/109 when applying the principle of equal treatment provided for in that provision.[486]

Article 11(1) Long-Term Residence Directive lists the areas in which equal treatment is to be enjoyed: access to employment, education, recognition of diplomas, social security, tax benefits, access to goods and services, freedom of association, and free movement within the territory of the Member State. This list is not exhaustive, as is confirmed in the second phrase of Article 11(5): Member States may decide to grant equal treatment with regard to areas not covered in the list of Article 11(1). They may also decide to grant access to additional benefits. Thus, this provision lays down a minimum standard on equal treatment and leaves room for granting equal treatment in other areas as well.

The Directive explicitly allows for several restrictions on equal treatment. According to Article 11(2), Member States may restrict equal treatment with regard to education, social security, tax benefits, access to goods and services and freedom of association to cases where the long-term resident or his family lives within the territory of the concerned Member State.[487]

The right of access to work may be restricted in a number of ways. First, third-country nationals may be excluded from activities which entail 'involvement in the exercise of public authority',[488] an exception formulated more broadly than the public service exception of Article 45(4) TFEU. Potentially far-

---

[486] Ibid.
[487] Literally: cases where the registered or usual place of residence of the long-term resident, of that of his family members for whom he claims benefits, lies within the territory of the Member State concerned.
[488] Article 11(1)(a) Long-Term Residence Directive.

reaching is that access to employment may also be restricted in cases where preferential treatment is given to nationals, EU, or EEA citizens.[489] Although this provision allows Member States to uphold a sharp distinction between nationals and third-country nationals regarding access to work, this requirement is subject to a standstill clause: distinctions may only be maintained in accordance with existing legislation.

Regarding education, Member States may restrict access by way of requiring proof of appropriate language proficiency or other educational prerequisites.[490] A further important restriction concerns access to social assistance. Equal treatment in respect of social benefits and social protection may be limited to core benefits.[491] Although the notion of 'core benefits' is not defined, Recital 13 of the Preamble of the Directive stipulates that this notion covers at least minimum income support, assistance in the case of illness, pregnancy, parental assistance and long-term care. In the *Kamberaj* judgment, the Court stressed that, since the integration of third-country nationals who are long-term residents in the Member States and the right of those nationals to equal treatment in the sectors listed in Article 11(1) of the Long-Term Residence Directive is the general rule, the derogation provided for in Article 11(4) thereof must be interpreted strictly.[492]

4.7.6. PROTECTION AGAINST EXPULSION FOR REASONS OF PUBLIC ORDER AND PUBLIC SECURITY IN THE FIRST MEMBER STATE

Third-country nationals who qualify for long-term resident status must be granted a long-term resident EU residence permit.[493] According to Article 8(2) Long-Term Residence Directive, the permit shall be valid for at least five years. It shall, upon application, be automatically renewable on expiry. The ruling of the Court in *Iida* made clear that for acquisition of a long-term residence permit an application is necessary.[494]

Clearly, the residence permit does not embody the long-term resident status, but merely certifies it. If a holder of the long-term resident status forgets to apply for renewal of the permit, he will not lose his status, as this ground for losing the status is not mentioned in Article 9. Further, as the latter provision explicitly states in paragraph 6, the expiry of a long-term resident's EU residence permit shall in no case entail the withdrawal or loss of long-term resident status.

---

[489]   Article 11(3)(a) Long-Term Residence Directive.
[490]   Article 11(3)(b) Long-Term Residence Directive.
[491]   Article 11(4) Long-Term Residence Directive.
[492]   ECJ 24 April 2012, *Kamberaj*, Case C-571/10, para. 86.
[493]   Article 8(2) Long-Term Residence Directive.
[494]   ECJ 8 November 2012, *Iida v. Germany*, C-40/11, para. 47.

As a result of disagreement among the negotiating Member States on the issue of guaranteeing protection approximating that of EU citizens to long-term residents whose behaviour is considered to affect public policy or public security, the Directive uses ambiguous and inconsistent terms regarding protection against expulsion. In order to examine this rather complicated matter, it is probably most fruitful to distinguish between the possibilities of invoking public policy and public security exceptions in the various stages of acquisition and loss of long-term resident status. These stages can be found in Article 6, on the acquisition of the long-term residence status; Article 9, on the withdrawal and loss of the long-term residence status; and Article 12, on expulsion. Throughout these stages the guiding question is whether or not a protection equal to that of EU citizens is granted.

What are the criteria for obtaining a long-term resident status? As described in section 4.7.4, Article 6 of the Directive allows for refusing the status of long-term resident on grounds of public policy or public security. The phrasing of this provision is very similar to that of Article 6 of the Family Reunification Directive, which is, as was described in section 4.2.10, a watered-down version of a draft clearly referring to the standard used in relation to EU citizens. Though one must take care when interpreting vague terms like those unavoidably used in provisions on public order and public policy, it can presumably be taken as a fact that the criteria for granting a long-term resident status provide Member States with more discretion than they would have had if EU citizens were concerned. But once the status is acquired, another regime of protection from expulsion comes into being.

Article 12 Long-Term Residence Directive pronounces in terms similar to those of the Citizens Directive (which reflects the Court's jurisprudence on the protection of expulsion of EU citizens) that Member States may take a decision to expel a long-term resident solely

> where he/she constitutes an actual and sufficiently serious threat to public policy or public security.[495]

Further, the decision may not be based on economic considerations,[496] and in wordings similar to that of Article 28(1) Citizens Directive, the Long-Term Residence Directive obliges Member States, before taking a decision to expel, to have regard to: (a) the duration of residence in their territory, (b) the age of the person concerned, (c) the consequences for the person concerned and family members, and (d) links with the country of residence or absence of links with the country of origin.

---

[495]   See Article 27 (2) Citizens Directive.
[496]   See for comparison Article 27(1).

Although this provision of the Directive is less elaborate than Articles 27 and 28 Citizens Directive, it seems fair to assume that Article 12 Long-Term Residence Directive aims at protection as near as possible to protection against expulsion of EU citizens who have not yet acquired a permanent status.[497]

In paragraph 80 of the *Ziebell* judgment, the Court referred to Article 12 Long-Term Residence Directive. In the subsequent paragraphs, the Court made a number of observations which referred to its case law on the EEC-Turkey Association treaty, but which appear to be framed in the context of explaining the import of Article 12 for Turkish nationals. These observations are fully in line with the protection offered by Article 17 Citizens Directive to Union citizens. It is not very likely that the Court could still attach a lesser level of protection to Article 12 Long-term Residence Directive, if it were to be applied to third-country nationals other than Turkish citizens.

The protection offered by Article 12 Long-Term Residence Directive is complicated due to the provisions in Article 9 on the withdrawal or loss of the status. Article 9(3) stipulates that:

> Member States may provide that the long-term resident shall no longer be entitled to maintain his/her long-term resident status in cases where he/she constitutes a threat to public policy, in consideration of the seriousness of the offence he/she committed, but such threat is not a reason for expulsion within the meaning of Article 12.

If a Member State makes use of this option, the anomaly is created of a person who is protected against expulsion under Article 12 without being entitled to maintain the long-term resident status. For reasons of convenience we will refer to a person in this situation as the 'limbo man'. How must we come to terms with this? Does the 'limbo man', in spite of losing his status, still retain the quality of a long-term resident in the sense of Article 12, or is he merely to be tolerated under national immigration rules?

Article 9(7) Long-Term Residence Directive holds that where the withdrawal or loss of the status of long-term resident does not lead to removal, and the third-country national is not considered to be a threat to public policy or security, he must be *authorised to remain* in the territory if he fulfils the conditions provided for in its national legislation and/or he does not constitute a threat to public policy or public security. Thus, the Directive further weakens the position of the 'limbo man' by firstly conditioning his right to 'remain' on provisions of national legislation, and secondly, by repeating a requirement of not constituting a threat to public policy or public security, without any guarantee that this is the very same requirement as the one of Article 12. The net result of these combined provisions could be that persons with long-term resident status who pose a threat

---

[497] Article 28(2) and (3) offers additional protection to EU citizens with respectively a permanent residence right and with more than 10 years legal residence.

to public policy insufficiently serious to be liable to expulsion in accordance with Article 12, may first be stripped of their status, after which they can no longer invoke the protection of Article 12, and may subsequently be expelled in accordance with national legislation and/or for reasons of public policy or public security.

Two questions fight for priority: (a) is this understandable? (b) Is this permissible? It goes without saying that the underlying logic of this system is hard to comprehend. The question of whether it is permissible deserves more attention. We may recall the manner in which the Court of Justice looked at the Family Reunification Directive from the perspective of principles of Union law.[498] In that judgment, the Court considered that the use of options to derogate from the rule laid down in the Directive does not authorise Member States to neglect principles of Union law on fundamental rights. Accordingly, we may presume that the option of creating a 'limbo man' does not absolve Member States from abiding by Union law principles securing fundamental rights like the right to non-discrimination and the right to private and family life. Further, the principle of effectiveness may be at stake. This principle was applied to the Long-Term Residence Directive by the Court in an infringement procedure brought by the Commission against the Netherlands.[499] These principles of Union law could, arguably, lead to an interpretation according to which the contended provisions are considered void, or at least to an interpretation making them harmless. This book is not the place for an extensive elaboration on how these principles should be applied with regard to this particular phenomenon. But, briefly summarised, the main line of thought should be that the option of a 'limbo man' undermines the effectiveness of the protection against expulsion laid down in Article 12, that the system leads to disproportionate and unjustified differences between persons in their rights to protection of private life in different Member States if some Member States apply the option and others do not, and finally, that the system may, in concrete cases, be irreconcilable with the right to remain under Article 8 ECHR, as explained in Chapter 5.

4.7.7. WITHDRAWAL AND LOSS OF THE STATUS IN THE FIRST MEMBER STATE

Apart from reasons of public policy and security, the status of long-term resident can be withdrawn or lost on a variety of grounds (Article 9). The Directive uses the terms 'withdrawal' and 'loss' without defining what the difference between the two concepts is. The wording of the text suggests that 'loss' might mean loss of the status by law (*ipso jure*). Article 10(1) endorses this view, as it stipulates

---

[498] ECJ 27 June 2006, *Parliament v. Council*, Case C-540/03 (see, extensively, Chapter 2.5.4).
[499] ECJ 26 April 2012, *Commission v. the Netherlands*, Case C-508/10. para. 73.

that reasons must be given for any decision rejecting a status or withdrawing a status. It appears that for loss of a status no reasons have to be given, which could be explained from the assumption that 'loss' means loss by law.

Article 9 avoids the terms 'loss' or 'withdrawal' when it comes to the material provisions. It mentions the grounds on which long-term residents are no longer 'entitled to maintain long-term residence status', leaving the question unanswered as to whether these constitute reasons either for loss or for withdrawal.

The enumeration, in Article 9, of grounds on which entitlement to maintaining long-term residence status terminates, is exhaustive. Mandatory withdrawal or loss will take place in the cases of:

- the detection of fraudulent acquisition of the status;
- the adoption of an expulsion measure under the conditions of Article 12 (see section 4.7.6, above); and
- acquiring long-term residence status in another Member State.

In the following cases, the norm is formulated in a mandatory way, but Member States are allowed to provide differently for specific reasons:

- a period of absence from the territory of the Member State of more than 6 years; and
- absence of the territory of the EU for more than 12 consecutive months,

In cases of loss of status because of the absence of the territory or acquiring status in another Member State, there must be a facilitated procedure for the re-acquisition of the status. These procedures shall, in particular, apply to the cases of persons who have resided in a second Member State for study.[500]

4.7.8. RESIDENCE RIGHTS IN OTHER MEMBER STATES

Apart from protection against expulsion and equal treatment, long-term resident status confers upon long-term residents a right of residence in other Member States. In itself, the granting of free movement rights by the Directive is a breakthrough in the EU regime on the internal free movement of third-country nationals. In section 1.6.3 we saw that the internal free movement of third-country nationals within the continental part of the EU is *de facto* secured by the lifting of internal border controls. Further, Article 21 of the Schengen Implementation Convention grants third-country nationals lawfully residing in one of the Member States a circulation right for three months within the

---

[500] Article 9(5) Long-Term Residence Directive.

territories of the other Member States. In addition to these short-term movement rights, the Long-Term Residence Directive now offers a right to residence in other Member States for more than three months.

At first sight, the rights provided by the Long-Term Residence Directive look promising, as the purposes for which lawful residence in a second Member State is allowed are similar to those of EU citizens:

(a) to exercise an economic activity in an employed or self-employed capacity;
(b) for studies or vocational training; and
(c) for other purposes.

However, in contrast to the free movement rights of EU citizens, the rights granted to third-country national workers are heavily conditioned, such, that their position is, in many respects, barely different to a situation without the Long-Term Residence Directive. For all categories, Article 15 allows the second Member State to require the status holder to fulfil three optional conditions:

– stable and regular resources which are sufficient to maintain the long-term residents themselves and the members of their families. The Member State must evaluate these resources by reference to their nature and regularity, and may take into account the level of minimum wages and pensions; workers may be asked to show evidence that they have or will have an employment contract; self-employed persons may be asked to show that they have appropriate funds and the necessary documents and permits;
– sickness insurance covering all risks in the second Member State normally covered for its own nationals in the Member State concerned; and
– compliance with integration measures, in accordance with national law. This condition may not be imposed where the third-country nationals concerned have been required to comply with integration conditions in order to be granted long-term resident status in the first Member State, although any person may be required to attend language courses.

Further, residence in the second Member State may, according to Article 17, be refused if the long-term resident constitutes a threat to the public policy or public security of the second Member State.

Apart from these general conditions, the Long-Term Residence Directive provides for many optional restrictions, especially for employed or self-employed persons. The exercise of economic activity may, according to Article 14, be made dependent on the state of the labour market. For reasons of labour market policy, Member States may give preference to Union citizens, to third-country nationals who can derive the right to exercise an economic activity from EU legislation (such as family members of EU citizens), as well as to third-country nationals who reside legally and receive unemployment benefits in the Member State concerned. Thus, the migrating long-term resident may be placed at the lowest point on a scale of priority in the host Member State, after nationals, EU citizens and third-country nationals – long-term residents or not – who are already legally residing in the host Member State. This is normally the position of any third-country national wishing to work in an EU Member State, and appears to be a striking example of an empty right. However, it must be borne in mind that Member States are not *obliged* to set such conditions. There are more options for the second Member States to restrict the right of long-term resident workers. The rights of seasonal workers and cross-border workers may be conditioned by the Member States. Further, Member States may limit the total number of third-country nationals entitled to be granted a right of residence, provided that such limitations were already provided for in existing legislation at the time of the adoption of the Directive. Finally, Member States may, for a maximum of 12 months, provide that workers shall have restricted access to employed activities different than those for which they have been granted their residence permit.

The scope of the right to exercise economic activity under the Directive does not extend to providers of cross-border services, nor to employed workers posted by a service provider for the purposes of the cross-border provision of services. The position of the latter category is covered by the right to provide services under Article 56 TFEU, if the employer is an EU national or an EU enterprise (see sections 2.3.5 and 2.3.6, above). So, many restrictions are possible with regard to workers.

The other two categories provide less room for derogation. In respect of students and candidates for vocational training, Article 15 allows the Member State to require that the persons concerned provide evidence of enrolment in an accredited establishment in order to pursue studies or vocational training. Further, an income requirement is foreseen. As was shown in section 4.5, similar conditions are laid down in the Students Directive for third-country nationals who do not possess long-term resident status. Although the additional value of the Long-Term Residence Directive for students is limited, it cannot be said that long-term resident status holders are substantially hindered in their right to study or follow a vocational training in other Member States.

The only true novelty appears to be the right to stay in another Member State for 'other purposes' on the mere basis of having sufficient income and sickness insurance. Obviously, this category covers a wide range of residence purposes, and may include such categories as retired long-term residents who simply wish to live in another Member State, or long-term residents wishing to join family members. In doing so, a long-term resident may use the income earned in the first Member State to settle in another Member State. But also for this category, the second Member State is allowed to require compliance with integration measures, unless such a condition was already set in the first Member State for obtaining long-term resident status.

If the long-term resident complies with the conditions for being granted residence in the second Member State, this state must issue him a renewable residence permit.[501] As soon as this permit has been issued, the long-term resident is entitled to equal treatment with nationals of the second Member State in the same areas and under the same conditions as applying to long-term residents residing in the first Member State, except for the restrictions on access to the labour market allowed under Article 14.[502] Naturally, after having been legally resident in the second Member State for a period of five years, the person concerned becomes eligible for long-term residence status in the second Member State, implying that the additional restrictions enumerated in Article 14 may no longer be invoked towards him.

If the second Member State refuses residence, or withdraws the residence permit before the long-term resident obtains the status of long-term resident in the second Member State, the first Member State is under the obligation to immediately readmit the long-term resident.[503] The second Member State may also, on serious grounds of public policy or security, expel the third-country national from the territory of the Union.[504]

4.7.9. PROTECTION AGAINST EXPULSION FOR REASONS OF PUBLIC ORDER AND PUBLIC SECURITY IN THE OTHER MEMBER STATE

Similar to the withdrawal of long-term resident status on grounds of public policy and public security, these exceptions have led to a complicated set of provisions with regard to residence rights in the *second* Member State. Again, a distinction is made in the Directive between the withdrawal of the permit and grounds for expulsion. For withdrawal of the residence permit in the second Member State, it is sufficient that it is established that the concerned person 'constitutes a threat to public policy or public security'. Only the severity or type of the offence needs to be taken into account (Article 22(1)(a), in connection with Article 17). However, with regard to expulsion, Article 22(3) of the Directive obliges the second Member State to take into account the more robust criteria of Article 12, which are similar to the criteria for expelling EU citizens who have no permanent residence permit. In cases of withdrawal of the permit, the first Member State shall, according to Article 22(2), immediately readmit the person. In cases of expulsion from the territory of the Union, the second Member State shall consult the first Member State.

---

[501]   Article 19(2) Long-Term Residence Directive.
[502]   Article 21(1) Long-Term Residence Directive.
[503]   Article 22 Long Term Residence Directive.
[504]   Article 22(3) Long-Term Residence Directive.

4.7.10. WITHDRAWAL AND LOSS OF RESIDENCE PERMIT IN THE OTHER MEMBER STATE

Apart from the reasons of public policy and security, the residence permit in the second Member State may, according to Article 22(1) Long-Term Residence Directive, be withdrawn or not renewed:

- where the conditions regarding the grounds for residence as listed in Article 14 (the exercise of an economic activity, study or vocational training or other purposes), or the requirements of sufficient income, housing and sickness insurance of 15 are no longer met; and
- where the third-country national is not lawfully resident in the Member State concerned (which may be the case if renewal is asked for after expiration of the permit).

If the residence permit is terminated on these grounds, the first Member State shall immediately readmit the person concerned without formalities.

4.7.11. FAMILY MEMBERS

The acquisition of a long-term resident status in the first Member State does not extend to the family members of the holder of a long-term residence permit. As long as the third-country national resides in the first Member State, the legal position of his family members is determined by the Family Reunification Directive. In contrast, the right of a long-term resident to settle in another Member State extends to his family members. According to the Preamble, when a long-term resident wants to settle in another Member State, family members should be able to join him in order to preserve family unity and to avoid hindering the exercise of the long-term resident's right of residence.[505] However, the free movement rights of family members are not fully comparable to the rights of family members of EU citizens.

The circle of family members who have a clear right join the long-term resident status holder in the second Member State is limited to the core family, as defined in Article 4(1) Family Reunification Directive, provided that they fulfil the conditions of that provision. However, the right to join only extends to the family *already constituted* in the first Member State, implying that members of the family not yet constituted in the first Member State must comply with the conditions of the Family Reunification Directive in the second Member State.[506]

---

[505] Long-Term Residence Directive, Preamble, Recital 20.
[506] Article 16(1) Long-Term Residence Directive.

Members of the family constituted in the first Member State, who do not belong to the categories of Article 4(1) Family Reunification Directive, have no self-evident right to join the long-term resident status holder in the second Member State: they 'may be authorised' to do so, although the preamble of the Long-Term Residence Directive does call upon Member States to pay special attention to the situation of disabled adult children and first degree relatives in the direct ascending line who are dependent on them.[507]

Since Article 16(1)(2) Long-Term Residence Directive only refers to the first paragraph of Article 4 Family Reunification Directive, it follows that for the right of members of the constituted family to join the long-term resident in another Member State, none of the derogations enumerated in the other paragraphs of Article 4 FRD may be invoked if the first Member State did not do so. Thus, the second Member State may not invoke the facultative exceptions of Article 4(4), (5) and (6), respectively, in order to exclude children born out of a polygamous marriage, spouses and sponsors who have yet to reach the age of 21, or children above the age of 15.

According to Article 16(4), the second Member State may require a travel document, evidence that the family members resided with the long-term resident status holder in the first Member State. Further, an income requirement may be set, which may either be fulfilled by the family members themselves or by the long-term resident.

Although the rights of family members are limited, their possibilities are wider in the reverse situation, namely when the family member, him or herself, has a long-term resident status and wants to move to another Member State where a family member lives with whatever status. As the Long-Term Residence Directive offers the possibility for the long-term resident to reside in another Member State for the broad category of 'other purposes', this may include the purpose of family reunification or family formation for all conceivable relationships with a family member with whatever status in another Member State. Consider the example of a Chinese long-term resident in Member State A, who wishes to join his unmarried partner of Chinese nationality in Member State B. If the moving family member has acquired the position of long-term resident himself, and he meets the conditions set by the second Member State, he can join his unmarried partner in Member State B, even though their relationship does not fall under the definition of family members contained in the Family Reunification Directive. This construction might be possible for all kinds of other family relationships, like unmarried (same-sex) partners, brothers or sisters, adult children and their parents. Whether successful use can be made of this construction will primarily depend on the manner in which the second Member State has made use of the possibility to set additional conditions for residence, such as an income and/or integration requirement.

---

[507] Long-Term Residence Directive 2003/109, Preamble, Recital 20.

4.7.12. THE RIGHTS OF THE LONG-TERM RESIDENT UNDER THE DIRECTIVE PUT IN PERSPECTIVE

The basic principle of the Directive on long-term residents is that the legal status of third-country nationals should be approximated to that of Member State nationals, and that a person who holds a long-term residence permit should be granted, in that Member State, a set of uniform rights which are as near as possible to those enjoyed by citizens of the European Union. This principle, formulated during the European Council in Tampere in 1999, has been confirmed in the Preamble of the Directive. Although the standard of 'near-equality' is somewhat imprecise, it is clear that in various aspects, the legal status of long-term resident third-country nationals does not approximate that of EU citizens.

As regards the right to equal treatment with nationals, the legal position of third-country nationals remains weaker than that of EU citizens residing in another Member State. The areas in which equal treatment must be enjoyed are listed exhaustively, and are subject to several options of derogation. These restrictions are most apparent regarding access to employment and access to social security. Other examples of inequality are the various possibilities to withdraw a residence permit and to expel long-term residents, in accordance with Articles 9 and 12; the option to impose 'integration' requirements for being able to obtain long-term resident status or to move to another Member State; and the additional limitations to access to the labour market in the second Member State.

One must keep in mind that in some respects, third-country nationals can derive more favourable rights from other instruments. Turkish migrants who fall within the scope of Decision 1/80 of the Association Council can derive the right to free access to the labour market after four years of legal employment.[508] This is not only one year earlier than prescribed by the Long-Term Residence Directive in Article 4(1), but is also a right which is not subject to the broadly formulated possibility to exclude equal access to employment in the public service or the restrictions of Article 11(3) regarding preferential treatment of nationals, EU or EEA citizens.[509] Other categories of third-country nationals who may be entitled to a stronger resident status are family members of EU citizens making use of their right to free movement, and nationals from EEA countries.

The fact that these last categories may now also benefit from the Long-Term Residence Directive can create additional rights. Arguably most notorious is that

---

[508]   Article 6(1) Decision 1/80 of the Association Council.

[509]   Other examples of instruments which offer certain groups more favourable rights are the ILO convention and EEA Agreement. See, more extensively, L. Halleskov, 'The Long-Term Residents Directive: A Fulfilment of the Tampere Objective of Near-Equality?' *EJML* Vol. 7 (2005), pp. 191–192.

third-country national family members of EU citizens, once they have obtained the status of long-term resident, can acquire an independent right to move to another Member State, while this possibility is, under the free movement regime, dependent on accompanying the Union citizen. The same holds for the right of Turkish migrants to move to another Member State.

4.7.13. LONG-TERM RESIDENCE: FINAL REMARKS

Much of the practical effect of the Long-Term Residence Directive will depend on the extent to which Member States make use of the possibilities of derogation in implementing the Directive. The indeterminacy of the foreseeable consequences of the Directive further lies in the rather broad and sometimes ambiguous terms in which certain provisions have been formulated, most notably concerning the circumstances under which the enjoyment of rights may be restricted, or under which the status of long-term residence may be withdrawn. In its evaluation report on the implementation of the Directive the Commission identifies several possible problematic issues.[510] The Commission encountered problems with respect to the exclusion of third-country nationals who have been admitted solely on temporary grounds (Article 3(2)(e)). According to the report, some Member States apply a very broad interpretation, and define the status of certain categories of third-country nationals as temporary, even though their residence permit may be renewed for a potentially indefinite period. Other issues raised by the Commission are the transposition of the term 'lawful residence' by excluding, as a matter of principle, visas and other forms of authorisation to stay; the high fees levied by some Member States; and the refusal of a resident permit based on grounds of public order or public security.

Apart from the Member States' attitude regarding the implementation of the Directive, the manner in which national courts and the European Court of Justice will fulfil their role as supervisory organs will prove crucial to outlining the contents of the long-term resident status.

FURTHER READING

M.H.A. Strik, C.A.F.M. Grütters (eds.), *The Blue Card Directive, Central Themes, Problem issues and Implementation in selected Member States*, Oisterwijk, Wolf legal Publishers, (2013).

---

[510] Report from the Commission to the European Parliament and the Council on the application of Directive 2003/109/EC concerning the status of third-country nationals who are long-term residents, COM(2011) 585 final.

S. Peers, E. Guild, D. Acosta Arcarazo, C.A. Groenendijk, v. Moreno – Lax, *EU Immigration and Asylum Law, Vol. 2, EU Immigration Law*, Leiden, Martinus Nijhoff, (2012).

Diego Acosta Arcarazo, *The Long-Term Residence Status as a Subsidiary Form of EU Citizenship*, The Hague, Martinus Nijhoff, (2011).

P.E. Minderhoud & E. Guild, The First Decade of EU Migration and Asylum Law, Leiden, Martinus Nijhoff, (2012).

Yves Pascouau in collaboration with Henri Labayle, *Conditions for family reunification under strain. A comparative study in nine EU member states; King Baudouin Foundation, European Policy Centre*, Odysseus Network, November (2011).

Anja Wiesbrock, *Legal Migration to the European Union. Ten years after Tampere, Nijmegen,* Wolf Legal Publishers (2009).

Laura Block and Saskia Bonjour, *Fortress Europe or Europe of Rights? The Europeanisation of Family Migration Policies in France, Germany and the Netherlands*, EJML, 203–224, (2013).

Anne Staver, *Free Movement and the Fragmentation of Family Reunification Rights*, EJML, 69–89 (2013).

Julien Hardy, 'The objective of Directive 2003/86 is to Promote the Family Reunification of Third Country Nationals', EJML, 439–452, (2012).

C.A. Groenendijk, *Are third-country nationals protected by the Union law prohibition of discrimination on grounds of nationality?* In K. Barwig & R. Dobbelstein (eds.), Den Fremden akzeptieren. Festschrift für Gisbert Brinkmann (Schriften zum Migrationsrecht, 6) (131–142). Baden-Baden: Nomos (2012).

C.A. Groenendijk, *Pre-departure Integration Strategies in the European Union. Integration or Immigration Policies?* EJML, 1–30, (2011).

Arjen Leerkes, Isik Kulu-Glasgow, *Playing Hard(er) to Get: the State, International Couples and the Income Requirement*, EJML, 95–121, (2011).

John Handoll, *Art. 12 Council Directive 2003/109/EC*, in Kay Hailbronner (ed.) EU Immigration and Asylum law: a Commentary, marginal no. 7, (2010).

Steve Peers, *EU Migration Law and Association Agreements*, in Bernd Martenczuk & Servaas van Thiel (eds.) Justice, Liberty, Security: New challenges for EU external relations, 53–88, (2008).

Louise Halleskov, *The Long-Term Residents Directive: A Fulfillment of the Tampere Objective of Near-Equality?* EJML 2005, 192–99.

Steve Peers, *Implementing Equality? The Directive on Long Term Resident Third Country Nationals*, 29 EUR. L. REV. 427, 452 (2004).

5. FAMILY REUNIFICATION AND PROTECTION OF SETTLED MIGRANTS UNDER ARTICLE 8 ECHR

5.1. INTRODUCTION

The right to respect for private and family life laid down in Article 8 of the European Convention of Human Rights plays a central role in migration law. When people get on the move, preserving or restoring the unity of the family is often one of the primary issues at stake.

In this chapter, the focus will be on the import of Article 8 for family reunification. In the former chapters, family reunification came to the fore as a right provided for in Union law. Both the Citizens' Directive and the Family Reunification Directive formulate an entitlement to family reunification under fairly clear conditions. There are, however, situations in which migrant family members wishing to reunite in a Member State cannot invoke EU instruments, because their situation is outside the scope of Union law. First, there are Member States where the Family Reunification Directive is not applicable, like the UK, Ireland and Denmark. Second, EU law is not applicable to the own nationals of a host Member State, who desire their family members from a third country to join them. They cannot invoke the Family Reunification Directive, as EU citizens are excluded from its scope of application in Article 3(3). Nor can they rely on the Citizens' Directive inasmuch as they did not use their right to free movement within the EU. In such situations, the European Convention of Human Rights may be an important instrument offering basic safeguards for the respect of family life and private life. As all Member States have ratified the ECHR, everyone within the jurisdiction of a Member State may issue a complaint with the European Court of Human Rights in Strasbourg against violation of the Convention.

True, the possibility to complain to the ECtHR exists also in situations that are covered by Union law. However, the protection offered by EU law is often stronger than the protection provided by the ECHR. Thus, a complaint to the ECtHR will only be attractive in such situations if Union law does not grant relief. See sections 1.3 and 1.7.2, above, for a discussion of the differences between EU law and international protection by human rights Conventions like the ECHR.

At present, family reunification is a major source of immigration in Europe. The boom of – mostly individual – labour migration in the 1960s and 1970s has – particularly in the Northern and Western European countries – greatly enhanced the phenomenon of family reunification in recent decades. Over time, it became increasingly apparent that labour migration was not a temporary matter but that migrants who came in as workers wished to settle permanently in the host country, and, if possible, be reunited with their families residing in the home state.

It is in this historical context, that the interpretative development of the European Court of Human Rights on Article 8 ECHR in relation to migration matters, must be situated. Initially, it still was an issue whether the right to respect for family life could have an impact on residence rights of migrants at all. When the European Court of Human Rights took the rather revolutionary step, in 1985,[511] to recognise that the right to stay together as a family in an immigration country may be affected by Article 8, the Court was cautious not to go too far in placing new responsibilities on the shoulders of the contracting states. In the first 10 years after 1985, the Court concentrated on holding states accountable for the consequences of an earlier decision to admit a foreigner to live with his family on their territories. Once states have allowed family life to develop within their borders, this may not be arbitrarily disrupted by expelling one or more family members. At a later stage, the Court, on rare occasions, extended the impact of Article 8 to situations in which family life had not yet been allowed to develop within the borders of a state. Only then, did the scope of Article 8 begin to touch upon 'family reunification' proper, which pertains to reuniting an immigrant with his family members living in another country.

In the meantime, the Court had also started to extend the influence of Article 8 to other types of migration matters, which were less clearly connected with the preservation of family unity, but were related to the right of settled migrants to remain in the country with which they had established strong social and cultural ties. In doing so, the Court took recourse to the right to private life, which became a core concept governing the cross-border movement of persons. Accordingly, the bearing of Article 8 on migration issues has tended to become wider and more fundamental.

This chapter focuses on the ECtHR's rich case law on the meaning of Article 8 ECHR on the residence rights of migrants. Unavoidably, it is a rather polymorphous chapter, which can be appreciated in different ways. Partly, it is a historical account of how the Court has hesitantly proceeded in the direction of acknowledging a right to family reunification under Article 8 ECHR. It is also the story of the Court's internal struggle with how to appreciate the residence status of migrants who are born and have lived their entire lives in the host state;

---

[511] ECtHR 28 May 1985, *Abdulaziz, Balkandali and Cabales v. United Kingdom*, Nos. 9214/80, 9473/81 and 9474/81.

and how this status should relate to potential dangers the migrant may pose to the host state due to criminal activity. Attention is paid, further, to the gradual, sometimes reluctant, societal acceptance of unmarried and same-sex partnerships; on the vulnerable position of migrant children; and on the residence rights of divorced migrants.

When using the term 'family reunification' in this chapter, we refer to both the reunion of family members who have been separated as a consequence of the emigration of one or more family members, and the reunion of family members in a new country when the family has been formed after immigration. In other words: unless explicitly stated otherwise, we do not distinguish between family reunification and family formation.

5.2. OTHER RELEVANT HUMAN RIGHTS SOURCES

None of the relevant human rights treaties recognise a general individual claim to family reunification, nor an unconditional right for family members not to be separated.[512] Nevertheless, human rights treaties are of great importance for migrants claiming a right of residence for the purpose of being able to live together with their families. Article 8 of the ECHR, recognising the right to respect for family life and private life, has been interpreted by the ECtHR as obliging States Parties to strike a fair balance between, on the one hand, their legitimate interests in controlling immigration, and, on the other hand, the interests of family members wishing to reunite or to stay with persons on their territories. As a result, states can be obliged to allow persons to enjoy, or to continue to enjoy, family life on their territories. The comparable provision in the ICCPR, Article 17, has been interpreted more or less similarly by the Human Rights Committee. Other human rights provisions that may be of potential importance for migrants with a family life are the provisions on the protection of the family in Article 23 ICCPR and the protection of the child in Article 24 ICCPR. The latter provisions do not have a counterpart in the ECHR, although Article 12 ECHR does secure the right to marry and to found a family.

Specific provisions protecting children are laid down in the Convention on the Rights of the Child (CRC). Although the content of some provisions of the CRC appear to have great potential impact on matters of family life and family

---

[512] In some European countries, such a right was recognised in one form or another. In Germany, the Constitutional Court (*Bundesverfassungsgericht*) decided that a quota system for family reunification would be unconstitutional (BverfG 12.5.1987, E 76, 1 II). In France, the Council of State (*Conseil d' État*) decided, in 1978, that family reunification for aliens who are legally residing in France is a general principle of law. In 1995, the Constitutional Court of Italy ruled that family reunification is a constitutional right of workers. In the meantime, the coming into being of the Family Reunification Directive has put beyond doubt that there is, under EU law, a right to family reunification for third-country nationals.

reunification, a general complication regarding the CRC is that authoritative interpretations on an international scale are difficult to find, since there is no international body with a competence to consider individual complaints attached to the CRC. With regard to women, a source of potential importance is the Convention on the Elimination of All Forms of Discrimination against Women. Although a Committee competent to receive communications from individuals was established under the Optional protocol of 6 October 1999, as yet this Committee has not expressed any views on the impact of the treaty on family reunification-related cases.

At the level of the European Union, the Charter of Fundamental Rights of the EU is an effective tool for securing human rights, as has been set out in section 1.7. In the Charter, the right to respect for private and family life is laid down in Article 7, the right to marry and to found a family in Article 9, the equality of men and women in Article 23, the protection of children in Article 24 and the right to legal, economic and social protection of the family in Article 33. The Charter is only applicable in situations covered by Union law. In contrast, the primary importance of Article 8 ECHR emerges when a situation is not covered by Union law.[513]

In the following sections, we will concentrate on the state of the law under the European Convention of Human Rights.

5.3. RESPECT FOR FAMILY LIFE UNDER ARTICLE 8 ECHR – POSITIVE AND NEGATIVE OBLIGATIONS

Article 8 ECHR holds that 'everyone has the right to respect for his private and family life, his home and his correspondence'. Interference with the exercise of these rights is not permitted according to paragraph 2, 'except such as is in accordance with the law and is necessary in a democratic society in the interests of national security, public safety or the economic well-being of the country, for the prevention of disorder or crime, for the protection of health or morals, or for the protection of the rights and freedoms of others'. In this chapter, we will not explicitly deal with the right to respect for the home and correspondence, and limit ourselves to private life and family life – as far as it is relevant in relation to migration issues.

Article 8 ECHR obliges the States Parties not only to refrain from arbitrary interference with the exercise of family life of migrants residing on their territory (which can be labelled as a *negative obligation*), but also to *enable* family ties to develop and to take appropriate measures to reunite the family (which can be

---

[513] See also, more elaborately, section 1.7.

labelled as a *positive obligation*).[514] Though it is, as such, meaningful to draw attention to the existence of positive obligations in order to demonstrate that Article 8 requires more from states than merely an approach of abstinence, it would not be fruitful to build a dogmatic view on a sharp distinction between positive and negative obligations. A strict distinction would be fairly artificial as a simple example may illustrate. If a person knocks on our door and we do not open, we abstain from an active act, but if the person would have his feet between a half-opened door, which we try to close by pushing the door, we are performing an active deed. In both cases the effect and the purpose is exactly the same, that is, to prevent a person from entering. Accordingly, it is consistently repeated in the ECtHR case law that the boundaries between positive and negative obligations cannot be precisely defined. In the *Gül* case, for instance, the Court considered that:

> [T]he essential object of Article 8 is to protect the individual against arbitrary action by the public authorities. There may in addition be positive obligations inherent in effective 'respect' for family life. However, the boundaries between the State's positive and negative obligations under this provision (Article 8) do not lend themselves to precise definition. The applicable principles are, nonetheless, similar. In both contexts regard must be had to the fair balance that has to be struck between the competing interests of the individual and of the community as a whole; and in both contexts the State enjoys a certain margin of appreciation.[515]

Hence, a balance must always be struck, regardless of whether positive or negative obligations are involved. That does not, however, mean that the balancing act must always be performed identically. The Court does differentiate, at least in the construction of its reasoning, between cases of expulsion and cases of admission. Once family life involving one or more foreigners has been accepted as existing on a state's territory, the termination of permission for legal residence of the family members is tested against the criteria of the second paragraph of Article 8. Thus, it must be considered whether there is interference, whether this interference is in accordance with the law, and whether the interference is proportionate to a legitimate aim, as described in the second paragraph of the Article.

But when family members seek residence in the territory for the first time, the Court confines its task to examining whether the refusal of the residence permit or the visa strikes a fair balance between the competing interests (also called the 'fair balance' test). The application of the latter test has rarely led to the conclusion that Article 8 has been violated. This is probably so because the Court, in balancing the competing interests of the migrant and the state in cases

---

[514] ECtHR 10 April 2003, *Mehemi v. France*, No. 53470/99, para. 45; see also ECtHR 27 November 1992, *Olsson v. Sweden* (No. 2), No. 13441/87, para. 90.
[515] ECtHR 19 February 1996, *Gül v. Switzerland*, No. 23218/94, para. 38.

of first admission, departs from the view that Article 8 'does not entail a general obligation for a State to respect immigrants' choice of the country of their residence and to authorise family reunion in its territory.'[516]

In examining the meaning of Article 8 ECHR for residence rights of migrants in the next sections, we will distinguish the following questions:

– When does family life or private life, in the meaning of Article 8, exist?
– When does a decision or measure constitute interference with private or family life?
– When is such interference justified?
– When is there a positive obligation to provide for family reunification?

5.4. FAMILY LIFE

In the *Al-Nashif* judgment, the Court gave a general characterisation of the concept of family life, which can be seen as an up-to-date summary of the case law so far:

> The existence or non-existence of 'family life' is essentially a question of fact depending upon the reality in practice of close personal ties. Nevertheless, it follows from the concept of family on which Article 8 is based that a child born of a marital union is *ipso jure* part of that relationship; hence from the moment of the child's birth and by the very fact of it, there exists between him and his parents a bond amounting to 'family life' which subsequent events cannot break save in exceptional circumstances. In so far as relations in a couple are concerned, 'family life' encompasses both families based on marriage and also *de facto* relationships. When deciding whether a relationship can be said to amount to 'family life', a number of factors may be relevant, including whether the couple live together, the length of their relationship and whether they have demonstrated their commitment to each other by having children together or by any other means.[517]

From this description it is apparent that the Court does not wish to define 'family life' in narrow terms. Legal criteria are not decisive; what counts is the existence in reality of close personal or emotional ties. Although family life clearly encompasses the bond between children and their parents and the relationship between married or unmarried couples, it may also cover the relationship between other persons, irrespective of whether or not their relationship is defined by legal or genetic ties. In the case of *Marckx*, for example,

---

[516] See, for the first time, ECtHR 28 May 1985, *Abdulaziz, Balkandali and Cabales v. United Kingdom*, Nos. 9214/80, 9473/81 and 9474/81, para. 68. For a more recent example, see, for instance, ECtHR 28 June 2011, *Nunez v. Norway*, No. 55597/09, para. 70.
[517] ECtHR 20 June 2002, *Al-Nashif*, No. 50963/99, para. 112.

the European Court decided that the bond between a child and a grandparent falls within the scope of family life.[518] According to the Court, the existence of 'family life' cannot be relied on by a person in relation to adults who do not belong to the core family and who have not been shown to have been dependent members of the person's family.[519] However, it is established case law of the Court that family life exists between family members not belonging to the core family of parents and minor children, subject to the proviso that there must exist more than normal emotional ties. Such ties may be demonstrated by factual circumstances, such as belonging to the same household.[520] The main test seems to be that there is a reality in practice of sufficiently close personal ties.

The term 'family life' relates not only to married couples, but also to couples to be, and may be independent of the question whether people have been cohabiting,[521] or whether there has been no cohabitation as a result of a criminal conviction and expulsion.[522] In the case of *Kroon*, the Court considered that, 'although, as a rule, living together may be a requirement for such a relationship, exceptionally other factors may also serve to demonstrate that a relationship has sufficient constancy to create *de facto* 'family ties''[523] Nor is the legal validity of a marriage a decisive factor. In the case of *Cabales*, in which the persons in question believed themselves to be married and genuinely wished to cohabit and lead a normal family life, the Court considered that the committed relationship was sufficient to attract the application of Article 8.[524] As the Court established in *Al Nashif*, cited above, *de facto* relationships may also constitute family life. In the case of *Üner v. The Netherlands*,[525] the Court had no difficulty in accepting that the expulsion of an unmarried partner of a Dutch woman constituted interference with the applicant's right to respect for his family life.

---

[518] ECtHR 13 June 1979, *Marckx*, No. 6833/74, para. 45: 'In the Court's opinion, 'family life', within the meaning of Article 8, includes at least the ties between near relatives, for instance those between grandparents and grandchildren, since such relatives may play a considerable part in family life. 'Respect' for family life so understood implies an obligation for the State to act in a manner calculated to allow these ties to develop normally.'

[519] ECtHR 9 October 2003, *Slivenko a.o. v. Latvia* (Grand Chamber), No. 48321/99 para. 97; see also *Kwakye-Nti and Dufie v. the Netherlands*, No. 31519/96, 7 November 2000; and, more recently, *Anam v. the United Kingdom*, No. 21783/08, 7 June 2011.

[520] For instance: EcomHR 19 July 1968, *X v. Federal Republic of Germany*, No. 3110/67 (concerning an uncle and nephew); ECtHR 3 July 2001 (Dec) *Javeed*, No. 47390/99; ECtHR 28 February 2006 (Dec), *Z. and T. v. UK*, No. 27034/05.

[521] ECtHR 28 May 1985, *Abdulaziz, Balkandali and Cabales v. United Kingdom*, Nos. 9214/80, 9473/81 and 9474/81, para. 62.

[522] ECtHR 13 July 1995, *Mehemi v. France*, No. 19465/92.

[523] ECtHR 27 October 1994, *Kroon v. The Netherlands*, No. 18535/91, para. 30.

[524] ECtHR 28 May 1985, *Abdulaziz, Balkandali and Cabales v. United Kingdom*, Nos. 9214/80, 9473/81 and 9474/81, para. 63.

[525] ECtHR 18 October 2006, *Üner v. The Netherlands*, No. 46410/99, para. 61.

In a judgment of 2010, the Court acknowledged that homosexual relationships are within the scope of family life, thereby referring to a rapid evolution of social attitudes towards same-sex couples in many Member States.[526]

> In view of this evolution, the Court considers it artificial to maintain the view that, in contrast to a different-sex couple, a same-sex couple cannot enjoy 'family life' for the purposes of Article 8. Consequently, the relationship of the applicants, a cohabiting same-sex couple living in a stable *de facto* partnership, falls within the notion of 'family life', just as the relationship of a different-sex couple in the same situation would.

However, the Court is of the opinion that states are still free to restrict access to marriage to different-sex couples. States enjoy a certain margin of appreciation as regards the exact status conferred by alternative means of recognition of the family life of same-sex couples.[527]

Family life exists *ipso jure* between children and parents. From the moment of the child's birth, and by the very fact of it, there exists between him and his parents a bond amounting to 'family life', which subsequent events cannot break, save in exceptional circumstances.[528] The Court does not readily accept that such exceptional circumstances have occurred. Family life was not considered to be broken, even where the father recognised the child only after 10 months, did not maintain that child and scarcely saw him,[529] nor where the father was in prison or resided in the country of origin, and where the child was taken care of by his sister.[530] It is, moreover, irrelevant whether the relationship between child and parent is lawful. In the case of *Keegan*, the bond between a husband with a child who had been adopted without the biological father's consent, constituted family life.[531]

---

[526] ECtHR 24 June 2010, *Schalk and Kopf v. Austria*, No. 30141/04, para. 94. Earlier, the Court accepted that such relations may be covered by the concept of private life. The Court considered the punishability of (some) homosexual acts a violation of private life: ECtHR 22 October 1981, *Dudgeon*, No. 7525/76; ECtHR 26 October 1988, *Norris*, No. 10581/83; ECtHR 22 April 1993, *Modinos*, No. 15070/89. A refusal to change the public registration in connection with changed sex of transsexuals is considered an issue of private life, regardless of whether this has consequences for the possibility to marry: ECtHR 17 October 1986, *Rees*, No. 9532/81; ECtHR 27 September 1990, *Cossey*, No. 10843/84.
[527] *Schalk and Kopf v. Austria*, para.108.
[528] ECtHR 28 November 1996, *Ahmut v. The Netherlands*, No. 21702/93, para. 60: '(.) from the moment of the child's birth and by the very fact of it, there exists between him and his parents a bond amounting to *family life* (...), which subsequent events cannot break save in exceptional circumstances.' See also ECtHR 19 February 1996, *Gül v. Switzerland*, No. 23218/94, para. 32; and, less restrained, EctHR 21 June 1988, *Berrehab v. The Netherlands*, No. 10730/84, para. 21.
[529] ECtHR 24 April 1996, *Boughanemi v. France*, No. 22070/93.
[530] ECtHR 7 August 1996, *C. v. Belgium*, No. 21794/93.
[531] In ECtHR 26 May 1994, *Keegan v. Ireland* No. 16969/90.

An issue deserving special attention is the relevance of the age of minority. In immigration matters, the protection of family life with children is normally based on their dependency on the parents because of their young age.[532] However, the fact that the children attain the age of majority does not affect the family bond as such.[533] Even when children are no longer dependent on their parents, family relations will continue to exist and have a bearing on the question of whether a person's right to family life is interfered with.[534]

5.5. PRIVATE LIFE

Article 8 ECHR protects not only the right to respect for family life, but also the right to respect for private life. Where the concept of family life refers to close personal ties between family members, private life entails the sphere of actions and relationships emanating from, and connected to, one person. Although the right to private life in expulsion cases is often considered together with the right to family life, migrants without a firm claim to family life may additionally rely on their right to private life, for example, on account of the length of stay in the host country.[535] In earlier case law, where second-generation immigrants challenged expulsion on grounds of criminal behaviour, the Court consistently considered that:

> [I]ts task consists of ascertaining whether the deportation in issue struck a fair balance between the relevant interests, namely the applicant's right to respect for his *private and family life*, on the one hand, and the prevention of disorder or crime, on the other.[536]

The judgment in *Slivenko v. Latvia* was the first in which the Court expressly acknowledged that the right to private life may have autonomous standing in cases involving the expulsion of settled migrants. It considered that, regardless of the existence of family life, the removal of persons from the country where 'they had developed, uninterruptedly since birth, a network of personal, social

---

[532] E.g. ECtHR 17 February 2009, *Onur v. United Kingdom*, No. 27319/07, para. 45.

[533] ECtHR 18 February 1991, *Moustaquim v. Belgium*, No. 12313/86.

[534] ECtHR 24 April 1996, *Boughanemi v. France*, No. 22070/93; ECtHR 7 August 1996, *C. v. Belgium*, No. 21794/93; ECtHR 29 January 1997, *Bouchelkia v. France*, No. 23078/93; ECtHR 13 July 1995, *Mehemi v. France*, No. 19465/92; ECtHR 26 September 1997, *El Boujaïdi v. France*, No. 25613/94; ECtHR 21 October 1997, *Boujlifa v. France*, No. 25404/94.

[535] E.g. ECtHR 26 September 1997, *El Boujaïdi v. France*, No. 25613/94, para. 33; ECtHR 21 October 1997, *Boujlifa v. France*, No. 25404/94, para. 36.

[536] ECtHR 24 April 1996, *Boughanemi v. France*, No. 22070/93, para. 42, emphasis added; see also ECtHR 26 September 1997, *El Boujaïdi v. France*, No. 25613/94, para. 40; ECtHR 21 October 1997, *Boujlifa v. France*, No. 25404/94, para. 35; ECtHR 4 October 2001, *Adam v. Germany* (adm. dec.), No. 43359/98.

and economic relations that make up the private life of a human being', amounted to interference with their 'private life' and their 'home'.[537] Because this case concerned the rather specific situation of the expulsion of persons belonging to the Russophone minority in one of the Baltic states, its immediate importance for the residential status of all settled or second-generation immigrants, was not completely clear.

In the Grand Chamber judgment in *Üner*, the Court unequivocally affirmed that the right to private life may obstruct the removal of a settled migrant on grounds of public order, and clarified the relationship between the concepts of private and family life:

> [N]ot all migrants, no matter how long they have been residing in the country from which they are to be expelled, necessarily enjoy 'family life' there within the meaning of Article 8. However, as Article 8 also protects the right to establish and develop relationships with other human beings and the outside world (…) and can sometimes embrace aspects of an individual's social identity (…), it must be accepted that the totality of social ties between settled migrants and the community in which they are living constitute part of the concept of 'private life' within the meaning of Article 8. Regardless of the existence or otherwise of a 'family life', therefore, the Court considers that the expulsion of a settled migrant constitutes interference with his or her right to respect for private life. It will depend on the circumstances of the particular case whether it is appropriate for the Court to focus on the 'family life' rather than the 'private life' aspect.[538]

Through defining the concept of private life as embodying 'the totality of social ties between settled migrants and the community in which they are living', the Court substantially widened the application of Article 8 ECHR to expulsion cases. As any *settled migrant* may be expected to have developed such ties with the host country, their expulsion will normally constitute interference with the right to respect for private life. This wide conception of private life was also apparent in the case of *İletmiş v. Turkey*, referred to in chapter 2.3, where the Court considered in fairly broad wordings that 'freedom of movement, particularly across borders, (…) [is] essential to the full development of a person's private life, especially when, (…) the person has family, professional and economic ties in several countries.'[539]

It will depend on the circumstances of the particular case whether it is appropriate for the Court to focus on the 'family life' rather than the 'private life' aspect. In the *Samsonnikov* case, for instance, the Court found it unnecessary to determine the matter conclusively, since in practice, the factors to be examined

---

[537] ECtHR 9 October 2003, *Slivenko a.o. v. Latvia* (Grand Chamber), No. 48321/99, paras. 96–97.
[538] ECtHR 18 October 2006, *Üner v. The Netherlands*, No. 46410/99 (Grand Chamber), para. 59.
[539] ECtHR 6 December 2005, *İletmiş v. Turkey*, No. 29871/96, para. 50.

in order to assess the proportionality of the deportation measure are essentially the same, regardless of whether family or private life is engaged.[540]

5.6. INTERFERENCES AND JUSTIFICATIONS

In establishing whether the termination of lawful residence of a non-national is allowed under Article 8, the Court will normally first examine whether the state has interfered with one's family or private life. For some time, the former European Commission on Human Rights considered the right to respect for family life not interfered with in situations where the family members could enjoy family life in the country of origin.[541] The Court, however, applies a lower threshold. In the case of *Berrehab*, the Court considered that while the separation of a father and child as a result of a refusal to grant a new residence permit to the father would not make it, in 'theory', impossible for the father and child to maintain regular contact, the refusal of a permit amounted to interference with the exercise of the right to family life.[542] In the cases that followed *Berrehab*, the Court, without additional reasoning, consistently concluded that the termination of residence of a family member constituted interference in the enjoyment of family life. It appears that the question of whether it is possible to continue family life in another country is no longer considered relevant to the question whether of there is interference, but is dealt with by the Court in examining the question of whether the interference is 'necessary in a democratic society'.

Interference is only permitted if it meets the conditions laid down in the second paragraph of Article 8 ECHR: it must be 'in accordance with the law and necessary in a democratic society in the interests of national security, public safety or the economic well being of the country, for the prevention of disorder, for the protection of health or morals, or for the protection of the rights and freedoms of others'. The term 'in accordance with the law' requires that interference is based on a norm which must be made public, and has to be precisely formulated. Since the *Al Nashif* case, the Court worked out the requirement of 'in accordance with the law' by developing a concept of 'quality of law'.[543] It follows from this concept, firstly, that it must be examined whether the disputed measure has any basis in domestic law. If there is a domestic legal basis, its quality must meet a certain standard regarding accessibility and

---

[540] ECtHR 3 July 2012, *Samsonnikov v. Estonia*, No. 521788/10, para. 82.

[541] For an overview of older case law of the Commission on Human Rights, see H. Storey, 'The Right to Family Life and Immigration Case Law at Strasbourg', *The International and Comparative Law Quarterly*, Vol. 39, No. 2 (April 1990), pp. 328–344.

[542] ECtHR 28 May 1988, *Berrehab v. The Netherlands*, No. 10730/84, para. 23.

[543] ECtHR 21 June 2002, *Al Nashif v. Bulgaria*, No. 50964/99, para. 119. See also ECtHR 8 June 2006, *Lupsa v. Romania*, No. 10337/04; ECtHR 6 December 2007, *Liu and Liu v. Russia*, No. 42086/05; and ECtHR 24 April 2008, *C.G. and others v. Bulgaria*, No. 1365/07.

foreseeability. Further, there must be safeguards to ensure that discretion left to the executive is exercised in accordance with the law and without abuse, also in situations where national security is at stake.

Regarding the legitimate aims for restricting the right to private or family life enumerated in Article 8(2) ECHR, the Court often presumes 'economic well-being' as ground for the justification of immigration law measures.[544] This is understandable, as an important rationale behind immigration policies is to safeguard the national labour market and social security system. When the expulsion is based on criminal activities of the immigrant, the Court ordinarily assumes the legitimate aim to consist of the prevention of 'disorder' or crime.[545]

Whether interference can be considered 'necessary' depends on the question of whether the measure is justified by a pressing social need, and, in particular, whether it is proportionate to the legitimate aim pursued.[546] This means that the state must establish why, in its assessment of the interests of the state and those of the person in question, it was necessary to let the interests of the state prevail. Ever since the *Boughanemi* case, the Court's examination of whether interference can be considered necessary departs from the question of whether a fair balance has been struck between the relevant opposing interests.[547]

To a considerable extent, ensuing case law of the Court on Article 8 ECHR in relation to the residence rights of migrants can be conceived as a continuous search for, and refinement of, the relevant interests and the respective weight attached to those interests. In the vast majority of cases, whether it concerns the expulsion of second-generation immigrants or recently settled migrants; whether it concerns expulsion for reasons of public order or the economic well-being of the country; whether it concerns family reunification or the termination of legal residence; the crucial test is whether the expulsion (or non-admittance) strikes a fair balance between the interests of the state and those of the individual concerned.

In the following sections, an overview is presented of the manner in which the Court has dealt with three typical situations where residence rights of migrants are at stake: (1) the situation in which a state decides to terminate legal residence of a person after divorce or separation when a child is involved; (2) the situation in which a state decides to terminate lawful residence on grounds of public order; and (3) the situation in which an immigrant with legal stay in a host state wishes to be united with a family member residing in the country of origin or in a third country.

---

[544] E.g. ECtHR 28 May 1988, *Berrehab v. The Netherlands*, No. 10730/84; ECtHR 31 January 2006, *Rodrigues da Silva and Hoogkamer v. The Netherlands*, No. 50435/99, para. 44.

[545] E.g. ECtHR 2 August 2001, *Boultif v. Switzerland*, No. 54273/00.

[546] E.g. ECtHR 28 May 1988, *Berrehab v. The Netherlands*, No. 10730/84, para. 28.

[547] ECtHR 24 April 1996, *Boughanemi v. France*, No. 22070/93.

5.7. TERMINATION OF LAWFUL RESIDENCE AFTER DIVORCE OR SEPARATION WHEN A CHILD IS INVOLVED

The leading case in situations of termination of lawful residence after the separation of two persons where a child is involved is *Berrehab*.[548] The *Berrehab* case evolved around the question of whether a Moroccan father was entitled to continued residence in the Netherlands in order to be able to maintain family relations with his young Dutch daughter after he separated from his wife. In determining whether the interference with family life – caused by refusing the renewal of his residence permit – was justified, the Court expressed concerns with regard to the distance between the Netherlands and Morocco, the travel expenses, and the fact that family life with a young child can only be maintained in direct contact. The Court found of particular interest that the case involved a very young child, and that continuous contact was necessary to maintain the relationship with the father. In considering the interests of the Netherlands, the Court noted that Berrehab was engaged in salaried employment until he was prevented from working due to the termination of his residence, and that he constituted no threat to the public order of the Netherlands. Having regard to these circumstances, the Court concluded that a proper balance was not achieved between the interests involved, and that Article 8 ECHR was violated. Thus, the father was allowed to stay in the Netherlands for the purpose of maintaining contact with his daughter.

In later cases, the Court has maintained this line of jurisprudence, also where the contacts between father and child were less intense and frequent than in the *Berrehab* case. In the judgment in *Ciliz*,[549] the right of a divorced father to see his child was disputed by the child's mother, who was appointed as guardian. The Court found that the decision to expel the father while the proceedings concerning a formal access arrangement with his son were still pending, frustrated the examination by the domestic authorities of the feasibility and desirability of the father's access to his son. The decision-making process concerning both the question of the applicant's expulsion and the question of access to his son did not afford the requisite protection of Mr. Ciliz's interests, as safeguarded by Article 8 ECHR.

The case of *Rodrigues da Silva and Hoogkamer v. The Netherlands*[550] involved a Dutch girl, Rachael, and a Brazilian mother who was illegally staying in the Netherlands, and who wished to remain with her daughter. The Dutch father, who had split up with the mother, was granted parental authority over Rachael. The Dutch Child Care and Protection Board was of the opinion that granting

---

[548] ECtHR 28 May 1988, *Berrehab v. The Netherlands*, No. 10730/84.
[549] ECtHR 11 July 2000, *Ciliz v. The Netherlands*, No. 29192/95.
[550] ECtHR 31 January 2006, *Rodrigues da Silva and Hoogkamer v. The Netherlands*, No. 50435/99.

parental authority to the father was in the interest of the child because it could prevent her from being taken to Brazil by her mother. The Court noted that, from a very young age, Rachael had been raised jointly by the mother and her paternal grandparents, with her father playing a less prominent role. She spent three to four days a week with her mother, and had very close ties with her. The refusal of a residence permit and the expulsion of the mother to Brazil would, in effect, break those ties, as it would be impossible for them to maintain regular contact. This would be all the more serious given that Rachael, who was only three years old at the time of the final decision, needed to remain in contact with her mother. In view of the far-reaching consequences which an expulsion would have on the responsibilities of the mother, as well as on her family life with her young daughter, and taking into account that it was clearly in Rachael's best interests for the mother to stay in the Netherlands, the Court considered that in the particular circumstances of the case, the economic well-being of the country did not outweigh the applicant's rights under Article 8 ECHR, despite the fact that the first applicant was residing illegally in the Netherlands at the time of Rachael's birth. Indeed, by attaching such paramount importance to this latter element, the Court considered the authorities to have indulged in 'excessive formalism'.[551]

Paradoxically, guardianship over a child may impact negatively on a person's claim to residence. The expulsion of a parent without legal residence, but with custody of a child, will not normally intrude sufficiently upon the family bond, because the parent may take the child with him or her to the country of origin. Even if the child has the nationality of the host country, there is no self-explaining right for the guardian to live in that country as well.[552] A lack of guardianship means, however, that the child may not be removed from the host state, because the other parent who has custody is legally resident there. Expulsion may then unjustifiably intrude upon the family bond, provided that the parent without custody established regular contact with the child, or at least is undertaking concrete steps to secure such contact. Because guardianship is, in a majority of cases, still accorded to the mother, this puts mothers in a disadvantageous position compared to fathers.

5.8. CHILDRENS' INTERESTS AND THE WEIGHT OF ILLEGAL OR FRAUDULENT STAY

According to standing case law, an important consideration in the weighing of interests is whether family life was created at a time when the persons involved were aware that the immigration status of one of them was such that the

---

[551] Ibid, para. 44.
[552] E.g. EComHR 30 November 1994, *Maikoe and Baboelal v. The Netherlands*, appl. 22791/93.

persistence of that family life within the host state would, from the outset, be precarious. Where this is the case, the removal of the non-national family member will be considered incompatible with Article 8 only in exceptional circumstances.[553]

Such exceptional elements were seen by the Court in the above-mentioned case of *Rodrigues da Silva and Hoogkamer,* where the Dutch authorities were even deemed to have indulged in 'excessive formalism' by attaching paramount importance to the fact that the mother was residing illegally in the Netherlands during the birth of her daughter. It is not fully clear on what grounds the situation of the applicants in this case was considered so extraordinary that it could not be held against the mother that she was fully aware of her precarious immigration status when she had the child, like it has been held against many other immigrants in similar positions. What importance is attached to the best interests of the child?

Children, especially young children, are, by definition, not in the position to be aware of any immigration status of their parents. In general, the conduct of parents should not be held against their children. From that point of view, it would be easier to understand the Court, if the Court were to outright say that family life, even if created at a time when the persons involved were aware of the precarious immigration situation of one of them, should result in protection against the disruption of family life by expulsion of the partner who stayed in the host country without permission, if the best interests of children involved require so.

A judgment going in that direction was *Nunez v. Norway,*[554] which concerned a Dominican woman who had come to Norway with a new identity after she had previously been deported and was prohibited re-entry for shoplifting. On the basis of the new passport, she was granted lawful residence. From a relationship with a Dominican man, settled in Norway, she had two daughters, born in 2002 and 2003. In 2001, the fraud was discovered by the authorities. In 2002, her permits were revoked. In 2005, she and her partner separated. In 2005 it was decided that Mrs. Nunez should be expelled and prohibited re-entry for a period of two years. In 2007, the City Court of Oslo awarded sole parental responsibility and the daily care of the children to the father until the return of the mother. The mother complained to the ECtHR on the ground of a violation of Article 8.

The Court found that the residence of Mrs. Nunez in Norway had at no time been lawful. She had given misleading information about her identity, her previous stay in Norway and her criminal conviction. 'She had thus lived and worked in the country unlawfully throughout, and the seriousness of the offences does not seem to have diminished with time'. However, noting that the

---

[553] See ECtHR 28 May 1985, *Abdulaziz, Cabales and Balkandali,* No. 9214/81, 9473/81, 9474/81, para. 68; ECtHR 26 January 1999 (Dec.), *Jerry Olajide Sarumi v. UK,* No. 43279/98; ECtHR 22 May 1999 (Dec.), *Andrey Sheabashov v. Latvia,* No. 50065/99; ECtHR 24 November 1998 (Dec.) *Mitchell v. UK,* No. 40447/98.

[554] ECtHR 28 June 2011, *Nunez v. Norway,* No. 55597/09.

applicant was the children's primary carer from their birth until the father was awarded custody, and that she was, together with the father, the most important person in the children's lives, the Court considered:

> Having regard to all of the above considerations, notably the children's long lasting and close bonds to their mother, the decision in the custody proceedings, the disruption and stress that the children had already experienced and the long period that elapsed before the immigration authorities took their decision to order the applicant's expulsion with a re-entry ban, the Court is not convinced in the concrete and exceptional circumstances of the case that sufficient weight was attached to the best interests of the children for the purposes of Article 8 of the Convention. Reference is made in this context also to Article 3 of the UN Convention on the Rights of the Child, according to which the best interests of the child shall be a primary consideration in all actions taken by public authorities concerning children (…). The Court is therefore not satisfied that the authorities of the respondent State acted within their margin of appreciation when seeking to strike a fair balance between its public interest in ensuring effective immigration control, on the one hand, and the applicant's need to be able to remain in Norway in order to maintain her contact with her children in their best interests, on the other hand.

In a similar case, but regarding a father, the Court came to a different result. The case of *Antwi v. Norway* was about a Ghanaian man who entered Norway on a false Portuguese passport and got a residence permit.[555] He cohabited with a Norwegian woman of Ghanaian origin and had a daughter in 2001, having Norwegian nationality. In 2005, his true identity was discovered. In 2006 it was decided that he should be expelled and prohibited re-entry for a period of five years. The Court noted that the daughter was a Norwegian national who, since her birth, had spent her entire life in Norway, was fully integrated into Norwegian society, and spoke Norwegian with her parents at home. However, the Court saw no reason to call into doubt the Norwegian High Court's findings to the effect that, both parents having been born and brought up in Ghana and having visited the country three times with their daughter, there were no insurmountable obstacles in the way of the applicants settling together in Ghana, or, at least, to maintaining regular contact. Further, it did not emerge, according to the Court, that the daughter had any special care needs or that her mother would be unable to provide satisfactory care on her own. So, expulsion of the father with a five-year re-entry ban would not entail a violation of Article 8 of the Convention. In a separate opinion, Judges Sicilianos and Trajkovska argued that this outcome seemed to contradict the *Nunez* judgment (paras. 9 and 10).

These cases show that weighing the best interests of the child may lead to different outcomes, which are hard to predict. The children's interests are balanced against the negative aspects of the conduct of the parents, even if the

---

[555] ECtHR 14 February 2012, *Antwi v. Norway*, No. 26940/10.

children had no influence on it. Further, it appears that the need of a child for a mother is weighed heavier than the need for a father. Moreover, the fact that the children have the nationality of the host state plays a negligible role (see also section 5.11).

5.9. TERMINATION OF LAWFUL RESIDENCE ON GROUNDS OF PUBLIC ORDER

Initially, the issue of terminating lawful residence of a person with a criminal record came only to the attention of the Court in cases concerning 'second-generation immigrants': children of immigrants, either born in the territory of a Member State of the ECHR, or residing in that territory with their parents. Since the first 'second-generation' judgment, *Moustaquim*, judges of the Court have constantly been debating the issue as to what weight must be attached to long-term lawful residence of a second-generation immigrant, born and having grown up in the host country – or born elsewhere, but otherwise in a similar position.[556] One of the representatives of the trend to attribute almost decisive importance to long-term residence in favour of a right to continued residence was the Dutch Judge Martens. In his dissenting opinion in *Boughanemi*,[557] he accepted the thesis, also advocated by Judges De Meyer and Morenilla, that 'the idea that integrated aliens – that is aliens who have lived all, or practically all, their lives within a State – should no more be expelled than nationals. (…) Under this approach expulsion of an integrated alien *per se* constitutes a violation, whatever the crime committed.' Only under very exceptional circumstances could such an expulsion be justified, according to Martens. A majority of the Court did not follow Martens and his fellow judges in their approach. In the late 1990s it even appeared that the Court had adopted a diametrically opposed position. The ECtHR considered Article 8 to be violated in two earlier cases of *Beldjoudi* (1992) and *Nasri* (1995), and for the last time, with regard to *Mehemi* (1997),[558] but no violation was found in the cases of *Boughanemi* (1996), *C.* (1996), *El Boujaïdi* (1997), *Boujlifa* (1997), *Dalia* (1998), *Baghli* (1999), *Adam* (2001), *Yildiz* (2002), *Yilmaz* (2003), and *Benhebba* (2003).[559]

---

[556] ECtHR 18 February 1991, *Moustaquim v. Belgium*, No. 12313/86.
[557] ECtHR 24 April 1996, *Boughanemi v. France*, No. 22070/93.
[558] ECtHR 26 March 1992, *Beldjoudi v. France*, No. 12083; ECtHR 13 July 1995, *Nasri v. France*, No. 19465/92; ECtHR 26 September 1997, *Mehemi v. France*, No. 25017/94.
[559] ECtHR 24 April 1996, *Boughanemi v. France*, No. 22070/93; ECtHR 7 August 1996, *C. v. Belgium*, No. 21794/93; ECtHR 26 September 1997, *El Boujaïdi v. France*, No. 25613/94; ECtHR 21 October 1997, *Boujlifa v. France*, No. 25404/94; ECtHR 19 February 1998, *Dalia v. France*, No. 26102/95; ECtHR 30 November 1999, *Baghli v. France*, No. 34374/97; ECtHR 4 October 2001, *Adam v. Germany* (adm. dec.), No. 43359/98; ECtHR 31 October 2002, *Yildiz v. Austria*, No. 37295/97; ECtHR 17 April 2003, *Yilmaz v. Germany*, No. 52853/99; ECtHR 10 July 2003, *Benhebba v. France*, No. 53441/99.

Since *Benhebba* however, the Court developed a new set of criteria for deciding cases in which second-generation migrants were expelled on grounds of their criminal conduct. This emerged after the Court had to take a stance, in 2001, in another category of cases where public order was at issue. This other category concerns the *first-generation* immigrants, which we will have to elaborate on before we return to the position of the second generation. In the case of *Boultif v. Switzerland*, concerning an Algerian spouse of a Swiss woman challenging his expulsion for having committed crimes, the Court felt called upon to establish guiding principles for cases:

> where the main obstacle to expulsion are the difficulties for the spouses to stay together, and in particular, for a spouse and/or children to live in the other's country of origin.[560]

In *Boultif*, the Court paid considerably more attention to the position and interests of other family members than in its previous judgments. It formulated eight criteria for examining whether an expulsion measure can be considered necessary in a democratic society[561]:

- the nature and seriousness of the offence committed by the applicant;
- the length of the applicant's stay in the country from which he is going to be expelled;
- the time elapsed since the offence was committed, as well as the applicant's conduct in that period;
- the nationalities of the various persons concerned; and
- the applicant's family situation, such as the length of the marriage, and other factors expressing the effectiveness of a couple's family life;
- whether the spouse knew about the offence at the time when he or she entered into a family relationship;
- whether there are children in the marriage, and if so, their ages; and
- the seriousness of the difficulties which the spouse is likely to encounter in the country of origin.

Boultif, an Algerian national, had, for a relatively short period, resided lawfully with his Swiss wife in Switzerland when he committed, together with another person, the offences of robbery and damage to property, by attacking a man. He was sentenced to two years' imprisonment. Subsequently, the Swiss authorities refused to renew his residence and Mr. Boultif was ordered to leave the country. In examining whether the expulsion was permitted under paragraph 2 of Article 8 ECHR, the Court took note of the fact that Mr. Boultif had not

---

[560] ECtHR 2 August 2001, *Boultif v. Switzerland*, No. 54273/00, para. 48.
[561] Ibid.

committed any crime since his conviction, and that he was released prematurely from prison since his conduct was without blemish. However, of apparently greater importance to the Court, was the question of whether the applicant and, in particular, his Swiss wife, could establish family life elsewhere:

> It is true that the applicant's wife can speak French and has had contacts by telephone with her mother-in-law in Algeria. However, the applicant's wife has never lived in Algeria, she has no other ties with that country, and indeed she does not speak Arabic. In these circumstances she cannot, in the Court's opinion, be expected to follow her husband, the applicant, to Algeria.[562]

This fairly liberal approach was also applied in the cases of *Amrollahi*,[563] *Yildiz*,[564] and *Mokrani*.[565] But in 2006, the Grand Chamber of the Court followed a new line, when it rejected an application of a Turkish citizen, in the case of *Üner v. The Netherlands*. Üner had come to the Netherlands with his mother and two brothers when he was 12 years old, in order to join his father, who had already been living there for 10 years. He cohabited with a Dutch woman with whom he had two children. In examining whether the expulsion and exclusion of Üner was proportionate to the aim pursued, the Court reiterated the *Boultif* criteria and added two further criteria to be taken into account:[566]

- the best interests and well-being of the children, in particular the seriousness of the difficulties which any children of the applicant are likely to encounter in the country to which the applicant is to be expelled; and
- the solidity of social, cultural and family ties with the host country and with the country of destination.

Although the Court listed two additional criteria reflecting the interest the person concerned and his or her children may have to remain the country, it transpires from the Court's reasoning in the *Üner* case, that even though all listed circumstances must be taken into consideration, the seriousness of the committed crime(s) is accorded predominant weight. While the Court would not wish to underestimate the practical difficulties entailed for his Dutch partner in following Üner to Turkey, it considered that in the particular circumstances of the case, the family's interests were outweighed by the other considerations:

> The Court considers at the outset that the applicant lived for a considerable length of time in the Netherlands, the country that he moved to at the age of twelve, together

---

562 Ibid, para. 53.
563 ECtHR 11 July 2002, *Amrollahi v. Denmark*, No. 56811/00.
564 ECtHR 31 October 2002, *Yildiz v. Austria*, No. 37295/97.
565 ECtHR 15 July 2003, *Mokrani v. France*, No. 52206/99.
566 ECtHR 18 October 2006, *Üner v. The Netherlands*, No. 46410/99, para. 58.

with his mother and brothers in order to join his father, and where he held a permanent residence status. Moreover, he subsequently went on to found a family there. In these circumstances, the Court does not doubt that the applicant had strong ties with the Netherlands. That said, it cannot overlook the fact that the applicant lived with his partner and first-born son for a relatively short period only, that he saw fit to put an end to the cohabitation, and that he never lived together with his second son. As the Chamber put it in paragraph 46 of its judgment, '… the disruption of their family life would not have the same impact as it would have had if they had been living together as a family for a much longer time.' Moreover, while it is true that the applicant came to the Netherlands at a relatively young age, the Court is not prepared to accept that he had spent so little time in Turkey that, at the time he was returned to that country, he no longer had any social or cultural (including linguistic) ties with Turkish society.

As to the criminal conviction which led to the impugned measures, the Court is of the view that the offences of manslaughter and assault committed by the applicant were of a very serious nature. While the applicant claimed that he had acted in self-defence – a claim that was in any event rejected by the trial courts – (…), the fact remained that he had two loaded guns on his person. Taking his previous convictions into account, the Court finds that the applicant may be said to have displayed criminal propensities. Having regard to Dutch law and practice relating to early release (…), the Court is, furthermore, not inclined to attach particular weight to the fact that the applicant was released after having served two-thirds of his sentence.[567]

Illustrative for the strongly opposing views conceivable with respect to the appreciation of Üner's case was the dissenting opinion of Judges Costa, Zupančič and Türmen:

> First of all, in general terms, we believe that foreign nationals – in any case those who, like Mr. Üner, have been residing legally in a country – should be granted the same fair treatment and a legal status as close as possible to that accorded to nationals. This objective has been set forth and reiterated in numerous instruments at European level within both the European Union and the Council of Europe, and to some extent at global level. (…)
>
> Of course, we are not arguing that all these international instruments[568] – which, moreover, do not all have the same legal force – mean that foreign nationals can never be expelled, as is the case with nationals under Article 3 of Protocol No. 4. That would be ridiculous. But we do believe that Article 8 of the Convention must be construed in the light of these texts. In our view, the judgment does not quite do that, as it does not, we believe, draw the correct inferences from the international instruments which it cites.

---

[567] Ibid, paras. 62–63.

[568] The dissenting judges referred to the conclusions of the Presidency of the Tampere European Council on 15 and 16 October 1999, to the Committee of Ministers Recommendation Rec (2000)15, Parliamentary Assembly Recommendation 1504 (2001) and Committee of Ministers Recommendation Rec (2002)4, and to the 1989 United Nations Convention on the Rights of the Child.

(…) The nature and seriousness of the offence committed by the applicant were, as we have said, factors contributing to his expulsion (…). On the other hand, the length of the applicant's residence in the Netherlands (seventeen years prior to his expulsion) militated in his favour. Furthermore, almost five years had passed since the applicant had committed the offence, and his conduct in prison does not appear to have caused any problems. His partner and children, as mentioned, are Netherlands nationals. The couple's relationship had begun seven years before he was expelled and the ties were strong (a stable relationship and two children). It seems clear, too, that the applicant's partner would have faced considerable difficulties had she been forced to move with him to a country which was completely alien to her.

In short, apart from the seriousness of the offence, all the 'Boultif criteria' seem to us to point to a violation of Article 8. Paradoxically, even those added by the judgment in this case (…) tend in the same direction (…). Hence, the only way in which the finding of a non-violation can possibly be justified, when the 'Boultif criteria' – especially in their extended form – are applied, is by lending added weight to the nature and seriousness of the crime.[569]

Since the *Üner* judgment of the Grand Chamber, the Court followed a fairly restrictive line with regard to similar applications in, amongst others, the cases of *Kilic, Kaya, Chair,* and *Samsonnikov.*[570] However, in the cases of the Nigerians, *Omojudi,* and *Udeh,* a violation of Article 8 was found.[571] Two factors seemed to be decisive in the two latter cases: First, the absence of a pattern of criminal offences (*Omojudi* had been sentenced for using a false passport in 1989 and for touching a woman's breast without her consent in 2006; *Udeh* committed only one serious offence, and his conduct in prison and after his release was irreproachable); second, the circumstance that they had children with the nationality of the host state. Here the emphasis, which was, in the *Boultif* case, placed on the interests of the spouse having the nationality of the host state, shifted to the interests of the children. This was so, in the case of *Udeh,* even though he was divorced and his children stayed with his ex-wife. He had access to his children for one afternoon every two weeks. The Court observed in para. 52:

(…) that the twin daughters, who have Swiss nationality, were born in 2003. The first applicant's removal is likely to result in their being brought up separated from their father. According to the Federal Court, the second, third and fourth applicants could hardly be obliged to follow the first applicant to Nigeria. In any event, the Court takes the view that it is in the daughters' best interests to grow up with both parents and, as the latter are now divorced, the only way for regular contact to be maintained

---

[569] Joint dissenting opinion of Judges Costa, Zupancic and Türmen, ECtHR 18 October 2006, *Üner v. The Netherlands*, No. 46410/99, pts. 5, 9, 14, 16.

[570] ECtHR 22 January 2007, *Kilic v. Denmark* (adm. dec.), No. 20277/05; ECtHR 28 June 2007, *Kaya v. Germany*, No. 31753/02; ECtHR 6 December 2007, *Chair and J.B. v. Germany*, No. 69735/01, ECtHR 3 July 2012, *Samsonnikov v. Estonia*, No. 521788/10.

[571] ECtHR 24 November 2009, *Omojudi v. UK*, No. 1820/08; ECtHR 16 April 2013, *Udeh v. Switzerland*, No. 12020/09.

between the first applicant and his two children is to authorise him to remain in Switzerland, given that the mother could not be expected to follow him to Nigeria with their two children.

The *Udeh* judgment illustrates that the nationality of the child of a settled migrant may play a role in cases where the migrant is threatened with expulsion, where it is normally not taken into account in cases of first admittance (see section 5.8).

With regard to the *second generation*, similar opposing views existed as they were expressed in the *Üner* judgment. The approach favouring the protection of residence rights of the second generation on a near-equal basis with nationals was not followed by a majority of the Court, which instead granted states considerable discretion in expelling settled migrants on grounds of public order. In 2003, however, the Court began adapting its doctrine on settled migrants to the new '*Boultif* line'.

The first connection between the *Boultif* criteria and the 'second generation' was made in the *Yildiz v. Austria* case.[572] Here, the Court applied the *Boultif* criteria to a situation where the expellee was not married to a national of the expelling state, but to a woman of his own nationality, born in the expelling state, having lived there all her life. According to the Court, the Austrian authorities failed to establish whether Yildiz's wife could be expected to follow him to Turkey, whether she spoke Turkish, or had maintained any links with the country. The Court established that the expelling state was under an obligation to investigate whether the spouse or another relevant family member could be expected to follow the expellee. The case was atypical to the extent that the criminal behaviour was not performed by the second-generation migrant herself, but by her husband, a first-generation migrant.

The *Mokrani* case concerned a more typical situation, where the second-generation migrant himself was reproached criminal behaviour. The Court referred to the *Boultif* judgment, and stated that the Boultif criteria must *a fortiori* be applied to immigrants of the second generation or aliens who entered as very young children in so far as they have founded a family in the receiving country.[573] If there is no actual family life with spouse and/or children, the Court will only apply the first of the three of the *Boultif* criteria:

- the nature and seriousness of the offence committed by the applicant;
- the length of the applicant's stay in the country from which he is going to be expelled; and
- the time elapsed since the offence was committed, as well as the applicant's conduct in that period.

---

[572]   ECtHR 31 October 2002, *Yildiz v. Austria*, No. 37295/97.
[573]   ECtHR 15 July 2003, *Mokrani v. France*, No. 52206/99, para. 31.

But in all 'second generation' cases the Court will, additionally, pay attention to the fact that the second-generation immigrants have passed the essential part of their lives in the receiving country where they received their education, developed most of their social ties and their identities. Relevant, further, is whether they have ties with the country of origin other than their nationality.[574] Similar to the *Üner* judgment, however, in applying those criteria to second-generation cases, the Court remained prepared to attach primary importance to the threat the immigrant would pose to the expelling country.

A new development followed in 2008 with the Grand Chamber judgment on *Maslov v. Austria*.[575] In the chamber judgment of 2007, the Court concluded, by four votes to three, that Article 8 ECHR had been violated by Austria in deciding to expel a 16-year-old Bulgarian second-generation migrant on account of having committed a large range of relatively minor offences, mostly relating to burglary.[576] The case was referred to the Court's Grand Chamber, which produced a much more outspoken judgment and concluded, by sixteen votes to one, that Article 8 ECHR had been violated. The Grand Chamber applied the criteria set out in the *Mokrani* judgment, referred to above, together with the relevant additional criteria of the *Üner* judgment. But the Court also added important explanations as to the relevance of the age of the person concerned:

> In a case like the present one, where the person to be expelled is a young adult who has not yet founded a family of his own, the relevant criteria are:
> – the nature and seriousness of the offence committed by the applicant;
> – the length of the applicant's stay in the country from which he or she is to be expelled;
> – the time elapsed since the offence was committed and the applicant's conduct during that period;
> – the solidity of social, cultural and family ties with the host country and with the country of destination.

> The Court would also clarify that the age of the person concerned can play a role when applying some of the above criteria. For instance, when assessing the nature and seriousness of the offences committed by an applicant, it has to be taken into account whether he or she committed them as a juvenile or as an adult (…).
> In turn, when assessing the length of the applicant's stay in the country from which he or she is to be expelled and the solidity of the social, cultural and family ties with the host country, it evidently makes a difference whether the person concerned had already come to the country during his or her childhood or youth, or was even born there, or whether he or she only came as an adult. This tendency is also reflected in various Council of Europe instruments, in particular in Committee of Ministers Recommendations Rec (2001)15 and Rec (2002)4.[577]

---

[574]   Ibid.
[575]   ECtHR 23 June 2008, *Maslov v. Austria* (Grand Chamber), No. 1638/03.
[576]   ECtHR 22 March 2007, *Maslov v. Austria* (Chamber), No. 1638/03.
[577]   ECtHR 23 June 2008, *Maslov v. Austria* (Grand Chamber), No. 1638/03, paras. 71–73.

From these general criteria, the Court inferred that settled migrants should enjoy a privileged position as regards their right to reside in the host country:

> In short, the Court considers that for a settled migrant who has lawfully spent all or the major part of his or her childhood and youth in the host country very serious reasons are required to justify expulsion. This is all the more so where the person concerned committed the offences underlying the expulsion measure as a juvenile.[578]

In applying the principles to the circumstances of the case, the young age, the juvenile character of the offences and the fact that they were mostly non-violent were taken into account. Further, the Court attached due weight to the rights of the child:

> In the Court's view, the decisive feature of the present case is the young age at which the applicant committed the offences and, with one exception, their non-violent nature. (...) Without underestimating the seriousness of and the damage caused by such acts, the Court considers that they can still be regarded as acts of juvenile delinquency.
> The Court considers that where offences committed by a minor underlie an exclusion order regard must be had to the best interests of the child. (...) The Court considers that the obligation to have regard to the best interests of the child also applies if the person to be expelled is himself or herself a minor, or if – as in the present case – the reason for the expulsion lies in offences committed when a minor. (...)
> The Court considers that, where expulsion measures against a juvenile offender are concerned, the obligation to take the best interests of the child into account includes an obligation to facilitate his or her reintegration. In this connection the Court notes that Article 40 of the Convention on the Rights of the Child makes reintegration an aim to be pursued by the juvenile justice system (...). In the Court's view this aim will not be achieved by severing family or social ties through expulsion, which must remain a means of last resort in the case of a juvenile offender. It finds that these considerations were not sufficiently taken into account by the Austrian authorities.
> In sum, the Court sees little room for justifying an expulsion of a settled migrant on account of mostly non-violent offences committed when a minor (...). Conversely, the Court has made it clear that very serious violent offences can justify expulsion even if they were committed by a minor (...).[579]

This approach can also be recognised in subsequent case law of the Court. The judgment on *Bousarra v. France*[580] concerned a single condemnation for trafficking in cannabis followed by irreproachable conduct. The Court found that deportation would be in violation of Article 8. In *A.A. v. UK*,[581] a serious

---

[578] Ibid, para. 75.
[579] Ibid, paras. 81–84.
[580] ECtHR 23 September 2010, *Bousarra v. France*, No. 25672/07.
[581] ECtHR 20 September 2011, *A.A. v. UK*, No. 8000/08.

offence was committed (rape, together with a group of boys, of a 13-year-old girl), but there were no further offences, and the conduct of A.A. after his release from prison was 'exemplary'.

In sum, the European Court of Human Rights has developed a comprehensive body of case law in which increasingly more precisely circumscribed criteria are formulated regarding how cases of settled immigrants having committed criminal offences should be approached. In weighing the relevant criteria, however, the Court has not always followed a consistent line. In relation to first generation immigrants, the Court returned from a fairly liberal *intermezzo* launched in the *Boultif* judgment – attaching considerable importance to the interests of all family members affected by the decision – to the more restrictive approach of the *Üner* Grand Chamber judgment, in which the appraisal of the seriousness of the crimes committed was put far ahead of the other criteria to be assessed. In cases involving the second generation of immigrants, the Court has incrementally formulated relevant indicators reflecting the social and cultural ties immigrants have developed with the host country, but it has also underlined that very serious violent offences can justify expulsion, even of minors who were born and raised in the host state, and who have not developed ties with the country of their nationality.

5.10. STATE OBLIGATIONS TO ACCEPT NEW IMMIGRANTS TO RESIDE FOR REASONS OF FAMILY LIFE

The situation of termination of previous lawful residence, described in the previous section of this chapter, must be distinguished from the situation in which a migrant claims a first right of entry or residence. There is, in the Court's opinion, hardly any obligation on the side of states to accept the entry and residence of new immigrants in their territories for reasons of family life. Under Article 8 ECHR, a right to family reunification has never been expressly recognised. This does not mean that a development of the Court's case law towards recognition of such a right is inconceivable. At any rate, there are two cases (*Sen* (2001)[582] and *Tuquabo-Tekle* (2005))[583] in which the refusal to allow the reunion with a child who was left behind in the country of origin by its parents, was found to constitute a violation of Article 8 ECHR. There have been further cases from which criteria may be derived in ascertaining under what conditions states are under a duty to allow family reunification on their territories.

---

[582]   ECtHR 21 December 2001, *Şen v. The Netherlands*, No. 31465/96.
[583]   ECtHR 1 December 2005, *Tuquabo-Tekle a.o. v. The Netherlands*, No. 60665/00.

In the *Abdulaziz* judgment, the Court held that the duties imposed by Article 8 ECHR cannot be considered as extending to a general obligation on the part of a contracting state to respect the choice by married couples of the country of their matrimonial residence and to accept the non-national spouses for settlement in that country.[584] The Court observed that this was not a case concerning immigrants who already had a family that they left behind in another country, but that it was only after becoming settled in the United Kingdom that the couple had entered into a contract of marriage. The Court further observed that the applicants had not shown that there were obstacles to establishing family life in their own home countries, or that there were special reasons why they could not be expected to establish family life there. In addition, the applicants knew that their husbands residing in the United Kingdom did not have a right to remain there permanently. The Court found that there was, accordingly, no 'lack of respect' for family life and, hence, no breach of Article 8.[585]

The question of whether contracting states would ever be obliged to accept the settlement of non-national family members, and if so, under what circumstances, remained unanswered for a long period. One could, reasoning *a contrario* on the basis of the *Abdulaziz* judgment, assume that the Court would be prepared to accept such an obligation in one of the following situations:

1. when a family already exists before the person seeking a reunion emigrates to the host country;
2. when there are obstacles to establish family life in the home country; or
3. when there are special reasons why it cannot be expected from the persons involved to establish family life elsewhere.

In the *Gül* case, it appeared that only the second factor counted for the Court.[586] The application was filed by Mr. Gül, a Kurdish asylum seeker who had left Turkey and was granted humanitarian stay in Switzerland, where he resided, together with his wife and daughter, who was born there. He wished his minor son, Ersin, who had been left behind in Turkey, to join the family in Switzerland. There clearly was a situation as described under point one above: family life already existed before Mr. and Mrs. Gül left Turkey. Apparently, the Gül family was of the opinion that they could not be expected to abandon the residence rights they acquired in Switzerland, and that it would therefore be reasonable to allow their minor son to join them. However, the Court followed another path. In paragraph 38 of the judgment, it extended its statement in the *Abdulaziz* case,

---

[584] ECtHR 28 May 1985, *Abdulaziz, Balkandali and Cabales v. United Kingdom*, Nos. 9214/80, 9473/81 and 9474/81, para. 68.
[585] Ibid, paras. 68–69.
[586] ECtHR 19 February 1996, *Gül v. Switzerland*, No. 23218/94.

which was then limited to the situation of spouses, to family reunification in general:

> Moreover, where immigration is concerned, Article 8 cannot be considered to impose on a State a general obligation to respect the choice by married couples of the country of their matrimonial residence and to authorise family reunion in its territory. In order to establish the scope of the State's obligations, the facts of the case must be considered (…).[587]

The Court limited its scrutiny of the facts to one single issue: the question of whether allowing Ersin to join his family in Switzerland would be the *only way* for Mr. Gül to develop family life with his son. The Court considered that this was not the case, and accordingly, found no violation of Article 8:

> In view of the length of time Mr. and Mrs. Gül have lived in Switzerland, it would admittedly not be easy for them to return to Turkey, but there are, strictly speaking, no obstacles preventing them from developing family life in Turkey.[588]

The *Gül* approach is truly restrictive, as it rules out the possibility that a host state might become responsible for securing the enjoyment of family life of immigrants who have previously been allowed lawful residence. Only in situations that nearly amount to '*force majeure*', would a state be compelled to give permission for family members to join the immigrant.

An equally restrictive approach, along slightly different lines, was adhered to in the *Ahmut* case.[589] A Dutch father of Moroccan origin, Salah Ahmut, requested family reunification with his son, Souffiane, who was nine years old when Salah had arrived in the Netherlands. In the course of Souffiane's application for a residence permit, he was sent back to Morocco by his father, to a boarding school, because it was, at that time, unclear whether Souffiane would be allowed to remain in the Netherlands, and the time had come to make choices with regard to his education. The Court concluded that Article 8 was not violated by the refusal of the Dutch government to allow Souffiane to return to the Netherlands:

> The fact of the applicants' living apart is the result of Salah Ahmut's conscious decision to settle in the Netherlands rather than remain in Morocco. In addition to having had Netherlands nationality since February 1990, Salah Ahmut has retained his original Moroccan nationality (…). Souffiane has Moroccan nationality only (…). It therefore appears that Salah Ahmut is not prevented from maintaining the degree of family life, which he himself had opted for when moving to the Netherlands in the

---

[587] Ibid, para. 38.
[588] Ibid, para. 42.
[589] ECtHR 28 November 1996, *Ahmut v. The Netherlands*, No. 21702/93.

first place, nor is there any obstacle to his returning to Morocco. Indeed, Salah Ahmut and Souffiane have visited each other on numerous occasions during the latter's return to that country.

It may well be that Salah Ahmut would prefer to maintain and intensify his family links with Souffiane in the Netherlands. However, as noted in paragraph 65, above, Article 8 does not guarantee a right to choose the most suitable place to develop family life.[590]

Thus, the Court developed several arguments justifying a restrictive approach regarding claims to family reunification. Rephrasing the Court's considerations in its judgments in *Gül* and *Ahmut*, the picture emerges that by settling in a new country, immigrants consciously take the risk that they will not be enabled to have their families with them. If they wish to live together with their family, they should do that in their own countries. Only if that is absolutely impossible, may the host state be held responsible for not awarding residence to their family members. Otherwise, immigrants should be satisfied with maintaining a lower degree of family life in the form of regular visits. Article 8 ECHR does not embody a right to choose the most suitable place to develop family life.

However, a twist in the Court's case law came about with its judgment on *Şen v. The Netherlands*.[591] A Turkish national, Zeki Şen, came to the Netherlands in 1977, at the age of 12, for reasons of family reunification. In 1982 he married a woman residing in Turkey, who initially remained in Turkey after the marriage. They had a daughter, Sinem, in 1983, who was born in Turkey. In 1986, the mother came to the Netherlands to reunite with her husband, but Sinem was left behind, and was entrusted to the care of her mother's sister. In 1990 a second child was born in the Netherlands. Between themselves, the parents initially disagreed on whether Sinem should come to the Netherlands. The father objected, but the mother persisted. Finally, in 1992, the father applied for an entry clearance for Sinem. The Dutch government refused the entry clearance, stating, amongst others, that Sinem no longer *de facto* belonged to the family of her parents. The Şen family appealed unsuccessfully to the Dutch judicial authorities. In 1994, a third child was born in the Netherlands. In the proceedings before the ECtHR, the Dutch government referred to the *Ahmut* judgment, stressing that the applicants were not prevented from living their family life in the form they had chosen themselves by leaving Sinem behind.

In its judgment, the Court used completely different language than in its judgments in *Gül* and *Ahmut*. It considered that there was a 'major impediment'[592] for the Şen family to return to Turkey. The parents had lawfully lived in the Netherlands for many years, and two of their children were born there, and went to school and had lived their whole lives in the cultural environment of the

---

[590]   Ibid, paras. 70–71.
[591]   ECtHR 21 December 2001, *Şen v. The Netherlands*, No. 31465/96.
[592]   In the original French text: *'obstacle majeur'*.

Netherlands. In those circumstances, the transfer of Sinem to the Netherlands was considered as the most adequate means to develop family life with her, while her young age constituted a particular necessity for enabling her integration in the family nucleus with her parents. The Court rejected the idea that the parents' decision to leave Sinem behind in Turkey could be held to be a final one, and considered it irrelevant that the parents had not been able to prove that they had taken financial care of Sinem while she was in Turkey. In its final consideration, the Court attached decisive importance to the fact that the Dutch government forced the parents to choose between abandoning the position they had acquired in the Netherlands and leaving their daughter in Turkey.[593]

In contrast with the *Gül* and *Ahmut* approach, the Court now acknowledged that the established position of the settled parent immigrants could oblige the host country to allow children to join them. This was the first judgment of the Court in which an obligation to admit a family member, who had never lived in the host country, was established under Article 8 ECHR. It is also the first judgment in which the obstacle for developing family life in the country of origin was expressly found in the fact that the family had developed strong ties with the host country. Similar to the *Berrehab* case, the Court attached particular weight to the young age of Sinem and her need to grow up in her parental family. In *Şen*, part of the *Abdulaziz* considerations that had been cast aside in the cases of *Gül* and *Ahmut* appeared to be rehabilitated – i.e. the part where an obligation to accept the settlement of non-national family members may exist if there are special reasons why it *cannot be expected* of the persons involved to establish family life elsewhere.

In the first four years after the *Şen* judgment, the Court delivered a number of non-admissibility decisions in cases of family reunion with children left behind in their countries of origin, where the Court used language suggesting more affinity with the *Gül* en *Ahmut* judgments than with its judgment in *Şen*. Repeatedly, the Court considered that 'Article 8 does not guarantee a right to choose the most suitable place to develop family life', suggesting that family reunification is not a paramount concern under Article 8 ECHR.[594] In short, the Court appeared to distance itself from the *Şen* judgment.

However, in 2005 the Court reaffirmed the *Şen* approach in *Tuquabo-Tekle*, another case against the Netherlands.[595] A mother, who had fled Eritrea in 1990 and established herself in the Netherlands in 1993, asked permission, in 1997, for her 15-year-old daughter, Mehret, to join her in the Netherlands. The mother had originally fled to Norway, where she was granted a residence permit on humanitarian grounds. Her son had joined her there in 1991, but for practical

---

[593]   ECtHR 21 December 2001, *Şen v. The Netherlands*, No. 31465/96, paras. 39–41.
[594]   See, especially, ECtHR 13 May 2003, *Chandra v. The Netherlands*, No. 53102/99; ECtHR 18 March 2003, *Ebrahim v. The Netherlands*, No. 59186/00; and ECtHR 25 March 2003, *I.M. v. The Netherlands*, No. 41226/98.
[595]   ECtHR 1 December 2005, *Tuquabo-Tekle a.o. v. The Netherlands*, No. 60665/00.

reasons, it was not, at that time, possible to let her daughter come as well. Later, the mother married a Dutch former refugee and moved to the Netherlands, where two children were born to the new couple. The Dutch authorities refused permission for the daughter to come over. As it had earlier done in the case of Şen, the Court did not apply the test of whether it would be impossible for the family to reunite elsewhere, but examined whether Mehret coming to the Netherlands would be the most adequate means to develop family life:

> As regards the question to what extent it is true that Mehret's settling in the Netherlands would be the most adequate means for the applicants to develop family life together, the Court observes that the present application is very similar to the case of Şen v. The Netherlands (…), in which it found a violation of Article 8 of the Convention. That case also concerned parents with settled immigrant status in the Netherlands who chose to leave a daughter (Sinem) behind in the care of relatives in her country of origin (Turkey) for a number of years before they applied to be reunited with her. At this juncture, the Court would remark that it is questionable to what extent it can be maintained in the present case, as the Government did, that Mrs. Tuquabo-Tekle left Mehret behind of 'her own free will', bearing in mind that she fled Eritrea in the course of a civil war to seek asylum abroad following the death of her husband. Be that as it may, it is, in any event, the case that Mrs. Tuquabo-Tekle and her husband, just like Mr. and Mrs. Şen, have been lawfully residing in the Netherlands for a number of years, even opting for, and obtaining, Netherlands nationality. In addition, and also just as in the Şen case, two children have been born to the couple in the Netherlands: Tmnit in 1994 and Ablel in 1995. These two children have always lived in the Netherlands and its cultural and linguistic environment, have Netherlands nationality, and attend school there. Consequently, they can only have minimal ties, if any, to their parents' country of origin (see Şen, cited above, §40).
>
> It was precisely these circumstances which led the Court to conclude in the case of Şen that a major impediment existed to that family's return to Turkey, and that allowing Sinem to come to the Netherlands would be the most adequate way in which the family could develop family life with her.[596]

A point of difference with the Şen case, where the daughter was 9 years old, was that Mehret was already 15 at the time of the request for family reunification, and therefore presumably less dependent on her mother. The Court noted, however, that the question of dependency not only hinged on the age of the child. The Court found it of relevance that Mehret had reached an age where she could be married off, and that, in accordance with Eritrean custom, she had, moreover, been taken out of school – factors making it pertinent for her to be allowed to join her family in the Netherlands. The Court agreed with the Dutch Government that this context did not, in itself, warrant the conclusion that the Netherlands was under a positive obligation to allow Mehret to reside in its

---

[596]   Ibid, paras. 47–48.

territory. Even so (and bearing in mind that she was, after all, still a minor), the Court accepted, in the particular circumstances of the case, that Mehret's age at the time the application for family reunion was lodged, was not an element that should lead it to assess the case differently from that of Şen.[597]

Summarising, one sees two conflicting approaches in the Court's case law on requests for family reunification with relatives residing abroad. Under the first approach, represented by the judgments in *Gül* and *Ahmut*, an obligation to allow family members to reunite is acknowledged only if there is no possibility of enjoying family life in the home country.[598] Under the other approach, followed in the cases of *Şen* and *Tuquabo-Tekle*, different language is used, and the decisive tests appears to be whether reunification in the host country is the most 'adequate means to develop family life' or whether there would be – in the light of all the circumstances – a 'major impediment' to enjoy family life in the home country. It does appear that the Court's case law is not always consistent, which may be explained from internal disagreements between judges on this sensitive issue. What is clear, nonetheless, is that the Court has made some important steps in the direction of recognising a right to family reunification.

5.11. IS THERE A NATIONALITY-LINKED RIGHT TO LIVE WITH ONE'S FAMILY IN ONE'S OWN COUNTRY?

In many of the cases described above, the nationalities of the various family members involved played a role, the impact of which was sometimes important, in other instances, almost negligible. In the case of *Boultif*, for instance, the Swiss nationality of the spouse was practically decisive for the Court in barring Boultif's expulsion from Switzerland. But in the *Ahmut* case, the Dutch nationality of the father, wishing his Moroccan son to live with him in the Netherlands, was not deemed to be of particular relevance, apparently because he had also retained his Moroccan nationality.[599] Is there no natural right of a national to live on the soil of his country and to have his family with him?

According to Article 3(2) Fourth Protocol ECHR, no one shall be deprived of the right to enter the territory of the state of which he is a national. Additionally, the first paragraph of Article 3 says that no one shall be expelled, by means either of an individual or a collective measure, from the territory of the state of which he is a national. Both prohibitions are framed in absolute terms. No exceptions are allowed, apart from the possibility of derogation in times of emergency, as

---

[597]   Ibid, para. 50.
[598]   See also ECtHR 25 March 2014, *Biao v. Denmark*, No. 38590/10, paras. 57, 58.
[599]   ECtHR 28 November 1996, *Ahmut v. The Netherlands*, No. 21702/93, para. 70.

provided by Article 15 ECHR.[600] Thus, a very strong right to enter and to remain in one's own country is linked to having the nationality of that country.[601] In principle, the right to enter the country of one's own nationality ensures that everyone with a nationality is secured a place of residence. It is a tragic fact that this freedom is neither of any avail to stateless persons, nor to persons who are *de facto* in the situation of a stateless person because they are unable to provide satisfactory proof of their nationality.

The ECtHR has predominantly examined the right to enter one's own country in situations where persons were expelled from their own countries or formally barred from entry as a consequence of entry bans.[602] In such situations, there are objective obstacles, in the form of law, for persons to be able to remain or to return to their own countries. The question may rise as to whether Article 3 Fourth Protocol ECHR is only applicable in situations where there are objective obstacles to enter or remain in a country, such as formal expulsion orders or entry bans, or whether the right may also be violated as a result of measures which do not specifically purport to prevent a person from living in his own country, but have the effect of indirectly dissuading a person from making use of his right to live in his country or of making it *de facto* impossible to do so.

This question comes to the fore especially when foreign family members enter the stage. If a non-national family member is expelled or not allowed entry, this may *de facto* prevent a national from remaining in his own country, because to do so would result in the break-up of the family. Two opposite approaches to this issue are conceivable. Is the residence right linked to nationality so strong that it extends to family members, regardless of the nationality that they may or may not have? Or is the wish to control entry and residence of foreigners so strong that, as a consequence, nationals may be required by their government to enjoy family life with foreigners in a state other than their own?

The former European Commission of Human Rights was a clear proponent of the latter approach. In the case of *Maikoe and Baboelal v. The Netherlands*, a woman of Surinam nationality who was ordered to be expelled from the Netherlands, where she had been residing legally together with her husband and daughter, both of Dutch nationality, complained that her expulsion would also entail the *de facto* expulsion of her daughter, thereby violating her daughter's

---

[600] Unlike the ECHR, Article 12(4) ICCPR contains a qualified right to enter one's own country: 'No one shall be *arbitrarily* deprived of the right to enter his own country', emphasis added.

[601] Note that the word 'expulsion' in Article 3 Fourth Protocol ECHR does not cover extradition. The provision does not, accordingly, prevent the extradition of persons for the purpose of standing trial or the execution of a sentence imposed upon him; see Council of Europe Committee of Experts, 'Explanatory reports on the Second to Fifth Protocols to the European Convention for the Protection of Human Rights and Fundamental Freedoms', Doc. H (71) 11, Strasbourg (1971), paras. 21, 13. See also EComHR 24 May 1974, *I.B. v. Federal Republic of Germany*, No. 6242/73, para. 13.

[602] E.g. ECtHR 25 October 2005, *Nagula v. Estonia* (adm. dec.), No. 39203/02; ECtHR 9 October 2003, *Slivenko v. Latvia*, No. 48321/99.

right not to be expelled from her own country. The Commission did not spend many words in dismissing the complaint, and merely observed that 'the Dutch authorities have not ordered her [the daughter's] expulsion' and that, accordingly, the complaint must be considered ill-founded.[603] This approach was much in line with – and perhaps instigated by – a decision taken a few months earlier. In the case of *C.B. v. Germany*, concerning a German national living in France, who had been served an arrest warrant by the German authorities, and who had complained that the outstanding arrest warrant prevented him from entering Germany, the Commission considered that Article 3 Fourth Protocol ECHR 'relates not to measures which affect an applicant's desire to enter a country.'[604]

Albeit somewhat less outspoken, the European Court of Human Rights has shown similar reluctance in accepting that the expulsion of a non-national family member can have an impact on the right of a national to remain in his country. In the case of *Schober v. Austria*, the Austrian police had imposed a residence ban on a Slovakian woman who lived in Vienna, together with her Austrian husband, after the couple had been convicted for setting fire to a number of shops of a food store company. She was subsequently deported to Slovakia. Before the Court, her husband complained that the residence ban imposed on his wife had the direct effect of forcing him either to renounce his marriage or to leave his country of origin. The complaint was based both on the prohibition of expulsion of nationals *and* the freedom to choose a residence within the territory of a state in which one is lawfully present (Article 2 Fourth Protocol). Interestingly, the Court did not exclude that the residence ban against his wife could constitute a *de facto* restriction on his right to choose his residence, but considered the restriction justified for reasons of public order. Contrary to the right to remain in one's own country, the right to choose a residence is not an absolute right. Regarding the right to remain in one's own country, the Court found the complaint not to 'disclose any appearance of a violation of Article 3(1) Fourth Protocol.'[605]

The reluctance of the Court not to apply analogous considerations to the right to remain in one's own country may be explained by the fact that this right is absolute, meaning that any finding of an interference would automatically amount to a violation. Still, it cannot be excluded definitely that the expulsion of a family member may obstruct a person's right to stay in his country of nationality. While Mr. Schober clearly had a choice to not follow his wife to Slovakia, this may be different when children are involved.

In the case of *Rodrigues da Silva and Hoogkamer*,[606] discussed in sections 5.7 and 5.8, above, the Brazilian mother of a Dutch child, Rachael, was challenging

---

[603] EComHR 30 November 1994, *Maikoe and Baboelal v. The Netherlands*, No. 22791/93.
[604] EComHR 11 January 1994, *C.B. v. Germany*, No. 22012/93.
[605] ECtHR 9 November 1999, *Schober v. Austria*, No. 34891/97.
[606] ECtHR 31 January 2006, *Rodrigues da Silva and Hoogkamer v. The Netherlands,* No. 50435/99.

her expulsion from the Netherlands. The issue was not looked at as a matter pertaining to the nationality of the child under the absolute rights laid down in Article 3 Fourth Protocol ECHR. Neither the parties nor the Court took into consideration that the expulsion of the mother might compel her, as the caring parent for her daughter, to take the Dutch child away from the Netherlands. Instead, the Court was asked to investigate the case under the right to respect for family life, secured in the non-absolute Article 8 ECHR. Though one must be careful to draw conclusions from this case, in which the relevance of the Fourth Protocol was not considered, the Human Rights Court does appear to accept, albeit under exceptional circumstances, that a child's right to live in his own country may entail that his foreign caring parents must be allowed a right to residence. In the cases of *Omojudi* and *Udeh*,[607] the nationality of the children was taken into account in balancing the interests of settled migrants threatened with expulsion. However, in the case of *Antwi v. Norway*, the Norwegian nationality of Mr. Antwi's daughter played no role in the considerations of the Court.[608] Thus, the picture is variable.

Concluding, one can say that the absolute right to enter one's own country and to remain there does not extend, under present ECtHR jurisprudence, to a firm claim for minor children to share this right with parental carers, regardless of their nationality. It can be even less contended that a general right exists connected to the nationality of a person to have one's family united in his own country. Accordingly, a citizen may be compelled to choose between his right to live in his own country and his right to live with his own family elsewhere.

5.12. SUFFICIENT MEANS OF SUBSISTENCE

A note must be made concerning the requirement of having 'sufficient means of subsistence', which features quite commonly in national legislation of European countries regarding conditions for family reunification. For a long time, imposing a requirement of sufficient resources did not appear to be a relevant issue under Article 8 ECHR. The Court has not considered the requirement of sufficient means of subsistence as a relevant factor for establishing whether an interference with a migrant's family or private life is justified. It has not, for instance, determined whether, and under what circumstances, that requirement may be imposed; whether the required amount is of any relevance; whether a remote chance of success on the labour market or a genuine effort at obtaining income would be sufficient for meeting such requirement; whether account should be taken of the presence of young children in imposing an income

---

[607]   ECtHR 24 November 2009, *Omojudi v. UK*, No. 1820/08; ECtHR 16 April 2013, *Udeh v. Switzerland*, No. 12020/09.
[608]   ECtHR 14 February 2012, *Antwi v. Norway*, No. 26940/10.

requirement; or whether, given the interest of economic well-being of the country, it is reasonable to expect that only the person residing there – as opposed to the family member residing abroad – has any income.

In 2006, the question of whether the refusal of family reunification on grounds of non-compliance with the requirement of sufficient means of subsistence can raise an issue under Article 8 ECHR was, for the first time, addressed by the Court in its non-admissibility decision in the case of *Haydarie v. The Netherlands*.[609] In *Haydarie*, the Court did not consider it unreasonable to impose an income requirement in a situation where there might be obstacles for the mother, who had legal residence in the Netherlands, and her children, to live in the country of origin, Afghanistan. The Netherlands authorities had stated that they would not maintain the income requirement if the mother could demonstrate to having made serious but unsuccessful efforts to comply with it. In principle, the Court did not consider 'unreasonable a requirement that an alien who seeks family reunion must demonstrate that he/she has sufficient independent and lasting income, not being welfare benefits, to provide for the basic costs of subsistence of his or her family members with whom reunion is sought.' With regard to the question of whether such a requirement was reasonable in the case at hand, the Court observed that it had not been demonstrated that the mother had in fact actively sought gainful employment after the date on which she became entitled to work in the Netherlands, but that she had instead preferred to care for her wheelchair-bound sister at home. Nor had it been demonstrated that it would have been impossible for the mother to call in and entrust the care for her sister to an agency providing care for disabled persons. According to the Court, it could not be said that the Netherlands failed to strike a fair balance between the applicants and its own interest in controlling immigration.

The Court regrettably did not consider in depth the issue of the alleged impossibility for the family members to enjoy their family life in Afghanistan. If it were, in this case, established that objective obstacles existed for the family to reunite in their own country, the question might arise as to how reasonable it is to make it impossible – temporarily or permanently – for a family to enjoy family life in the only remaining available country – the Netherlands – on the sole ground that the family has no income. Nor was the Court very outspoken on the question of the circumstances under which it would let the right to family life prevail over the Dutch interest not to be burdened with families having insufficient resources of their own. To strike such a balance might involve answering a number of important questions. How seriously and how long must the person concerned have looked for work? To what extent must any arguments regarding the difficult position on the labour market be taken in to account? Is there any relevance in the personal situation of the family members who are waiting abroad for reunification? It appears that the Court was hesitant in

---

[609]   ECtHR 20 October 2005, *Haydarie a.o. v. The Netherlands*, No. 8876/04.

delving deeply into the impact the imposition of an income requirement might have on the possibility of enjoying family life and – possibly – its corollary implications for family reunification with holders of an asylum permit.

In its judgment in the case of *Konstantinov v. The Netherlands*, the Court confirmed the line set out in the *Haydarie* decision.[610] In this case, the Court did explicitly test whether there were insurmountable obstacles for the exercise of family life outside the Netherlands, but it found that this was not the case. From the Court's reiteration of general principles to be applied to cases such as this, it appears that the question of whether there are insurmountable obstacles for the exercise of family life outside the country concerned is only one factor in the establishment of whether family reunification should be granted, while compliance with requirements of immigration control, is another.[611]

5.13. NON-DISCRIMINATION WITHIN THE AMBIT OF FAMILY LIFE

Already since the first judgment of the ECtHR on family life in 1985, it is established case law that a claim of discrimination may be founded even when Article 8 ECHR, taken alone, is not violated.[612] It is, however, necessary that the facts at issue fall within the ambit of Article 8. Under Article 14 ECHR, the enjoyment of the rights and freedoms set forth in the ECHR shall be secured without discrimination on any ground such as sex, race, colour, language, religion, political or other opinion, national or social origin, association with a national minority, property, birth or other status. This provision complements the other substantive provisions of the ECHR and has no independent existence. In the *Abdulaziz* case, three women settled in the UK, wishing to be reunited with their husbands staying abroad, had complained of a violation of Article 14, taken together with Article 8. It was easier for a man settled in the United Kingdom than for a woman so settled to obtain permission for his or her non-national spouse to enter or remain in the country for settlement. According to the UK government, the applicable rules had the aim of protecting the domestic labour market. On average, there was been a greater percentage of men of working age than of women of working age who were 'economically active'. However, the Court did not deem these arguments convincing.

> Whilst the aforesaid aim was without doubt legitimate, this does not in itself establish the legitimacy of the difference made in the 1980 Rules as to the possibility for male

---

[610] ECtHR 25 April 2007, *Konstantinov v. The Netherlands*, No. 16351/03, para. 50.
[611] Ibid, para. 48.
[612] ECtHR 28 May 1985, *Abdulaziz, Balkandali and Cabales v. United Kingdom*, Nos. 9214/80, 9473/81 and 9474/81, para. 71.

and female immigrants settled in the United Kingdom to obtain permission for, on the one hand, their non-national wives or fiancées and, on the other hand, their non-national husbands or fiancés to enter or remain in the country.

Although the Contracting States enjoy a certain 'margin of appreciation' in assessing whether and to what extent differences in otherwise similar situations justify a different treatment, the scope of this margin will vary according to the circumstances, the subject matter and its background (...).

As to the present matter, it can be said that the advancement of the equality of the sexes is today a major goal in the Member States of the Council of Europe. This means that very weighty reasons would have to be advanced before a difference of treatment on the ground of sex could be regarded as compatible with the Convention.

The Court found that Articles 14 and 8 were violated because of discrimination on ground of sex. In later judgments and decisions on Article 14, the Court has developed an approach in which one of the primary questions is whether there is a difference in the treatment of persons in analogous or relevantly similar situations. In the case of *Bah v. the UK*, the Court summarised its jurisprudence:

The Court has also established in its case law that only differences in treatment based on an identifiable characteristic, or 'status', are capable of amounting to discrimination within the meaning of Article 14 (...). Moreover, in order for an issue to arise under Article 14 there must be a difference in the treatment of persons in analogous, or relevantly similar, situations (...). Such a difference of treatment is discriminatory if it has no objective and reasonable justification; in other words, if it does not pursue a legitimate aim or if there is not a reasonable relationship of proportionality between the means employed and the aim sought to be realised. The Contracting State enjoys a margin of appreciation in assessing whether and to what extent differences in otherwise similar situations justify a different treatment (...).[613]

Though these criteria are clear and comprehensible, practice shows that they cannot prevent a changeable outcome. The question of who is the appropriate comparator to the applicant may be diversely appreciated. Further, the issue of whether there is an 'objective and reasonable' justification for making a distinction is subject to widely diverse interpretations. In this section, only the case law regarding family reunification is discussed.[614] In the *Hode and Abdi* case,[615] about the requirements for family reunification with a refugee, the outcome was different from the case of *Biao v. Denmark*, about the requirements for family reunification with Danish citizens, while it could be contended that there were many similarities between the cases.

---

[613]   ECtHR 27 September 2011, *Bah v. the UK*, No. 56328/07, para. 36.
[614]   See, further, e.g. ECtHR 18 February 1991, *Moustaquim v. Belgium*, No. 12313/86; ECtHR 25 October 2005, *Niedzwiecki v. Germany*, No. 58453/00.
[615]   ECtHR 6 November 2012, *Hode and Abdi v. the UK*, No. 22341/09.

The case of *Hode and Abdi* was about British rules that required the spouses of refugees, in order to be admitted to the UK, to be married before the refugee left the country of origin. The applicants argued that this was discriminatory because a similar condition was not imposed on other migrants with temporary leave in the UK, like students and workers. The ECtHR considered:

> The Court notes that the requirement to demonstrate an 'analogous situation' does not require that the comparator groups be identical. Rather, the applicants must demonstrate that, having regard to the particular nature of their complaints, they had been in a relevantly similar situation to others treated differently (...). In the present case, the applicants are complaining that at the relevant time the Immigration Rules did not permit refugees to be joined in the United Kingdom by spouses where the marriage took place after the refugee had left the country of permanent residence. The Court therefore considers that refugees who married before leaving their country of permanent residence were in an analogous position as they were also in receipt of a grant of refugee status and a limited period of leave to remain in the United Kingdom. In fact, the only relevant difference was the time at which the marriage took place. Moreover, as students and workers, whose spouses were entitled to join them, were usually granted a limited period of leave to remain in the United Kingdom, the Court considers that they, too, were in an analogous position to the applicants for the purpose of Article 14 of the Convention.[616]

The Court saw no justification in the arguments brought by the UK government for treating refugees who married post-flight differently from those who married pre-flight. Accordingly, Articles 14 and 8 ECHR were violated.

The *Biao* case was about Danish legislation, according to which family reunion could only be granted to naturalised Danish citizens if both spouses were over 24 years old and their aggregate ties to Denmark were stronger than the spouses' attachment to any other country.[617] A Ghanaian man had obtained Danish nationality eight years after his entry to Denmark. He had been married to a Danish wife before, but soon after his naturalisation, he married a Ghanaian woman. She was refused entry and residence in Denmark on the ground that it had not been established that the spouses' aggregate ties to Denmark were stronger than their aggregate ties to Ghana. It was not contested that Mr. Biao was in an analogous position with other Danish nationals and that he was treated differently. For, Danish citizens by birth and naturalised Danish citizens who had possessed this nationality for at least 28 years, were exempted from this requirement. The discussion concentrated on whether there was an objective and reasonable justification for this 28-year rule. The Court acknowledged that the 28-year rule affected persons who acquired Danish nationality later in life with a far greater impact than persons born with Danish nationality:

---

[616]   *Hode and Abdi v. the UK*, para. 50.
[617]   ECtHR 25 March 2014, *Biao v. Denmark*, No. 38590/10.

In fact, this group of Danes' chances of reuniting with a foreign spouse in Denmark, and creating a family there, were significantly poorer and, it appears, almost illusory where the residing partner acquired Danish citizenship as an adult, since they either had to wait 28 years after that date, or they had to create such strong aggregate bonds in other ways to Denmark, despite being separated, that they could fulfil the attachment requirement.

In these circumstances, the Court must conclude that persons who acquire Danish nationality later in life have very little benefit from the 28-year exemption. It is even difficult to imagine how a person acquiring Danish nationality at the average age for creating a family can expect to do so with a foreign spouse in Denmark.[618]

However, in accordance with earlier case law, the Court did not see it as its task to review the relevant legislation in abstract. Therefore, it limited itself to determining, in the concrete case of Mr. Biao, whether 'at the relevant time in 2004 there was a lack of reasonable relationship of proportionality between the means employed and the aim sought to be realised by the 28-year rule.' The Court noted that the spouses communicated in the Hausa and Twi languages, and that Mr. Biao had been a Danish national for less than two years when he was refused family reunion.

To refuse to exempt the applicant from the attachment requirement after such a short time cannot, in the Court's view, be considered disproportionate to the aim of the 28-year rule, namely to exempt from the attachment requirement a group of nationals who, seen from a general perspective, had lasting and long ties with Denmark, so that it would be unproblematic to grant family reunion with a foreign spouse, because it would normally be possible for such spouse to be successfully integrated into Danish society.

Accordingly, the majority of the Court (four judges) found, in this concrete case, no violation of Article 14, taken together with Article 8. In an extensive joint dissenting opinion, three judges opposed this finding. They argued that the majority judgment overemphasised 'the watershed between the factual situation, on the one hand, and the law owing to which this situation had been created, on the other.'

In this context, the paramount concern of a human rights court should be whether such criteria have the disparate adverse impact of a stereotype on a minority group, no less important than the actual individual impact, which in every case is absolutely necessary for victim status to obtain. The difference in the treatment of a group raises fundamental human rights concerns, especially if it reflects or reinforces existing patterns of social stereotyping related to one or other 'natural feature'. It is impossible to think of Article 14 of the Convention as permitting second-class citizenship, especially within the ambit of Convention rights (such as those consolidated in Article 8).[619]

---

618   *Biao v. Denmark*, paras. 101, 102.
619   Joint dissenting opinion of judges Sajó, Vučinič and Kūris in the *Biao* judgment, point 8.

The divided views of the judges in the Biao case illustrate how divergent the conceptions of discrimination can be, and how difficult it is to reach consensus in this field on the basis of purely legal arguments. In migration cases there is often a hidden issue of ethnic discrimination, which may easily create dissension. Two judges belonging to the majority wrote a concurring opinion in which they stressed that criticising the Danish 28-year rule was beyond the task of the Court.[620] In contrast, the dissenters in the *Biao* judgment expressly stated that the case was about discrimination based on ethnic or national origin, for which the standard of *D.H. and others v. the Czech republic* should have been applied.[621] In the *D.H. and others* judgment, about the difference in schooling between Roma children and other children, the Grand Chamber of the Court formulated criteria for the approach of discrimination on the basis of a person's ethnic origin.

> The Court has established in its case law that discrimination means treating differently, without an objective and reasonable justification, persons in relevantly similar situations (…). However, Article 14 does not prohibit a Member State from treating groups differently in order to correct 'factual inequalities' between them; indeed in certain circumstances a failure to attempt to correct inequality through different treatment may in itself give rise to a breach of the Article (…). The Court has also accepted that a general policy or measure that has disproportionately prejudicial effects on a particular group may be considered discriminatory notwithstanding that it is not specifically aimed at that group (…), and that discrimination potentially contrary to the Convention may result from a *de facto* situation (…).

> Discrimination on account of, *inter alia*, a person's ethnic origin is a form of racial discrimination. Racial discrimination is a particularly invidious kind of discrimination and, in view of its perilous consequences, requires from the authorities special vigilance and a vigorous reaction. It is, for this reason, that the authorities must use all available means to combat racism, thereby reinforcing democracy's vision of a society in which diversity is not perceived as a threat but as a source of enrichment (…). The Court has also held that no difference in treatment which is based exclusively or to a decisive extent on a person's ethnic origin is capable of being objectively justified in a contemporary democratic society built on the principles of pluralism and respect for different cultures (…).[622]

Apparently, some observers may see a suspect distinction on the basis of ethnic origin, whereas others just see an acceptable form of migration policy. In general, it cannot be denied that migration policy has, by definition, 'prejudicial effects on a particular group', as meant in para. 175 of the *D.H. and others* judgment. As was set out above in section 1.2.7, migration law is always based on a distinction on grounds of nationality, which is normally not considered to amount to

---

[620] Concurring opinion of judges Raimondi and Spano.
[621] ECtHR 13 November 2007, *D. H. and others v. the Czech Republic*, No. 57325/00.
[622] *D.H. and others v. the Czech republic*, paras. 175, 176.

discrimination.[623] Although the Court is of the opinion that very weighty reasons would have to be put forward before a difference of treatment based exclusively on the ground of nationality could be regarded as compatible with the Convention,[624] it emerges from the above-cited case law that migration law, *as such*, is not seen by the Court as a *prima facie* discriminatory differentiation.

On the other hand, the mere fact that a distinction is made in the framework of migration law, does not exclude the possibility that such a distinction is discriminatory. In particular cases, the detrimental effects of a certain policy on a certain group may be disproportional, and thus, discriminatory.

In the *Kiyutin* judgment,[625] the ECtHR classified a migration policy excluding HIV positive spouses from family reunification as discriminatory. An Uzbek man was married to a Russian female. The couple had a daughter. He was required by the Russian authorities to undergo a medical examination during which he tested positive for HIV. On account of that circumstance, his application for a residence permit was refused. The Court found that Mr. Kiyutin was in a situation analogous to that of other foreign nationals for the purpose of an application for a residence permit on account of their family ties in Russia.

> (…), the Court finds that, although the protection of public health was indeed a legitimate aim, the Government were unable to adduce compelling and objective arguments to show that this aim could be attained by the applicant's exclusion from residence on account of his health status. A matter of further concern for the Court is the blanket and indiscriminate nature of the impugned measure.
> (…)
> Taking into account that the applicant belonged to a particularly vulnerable group, that his exclusion has not been shown to have a reasonable and objective justification, and that the contested legislative provisions did not make room for an individualised evaluation, the Court finds that the Government overstepped the narrow margin of appreciation afforded to them in the instant case. The applicant has therefore been a victim of discrimination on account of his health status, in violation of Article 14 of the Convention taken together with Article 8.[626]

While it is difficult to predict the outcome of a complaint on violation of Article 14, together with Article 8, the case law of the ECtHR shows that such an application is by no means *a priori* chanceless.

---

[623] See, e.g., Article 1(3) Convention on the Elimination of All Forms of Racial Discrimination.
[624] See ECtHR 16 September 1996, *Gaygusuz v. Austria*, No. 17371/90, para. 42; ECtHR 30 September 2003, *Koua Poirrez v. France*, No. 40892/98; ECtHR, 18 February 2009, *Andrejeva v. Latvia*, No. 55707/00.
[625] ECtHR 10 March 2011, *Kiyutin v. Russia*, No. 2700/10.
[626] Ibid. paras. 72, 74.

5.14 CONCLUDING REMARKS

The extensive case law of the European Court of Human Rights on the meaning of Article 8 ECHR for claims relating to residence rights displays a sincere and balanced outlook on the quality of private and family life of migrants. Although the doctrine of the Court is developing incrementally, the discernable trend is in the direction of recognising rights to family reunification and rights to remain. Throughout the whole process of doctrinal debate within the Court, we may discern two opposite appreciations of the phenomenon of family life and migration. On the one hand, we see a perception laying primary responsibility with the migrant who, by the very decision to migrate, wilfully took the risk that he might not be able to share life with his family in the new country. On the other hand, we see an approach under which the responsibility is laid upon the host country to recognise that to allow migrants to reside on its territory may entail a legitimate claim to family reunion.

These conflicting approaches are also discernable with regard to criminal behaviour of settled immigrants. One opinion is, in extreme terms, that even settled immigrants no longer deserve to remain on the territory once they have seriously misbehaved and that the consequences for their family life comes at their own risk. The other is, that misbehaving migrants should, in principle, be treated equal to misbehaving nationals, and that their families should not be 'punished' for their criminal acts.

FURTHER READING

Fulvia Staiano, *Good Mothers, Bad Mothers: Transnational Mothering in the European Court of Human Rights' Case Law,* EJML, 2013, 155–182.

Ersin, Souffiane, Sinem and Mehret. *Strasbourg Case Law on the Right of Foreign Children to Join their Parents*, EJML, 2009, 271–293.

Betty de Hart, *Love thy Neighbour, Family Reunification and the Rights of Insiders*, EJML, 2009, 235–252.

Sarah van Walsum, *Against All Odds. How Single and Divorced Migrant Mothers were Eventually able to Claim their Right to Respect for Family Life*, EJML, 2009, 295–311.

PART III
FORCED MIGRATION

6. THE COMMON EU ASYLUM SYSTEM

6.1. ASYLUM IN INTERNATIONAL LAW

The word asylum originates from the Greek word '*asylon*', meaning 'inviolable' or 'free from seizure'. In ancient times, it referred to a place where a fugitive could find sanctuary and where the pursuer was prohibited from retrieving him. In international law, asylum refers to protection granted by a state to an individual against persecution or harm done by another state, normally the individual's home state.[627] Two forms of asylum are generally distinguished. Territorial asylum refers to asylum accorded by a state to persons within its territory. Diplomatic asylum refers to asylum granted by a state in a foreign country, normally on the premises of an embassy or consulate.[628] Some recent sensational instances notwithstanding, the practice of diplomatic asylum has gradually fallen in disuse.[629] This book discusses only territorial asylum, which has become the dominant form of asylum throughout the world.

Traditionally, the 'right of asylum' was understood as the right, belonging to the state, to grant asylum to a national of another state. It thus signified the right of the state that had granted the asylum to refuse a request for extradition made by the pursuing state. The International Court of Justice explained, in the 1950 *Asylum Case*, that the competence of a state to grant territorial asylum derives directly from the principle of territorial sovereignty, and that such a grant must therefore be respected by other states, including the fugitive's home state.[630]

In current international law, the 'right of asylum' is understood primarily as a human right, a right belonging to the individual that may either be invoked

---

[627] A. Grahl-Madsen, *The Status of Refugees in International Law*, Vol. II, Leiden: Sijthoff (1972), p. 3; A. Grahl-Madsen, *Territorial Asylum*, Stockholm: Almqvist and Wiksell (1980), p. 1; F. Morgenstern, 'The Right of Asylum', 26 *British Yearbook of International Law* (1949), p. 327; G.S Goodwin-Gill and J. McAdam, *The Refugee in International Law*, Oxford University Press (2007), pp. 355–358.

[628] Grahl-Madsen (1980), p. 1; F. Morgenstern, "Extra-Territorial' Asylum', 25 *British Yearbook of International Law* (1948), p. 236. Asylum granted in a foreign territory may also be referred to as extraterritorial asylum.

[629] M. den Heijer, 'Diplomatic Asylum and the Assange Case', 26 *Leiden Journal of International Law* (2013), pp. 399–425.

[630] *Colombian-Peruvian asylum case*, Judgment, 20 November 1950, ICJ Reports 1950, p. 266 at p. 274. See also UN General Assembly, *Declaration on Territorial Asylum*, 14 December 1967, A/RES/2312(XXII); and Council of Europe, *Declaration on Territorial Asylum*, 18 November 1977.

against the state where asylum is sought, or against the pursuing state. According to Article 14 of the Universal Declaration of Human Rights (UDHR), everyone has the right to seek and to enjoy, in other countries, asylum from persecution. This provision does not refer to a right to be *granted* asylum, hence preserving the decision to admit a person fleeing from persecution to the sovereign domain of the state.[631] Article 14 UDHR thus gives expression to the rights, firstly, to escape persecution ('the right to seek asylum') and, secondly, not to be extradited once asylum has been granted ('the right to enjoy asylum').

Contrary to the other rights mentioned in the Universal Declaration, a right to seek and enjoy asylum has not, however, been formulated in any of the human rights treaties that were adopted under the auspices of the United Nations. Nor is the concept to be found in the European Convention on Human Rights.[632]

The institution of asylum has found a basis, nonetheless, in human rights law. The 1951 Convention Relating to the Status of Refugees and the 1967 Additional Protocol (Refugee Convention, also referred to as Geneva Convention) created a framework for the protection of refugees. A key right laid down in the Refugee Convention is the right to be protected from *refoulement*, which is the right of a refugee not to be returned to his or her country of origin, or any other country for that matter, where he or she is at risk of being subjected to serious harm. Apart from prohibiting *refoulement*, the Refugee Convention lays down a refugee rights regime that ought to secure a minimum standard of treatment of refugees.

Traditionally, the French term *refoulement* refers to the obligation of states, under Article 33(1) of the Refugee Convention, not to return a refugee to a country where his life or freedom is threatened. A second explicit prohibition of *refoulement* was later formulated in Article 3 of the 1984 Convention against Torture and Other Cruel, Inhuman or Degrading Treatment or Punishment (CAT).

Apart from the explicit prohibitions of *refoulement* in the Refugee Convention and CAT, other human rights, which do not expressly refer to the expulsion of a person, have been interpreted as entailing a prohibition of *refoulement*. Thus, Article 7 ICCPR, prohibiting exposure to torture or cruel, inhuman or degrading treatment or punishment, has been interpreted by the Human Rights Committee (HRC) as 'implicitly' prohibiting *refoulement*. Likewise, the ECtHR has considered Article 3 ECHR to be applicable to situations where a person is expelled to a territory where he may be subjected to proscribed harm. Apart from protecting individuals from *refoulement*, international human rights form a universal standard of treatment that is also to be accorded to any person who a state admits to its territory.

---

[631] H. Lauterpacht, *International Law and Human Rights*, Hamden: Archon Books (1968 reprint), pp. 421–422.

[632] The Inter-American Human Rights Convention does mention the right to seek and be granted asylum in Art. 22(7).

International law on asylum therefore rests on two primary pillars: the specific refugee rights regime of the Refugee Convention and the general human rights standard, as informed by international and regional treaties. These two regimes are also the main sources of the evolving protection regime for persons who seek asylum under European Union law. Article 78 TFEU, the legal basis for adopting measures on asylum, sets forth that the common policy on asylum must be in accordance with the Refugee Convention and 'other relevant treaties'. A significant development further, is that the Charter of Fundamental Rights of the EU recognises the 'right to asylum' in Article 18, making asylum a subjective and enforceable right within the Union's legal order, even though the precise contours of that right remain to be determined.[633] Additionally, the Charter explicitly prohibits *refoulement* in Article 19(2).

The present chapter discusses the coming into being of the Union's rules on asylum, their functioning, and how they relate to international standards on asylum, as stemming from the Refugee Convention and general human rights treaties – chiefly the European Convention on Human Rights. Chapters 7 and 8 discuss the two core international protection (or: asylum) statuses guaranteed within the common EU asylum system: protection in accordance with the Refugee Convention (refugee status), and other forms of international protection that mainly derive from generally applicable human rights standards (subsidiary protection).

6.2. THE HARMONISATION OF EU ASYLUM LAW

The 1997 Amsterdam Treaty created a legal basis for the Community legislature to adopt binding measures in the field of asylum (ex Article 63 TEC). As a result, a series of Directives and Regulations was adopted which together form the Common European Asylum System (CEAS). The CEAS was built in two stages. The first series of instruments was adopted in the years 2001–2005, laying down a mechanism for allocating asylum seekers between the Member States; minimum standards for the reception of asylum seekers; minimum standards for asylum procedures; and minimum standards for granting asylum. The second phase of developing a common asylum policy aimed at upgrading some of these instruments, and was completed in 2013.

Although Article 78 TFEU, the current legal basis for developing a common policy on asylum, as introduced by the Lisbon Treaty, has given the EU the

---

[633] M.-T. Gil-Bazo, 'The Charter of Fundamental Rights of the European Union and the Right to be Granted Asylum in the Union's Law', 27 *Refugee Survey Quarterly* (2008), pp. 33–52. Although the Court of Justice EU dealt with the scope of Article 18 of the Charter in the *N.S.* case, it refrained from giving it substance, in the particular context of that case, beyond that of Article 4 of the Charter (the prohibition of torture and inhuman or degrading treatment): ECJ 21 December 2011, *N.S. and M.E.*, Joined Cases C-411/10 and C-493/10, para. 114.

competence to harmonise asylum law fully if it wishes, the Member States have as of yet been unable to agree on a fully integrated asylum system. The CEAS rules are part of the legal order of the European Union and, consequently, form an integral part of the legal systems of the Member States, which their courts are bound to apply.

In many respects, the EU asylum system provides for clear and precise rules that the Member States must respect in offering asylum protection. As will be explained in the coming chapters, the CEAS provides for a right to have an asylum claim processed according to minimum procedural standards, and a right to be granted refugee status or subsidiary protection status if the conditions are fulfilled. According to the Tampere conclusions of the European Council of 1999, the The Hague Programme of 2005 and The Stockholm Programme of 2010, Community rules should develop into a system where 'individuals, regardless of the Member State in which their application for asylum is lodged, are offered an equivalent level of treatment as regards reception conditions, and the same level as regards procedural arrangements and status determination.'[634] Despite the revisions of the asylum instruments in the second phase, full harmonisation in that sense has not yet been achieved, as most instruments still leave considerable discretion for the Member States to organise their own asylum systems. However, the impact of the common rules must not be underestimated. Not only because they contain, for instance, a clear and binding choice as to the interpretation of the Refugee Convention, but also because they offer the possibility for an interpretative development of the system by the case law of the Court of Justice, which may go beyond what the legal provisions appear to say at first glance. In this regard, we may recall the development described in Chapters 2 and 3, of how the Court's jurisprudence created a comprehensive sphere of principles and rights.

6.2.1. TOWARDS HARMONISATION OF ASYLUM POLICIES

Reflection on the harmonisation of asylum policies in Europe commenced in the mid-1980s, when policymakers across Europe realised that the creation of a Single Market with the abolishment of internal borders, as envisaged by the Single European Act (1986) and brought about by the Schengen Conventions of 1985 and 1990 and the entry into force of the 1992 Maastricht Treaty, could have a profound impact on national asylum policies (see also section 1.5).

---

[634] Presidency Conclusions, Tampere European Council, 15–16 October 1999, 16 October 1999, para. 15; The Hague Programme: Strengthening Freedom, Security and Justice in the European Union, (2005) OJ C 53/1, para. 1.3; and The Stockholm Programme – An Open and Secure Europe Serving and Protecting Citizens, (2010) OJ C 115/1, para. 6.2.1.

Policymakers feared that the abolishment of border controls would put incentives in place for asylum seekers to 'shop' for asylum: once inside the territory of the European Community, it would be possible for asylum seekers to travel unchecked and to apply for asylum in those Member States with the most generous reception conditions, procedural arrangements or protection statuses. It would also be easier for asylum seekers to apply for asylum in more than one Member State: once an initial claim for asylum in a Member State failed, the absence of border controls and coordinated policies could encourage asylum seekers to lodge a subsequent claim in a second Member State.

To reduce the risk of such secondary movements within the EU, additional measures dealing with asylum seekers were deemed indispensable. European asylum law therefore took off primarily as 'flanking measures'. The goal was to control the movement of asylum seekers on European territory. Therefore, clear rules should be developed for determining the Member State responsible for the examination of an asylum application. Further, standards relating to the reception of asylum seekers, asylum procedures, and the rules on the recognition and content of refugee status, should be approximated.

The first result of this impetus to coordinate asylum policies in Europe was the establishment of a mechanism to determine which state was responsible for processing asylum applications. This mechanism was first laid down in the 1990 Schengen Implementation Convention, and replaced by a concurring mechanism in the Dublin Convention, which entered into force in 1997 between the original 12 signatory states.[635] The name of the Dublin Convention has survived the Convention itself: as we will learn in section 6.3, the EU Regulation replacing the Dublin Convention is still referred to as the 'Dublin Regulation', although it was established in Brussels.

The 1992 Treaty on European Union formally recognised asylum to be a 'matter of common interest' of the EU, and placed asylum policies in the intergovernmental Third Pillar of the Union.[636] Third Pillar discussions during the post-Maastricht era (1993–1999) resulted in the adoption of a number of non-binding conclusions, recommendations and common positions, which did touch upon important aspects of asylum, but did not enhance basic rights of asylum seekers and refugees, and were unsuccessful in truly converging asylum

---

[635] See Articles 28–38 Convention Implementing the Schengen Agreement of 14 June 1985 between the Governments of the States of the Benelux Economic Union, the Federal Republic of Germany and the French Republic, on the Gradual Abolition of Checks at their Common Borders (Schengen Implementation Agreement), 19 June 1990. Convention Determining the State Responsible for Examining Applications for Asylum lodged in one of the Member States of the European Communities, 15 June 1990, OJ C 254/1, 19 August 1997. On the Dublin Convention, see, extensively, C. Marinho (ed.), *The Dublin Convention on Asylum; Its Essence, Implementation and Prospects*, Maastricht, European Institute of Public Administration (2000).
[636] Former Article K1 TEU.

policies.[637] On the contrary, mainly as a result of a sharp increase of asylum applications in Europe from 1990 onwards, multiple Member States decided to unilaterally restrict their asylum systems, in the hope that asylum seekers would knock on another Member State's door.[638]

From the mid-1990s onwards, Member States became increasingly aware of the shortcomings of intergovernmental cooperation under the Third Pillar. The lack of effective instruments and the cumbersome negotiating processes eventually prompted European governmental leaders to *communautarise* immigration and asylum policies, resulting in a new Title IV in the 1997 Amsterdam EC Treaty, dealing with visas, asylum, immigration and other policies related to the free movement of persons (ex Articles 61–69 TEC).

The transfer of asylum policies from the Third to the First Pillar made the issuing of binding legislation possible, together with judicial control asserted by the Court of Justice. Article 63 TEC dealt explicitly with asylum: it obliged Member States to adopt, before the 1st of May 2004, measures in this field; Article 63 sub (1) and (2) listed the precise subject matters on which results had to be achieved (new Article 78 TFEU).

The negotiating process on this new legislative programme started with the European Council summit in Tampere (1999), which, in its conclusions, worded, for the first time, the ambition to create a Common European Asylum System (CEAS).[639] At Tampere, it was decided to construct the CEAS in two stages. The first stage, which had to be completed before 1 May 2004, was to consist of a range of instruments laying down minimum standards, allowing Member States to retain national procedures and interpretations of certain concepts and to deviate in favour of the individual seeking protection. The second stage, to be started after 2004, was supposed to restrict discretion offered to Member States, thus arriving at common standards – most notably, a common asylum procedure and a uniform asylum status.

The Tampere summit resulted in the European Commission presenting a range of draft Directives and Regulations to the Council, elaborating the subjects listed in Article 63 EC. In contrast to the speed with which the Commission

---

[637] Most notable examples of these non-binding instruments are the Resolution on minimum guarantees for asylum procedures (OJ C 274/13, 19 September 1996) and a Joint Position on the harmonised application of the refugee definition of the 1951 Convention (OJ L-63/10, 13 March 1996). Furthermore, in the aftermath of the Bosnian civil war, a Resolution on burden-sharing with regard to admission of displaced persons in situations of mass influx was adopted (OJ C 262/1, 7 October 1995). See, on the post-Maastricht measures in the field of asylum, extensively, K. Hailbronner, *Immigration and Asylum Law and Policy of the European Union*, The Hague: Kluwer (2000), pp. 353–465.

[638] For figures and comments, see, more extensively, E. Thieleman, 'Why Asylum Policy Harmonisation Undermines Refugee Burden-Sharing', 6 *European Journal of Migration and Law* (2004), pp. 47–65.

[639] Presidency Conclusions, Tampere European Council, 15–16 October 1999, 16 October 1999, para. 13.

came up with proposals, negotiations in the Council turned out to be rather cumbersome, mostly due to the unanimity requirement and the fact that several Member States were anxious to avoid undue encroachment of the Community on their national asylum arrangements. This resulted in most of the Commission's proposals being adjusted downwards with regard to individual rights of asylum seekers and refugees, and arguably a lower standard of harmonisation than was initially pursued.[640]

After the first phase instruments were adopted and their functioning and application by the Member States evaluated,[641] the second stage of harmonising asylum policies in Europe was set in motion in 2008. The European Commission presented proposals to revise the existing secondary legislation.[642] By virtue of the 2007 Lisbon Treaty, these proposals were now subject to the 'ordinary legislative procedure', i.e. qualified majority in the Council and joint legislative power of European Parliament (formerly co-decision).[643] The Lisbon Treaty had introduced Article 78 TFEU as the new legal basis for the common policy of asylum. That provision no longer refers to 'minimum standards', but to 'uniform

---

[640] Regulation 343/2003 establishing the criteria and mechanisms for determining the Member State responsible for examining an asylum application lodged in one of the Member States by a third-country national (Dublin Regulation); Directive 2003/9/EC laying down minimum standards for the reception of asylum seekers (Reception Conditions Directive); Directive 2004/83/EC on minimum standards for the qualification and status of third-country nationals or stateless persons as refugees or as persons who otherwise need international protection and the content of the protection granted (Qualification Directive); Directive 2005/85/EC on minimum standards on procedures in Member States for granting and withdrawing refugee status (Procedures Directive). For an extensive appraisal of the relation between the first phase asylum instruments and international law: H. Battjes, *European Asylum Law and International Law*, Leiden/Boston: Martinus Nijhoff (2006).

[641] COM (2007) 299 final, SEC (2007) 742, Report from the Commission to the European Parliament and the Council on the evaluation of the Dublin system; COM(2007) 745 final Report from the Commission to the Council and to the European Parliament on the application of Directive 2003/9/EC of 27 January 2003 laying down minimum standards for the reception of asylum seekers; COM(2010) 465 final, Report from the Commission to the European Parliament and the Council on the application of Directive 2005/85/EC of 1 December 2005 on minimum standards on procedures in Member States for granting and withdrawing refugee status; COM(2008) 360 final, Policy Plan on Asylum 'An integrated approach to protection across the EU'. See also COM (2007) 301 final, Green Paper on the future of the Common European Asylum System.

[642] COM(2008) 820 final, Proposal for a Regulation of the European Parliament and of the Council establishing the criteria and mechanisms for determining the Member State responsible for examining an application for international protection lodged in one of the Member States by a third-country national or a stateless person (recast); COM(2008) 815 final, Proposal for a Directive laying down minimum standards for the reception of asylum seekers (recast); COM(2009) 554 final, Proposal for a Directive of the European Parliament and of the Council on minimum standards on procedures in Member States for granting and withdrawing international protection (recast); COM(2009)551 final, Proposal for a Directive of the European Parliament and of the Council on minimum standards for the qualification and status of third-country nationals and stateless persons as beneficiaries of international protection and the content of the protection granted (recast).

[643] See Articles 78(2) and 294 TFEU.

statuses' and 'common procedures'. The Council and Parliament had difficulty, however, agreeing on truly common standards, and in respect of two Directives, the Commission tabled amended proposals to facilitate the discussions.[644] Yet, in June 2013 all second phase instruments had been adopted. Although not setting forth a uniform system of protection, they may be expected to further converge asylum law and practice within the EU.

6.2.2. LEGAL BASIS AND SCOPE OF THE COMMON EUROPEAN ASYLUM SYSTEM

Article 78(2) TFEU sets forth that measures for a common European asylum system must comprise: (a) a uniform status of asylum for third-country nationals, valid throughout the Union; (b) a uniform status of subsidiary protection for third-country nationals; (c) a common system of temporary protection in the event of a massive inflow; (d) common asylum procedures; e) criteria and mechanisms for determining which Member State is responsible for considering an application for asylum; (f) standards concerning reception conditions; and (g) cooperation with third countries for the purpose of managing inflows of asylum seekers.

The text of Article 78 distinguishes between matters of 'asylum' and 'subsidiary protection' – the former referring to the protection of refugees, and the latter, to the protection of persons under human rights treaties of general applicability. The secondary EU instruments on asylum employ the term 'international protection' to refer to both types of protection, and do not define the term 'asylum'.[645] Contrary to the language used in Article 78, 'asylum' is the common word to denote all forms of protection of forced migrants, and may therefore be used interchangeably with 'international protection'.

Also relevant is Article 80 TFEU, which applies to all the Union's policies on border checks, asylum and immigration, and which stipulates that those policies are governed by the principle of solidarity and fair sharing of responsibility, including its financial implications.

The common European asylum system, as envisaged by Article 78 TFEU, only applies to third-country nationals and stateless persons – in other words,

---

[644] COM(2011) 319 final, amended proposal on recasting the Procedures Directive; COM(2011) 320 final, amended proposal on recasting the Reception Conditions Directive.

[645] The first phase asylum Directives had defined 'applications for asylum' as requests for refugee status, and 'asylum seekers' as persons who had requested refugee status (Article 2 Directive 2003/9/EC, Article 2 Reg. 343/2003 and Article 2 Directive 2005/85/EC). The revised Directives employ instead the terms 'application for international protection' (referring to refugee status and subsidiary protection) and 'applicant' (referring to persons who have made an application for international protection).

persons who do not possess the nationality of one of the EU Member States. Member State nationals who apply for asylum in another Member State therefore fall outside the scope of the common European asylum system. These 'internal' asylum seekers are instead covered by the Protocol on asylum for nationals of Member States of the European Union, which is annexed to the TEU and TFEU.[646] This protocol stipulates that, given the level of fundamental rights protection by the Member States, all Member States must be regarded as safe countries in relation to asylum matters. Accordingly, Member States will normally have to declare asylum applications lodged by a national of another Member State inadmissible. Only in exceptional circumstances may Member States take such applications into consideration: when another Member State makes use of the possibility provided by Article 15 ECHR to derogate from its human rights obligations in times of war or public emergency; or when the special procedure under Article 7(1) EU Treaty, which applies to situations in which there is a clear risk that a Member State is in serious breach of fundamental rights or the rule of law, has been initiated or completed.[647] However, Member States may, apart from these situations, unilaterally decide to process an application, but must then do so on the presumption that it is unfounded, and inform the Council.[648]

In itself, the exclusion of EU citizens from the scope of the common European asylum system may be seen as understandable, given its underlying rationale – which is primarily to set common rules for entry of third-country nationals and to control their movement within the EU once they have crossed the common external border. The Directives and Regulations making up the common European asylum system do not prevent Member States from providing for rules on asylum applicable to EU citizens. On the other hand, the Protocol on asylum for nationals of Member States does raise a threshold for EU citizens to obtain asylum in another Member State. This may be problematic from the perspective of the Refugee Convention and the other relevant human rights treaties that apply equally to EU citizens and non-EU citizens. It cannot be definitely excluded that, also in times of peace, there may be cases where EU citizens do qualify as refugees. In such situations, the Protocol on asylum may not be implemented in a manner effectively depriving a refugee from being entitled to protection in another Member State.[649] Presumably, therefore, the

---

[646] Protocol 24 on asylum for nationals of Member States of the European Union (also known as *the Aznar Protocol*).

[647] *Ibid*, sole Article, sub (a), (b) and (c).

[648] *Ibid*, sole Article, sub (d).

[649] The one Member State which made a reservation to the Protocol on asylum for nationals of Member States annexed to the Amsterdam Treaty was Belgium, stipulating that 'it shall, in accordance with its obligations under the [Refugee Convention], (...) carry out an individual examination of any asylum request made by a national of another Member State.' Belgium did not repeat that declaration under the Lisbon Treaty, however. See Declaration No. 56 by

only clear limitation to receiving an asylum application from a national of another Member State established by the Protocol is the procedural duty to inform the Council.[650]

A further limitation to the personal scope of the common European asylum system is that the measures adopted under the CEAS only apply to persons who *apply for international protection*.[651] 'International protection' is defined in the Qualification Directive as refugee status and subsidiary protection status.[652] These two statuses derive from the Refugee Convention and human rights treaties of general applicability, respectively, and are dealt with in detail in the next two chapters. It follows that requests for another kind of protection – such as on national grounds for asylum – fall outside the scope of the common European asylum system. Member States may, however, apply the provisions of the Reception Conditions Directive and Procedures Directive also to persons who apply for another type of protection.[653] Further, since at the time of lodging of the application it will normally not be clear what kind of protection a person seeks or to which they are entitled, there is a presumption that asylum applications amount to a request for international protection, unless another kind of protection is explicitly requested.[654]

The common European asylum system is only applicable to applications that are made in the territory, including at the border, in the territorial waters or in the transit zones of the Member States.[655] Hence, asylum seekers who have landed at an international airport in a Member State but not yet passed border control can invoke protection under the common European asylum system. On the other hand, persons who are rescued or intercepted in the high seas fall outside the common European asylum system, although they are protected against arbitrary returns under human treaties.[656] It is also specified that the asylum Directives do not apply to requests for diplomatic asylum, i.e. applications made at diplomatic or consular representations of a Member State in a third country.[657]

Belgium on the Protocol on asylum for nationals of Member States of the European Union, Annex to the Treaty of Amsterdam.

[650] Cf. G. Noll, *Negotiating Asylum. The EU acquis, Extraterritorial Protection and the Common Market of Deflection*, The Hague, Martinus Nijhoff Publishers (2000), p. 553.

[651] Article 1 Regulation No. 604/2013, Article 3 Directive 2013/32/EU, Article 3 Directive 2013/33/EU, Article 1 and 2(h) Directive 2011/95/EU.

[652] Article 2(a) Directive 2011/95/EU.

[653] Article 3(3) Directive 2013/32/EU, Art. 3(4) Directive 2013/33/EU.

[654] Cf. Article 2(h) Directive 2011/95/EU and Article 2(b) Directive 2013/32/EU.

[655] Article 3(1) Directive 2013/32/EU, Article 3(1) Directive 2013/33/EU. Note that the Dublin Regulation does not refer to applications made in the territorial waters (Article 3(1) Regulation No. 604/2013), and that the Qualification Directive (Directive 2011/95/EU) is silent on its territorial scope.

[656] ECtHR 23 February 2012, *Hirsi v. Italy*, No. 27765/09.

[657] Article 3(2) Directive 2013/32/EU, Article 3(2) Directive 2013/33/EU.

6.2.3. OVERVIEW OF SECONDARY ASYLUM LEGISLATION

Legislation has been adopted on all fields listed in Article 78(2)(a)-(f) TFEU. These measures are the following:

- *the Temporary Protection Directive* (Directive 55/2001/EC)[658]
  (Possibility for the Council to decide on temporary protection in a situation of mass influx)
- *the Reception Conditions Directive* (Directive 2013/33/EU)[659]
  (What are the standards for the reception of asylum seekers?)
- *the Dublin Regulation* (Regulation 604/2013)[660]
  (Which Member State is responsible for examining the asylum claim?)
- *the Qualification Directive* (Directive 2011/95/EU)[661]
  (Who is eligible for protection and what is the content of protection?)
- *the Procedures Directive* (Directive 2013/32/EU)[662]
  (What are the rules of procedure for the examination of asylum claims?)

Except for the Dublin Regulation, all legislative measures have been moulded as Directives, giving Member States a certain amount of time to transpose the provisions into domestic legislation. The transposition period of the recast of the Qualification Directive ended on 21 December 2013; that of the recasts of the Procedures Directive and Reception Conditions Directive ends on 21 July 2015. Until that time, the first phase instruments remain in force.

Denmark, Ireland and the United Kingdom do not take part in all asylum instruments. With regard to the first phase instruments, the United Kingdom opted into all asylum legislation, Ireland opted into all instruments except the Reception conditions Directive, and Denmark participated only in the Dublin Regulation. The willingness of these Member States to partake in the second phase instruments is even smaller. Denmark has opted out of all asylum

---

[658] Directive 55/2001/EC of 20 July 2001, on minimum standards for giving temporary protection in the event of a mass influx of displaced persons and on measures promoting a balance of efforts between Member States in receiving such persons and bearing the consequences thereof.

[659] Directive 2013/33/EU of 26 June 2013 laying down standards for the reception of applicants for international protection.

[660] Regulation No 604/2013of 26 June 2013 establishing the criteria and mechanisms for determining the Member State responsible for examining an application for international protection lodged in one of the Member States by a third-country national or a stateless person.

[661] Directive 2011/95/EU of 13 December 2011 on standards for the qualification of third-country nationals or stateless persons as beneficiaries of international protection, for a uniform status for refugees or for persons eligible for subsidiary protection, and for the content of the protection granted.

[662] Directive 2013/32/EU of 26 June 2013 on common procedures for granting and withdrawing international protection.

instruments, and Ireland and the United Kingdom only take part in the revised Dublin Regulation. This means that, also after the transposition period of the revised Directives expires, the United Kingdom and Ireland remain bound by the first phase Qualification Directive (2004/83/EC) and Procedures Directive (2005/85/EC), and that the United Kingdom remains bound by the first phase Reception Conditions Directive (2003/9/EC).

6.2.4. THE INTERRELATED CHARACTER OF THE REGULATION AND THE DIRECTIVES

In practice, the Regulations and Directives on asylum, which may be conceived as different chapters of one coherent law, relate to each other as follows.

A third-country national who applies for asylum on the territory or at the border of a Member State has the status of 'applicant for international protection', and is allowed to remain in the Member State until a decision on his application is taken.[663] He has the right to have his asylum application processed by one of the Member States.[664] The *Dublin Regulation* determines the Member State responsible for examining the asylum request. If the asylum seeker is present in another Member State than the Member State responsible, he can be transferred to the responsible Member State in accordance with the procedural provisions of the Dublin regulation. Until a decision on the asylum application has been taken, including the time necessary for effectuating a possible Dublin transfer,[665] the asylum seeker is entitled to the reception conditions laid down in the *Reception Conditions Directive*. These conditions relate to free movement, housing, employment, schooling, healthcare, *etc.*

The asylum seeker is entitled to have his application processed according to the procedural standards laid down in the *Procedures Directive*. These include such rights as legal assistance, a right to appeal and a right to remain in the territory pending the appeals procedure.[666]

The asylum procedure is meant to establish whether the third-country national should be granted international protection. The *Qualification Directive* defines international protection as 'refugee status' and 'subsidiary protection status',[667] and lays down the eligibility criteria for these two statuses. Refugee status, as described in the Qualification Directive, closely resembles the refugee definition in the Refugee Convention. Subsidiary protection covers other forms of protection, as guaranteed by human rights treaties of general applicability, such as the European Convention on Human Rights. If an asylum applicant

---

[663]   Article 9(1) Directive 2013/32/EU.
[664]   Article 3(1) Regulation No 604/2013.
[665]   ECJ 27 September 2012, *Cimade and GISTI*, Case C-179/11.
[666]   Articles 20 and 46 Directive 2013/32/EU.
[667]   Article 2(1) Directive 2011/95/EU.

qualifies for international protection, he must be granted refugee status or subsidiary protection status. The Qualification Directive also describes what the content of that status is, i.e. to what rights the refugee and subsidiary protection beneficiary are entitled. This includes, for persons with refugee status, a residence permit that is valid for at least three years; and for beneficiaries of subsidiary protection, a residence permit that is valid for at least one year.[668] The statuses of the Qualification Directive are extensively described in Chapters 7 and 8.

In parallel to this system, the Temporary Protection Directive provides an alternative protection scheme which applies only in cases of 'mass influx of displaced persons', by which large refugee streams stemming from international crises are meant, such as occurred in the aftermath of the Yugoslavian civil war in the 1990s. The Temporary Protection Directive contains a mechanism that makes it possible to grant these displaced persons temporary protection without obliging them to lodge a claim for asylum. After the expiry of the temporary period, these persons can either return to their country of origin or apply for asylum according to the normal procedures. The temporary protection mechanism is meant to ensure that national immigration services will not collapse under huge numbers of applications.

Apart from the specific EU asylum instruments, other pieces of EU migration law are also relevant for asylum applicants or asylum status holders. Firstly, in the context of entry into the Schengen area, the Schengen Borders Code contains several favourable provisions aimed at upholding the special rights of refugees and other persons requesting international protection who present themselves at the Schengen external border, to the effect of exempting them from the ordinarily applicable conditions of entry.[669] This ensures that asylum seekers who do not meet the entry conditions such as possessing a valid passport or visa, may, nonetheless, be granted entry.

Secondly, Chapter V of the Family Reunification Directive (2003/86/EC) contains more favourable provisions for granting family reunification to persons who have been recognised as refugees in accordance with the Qualification directive. This special regime does not, however, apply to beneficiaries of subsidiary protection (see, extensively, section 4.2.17).

Thirdly, persons who have been accorded refugee or subsidiary protection status can obtain, after five years of legal residence in a Member State, the status of long-term resident, in accordance with the Long-Term Residence Directive (2003/109/EC), as amended by Directive 2011/51/EU (see, extensively, section 4.7). The status of long-term resident confers a right to equal treatment in the Member State granting that status and enhanced protection against expulsion. Further, the status brings a conditional right to move to another

---

[668] Article 24 Directive 2011/95/EU.
[669] See Articles 3(b), 5(4)(c) and 13(1) Regulation No 562/2006.

Member State. A hiatus in respect of the latter right is that EU law does not oblige the receiving Member State to guarantee the rights and benefits accruing to the protected status as refugee or subsidiary protection beneficiary. This issue is instead – partly – regulated by the European Agreement on Transfer of Responsibility for Refugees, adopted in the framework of the Council of Europe, which is ratified by only 13 European states.[670] That treaty sets forth the basic rule that responsibility for a refugee is considered to be transferred to a second state, following 'two years of actual and continuous stay in the second state' (Article 2). The responsibility pertains to the issuing of a travel document, the facilitation of family reunification, and, implicitly, granting the refugee all the rights and freedoms flowing from the Refugee Convention.[671] The Agreement does not apply to persons with subsidiary protection status.

Fourthly, in the context of expulsion, the Returns Directive (2008/115/EC), which lays down the rules for returning illegally staying third-country nationals, applies to asylum seekers as soon as a negative decision on their asylum application has entered into force.[672] In *Arslan*, the Court of Justice explained that an asylum seeker has the right to remain in the territory of the Member State concerned at least until his application has been rejected at first instance or until the outcome of any action brought against that decision is known, and cannot, therefore, until such time, be considered to be 'illegally staying' within the meaning of the Returns Directive.[673] But once a refusal of the asylum application enters into force, the (failed) asylum seeker can no longer invoke his status as 'applicant for international protection', and is susceptible to expulsion, according to the terms of the Returns Directive.

In the remainder of this chapter, the Dublin Regulation, the Reception Conditions Directive, the Procedures Directive and the Temporary Protection Directive, are discussed. Chapters 7 and 8 focus on the two key asylum statuses in international law and their incorporation within EU law: refugee status and subsidiary protection status. Even though the first phase asylum instruments remain binding on some Member States, we discuss only the revised second phase instruments.[674]

---

[670] Extensively: S. Peers, 'Transfer of International Protection and European Union Law', 24 *IJRL* (2012), pp. 527–560.

[671] Articles 5 and 6 European Agreement on Transfer of Responsibility for Refugees, ETS No. 107 and explanatory report, para. 31.

[672] Recital 9 and Article 2(1) Directive 2008/115/EC.

[673] ECJ 30 May 2013, *Arslan*, Case C-534/11, paras. 48–9.

[674] For the first phase instruments, see P. Boeles et al., *European Migration Law*, Intersentia (2009); H. Battjes, *European Asylum Law and International Law*, Leiden/Boston: Martinus Nijhoff (2006); S. Peers and N. Rogers (eds.), *EU Immigration and Asylum Law: Text and Commentary*, Leiden/Boston: Martinus Nijhoff (2006); K. Hailbronner (ed.), *European Immigration and Asylum Law: A Commentary*, Oxford: Hart (2010).

6.3. DUBLIN REGULATION

The Dublin Regulation (Reg. 604/2013) – named after its predecessor, the Dublin Convention – establishes 'the criteria and mechanisms for determining the Member State responsible for examining an asylum application lodged in one of the Member States by a third-country national.' The system of distributing asylum seekers among EU Member States is a key distinctive feature of the common EU asylum system and, contrary to the other fields of asylum, is governed by a fully harmonised set of rules in the form of a Regulation which should be applied directly by the Member States, i.e. without transposition into national law. The transfer of asylum seekers pursuant to the Dublin Regulation is also one of the most controversial aspects of EU asylum law. This is mainly due to the divergent standards of reception in the Member States. As is extensively discussed below, the transfer of asylum seekers to Greece was prohibited by the European Court of Human Rights and the Court of Justice in 2011.[675] Although these judgments provoked discussions on revising the allocation mechanism, the 2013 recast of the Dublin Regulation has not fundamentally altered the allocation criteria.

The key aim of the Dublin Regulation is to reduce secondary movements of asylum seekers within the EU. It serves to prevent the phenomenon of 'asylum shopping', i.e. asylum seekers lodging multiple or subsequent applications in more than one Member State. It also addresses the potential problem of 'refugees in orbit', i.e. persons who claim, or are entitled to, protection without any Member State acknowledging responsibility for examining or accepting the claim.

The legal basis for the Dublin Regulation is Article 78(2)(e) TFEU. The 2013 recast of the Dublin Regulation entered into force on 19 July 2013, and applies to applications lodged from 1 December 2013 onwards.[676] Older applications are distributed according to the former Dublin Regulation (Reg. 343/2003). The United Kingdom and Ireland have opted in to the Regulation. Denmark does not take part in the Regulation. Denmark does, however, apply the former Dublin Regulation, following an international agreement that it concluded with the EC in 2006,[677] and may notify the Commission of a decision to implement the content of the revised Regulation.

Non-EU members, Norway, Iceland, Switzerland and Liechtenstein, took part in the existing Dublin *acquis* by virtue of separate international agreements, and must, under these agreements, accept its development without exception.

---

[675] ECtHR 21 January 2011, *M.S.S. v. Belgium and Greece*, No. 30696/09; ECJ 21 December 2011, *N.S. and M.E.*, Joined Cases C-411/10 and C-493/10.
[676] Article 49 Regulation 604/2013.
[677] Council Decision 2006/188/EC of 21 February 2006.

These countries must notify to the Commission whether or not to accept the revised Regulation.[678]

6.3.1. THE ALLOCATION CRITERIA

Article 3(1) Dublin Regulation sets forth that the Member States *shall examine* any application for international protection by a third-country national, and that the application shall be examined by *a single* Member State. This provision is not only relevant because it establishes the principle of a single responsible Member State. It is also important because it establishes a clearly defined right for the asylum seeker to have his application examined.

To determine the Member State responsible, Chapter III (Articles 7–15) lays down a hierarchy of criteria. This hierarchy works as a kind of checklist, in which the order in which the provisions are placed is determinative for allocating an asylum seeker to a Member State (Article 7(1)). The first listed provision that matches the factual situation points out the Member State responsible.

The criteria can be grouped into three overarching principles of allocation.

6.3.1.1. *Special Guarantees for Minors and Families*

Articles 8–11 contain preferential criteria for unaccompanied minors and applicants who have family members who are already present in a Member State. According to Article 8(1)(2), if the asylum applicant is an unaccompanied minor, the Member State responsible is that where a family member, a sibling or a relative who can take care of him or her, is legally present.[679] If the unaccompanied minor has no family members or relatives present in the Member States, the Member State where the unaccompanied minor has lodged his asylum claim is responsible, provided that it is in the best interests of the

---

[678] Agreement between the European Community and the Republic of Iceland and the Kingdom of Norway concerning the criteria and mechanisms for establishing the State responsible for examining a request for asylum lodged in a Member State or in Iceland or Norway, OJ L 93, 3 April 2001, p. 40; Agreement between the European Community and the Swiss Confederation concerning the criteria and mechanisms for establishing the State responsible for examining a request for asylum lodged in a Member State or in Switzerland, OJ L 53, 27 Feb. 2008, p. 5; Protocol between the European Community, the Swiss Confederation and the Principality of Liechtenstein to the Agreement between the European Community, and the Swiss Confederation concerning the criteria and mechanisms for establishing the State responsible for examining a request for asylum lodged in a Member State or in Switzerland; OJ L 161, 24 June 2009, p. 8. According to the 'guillotine' clause in these agreements, a failure by one of these countries to accept the amended regulation terminates the participation of that country in the Dublin system, unless the Joint/Mixed Committee established by the agreements decides otherwise by unanimity.

[679] See for the definition of family members and relatives Article 2(g) and (h).

minor Article 8(4). The Court of Justice explained, in respect of this latter rule in the former Dublin Regulation, that, if the unaccompanied minor has lodged asylum applications in more than one Member State, the Member State responsible is the one where the minor is present (normally the last Member State). This was derived from the best interests of the child principle, which, according to the Court, implied that unaccompanied minors should not, as a rule, be transferred to another Member State.[680]

Articles 9 and 10 ensure that asylum applicants must be reunited with a family member who either has been granted international protection or who has an outstanding asylum application in a Member State, provided both family members so desire. Lastly, Article 11 provides for the maintenance of family unity in the case that family members apply for asylum simultaneously in the same Member State, and where applying the Dublin criteria would otherwise result in their separation.

6.3.1.2.   The Member State that has Facilitated Legal Entry into the Union

Articles 12 and 14 appoint responsibility to the Member State which has issued a valid residence document or visa to the applicant (Article 12), or which the applicant entered and has waived the visa requirement (Article 14).

6.3.1.3.   The Member State where Illegal Entry into the Union was Effectuated

Article 13 appoints, as Member State responsible, the one whose borders were irregularly crossed by an applicant having come from a non-Member State. Note that this criterion takes precedence over the Member State that waived the visa requirement (Article 14).

If none of these criteria apply, Article 3(2) provides as residual rule, that the first Member State in which the application was lodged, is responsible. This rule should be read together with Article 15, setting forth the same principle in respect of applications made in an international transit area of an airport of a Member State.

The allocation criteria reflect the general principles that the responsibility for examining an application should lie with the Member State that played the greatest part in the applicant's entry into and residence in the Union, with some exceptions designed to protect minors and family unity. Although humanitarian considerations and asylum seekers' preferences do play a role in the order of criteria, the Member States clearly wanted to prevent, as far as possible, the phenomenon of asylum seekers travelling through Europe in order to seek asylum in the country of their choice.

---

[680]   ECJ 6 June 2013, *MA and Others*, Case C-648/11.

6.3.2. THE OBLIGATION TO BE A SAFE STATE

One of the premises of the Dublin mechanism is that all Member States are safe countries in which transferred asylum applicants will be granted appropriate protection according to international agreed standards.[681] In *T.I. v. United Kingdom*, the ECtHR made clear, however, that when a Member State carries out the Dublin mechanism and transfers an applicant to another state, it is not relieved from the duty to ensure that the transfer does not result in exposure to a real risk of ill-treatment (the prohibition of *refoulement*), as laid down in Article 3 ECHR.[682]

Hence, human rights considerations may oblige Member States to set aside the Dublin criteria. The *T.I.* decision concerned the application of the Dublin Convention, and dated from before the adoption of the CEAS. Presently, a Member State which is not 'safe' in guaranteeing *non-refoulement* and adequate standards of reception, is not only infringing on the standards of the ECHR, but also on the standards of the common European asylum system. In other words, there is a EU obligation to be a safe state. In the immediate aftermath of adoption of the Dublin regulation, the taking back of asylum seekers by Greece came to the fore as potentially in conflict with the prohibition of (indirect) *refoulement*. This was due to a lack of reception capacity in Greece, and a policy whereby asylum seekers who had left Greece without notifying the authorities were deemed to have their application withdrawn and would normally not be entitled, upon return, to have their asylum application examined on the merits.[683]

Although the ECtHR had first declared, in 2008, a complaint under Article 3 ECHR against the transfer of an asylum seeker from the United Kingdom to Greece inadmissible,[684] the ECtHR's Grand Chamber, in its 2011 judgment in *M.S.S. v Belgium and Greece*, found violations of Article 3 ECHR on the part of Greece for subjecting an asylum seeker transferred to it by Belgium to a manifestly deficient asylum procedure and humiliating detention and living conditions; and on the part of Belgium, for exposing him to such treatment. The ECtHR referred to a range of reports and materials, on the basis of which it considered that the Belgian authorities should have known that M.S.S. had no guarantee that his asylum application would be seriously examined by the Greek

---

[681] Preamble, Recital 3.

[682] ECtHR 7 March 2000, *T.I. v. United Kingdom* (dec.), No. 43844/98.

[683] The UNHCR has repeatedly highlighted certain aspects of the asylum legislation in Greece and their consequences for asylum seekers returned to Greece, pursuant to the Dublin Regulation, see, e.g., UNHCR, 'Council Regulation (EC) No. 343/2003 of 18 February 2003 establishing the criteria and mechanisms for determining the Member State responsible for examining an asylum application lodged in one of the Member States by a third country national (the 'Dublin II Regulation'): Updated UNHCR memorandum on the law and practice of Greece', Geneva, 30 November 2005; UNHCR, 'UNHCR position on the return of asylum-seekers to Greece under the 'Dublin regulation'', Geneva, 15 April 2008.

[684] ECtHR 2 December 2008, *K.R.S. v. the United Kingdom* (dec.), No. 32733/08.

authorities.[685] The Court of Justice, in the case of *NS and ME*, took over that reasoning by considering that Article 4 of the EU Charter of Fundamental Rights, laying down the prohibition on torture or inhuman or degrading treatment, precludes the transfer of an asylum seeker from one Member State to another Member State, pursuant to the Dublin Regulation, if there are systemic deficiencies in the asylum procedure and reception conditions in the receiving Member State that give rise to a real risk of the asylum seeker being subjected to inhuman or degrading treatment.[686] The Court of Justice explained that in such a scenario, the Member State that is prevented from transferring may either decide to examine the application itself or continue to examine the criteria of the Regulation in order to identify whether another (third) Member State can be designated as responsible.[687]

The revised Dublin Regulation corresponds to these fundamental notions. The Court's dictum in *NS and ME* is rehearsed in Article 3(2). Although that provision makes it mandatory to first establish, in a situation where transfer is impossible, whether another (third) Member State can be designated as responsible, the discretionary clause of Article 17 also makes it possible for the determining Member State to examine the asylum application itself.

After Greece was declared unsafe for asylum applicants by both the European Court of Human Rights and Court of Justice in 2011, attention shifted to other Member States at the EU's eastern and southern borders which allegedly also lacked the capacity, resources and/or experience in dealing with asylum applications. In 2013, the ECtHR reviewed extensively the conditions for asylum seekers in Italy and Hungary. Even though the Court pointed to shortcomings in the Italian reception system, and noted that the situation of asylum seekers in Hungary had been 'alarming', it concluded, in both cases, that the transfer would not violate Article 3 of the European Convention on Human Rights.[688]

6.3.3. THE HUMANITARIAN AND DISCRETIONARY CLAUSES

Apart from the exceptional situation where a Dublin transfer conflicts with Article 3 ECHR or Article 4 of the EU Charter of Fundamental Rights, the

---

[685] ECtHR 21 Jan. 2011, *M.S.S. v Belgium and Greece*, No. 30696/09.

[686] ECJ 21 December 2011, *N.S. and M.E.*, Joined Cases C-411/10 and C-493/10.

[687] *N.S. and M.E.*, para. 107.The possibility of finding another responsible Member State is, however, qualified by the obligation to provide the asylum seeker with clarity within a reasonable time. See also ECJ 14 November 2013, *Puid*, Case C-4/11.

[688] ECtHR 2 April 2013, *Mohammed Hussein and Others v. the Netherlands and Italy* (dec.), No. 27725/10; ECtHR 6 June 2013, *Mohammed v. Austria*, No. 2283/12. The European Court had earlier considered the detention of asylum seekers in Hungary to be in violation of Article 5 ECHR: ECtHR 20 September 2011, *Lokpo and Touré v. Hungary*, No. 10816/10; and ECtHR 23 October 2012, *Hendrin Ali Said and Aras Ali Said v. Hungary*, No. 13457/11.

Dublin Regulation foresees two further possibilities for setting the allocation criteria aside. Article 16 contains a special guarantee for an applicant who is dependent, on account of pregnancy, a newborn child, serious illness, severe disability or old age, on the assistance of a child, sibling or parent that is legally resident in a Member State (or *vice versa*: the child, sibling or parent is dependent on the applicant), and whose position is not covered by Articles 8–11. In such a situation, the Member States 'shall normally' keep or bring together these family members, normally in the Member State where the family member of the applicant is legally resident (Article 16(2)). The words 'shall normally', as now contained in Article 16(1), were interpreted by the Court of Justice in the context of the former Dublin Regulation as creating an obligation, in case the conditions of dependency are satisfied, of bringing the family members together, unless an exceptional situation exists.[689] It can be inferred from the words 'keep or bring together' that the clause applies to both the situation where the family members are present in different Member States and where they are present in the same Member State. An important difference with the ordinary allocation criteria for family members (Articles 9–10) is that Article 16 applies to the wider category of family members who are 'legally resident', thus not requiring that their stay is asylum-related.

Article 17(1) is the general discretionary clause under which each Member State that receives an asylum request may examine it, even though another Member State could be responsible. The exercise of that option is not subject to any particular condition.[690] The clause may be used for humanitarian reasons that are not yet covered by the ordinary allocation criteria or Article 16, or for political or practical considerations, for example, when processing a claim would be less resource intensive than going through the process of transferring the asylum seeker to another Member State.[691]

Wider humanitarian reasons may, furthermore, be invoked by a Member State in requesting another Member State to take charge of an applicant in order to bring together 'any family relations' (Article 17(2)). It can be inferred from the discretionary language of that provision that the making of such a request is not mandatory. Nor is it mandatory for the petitioned Member State to accept to the request, although in case of refusal, that Member State must state reasons.

---

[689]   ECJ 6 November 2012, *K. v Bundesasylamt*, Case C-245/11, paras. 27, 46.

[690]   Cf. ECJ 30 May 2013, *Halaf*, Case C-528/11, paras. 36–37 (in respect of the former 'sovereignty clause' of Article 3(2) Regulation No. 343/2003).

[691]   The corresponding 'sovereignty clause' of the former Dublin regulation was used for both sets of reasons: Commission Staff Working Document, 'Annex to the Communication on the Evaluation of the Dublin System', COM(2007) 299 final, Brussels, 6 June 2007, p. 21 Also see European Commission, 'Report on the evaluation of the Dublin system', COM(2007) 299 final, Brussels, 6 June 2007, p. 7.

6.3.4. PROCEDURAL AND ADMINISTRATIVE PRINCIPLES: TAKING CHARGE AND TAKING BACK

Chapter V of the Dublin Regulation sets forth the obligations of the Member State responsible. The two basic obligations are firstly, to either *take charge* of an asylum seeker who lodged his application in a different Member State or to *take back* an asylum seeker who lodged his application in the Member State responsible, but who subsequently left for another Member State, regardless of whether the application is still under consideration or has been withdrawn or rejected (Article 18(1)). Secondly, the responsible Member State must complete the examination of the application, or, in case the application had already been rejected, provide effective remedies against the rejection (Article 18(2)).

Chapter VI of the Regulation lays down detailed rules on the cooperation between Member States for effectuating transfers. Both the procedure on taking charge (Articles 21–22, 29) and that on taking back (Articles 23–25, 29) provide for certain time limits within which requests for a transfer must be lodged, within which replies must be given, and within which the transfer must be executed. Save in exceptional instances, failure to comply with these limits places responsibility for the asylum seeker with the defaulting state. As regards the date on which the period within which the transfer must be carried out begins to run, the Court of Justice has held that if domestic legislation allows for judicial appeal against the transfer with suspensive effect, the period for implementing the transfer begins to run from the time a judicial decision on the merits has been taken.[692] This has been made explicit in Article 29(1) of the recast Regulation. Moreover, Article 27(3) now provides that appeals must suspend the transfer, either automatically or upon request. If the asylum seeker withdraws his asylum application before the responsible Member State has agreed to take charge of the applicant, the Regulation is no longer applicable and the transfer must be discontinued.[693]

Compared to the former Dublin Regulation, the recast contains stricter procedural safeguards for the asylum seeker who is subjected to a Dublin procedure. He has the right to be informed about the Dublin procedure (Article 4), the right to a personal interview (Article 5), special guarantees if he is a minor (Article 6), and the right to appeal a transfer decision (Article 27), including, as noted above, the right to remain pending the appeal (Article 27(3)). The Court of Justice clarified, further, that until a person is actually transferred to the Member State responsible, the transferring Member State is obliged to grant the rights and benefits provided for in the Reception Conditions Directive.[694]

---

[692]   ECJ 29 January 2009, *Petrosian*, Case C-19/08.
[693]   ECJ 3 May 2012, *Kastrati*, C-620/10.
[694]   ECJ 27 September 2012, *Cimade and GISTI*, Case C-179/11.

Article 28(1) sets forth the principle that persons may not be detained for the sole reason that they are subject to a Dublin procedure. Detention is only allowed if four conditions are fulfilled: there must be a significant risk of absconding, detention may only occur on the basis of an individual assessment, detention must be proportional, and no other less coercive alternative must be available (Article 28(2)). Moreover, Article 28(3) sets limits to the duration of detention. If a person is detained in order to secure a Dublin transfer, the request for taking back or taking charge must be made within one month after the application was lodged; the requested state must reply within two weeks; and the transfer must be executed within six weeks of acceptance of the request, or from the time a judicial decision on appeal has been taken. Failure to meet these deadlines means that the person must be released.

6.3.5. EURODAC: FINGERPRINTS FOR DUBLIN

The 'Dublin system' comprises, apart from the Dublin Regulation, the Eurodac Regulation (Regulation No. 603/2013) and the Dublin Implementing Regulation (Regulation No. 1560/2003).[695] The Dublin Implementation Regulation lays down detailed administrative rules for Member State cooperation in taking charge of, or taking back, asylum seekers. Eurodac is a central data unit in which fingerprints of asylum seekers are stored and compared, in order to detect asylum seekers residing in another Member State than the Member State responsible. The Eurodac Regulation was revised simultaneously with the Dublin regulation in 2013.[696]

The Eurodac Regulation obliges Member States to take fingerprints from two categories of persons: i) all persons who apply for asylum (Article 9), and ii) all third-country nationals who illegally cross their borders (Article 14). Member States may, further, collect fingerprint data from third-country nationals who are found illegally staying on their territories (Article 17). The Member States must transmit the fingerprints and other relevant data promptly to Eurodac. If registration in the Eurodac unit produces a 'hit' with a fingerprint stored earlier, Member States can, according to the allocation criteria of the Dublin Regulation, act to establish which Member State is responsible. Eurodac has been in operation since January 2003, and is highly instrumental in the effective functioning of the Dublin mechanism. In 2012, data of 285,959 asylum seekers

---

[695] The Dublin Implementing Regulation was amended by Regulation No. 118/2014.

[696] The new Eurodac Regulation applies from 20 July 2015. Until that time, Eurodac Regulation No. 2725/2000 is in force. The new Eurodac Regulation has incorporated the provisions of the Eurodac Implementing Regulation (No. 407/2002), which is repealed with effect from 20 July 2015.

was recorded in Eurodac, with 'hits' detected in 27% of cases.[697] Around 50% of the requests for a transfer are based on hits in Eurodac.[698]

A new – and controversial[699] – feature of the recast of the Eurodac Regulation is the access to Eurodac data for law enforcement purposes.[700] National law enforcement authorities and Europol may compare fingerprint data with the data stored in Eurodac if such comparison is necessary for combatting terrorism or serious crime.[701]

6.3.6. NOTES ON THE DUBLIN SYSTEM

The Dublin Regulation has certainly been instrumental in addressing the troublesome phenomena of 'asylum shopping' and 'refugees in orbit'. Yet, there are some drawbacks in the Dublin system. Although the mechanism is based on criteria which, in themselves, are neutral and aimed at the fair distribution of asylum applicants among Member States,[702] it has become evident that they do not distribute asylum seekers evenly among the Member States. Even though traditional asylum countries such as Germany, France, Sweden and the United Kingdom continue to receive by far the largest number of asylum applicants in the EU,[703] the allocation criteria do have some effect of shifting the burden to countries at the EU southern and eastern external borders. This is primarily a result of Article 13, assigning responsibility to the Member State whose borders are irregularly crossed by an applicant coming from a non-Member State. Statistics show that Poland, Italy, Greece (before transfers were suspended), Spain, Hungary and Malta have significantly more incoming than outgoing Dublin transfers.[704]

---

[697] Annual report on the activities of the EURODAC Central Unit in 2012, COM(2013) 485 final, para. 2.2.
[698] Report on the evaluation of the Dublin system, COM(2007) 299 final, para/ 2.2.
[699] According to the European Data Protection Supervisor, this use of Eurodac is a serious intrusion into the rights of a vulnerable group of people in need of protection, because, amongst other reasons, 'if a fingerprint is found at a crime scene, asylum seekers can potentially be identified through EURODAC data while other individuals cannot because similar data is not available for all other groups of society.' Opinion of the European Data Protection Supervisor of 5 September 2012 on the amended proposal for a Regulation of the European Parliament and of the Council on the establishment of 'EURODAC' for the comparison of fingerprints for the effective application of Regulation (EU) No [.../...].
[700] Arts. 1(2), 5–7 and 19–22.
[701] Art. 20.
[702] Preamble, Recital 5.
[703] Eurostat, Asylum applicants and first instance decisions on asylum applications: 2012, Issue number 5/2013.
[704] Report on the evaluation of the Dublin system, COM(2007) 299 final, para. 3. The ratio between incoming and outgoing transfers was 1196–148 in Poland, 419–47 in Italy, 350–6 in Greece, 315–52 in Spain, 160–6 in Hungary and 39–1 in Malta.

Nor do the allocation criteria reflect the guiding principle established by UNHCR in 1979 that the identification of the country responsible for examining an asylum request should, as far as possible, be informed by the intentions of the asylum seeker as regards the country in which he wishes to request asylum.[705] One can argue that if primacy were to be given to the country of preference of asylum seekers – or simply to the country where the asylum application was first lodged – this would not only reduce time and costs involved in establishing which Member State would be responsible, but could also increase the chances of successful integration, since a willingness to integrate is likely to be greater in the asylum seeker's country of first choice. Such a system could, further, be instrumental in reducing the amount of asylum seekers who abscond from the country responsible in order to live in another Member State illegally. On the other hand, the main disadvantage of having a system based solely or primarily upon the asylum seekers' own preferences is that this could place too heavy a burden on those Member States employing the most generous procedures and eligibility criteria.[706]

The recast of the Dublin Regulation has only partially addressed the fundamental issue of Member States that are too unsafe to receive Dublin transfers, as has been the case with Greece since 2011. Although Article 3(2) now clarifies that transfers must be discontinued in such a scenario, the European Commission had wanted to go a step further by introducing a clause in the Dublin Regulation that would allow a Member State faced with an exceptional burden on its reception capacities to request for the suspension of Dublin transfers.[707] The Council could not, however, agree on that clause, and introduced instead the so-called 'early warning mechanism', which allows for the close involvement and monitoring of the Commission and the European Asylum Support Office in a Member State if the application of the Regulation is jeopardised due to 'particular pressure being placed on a Member State's asylum system and/or problems in the functioning of the asylum system' (Article 33). That mechanism does not provide for the suspension of transfers however, leaving it to national decision-makers and courts to examine, in each individual case, whether a transfer meets the requisite human rights standards.

Further, the evaluation report on the functioning of the Dublin mechanism published by the European Commission in 2007 shows that the Dublin Regulation does not work as effectively as envisaged. Although the mechanism

---

[705]   UNHCR Executive Committee Conclusions No. 15 (XXX) Refugees without an asylum country (1979), para. h(iii).

[706]   This was also the argument the Commission used in defence of its original proposal; see 'Proposal for a Council regulation establishing the criteria and mechanisms for determining the Member State responsible for examining an asylum application lodged in one of the Member States by a third country national', Brussels, 26 July 2001, COM(2001) 447 final, para. 2.2.

[707]   COM(2008) 820 final, Art. 31.

for determining the Member State responsible and the cooperation between Member States appear to function generally satisfactorily, a relatively low rate of transfers is actually effected. The main reason for this low number appears to be that asylum seekers often abscond after they have been informed that they will be transferred to another Member State.[708]

Some Member States have tried to diminish this risk by detaining asylum seekers during the responsibility determination process. The new provision on detention in the recast of the Dublin Regulation (Article 28) now rules out, however, the automatic detention of persons who are subject to the Dublin procedure, enlivening such a competence only when there is a significant risk of absconding, and provided other conditions are met.[709]

6.4. RECEPTION CONDITIONS DIRECTIVE

The Reception Conditions Directive (Directive 2013/33/EU) lays down standards for the reception of asylum seekers within the Member States. A key aim of the Directive is to limit secondary movements of asylum applicants within the EU influenced by disparities in reception conditions in Member States.[710] The Directive should, according to the Preamble, lay down reception standards that ensure a dignified standard of living and comparable living conditions in all Member States.[711]

In this regard, the Directive can also be seen as observing the Refugee Convention. As will be explained in Chapter 7, the Refugee Convention provides for a specific set of rights to the category of refugees who are physically present in a state's territory, irrespective of their legal status.[712] Since asylum seekers might be refugees in the process of being recognised as such, it is appropriate to grant asylum seekers at least the rights, which, according to the Refugee Convention, should be conferred upon refugees falling under this category. In particular, refugees who do not have a legal status must, according to the Refugee Convention, be free to practise their religion, have certain property rights, have access to elementary education, have the right to administrative assistance and the right to be issued identity papers.[713] As we will see, the Reception Conditions Directive generally complies with this standard, and does, in fact, grant a

---

[708] Report on the evaluation of the Dublin system, COM(2007) 299 final, para. 2.3.1.
[709] On the detention of asylum seekers, see also sections 6.4.2 and 9.4.2.
[710] Preamble, Recital 12.
[711] Preamble, Recital 11.
[712] See section 7.6. Arguably, refugees who are allowed to stay in the country pending the asylum procedure can also be considered 'lawfully present', and may therefore be entitled to additional Refugee Convention rights, such as the right to be engaged in self-employment (Article 18). See, on this argument, extensively, J.C. Hathaway, *The Rights of Refugees under International Law*, Cambridge University Press (2005), pp. 173–186.
[713] See in particular Articles 4, 13, 14, 22, 25 and 27 Refugee Convention.

number of rights to asylum seekers which states under the Refugee Convention are only obliged to grant to refugees who have expressly been permitted residence.

A further benchmark in respect of living conditions of asylum applicants, are generally applicable fundamental rights. In *M.S.S. v. Belgium and Greece*, the ECtHR considered that Greece had violated Article 3 ECHR because it had failed to assist an asylum seeker who had spent months living in the street in a state of the most extreme poverty, unable to cater for his most basic needs: food, hygiene and a place to live. This attained the level of severity required to fall within the scope of Article 3 ECHR.[714] The Court of Justice has held that it follows from the general scheme and purpose of the Reception Conditions Directive, as well as from Article 1 of the EU Charter of Fundamental Rights, under which human dignity must be respected and protected, that the Member States must grant a level of benefits which is sufficient to ensure a dignified standard of living and adequate health.[715]

The legal basis for the Reception Conditions Directive is Article 78(2)(f) TFEU. The Directive covers all third-country nationals and stateless persons who make an application for international protection, as long as they enjoy the status of applicant in a Member States (Article 3(1)). This means that as soon as the asylum seeker makes his application for asylum, he is entitled to the conditions enumerated in the Directive, which includes the admissibility stage of the asylum procedure and the period in which a request for transfer, pursuant to the Dublin Regulation, is made.[716] A person ceases to be an asylum applicant when a final decision on his application is taken. A 'final decision' must be understood as a decision that can no longer be challenged under national law, i.e. including appeals procedures before judicial bodies.[717] Family members of the applicant who have not, themselves, lodged an asylum application are only treated on equal footing with the applicant under the Directive if the national law of the Member State so provides.

The United Kingdom, Ireland and Denmark do not take part in the Reception Conditions Directive. Denmark does not participate in any asylum Directive. Ireland already refused to participate in the first phase Reception Conditions Directive (2003/9/EC), since it was particularly firm in refusing to accept that the right to work could be extended to asylum seekers. The UK did opt in to the first phase Reception Conditions Directive, which implies that it remains bound by that Directive, also when the transposition period of the recast Directive expires on 20 July 2015.

---

[714]   *M.S.S. v. Belgium and Greece*, para. 263. Cf. ECtHR 18 April 2013, *Mohammed Hussein v. the Netherlands and Italy*, No. 27725/10, where the Court, in respect of the treatment of a pregnant asylum seeker, did not find a violation of Article 3 ECHR on the part of Italy.

[715]   ECJ 27 February 2014, *Saciri*, Case C-79/13, para. 35.

[716]   ECJ 27 September 2012, *Cimade and GISTI*, Case C-179/11.

[717]   See Article 2(e) Procedures Directive.

Even though the recast Directive speaks of 'standards' for reception, and thus no longer of 'minimum standards' as in the first phase Directive, it does not aim at fully harmonising reception conditions. To ensure agreement in the Council, the Directive grants Member States flexibility in integrating the reception conditions into their national legal systems.[718] Article 4 expressly allows Member States to retain or introduce more favourable standards.

6.4.1. RECEPTION CONDITIONS

Chapter II of the Reception Conditions Directive lays down the reception standards. Instead of commenting on the entire range of provisions, we will highlight the most noteworthy ones:

6.4.1.1. *Documentation*

Article 6 obliges Member States to provide asylum seekers with a document certifying their status as asylum seekers or testifying that they are allowed to remain in the territory of the Member State pending the asylum procedure.

6.4.1.2. *Freedom of Movement and Residence*

Article 7 lays down the principle that asylum seekers are free to move within the territory of the host Member State, but this principle is subject to a number of exceptions. Member States are free, in the first place, to determine that an asylum seeker may only freely move in a specific area (paragraph 1), provided that this area is not restricted to such a degree that it violates the right to privacy and impedes access to benefits guaranteed by the Reception Conditions Directive. Secondly, Member States can also designate the specific place of residence of the asylum seeker, whenever such designation is needed for reasons of public interest, public order or for the swift processing of an application (paragraph 2). This provision allows for the placement of asylum seekers in special accommodation centres.

6.4.1.3. *Education*

Article 14 guarantees the right to education for minor asylum seekers.

6.4.1.4. *Employment*

Article 15 deals with the controversial issue of access to employment for asylum seekers. The provision embodies a political compromise between those Member

---

[718]   Cf. Amended proposal, COM(2011) 320 final, p. 3, 5.

States that wanted to exclude or severely restrict the right to employment for asylum applicants, and those who wanted to grant asylum seekers unrestricted access to employed activities. The two opposing interests are that, on the one hand, access to employment fosters integration in the host society and promotes self-sufficiency among asylum seekers, and, on the other hand, that access to labour is normally only accorded to persons who are legally resident.

The agreed text lays down that Member States must grant access to the labour no later than nine months after the application was lodged. Member States may set conditions for such access (such as regarding type and maximum duration of work or the requirement of a work permit),[719] but these conditions may not impair the effectiveness of the right to work (Article 15(2)). The right of access to the labour market may not be withdrawn during appeals procedures with suspensive effect – i.e. appeals that allow for applicants to stay in the Member State (Article 15(3)).

6.4.1.5.   Material Reception Conditions

Articles 17 and 18 govern the material reception conditions of asylum seekers. Material reception conditions include housing, food and clothing that can be provided in kind or in the form of a financial allowance or voucher (Article 2(g)). According to Article 17(1–4), the basic rule is that Member States must ensure an 'adequate standard of living' (Article 17(2)). This standard is rather vague and susceptible to different interpretation.[720] The provision of material reception conditions may be made subject to the requirement that the applicant does not have sufficient means to provide for himself (Article 17(3)). Article 18 provides specific modalities for the right to housing. If a Member State opts to grant the material reception conditions in the form of financial allowances or vouchers, those allowances must be provided from the time the asylum application is made.[721]

6.4.1.6.   Healthcare

Article 19 obliges Member States to ensure that asylum seekers receive the necessary healthcare, at least including emergency care and essential treatment of illness and of serious mental disorders, again, under the provision that applicants do not have sufficient means to bear these costs themselves (Article 15(3)). There is, accordingly, no right of access to healthcare on equal

---

[719]   See Explanatory Memorandum annexed to the Commission's proposal, COM(2001), 181 Final, 3 April 2001, p. 14. It appears that Member States make use of these derogations extensively; see Commission Evaluation Report, COM(2007) 745 final, para. 3.4.3.

[720]   See, however, ECJ 27 February 2014, *Saciri*, Case C-79/13, para. 35, referring to Article 1 of the EU Charter of Fundamental Rights.

[721]   Ibid, para. 52.

footing with nationals. What exactly, the minimum threshold entails of 'necessary' healthcare and 'essential treatment of illness' remains unclear.

For vulnerable persons, Articles 21 to 25 contain, complementary to the general provisions on reception conditions, a number of additional conditions. Vulnerable persons are described as 'minors, unaccompanied minors, disabled people, elderly people, pregnant women, single parents with minor children, victims of human trafficking, persons with serious illnesses, persons with mental disorders and persons who have been subjected to torture, rape or other forms of psychological, physical or sexual violence' (Article 21). To make these provisions effective, Article 22 stipulates that the asylum procedure must include a preliminary identification of whether the applicant has special reception needs.

As will often be the case, asylum seekers fleeing from persecution may have suffered traumatic experiences. The Directive obliges Member States to pay due regard to the conditions in which asylum seekers may find themselves, which might oblige Member States to provide specialised forms of treatment, such as mental healthcare and qualified counselling, or, in the case of unaccompanied minors, placement with adult relatives, foster families, or in suitable accommodation centres. The obligation to make these special arrangements available may preclude the placement of vulnerable persons in a detention facility – if that facility is not equipped with the necessary utilities.

6.4.2. DETENTION OF ASYLUM SEEKERS

Articles 8–11 of the Reception Conditions Directive, which were newly inserted in the recast, deal with the controversial issue of detention of asylum seekers. International law does not, as a matter of principle, prohibit the detention of asylum seekers. Although Article 26 Refugee Convention provides that refugees lawfully staying in a state have the right to move freely within the state's territory, Article 31(2) Refugee Convention makes it possible to restrict free movement of refugees on account of illegal entry or presence, if such restriction is necessary, and until their status is regularised or they have been admitted to another country. It is generally accepted that detention of asylum seekers under that provision is allowed to verify the identity of the asylum seeker, in particular, in the case of loss or destruction of travel documents and to prevent him from absconding.[722] More contested is whether that provision also allows for detention merely for conducting the actual asylum procedure.[723] It follows from

---

[722] A Grahl-Madsen, *The Status of Refugees in International Law*, vol. II: Asylum, Entry and Sojourn (Leiden, A. W. Sijthoff, 1972), p. 418; UNHCR EXCOM Conclusion No 44 (XXXVII).

[723] See the discussion in JC Hathaway, *The Rights of Refugees under International Law*, Cambridge University Press, Cambridge, 2005, pp. 415 et seq.; Zimmerman (red.), *The 1951 Convention relating to the Status of refugees and its 1967 Protocol: A Commentary*, Oxford University Press 2011, p. 1272–1273; UNHCR, Saadi v United Kingdom: Written Submission,

the term 'necessary' in Article 31(2), that detention can only be exceptionally resorted to for a legitimate purpose, and that detention for the mere convenience of the authorities is not permitted. The most recent UNHCR guidelines on the issue stipulate that illegal entry is an insufficient basis for detention.[724]

The ECtHR has not, up to now, set very strict limits to the detention of asylum seekers if their detention forms part of a procedure to decide on their right to enter the territory. In *Saadi v. The United Kingdom*, the ECtHR held that the detention of asylum seekers to prevent them from effectuating illegal entry is permitted under the first limb of Article 5(1)(f) ECHR ('detention of a person to prevent his effecting an unauthorised entry'), provided the detention is not arbitrary.[725] To avoid being branded as arbitrary, the detention must: i) be carried out in good faith; ii) it must be closely connected to the purpose of preventing unauthorised entry; iii) the place and conditions of detention should reflect the fact that asylum seekers are not criminals; and iv) the length of the detention should not exceed that reasonably required for the purpose pursued.[726]

Accordingly, the ECtHR does not require the detention to be necessary or that it is only applied if no less coercive alternatives are available.[727] The ECtHR clarified, however, that this does not mean that all Contracting States may lawfully detain immigrants pending their asylum claim, but that this is chiefly a matter of national law. If national law provides for a right of entry of asylum seekers, or when an asylum seeker has been granted formal authorisation to enter or stay, the first limb of Article 5(1)(f) can no longer be invoked as justified ground for detention.[728]

The Reception Conditions Directive sets somewhat stricter criteria for the detention of asylum seekers. It follows from Article 8(1) and (2) of the Reception Conditions Directive that the automatic detention of asylum applicants is prohibited: detention must be 'necessary', be based on an individual assessment, and may only occur if other less coercive measures are unavailable. Apart from these general requirements, Article 8(3) contains an exhaustive list of six permissible grounds for detention. Presumably, these grounds inform the necessity requirement of paragraph 2. The grounds are: i) detention in order to determine the identity or nationality of the applicants; ii) detention in order to determine the elements on which the application is based which could not otherwise be obtained, in particular, when there is a risk of absconding; iii) detention in order to decide on the right to enter the territory; iv) detention when

---

paras. 26–27; UNHCR's Guidelines on Applicable Criteria and Standards relating to the Detention of Asylum-Seekers, February 1999.

[724] UNHCR's Guidelines on the Applicable Criteria and Standards relating to the Detention of Asylum Seekers and Alternatives to Detention, 2012.

[725] EHRM 29 January 2008, *Saadi v the United Kingdom*, nr. 13229/03, Grand Chamber.

[726] Ibid, para. 74.

[727] Ibid, paras. 72, 73.

[728] ECtHR 23 July 2013, *Suso Musa v Malta*, no. 42337/12, para. 97.

a return procedure under the Returns directive is already on-going and the asylum application is made merely to delay or frustrate the return procedure; v) detention for reasons of national security or public order; and vi) detention in accordance with the Dublin Regulation.

The possibility to detain an asylum applicant in order to decide on his right to enter the territory (Article 8(3)(c)) is rather wide, but it must be read together with Articles 43, 31(8) and 33 of the Procedures Directive, from which it follows that an asylum applicant may only be subjected to a border procedure in order to decide on his right of entry under prescribed grounds, which relate to establishing the admissibility of the application, grounds of public order, abuse and manifestly ill-founded applications.

Article 9 contains guarantees for detained applicants, including the right of judicial review. Article 10 sets forth the requisite detention conditions. Although the Commission had proposed that detention may only take place in specialised detention facilities, the Council has maintained, in the Directive, the possibility of resorting to prison accommodation if no specialised detention facilities are available.

Upon instigation of the Council, the possibility of detaining minors is also provided in Article 11, albeit only as a measure of last resort, and by taking into account the minor's best interests (Article 11(2)). The ECtHR has, in deviation from the *Saadi* criteria, set more stringent conditions for the placement of minors in immigration detention, including the requirements of detention as last resort, and that the conditions must be adapted to children (see, on immigration detention, further, section 9.4.6).[729]

6.4.3. REDUCTION AND WITHDRAWAL OF RECEPTION CONDITIONS

The reception conditions may be withdrawn or restricted in a number of situations (Article 20). The rationale behind Article 20 is that Member States must be able to sanction those asylum seekers who abuse the reception system. These cases of abuse – or non-compliance with the system – include the situation where an asylum seeker abandons the place of residence where he or she was designated to stay (Article 20(1)(a)); where an asylum seeker fails to comply with reporting duties or with requests to provide information (Article 20(1)(b)); and where the asylum seeker has lodged a subsequent application (Article 20(1)(c)). Material reception conditions may also be reduced if the applicant has not lodged his asylum claim 'as soon as reasonably practicable after arrival' (Article 20(2)). This provision was inserted at the behest of a number of Member

---

[729] ECtHR 5 April 2011, *Rahimi v. Greece*, No. 8687/08; ECtHR 19 January 2012, *Popov v. France*, No. 39472/07 and 39474/07.

States. Lastly, material reception conditions may be reduced or withdrawn where an applicant has concealed financial resources (Article 20(3)). All decisions of reduction and withdrawal must be in conformity with the principle of proportionality (Article 20(5)), by taking into account the situation of the persons concerned – and especially the situation of vulnerable persons.

Importantly, the reduction or withdrawal of reception conditions may not impede access to healthcare or a dignified standard of living (Article 20(5)). The United Kingdom House of Lords has, likewise, recalled that reception conditions may not be denied to asylum seekers when this would result in the provision of treatment below the standard of 'human treatment', as guaranteed by Article 3 ECHR. Accordingly, and having regard to the circumstances of each case, the House of Lords considered the refusal of housing, food and other conditions to three asylum seekers on the ground that they had failed to make their claims as soon as practicable, to be in violation of Article 3 ECHR.[730]

Asylum seekers faced with a negative decision relating to the granting of benefits – including the refusal, withdrawal or reduction of benefits – must have the possibility of an appeal before a judicial body (Article 26).

6.4.4. NOTES ON THE RECEPTION CONDITIONS DIRECTIVE

The Reception Conditions Directive guarantees the key material, economic and social conditions that ensure a basic standard of living for asylum seekers awaiting a decision on their application in one of the Member States. The *de minimis* rule of an 'adequate standard of living' reflects the ECtHR's position that Contracting States must have due regard to the vulnerability of asylum seekers, and must prevent a situation of serious deprivation or want incompatible with human dignity.[731] The Directive also guarantees the rights accruing to refugees who do not have a residence status as laid down in the Refugee Convention, with as possible exception, the lack of an express right to be issued an identity paper, laid down in Article 27 Refugee Convention.[732]

Nonetheless, the revised Directive still leaves a wide amount of discretion to Member States and does not secure full integration of reception standards. The

---

[730] House of Lords 3 November 2005, *Regina v. Secretary of State for the Home Department*, [2005] UKHL 66; see, e.g., §7: 'A general public duty to house the homeless or provide for the destitute cannot be spelled out of Article 3 [ECHR]. But I have no doubt that the threshold may be crossed if a late applicant with no means and no alternative sources of support, unable to support himself, is, by the deliberate action of the state, denied shelter, food or the most basic necessities of life' (Lord Bingham of Cornhill).
[731] *M.S.S. v Belgium and Greece*, paras. 253, 263.
[732] Article 6 of the Directive holds that asylum seekers are to be provided with a document certifying the status of asylum seeker, which need not certify the identity of the asylum seeker (Article 6(3)).

initial ambition of the European Commission to aim for high standards of reception conditions, and in some respects, equal treatment with nationals, has been lowered, amongst other reasons, for a fear of some governments of unduly high financial implications. A key improvement of the 2013 revision of the reception conditions regime is, however, the clarification of circumstances under which detention of asylum seekers is permitted. That detention may only occur under prescribed grounds and if it meets the principles of proportionality and necessity filled a gap within the existing EU asylum *acquis* on the issue of asylum detention. The limits to detention are of considerable practical relevance in view of the wide use of detention – and in some instances, automatic detention – of asylum seekers in some Member States.[733]

6.5. THE PROCEDURES DIRECTIVE

The Procedures Directive (2013/32/EU) lays down common procedures for granting and withdrawing international protection. International protection means refugee status and subsidiary protection status as defined in the Qualification Directive.[734] The Procedures Directive lays down the procedural framework for examining whether an asylum applicant meets the qualification criteria for granting (or withdrawing) international protection as set forth in the Qualification Directive.

Negotiations in the Council on both the first phase and the revised Procedures Directive proved cumbersome. In both instances, amended proposals by the European Commission were needed to facilitate a breakthrough.[735] The revised Directive applies to applications for international protection lodged after 20 July 2015. Earlier applications are governed by the former Directive 2005/85/EC. Member States are, however, given more time to implement the Directive's provisions that set strict limits to the duration of the examination procedure. These provisions apply to applications lodged after 20 July 2018.[736] The legal basis of the Directive is Article 78(2)(d) TFEU. Neither Ireland, the UK nor Denmark take part in the Directive. Since Ireland and the UK did opt in to the first phase Directive, they remain bound by that Directive after it is repealed for the other Member States.

Despite the ambition to establish a 'common asylum procedure' and the reference in the Directive's title to 'common procedures', the procedural

---

[733] Parliamentary Assembly of the Council of Europe, 'The detention of asylum seekers and irregular migrants in Europe', doc. 12105, 11 January 2010.
[734] Article 2(i) Directive 2013/32/EU; Articles 13 and 18 Directive 2011/95/EU.
[735] See, for the first phase Directive (2005/85/EC): COM(2000) 578 final (Original Proposal) and COM(2002) 326 final (Amended Proposal); and for the revised Directive: COM(2009) 554 final (Original Proposal) and COM(2011) 319 final (Amended Proposal).
[736] Article 52(2) Directive 2013/32/EU.

standards retain flexibility to accommodate the particularities of national legal systems. This reflects the differences that exist between the administrative frameworks for handling asylum applications in the Member States.[737] Because asylum procedures are normally part of general administrative law systems, the imposition of common European procedural standards can have a profound impact on domestic constitutional and administrative arrangements. The flexibility provided in the Directive concerns, *inter alia*, the rules on decisions on the right to enter the territory, the possibility to postpone the taking of a decision where the situation in the country of origin is temporarily uncertain, and grounds for examining applications at the border. Article 5 allows Member States to introduce or maintain more favourable standards. Similar to the Reception Conditions Directive and the Dublin Regulation, the Procedures Directive applies only to applications for international protection, although Member States may apply the Directive's standards in any protection procedure they employ (Article 3(3)).

6.5.1. THE RIGHT TO A FAIR ASYLUM PROCEDURE

A further factor explaining the difficulty to arrive at common acceptable procedural standards is that there is no obvious legal framework setting forth the manner of examination of asylum claims. The Refugee Convention does not indicate what type of procedures are to be adopted for the determination of refugee status, leaving it to each Contracting State to establish the procedure that it considers most appropriate, having regard to its particular constitutional and administrative structure.

However, some procedural standards flow implicitly from the prohibition of *refoulement* of Article 33 Refugee Convention and Article 3 ECHR. The ECtHR has consistently held that, in view of the absolute character of Article 3 ECHR and the irreparable harm that might occur, a rigorous scrutiny must necessarily be conducted of an individual's claim that his or her deportation to a third country will expose that individual to ill-treatment.[738] This implies, *inter alia*, that an applicant must be given opportunity to state his case and that relevant evidence must be seriously examined by the authorities. UNHCR has issued more specific requirements for conducting asylum examinations, including on such issues as the availability of interpreters and legal assistance, evidentiary

---

[737] On the negotiating process more extensively: D. Ackers, 'The Negotiations on the Asylum Procedures Directive', *EJML* Vol. 7, No. 1 (2005), pp. 1–33.

[738] ECtHR 30 October 1991, *Vilvarajah v. The United Kingdom*, No. 13163/87, para. 108; ECtHR 11 July 2000, *Jabari v. Turkey*, No. 40035/98, paras. 39–40; ECtHR 4 February 2005, *Mamatkulov v. Turkey*, Nos. 46827/99 and 46951/99, para. 123.

standards, the right to remain in the territory pending the procedure and the treatment of vulnerable categories of asylum seekers.[739]

In combination with the prohibition of *refoulement*, the right to an effective remedy (Article 13 ECHR) further sets requirements on the intensity of judicial review and the suspensive effect of appeals.[740] Although Contracting States are afforded some discretion as to the manner in which they organise national remedies, the ECtHR holds that there must be an independent and rigorous scrutiny of any claim that there exist substantial grounds for fearing a real risk of treatment contrary to Article 3 ECHR.[741] In more general terms, Article 16(1) Refugee Convention states that refugees must have free access to courts. This right also accrues to refugees who have not yet been formally been admitted to the state, and may thus be invoked to appeal against a negative decision on refugee status.[742]

It must be presumed that the above standards are also reflected in the EU Charter of Fundamental Rights, which prohibits torture and inhuman treatment in Article 4, prohibits *refoulement* in Article 19(2), and lays down the right to an effective remedy and to a fair trial in Article 47.[743] A general point made by the Court of Justice in its nascent case law on the fairness of asylum procedures is that the effectiveness of the remedy depends on the administrative and judicial system of each Member State as a whole.[744] Likewise, the ECtHR holds that the aggregate of remedies determines their effectiveness in the meaning of Article 13 ECHR.[745] Generally, the fairness and permissibility of particular national procedural rules or practices should not be examined in isolation, but in the context of the entire asylum procedure, including the administrative as well as appeals phase. Shortcomings in one step or phase may be compensated or repaired in a subsequent procedure.[746] The ECtHR has, further, held that applicants may generally be expected to comply with domestic procedural rules such as on time limits and formal requirements, although such rules must not be

---

[739] UNHCR Handbook, para. 189–219; UNHCR EXCOM Conclusion no. 8 (XXVIII) of 12 October 1977.

[740] E.g. ECtHR 5 February 2002, *Conka v. Belgium*, No. 51564/99; ECtHR 26 April 2007, *Gebremedhin v. France*, No. 25389/05. See extensively T. Spijkerboer, 'Subsidiarity and 'Arguability': the European Court of Human Rights' Case Law on Judicial Review in Asylum Cases', 21 *International Journal of Refugee Law* (2009), pp. 1–27.

[741] E.g. ECtHR 12 April 2005, *Shamayev and Others v. Georgia and Russia*, No. 36378/02, para. 448, ECtHR 11 July 2000, *Jabari v. Turkey*, No. 40035/98, para. 50.

[742] J.C. Hathaway, *The Rights of Refugees under International Law*, Cambridge University Press (2005), p. 645.

[743] M. Reneman, *EU Asylum Procedures and the Right to an Effective Remedy*, Oxford: Hart, 2014.

[744] CJEU 28 July 2011, *Samba Diouf*, Case C-69/10, para. 46; CJEU 31 January 2013, *H.I.D.*, Case C-175/11, para. 102.

[745] *M.S.S. v Belgium and Greece*, para. 289, ECtHR 26 April 2007, *Gebremedhin v France*, No. 25389/05, para. 53.

[746] Reneman (2014), pp. 110–111.

applied so inflexibly as to deny a realistic opportunity to prove an asylum claim.[747]

The revised Procedures Directive aims at ensuring full respect of fundamental rights, as it is informed by developing case law of the Court of Justice EU and the European Court of Human Rights, especially concerning the right to an effective remedy.[748]

6.5.2. BASIC PRINCIPLES AND GUARANTEES

Chapter II of the Procedures Directive (Articles 6–30) lists the principles and guarantees to be respected during the examination of the asylum application. Some of these provisions apply only to the procedure at first instance, i.e. the examination of the application by a determining authority of the state; some of these provisions apply only to appeals procedures, i.e. the subsequent procedure before a court; and some provisions apply to both stages of the procedure. The requirements are framed in terms of individual rights and positive obligations of Member States.[749] Most notable are:

- The right of access to the procedure (Article 6);
- The right to remain in the Member State pending the examination in first instance (Article 9), which reflects the case law under Articles 3 and 13 ECHR that an asylum seeker may not be expelled before his claim that he will be subjected to ill-treatment upon return is examined;[750]
- The rule that eligibility for refugee status must be examined before eligibility for subsidiary protection (Article 10(2));
- The obligation to conduct an 'appropriate' examination (Article 10(3)), based, among others, on the principles of individuality, objectiveness and impartiality;
- The obligation to give a decision in writing (Article 11(1)) and, in case of rejection, with stating reasons (Article 11(2));
- The right of the applicant to be informed about the procedure and the decision taken in a language they understand (Article 12(a)(f));
- The right of the applicant to receive the services of an interpreter (Article 12(b));
- The right of the applicant to be invited to a personal interview (Articles 14–17);

---

[747] ECtHR 19 February 1998, *Bahaddar v. The Netherlands*, No. 25894/94, para. 45.
[748] COM(2011) 319 final, para. 3.1.
[749] Chapter II also deals with obligations for asylum applicants; see especially Article 13.
[750] See, e.g., ECtHR 23 February 2012, *Hirsi v. Italy*, No. 27765/09, para. 205; ECtHR 21 January 2011, *M.S.S. v. Belgium and Greece*, No. 30696/09, para. 293; ECtHR 22 September 2009, *Abdolkhani and Karimnia v. Turkey*, No. 30471/08, para. 113.

- The right to be medically examined if relevant for establishing past persecution or serious harm, although Member States may require the applicant to arrange for such examination himself (Article 18);
- The right to (under conditions: free) legal assistance and representation (Articles 20–23);
- Additional safeguards for unaccompanied minors and other persons in need of special procedural guarantees (Articles 24–25);
- The right of the applicant not to be held in detention on the sole reason that he/she is applying for asylum, with a reference to the detailed rules on detention of asylum seekers in the Reception Conditions Directive (Article 26);
- The obligation to allow UNHCR to visit applicants and to review the particulars of the procedure (Article 29).

6.5.3. PROCEDURES AT FIRST INSTANCE

Chapter III of the Directive (Articles 31–43) is devoted to the procedure at first instance, i.e. the procedure in which a determining authority – normally the immigration service – examines and decides upon the application. Chapter III provides a rather complex array of special situations in which Member States may decide not to examine a request, may consider applications inadmissible or may apply extraordinary procedures. This complexity reflects the wide variety in Member State procedural practices, but also stems from a common desire to process asylum applications as fast and efficiently as possible. Hereunder, we discuss the most notable procedural concepts.

6.5.3.1. Duration of the Examination Procedure

Contrary to the first phase Directive, the recast lays down strict time limits for concluding any examination procedure, although these provisions are subject to an extended transposition deadline of 20 July 2018.[751] The examination must be completed within six months, with the possibility of extension of nine months in three situations: i) if complex issues of fact and/or law are involved; ii) if a large number of applications is received; or iii) if the delay can be attributed to the applicant. Further, by way of exception, and in duly certified circumstances, Member States may exceed these time limits by a maximum of three months (Article 31(3)).

Article 31 also provides for the possibilities of *postponement, prioritisation* and *acceleration* of the examination. Article 31(4) refers to the procedural practice in some Member States of postponing the examination in case the

---

[751] Article 51(2).

situation in the country of origin is temporarily uncertain. Such postponement may last up to 21 months from the lodging of the application (Article 31(5)).

The Directive does not set a minimum duration for examining a claim. It follows from the case law of the ECtHR, however, that accelerated procedures can be problematic under Articles 3 and 13 ECHR, because they may complicate, for example, the procurement of necessary evidence, the conducting of a medical examination, contact with a lawyer, or the translation of documents.[752] The Directive allows the prioritisation of an examination 'in particular' in two situations: i) where the application is likely to be well-founded, and ii) where the applicant is vulnerable or in need of special procedural guarantees (Article 31(7)). Presumably, 'prioritisation' does not refer to a shorter duration of the actual examination, but an earlier start of the examination. It follows from the words 'in particular' that prioritisation may also occur in other situations. In respect of the corresponding provision on prioritisation in the former Directive, which was, however, formulated in slightly different terms, the Court of Justice considered that other applications could also be prioritised, including categories of asylum applications that are defined on the basis of the nationality of the applicant.[753]

Acceleration of the examination is possible in 10 exhaustively listed situations (Article 31(8)). These circumstances concern manifestly ill-founded applications, situations of abuse, subsequent applications and applicants who endanger national security or public order. When accelerating the procedure, the basic guarantees of Chapter II must continue to apply.[754] The Directive does not specify what acceleration exactly entails and leaves it to Member States to lay down time limits in national law (Article 31(9)). Minors and persons with special procedural needs may only be subjected to an accelerated procedure if certain conditions are met.[755]

6.5.3.2. Inadmissible Applications – Countries of First Asylum and Safe Third Countries

Article 33 Procedures Directive classifies five categories of applications as inadmissible. When it is established that an application falls into one of these categories, Member States are 'not required' to examine the asylum claim, and may, hence, derogate from the basic principles and guarantees of Chapter II of the Directive, although a personal interview must be granted.[756] The first category is comprised of cases, which, according to the Dublin Regulation, fall under the responsibility of another Member State (Article 33(1)).

---

[752] ECtHR 2 February 2012, *I.M. v. France*, No. 9152/09.
[753] ECJ 6 May 2008, *H.I.D.*, Case C-175/11.
[754] But see Art. 17(5).
[755] Articles 24(3) and 25(6).
[756] Article 34.

The other categories include the *first country of asylum* concept and the *safe third country* concept. These concepts reflect the idea that Member States are not obliged to examine asylum claims when applicants can receive protection in a non-Member State. A first country of asylum means a third country where the applicant has been recognised as refugee or has otherwise enjoyed sufficient protection, provided that the applicant will be readmitted to that country. The applicant must, however, be allowed to challenge the application of the concept in his case (Article 35).

A safe third country means a third country where the applicant has not before enjoyed protection, but where he will be treated in accordance with a range of international standards which reflect the principles that asylum seekers must, in all circumstances, be treated in accordance with the Refugee Convention, and that the third country must respect the prohibition of *refoulement*. Furthermore, there must be a connection between the country and the applicant, making it reasonable for that person to go that country, the safety must be subject to rebuttal, and the person must be admitted to that country (Article 38).

The criteria for applying the safe third country concept must be read against the background of relevant case law of the ECtHR on returning asylum seekers to a supposedly safe third country. In *Hirsi v. Italy*, concerning the interception at sea and summary return by Italy of nationals from Eritrea and Somalia to Libya, the ECtHR dismissed the argument brought by Italy that Libya was a safe host country. It found a violation of Article 3 ECHR because refugees enjoyed no special protection in Libya, and because they were, like other irregular migrants, at risk of arrest and detention under inhuman circumstances or even torture, and subjected to precarious living conditions and xenophobic and racist acts.[757] The Court further concluded that the applicants were exposed to the risk of arbitrary repatriation to Eritrea and Somalia, because: i) Libya had not ratified the Refugee Convention, ii) Libya did not provide for refugee status determination or an equivalent asylum procedure, iii) UNHCR played a marginal role in Libya, and iv) there was evidence of actual forced returns of asylum seekers and refugees.[758]

These criteria jointly informed the risk of onward removal from Libya to Eritrea and Somalia in violation of Article 3 ECHR.[759] It is, further, clear from the *Hirsi* judgment, that asylum seekers must be granted the opportunity to effectively challenge the safety of the third country.

---

[757]   *Hirsi v. Italy*, para. 125.
[758]   Para. 153–5.
[759]   See, on the safe third country concept, extensively: S.H. Legomsky, 'Secondary Refugee Movements and the Return of Asylum Seekers to Third Countries: The Meaning of Effective Protection' (2003) 15 *IJRL* 567–677; M. Foster, 'Protection Elsewhere: The Legal Implications of Requiring Refugees to Seek Protection in Another State' (2007) 28 *Michigan Journal of International Law* (2007) 223–286; M.-T. Gil-Bazo, 'The Practice of Mediterranean States in the context of the European Union's Justice and Home Affairs External Dimension. The Safe Third Country Concept Revisited' (2006) 18 *IJRL* 571–600.

6.5.3.3. Safe Countries of Origin

The recast maintains the possibility for Member States to designate in their national law countries as a *safe country of origin* (Article 37). The criteria for such designation must reflect, *inter alia*, the absence of a risk of persecution or ill-treatment in the meaning of the Refugee Convention and Article 3 ECHR.[760] Member States making use of the safe country of origin concept may not, however, automatically apply it in respect of individual applicants, because the safety must allow for rebuttal (Article 36). The standard for rebuttal (the applicant must submit 'serious grounds for considering the country not to be safe country') can raise issues under Article 3 ECHR, as it possibly deviates from the ordinary standard used by the ECtHR that in case the applicant adduces 'evidence capable of proving that there are substantial grounds for believing that there is a real risk of ill-treatment', it is for the authorities to dispel any doubts about it.[761] It can be inferred from the wording in Article 36(1) ('after an individual examination') that the procedure leading to the application of the safe country of origin concept is subject to the ordinary examination procedure, and must therefore respect the basic principles and guarantees of Chapter II of the Directive.

It was envisaged in the former Procedures Directive that the Council would adopt a minimum list of third countries that all Member States had to treat as safe countries of origin.[762] The ECJ annulled that provision however, in considering that the adoption of such a list must be seen as forming part of the second stage of establishing a common European asylum policy, and that accordingly, the co-decision procedure should apply to the adoption of such a list.[763] Although the ECJ annulled the provisions on the procedure for establishing a common list, it did not annul the substantive provisions on the concept of safe countries of origin, which means that Member States may continue to apply or introduce the concept in their national procedures. The revised Directive did not reintroduce the idea of a common EU list of safe countries of origin.

6.5.3.4. Special Procedures: European safe Third Countries, Subsequent Applications and Border Procedures

The Directive mentions three further procedures in which special rules apply.

Firstly, Member States may make use of the *European safe third country* concept, under which no, or no full, examination in accordance with the basic

---

[760] Annex I Directive 2013/32/EU.
[761] E.g. ECtHR 28 February 2008, *Saadi v. Italy*, No. 37201/06, para. 129.
[762] Art. 29 Directive 2005/85/EC.
[763] ECJ 6 May 2008, *Parliament v. Council*, C-133/06.

principles and guarantees of Chapter II of the Directive, is required (Article 39). The concept may be applied to an applicant if: i) he seeks to enter or has entered the Member State from that third country, ii) the third country has ratified both the Refugee Convention and the ECHR (and is therefore a member of the Council of Europe but not (yet) a EU Member State) and has in place an asylum procedure prescribed by law, and iii) the third country readmits the applicant. Further, the applicant must be allowed to challenge the safety in his circumstances. Together with the provisions on the establishment of lists of safe countries of origin, the ECJ annulled the provision in the former Procedures Directive on the set up of a list by the Council of European safe third countries, on the grounds that such a list must be established in accordance with the co-decision procedure.[764] The revised Directive no longer foresees in the adoption of a common list.

Secondly, some derogations from procedural guarantees are allowed in respect of *subsequent applications* (Article 40). These reflect the concern of Member States that the possibility to lodge a fresh application is merely used to frustrate expulsion. Two scenarios are distinguished. If a preliminary examination reveals no new elements or findings relevant for the examination, no further examination is required and the subsequent application must be considered inadmissible.[765] If the preliminary examination concludes that new elements or findings have arisen, the application must be further examined according to the normal procedural standards of Chapter II. In order to prevent subsequent applications to have the effect of making removals impossible, Article 41 contains exceptions from the right to remain pending the asylum procedure. No right to remain exists if: a first subsequent application is not further examined because no new elements of findings have arisen, or if a further subsequent application is brought after a final decision on the first subsequent application. In these two situations, a right to remain neither exists when an appeal is brought, until a court has ruled that the applicant may remain on the territory (Article 41(2)(c)).

Thirdly, the *border procedure* of Article 43 allows Member States to decide on applications at the border or transit zones. This border procedure may only be applied in two situations: i) to decide whether an application can be declared inadmissible in accordance with Article 33, provided the application is made at such location; and ii) to decide on the substance of an application (wherever it is lodged) in one of the ten exhaustively listed situations in Article 31(8), as already described above in respect of accelerated procedures. These circumstances concern manifestly ill-founded applications, situations of abuse, subsequent applications and applicants who endanger national security or public order. A border procedure must be conducted in accordance with the basic principles and

---

[764] ECJ 6 May 2008, *Parliament v. Council*, C-133/06.
[765] Article 40(2) and (5) and Article 33(2)(d).

guarantees of Chapter II. If a decision has not been taken within four weeks, the applicant must be granted entry to the territory of the Member State. The border procedure thus presumes, in accordance with Article 2(p) of the Directive, that the right of the applicant to remain in the territory pending the examination of the application (Article 9) can be limited to the border. This provision must be read together with Article 8(3)(c) of the Reception Conditions Directive, which allows for the detention of asylum applicants in the context of a procedure on the applicant's right to enter the territory.

6.5.4. WITHDRAWAL AND APPEALS PROCEDURES

Articles 44–45 of the Procedures Directive lay down the procedural rules concerning the withdrawal of refugee status. Such proceedings may be started when new elements or findings arise which indicate that the grant of international protection must be reconsidered (Article 44). Article 45 lays down the safeguards that must be respected during such a procedure.

Article 46 Procedures Directive ensures that applicants have the right to an effective remedy before a court or tribunal against a decision on their asylum application. At first sight, the sorts of decisions which must be open to judicial challenge appear to be listed exhaustively, but the words 'a decision taken on their application for asylum' in Article 46(1)(a) suggest an interpretation that other decisions on asylum applications must also be open to judicial review. The Court of Justice explained, in *Samba Diouf*, that the decisions against which a remedy must exist are those that entail rejection of the application for either substantive or formal reasons.[766] Decisions pertaining to the organisation of the procedure (such as a decision to prioritise or accelerate the procedure) are not covered by Article 46. In so far as the latter type of decisions may affect the examination of the merits of the application however, they must be subject to judicial review in the action against the final decision rejecting the application. Article 46(2) specifies that decisions entailing the granting of subsidiary protection but refusal of refugee status must also allow for a remedy, unless the content of these statuses is the same in the Member State concerned. As is explained in the next two chapters, Member States may provide for lesser rights and benefits accruing to subsidiary protection status compared to refugee status.[767]

In conformity with the approach of the ECtHR in respect of *non-refoulement* in the context of Article 3 ECHR, Article 46(3) provides that at least in appeals in first instance, courts must conduct a 'full and *ex nunc*' assessment, i.e. take into

---

[766] ECJ 28 July 2011, *Samba Diouf*, Case C-69/10.
[767] See Chapters 7 and 8.

account facts and points of law that came to light after the decision by the determining authority was taken.[768]

As a rule, appeals procedures must provide for automatic suspensive effect, i.e. allow applicants to remain in the territory from the moment the appeal is brought and pending the outcome (Article 46(5)). This rule also corresponds to the case law of the ECtHR, which has frequently underlined that the effectiveness of a remedy against expulsion that arguably violates Article 3 ECHR requires that the remedy has 'automatic suspensive effect'.[769] In a limited number of situations however, including subsequent applications that have been declared inadmissible, Member States may also provide that courts decide, either upon request of the applicant or *ex officio*, whether the appeal entails a right to remain pending the outcome (Article 46(6)).

6.5.5. NOTES ON THE PROCEDURES DIRECTIVE

Although the revised Procedures Directive still contains a patchwork of extraordinary procedures and exceptions through which Member States retain considerable flexibility in arranging national procedures, it also aims at incorporating procedural human rights obligations that stem from the ECHR and EU Charter of Fundamental Rights. Thus, the Directive guarantees a right to remain pending the procedure, a right to (free) legal assistance, suspensive effect of appeals and the right to challenge the application of the concepts of safe country of origin, first country of asylum, safe third country and European safe third country.

The Procedures Directive is the first internationally agreed upon instrument that lays down such minimum requirements for asylum procedures. Moreover, the Procedures Directive must also be interpreted in accordance with provisions of the EU Charter of Fundamental Rights and general principles of EU law, amongst which the prohibition of *refoulement* and the right to an effective judicial remedy. These rights and principles are informed by, *inter alia*, the case law of the ECtHR and other human rights treaty monitoring bodies.[770] This implies that the precise content of safeguards contained in the Directive and the possibility to derogate from certain standards may well be given further substance.

---

[768] See, e.g., ECtHR 11 January 2007, *Salah Sheekh v. The Netherlands*, No. 1948/04, para 136 and ECtHR 29 January 2013, *S.H.H. v. The United Kingdom*, No. 60367/10, para. 72: 'A full and *ex nunc* assessment is called for as the situation in a country of destination may change over the course of time. Even though the historical position is of interest insofar as it may shed light on the current situation and its likely evolution, it is the present conditions which are decisive and it is therefore necessary to take into account information that has come to light since the final decision taken by the domestic authorities.'

[769] ECtHR 26 April 2007, *Gebremedhin v. France*, No. 25389/05, para. 66.

[770] See, more extensively, section 1.7.

6.6. THE TEMPORARY PROTECTION DIRECTIVE

During the 1990s, the conflicts in the former Yugoslavia demonstrated the need for a joint and comprehensive mechanism to deal with mass influxes of displaced persons. The Temporary Protection Directive (2001/55/EC) was set up to provide such a response mechanism. The Directive was the first legal instrument adopted in the legislative Tampere programme. Contrary to the other first phase Directives, it was not deemed necessary to revise it. The Directive is specifically designed to deal with situations of large numbers of displaced persons coming to the EU from a specific country or geographical area that is plagued by armed conflict or endemic violence.[771]

The Council has not, to date, set the Directive's mechanism in motion, even though calls were made to apply the Directive in response to the mass exodus of migrants and asylum seekers from Libya in 2011 and from Syria in 2012–14.[772]

The Directive serves three goals:

– to provide protection to large numbers of displaced persons who are (temporarily) unable to return to their country of origin;
– to prevent flooding of the asylum systems of Member States; and
– to ensure some form of burden sharing between Member States.

The exceptional character of the temporary protection mechanism is highlighted by the fact that the protection mechanism will only be set in motion after the Council has decided, by qualified majority, that a situation of mass influx exists (Article 5(1)). Such a decision is taken upon a Commission proposal. The decision is binding upon all Member States and describes to which group of persons temporary protection will apply and when protection should commence (Article 5(3)).

The fundamental difference between temporary protection and the normal protection scheme is that persons eligible for temporary protection – those indicated in the Council's decision – do not have to apply for asylum in the Member States, but are entitled to protection as soon as they are taken in by a Member State. The Council does not oblige the Member States to admit a specific number of persons. Instead, Chapter VI of the Directive calls upon Member States to receive persons eligible for temporary protection in a spirit of

---

[771] On the Temporary Protection Directive, extensively: K. Franssen, *Tijdelijke bescherming van asielzoekers in de EU. Recht en praktijk in Duitsland, Nederland en het Verenigd Koninkrijk en richtlijn 2001/55/EG*, Amsterdam: Boom (2011). See also K. Kerber, 'The Temporary Protection Directive', 4 *European Journal of Migration and Law* (2002), pp. 193–214.

[772] See, in respect of the Libya crisis: COM(2011) 248 final, para. 2.1 and Parliamentary Assembly of the Council of Europe, Resolution 1805 (2011), para. 14; and in respect of Syria: UNHCR Briefing note 16 October 2012, 'As Syria crisis continues, UNHCR urges EU States to uphold Common Asylum System principles'.

'Community solidarity' (Article 25(1)). To this end, Member States are to inform the Council about their reception capacities, which serves as basis for the distribution of persons among the Member States. When the number of displaced persons exceeds the indicated reception capacities, the Council has to re-examine the situation and to ask for additional support from the Member States (Article 25(3)).

Article 4(1) provides that the normal duration of temporary protection is one year, with a possible automatic extension of two six monthly periods for a maximum of one year. After this period, the Council may decide to extend the protection regime for another year (Article 4(2)). The maximum possible duration of temporary protection is, therefore, three years. The Council can at any time, however, decide to terminate the protection, provided that the situation in the country of origin is safe (Article 6).

During the duration of temporary protection, beneficiaries are granted the rights listed in Chapter III of the Directive. They are entitled to a residence permit for the duration of protection (Article 8); they have the right to engage in employed or self-employed activities (Article 12); they must have access to suitable accommodation (Article 13(1)), they must receive – if necessary – assistance in terms of social welfare, means of subsistence and emergency medical care (Article 13(2)); minors must have access to education (Article 14); and unaccompanied minors must receive the necessary representation and must be placed in an accommodation involving some form of supervision (Article 16). Article 15(2) provides for the reunification of family members who enjoy temporary protection in different Member States. Article 15(3) provides the right to family reunification when a sponsor enjoys temporary protection in a Member State, whereas his or her family members reside outside EU territory. These rights are subject to various possibilities of derogation.

When enjoying temporary protection, beneficiaries do have the right to apply for asylum according to the normal procedures (Article 17). Since the Reception Conditions Directive would normally apply to 'regular' asylum applicants, Article 19(1) allows Member States not to grant persons who make use of this possibility asylum applicant status, thereby withholding from them the rights provided by the Reception Conditions Directive (see also Article 3(3) Directive 2013/33/EU). Article 19(2) ensures that when refugee or subsidiary protection status is not granted after the examination of the application in the regular procedure, temporary protection beneficiaries continue to enjoy protection according to the provisions in the Temporary Protection Directive.

When the duration of temporary protection ends, former beneficiaries are to be treated according to the domestic asylum laws applicable in the Member State concerned (Article 20). The Directive expressly urges Member States to provide for voluntary returns (Article 21(1)), but does not exclude the possibility of enforced returns when the duration of temporary protection has ended and the beneficiary is not eligible for admission on regular grounds (Article 22). These enforced returns must be conducted with due respect for human dignity, without, however, defining what this dignity amounts to (Article 22(1)).

The United Kingdom and Ireland participate in the Directive; Denmark decided not to take part.[773]

6.7. PRACTICAL COOPERATION AND BURDEN SHARING

6.7.1. THE EUROPEAN ASYLUM SUPPORT OFFICE

In order to support Member States in asylum matters, the European Asylum Support Office (EASO) was created by Regulation 439/2010 on the basis of Articles 74 and 78(1) and (2) TFEU. Article 74 TFEU allows for the adoption of measures to ensure administrative cooperation between the Member States in the Area of Freedom, Security and Justice. The European Asylum Support Office was officially inaugurated in Malta on 19 June 2011. The agency has no power to take decisions on individual asylum requests.[774] Nor was it set up to monitor the asylum policies of the Member States. Although Member States recognised the importance of better cooperation in the field of asylum, they wanted to preserve the domain of individual decision-making as part of national sovereignty.[775]

EASO's mandate consists of three pillars. The first is support for practical cooperation on asylum (Articles 3–7). This includes the gathering, drafting and managing of country of origin information that can be used by Member States in the asylum procedure (Article 4). Article 4(e) also allows EASO to analyse country of origin information, but such analysis 'shall not purport to give instructions to Member States about the grant or refusal of applications for international protection'. EASO is also responsible for coordinating relocation. Relocation is the term used for the intra-EU transfer of recognised international protection beneficiaries. Such relocation can be organised if a Member State is faced with 'specific and disproportionate pressure on its asylum and reception system' (Article 5). Participation in relocation is not obligatory, but requires agreement of the Member States. A first pilot project concerned the intra-EU relocation from Malta, resulting in 277 persons being relocated to primarily Germany and France in 2011.[776] The reluctance of Member States to participate

---

[773] Although initially refusing to take part, Ireland opted in on 2 October 2003. See Council Decision 2003/690/EC.

[774] Recital 14 of the Preamble.

[775] See, on the creation of EASO, F. Comte, 'A New Agency is Born in the European Union: The European Asylum Support Office', 12 *European Journal of Migration and Law* (2012), pp. 373–405.

[776] EASO fact-finding report on intra-EU relocation activities from Malta, July 2012.

in (obligatory) relocation reflects the absence of a tradition in most European states to resettle refugees. Contrary to 'resettlement countries' such as the United States, Canada, Australia and New Zealand, which receive a substantial part of their total of refugees through specific annual resettlement programmes (in which refugees are pre-screened in regions of origin before being relocated to the host country), European countries traditionally receive refugees in the context of spontaneous arrivals.[777] The training of asylum decision-makers is a further form of ensuring practical cooperation, including through the 'European asylum curriculum', which provides common vocational training for employees of the immigration and asylum services in the Member States (Article 6).

The second pillar is support for Member States subject to particular pressure. The complex definition of 'particular pressure' in Article 8 reflects the difficulty to arrive at a common understanding of when a Member State is in a position that warrants support from other Member States. EASO should gather information on sudden arrivals of large numbers of third-country nationals and on asylum capacities in Member States (Article 9), and should coordinate support actions, but only at the request of the Member States (Article 10). Such support can take the form of the deployment of Asylum Support Teams in a Member State. These teams are formed by experts of the Member States, such as interpreters or country of origin experts (Articles 13–23). The first Asylum Support Teams were deployed in Greece in 2011 with a view to assisting Greece in setting up a 'modern and efficient asylum and reception system'.[778]

The third pillar is the contribution to the implementation of the CEAS. This relates to the gathering and exchange of information, reports and other documents with a view to improving the quality, consistency and effectiveness of EU asylum law and policy. This includes the drawing up of an annual report on the situation of asylum in the Union (Article 12).[779]

EASO has a management board, responsible for directing and managing the agency, in which the Member States and the European Commission are represented, with a voting right to each Member State and two voting rights for the Commission. EASO is led by an Executive Director, who is responsible for day-to-day management. It is further assisted by a Consultative Forum consisting of representatives of civil society and UNHCR.[780] The United Kingdom and Ireland take part in the regulation and are represented on the

---

[777] With the exception of Scandinavian countries, The United States and Canada together admitted nearly nine out of ten resettled refugees in 2012, see UNHCR Global Trends, 2012.

[778] Press release European Commission 1 April 2011, 'EU support to Greece: Asylum Support Teams are being deployed'. Also see EASO press release 7 March 2013, 'EASO and the Greek government sign agreement to extend EASO support to Greece until December 2014'.

[779] See EASO, 2011 Annual Report on the Situation of Asylum in the European Union and on the Activities of the European Asylum Support Office, 20 July 2012; EASO, Annual Report on the Situation of Asylum in the European Union 2012, 8 July 2013.

[780] Articles 24–31, 51.

Management Board, but may not vote on issues relating to asylum instruments to which they are not bound. Denmark does not take part in the regulation and has no voting rights, although EASO may facilitate cooperation with Denmark.[781]

6.7.2. FINANCIAL BURDEN SHARING

The creation of a well-functioning financial burden sharing mechanism was the original idea behind the setting up of the European Refugee Fund (ERF) in 2000.[782] The annual budget of this Fund,[783] around € 100 million in 2013 – considerably less than the original annual budget proposed by the Spanish Presidency of the Council in 1999 which amounted to € 3 billion – is, however, neither sufficient nor meant to cover the totality of expenses of Member States for receiving asylum seekers and providing assistance to refugees and subsidiary protection beneficiaries. The total estimated costs for the reception of asylum seekers in 2012 was, for example, € 403 million in Belgium, € 426 million in the Netherlands, and € 555 million in Sweden.[784]

The European Refugee Fund redistributes some of these expenses by 'supporting and encouraging the efforts made by the Member States in receiving and bearing the consequences of receiving refugees and displaced persons.'[785] Financial redistribution is achieved through allocating more funds to new Member States and to distribute resources in proportion to the number of asylum seekers and protection beneficiaries admitted in a Member State.[786] The Fund may also be used to finance emergency measures such as in the context of the Temporary protection directive or other situations of particular pressure.[787]

The Fund further incorporates the joint EU resettlement programme, by allocating a fixed amount of € 4,000–6,000 to the Member States for each resettled person.[788] Funding is only allocated if resettlement takes place in accordance with pre-established EU resettlement priorities. As of 1 January

---

[781] Article 48.
[782] Council Decision 2000/596/EC of 28 September 2000 establishing a European Refugee Fund; Council Decision 2004/904/EC of 2 December 2004 establishing the European Refugee Fund for the period 2005 to 2010; Council Decision 573/2007/EC of 23 May 2007 establishing the European Refugee Fund for the period 2008 to 2013.
[783] Article 12 Council Decision 573/2007/EC.
[784] European Migration Network, Ad-hoc Query on the total costs estimated for 2012 for the reception of asylum seekers, 24 April 2012.
[785] Article 2 Council Decision 573/2007/EC.
[786] Ibid, Article 13(1) and (2).
[787] Ibid, Article 5.
[788] See Decision 281/2012/EU amending the European Refugee Fund.

2014, the European Refugee Fund has been replaced by the Asylum and Migration Fund.[789]

FURTHER READING

H. Battjes, *European Asylum Law And International Law*, Leiden/Boston: Martinus Nijhoff (2006).

Boccardi, *Europe and Refugees: Towards an EU Asylum Policy*, The Hague: Kluwer Law International (2002).

K. Hailbronner (ed.), *European Immigration Law*, Munich: C.H. Beck (2010).

S. Peers and N. Rogers (eds.), *EU Immigration and Asylum Law: Text and Commentary*, Leiden/Boston: Martinus Nijhoff (2006).

M. Reneman, *EU Asylum Procedures and the Right to an Effective Remedy*, Oxford: Hart Publishing, 2014.

L. Slingenberg, *Between Sovereignty and Equality. The Reception of Asylum Seekers under International Law*, Oxford: Hart Publishing, 2014.

C. Smyth, *European Asylum Law and the Rights of the Child*, Oxford: Routledge, 2014.

---

[789] COM(2011) 751 final, Proposal for a regulation establishing the Asylum and Migration Fund.

7. REFUGEE PROTECTION

7.1. INTRODUCTION

Refugee protection refers to protection as a refugee in accordance with relevant international legal instruments. The 1951 Convention relating to the Status of Refugees[790] and the 1967 Additional Protocol[791] (hereafter referred to jointly as Refugee Convention, unless indicated differently) provide the cornerstone of the international legal regime for the protection of refugees.[792] In addition, refugee protection can be based on regional instruments, including the 1969 OAU Convention governing Specific Aspects of Refugee Protection in Africa,[793] and, in Latin America, the 1984 Cartagena Declaration.[794]

In the European Union, refugee protection is part of the Common European Asylum System, which is based on a full and inclusive application of the Refugee Convention.[795] According to the Treaty on the Functioning of the EU and case law of the Court of Justice of the European Union (CJEU), all legal and policy measures on asylum must be in accordance with the Refugee Convention. This includes measures on the qualification and treatment of persons as beneficiaries of refugee protection, as stipulated in the Qualification Directive.[796]

The Qualification Directive (2011/95/EU) aims to ensure that Member States 'apply common criteria for recognising applicants for asylum as refugees within the meaning of Article 1 of the Geneva [Refugee] Convention'.[797] The standards for the definition and the content of refugee protection laid down in the

---

790   The 1951 Convention relating to the Status of Refugees, 189 U.N.T.S. 137.
791   The 1967 Protocol relating to the Status of Refugees, 606 U.N.T.S. 267.
792   Qualification Directive, Recital 4.
793   1969 OAU Convention Governing Specific Aspects of Refugee Problems in Africa, 1001 U.N.T.S. 45.
794   1984 Cartagena Declaration on Refugees, Colloquium on the International Protection of Refugees in Central America, Mexico and Panama, 22 November 1984. Although not legally binding, the definition of a refugee contained in the Cartagena Declaration has been included either verbatim or with slight variations in the national legislation of many States in Latin America. Importantly, both instruments broaden the refugee protection regime to include people fleeing objective situations such as external or foreign aggression, domination, or occupation; generalized violence; internal conflicts; massive human rights violations; and events seriously disturbing public order.
795   Qualification Directive, Recital 3.
796   European Union, *Consolidated version of the Treaty on the Functioning of the European Union*, 13 December 2007, 2008/C 115/01, Article 78(1).
797   Qualification Directive, Recital 24.

Qualification Directive (2011/95/EU) are to guide Member States in the application of the Refugee Convention.[798]

In this regard, the United Nations High Commissioner for Refugees (UNHCR) may provide 'valuable guidance' when determining refugee status.[799] In the case of *Halaf* (C-528/11), the Court of Justice referred to UNHCR's documents as particularly relevant in the light of the role conferred on UNHCR by the Refugee Convention.[800] In a wide variety of resources UNHCR regularly comments on the Convention and gives its views on interpreting and applying the Refugee Convention.[801] Most important is the *UNHCR Handbook on Procedures and Criteria for Determining Refugee Status*, complemented and updated by its Guidelines on International Protection.[802] Other important UNHCR documents include the various thematic and country related notes or papers, including guidelines on eligibility for international protection[803] and interventions in court.[804] It is noteworthy that neither UNHCR's Handbook and Guidelines on International Protection nor any of its other documentation is legally binding for States Parties to the

---

[798]   Qualification Directive, Recital 23.

[799]   Qualification Directive, Recital 22.

[800]   Case C-528/11, *Halaf*, 30 May 2013, para. 44.

[801]   UNHCR's authority to give its views on the interpretation and application of the Refugee Conventions stems from its mandate and supervisory responsibility. UNHCR's mandate is primarily based on its Statute, UN General Assembly, *Statute of the Office of the United Nations High Commissioner for Refugees*, 14 December 1950, A/RES/428(V). UNHCR's responsibility to supervise the Refugee Convention is based on Paragraph 8(a) of its Statute, as well as the Preamble of the Refugee Convention. Further, in accordance with Article 35 Refugee Convention, States Parties are obliged to cooperate with UNHCR in the exercise of its functions, in particular, its supervisory responsibility. See also, UN High Commissioner for Refugees (UNHCR), *Note on the Mandate of the High Commissioner for Refugees and his Office*, October 2013. Volker Turk, Summary of Introductory Remarks, International Journal of Refugee Law Vol. 25 No. 2 pp. 394–398.

[802]   UNHCR's Handbook was issued at the request of Member States of the Executive Committee of the High Commissioner's Programme, and first published in 1979. It was re-edited in 1992 and reissued in 2011. Since 2001 the Handbook has been complemented by UNHCR's Guidelines on International Protection. As of 1 March 2014, 10 Guidelines on International Protection have been issued and concern key components of refugee status determination.

[803]   UNHCR's guidelines on eligibility for international protection are legal interpretations of the refugee criteria in respect of specific profiles on the basis of assessed social, political, economic, security, human rights and humanitarian conditions in the country or territory of origin concerned. The pertinent international protection needs are analysed in detail, and recommendations made as to how the applications for protection relate to relevant principles and criteria of international refugee law, as per the relevant legal instruments, in particular, the 1951 Convention and 1967 Protocol, but also the Qualification Directive. The Guidelines are based on in-depth research, information provided by UNHCR's global network of field offices and material from independent country specialists, researchers and other sources, rigorously reviewed for reliability. These Guidelines are aimed to assist decision-makers in assessing the international protection needs of asylum seekers.

[804]   UNHCR documentation is accessible via www.refworld.org.

Convention and that their impact arguably depends on the quality of reasoning.[805]

The current chapter describes the refugee protection regime based on the Refugee Convention, and regulated in, and developed under, the Qualification Directive, including through case law of the Court of Justice of the European Union. This Directive provides common standards for the qualification of persons as beneficiaries of international protection, i.e. as refugees or as persons eligible for subsidiary protection, as well as the content of such protection. Chapter I of the Qualification Directive concerns a general provision and a list of definitions. Chapter II deals with criteria relevant for both refugee protection and subsidiary protection, whereas Chapter III specifically deals with the qualification for being a refugee, for ceasing to be a refugee and for being excluded from being a refugee. Chapter IV then concerns provisions regarding the granting of refugee status and the ending thereof. Chapter V focuses on the qualification of subsidiary protection, followed, in Chapter VI, with provisions concerning the grant and end of subsidiary protection status. Chapter VII finally regulates the content of international protection, i.e. for both refugee status and subsidiary protection status.

As mentioned, the Qualification Directive provides for common, rather than minimum, standards for international protection. Nevertheless, Member States retain the right to introduce more favourable standards both for the qualification for protection and for the content thereof.[806]

Because of the primacy of the Refugee Convention, this chapter continues, in paragraph 7.2, with proving some background to the Refugee Convention. This is followed, in paragraph 7.3, by a discussion of the refugee definition; and, in paragraph 7.4, common criteria for international protection. In paragraph 7.5 issues relevant for assessing international protection, including evidentiary issues, the burden of proof and the benefit of the doubt, are addressed. This is followed, in paragraph 7.6, by cessation, exclusion and the ending of refugee status; and, finally, in paragraph 7.7, the content of refugee status. Chapter 8 subsequently deals specifically with subsidiary protection.

7.2. BACKGROUND TO THE REFUGEE CONVENTION

Because refugee protection in the European Union is primarily based on the Refugee Convention, it is relevant to provide a brief background to the Convention, including its history, object and purpose, and structure and content.

---

[805] Advocate General Sharpston in her Opinion in Case, C-31/09, *Bolbol*, 4 March 2010, para. 16, referred to UNHCR's persuasive, but not binding, statements.
[806] Qualification Directive, Article 3.

The Refugee Convention was adopted in 1951 entered into force on 22 April 1954. In 1967 a Protocol relating to the Status of Refugees was adopted as an instrument independent of, but very much related to, the Refugee Convention of 1951.[807] The objective of the Additional Protocol is to ensure equal status of all refugees in need of international protection, irrespective of a date clause that is contained in (Article 1A of) the Refugee Convention.[808] The Protocol entered into force on 4 October 1967.[809] According to Article 1(1) of the Protocol, the States Parties are obliged to apply Articles 2 to 34 of the Refugee Convention without the temporal limitation contained in Article 1A(2) of the Refugee Convention and without a geographical limitation contained in Article 1B of the Refugee Convention, except when states had already declared to opt for such a (geographical) limitation in accordance with the Refugee Convention.[810] A total of 148 states are party to both the Refugee Convention and the Protocol.[811]

The Preamble of the Refugee Convention affirms the principle that human beings shall enjoy fundamental rights and freedoms without discrimination, and contains a specific reference to the Universal Declaration of Human Rights. The Preamble stresses the social and humanitarian nature of the refugee problem. The Refugee Convention has a clear humanitarian character[812] and should be regarded as a human rights treaty.[813] Its object and purpose is the protection of fundamental (human) rights of people who are no longer protected by their own country and need to find protection elsewhere.

The Convention establishes a variety of rights and prescribes certain standards of treatment for refugees.[814]Article 1 Refugee Convention provides the

---

[807] G.S. Goodwin-Gill & J. McAdam, *The Refugee in International Law*, p. 507–508; Hathaway, James C., *The Rights of Refugees under International Law*, p. 111.

[808] Lauterpacht, Sir Elihu and Daniel Bethlehem, 'The scope and content of the principle of *non-refoulement*: Opinion', in: Erika Feller, Volker Türk and Frances Nicholson (eds.), *Refugee Protection in International Law, UNHCR's Global Consultations on International Protection*, p. 102.

[809] For more background information on the drafting and adoption of the 1967 Protocol: Bem, Kazimierz, 'The Coming of a 'Blank Cheque' – Europe, the 1951 Convention, and the 1967 Protocol', *IJRL* Vol. 16 (2004) No. 4, pp. 609–627.

[810] Three states – Cape Verde, the United States of America and Venezuela – are only party to the Protocol. Two states are only a party to the Refugee Convention: Madagascar and Saint Kitts and Nevis. There are currently four States parties that still apply the geographical limitation: the Republic of Congo (i.e. Congo Brazzaville), Madagascar, Monaco, and Turkey.

[811] Updated 1 March 2014.

[812] Lauterpacht, Sir Elihu and Daniel Bethlehem, 'The scope and content of the principle of *non-refoulement*: Opinion', in: Erika Feller, Volker Türk and Frances Nicholson (eds.), *Refugee Protection in International Law, UNHCR's Global Consultations on International Protection*, pp. 106 and 107.

[813] Hathaway, James C., *The Rights of Refugees under International Law*, p. 5: 'refugee law is a remedial or palliative branch of human rights law'; and p. 53: 'the first two operative paragraphs of the Preamble to the Refugee Convention unequivocally establish the human rights purposes of the treaty.'

[814] The 'human rights purposes' of the Refugee Convention were reaffirmed by its States Parties in a Declaration adopted at the Ministerial Meeting of State parties to mark the fiftieth

definition of the term 'refugee' and is divided into six sub-articles, numbered 1A to 1F. Articles 1A and 1B are the so-called inclusion clauses and define who is a refugee. Article 1C contains the cessation clauses stipulating the circumstances in which a refugee ceases to be a refugee. Articles 1D, 1E and 1F contain the exclusion clauses, according to which a person shall be excluded from being a refugee. If a person is a 'refugee' in accordance with Article 1 of the Refugee Convention, he has a number of rights in accordance with Articles 3 to 34 of the Refugee Convention, and the obligation to conform to the laws and regulations of the country of refuge (Article 2). The rights listed in the Refugee Convention can be divided into five categories. Each category relates to a level of attachment of the refugee to the country of refuge and determines a refugee's entitlements. While all refugees benefit from a number of core rights, additional rights accrue as a function of the nature and duration of the attachment to the country of refuge.[815] It is important to note that the rights of refugees are also governed by general international human rights law, laying down fundamental standards for the treatment of all human beings, including refugees.[816] The Refugee Convention does not provide for a right of the refugee to be granted a residence permit in the country of refuge. This remains the sovereign authority of the country of refuge.[817] Contrary to the Refugee Convention, the purpose of the Qualification Directive is, *inter alia*, to provide a uniform status for refugees (Article 1).

7.3.   THE DEFINITION OF A REFUGEE

Article 2(d) of the Qualification Directive defines a refugee for the purpose of the Directive. The wording of the definition corresponds largely with the principal definition of a refugee included in Article 1A(2) Refugee Convention.[818] According to Article 1A(2) Refugee Convention, a refugee is any person who:

owing to a well-founded fear of being persecuted for reasons of race, religion, nationality, membership of a particular social group or political opinion, is outside the country of his nationality, and is unable or, owing to such fear, is unwilling to

---

anniversary of the Refugee Convention in 2001. See Declaration of States Parties to the 1951 Convention and/or its 1967 Protocol Relating to the Status of Refugees, Ministerial Meeting of States Parties, Geneva, Switzerland, 12–13 December 2001, Preamble, paragraph 2; and operative paragraphs, para. 2, available as UN doc. HCR/MMSP/2001/09, 16 January 2002 and published in Feller, Erika, Volker Türk and Frances Nicholson (eds.), *Refugee Protection in International Law, UNHCR's Global Consultations on International Protection*, pp. 81–84.

[815]   J.C. Hathaway, *The Rights of Refugees under International Law*, p. 154.

[816]   See, more extensively, Alice Edwards, 'Human Rights, Refugees, and The Right 'To Enjoy' Asylum', *International Journal of Refugee Law*, Vol. 17 (2005), pp. 293–330.

[817]   Refugee Convention, Article 12.

[818]   Qualification Directive, Recital 24 stipulates, in this regard, that '[i]t is necessary to introduce common criteria for recognizing applicants for asylum as refugees within the meaning of Article 1 of the Geneva [Refugee] Convention.'

avail himself of the protection of that country; or who, not having a nationality and being outside the country of his former habitual residence, is unable or, owing to such fear, is unwilling to return to it.

A notable difference between this principal definition and the one contained in Article 2(d) Qualification Directive is that the latter refers only to third-country nationals, thereby excluding EU citizens from the Directive. This limitation is in accordance with the Protocol on Asylum for Nationals of Member States of the European Union ('Aznar Protocol') annexed to the founding treaties.[819] The compatibility of this limitation with the principle of non-discrimination among refugees regarding the country of origin under Article 3 Refugee Convention is doubtful. A conflict with the Refugee Convention may be avoided as paragraph (d) of the Aznar Protocol's only article allows Member States to unilaterally decide to treat the asylum application of a EU citizen as admissible.[820]

7.3.1.   GENERAL OBSERVATIONS

From the refugee definition follow five general observations.

First, a person is a refugee as soon as he fulfils the criteria contained in the definition. This necessarily occurs prior to the moment his status, as a refugee, is formally determined. Accordingly, recognition of his refugee status does not make him a refugee, but declares him to be one.[821] This implies that asylum seekers claiming to be refugees must benefit from core rights applicable to all refugees, irrespective of their level of attachment to the country of refuge. The Qualification Directive confirms the declaratory character of the recognition of a person as a refugee.[822] The Directive, however, seems to delay the acquisition of rights until refugee status has been granted. Many of the rights provided to refugees in accordance with the Qualification Directive are only provided once refugee status has been granted. Nevertheless, Article 20(1) Qualification Directive makes clear that the content of international protection 'shall be without prejudice to the rights laid down in the Geneva [Refugee] Convention. The content of international protection as a refugee is further explained in section 7.6.

Second, the definition protects persons who do not have a nationality, i.e. stateless persons. When explaining the Refugee Convention, we will include both nationals and stateless person and will refer to a person's country or origin rather than the country of nationality or former habitual residence.

---

[819] Qualification Directive, Recital 20.
[820] Notably, the application shall be dealt with on the presumption that it is manifestly unfounded and the European Council shall be informed immediately. See also section 8.3.
[821] *UNHCR Handbook*, para. 28.
[822] Qualification Directive, Recital 21. Also, Qualification Directive, Article 20(1).

Third, the definition is limited to persons who are outside their country of origin. To be a refugee, one needs to have crossed an international border. This is also referred to as the condition of alienage. Therefore, refugee protection cannot be claimed at embassies located within the country of origin. Under international law, embassies or other legations are part of the territory of the host country.

Fourth, the definition implies that the risk of persecution stems from a persecutor. Thus, the risk of persecution must be linked to human activities. Victims of hunger – unless people are intentionally starved – or natural disasters, are not refugees in accordance with the Refugee Convention.

Fifth, the fear of persecution must be linked to one of the reasons mentioned in the definition. This implies, amongst others, that victims of the indiscriminate effects of violence will normally not be refugees. This may be different in the context of subsidiary protection (see chapter 8.3.2).

7.3.2. WELL-FOUNDED FEAR

The concept of well-founded fear is the backbone of the refugee definition. It requires that there is a risk of persecution based on at least one of the reasons or grounds mentioned in the definition and in absence of protection from the country of origin. Neither the Refugee Convention nor the Qualification Directive elaborate upon the level of risk or on the evidentiary standard applicable beyond requiring that the risk must be well-founded. In this regard, the Court of Justice has noted that to 'ascertain whether or not the circumstances established constitute such a threat that the person concerned may *reasonably fear*, in the light of his individual situation, that he will in fact be subject to acts of persecution' [emphasis added].[823] The standard of 'reasonable possibility or chance' appears widely accepted.[824]

'Risk' implies a possibility of persecution in the future. It is not, therefore, necessary that the person has been persecuted in the past, although past experiences of persecution or serious harm 'is a serious indication of the applicant's well-founded fear of persecution' (see further section 7.5).[825]

The word 'fear' is somewhat unfortunate, as it suggests that the definition rests on a subjective component. While the emotion of fear is subjective, for purposes of refugee status determination the fear must be well-founded, implying that it must have an objective basis. There are varying degrees to which the subjective and objective element of the fear criterion may be weighed in an individual case. Where a person does not express an emotion of fear, objectively

---

[823] ECJ 5 September 2012, *Y and Z*, Cases C-71/11 and C-99/11, para. 76.
[824] UNHCR Handbook, para. 42. Also, Vanessa Holzer, *The 1951 Refugee Convention and the Protection of People Fleeing Armed Conflict and Other Situations of Violence*, September 2012, PPLA/2012/05, p. 14 (footnote 80 and 81).
[825] Qualification Directive, Article 4(4). Also, *UNHCR Handbook* para. 45.

the circumstances may, nonetheless, justify his recognition as a refugee, because they indicate there is a risk. Conversely, there may be instances where objective circumstances in themselves do not appear to be sufficient to indicate a risk, but where these circumstances, in conjunction with the individual's own background, belief system and activities, may indeed be considered as substantiating a well-founded fear for that individual, although the same objective circumstances might not be so considered for another.[826] So, it is not the frame of mind of the person concerned which is decisive for his claim, but the objective yardstick by which it is measured.[827] Fear, as a purely emotional state of mind, is neither decisive nor sufficient for claiming refugee protection.

The definition of a refugee is individualised as it refers to a person. A claim for protection as a refugee must be based on facts and circumstances that directly relate to the individual. The applicant must show that he personally has a well-founded fear of persecution. The well-founded fear may be based on a variety of personal facts as well as on general facts and circumstances that somehow relate to the individual concerned. It may also be based on experiences of others who are in a similar situation, such as family members or fellow political activists.[828] This does not exclude the possibility that a well-founded fear may be based on the fact that the individual concerned belongs to a group that as a whole is targeted. In such a case the fear or risk of collective persecution may be sufficient to warrant refugee protection for a whole group. The relevant question in such a situation is whether the group is targeted on a scale sufficient to determine that each individual member has a well-founded fear of persecution without any additional grounds being required, provided that there is a connection with one of the persecution grounds (see sections 7.3.3. and 7.3.5).

7.3.3. ACTS OF PERSECUTION

Neither the Refugee Convention nor the Qualification Directive define the term 'persecution'. Article 9 Qualification Directive, however, elaborates on 'acts of persecution', characterising such acts as either a single act that is 'sufficiently serious by its nature or repetition as to constitute a severe violation of basic human rights' (Article 9(1)(a)), or by 'accumulation of various measures, including violations of human rights which is sufficiently severe as to affect an individual in a similar manner' (Article 9(1)(b)).[829]

The meaning of 'persecution' is linked to Article 33(1) Refugee Convention. From this article, it may be inferred that a threat to life or freedom amounts to

---

[826] *UNHCR Handbook* paras. 37 to 40.
[827] A. Grahl-Madsen, *The Status of Refugees in International Law,* Vol. I, Sijthoff, Leiden, 1966, p. 174.
[828] *UNHCR Handbook*, para. 43. See also Qualification Directive, Article 4(3).
[829] *UNHCR Handbook*, para. 53.

persecution, as a refugee may not, according to that provision, be returned to a country where his life or freedom is threatened.[830] UNHCR goes further and states that other, serious, human rights violations may also amount to persecution, without specifying what human rights or what 'type' of violations.[831]

Both the Refugee Convention and the Qualification Directive acknowledge that human rights and the seriousness of a violation thereof are at the heart of 'persecution'.

The concept of 'basic human rights' referred to in the Qualification Directive is not further defined, although by way of example, reference is made to 'rights from which derogation cannot be made under Article 15(2) of the European Convention on Human Rights and Fundamental Freedoms'.[832] This reference to non-derogable rights, as listed in the ECHR, has been criticised as too restrictive and European focused.[833] The Court of Justice appears to agree. In the case of *Y and Z* (C-71/11 and C-99/11) the Court concluded that reference to non-derogable rights, as listed in Article 15(2) ECHR and in Article 9(1) Qualification Directive, is meant as 'a way of guidance, for the purpose of determining which acts must in particular be regarded as constituting persecution.'[834] Further, a restrictive interpretation of persecution would be difficult to reconcile with the various types of acts of persecution listed in a non-exhaustive way in Article 9(2) Qualification Directive.[835]

The seriousness of a violation is determined by the nature of the act or its repetition and the effect the act has on a person's human right(s). Acts of physical or mental violence, including acts of sexual violence; legal, administrative, police, and/or judicial measures which are discriminatory by nature or their way of implementation; prosecution or punishment which is disproportionate or discriminatory, or the denial of judicial redress that leads to disproportionate or discriminatory punishment; and acts of a gender- or child-specific nature, are

---

[830]   *UNHCR Handbook*, para. 51.

[831]   *UNHCR Handbook*, para. 51.

[832]   Article 15(2) ECHR: 'No derogation from Article 2, except in respect of deaths resulting from lawful acts of war, or from Articles 3, 4 (paragraph 1), and 7 shall be made under this provision'. This refers to the right to life (Article 2); the prohibition of torture and inhuman or degrading treatment of punishment (Article 3); the prohibition of slavery and forced labour (Article 4); and no punishment without law (Article 7).

[833]   Hemme Battjes, *European Asylum Law and International Law*, p. 233; Maarten den Heijer, 'Whose Rights and Which Rights? The Continuing Story of Non-Refoulement under the European Convention on Human Rights', *EJML* 2008, 277; Kees Wouters, *International Legal Standards for the Protection from Refoulement*, Intersentia, Antwerp: 2009, p. 61. Also, UNHCR, *UNHCR statement on religious persecution and the interpretation of Article 9(1) of the EU Qualification Directive*, 17 June 2011, C-71/11 & C-99/11, para. 4.1.2.

[834]   ECJ 5 September 2012, *Y and Z*, Cases C-71/11 and C-99/11, para. 57.

[835]   UNHCR, *UNHCR statement on religious persecution and the interpretation of Article 9(1) of the EU Qualification Directive*, 17 June 2011, C-71/11 & C-99/11, para. 4.1.6.

listed in Article 9(2) Qualification Directive.[836] Further, Recital 30 Qualification Directive also mentions genital mutilation, forced sterilisation and forced abortion as possible acts of persecution. The relevance of the effect of an act on a person's human right(s) for the act to amount to persecution, was addressed by the Court of Justice EU in the case of *X, Y and Z* (C-199/12, C-200/12 and 201/12). In this case, the Court was asked whether a legislative act could amount to persecution, in particular, whether the criminalisation of consensual same-sex relations between adults constitutes an act of persecution within the meaning of the Qualification Directive. According to the Court,

> the mere existence of legislation criminalising [consensual same-sex relations between adults] cannot be regarded as an act affecting the applicant in a manner so significant that it reaches the level of seriousness necessary for a finding that it constitutes persecution.[837]

What is relevant, according to the Court, is how the law is applied in practice, in particular, regarding the sanctions that are attached to the law, which would infringe basic human rights.[838]

Clearly, for human rights violations to amount to persecution, they must be serious. In the case of *Y and Z* (C-71/99 and C-99/11) the Court of Justice concluded, for example, that not every interference with the right to religious freedom constitutes an act of persecution, but that there must be a severe violation having a significant effect on the person concerned.[839] For a violation to be severe or serious to amount to persecution the Court noted that account should be made of the 'intrinsic severity [of the act] as well as the severity of their consequences for the person concerned.'[840]

As such, discrimination will not always amount to persecution. Differences in treatment of various groups will exist to a greater or lesser extent in many countries. Persons who receive less favourable treatment as a result of such differences are not necessarily victims of persecution. UNHCR has further qualified the notion of discrimination amounting to persecution by way of the following examples: when it seriously restricts the person's right to earn his livelihood, his right to practice his religion, or his access to normally available educational facilities.[841]

Article 9(2)(e) also mentions explicitly as an act of persecution, the 'prosecution or punishment for refusal to perform military service in a conflict, where performing military service would include crimes or acts falling within the scope of the grounds for exclusion as set out in Article 12(2)'. Therefore,

---

[836]   Qualification Directive, Article 9(2) (a), (b), (c), (d) and (f).
[837]   ECJ 7 November 2013, *X, Y and Z*, Cases C-199/12, C-200/12, and C-201/12, para. 55.
[838]   Ibid, paras. 57–61.
[839]   ECJ 5 September 2012, *Y and Z*, Cases C-71/99 and C-99/11, paras. 58, 59.
[840]   Ibid, para. 65.
[841]   *UNHCR Handbook*, para. 54.

conscientious objectors and draft evaders may be eligible for refugee protection, provided they object or evade military service in a conflict, and where performing military service would lead to the commission of excludable acts under Article 12(2) Qualification Directive (which incorporates Article 1F Refugee Convention). UNHCR has a different view, according to which the prosecution or punishment for the refusal to perform military service amounts to persecution if the refusal is based on ethical convictions and the prosecution or punishment is disproportionate or discriminatory.[842]

7.3.4.   REASONS FOR PERSECUTION

To be a refugee the person must have a well-founded fear of persecution for one (or more) of the five characteristics or qualities of the persecuted person, mentioned in Article 1A(2) of the Refugee Convention. These 'reasons' for persecution are also known as the Convention grounds, and are:

– race;
– religion;
– nationality;
– membership of a particular social group;
– political opinion.

When assessing the reasons for persecution, Member States are required to take into account a number of elements listed in Article 10 Qualification Directive and addressed below.

Race has to be understood in its widest sense, and includes considerations of colour, descent, or membership of a particular ethnic group.[843]

Nationality has overlap with race and not only refers to citizenship, but also to membership of a cultural, ethnic or linguistic group.[844] It may, further, refer to a group with a common geographical background, political origin or a relationship with the population of another state.[845] This rather broad interpretation of the concept of nationality is explained from the purpose of

---

[842]   *UNHCR Handbook*, paras. 167 to 174. UNHCR, Guidelines on International Protection No. 10: Claims to Refugee Status related to Military Service within the context of Article 1A(2) of the 1951 Convention and/or the 1967 Protocol relating to the Status of Refugees, HCR/GIP/13/10, 3 December 2013. The Guidelines identify five types of claims related to military service that may be grounds for refugee protection: (1) objection to state military service for reasons of conscience; (2) objection to military service in conflict contrary to the basic rules of human conduct; (3) conditions of state military service; (4) forced recruitment and/or conditions of service on non-state armed groups; and (5) unlawful child recruitment.
[843]   Qualification Directive, Article 10(1)(a). *UNHCR Handbook*, para. 68.
[844]   *UNHCR Handbook*, para. 74.
[845]   Qualification Directive, Article 10(1)(c).

refugee protection. On the one hand, it is not to be expected that a government will persecute its own citizens merely for having the nationality of that state. On the other hand, if a government persecutes people for having a foreign nationality, these people may be expected to find protection within their own country, in which case they cannot be defined as refugees.

Religion not only refers to well-known global religions such as Judaism, Christianity, Islam, Hinduism and Buddhism, but to any kind of religious community. According to Article 10(1)(b) Qualification Directive, the concept of religion shall, in particular, include the holding of theistic, non-theistic and atheistic beliefs; the participation in, or abstention from, formal worship in private or in public, either alone or in community with others; other religious acts or expressions of view; or forms of personal or communal conduct based on or mandated by any religious belief. In general, it refers to a person's right to freedom of thought, conscience and religion, and includes the freedom to change religion; to manifest religion, in public or in private; to teach, practice, worship; and observe religion. It can also refer to a person's right to have no religion.[846] In the case of *Y and Z* (C-71/11 and C-99/11) the Court of Justice confirmed the wide interpretation of the concept of religion considering that it is 'unnecessary to distinguish acts that interfere with the 'core areas' ('*forum internum*') of the basic right to freedom of religion, which do not include religious activities in public ('*forum externum*'), from acts which do not affect those purported 'core areas".[847] As such, according to the Court, a person cannot be expected to refrain from religious activities in public to avoid persecution.[848]

In general, there is no obligation on the part of individuals to exercise restraint, be discreet, or conceal their belief, opinion or identity in order to avoid persecution. This is an issue that is not only relevant in the context of 'religion', but also relevant in the context of other reasons for persecution, in particular, membership of a particular social group and political opinion. In the case of *X, Y and Z* (C-199/12, C-200/12 and C-201/12) the Court of Justice concluded that 'an applicant for asylum cannot be expected to conceal his [sexual orientation] in his country of origin in order to avoid persecution.'[849] Further, the UK Supreme Court has adopted the same principle in a case involving a claim for refugee protection for reasons of political opinion.[850]

---

[846]   *UNHCR Handbook*, paras. 71 to 73.

[847]   ECJ 5 September 2012, *Y and Z*, Cases C-71/11 and C-99/11, para. 62.

[848]   Ibid, paras. 79 and 80.

[849]   ECJ 7 November 2012, *X, Y and Z*, Cases C-199/12, C-200/12, para. 71. See also, *HJ (Iran) and HT (Cameroon) v. Secretary of State for the Home Department*, [2010] UKSC 31, United Kingdom: Supreme Court, 7 July 2010.

[850]   *RT (Zimbabwe) and others v. Secretary of State for the Home Department*, [2012] UKSC 38, United Kingdom: Supreme Court, 25 July 2012, in particular, paras. 22, 43 and 45. By way of analogy, the UK Supreme Court applied the principle that no restraint, discretion or concealment of a belief, opinion or identity can be expected of a person in order to avoid persecution, including when the person has no political belief and is obliged to pretend to

Membership of a particular social group is difficult to define, and is often regarded as a kind of residual category, although it still should be a group with distinguishable characteristics and may not be interpreted so broadly that the requirement that the fear of persecution is based on one of the reasons mentioned is no longer an independent requirement. This implies, in other terms, that the social group must exist independently of the persecution: the defining characteristic of the social group cannot be the fact that they fear persecution. For example, Chinese women fearing persecution because of the one-child policy in China are not a social group simply because they share a fear of persecution. A particular social group is often defined by focusing either on the group's internal characteristic or its external perception.[851] The Qualification Directive combines both in its definition of 'a particular social group', requiring cumulatively that the group has an internal or shared characteristic or belief, or common background; *and* being perceived as different by the surrounding society.[852]

Sexual orientation and/or gender identity are specifically mentioned as characteristics that may define a particular social group.[853] This is not without relevance, as in many parts of the world individuals are experiencing serious human rights violations due to their actual or perceived sexual orientation and/ or gender identity.[854] A person's sexual orientation and/or gender identity is so fundamental to a person's identity that it is an innate or immutable characteristic that cannot be concealed or renounced.[855]

Political opinion refers to the holding of an opinion, thought or belief that differs from his persecutors' opinion, polices or methods. Arguably, the term 'political' must be interpreted broadly, and may refer to any type of opinion on the state, society or public cause. Political opinion also includes being politically

---

support a political regime in order to avoid the persecution that he would suffer if his political neutrality were disclosed.

[851] This is often referred to as the 'protected characteristics approach' *versus* the 'social perception approach'; see UNHCR, Guidelines on International Protection No. 2: 'Membership of a particular social group' within the context of Article 1A(2) of the 1951 Convention and/or its 1967 Protocol relating to the Status of Refugees, HCR/GIP/02/02, 7 May 2002, paras. 5 to 13.

[852] Qualification Directive, Article 10(1)(d). UNHCR acknowledges the validity of each approach separately in line with established state practice; see UNHCR, Guidelines on International Protection No. 2: 'Membership of a particular social group' within the context of Article 1A(2) of the 1951 Convention and/or its 1967 Protocol relating to the Status of Refugees, HCR/ GIP/02/02, 7 May 2002, paras. 5 to 9; and UNHCR, *UNHCR public statement in relation to decisions J.E.F. and A.O. by the Cour nationale du droit d'asile*, 12 June 2012, para. 2.1.3.

[853] Qualification Directive, Article 10(1)(d) final indent. Also, Qualification Directive, Recital 30.

[854] UNHCR, Guidelines on International Protection No. 9: Claims to Refugee Status based on Sexual Orientation and/or Gender Identity within the context of Article 1A(2) of the 1951 Convention and/or its 1967 Protocol relating to the Status of Refugees, HCR/GIP/12/09, 23 October 2012, paras. 1 to 4.

[855] ECJ 7 November 2013, *X, Y and Z*, Cases C-199/12, C-200/12, and C-201/12, para. 70.

neutral and not holding or having a political opinion.[856] To fear persecution for reasons of political opinion presupposes that the opinion has come to the attention of the persecutors. There is a variety of ways as to how the persecutor may become aware of a person's political opinion, such as a publication, a speech, a conversation, or participation in a demonstration or wearing certain clothes. There may, however, also be situations in which the applicant has not given any expression to his opinions, but where his convictions are so strong that there may be an assumption that these opinions will sooner or later find expression, and that the applicant will, as a result, come into conflict with the authorities. Where this can be reasonably be assumed, the applicant can be considered to have fear of persecution for reasons of political opinion.[857]

In the explanations above regarding the various reasons for persecution it was presumed that an individual actually has the characteristic for which he is persecuted. There may, however, also be situations where the individual concerned does not, in reality, have such a characteristic, but may be *perceived* as having one or is attributed one. In such situations the person concerned may also be recognised as a refugee as is recognised by Article 10(2) Qualification Directive.[858]

7.3.5. CONNECTION BETWEEN ACTS OF PERSECUTION AND THE REASONS FOR PERSECUTION

A refugee must have a well-founded fear of being persecuted *for reasons of* one of the five characteristics mentioned in the definition. The phrase 'for reasons of' implies a nexus between the well-founded fear of persecution and one (or more) of the grounds listed in the refugee definition. The Qualification Directive (2011/95/EU) refers to a 'connection' between the reasons and the act of persecution or the absence of protection against such acts in Article 9(3) and, in Recital 29, to a 'causal link'. How should this connection be interpreted, or, what kind of causality is required between the act of persecution or the absence of protection and the reasons?

One may argue that the (perceived) characteristic of the refugee must be the main reason or the direct cause for the persecution. However, such conception would imply a high standard of proof for the refugee, who must then show that he was persecuted for precisely one of the grounds. Because the text of the refugee definition does not compel the adoption of such a strict standard, it

---

[856] UNHCR, *UNHCR intervention before the Supreme Court of the United Kingdom in the case of RT (Zimbabwe) and others (Respondents) v Secretary of State for the Home Department*, 25 May 2012, 2011/0011, para. 8.
[857] *UNHCR Handbook*, para. 82.
[858] Also, *UNHCR Handbook*, para. 80.

appears appropriate to assume that it is also sufficient that the ground must be just one of the perhaps many reasons for the persecution.

Further, the connection between a well-founded fear of persecution and the reasons for persecution should not be interpreted as requiring that the persecutor must have the *intention* to persecute because of one of these reasons. To require an element of intent would again imply a high standard of proof for the refugee, and does not follow from the text of the Convention. Obviously, the motives of the persecutor may be relevant in establishing whether a person has a well-founded fear of persecution, but the precise motives may be difficult to establish, and they may, moreover, be related to acts and expressions of the individual which do not necessarily correspond to that person's true beliefs or characteristics.

When the fear of persecution emanates from non-state actors, the connection with the persecution reasons may be linked to the state as the responsible protector, if the state is unwilling or unable to provide protection precisely because of one of these five reasons. An example is the problem of domestic violence, whereby a woman is abused by her husband, and where the woman, on that account, has a well-founded fear of being subjected to inhuman treatment. There may be a variety of reasons as to why she is maltreated, none of which are linked to one of the reasons for persecution, as far as the husband is concerned. Nevertheless, the woman may be a refugee if the state is unwilling or unable to protect her, for example, because domestic violence against women is accepted in society or even approved by law. In that case, the reason for persecution is that women in that country belong to a particular social group, of – most likely – women who have transgressed the social mores of society, which is not protected by the state against domestic violence. Another reason the state may fail to provide protection can be that the woman belongs to a certain ethnic or religious minority, and for that reason, is discriminated by the police authorities, in, for example, refusing to provide assistance or instigate prosecution. In this case, the reason for persecution is the woman's ethnicity or religion.

7.3.6. PEOPLE FLEEING ARMED CONFLICT

Before addressing in the next paragraph common criteria for international protection it is important to focus briefly on the protection of people fleeing armed conflict. In mid-2013 the majority of refugees came from countries that are experiencing conflict.[859] There is concern that many persons fleeing these

---

[859] In mid-2013, Afghanistan, the Syrian Arab Republic, Somalia, Sudan and the Democratic Republic of the Congo were the top five source countries of refugees. Together they accounted for 60% of all refugees worldwide. See UNHCR, Mid-Year Trends 2013, 19 December 2013.

conflicts meet the criteria for refugee protection but are not recognised as such, and are not granted refugee status.[860]

The second half of the 20th century saw a steep rise in the number of internal armed conflicts involving a diversity of armed actors along with different modes of violence. The Refugee Convention is the primary instrument for providing international protection, including to those fleeing armed conflict. Nothing in the text, context or object and purpose of the Convention hinders its application to persons fleeing armed conflict. According to UNHCR, persons compelled to leave their country because of an armed conflict are not normally considered to be refugees under the Refugee Convention.[861] In part, this is because of the difficulty in assessing a well-founded fear and establishing the link between one or more Convention grounds and the well-founded fear of persecution.

A person's risk of being persecuted must be assessed in the context of the overall situation in the country of origin, taking into account general, as well as individual, circumstances. In a situation of armed conflict, whole communities may suffer or be at risk of persecution. The fact that many or all members of particular communities may be equally at risk may well determine that the individual's fear of being persecuted is well-founded. There is no basis in the Refugee Convention for holding that in armed conflict situations; a person needs to establish a risk of persecution over and above that of others caught up in such situations. There is nothing in the text of the Refugee Convention to suggest that a refugee has to be singled out for persecution, either generally or over and above other persons at risk of being persecuted. A person may have a well-founded fear of persecution that is shared by many others.

Determining which Convention ground or grounds is of relevance for a person fleeing armed conflict is not easy. When assessing international protection for persons fleeing armed conflict, each – and more than one – of the Convention grounds may be relevant. An analysis of the causes, character and impact of the conflict is necessary to determine the relevant ground(s) and the connection with the well-founded fear of persecution. The conflict may be motivated or driven by ethnic, religious, political, or social divisions; or may impact people along ethnic, religious, political, social or gender lines.

In some armed conflicts harm may appear to be indiscriminate. However, the underlying causes, character and/or impact of the violence causing harm may reveal that it is, in fact, discriminate. For example, on the face of it, civilians

---

860   UNHCR, *Safe at Last? Law and Practice in Selected EU Member States with Respect to Asylum-Seekers Fleeing Indiscriminate Violence*, 27 July 2011, p. 101.

861   UNHCR, *Handbook and Guidelines on Procedures and Criteria for Determining Refugee Status under the 1951 Convention and the 1967 Protocol Relating to the Status of Refugees*, December 2011, HCR/1P/4/ENG/REV.3, para. 164. Also, UN High Commissioner for Refugees (UNHCR), *Summary Conclusions on International Protection of Persons Fleeing Armed Conflict and Other Situations of Violence; Roundtable 13 and 14 September 2012, Cape Town, South Africa*, 20 December 2012, para. 6.

in a particular conflict may appear to be at a general risk of harm from bombing. However, such a method of warfare may also be used to target particular groups of civilians or the areas where they reside or gather, because of their real or perceived ethnic, religious, political, or social profiles.[862] Where this is the case, these acts may be persecutory and linked to a Convention ground. Notably, too, violence may be both generalised (for example, because it is experienced throughout the territory) and discriminate (for example, because there are targeted attacks against particular groups) at the same time.[863]

7.4. COMMON CRITERIA FOR INTERNATIONAL PROTECTION

The Qualification Directive contains in Articles 4–8 common provisions on the assessment of claims for international protection. These provisions apply not only in determining whether one qualifies for refugee status, but also to subsidiary protection. It is likely to assume that the interpretation of these provisions is not only guided by the Refugee Convention, but also by the prohibition of *refoulement,* as developed in general human rights law, including in the case law of the ECtHR. The current section describes the legal concepts mentioned in Articles 5–8 of the Directive. Section 7.5 describes matters relating to evidence and proof, which are regulated in Article 4 of the Directive.

7.4.1. INTERNATIONAL PROTECTION '*SUR PLACE*'

The prospective nature of the concept of 'well-founded fear' and 'real risk' implies that the risk of persecution or serious harm may also arise after the person concerned has left his or her country of origin. This situation originates from the French concept '*refugié sur place*', indicating that a person can become a refugee 'on the spot', when he already finds himself in the host country. The Qualification Directive recognises this concept in Article 5 for both refugee and subsidiary protection.

---

[862] See, in this regard, UNHCR's assessment of the conflict in Syria, UNHCR, *International Protection Considerations with regard to people fleeing the Syrian Arab Republic, Update II,* 22 October 2013, para. 14 (ft. 56). Also, Vanessa Holzer, The 1951 Convention and the Protection of People Fleeing Armed Conflict and Other Situations of Violence, UNHCR: PPLA/2012/05, September 2012, pp. 22 and 23.

[863] UNHCR, *Summary Conclusions on International Protection of Persons Fleeing Armed Conflict and Other Situations of Violence; Roundtable 13 and 14 September 2012, Cape Town, South Africa,* 20 December 2012, para. 17.

There are two ways international protection *sur place* can arise.[864] First, based on events which have taken place since the individual left the country of origin (Article 5(1)), and, second, as a result of activities which the individual has engaged in since he or she left the country of origin, 'in particular where it has been established that the activities relied upon constitute the expression and continuation of convictions or orientations held in the country of origin' (Article 5(2)). This could be taken to mean that the latter situation can only give rise to international protection if the conduct is the continuation of actions, convictions or orientations already held in the country of origin.[865] The Qualification Directive even goes on to state in Article 5(3), specifically in the context of refugee protection, that for subsequent applications 'Member States may determine that an applicant who files a subsequent application should not normally be granted refugee status if the risk of persecution is based on circumstances which the applicant has created by his or her own decision since leaving the country of origin.' This restrictive language must be explained from a concern on the part of Member States that persons could otherwise 'fabricate' their own refugee status.

The words 'in particular' in Article 5(2) suggest, however, that continuation is no absolute requirement.[866] Article 5(3), moreover, mentions that the provision is without prejudice to the Refugee Convention. This is reference is important, because the wording of Article 1A(2) Refugee Convention does not appear to leave much room for applying a continuation requirement, as incorporated in the Qualification Directive. What is relevant for being able to be defined as a refugee is that there is a risk (well-founded fear) of persecution, irrespective of when or how this risk was developed, and irrespective of whether it was deliberately created or not.[867]

Further, and this is recognised in the Directive because Article 5(3) only refers to refugee status, it is consistent case law of the ECtHR that it does not matter as a matter of principle, in the examination of whether there is a real risk of ill-treatment upon return, at what moment in time the risk arises or why the person has chosen to engage in particular activities.[868]

---

[864] *UNHCR Handbook* paras. 95 and 96.
[865] On this requirement, see T.P. Spijkerboer and B.P. Vermeulen, *Vluchtelingenrecht*, pp. 63–64.
[866] See to this effect, Council of State (The Netherlands) 13 January 2010, LJN BL0267.
[867] James C. Hathaway, *The Law of Refugee Status*, pp. 33 to 39.
[868] See especially ECtHR 15 May 2012, *S.F. v. Sweden*, No. 52077/10 (concerning political activities employed in Sweden). Also see ECtHR 31 August 2004, *A.B. v. Sweden*, No. 24697/04 (concerning publication of a book in Sweden) and ECtHR 20 July 2010, *N. v. Sweden No.* 23505/09 (concerning a divorce and a Westernised way of life in Sweden).

7.4.2. ACTORS OF PERSECUTION AND SERIOUS HARM AND ACTORS OF PROTECTION

Acts of persecution or serious harm involve a persecutor. The basic presumption is that the state from which the person flees is held responsible, either for actively performing acts of persecution or serious harm, through its organs such as the police or military,[869] or for failure to protect against acts of persecution or serious harm performed by non-state actors. According to Article 6 Qualification Directive (2011/95/EU), actors of persecution or serious harm include:

(a) the state;
(b) parties or organisations controlling the state or a substantial part of the territory of the state; and
(c) non-state actors, if it can be demonstrated that the actors mentioned in points (a) and (b), including international organisations, are unable or unwilling to provide protection against persecution or serious harm, as defined in Article 7.

Article 7(1) Qualification Directive refers to 'actors of protection', and mentions exhaustively the state and parties or organisations, including international organisations, controlling the state or a substantial part of the territory of the state, provided they are willing and able to offer protection.[870]

Linking actors of persecution or serious harm with the availability of protection, the relevant question is whether the country of origin can avoid persecution or serious harm by providing protection. Regarding refugee protection, this corresponds with the definition of a refugee according to which a person is a refugee if he 'is unable or, owing to such fear, is unwilling to avail himself of the protection of that country' and respects the object and purpose of the Refugee Convention.[871]

It is essential that the protection provided is 'effective' and 'of a non-temporary nature'.[872] According to Article 7(2) Qualification Directive, such protection is generally provided when the actors of protection 'take reasonable steps to prevent the persecution or suffering of serious harm, *inter alia*, by operating an effective legal system for the detection, prosecution and punishment of acts constituting persecution or serious harm, and when the

---

[869] *UNHCR Handbook*, para. 65.
[870] Interestingly, Recital 26 Qualification Directive states that protection can be provided by parties or organisations that '*control a region or a larger area* within the territory of the state' [emphasis added].
[871] *UNHCR Handbook*, paras.100 and 106, emphasising that national protection takes precedence over international protection.
[872] Qualification Directive, Article 7(2).

applicant has access to such protection.' The wording of Article 7(2) Qualification Directive implies that actors of protection have an 'obligation of conduct', i.e. 'take reasonable steps', rather than an 'obligation of result'. This appears to be at variance with the principal requirements that protection is 'effective' and 'non-temporary', as well as that the protection must be such as to alleviate the risk of persecution or serious harm below being well-founded or real. This view was confirmed by the Court of Justice in the case of *Abdulla* (C-175/08, C-176/08, C-178/08, and C-179/08), considering that 'factors which formed the basis of the refugee's fear of persecution [have to be] permanently eradicated.'[873] The adequacy of non-state actors being capable of providing protection can be contested. Oftentimes, they do not have the competencies of a state or the capacity to enforce the rule of law. What is, however, relevant for the Court is that the country of origin, and thereby the relevant actor of protection, is able to ensure protection against acts of persecution or serious harm.[874]

In reality, when the actor of persecution or serious harm is an *agent* of the state, protection will probably be difficult to find,[875] unless there are effective legal remedies available to challenge the acts of such agents, or a non-state actor is controlling (a part of) the state's territory. If the risk emanates from *non-state actors* it may be more likely that the state is willing to provide protection. However, states do no always have the ability to do so,[876] in particular, when the non-state agents control a certain part of the country. If non-state agents are the actors of persecution or serious harm, the individual must at least try and seek protection from his government, unless it is evident that protection will not be afforded. A country without a functioning government may still produce refugees and others in need of international protection. What is relevant is that the person cannot avail himself of the protection of his country.[877] The main problem for a person to be defined as a refugee in the case of a failed state does not relate to the assessment of persecution or the identification of the persecutor as such, but concerns the persecution reasons, as it may be difficult to determine for what reasons the person is harmed.

---

[873] ECJ 2 March 2010, *Abdulla*, Cases C-175/08, C-176/08, C-178/08 and C-179/08, para. 73.

[874] Ibid, para. 68. For the incapability of multinational troops to provide protection (in Iraq) see ECtHR 2 March 2010, *Al-Saadoon and Mufdhi v. UK*, No. 61498/08, ECtHR 7 July 2011, *Al-Jedda v. UK*, No. 27021/08; ECtHR 7 July 2011, *Al-Skeini v. UK*, No. 55721/07.

[875] ECtHR 15 November 1996, *Chahal v. the United Kingdom*, No. 22414/93. ECtHR 6 March 2001, *Hilal v. the United Kingdom*, No. 45276/99.

[876] ECtHR 29 April 1997, *H.L.R. v. France*, No. 24573/97, para. 40.

[877] ECtHR 11 January 2007, *Salah Sheekh v. The Netherlands*, No. 1948/04, para. 147.

7.4.3. INTERNAL PROTECTION[878]

Apart from the possibility of receiving protection from a specific actor, a person may also be deemed to seek protection in another part of the country of origin.[879] Article 8(1) Qualification Directive considers an internal protection alternative available if, in a part of the country of origin, there is (a) no well-founded fear of being persecuted or no real risk of suffering serious harm; or (b) access to protection against persecution, or serious harm, provided that the person can 'safely and legally travel to and gain admittance to that part of the country and can reasonably be expected to settle there'. Further, based on up-to-date information, the general circumstances prevailing in the alternative part of the country of origin, and the personal circumstances of the individual, should be taken into account.[880] The criteria for internal protection correspond largely with the views of UNHCR, who has added that it must be reasonable for a person to relocate to an alternative part of the country of origin where he can lead a relatively normal life without facing undue hardship.[881] According to the Court of Justice, for protection in the country of origin to be regarded as effective or reasonable, basic human rights must be guaranteed.[882]

Further, according to the ECtHR, for relying on an internal protection alternative, the safety of the alternative area must be guaranteed:[883] the durability thereof, in terms of in practice being able to remain and settle in the area:[884] and the safe accessibility of the alternative area.[885]

---

[878] The concept of 'internal protection' is often referred to as the internal protection, flight or relocation alternative. See UNHCR, Guidelines on International Protection No. 4: 'Internal Flight or Relocation Alternative' within the Context of Article 1A(2) of the 1951 Convention and/or 1967 Protocol relating to the Status of Refugees, HCR/GIP/03/04, 23 July 2004. Also, James C. Hathaway and Michelle Foster, 'Internal protection/relocation/flight alternative as an aspect of refugee status determination', in: Erika Feller, Volker Turk and Frances Nicholson (eds.), *Refugee Protection in International Law*, pp. 357–417.

[879] *UNHCR Handbook*, para. 91: 'the fear of being persecuted need not always extend to the whole territory of the refugee's country of nationality. Thus in ethnic clashes or in cases of grave disturbances involving civil war conditions, persecution of a specific ethnic or national group may occur in only part of the country.'

[880] Qualification Directive, Article 8(2).

[881] UNHCR, Guidelines on International Protection No. 4: 'Internal Flight or Relocation Alternative' within the Context of Article 1A(2) of the 1951 Convention and/or 1967 Protocol relating to the Status of Refugees, HCR/GIP/03/04, 23 July 2004, paras. 22 to 30.

[882] ECJ 2 March 2010, *Abdulla*, Cases C-175/08, C-176/08, C-178/08 and C-179/08, para. 71.

[883] The Court links the issue of safety to the strict standards of Article 3 ECHR, implying that there must be a real risk of prohibited ill-treatment or a real risk of indirect *refoulement* for the alternative area to be regarded as unsafe, ECtHR 11 January 2007, *Salah Sheekh v. The Netherlands*, No. 1948/04, para. 141. Also, ECtHR 28 June 2011, *Sufi and Elmi v. The United Kingdom*, Nos. 8319/07 and 11449/07, para. 266. ECtHR 27 June 2013, *S.A. v. Sweden*, No. 66523/10, para. 53.

[884] ECtHR 28 June 2011, *Sufi and Elmi v. The United Kingdom*, Nos. 8319/07 and 11449/07, para. 267.

[885] ECtHR 11 January 2007, *Salah Sheekh v. The Netherlands*, No. 1948/04, paras. 141 and 143.

7.5. EVIDENCE, PROOF AND THE BENEFIT OF DOUBT

In the above, it was discussed what circumstances give rise to refugee status and what common criteria apply to international protection in general. In a large number of asylum cases, however, the question is not central of whether the facts presented meet the standard of a well-founded fear for persecution or a real risk of ill-treatment, but whether one can believe that the facts and circumstances, as presented, are true. Refugee status determination by and large consists of two steps. In the first stage, relevant information is gathered, the factual circumstances are identified, and the credibility of the asylum seeker and his story are determined. The second step consists of a legal appraisal of that evidence, which entails determining whether the factual circumstances make a person eligible for protection.[886]

In refugee status determinations, it is often difficult to establish the factual circumstances, since documentary evidence is not always available. As the UNHCR Handbook notes, 'an applicant may not be able to support his statements by documentary or other proof, and cases in which an applicant can provide evidence of all his statements will be the exception rather than the rule.'[887] In most cases, a person fleeing persecution will have arrived with the barest necessities, very frequently even without personal documents, and there may be nobody around who may testify to support his story.[888] It is generally accepted that, because of the inherent difficulties asylum seekers face in proving a claim, the general legal principle that the burden of proof lies on the person submitting a claim is not appropriate for asylum cases.[889]

Efforts to establish the 'truth' may further be impeded by a range of factors influencing how the applicant cooperates with the asylum official.[890] The applicant may have reason to distrust any authority and be afraid to speak freely and give a full and accurate account of his case. Alternatively, he may have been threatened by a human smuggler not to disclose how he arrived in the country of asylum. He may also put forward a false story because he has been told it is a 'winning script' – even though he might have a promising asylum narrative of his own. It can also happen that the asylum seeker is ashamed or stressed about past experiences and is therefore reluctant to display complete openness.

---

[886] ECJ 22 November 2012, *M. M. v Minister for Justice, Equality and Law Reform, Ireland and Attorney General*, Case C-277/11, para. 64.

[887] UNHCR Handbook, para. 196.

[888] Ibid.

[889] E.g. B. Gorlick, 'Common Burdens and Standards: Legal Elements in Assessing Claims to Refugee Status', 15(3) *International Journal of Refugee Law* (2003), 357–376 at 362. UNHCR Handbook, para. 203.

[890] See, extensively, UNHCR Report, Beyond Proof, Credibility Assessment in EU Asylum Systems, May 2013.

Furthermore, cultural and linguistic differences between the asylum seeker and an asylum official may very well lead to misunderstandings and misinterpretations. On their part, asylum authorities are obviously hampered in collecting evidence, as they will not normally have access to the country of origin. All this makes the establishment of facts and circumstances a highly delicate affair.

Although Member States are, in principle, free to organise their own solutions to these problems, some outer limits to that freedom sprout from Union law, the case law of the ECtHR and UNHCR guidelines. These supranational standards govern the procedural phase of collecting evidence and establishing the facts. As was already highlighted in the previous chapter, the Asylum Procedures Directive lays down a range of procedural safeguards that take account of the inherent difficulties asylum seekers may face in bringing a claim. These range from more general safeguards, such as the obligation to examine asylum claims on an individual, objective and impartial basis, the right to an interpreter, the right to legal assistance and the training and competence of decision makers; to more specific guarantees, such as the obligation to ensure confidentiality of asylum interviews, the obligation that the interviewer is of the same sex as the applicant if the latter so requests, and the rule that the interviewer does not wear a military or law enforcement uniform.[891]

7.5.1. THE BURDEN OF PROOF

In addition to these procedural guarantees, the Qualification Directive sets forth some basic rules on the evidentiary assessment. Article 4(1) contains two rules relating to the burden of proof. Firstly, Member States may consider it the duty of the applicant to submit evidence in support of his claim. But, secondly, it is the duty of the Member State to cooperate with the applicant in determining the relevant elements of an asylum application. This is also referred to as the 'shared duty' of the state and the asylum seeker. The Court of Justice has explained that this duty means, in practical terms, that if, for any reason whatsoever, the evidence provided by an applicant is not complete, up-to-date or relevant, the Member State authorities must cooperate actively with the applicant, so that all the relevant evidence may be assembled. This reflects the fact that a Member State may be better placed than an applicant to gain access to certain types of documents.[892]

Union law on this issue corresponds with the consistent case law of the ECtHR that '[i]t is in principle for the applicant to adduce evidence capable of

---

891   Directive 2013/32/EU, Articles 10, 12, 14 and 15.
892   ECJ 22 November 2012, *M. M. v Minister for Justice, Equality and Law Reform, Ireland and Attorney General*, Case C-277/11, para. 66.

proving that there are substantial grounds for believing that expulsion entails a real risk of ill-treatment', and that, '[w]here such evidence is adduced, it is for the Government to dispel any doubts about it.'[893] Likewise, UNHCR's Handbook sets forth that 'while the burden of proof in principle rests on the applicant, the duty to ascertain and evaluate all the relevant facts is shared between the applicant and the examiner.'[894] It follows from all these sources that the Member State may not limit itself to statements and documentation presented by the applicant, but must actively contribute to the collection, assessment and appreciation of evidence.

The ECtHR judgment in *R.C. v Sweden* provides an example of this investigative duty on the part of the state. It concerned an applicant from Iran who had produced a medical certificate which stated that the scars around his ankles, kneecaps and neck could very well originate from the torture to which he claimed that he had been subjected in Iran, namely, that he had been chained around his ankles and that boiling water had been thrown at his chest. The Swedish authorities argued that the medical certificate did not prove that the applicant had been tortured, as the scars could also have a different cause. The ECtHR considered, however, in its assessment of whether there existed a real risk of ill-treatment contrary to Article 3 ECHR upon return, that the medical certificate gave a rather strong indication that the applicant's scars may have been caused by torture and that, in such circumstances, it was for the Swedish authorities 'to dispel any doubts that might have persisted as to the cause of such scarring'. The authorities should therefore have directed that an expert opinion be obtained as to the probable cause of the applicant's scars.[895]

The Court of Justice explained the burden of proof in a similar manner in the case of *X, Y and Z*, concerning three homosexual asylum seekers from Sierra Leone, Uganda and Senegal.[896] At the material time, legislation in these three countries criminalised homosexual activity. The Court held that where an applicant demonstrates the existence in his country of origin of legislation criminalising homosexual acts, it is for the national authorities to undertake, pursuant to Article 4 of the Qualification Directive, an examination of all the relevant facts concerning that country of origin, including the question of whether criminal sanctions are actually imposed on homosexuals in that particular country.[897]

---

[893] ECtHR 28 February 2008, *Saadi v. Italy*, No. 37201/06, para. 129; ECtHR 22 September 2009 *Abdolkhani and Karimnia v. Turkey*, no. 30471/08; ECtHR 9 March 2010, *R.C. v. Sweden*, No. 41827/07.

[894] UNHCR Handbook, para. 196.

[895] ECtHR 9 March 2010, *R.C. v. Sweden*, No. 41827/07, para, 53. Also see ECtHR 19 September 2013, *R.J. v. Sweden*, No. 10466/11.

[896] ECJ 7 November 2013, *X, Y and Z*, Cases C-199/12, C-200/12, and C-201/12.

[897] Ibid, paras. 58–61.

7.5.2. EVIDENCE

Evidence in asylum cases can take many forms: testimonies, an arrest warrant, a threat letter, an age test, a language analysis for determining the country or region of origin, identity papers, travel documents, baptismal certificates, *etc.* It is the shared duty of the applicant and the Member State to bring all the relevant materials on the table.

One type of evidence which Member State authorities must, as a rule, procure, are country of origin reports. These reports play an often-decisive role in the asylum procedure. Article 4(3)(a) Qualification Directive and Article 10(3) (b) Asylum Procedures Directive oblige Member States to obtain up-to-date information from various sources on the general situation prevailing in the country of origin. Such reports may in, and of, themselves constitute evidence of particular risks in the country of origin. Alternatively, they may serve to verify an applicant's statements. Country of origin reports are often compiled by the state authorities themselves, by NGOs and by international organisations, such as (agencies of) the United Nations.

In the context of expulsion and Article 3 ECHR, the ECtHR has set forth some parameters on how country of origin information is to be valued. Apart from the obvious point that such reports must be independent, reliable and objective, the weight to be attached to a country report depends on the authority and reputation of the author, on whether the conclusions are internally consistent and consistent with those of other reports and on whether the report directly addresses risks of ill-treatment falling in the scope of Article 3 ECHR.[898]

As is evident from *R.C. v Sweden*, discussed above, another type of evidence that plays a topical role in status determinations, are medical reports. Article 18 of the Asylum Procedures Directive specifies that, if relevant for the making of a decision, the Member State shall arrange for a medical examination of the applicant concerning signs of previous ill-treatment. This duty is, however, qualified by the phrase that '[a]lternatively, Member States may provide that the applicant arranges for such a medical examination' himself. There is, accordingly, no obligation on the part of the Member State to provide for a medical examination, but the applicant is always free to arrange for such an examination himself. If such examination is deemed relevant for making a decision, the examination is publicly paid. If it is not deemed relevant, the applicant remains free to undergo the examination and to present the results, but at his own cost.[899]

Medical evidence of past persecution or serious harm is especially relevant for a further evidentiary rule which is specified in Article 4(4) of the Qualification

---

[898]   ECtHR 17 July 2008, *NA. v. the United Kingdom*, No. 25904/07, ECtHR 20 June 2013, *Sidikovy v Russia*, No. 73455/11.

[899]   Directive 2013/32/EU, Article 18(2).

Directive, namely, the past persecution standard. According to this rule, proof of (threats of) past persecution or serious harm constitutes a 'serious indication' of the applicant's well-founded fear or real risk. Hence, someone who can demonstrate to having been tortured or otherwise ill-treated in the past or to having been threatened with such treatment, has a strong – albeit rebuttable – claim.[900]

This rule corresponds with several judgments of the ECtHR, in which evidence of past ill-treatment was an important factor in concluding that there was a real risk.[901] The case of *S.A. v Sweden* may serve as illustration. It concerned a male Sunni Muslim from Iraq who had been in a relationship with a female Shiah Muslim, whose family disapproved of the relationship. After having proposed to marry her, the woman was killed by her family and her hair and her hand with the engagement ring had been hung on the front door of her house, as a sign that the family had cleansed their honour. Afterwards, the man's house had been visited daily by the woman's relatives, and they had left a threatening letter stating that they wanted his head. The ECtHR considered that 'the events that led the applicant to leave Iraq strongly indicate that he would be in danger upon return to his home town.'[902] Eventually, however, no violation of the Convention was found, because a majority of judges considered that the man could internally relocate to another region in Iraq where the family would be unable to find him.

7.5.3. THE BENEFIT OF THE DOUBT

In many cases, even after the applicant has made a genuine effort – in cooperation with the authorities – to substantiate his story, there will still be a lack of evidence for some of his statements. Full proof cannot always be assembled and there may also be statements that are simply not susceptible of proof. In these situations, any gaps in documentary or other evidence may be compensated by giving the applicant the 'benefit of the doubt', provided that certain conditions are met.[903] These conditions relate chiefly to the *credibility* of the applicant and his story. Credibility can thus be a substitute for proof.[904]

---

[900] According to Article 4(4) Qualification Directive, this rule applies 'unless there are good reasons to consider that such persecution or serious harm will not be repeated.'

[901] ECtHR 17 July 2008, *NA. v. The United Kingdom*, No. 25904/07, ECtHR 9 March 2010, *R.C. v. Sweden*, No. 41827/07.

[902] ECtHR 27 June 2013, *S.A. v. Sweden*, No. 66523/10.

[903] UNHCR Handbook, paras. 203–204.

[904] See, further, M. Kagan, 'Is Truth in the Eye of the Beholder? Objective Credibility Assessment in Refugee Status Determination', 17 *Georgetown Immigration Law Journal* 2003, pp. 367–415; R. Thomas, 'Assessing the Credibility of Asylum Claims: EU and UK Approaches Examined', *European Journal of Migration and Law* 2006, pp. 79–96. J.A. Sweeney, 'Credibility, Proof and Refugee Law', *International Journal of Refugee Law* 2009, pp. 700–726; S. Norman, 'Assessing the Credibility of Refugee Applicants: A Judicial Perspective', *International Journal of Refugee Law* 2007, pp. 273–292.

The Union law equivalent of the benefit of the doubt principle is Article 4(5) Qualification Directive, which provides that statements which remain unsupported by evidence, shall not need confirmation if five conditions are cumulatively met:

- The applicant has made a genuine effort to substantiate his claim;
- A satisfactory explanation has been given regarding any lack of evidence;
- The statements are coherent and plausible and correspond with generally available information;
- The applicant has applied for asylum at the earliest possible time, unless there is good reason for not having done so; and
- The applicant is generally credible.

This rule is, by and large, in harmony with the case law of the ECtHR. The ECtHR pronounces as general principle that 'owing to the special situation in which asylum seekers often find themselves, it is frequently necessary to give them the benefit of the doubt when it comes to assessing the credibility of their statements and the documents submitted in support thereof.'[905] But the ECtHR also holds that 'when information is presented which gives strong reasons to question the veracity of an asylum seeker's submissions, the individual must provide a satisfactory explanation for the alleged discrepancies.'[906]

In the context of Article 3 ECHR, there is fairly detailed case law of the ECtHR on the issue of the applicant's credibility. Roughly, three general rules can be distilled from the often rather case specific reasoning of the Court.

Firstly, minor discrepancies and inconsistencies in the applicant's story need not put the applicant's general credibility in doubt. In *Said v. The Netherlands*, for example, the implausibility of the applicant's escape from the Eritrean army was not found relevant, as it was not in dispute that he was a deserter and, for that reason, at risk of arrest and inhuman treatment upon return.[907]

Secondly, major inconsistencies, vagueness and a lack of willingness to cooperate do detract from the applicant's credibility. Changing an asylum narrative pending the procedure, or in a subsequent procedure, does not speak in favour of the applicant.[908] Vague or general statements, as opposed to specific

---

[905]   Eg. ECtHR 20 July 2010, *N. v. Sweden*, No. 23505/09; ECtHR 5 September 2013, *I. v. Sweden*, No. 61204/09.

[906]   Ibid.

[907]   ECtHR 5 July 2005, *Said v. The Netherlands*, No. 2345/02. See also ECtHR 20 July 2010, *N. v. Sweden*, No. 23505/09; ECtHR 15 May 2012, *S.F. v. Sweden*, No. 52077/10; ECtHR 26 July 2005, *N. v. Finland*, No. 28885/02; ECtHR 6 March 2001, *Hilal v. The United Kingdom*, No. 45276/99; ECtHR 18 December 2012, *F.N. v. Sweden*, No. 28774/09.

[908]   ECtHR 8 March 2007, *Collins and Akaziebie v. Sweden*, No. 23944/05; ECtHR 15 May 2012, *H.N. v. Sweden*, No. 30720/09; ECtHR 1 October 2002, *Tekdemir v. The Netherlands*, No. 49823/99; ECtHR 16 March 2004, *Nasimi v. Sweden*, No. 38865/02.

assertions, detract from the applicant's credibility, as well as inconsistent statements about data, names and facts.[909] Equally, a complete absence of any form of evidence, false evidence, or the lack of a sound explanation as to why no evidence is presented, may seriously undermine the claim.[910]

Thirdly, it must be emphasised that credibility is no autonomous requirement for international protection. All that is required is that there is, objectively, a well-founded fear (or real risk). It may happen that an applicant with a highly incredible story still furnishes evidence, which proves the existence of a well-founded fear or real risk. In *I. v. Sweden*, for example, the ECtHR found that the statements of the applicant were not credible. He had claimed to have been ill-treated in Chechnya for reason of his journalistic activities, but could not produce any news articles written by him.[911] But he did present a medical report that noted that he had significant and visible scars on his body, which had probably been caused by torture. This was sufficient to conclude that there was a real risk of ill-treatment, contrary to Article 3 ECHR, because it was likely that he would be subjected to a body search upon return, resulting in the discovery of his scars. This could very well lead local security officials to conclude that he had taken active part in the second war in Chechnya, and that he had to be considered an enemy.

Accordingly, once it is established that one element of the applicant's statements gives rise to a well-founded fear or real risk, the credibility of other elements of his story is no longer at issue.

7.6. EXCLUSION, CESSATION AND ENDING OF REFUGEE STATUS

Article 1 of the Refugee Convention not only inclusively defines who is a refugee but also excludes several categories of persons from the refugee definition. These persons are not refugees in the meaning of the Refugee Convention and cannot, therefore, derive any rights from the Convention. Article 1C contains the 'cessation clauses'. These are based on the consideration that international

---

[909]   ECtHR 20 December 2011, *J.H. v. the United Kingdom*, No. 48839/09; ECtHR 10 February 2009, *S.M. v. Sweden*, No. 47683/08; ECtHR 17 January 2006, *Bello v. Sweden*, No. 32213/04.

[910]   ECtHR 20 March 1991, *Cruz Varas and others v. Sweden*, No. 15576/89, para. 78; ECtHR 28 February 2002, *Zubeyde v. Norway*, No. 51600/99; ECtHR 5 March 2002, *Avetissov v. Sweden*, No. 71427/01; ECtHR 19 March 2002, *Javanmardi and Ahmadi v. Sweden*, No. 65538/01; ECtHR 23 April 2002, *S.R. v. Sweden*, No. 62806/00; ECtHR 5 September 2013, *I. v Sweden*, No. 61204/09; ECtHR 22 October 2002, *Ammari v. Sweden*, No. 60959/00; ECtHR 8 December 2009, *Nduwayezu v. Sweden*; ECtHR 10 February 2009, *S.M. v. Sweden*, No. 47683/08.

[911]   ECtHR 5 September 2013, *I. v. Sweden*, No. 61204/09. Also see ECtHR 5 July 2005, *Said v. The Netherlands*, No. 2345/02; ECtHR 20 July 2010, *N. v. Sweden*, No. 23505/09.

protection should not be granted where it is no longer necessary or justified.[912] The refugee then ceases to be a refugee. Articles 1D, 1E and 1F contain the 'exclusion clauses'. These list the categories of persons who, for a range of different considerations, are, from the outset, to be excluded from the scope of the Refugee Convention.

The combined effect of the cessation and exclusion clauses is that, broadly speaking, refugee status may be lost or denied in four sets of circumstances: (a) due to voluntary acts of the individual; (b) because of changed circumstances; (c) because protection is accorded by another state or an international organisation; and (d) because of the (alleged) criminal nature of the individual.[913]

The Qualification Directive reiterates, with some additional textual clarifications, the cessation and exclusion clauses in respect of refugees in Articles 11 and 12. Under Union law, the legal effect of cessation or exclusion is that refugee status shall not be granted (Article 13), or, if the person in question was previously granted refugee status, that the status must be terminated (Article 14). The Court of Justice has considered that, in view of their character as exceptions, the exclusion clauses must be construed narrowly.[914] The argument is, furthermore, possible that exclusion from refugee protection constitutes a limitation on the exercise of the right to asylum guaranteed in Article 18 of the EU Charter of Fundamental Rights. Such a limitation is, according to Article 52(1) of the Charter, justified only if it meets the conditions of proportionality and necessity.[915]

7.6.1. CESSATION UNDER ARTICLE 1C

The cessation clauses of Article 1C Refugee Convention exhaustively enumerate the situations in which refugee status ends. These clauses are closely connected to the inclusive refugee definition of Article 1A(2). They refer to several elements of the definition that are no longer fulfilled: the well-founded fear criterion, the condition of alienage and the willingness to avail oneself of the protection of one's country of origin.

1) He has voluntarily re-availed himself of the protection of his country of nationality (Article 11(1)(a) Qualification Directive)

The first cessation clause refers to a refugee who remains outside the country of his nationality, but who has normalised the relationship with his country of nationality. The most frequent case of 're-availment of protection' will be where

---

[912] UNHCR Handbook para. 111.
[913] G.S. Goodwin-Gill and J. McAdam, *The Refugee in International Law*, OUP 2007, p. 135.
[914] ECJ 17 June 2010, *Bolbol*, Case C-31/09, para. 51.
[915] Article 52(1) EU Charter of Fundamental Rights.

the refugee wishes to return to his country of nationality and, to that purpose, obtains an entry permit or a national passport for the purposes of returning.[916] Obtaining a new passport can be considered as voluntarily terminating refugee status. Another circumstance in which a refugee can be considered to re-avail himself of the protection of his country of origin is when he regularly visits that country, for example, for holidays, or to establish business relations.[917] The situation of a refugee who actually returns to the country of his nationality is governed by the fourth cessation clause.

> 2) *Having lost his nationality, he has voluntarily reacquired it* (Article 11(1)(b) Qualification Directive)

The second cessation clause is similar to the first one. It applies to persons who have become a refugee as well as stateless. If such a person voluntarily reacquires the nationality that was previously lost, he must be considered to have normalised the relationship with his country of origin, and is therefore no longer in need of protection as refugee.[918]

> 3) *He has acquired a new nationality, and enjoys the protection of the country of his new nationality* (Article 11(1)(c) Qualification Directive)

The third cessation clause refers to the situation where another country, normally the country of refuge, has granted nationality to the refugee. If that country also provides the protection that is normally accorded to nationals, the person must be presumed to be able to avail himself of the protection of a state, and is therefore no longer in need of surrogate international protection under the Refugee Convention.

> 4) *He has voluntarily re-established himself in the country which he left or outside which he remained owing to fear of persecution* (Article 11(1)(d) Qualification Directive)

The fourth cessation clause applies to refugees who have returned to their country of origin or previous residence (in the case of stateless persons). The words 'voluntarily re-established' must be understood as return to the country of nationality or former habitual residence with a view to permanently residing there.[919]

---

[916] UNHCR Handbook, para. 122.

[917] Ibid, para. 125.

[918] See extensively UNHCR Handbook paras. 126–128; A. Zimmerman (ed), *The 1951 Convention Relating to the Status of Refugees and its 1967 Protocol: A Commentary*, OUP 2011, pp. 498–499.

[919] UNHCR Handbook, para. 134.

5 & 6) He can no longer, because the circumstances in connection with which he has been recognised as a refugee have ceased to exist, continue to refuse to avail himself of the protection of the country of his nationality (Article 11(1)(e) and (f) Qualification Directive)

Contrary to the first four cessation clauses, the fifth and sixth cessation clauses do not concern changes that have been brought about voluntarily by the refugee, but to fundamental changes in the country of origin, which can be assumed to remove the basis of the fear of persecution.[920] The fifth cessation clause refers to nationals whose reasons for becoming a refugee have ceased to exist. The sixth refers to stateless persons whose reasons for becoming a refugee have ceased to exist. The legal effect of both provisions is the same. A typical change in circumstances is a complete political change, as signified by democratic elections, declarations of amnesties, the repeal of oppressive laws, and/or the dismantling of security services.[921]

There is general consensus that these clauses may only be invoked if the change in the refugee's country of nationality or former habitual residence is fundamental, durable, and effective.[922] The Qualification Directive takes heed of this, and stipulates in Article 11(2) that 'Member States shall have regard to whether the change of circumstances is of such a significant and non-temporary nature that the refugee's fear of persecution can no longer be regarded as well-founded.' In *Salahadin*, the Court of Justice considered that '[t]he change of circumstances will be of a "significant and non-temporary" nature (…) when the factors which formed the basis of the refugee's fear of persecution may be regarded as having been permanently eradicated.'[923] This entails, according to the Court, the verification of whether the actor or actors of protection referred to in Article 7(1) of the Qualification Directive have taken reasonable steps to prevent the persecution, and that 'they therefore operate, *inter alia*, an effective legal system for the detection, prosecution and punishment of acts constituting persecution and that the national concerned will have access to such protection if he ceases to have refugee status.'[924]

The Court of Justice also found in *Salahadin* that, when considering cessation, a Member State must verify whether the person concerned has, beyond his original fear for persecution, no other reason to fear being persecuted.[925] A cessation decision in respect of a refugee, however, only concerns his refugee status, and does not have to take into account possible subsidiary grounds for

---

920   UNHCR Handbook, para. 135.
921   UNHCR, Note on the Cessation Clauses, 30 May 1997, EC/47/SC/CRP.30, para. 20.
922   UNHCR Handbook, para. 135; A. Zimmerman (ed.), *The 1951 Convention Relating to the Status of Refugees and its 1967 Protocol: A Commentary*, OUP 2011, p. 502.
923   ECJ 2 March 2010, *Salahadin*, Cases C-175/08, C-176/08, C-178/08 and C-179/08, para. 73.
924   Ibid, para. 76.
925   Ibid, paras. 91, 100.

protection.[926] A person whose refugee status is terminated on the basis of a cessation clause may, if he so wishes, apply for subsidiary protection.[927]

The second paragraph of the fifth and sixth cessation clauses in the Refugee Convention contains an exception for so-called 'statutory refugees', who are able to invoke 'compelling reasons arising out of previous persecution' for refusing to avail themselves of the protection of the country of nationality or their former habitual residence. Because the exception applies only to statutory refugees defined in Article 1A(1) of the Refugee Convention, i.e. persons considered to be refugees under treaties prior to the Refugee Convention, the exception has, at least formally, lost much of its significance. The exception was included at the time in respect of (especially Jewish) refugees from Germany and Austria, who, despite the change of regime in these countries after the Second World War, in view of the drafters of the Convention, could not be expected to return to the very country where they and their kin had suffered such atrocious forms of persecution, and with which they no longer wished to associate themselves as nationals.

UNHCR suggests, however, that the exception can also be applied to contemporary refugees, as it reflects a more general humanitarian principle of not returning a refugee who, due to trauma or fear of being confronted again with his former persecutors, cannot be expected to re-establish himself in his country of origin.[928] This has been acknowledged in Article 11(3) of the revised Qualification Directive, which reiterates the 'compelling reasons' proviso without restricting its scope to statutory refugees. This was in line with the practice of some Member States, including Belgium, France and Germany, of applying the proviso not only to pre-1951 refugees, but to all refugees.[929]

7.6.2.   EXCLUSION UNDER ARTICLE 1D

Article 1D Refugee Convention, which is incorporated into Article 12(1)(a) of the Qualification Directive, is intended to avoid overlapping competencies between different UN agencies that assist refugees.[930] It excludes refugees who fall under a protection mandate of another UN agency than UNHCR. In practice, this only refers to Palestinian refugees who are protected by the United Nations Relief and Works Agency for Palestine Refugees in the Near East (UNRWA). Article 1D

---

[926]   Ibid, para. 79.
[927]   Ibid, paras. 78–80.
[928]   UNHCR Handbook, para. 136; UNHCR, *The Cessation Clauses: Guidelines on Their Application*, 26 April 1999, para. 31.
[929]   A. Zimmerman (ed.), *The 1951 Convention Relating to the Status of Refugees and its 1967 Protocol: A Commentary*, OUP 2011, p. 531.
[930]   UNHCR, Revised Note on the Applicability of Article 1D of the 1951 Convention relating to the Status of Refugees to Palestinian Refugees, October 2009, para. 1.

consists of two paragraphs. The first one excludes persons 'who are at present receiving' protection or assistance from another UN agency. The second paragraph ensures that these persons shall be brought within the scope of the Refugee Convention, when 'such protection or assistance has ceased for any reason'. Because UNRWA is only active in the Middle-East,[931] the question can arise as to whether Palestinian refugees who claim asylum elsewhere can be considered to have left the protective mandate of UNRWA, and whether they may be required to re-avail themselves of UNRWA protection by returning to the Middle East.

The Court of Justice explained the scope of this exclusion clause on two occasions. In *Bolbol*, the Court considered that the clause only covers persons who have actually availed themselves of the assistance of UNRWA, and does not, therefore, apply to persons who are merely eligible for such assistance.[932] A person such as Ms. Bolbol, who had lived in the Gaza Strip but never availed herself of the assistance of UNRWA, and who had left for Hungary, where she claimed asylum, can therefore not be excluded from refugee status on the basis of Article 12(1)(a) Qualification Directive. The Court of Justice also clarified, in *Bolbol*, that the exclusion clause can apply to Palestinians who became refugees as a result of the 1948 Arab-Israeli conflict, as well as to Palestinians displaced following the 1967 Six-Day War. This finding was especially relevant for the United Kingdom, which had interpreted the words 'at present receiving' as referring only to Palestinians who were receiving UNRWA protection at the time the Refugee Convention was concluded, thereby limiting Article 1D to Palestinians who became displaced in 1948.[933] Descendants of Palestinian refugees can also come within the scope of Article 1D, because they fall within the protection mandate of UNRWA.[934]

In *El Kott*, the Court of Justice addressed the more fundamental issue of how to deal with Palestinians who withdraw themselves, forcedly or voluntarily, from UNRWA protection, and seek asylum elsewhere. The case concerned three Palestinians who had fled from the violence in UNRWA refugee camps in Lebanon and applied for asylum in Hungary. Contrary to Ms. Bolbol, these three Palestinians did receive assistance from UNRWA. The Court first noted that the mere absence or voluntary departure from UNRWA's area of operation is not sufficient to consider someone to be outside the scope of the exclusion clause, as this would mean that anyone physically absent from UNRWA territory can never be excluded, contrary to the rationale of Article 1D. The words 'who are at present

---

[931]   UNRWA's areas of operation are limited to the Gaza Strip, the West Bank, including East Jerusalem, Syria, Jordan, and Lebanon.

[932]   ECJ 17 June 2010, *Bolbol*, Case C-31/09, para. 51.

[933]   *El-Ali v Secretary of State for the Home Department* [2002] EWCA Civ 1103 (UK Court of Appeal).

[934]   UNHCR, Revised Note on the Applicability of Article 1D of the 1951 Convention relating to the Status of Refugees to Palestinian Refugees, October 2009, para. 4.

receiving protection' therefore includes persons who availed themselves of UNRWA protection 'shortly before' submitting their application in a Member State. Secondly, the second paragraph of Article 1D (corresponding with the second sentence of Article 12(1)(a) Qualification Directive), and in particular, the words 'when such protection or assistance has ceased for any reason', not only applies to a situation where UNRWA is abolished, but also when a person has been forced to leave UNRWA protection for reasons of personal safety and if UNRWA cannot guarantee his living conditions. This corresponds with the purpose of Article 1D that Palestinian refugees must anyhow receive effective protection.

Furthermore, because Article 1D Refugee Convention and Article 12(1)(a) Qualification Directive specify that persons whose protection by UNRWA has ceased, are *ipso facto* entitled to the benefits of the Convention and the Directive, respectively, they are, in principle, eligible for refugee status, provided other exclusion grounds are not applicable. They do not, therefore, need to show that they meet the refugee definition. This must be explained from the fact that these Palestinian refugees had already, by virtue of resolutions of the UN General Assembly, been considered in need of international protection.

The result is that when a Palestinian refugee claims asylum in a Member State, the first question will be whether he has availed himself of UNRWA assistance before his flight. If this is the case, the second question is whether he has left UNRWA's area of operations for a reason beyond his control and independent of his volition. To answer that question, the Member State must verify whether the safety of the individual was at serious risk in the UNRWA area. If that is the case, he cannot be excluded on the basis of Article 12(1)(a) Qualification Directive and must be granted refugee status, unless another exclusion ground applies.

The exclusion clause of Article 1D Refugee Convention only applies to refugee status. It is no ground for exclusion from subsidiary protection in the Qualification Directive. It follows that a claim for subsidiary protection of any Palestinian refugee must be examined on the basis of the ordinary eligibility requirements for subsidiary protection (see Chapter 8). In this assessment, the fact that a Palestinian refugee may avail himself of UNRWA protection may, however, well be relevant, as it may imply that there is a 'first country of asylum' or an 'internal protection alternative'.[935]

7.6.3. EXCLUSION UNDER ARTICLE 1E

Article 1E of the Refugee Convention, which is incorporated into Article 12(1)(b) of the Qualification Directive, contains an exclusion clause, which is, nowadays, of little relevance. It refers to persons who, in their new country of residence, are

---

[935] Directive 2013/32/EU, Article 35; Directive 2011/95/EU, Articles 7 and 8.

granted 'the rights and obligations which are attached to the possession of the nationality of that country'. Whereas under Article 1C(2) Refugee Convention refugee status ceases to exist when the refugee acquires the nationality of his country of residence as well as the protection of that country, Article 1E sees to a situation where the individual, by virtue of mere residence in a particular country, enjoys an effective status similar to nationals of that country.

The clause was inserted into the Refugee Convention to accommodate the situation of one specific group of refugees, namely, the ethnic Germans (*Volksdeutsche*) who had been living in Central and Eastern Europe, but who resettled in (and were in many cases expelled to) Germany after the Second World War. The drafters of the Convention considered that these persons, who numbered around 800,000 and who were granted citizenship rights by the post-war German government, should remain the primary responsibility of Germany, and should not be brought under the auspices of the UN.[936]

The general wording of Article 1E does allow for contemporary groups of refugees to be brought in its scope. The chief requirement is that a person is treated *de facto* as citizen of the country, which includes protection against expulsion.[937] It is not required that the person is granted full political rights such as the right to vote, but he must be treated as having a privileged status compared to other aliens residing in that country. This may apply to categories of aliens with a special bond with the host country such as former colonial subjects or persons with the same ethnic origin as the population of the host country. Article 12(1)(b) Qualification Directive reiterates Article 1E Refugee Convention, with the clarification that the rights and obligations must be 'equivalent' (and thus not necessarily 'equal') to those attached to nationality.

Like Article 1D, Article 1E of the Refugee Convention is not mentioned as a ground for exclusion from subsidiary protection.

7.6.4. EXCLUSION UNDER ARTICLE 1F

According to Article 1F Refugee Convention, which is incorporated into Article 12(2) Qualification Directive, the status of refugee does not accrue to any person with respect to whom there are serious reasons for considering that: (a) he has committed a crime against peace, a war crime, or a crime against humanity, as defined in the international instruments drawn up to make provision in respect of such crimes; (b) he has committed a serious non-political crime outside the country of refuge prior to his admission to that country as a

---

[936] Extensively: A. Zimmerman (ed.), *The 1951 Convention Relating to the Status of Refugees and its 1967 Protocol: A Commentary*, OUP 2011, p. 572–573.
[937] Ibid, p. 574.

refugee; or, (c) he has been guilty of acts contrary to the purposes and principles of the United Nations.

These are persons who, for reason of their questionable pasts, are deemed unworthy of protection as refugees.[938] A further rationale for their exclusion is that the institution of asylum should not allow fugitives to shelter from justice.[939] Exclusion on the basis of Article 1F may be considered as a penalty for acts committed in the past, and does not require that the person represents a present danger to the host Member State.[940]

The words 'serious reasons for considering' indicate that exclusion under Article 1F does not run parallel with the criminal standard of proof. To exclude a refugee, a previous criminal conviction is not required. Nor is it is necessary to establish someone's guilt beyond reasonable doubt. Mere suspicions are not sufficient, however. The established facts and circumstances must provide serious reasons from which a substantial suspicion arises that the individual can be held responsible for the act.[941] This also follows from Article 1F being an exclusion clause, which must, as the Court of Justice has held, be construed narrowly.[942]

Article 1F(a): he has committed a crime against peace, a war crime, or a crime against humanity, as defined in the international instruments drawn up to make provision in respect of such crimes

Article 1F(a) Refugee Convention (corresponding with Article 12(2)(a) Qualification Directive) mentions the three sets of international crimes that were recognised in Article 6 of the 1945 London Charter of the International Military Tribunal (the Nuremberg Charter): crimes against peace, war crimes and crimes against humanity.[943] Although the scope of Article 1F(a) is restricted to these three international crimes, the neutral reference to 'international instruments' indicates that the scope and definition of the crimes mentioned must also take account of further codifications of international crimes. There are a considerable number of treaties defining international crimes. Nowadays, reference is mostly made to the Statute of the International Criminal Court (ICC Statute).[944]

---

[938]   UNHCR Handbook, para. 147; ECJ 9 November 2010, *B and D*, Cases C-57/09 and C-101/09, para. 104.
[939]   Ibid.
[940]   Ibid, para. 103, 105.
[941]   UNHCR, Background Note on the Application of the Exclusion Clauses: Article 1F of the 1951 Convention Relating to the Status of Refugees, 4 September 2003, paras. 38–39; G.S. Goodwin-Gill and J. McAdam, *The Refugee in International Law*, OUP 2007, p. 165.
[942]   ECJ 17 June 2010, *Bolbol*, Case C-31/09, para. 51.
[943]   Charter of the International Military Tribunal. Annex to the Agreement for the prosecution and punishment of the major war criminals of the European Axis ('London Agreement'), 8 August 1945, 82 UNTS. 280.
[944]   Rome Statute of the International Criminal Court, 17 July 1998.

A *crime against peace* (or crime against aggression) is defined in Article 8 *bis* of the ICC Statute as 'the planning, preparation, initiation or execution, by a person in a position effectively to exercise control over or to direct the political or military action of a State, of an act of aggression which, by its character, gravity and scale, constitutes a manifest violation of the Charter of the United Nations.' It is clear from this definition that only governmental or military leaders, who are in a position to plan military actions, can qualify as potential perpetrators. This ground for exclusion therefore plays a role in exceptional cases only.[945]

War crimes involve grave breaches of international humanitarian law and can be committed by, or perpetrated against, civilian as well as military persons.[946] Attacks committed in times of an armed conflict against any person not, or no longer, taking part in hostilities, such as wounded or sick combatants, prisoners of war or civilians, are regarded as war crimes. Although war crimes were originally considered to arise only in the context of an international armed conflict, it is now generally accepted that war crimes may be committed in non-international armed conflicts as well. This is reflected in both the jurisprudence of the International Tribunal for the Former Yugoslavia and in Article 8 of the ICC Statute. Specific acts considered to be war crimes are, *inter alia*, wilful killing, torture or inhuman treatment, the taking of hostages and intentional attacks on civilians.[947]

Crimes against humanity are common crimes of notable gravity, committed as part of a widespread or systematic attack directed against any civilian population, such as murder, rape, torture, apartheid, and so on.[948] Genocide, which is not separately mentioned in Article 1Fa, will in many, if not all, cases amount to a crime against humanity.[949] The distinguishing feature of crimes against humanity is that they must be carried out as part of a widespread or systematic attack directed against the civilian population. Since such crimes can take place in peacetime as well as armed conflict, this is the broadest category under Article 1F(a).[950]

> *Article 1F(b): he has committed a serious non-political crime outside the country of refuge prior to his admission to that country as a refugee*

For a crime to lead to exclusion on the basis of Article 1F(b) Refugee Convention (corresponding with Article 12(2)(b) Qualification Directive), it must be serious, it

---

[945]   UNHCR, Background Note on the Application of the Exclusion Clauses: Article 1F of the 1951 Convention Relating to the Status of Refugees, 4 September 2003, para. 28.

[946]   Rome Statute of the International Criminal Court, Article 8.

[947]   Ibid.

[948]   Ibid, Article 7(1).

[949]   Ibid, Article 6; Convention on the Prevention and Punishment of the Crime of Genocide, 9 December 1948, Article 2.

[950]   UNHCR, Background Note on the Application of the Exclusion Clauses: Article 1F of the 1951 Convention Relating to the Status of Refugees, 4 September 2003, para. 13.

must be non-political and it must have been committed outside the country of refuge prior to the admission to that country as a refugee. According to UNHCR, in determining whether a particular offence is sufficiently serious, international rather than local standards are relevant.[951] However, in the absence of a clear dichotomy at the international level of what constitutes a serious crime and what does not, states obviously enjoy some discretion in considering a crime sufficiently serious to justify exclusion. It is safe to assume, however, that such crimes as murder, rape and armed robbery will qualify as serious offences, whereas petty theft will not.[952]

The political as opposed to common nature of a crime refers to the motives or objectives of the crime. For a crime to be non-political (common), it must be established that the crime was not committed out of genuine political motives but for reasons of personal gain.[953] It can, however, happen that crimes are grounded in a mix of political and personal motives. According to UNHCR, a serious crime should be considered non-political when other than political motives are the predominant feature of the specific crime committed. The political element of the offence should outweigh its common law character.[954] This is referred to as the predominance test. Egregious acts of violence will almost always fail the predominance test, as they will be disproportionate to any political objective. This is recognised in Article 12(2)(b) Qualification Directive, which specifies that 'particularly cruel actions, even if committed with an allegedly political objective, may be classified as serious non-political crimes.' The Court of Justice confirmed that terrorist acts, which are characterised by their violence towards civilian populations, even if committed with a purportedly political objective, are to be regarded as serious non-political crimes, and therefore form a basis for exclusion.[955]

For an act to lead to exclusion under Article 1F(b) Refugee Convention, it must have been committed outside the country of refuge and prior to admission as a refugee in that country. The rationale behind this limitation is that a person who commits a serious non-political crime after admission to the country of refuge is subject to the ordinary criminal laws of that country and may, moreover, be expelled from that country in accordance with Article 32(2) and 33(2) of the Refugee Convention. Article 12(2)(b) of the Qualification Directive specifies, however, that 'admission' means the time of issuing a residence permit based on the granting of refugee status. The Directive therefore does not restrict

---

[951]   UNHCR Background Note on the Application of the Exclusion Clauses: Article 1F of the 1951 Convention Relating to the Status of Refugees, 4 September 2003, para. 14.

[952]   Ibid.

[953]   A. Zimmerman (ed.), *The 1951 Convention Relating to the Status of Refugees and its 1967 Protocol: A Commentary*, OUP 2011, p. 600.

[954]   UNHCR Handbook, para. 152; UNHCR, Background Note on the Application of the Exclusion Clauses: Article 1F of the 1951 Convention Relating to the Status of Refugees, 4 September 2003, para. 41.

[955]   ECJ 9 November 2010, *B and D*, Cases C-57/09 and C-101/09, para. 81.

the temporal scope of the exclusion clause to non-political crimes committed while the applicant was physically outside the Member State in question, but extends it to crimes that could be committed after arrival in the territory of the Member State but before obtaining refugee status. Note however, that the crime must still have been committed outside the country of refuge.

> Article 1F(c) he has been guilty of acts contrary to the purposes and principles of the United Nations

Article 1F(c) Refugee Convention (corresponding with Article 12(2)(c) Qualification Directive) is only rarely invoked as ground for exclusion. The purposes and principles of the UN, which are set out in the Preamble and Articles 1 and 2 of the Charter of the United Nations, are formulated in broad and general terms, providing little guidance as to what acts may go contrary to them. Moreover, as most of the purposes and principles refer to the conduct of states, it is difficult to immediately recognise how individuals may act in breach of them. The common interpretation seems to be that Article 1F(c) includes only acts that offend the United Nations in a fundamental way, such as affecting international peace and security.[956] According to UNHCR, this implies that the personal scope of this clause is restricted to high officials of a state.[957]

One issue with contemporary relevance is to what extent terrorist acts may lead to exclusion on the basis of Article 1F(c). In the case of B. and D., the Court of Justice considered that, in principle, Article 12(2)(c) of the Qualification Directive applies to a person who has been involved in terrorist acts with an international dimension.[958] The Court noted that Resolutions 1373 (2001) and 1377 (2001) of the UN Security Council have made it clear that terrorist acts are contrary to the purposes and principles of the UN. Mere membership of a terrorist organisation is not, however, sufficient for exclusion, as is discussed below.[959] There may be some tension between this judgment and UNHCR's position that only terrorist acts that have significant implications for international peace and security, and that only the leaders of groups responsible for such atrocities, fall within the scope of Article 1F(c).[960] But this is a discussion which entertains only limited practical relevance, as the more general category of terrorist activity will – if committed outside the country of refuge prior to admission as a refugee – normally qualify for exclusion on the basis of Article 1F(b).

---

[956]   A. Zimmerman (ed.), *The 1951 Convention Relating to the Status of Refugees and its 1967 Protocol: A Commentary*, OUP 2011, p. 603–606; G.S. Goodwin-Gill and J. McAdam, *The Refugee in International Law*, OUP 2007, p. 186–189.

[957]   UNHCR Handbook, para. 163.

[958]   ECJ 9 November 2010, *B and D*, Cases C-57/09 and C-101/09, para. 83–84.

[959]   Ibid, para. 88.

[960]   UNHCR, Background Note on the Application of the Exclusion Clauses: Article 1F of the 1951 Convention Relating to the Status of Refugees, 4 September 2003, para. 49.

7.6.4.1. Individual Responsibility

A person is excludable under Article 1F Refugee Convention only when there are serious reasons for considering that he has *committed* (or is guilty of) one of the acts mentioned in Article 1F(a), (b) and (c).[961] The verb 'committed' must be seen as an equivalent of liability under criminal law for having committed a crime without grounds for rejecting individual responsibility being applicable.[962] In international criminal law, it is accepted that a person is criminally responsible for a crime not only if he has actually committed the act, but also if he has ordered or facilitated it, or participated in it in some other way.[963] According to the ICC Statute, individual criminal responsibility is further engaged because of having a command or superior responsibility.[964] More generally, any criminal liability presupposes that the acts have been committed with intent and knowledge.[965] Article 12(3) Qualification Directive recognises, albeit in succinct terms, these diverse principles of criminal responsibility, in specifying that exclusion also applies 'to persons who incite or otherwise participate in the commission of the crimes or acts' mentioned in Article 12(2) of the Directive.

To establish individual responsibility, certain States Parties to the Refugee Convention, including Canada and the Netherlands, have adopted the so-called 'personal knowing and participation test'.[966] The outcome of this test is no different than the above outlined way of establishing individual responsibility. According to this test, it must be determined that the individual concerned knew or ought to have known an excludable act was committed ('knowing participation') and that he was somehow involved in the act, because he committed the act, contributed to the act, instigated the act, aided or abetted the act or in any other way participated in the act, or because he was as a military commander or superior responsible for the act ('personal participation').

A controversial matter concerns the exclusion of persons merely on the basis of them having worked for a repressive regime or their membership of a terrorist group. In *B. and D.*, the Court of Justice held that the mere fact that a person is a

---

[961]   Note that the term 'guilty' in Article 1F(c) does not differ from the term 'committed' mentioned in Articles 1F(a) and (b). Furthermore, 'guilty' does not mean being found guilty after criminal proceedings. See UNHCR, Background Note on the Application of the Exclusion Clauses: Article 1F of the 1951 Convention Relating to the Status of Refugees, 4 September 2003, paras. 50–51.

[962]   UNHCR, Guidelines on International Protection No. 5: Application of the Exclusion Clauses: Article 1F of the 1951 Convention relating to the Status of Refugees, 4 September 2003, HCR/GIP/03/05, para. 18.

[963]   Rome Statute of the International Criminal Court, Article 25.

[964]   Ibid, Article 28.

[965]   Ibid, Article 30. Also see UNHCR, Guidelines on International Protection No. 5: Application of the Exclusion Clauses: Article 1F of the 1951 Convention relating to the Status of Refugees, 4 September 2003, HCR/GIP/03/05, para. 21.

[966]   T.P. Spijkerboer and B.P. Vermeulen, *Vluchtelingenrecht*, Ars Aequi 2005 p. 101.

member of a terrorist organisation cannot automatically mean that such a person must be excluded from refugee status. The authorities must also

> assess the true role played by the person concerned in the perpetration of the acts in question; his position within the organisation; the extent of the knowledge he had, or was deemed to have, of its activities; any pressure to which he was exposed; or other factors likely to have influenced his conduct.[967]

Member States may, however, but only after an assessment on a case-by-case basis has been made, apply the presumption that a person who has occupied a prominent position within a violent organisation or regime, has individual responsibility for acts committed by that organisation or regime.[968]

Presumably, the rule that exclusion is conditional on an assessment on a case-by-case basis of all relevant circumstances also implies that it must be verified whether there may be any defences to criminal responsibility or other grounds for rejecting criminal responsibility. International criminal law recognises such grounds as self-defence, mental illness, intoxication and being under the age of 18.[969]

In view of their different rationales however, not all principles of international criminal law may be relevant for questions of exclusion. For example, a contested matter is whether the fact that the individual has already served his sentence, or has been granted a pardon or benefited from an amnesty, stands in the way of exclusion from refugee status.[970] National judges in Belgium, Switzerland, France and the United Kingdom have considered, in the context of Article 1F(b), that such elements as service of a sentence, a lapse of time, or expressions of remorse are relevant in deciding on exclusion, even though these factors need not necessarily remove the grounds for exclusion.[971] Discussion on whether such factors should be relevant, or even decisive, forms part of the wider debate on the precise object and purpose of Article 1F. Is exclusion meant as penalty for persons who are undeserving of protection, irrespective of them already having served their sentence? Is exclusion meant to ensure criminal accountability? Is it meant to protect host societies from dangerous persons? Or is it meant to uphold societal support for the institution of asylum by preventing persons of questionable past to benefit from it? Probably, a

---

[967] ECJ 9 November 2010, *B and D*, Cases C-57/09 and C-101/09, para. 97.
[968] Ibid, para. 98. See also UNHCR, Guidelines on International Protection No. 5: Application of the Exclusion Clauses: Article 1F of the 1951 Convention relating to the Status of Refugees, 4 September 2003, HCR/GIP/03/05, para. 19.
[969] Rome Statute of the International Criminal Court, Article 31.
[970] UNHCR Handbook, para. 157.
[971] See, e.g., *Conseil du Contentieux des Étrangères* (Belgium) 18 May 2009, No. 27.479, paras. 3.9–3.10; *Conseil du Contentieux des Étrangères* (Belgium) 8 November 2011, No. 69656, p. 3; *Administratif Federal* (Switzerland), No. E-3549/2006, para. 5; *Conseil d'État* (France) 4 May 2011, *OFPRA, c./M.H.*, No. 320910B; Upper Tribunal (Asylum and Immigration Chamber) (United Kingdom), *AH v. Algeria*, [2013] UKUT 00382, para. 97.

combination of some or all these reasons forms the rationale of Article 1F. As noted above, however, the Court of Justice did find that the issue of whether a person represents a present danger to the host Member State is no relevant consideration for exclusion pursuant to Article 12(2)(b) or (c) of the Directive.[972]

7.6.5.   DENIAL AND TERMINATION OF REFUGEE STATUS

If a person meets all the elements of one of the cessation or exclusion clauses, refugee status in the meaning of the Qualification Directive must be terminated or may not be granted (Articles 14(1) and (3)(a) Qualification Directive). This seems only logical, but is controversial for two reasons.

First, UNHCR has considered that a decision on exclusion, especially in the context of serious non-political crimes in the meaning of Article 1F(b) Refugee Convention, requires a balance to be struck between the gravity of the offence in question and the consequences of exclusion.[973] If a person has a well-founded fear of very severe persecution, for example, persecution endangering his life or freedom, a crime must be very grave in order to exclude him.[974] The Court of Justice EU has, however, held that if a person is excludable from refugee status, a Member State is not required to undertake a separate assessment of proportionality.[975] Persons who fall under one of the exclusion clauses may simply not be granted refugee status in the meaning of the Directive, as this would run counter to 'the credibility of the protection system'.[976] The Court of Justice added, however, that exclusion from refugee status does not imply the adoption of a position on the separate question of whether that person can be deported to his country of origin.[977] Member States remain, after all, free to simply abstain from expulsion, and are, moreover, bound by the more generally applicable prohibition of *refoulement*, as laid down in human rights law and the Returns Directive.[978] Furthermore, Member States may grant a right of asylum under their national law to a person who is excluded from refugee status, pursuant to the Directive.[979] Under Union law therefore, exclusion from refugee status is mandatory and may not take into account considerations of proportionality, but Member States

---

[972]   ECJ 9 November 2010, *B and D*, Cases C-57/09 and C-101/09, para. 105.
[973]   UNHCR Handbook, para. 156; UNHCR Background Note on the Application of the Exclusion Clauses: Article 1F of the 1951 Convention Relating to the Status of Refugees, 4 September 2003, paras. 76 and 77. UNHCR, Guidelines on International Protection No. 5: Application of the Exclusion Clauses: Article 1F of the 1951 Convention relating to the Status of Refugees, 4 September 2003, HCR/GIP/03/05, para. 24.
[974]   Ibid.
[975]   ECJ 9 November 2010, *B and D*, Cases C-57/09 and C-101/09, para. 109.
[976]   Ibid, para. 115.
[977]   Ibid, para. 110.
[978]   Directive 2008/115/EC (see section 9.4.).
[979]   ECJ 9 November 2010, *B and D*, Cases C-57/09 and C-101/09, para. 121.

remain free to grant excluded persons a national form of residence on the basis of proportionality or other humanitarian considerations.

Second, the mandatory termination of refugee status, once a cessation clause becomes applicable, is difficult to reconcile with the practice of some Member States to not subject a refugee's status to frequent review. Member States' authorities do not normally check, on an everyday basis, whether a refugee is still in need of protection. Further, if the refugee has been granted permanent residence, the possibility to terminate the status of refugee is legally restricted or prevented in some Member States, despite the fulfilment of the conditions for cessation (or exclusion).[980] These national practices correspond with the idea that refugee status is not only a means to protect against persecution, but should also grant the refugee a sense of stability and the prospect of integrating into a new society.[981]

Article 14 Qualification Directive requires, however, that refugee status is terminated once a cessation (or exclusion) clause applies, irrespective of the duration of residence or other humanitarian considerations. It follows that a continued right of residence must then be based on grounds outside the Qualification Directive, such as national humanitarian grounds. This only changes when, after five years of residence, the refugee obtains long-term resident status in the meaning of the Long-Term Residence Directive.[982] Once that status is obtained, the conditions for withdrawal and loss of status of the Long-Term Residence Directive apply. Although these also include considerations of fraudulent acquisition of status and threat to public policy and security, the long-term residence status may not be withdrawn on the basis of any change of the circumstances that led to the granting of asylum. The logic of the EU asylum regime thus is that the continuation of refugee status will initially depend on a genuine need for protection, but that after a period of legal residence, the refugee should become entitled to a permanent status which approximates to that of the Member States' nationals. Whether this means that the Member States must routinely check – and in what time intervals – whether one still qualifies for refugee status is, as yet, undetermined.

Apart from cessation and exclusion, the Qualification Directive provides for two further grounds for terminating refugee status. The first one is if it transpires that the status was fraudulently obtained.[983] This clause is also mandatory, i.e. refugee status must be terminated if it is established that false information was decisive for granting refugee status. Secondly, Member States may terminate refugee status if: i) there are reasonable grounds for regarding the refugee as a danger to the security of the Member State; or ii) the refugee, having been convicted by a final judgment of a particularly serious crime, constitutes a

---

[980]   COM(2010)314 final, para 5.4.
[981]   UNHCR Handbook, para. 135; A. Zimmerman (ed.), *The 1951 Convention Relating to the Status of Refugees and its 1967 Protocol: A Commentary*, OUP 2011, p. 501.
[982]   See section 4.7.
[983]   Article 14(3)(b) Qualification Directive.

danger to the community of that Member State (Article 14(4)). This ground, even though it is facultative, has been critiqued, for it transforms the exception of Article 33(2) Refugee Convention into a ground for terminating refugee status.[984] Article 33(2) Refugee Convention sets forth the exceptions to the prohibition of *refoulement* of Article 33(1) Refugee Convention but upholds the person's status as refugee. The effect of Article 14(4) of the Directive is that a person who, for the reasons mentioned, constitutes a present danger to the host Member State, may forfeit his residence right and the other benefits of the Directive. He remains a refugee in the meaning of the Refugee Convention however, and must be treated as such until he is expelled from the Member State. To this effect, Article 14(6) of the Directive specifies that, as long as the person concerned is present in a Member State, he remains entitled to a number of rights of the Refugee Convention. This construction is legally awkward, but must be explained from the fact that the Directive grants stronger rights and benefits in a number of respects than the Refugee Convention. Articles 14(4) and (6) thus ensure that persons representing a danger to a Member State cannot benefit from the Directive's rights and benefits which are coupled to refugee status in the meaning of the Directive, but may not be denied their rights as Convention refugees.

7.7. CONTENT OF REFUGEE STATUS

What does refugee protection mean? To what rights are refugees entitled? Chapter VII of the Qualification Directive (Article 20–35) gives content to refugee status by listing a set of rights which, according to the Directive's Preamble, must ensure the availability of a minimum level of benefits, including adequate social welfare, means of subsistence and access to healthcare.[985] The rights set forth in the Directive apply both to refugees and persons eligible for subsidiary protection, unless the Directive indicates otherwise.[986]

The rights in the Directive are 'without prejudice to the rights laid down in the Geneva Convention'.[987] The refugee rights regime of the Qualification Directive is best to be seen not as displacing or repeating the rights of the Refugee Convention, but as expanding and complementing them. The Refugee Convention does not contain a genuine, or fully-fledged, right to asylum, in so far as that would mean a right of entry and residence. The Refugee Convention does, however, protect against *refoulement* to an unsafe country (Article 33(1)) and ensures a number of basic survival and dignity rights (Article 3–34). These include such rights as the right to

---

[984] Note, further, that Articles 14(4)(a) and (b) Qualification Directive speak not of termination of refugee status but of 'the status granted to a refugee'.

[985] Qualification Directive, Preamble, points 12, 45 and 46.

[986] Qualification Directive, Article 20(1).

[987] Qualification Directive, Article 20(1).

identity papers and a travel document, and rights in the spheres of employment, equal treatment and public relief. The Refugee Convention does not simply list a set of rights any refugee can invoke against the State Party in which he is present. Instead, the Refugee Convention attributes incrementally, in a fairly intricate way, different sets of rights to refugees, depending on their legal bond with the state.[988] This is based on the idea that the strength of the legal position of the refugee should be commensurate with the nature and duration of his ties with the host state.

The provisions of the Refugee Convention therefore differentiate on the basis of whether the refugee has no other bond with the state of refuge other than being within the state's *de facto* or *de jure* jurisdiction, whether he is 'physically present' within the territory of the country of refuge, whether he is 'lawfully present', whether he is 'lawfully residing', or whether he has some form of 'durable residence'. The distinction between these different forms of residence is not always easy to make, and in some respects, is contested. One question, for example, is whether 'lawful presence' includes refugees who are allowed to stay in the territory of the state pending the asylum procedure.[989] Among the basic rights to be accorded to any refugee, regardless of the nature of his legal bond with the state, are the prohibition of *refoulement*, the right to non-discrimination (Article 3), the right to be accorded the same treatment as is accorded to aliens generally (Article 7), and the right of access to court (Article 16).

The system of rights laid down in the Qualification Directive is of a somewhat different character. First, the Directive grants an unequivocal right of residence. It accordingly ensures that refugee status is a ground for residence in the Member States. Second, the Directive's rights do not accrue to a refugee incrementally, but are to be granted by Member States from the moment a person is granted refugee status. Third, the Directive does not simply reproduce the rights laid down in the Refugee Convention, but lists a distinct set of rights and benefits. Some of these can be traced back to the Refugee Convention, but others reflect common practices of Member States or general human rights standards, especially socioeconomic rights.[990] The rights regime of the Directive is a modern attempt at codifying the basic rights of refugees.

The rights of refugees under the Qualification Directive are:

Protection from refoulement (Article 21)

Refugees may not be subjected to *refoulement*, unless one of the exceptions of Article 21(2) applies. That paragraph recites the exceptions of Article 33(2)

---

[988] J.C. Hathaway, *The Rights of Refugees under International Law*, CUP 2005, p. 154.
[989] Ibid, p. 175–186.
[990] See more extensively A. Edwards, 'Human Rights, Refugees, and The Right 'To Enjoy' Asylum', *International Journal of Refugee Law*, Vol. 17 (2005), pp. 293–330.

Refugee Convention, i.e. there are reasonable grounds for considering the refugee as a danger to the security or the community of the Member State. If one of these exceptions applies, the Member State may also terminate the right of residence of the refugee (Article 21(3)). The possibility of expelling a refugee in accordance with these exceptions will be limited in practice, however, because Member States must, according to Article 21(1), respect 'the principle of *non-refoulement* in accordance with their international obligations'. Other international obligations, such as Article 3 ECHR, prohibit *refoulement*, irrespective of whether a person constitutes a danger to the host state.

Recall that the exception of constituting a danger to the host state may also be a ground for the denial of refugee status under the Directive (Article 14(4) Qualification Directive). When confronted with a refugee who can be considered to represent a danger to the Member State therefore, the Member may choose to refuse that person refugee status in accordance with Article 14(4) Qualification Directive, in which case the person cannot enjoy any of the Directive's benefits but is still to be regarded as Convention refugee. But the Member State may also choose to refuse only the residence permit and/or to serve an expulsion order, in which case the person continues to enjoy refugee status in the meaning of the Directive as well as the Refugee Convention, and thus enjoys the Directive's benefits until he is actually removed. In both scenarios, however, removal must also be tested against prohibitions of *refoulement* in general international law.

Maintaining family unity (Article 23)

Family members are defined in Article 2(j) of the Directive as spouses or partners in a stable relationship, and their minor children, provided that the family already existed in the country of origin and they are present in the Member State 'in relation to the application for international protection'. In respect of these family members, the Directive obliges Member States not only to maintain their unity, but also to grant a family member of a refugee who does not individually qualify for protection, the same rights as the refugee. Presumably, this provision applies only to family members who arrive (almost) simultaneously with the refugee in a Member State in order to claim asylum. Family members who arrive after the refugee has been granted refugee status fall within the regime of the Family Reunification Directive (chapter 4.2).

Residence permit (Article 24(1))

Refugees must be issued a residence permit, which must be valid for at least three years, and renewable.

Travel document (Article 25(1))

Refugees must be issued a refugee travel document (often termed 'refugee passport') under Article 28 of the Refugee Convention and the Schedule to the Refugee Convention, enabling them to travel internationally. This reflects the unlikelihood of a refugee obtaining a passport from his state of nationality. The cover of a refugee passport bears the date of approval of the Refugee Convention (28 July 1951), which also serves to identify the holder as a person in need of protection.

Access to employment (Article 26)

Refugees must have access to work.

Access to education (Article 27)

Minor refugees must have access to education on equal footing with nationals.

Social welfare (Article 29(1))

Refugees are entitled to 'the necessary social assistance' on equal footing with nationals.

Healthcare (Article 30)

Refugees must have access to healthcare under the same conditions as nationals.

Unaccompanied minors (Article 31)

Unaccompanied minor refugees must be ensured representation by a legal guardian or special organisation, must be placed under care, and must be assisted in the tracing of family members. These obligations are also listed in Article 22 of the Convention on the Rights of the Child, which sets out a number of special duties in respect of refugee children.

Access to accommodation (Article 32)

Refugees must have access to accommodation under equivalent conditions as other legally resident third-country nationals.

Freedom of movement (Article 33)

Refugees enjoy freedom of movement within the Member State under the same conditions as other legally resident third-country nationals.

Access to integration facilities (Article 34)

Refugees must have access to integration programmes.

When implementing the Directive's rights and benefits, Member States must take account of the specific situation of vulnerable persons, including minors.[991] It is, further, clear that refugees must be able to effectively enjoy the rights and benefits, and that the rights must be applied in line with the EU Charter on Fundamental Rights.[992] As was discussed in section 6.4, the Court of Justice held in *Saciri*, in the context of asylum applicants, that the provisions in the Reception Conditions Directive on material reception conditions had to be interpreted in conformity with Article 1 of the Charter, under which human dignity must be respected and protected.[993] There is no reason not to expect a similar reasoning to apply to persons whose status as refugee has been recognised.

FURTHER READING

H. Battjes, *European Asylum Law And International Law*, Leiden/Boston: Martinus Nijhoff (2006).

E. Feller, V. Türk and F. Nicholson, *Refugee Protection in International Law. UNHCR's Global Consultations on International Protection*, Cambridge University Press (2003).

M. Foster, *International refugee law and socio-economic rights: Refuge from deprivation*, Cambridge University Press (2007).

G.S. Goodwin-Gill and J. McAdam, *The Refugee in International Law*, Oxford University Press (2007).

K. Hailbronner (ed.), *European Immigration Law*, Munich: C.H. Beck (2010).

J.C. Hathaway, *The Rights of Refugees under International Law*, Cambridge University Press (2005).

J.C. Hathaway and M. Foster, *The Law of Refugee Status*, Cambridge University Press (forthcoming 2014).

S. Peers and N. Rogers (eds.), *EU Immigration and Asylum Law: Text and Commentary*, Leiden/Boston: Martinus Nijhoff (2006).

K. Wouters, *International Legal Standards for the Protection from Refoulement*, Antwerp: Intersentia (2009).

A. Zimmerman (ed.), *The 1951 Convention Relating to the Status of Refugees and its 1967 Protocol: A Commentary*, Oxford University Press (2011).

---

[991] Qualification directive, Article 20(3).
[992] See Qualification Directive, Preamble, points 41–47.
[993] Case C-79/13 *Saciri* [2014], para. 35.

8. SUBSIDIARY PROTECTION

8.1. INTRODUCTION

Subsidiary protection is the term used to describe the protection regime of the Qualification Directive for forced migrants who fall outside the framework of the 1951 Refugee Convention and the 1967 Protocol. It has its origin in the practice of states – influenced by the case law of international courts such as the European Court of Human Rights – of according protection against expulsion to persons who fail to meet the formal definition of 'refugee', but who are in a refugee-like situation. These forms of protection evolve around the prohibition of *refoulement* under, *inter alia*, Article 3 of the United Nations Convention against Torture, Articles 6 and 7 ICCPR, and Articles 2 and 3 ECHR.

In Europe, the region under scrutiny in this book, the European Court of Human Rights has unmistakably been the driving force behind the creation and fleshing out of *non-refoulement*. The ECtHR has shaped, since the beginning of the 1990s, a comprehensive body of binding case law on the basis of Article 3 ECHR, establishing an absolute prohibition from sending anyone to a place where he or she would be at risk of torture or inhuman or degrading treatment or punishment. The Union legislature followed up on this development by introducing 'subsidiary protection' in the first phase Qualification Directive (2004/83/EC), even though the former legal basis for measures in the field of asylum introduced by the Treaty of Amsterdam (Article 63 EC) only spoke of measures to be adopted with respect to the qualification of nationals of third countries as refugees. Importantly, whereas the ECtHR merely examines whether expulsion comes into conflict with Article 3 ECHR, the Qualification Directive has established a fully-fledged protection regime for those persons whose expulsion results in a risk of exposure to ill-treatment. This regime includes entitlement to a residence permit and a range of socio-economic rights. EU asylum law may thus be said to have complemented protection from *refoulement* with a status comparable to that accorded to refugees.

Article 78 TFEU sets forth that the common policy on asylum must include measures on subsidiary protection. The revised asylum instruments adopted in 2013, and discussed in Chapter 6, i.e. the Dublin Regulation, the Reception Conditions Directive and the Procedures Directive, therefore no longer distinguish – contrary to the first phase instruments – between applicants for refugee status and applicants for subsidiary protection status. The Qualification

Directive (2011/95/EU) is the key instrument setting forth the eligibility criteria for subsidiary protection. It also describes the content of subsidiary protection.

In a number of respects, the personal scope of the prohibition of *refoulement* under Article 3 ECHR is wider than that of the Refugee Convention. Because Article 3 ECHR protects *any* person who is within the jurisdiction of a state party (Article 1 ECHR), a person does not need to be a 'refugee' for invoking protection. This means, amongst other things, that it is not necessary that the risk of treatment is linked to one of the persecution grounds mentioned in the refugee definition. Further, the protection afforded by Article 3 ECHR is absolute. No exceptions are allowed for such reasons as public order or national security or activities of the person concerned.[994] Persons who are excluded from refugee protection on the basis of Article 1F Refugee Convention or who face expulsion in accordance with the exception of Article 33(2) Refugee Convention, may therefore still be protected by Article 3 ECHR. Another crucial difference between the protection regime of the ECHR and that of the Refugee Convention is that the ECtHR is competent to issue binding interpretations. In the region of the EU, the latter difference may, however, be assumed to be of diminishing importance, as the Refugee Convention will be interpreted in a binding manner by the CJEU, by way of interpreting the Qualification Directive.

Although the eligibility criteria for subsidiary protection laid down in the Qualification Directive are, for a good part, based on standards developed in the case law of the ECtHR, that case law is not necessarily decisive for the interpretation and application of the Directive. Firstly, the EU legislature chose, in respect of some issues, to expressly deviate from ECtHR case law. For example, the Directive's subsidiary protection regime is not 'absolute', because it does not cover persons who fall within one of the exclusion clauses of Article 1F of the Refugee Convention, nor persons who are a danger to the community or to the security of the Member State. Secondly, the ECHR is, as of yet, only of indirect relevance for interpreting the Qualification Directive, namely, through the general principles of Union law and the rights of the EU Charter of Fundamental Rights, which correspond to rights guaranteed by the ECHR. Article 4 of the Charter is the direct equivalent of Article 3 ECHR. Article 19(2) of the Charter is the EU equivalent of the prohibition of *refoulement*, as developed under Article 3 ECHR. Thirdly, it is not necessarily problematic if a situation arises in which there is a difference in personal scope between Article 3 ECHR and the EU subsidiary protection regime. In the case that only the Qualification Directive applies, the Member State will simply have to grant the person in question the higher level of rights and benefits under the Directive. In the case that only Article 3 ECHR applies, a person may not benefit from the higher standards under the Directive, but is still protected against expulsion under the ECHR.

---

[994] ECtHR 15 November 1996, *Chahal v. the United Kingdom*, No. 22414/93.

This chapter describes the subsidiary protection regime, as established in the Qualification Directive, but also pays systematic attention to the *non-refoulement* case law of the ECtHR. Even though the two regimes are not formally connected, the Qualification Directive has codified the case law of the ECtHR. There is, therefore, substantial substantive overlap between the Directive's eligibility criteria and ECtHR case law. Where such overlap is absent, it is important to remember that Article 3 ECHR continues to operate as a norm that independently protects against expulsion. Further, as the case law of the Court of Justice on subsidiary protection is still scarce, it is inevitable that this chapter draws heavily on the impressive body of case law of the ECtHR in the context of *non-refoulement*.

8.2. NON-REFOULEMENT IN HUMAN RIGHTS LAW

Before discussing the subsidiary protection regime of the Qualification Directive, we deem it helpful to elaborate briefly on the development on *non-refoulement* in general human rights law, in particular, in the case law of the ECtHR. That development was not self-evident, as the ECHR does not contain a right to asylum, nor does it refer explicitly to *non-refoulement*. Although the ECHR contains two specific provisions on the expulsion of aliens, namely Article 4 of Protocol No. 4 ECHR prohibiting collective expulsion and Article 1 of Protocol No. 7 on procedural safeguards in the event of expulsion, both these provisions see primarily to procedural standards to be respected in the case of deportation. The prohibition of collective expulsion has been interpreted by the ECtHR as entailing the right to an individual consideration of the person's circumstances before expulsion is effectuated.[995] These provisions are not concerned with the reasons for, or with the consequences of, expulsion.[996]

The ECtHR, however, held that the prohibition of *refoulement* is 'implicit' in Article 3 ECHR. In harmony with earlier decisions of the former European Commission on Human Rights,[997] and inspired by the explicit prohibition of *refoulement* of Article 3 of the Convention against Torture, the Court accepted,

---

[995] ECtHR 5 February 2002 *Čonka v Belgium*, No. 51564/99,; ECtHR 23 February 2012, *Hirsi Jamaa a.o. v. Italy*, No. 27765/09.

[996] Furthermore, not all EU Member States have ratified the Protocols laying down the two prohibitions; the prohibition of collective expulsion is, however, also laid down in Article 19(1) of the EU Charter of Fundamental Rights.

[997] EComHR 29 May 1961, *X. v Belgium*, No. 984/61; EComHR 26 March 1963, *X v Federal Republic of Germany*, No. 1802/62. Also see Parliamentary Assembly of the Council of Europe, Recommendation 434 (1965), para. 3: 'Considering Article 3 of the Convention for the Protection of Human Rights and Fundamental Freedoms which, by prohibiting inhuman treatment, binds Contracting Parties not to return refugees to a country where their life or freedom would be threatened.'

in *Soering* (1989), that Article 3 ECHR also governs the inter-state removal of a person, if such removal would result in proscribed ill-treatment. *Soering* concerned the extradition of a German national from the United Kingdom to the United States, where he had been an exchange student, and where he faced charges for murdering the parents of his girlfriend who had disapproved of their relationship.[998] The ECtHR accepted his complaint that extradition would expose him to a real risk of being sentenced to death and hence, experiencing the 'death row phenomenon', which would cause such tension and psychological trauma, also in view of its expected duration, to constitute treatment of a level of severity to be prohibited by Article 3 ECHR. The Court formulated, by way of general principle, that:

> the decision by a Contracting State to extradite a fugitive may give rise to an issue under Article 3 and hence engage the responsibility of that State under the Convention, where substantial grounds have been shown for believing that the person concerned, if extradited, faces a real risk of being subjected to torture or to inhuman or degrading treatment or punishment in the requesting country.[999]

In *Cruz Varas* (1991), concerning a Chilean political opponent of Augusto Pinochet's regime, whose asylum request had been refused by Sweden and was expelled to Chile, the ECtHR considered that this reasoning also applied to expulsion decisions and '*a fortiori* to cases of actual expulsion'.[1000] Any removal of a person from a Contracting State to another state, whether it concerns a criminal suspect (extradition) or an alien (expulsion), may thus be tested against Article 3 ECHR. Ever since, the ECtHR has reasoned that, notwithstanding the general right of states, as inherent in their sovereignty, to control the entry, residence and removal of aliens, and the fact that neither the Convention nor its Protocols confer the right to political asylum, 'expulsion by a Contracting State may give rise to an issue under Article 3, and hence engage the responsibility of that State under the Convention, where substantial grounds have been shown for believing that the person concerned, if deported, faces a real risk of being subjected to treatment contrary to Article 3.'[1001]

For a proper understanding of the impact of the ECtHR's case law on the prohibition of *refoulement*, it is useful to shortly reflect on the role of the Court, and its perception of that role, as it emerges from its case law. In general, it can be observed that the ECtHR has, over the years, become more active both in taking *measures preventing irreparable harm* and in independently *investigating relevant facts* underlying the applications brought before it.

---

[998] ECtHR 7 July 1989, *Soering v. The United Kingdom*, No. 14038/88.
[999] Ibid, para. 91.
[1000] Ibid, para. 70.
[1001] E.g. ECtHR 28 February 2008, *Saadi v. Italy*, No. 37201/06, paras. 124–125.

Groundbreaking was the judgment of the ECtHR in *Mamatkulov* of 2003, ruling that a request for the suspension of expulsion in accordance with Rule 39 of the Court's Rules of Procedure while an individual complaint is pending before the Court is binding for the State Party. Non-compliance with a request to adopt such an interim measure would be in breach of Article 34 of the ECHR, laying down the right for an individual to complain and the obligation of Contracting States not to hinder the effective exercise of that right.[1002] Illustrative of the development of the ECtHR's role, in this respect, is the difference in approach between the first judgment on Tamils in Sri Lanka (*Vilvarajah* 1991)[1003] and one of the last judgments on Tamils in Sri Lanka (*NA* 2008).[1004]

In the *Vilvarajah* case, there had been a *domestic* measure of the British judge, ordering that the expelled asylum seekers, whose applications had initially been refused by the United Kingdom authorities, should be brought back from Sri Lanka to the UK. The ECtHR itself had not been active in this respect, and it merely dealt with the question of whether the removal of the applicants had exposed them to a risk of inhuman treatment, and whether domestic law had provided sufficient legal remedies. In contrast, in the *NA. v. The UK* case, the ECtHR described how it had received, in 2007, an increasing number of requests for interim measures from Tamils, who were being returned to Sri Lanka from the United Kingdom and other Contracting States. The ECtHR applied Rule 39 in respect of no less than 342 Tamil applicants, who claimed that their return to Sri Lanka from the United Kingdom would expose them to ill-treatment in violation of Article 3 of the Convention. From this example, it transpires that the ECtHR nowadays actively takes preventive measures in order to secure the effectiveness of the protection offered by the Convention.

The ECtHR has also been engaged in independently establishing the facts, both in gathering documentary materials and in investigating the credibility of the statements of the applicant. The Court has consistently held that, in assessing conditions in the proposed receiving country, it will take as its basis all the material placed before it, or, if necessary, material obtained of its own motion (*proprio motu*). According to the Court, the establishment of a risk of ill-treatment in expulsion cases calls for a full and *ex nunc* assessment, as the situation in a country of destination may change over the course of time.[1005] In the *N. v. Finland*[1006] case, the ECtHR went so far as to carry out its own assessment of the facts by appointing two of its members as delegates in a fact-

---

[1002] ECtHR 6 February 2003, *Mamatkulov and Askarov v. Turkey*, Nos. 46827/99 and 46951/99, paras. 110 and 111.
[1003] ECtHR 30 October 1991, *Vilvarajah and Others v. The United Kingdom*, Nos. 13163 to -65/87 and 13447 to -8/87.
[1004] ECtHR 17 July 2008, *NA.v. The United Kingdom*, No. 25904/07.
[1005] ECtHR 11 January 2007, *Salah Sheekh v. The Netherlands*, No. 1948/04, para. 136.
[1006] ECtHR 26 July 2005, *N. v. Finland*, No. 38885/02.

finding mission, in order to take oral evidence from the applicant, his common-law wife, and a senior official in the Finnish Directorate of Immigration with extensive experience of processing asylum claims from the relevant part of Africa, and who had refused the applicant's request in the first instance.

Different from the European Convention, an 'explicit' prohibition of *refoulement* is laid down in the 1984 UN Convention against Torture. According to Article 3 of that Convention, no State Party shall expel, return (*refouler*) or extradite a person where there are substantial grounds for believing that he would be in danger of being subjected to torture. As noted above, the ECtHR's reasoning in *Soering* was partly modelled on Article 3 of the Convention against Torture. The scope of Article 3 of the Convention against Torture is, however, narrower than that of Article 3 ECHR, in that it only refers to torture, and not to inhuman or degrading treatment or punishment.

Like the ECHR, the ICCPR does not contain a provision specifically dealing with *non-refoulement*. The Human Rights Committee, in a much similar fashion as the ECtHR, has, nonetheless, considered that Articles 6 (the right to life) and 7 (the prohibition of torture or inhuman or degrading treatment) entertain a prohibition of *refoulement*, in the expulsion as well as extradition context.[1007]

Although subsidiary protection also entails protection from *refoulement* under the ICCPR and CAT, and both treaties are binding on all EU Member States and therefore relevant for this book, this chapter does not discuss the views of the HRC and the Committee Against Torture on cases involving *refoulement*, but focuses on the case law of the ECtHR, which covers roughly the same subject matter in a more comprehensive way.[1008] The relative popularity of the ECtHR as a forum for lodging complaints is, of course, explained from the fact that it issues binding judgments, whereas the Human Rights Committee and the Torture Committee are not judicial bodies, and lack the legal means to enforce their 'views'.

If a matter is within the scope of Union law, a Member State must also act in harmony with the EU Charter of Fundamental Rights. Article 19(2) of the Charter explicitly prohibits *refoulement*: 'No one may be removed, expelled or extradited to a State where there is a serious risk that he or she would be subjected to the death penalty, torture or other inhuman or degrading treatment or punishment.'

[1007] HRC, General Comment No. 31 (2004), CCPR/C/21/Rev.1/Add.13, para. 12; HRC 30 July 1993, *Kindler v Canada*, CCPR/C/48/D/470/1991.

[1008] On these other regimes: K. Wouters, *International Legal Standards for the Protection from Refoulement*, Antwerp: Intersentia (2009); J. McAdam, *Complementary Protection in International Refugee Law*, Oxford University Press (2007); H. Lambert, 'Protection Against Refoulement from Europe: Human Rights Law Comes to the Rescue', 48 *International and Comparative Law Quarterly* (1999) 515–544.

The explanations relating to the Charter clarify that this provision 'incorporates the relevant case law from the European Court of Human Rights regarding Article 3 of the ECHR.'[1009]

8.3. QUALIFICATION FOR SUBSIDIARY PROTECTION

A person eligible for subsidiary protection is defined in Article 2(f) of the Qualification Directive as *a third-country national or a stateless person who does not qualify as a refugee but in respect of whom substantial grounds have been shown for believing that the person concerned, if returned to his or her country of origin, would face a real risk of suffering serious harm as defined in Article 15 and is unable, or, owing to such risk, unwilling to avail himself or herself of the protection of that country.* Article 15 of the Directive completes the definition by exhaustively mentioning three types of 'serious harm':

– The death penalty or execution;
– Torture or inhuman or degrading treatment or punishment;
– Serious and individual threat to a civilian's life or person by reason of indiscriminate violence in situations of international or internal armed conflict.

The definition merits a few general observations. Firstly, Article 2(f) recites almost verbatim the standard formula used by the ECtHR in *refoulement* cases. Obviously, subsidiary protection draws on the case law of the ECtHR, which also informed the types of harm listed in Article 15.

Secondly, in excluding refugees from the definition of subsidiary protection, the Qualification Directive emphasises that the refugee regime remains the focal point for protection. Because it was specifically written to address the plight of fleeing persons, the refugee regime is accorded the status of *lex specialis* in the Directive. It follows logically from Article 2(f) that eligibility for refugee status should be examined prior to eligibility for subsidiary protection status. The duty to first determine whether the applicant qualifies as a refugee is explicitly formulated in Article 10(2) of the Procedures Directive.[1010] This duty is not only of practical importance in view of the substantive overlap between the eligibility criteria of the refugee definition and subsidiary protection, but also because the revised Qualification Directive continues to differentiate between the content of refugee status and subsidiary protection status. For that reason, the Procedures Directive lays down a right of appeal for persons who have been recognised as

---

[1009] Explanations relating to the Charter of Fundamental Rights [2007] OJ C303/2.
[1010] Directive 2013/32/EU. See section 6.5.

eligible for subsidiary protection, and who have thus been (expressly or impliedly) refused refugee status (Article 46(2)). If, however, a Member State makes use of its right to establish or maintain more favourable standards (Article 4 Qualification Directive) and offers the same rights and benefits to refugees and subsidiary protection beneficiaries, no right of appeal exists.[1011] Such a Member State will remain obliged to first examine refugee status, but a failure to do so cannot be challenged before a court.

Thirdly, in referring to third-country nationals and stateless persons, the definition once more affirms, in accordance with the Protocol on asylum for nationals of Member States of the European Union, that EU citizens fall outside the scope of the Union asylum regime.[1012] Both the categories of EU citizens and refugees remain, however, fully covered by the prohibitions of *refoulement* in the ECHR and the EU Charter of Fundamental Rights.

Fourthly, the definition of subsidiary protection must be read together with the common provisions for assessing applications for international protection laid down in Articles 4–8 of the Qualification Directive. These apply equally to refugee status determination and subsidiary protection status determination, and deal with the issues of assessments of facts and circumstances (Article 4), international protection *sur place* (Article 5), actors of persecution or serious harm (Article 6), actors of protection (Article 7) and internal protection (Article 8). These provisions build on, and must be interpreted in line with, both the Refugee Convention (and the sources for interpreting it) and the case law of the ECtHR. They were discussed in the previous chapter.[1013]

8.3.1. REAL RISK

To be granted subsidiary protection, the individual must show substantial grounds for believing that he would face a *real risk* of suffering serious harm. The real risk criterion is derived from the case law of the ECtHR. It is safe to assume that the criterion is to be given the same scope and meaning in the Qualification Directive.

Similar to the well-founded fear criterion of the refugee definition, a real risk sees to a forward-looking danger that can be objectively established. In *Soering*, the risk was defined by the ECtHR as a foreseeable or likely consequence of the extradition, and not as a certainty or high probability. Since *Vilvarajah*, the ECtHR has consistently held that the focus of the risk assessment must be on the

---

[1011] Article 46(2), second sentence Directive 2013/32/EU.
[1012] See section 6.2.2, and section 7.3.
[1013] ECtHR 7 July 1989, *Soering v. United Kingdom*, No. 14038/88.

'foreseeable consequences of the removal going beyond the mere possibility of being ill-treated'.[1014]

Crucial for determining whether a real risk exists are the circumstances informing it. As a general rule, the ECtHR posits that the level of risk must be determined on the basis of the general situation in the country of return as well as on the personal circumstances of the applicant.[1015] The ECtHR has specified that the assessment of whether there is a real risk must be made on the basis of all relevant factors which may increase the risk of ill-treatment. Even if a number of individual factors may not, when considered separately, constitute a real risk; taken cumulatively the same factors may give rise to a real risk.[1016]

In most cases where a violation of Article 3 ECHR is found by the ECtHR, the real risk is established on the basis of circumstances that are specific to the individual, often taken together with generally available information on the situation in the country of return. For instance, the ECtHR found that that a real risk of exposure to ill-treatment existed in cases concerning an Iranian woman who had committed adultery, against the background of international materials reporting the practice of punishment of adultery by stoning in Iran (*Jabari v. Turkey*);[1017] a deserter from the Eritrean army in the light of general public information that indicated that deserters in Eritrea were held in incommunicado detention and subjected to prolonged exposure to the sun in high temperatures (*Said v. the Netherlands*);[1018] a Tanzanian member of a rebel group who had been detained and ill-treated before his flight to the United Kingdom, and where international reports indicated widespread practices of the police in Tanzania ill-treating and beating detainees (*Hilal v. the United Kingdom*);[1019] and a Chechen man, whose father had been a high-ranking separatist and had been shot before his eyes, in the light of country reports providing a picture of regularly occurring human rights violations and a climate of impunity in Chechnya (*I.K. v. Austria*).[1020]

A more contested matter the extent to which the existence of a real risk may be deduced merely from a situation of general violence or from violence directed towards a particular group – thus lacking any specific individual characteristics. In *Vilvarajah*, the ECtHR held that 'special distinguishing features' needed to

---

[1014] ECtHR 30 October 1991, *Vilvarajah and others v. The United Kingdom*, Nos. 13163 to -65/87 and 13447 to -8/87, paras. 108 and 111; ECtHR 29 January 2013, *S.H.H. v. The United Kingdom*, No. 60367/10, para. 73.

[1015] *Vilvarajah*, para. 108, *NA.*, para. 113.

[1016] *NA.*, para 130; ECtHR 5 September 2013, *I. v. Sweden*, No. 61204/09, para. 66.

[1017] ECtHR 11 July 2000, *Jabari v. Turkey*, No. 40035/98.

[1018] ECtHR 5 July 2005, *Said v. The Netherlands*, No. 2345/02.

[1019] ECtHR 6 March 2001, *Hilal v. The United Kingdom*, No. 45276/99.

[1020] ECtHR 28 March 2003, *I.K. v. Austria*, No. 2964/12. See also ECtHR 5 September 2013, *I. v. Sweden*, No. 61204/09, where the Court found a violation of Article 3 ECHR in respect of the expulsion of a person of Chechen origin who had been engaged in journalistic activities in Chechnya, and who had previously been tortured.

exist in order to foresee that the applicants in that case would be subjected to proscribed ill-treatment.[1021] The Court considered the security and human rights situation for Tamils in Sri Lanka to be unsettling, but not sufficiently serious so as to create a risk that would go beyond the mere possibility of being ill-treated. Because the Tamil applicants had not shown that their personal circumstances were any worse than that of other members of the Tamil community, no violation of Article 3 was found. Throughout its case law, the ECtHR has indeed shown itself to be quite reluctant in accepting a real risk merely on the basis of situations of general violence such as in Colombia,[1022] Iraq,[1023] Afghanistan[1024] or Sri Lanka;[1025] or on the basis of persistent human rights violations of ethnic, religious or other minority communities, such as Turkmens in Iraq,[1026] Serbs in Croatia,[1027] gay people in Iran,[1028] or Christians in Iraq.[1029]

In theory, the phrase 'special distinguishing features' could be interpreted as implying an element of comparison. That would mean that the person concerned, if belonging to a group that is the target of violence or human rights violations, must be treated differently or substantially worse than other members of the group in order to have a real, personal and foreseeable risk. *Vilvarajah* can, however, also be read as requiring an applicant to show special distinguishing features, only if he could not otherwise show that the general situation in the country or of a minority group entails a real risk of ill-treatment. After all, countries or regions may experience varying degrees of general violence, and minority groups may be targeted with different intensities.

The latter interpretation has been confirmed in the ECtHR's later case law.[1030] The case of *Salah Sheekh v. the Netherlands* concerned an applicant from Somalia, belonging to the minority Ashraf clan. The Court started its assessment of the existence of a real risk of ill-treatment by considering that before leaving

---

[1021]   *Vilvarajah*, para. 112.
[1022]   ECtHR 29 April 1997, *H.L.R. v. France*, No. 24573/94.
[1023]   ECtHR 20 January 2009, *F.H. v. Sweden*, No. 32621/06, para. 93. Also see ECtHR 27 June 2013, *M.Y.H. a.o. v. Sweden*, No. 50859/10, paras. 56–58.
[1024]   ECtHR 20 September 2007, *Sultani v. France*, No. 45223/05, para. 67; ECtHR, *H. and B. v. The United Kingdom*, Nos. 70073/10 and 44539/11), para. 93.
[1025]   *NA.*, para. 125.
[1026]   ECtHR 26 April 2005, *Müslim v. Turkey*, No. 53566/99.
[1027]   ECtHR 14 October 2003, *Tomic v. The United Kingdom*, No. 17837/03.
[1028]   ECtHR 22 June 2004, *F. v. The United Kingdom*, No. 17341/03; ECtHR 9 December 2004, *I.I.N. v. The Netherlands*, No. 2035/04.
[1029]   ECtHR 20 January 2009, *F.H. v. Sweden*, No. 32621/06, para. 93. Also see ECtHR 27 June 2013, *M.Y.H. a.o. v. Sweden*, No. 50859/10, paras. 56–58.
[1030]   ECtHR 26 July 2005, *N. v. Finland*, No. 38885/02; and ECtHR 11 January 2007, *Salah Sheekh v. The Netherlands*, No. 1948/04, in which the Court, in paragraph 162 and 148 respectively, explicitly referred to its judgment in the *Vilvarajah* case regarding the issue of 'special distinguishing features' or terms of identical meaning. See, further, ECtHR 28 February 2008, *Saadi v. Italy*, No. 37201/06, para. 132; ECtHR 17 July 2008, *NA. v. The United Kingdom*, No. 25904/07, paras. 113–116.

Somalia, the applicant, as a member of a minority group, had been subjected to inhuman treatment because:

> members of a clan beat, kicked, robbed, intimidated and harassed him on many occasions and made him carry out forced labour. Members of the same clan also killed his father and raped his sister (…).[1031]

Furthermore, the Court considered that it was evident that members of the Ashraf and other minority groups would remain vulnerable to these types of human rights abuses, and were not the victims of indiscriminate violence, but clearly targeted.[1032] The Court then added that in the context of these findings:

> it cannot be required of the applicant that he establishes that *further* [italics; author] special distinguishing features, concerning him personally, exist in order to show that he was, and continues to be, personally at risk.[1033]

The conclusion that mere membership of a targeted group can be sufficient to establish a real, personal and foreseeable risk, was confirmed by the ECtHR in the case of *Saadi v. Italy*:

> in cases where an applicant alleges that he or she is a member of a group systematically exposed to a practice of ill-treatment, the Court considers that the protection of Article 3 of the Convention enters into play when the applicant establishes, (…), that there are serious reasons to believe in the existence of the practice in question and his or her membership of the group concerned.[1034]

Hence, if one can demonstrate to belong to a group that is 'systematically' exposed to ill-treatment, and provided there are no protection alternatives available, expulsion is prohibited. In a series of cases against Russia concerning the expulsion of Uzbek nationals who were members of the Hizb ut-Tahrir, a religious organisation recognised as extremist and banned in Uzbekistan, the ECtHR applied this reasoning. It considered that it would not insist that the applicant show further special distinguishing features, because reliable sources confirmed a continuing pattern of ill-treatment and torture on the part of the Uzbek authorities of members of the Hizb ut-Tahrir.[1035]

[1031] ECtHR 11 January 2007, *Salah Sheekh v. The Netherlands*, No. 1948/04, para. 146.

[1032] Ibid, paras. 146 and 148.

[1033] Ibid, para. 148.

[1034] ECtHR 28 February 2008, *Saadi v. Italy*, No. 37201/06, para. 132. See also ECtHR 20 September 2007, *Sultani v. France*, No. 45223/05, para. 67.

[1035] ECtHR 5 February 2013, *Zokhidov v Russia*, no. 67286/10, para. 138; ECtHR 3 July 2012, *Rustamov v Russia*, No. 11209/10, para. 128; ECtHR 12 May 2010, *Khodzhayev v Russia*, No. 52466/08), paras. 100–102; and ECtHR 8 November 2011, *Yakubov v Russia*, No. 7265/10, para. 89.

The ECtHR has also confirmed, in theory as well as practice, that the prohibition of expulsion can come into play merely on account of a situation of general violence. In *NA. v. The United Kingdom*, 17 years after *Vilvarajah*, the Court was again confronted with the situation of Tamils in Sri Lanka. This time the Court paid special attention to the implications of a situation of general violence on the determination of the existence of a real risk. As the Court apparently wished to clarify its position on this subject, it seems appropriate to cite the relevant passages at some length:

> [T]he foreseeable consequences of the removal of the applicant to the country of destination (…) must be considered in the light of the general situation there as well as the applicant's personal circumstances (…). In this connection, and where it is relevant to do so, the Court will have regard to whether there is a general situation of violence existing in the country of destination.
>
> However, a general situation of violence will not normally in itself entail a violation of Article 3 in the event of an expulsion (…). Indeed, the Court has rarely found a violation of Article 3 on that ground alone. (…)
>
> From the foregoing survey of its case law, it follows that the Court has never excluded the possibility that a general situation of violence in a country of destination will be of a sufficient level of intensity as to entail that any removal to it would necessarily breach Article 3 of the Convention. Nevertheless, the Court would adopt such an approach only in the most extreme cases of general violence, where there was a real risk of ill-treatment simply by virtue of an individual being exposed to such violence on return.[1036]

In *NA.*, concerning a Tamil who had been arrested six times between 1990 and 1997 on suspicion of being a member of Liberation Tigers of Tamil Eelam ('the LTTE'), and who had been ill-treated in detention before fleeing to the United Kingdom, the ECtHR arrived at a violation of Article 3 ECHR on the basis of a cumulative assessment of the climate of general violence, the treatment of members of the LTTE who were considered by the authorities to be of interest, and the applicant's personal history as a detainee.

In *Sufi and Elmi*, the ECtHR gave application proper to the notion that, exceptionally, general and indiscriminate violence can be of such intensity that anyone exposed to it is at real risk of ill-treatment. The case was exceptional in that it concerned expulsion to Mogadishu, the capital of Somalia, which was the theatre of rampant urban warfare in the years 2007–2011. The Court considered that:

> the large quantity of objective information overwhelmingly indicates that the level of violence in Mogadishu is of sufficient intensity to pose a real risk of treatment reaching the Article 3 threshold to anyone in the capital. In reaching this conclusion

---

[1036] ECtHR 17 July 2008, *NA. v. The United Kingdom*, No. 25904/07, paras. 113–116.

the Court has had regard to the indiscriminate bombardments and military offensives carried out by all parties to the conflict, the unacceptable number of civilian casualties, the substantial number of persons displaced within and from the city, and the unpredictable and widespread nature of the conflict.[1037]

Notable about *Sufi and Elmi* was, further, that the ECtHR dispelled the argument of the United Kingdom that the two applicants could safely relocate to other regions in Somalia, such as refugee camps in Southern Somalia. The Court observed, again on the basis of various reports, that the inhabitants of these camps were vulnerable to violent crime, exploitation, abuse and forcible recruitment; that due to extreme overcrowding, access to shelter, water and sanitation facilities was extremely limited; and that therefore, the conditions were sufficiently dire to amount to prohibited treatment under Article 3 ECHR.[1038] Similar to its assessment in respect of Mogadishu therefore, there was no need for the applicants to establish why they, specifically, would be at risk in one of the refugee camps.

That the ECtHR will only rarely establish a violation of Article 3 ECHR solely on the basis of general conditions is illustrated by its later judgment in *K.A.B. v. Sweden*, in which it considered that, despite on-going concerns about the security situation in Mogadishu and other parts of Somalia, the violence in Mogadishu had decreased to such an extent that there was no longer a real risk for anyone in the city.[1039]

8.3.2. SERIOUS HARM

Article 15 exhaustively lists three types of serious harm. These may be conceived as the three separate, but potentially overlapping, grounds for granting an applicant subsidiary protection status. Article 15 was not revised in the 2011 recast of the Directive.

Article 15(a): the death penalty or execution

The first category of harm is derived from the case law of the ECtHR on the basis of Article 2 ECHR (the right to life), read in conjunction with Protocol No. 6 ECHR (abolishment of the death penalty, except in time of war) and Protocol No. 13 ECHR (abolishment of the death penalty in all circumstances). Although the case law of the ECtHR in the context of non-*refoulement* has evolved primarily and overwhelmingly on the basis of Article 3 ECHR, the Court has consistently held that 'analogous considerations' apply to Article 2 ECHR and

---

[1037] ECtHR 28 June 2011, *Sufi and Elmi v. The United Kingdom*, nos. 8319/07 and 11449/07, para. 248.
[1038] Ibid, paras. 291–292.
[1039] ECtHR 5 september 2013, *K.A.B. v. Sweden*, No. 886/11, para. 91.

Protocols 6 and 13 ECHR where the return of an alien puts his or her life in danger, as a result of the imposition of the death penalty or otherwise.[1040] Before the ECtHR, the death penalty is usually at stake in the context of extradition, including many cases where extradition is sought by the United States. These cases often revolve around the issue of whether diplomatic guarantees offered by the receiving state obviate the risk of the death penalty being sought or executed. This matter is discussed in section 8.4. *Bader and Kanbor v Sweden* was the first judgment in which the Court found the prohibition of *refoulement* implicit in Article 2 to have been violated – in conjunction with Article 3 ECHR. The case concerned the expulsion from Sweden of a Syrian national who had been convicted *in absentia* in Syria, for complicity in a murder, and had been sentenced to death, and who was at serious risk of being executed upon return, as there were no assurances that he would receive a new trial and that the death penalty would not be sought or imposed.[1041]

It is somewhat unfortunate that the harm in Article 15(a) is narrowly defined as 'the death penalty or execution', thus omitting the more general language on the protection of life of Article 2 ECHR. The latter provision not only safeguards against arbitrary deprivation of life in the form of state authored punishment, but may also protect against foreseeable risk of loss of life as a result of murder, manslaughter, suicide, or general situations of lethal violence, such as in the context of (civil) war.[1042]

Apart from the right to life, the ECtHR has, albeit more reluctantly, also accepted that other Convention rights may imply a prohibition of expulsion. It has set a higher threshold for such provisions to entertain that effect, in requiring that there is 'a flagrant denial' of the right at issue in the receiving country.[1043] In *Othman*, the ECtHR accepted that this threshold was met. It concerned the high profile case of a radical Muslim cleric, who the United Kingdom definitely wanted to expel, but the Court concluded that this would violate Article 6 ECHR, since there was a real risk of a flagrant denial of justice if he were deported to Jordan, as the terrorism charges brought against him in Jordan

---

[1040] ECtHR 23 April 2002, *S.R. v. Sweden*, Appl. No. 62806/00; ECtHR 1 October 2002, *Tekdemir v. The Netherlands*, Appl. No. 49823/99; ECtHR 11 March 2003, *Razaghi v. Sweden*, Appl. No. 64599/01; ECtHR 26 October 2004, *B. v. Sweden*, Appl. No. 16578/03; ECtHR 17 January 2006, *Bello v. Sweden*, Appl. No. 32213/04; ECtHR 7 February 2006, *Gomes v. Sweden*, Appl. No. 34566/04; ECtHR 11 May 1999, *Sinnarajah v. Switzerland*, No. 45187/99.

[1041] ECtHR 8 November 2005, *Bader and Kanbor v. Sweden*, No. 13284/04.

[1042] ECtHR 29 June 2004, *Salkic and Others v. Sweden*, Appl. No. 7702/04; ECtHR 5 september 2013, *K.A.B. v. Sweden,* No. 886/11, para. 67.

[1043] *Soering*, para. 113; ECtHR 26 June 1992, *Drozd and Janousek v. France and Spain*, No. 12747/87, para. 110; ECtHR 16 October 2001, *Einhorn v. France*, No. 71555/01; ECtHR 6 February 2003, *Mamatkulov and Abdurasulovic v. Turkey*, Nos. 46827/99 and 46951/99, para. 85; ECtHR 11 March 2003, *Razaghi v. Sweden*, No. 64599/01; ECtHR 14 October 2003, *Tomic v. The United Kingdom*, No. 17837/03; ECtHR 22 June 2004, *F. v. The United Kingdom*, No. 17341/03; ECtHR 20 February 2007, *Al-Moayad v. Germany*, No. 35865/03.

would be based on evidence procured by torture.[1044] In *El-Masri v. Macedonia*, the Court established a violation of Article 5 ECHR on the part of Macedonia for having secretly handed over a terrorist suspect to the CIA. The CIA had subsequently flown him to the 'Salt Pit' in Afghanistan, where he was detained unlawfully and kept incommunicado before being released five months later, without charges having been brought, in a forest in Albania.[1045] This amounted to enforced disappearance and arbitrary detention, in flagrant violation of Article 5.

Whether other Convention provisions than Articles 5 and 6 – such as Articles 8 or 9 – also prohibit expulsion if it results in treatment proscribed by these provisions, is more contested.[1046] Such scenarios are not further discussed here.[1047]

At the time the first phase Qualification Directive was drafted, case law on a possible *refoulementwirkung* (for lack of a proper English noun) of other provisions than Articles 2 and 3 ECHR was less developed than it is now. Yet, the European Commission had proposed to include as ground for subsidiary protection in the Directive harm consisting of a 'violation of a human right, sufficiently severe to engage the Member State's international obligations'.[1048] This would seem to appropriately summarise the *refoulement* case law of the ECtHR. That proposal was, however, defeated in the Council, which opted instead for the narrow formula of the death penalty or execution. Nor did the EU legislature seize the opportunity, at the time of recasting the Directive, to incorporate the latest case law of the ECtHR on the matter. This has resulted in the Directive being more limited in scope in respect of types of harm that engage protection than the ECHR. Although not entitled to a protection status under EU law, persons to whom this hiatus applies may not, of course, be expelled, and Member States may choose to grant such persons a resident status, in accordance with their national legislation.

Article 15(b): torture or inhuman or degrading treatment or punishment

According to the Court of Justice EU, Article 15(b) corresponds, in essence, to Article 3 of the ECHR.[1049] The three types of ill-treatment mentioned in

1044 ECtHR 17 January 2012, *Othman (Abu Qatada) v. The United Kingdom*, No. 8139/09.
1045 ECtHR 13 December 2012, *El-Masri v. the Former Yugoslav Republic of Macedonia*, No. 39630/09.
1046 ECtHR 14 October 2003, *Tomic v. The United Kingdom*, No. 17837/03; *F. v. The United Kingdom*; *Razaghi v. Sweden*; *Gomes v. Sweden*; *Z. and T. v. The United Kingdom*; ECtHR 19 January 1999, *Ould Barar v. Sweden*, No. 42367/98.
1047 See M. den Heijer, *'Whose Rights and Which Rights? The Continuing Story of Non-Refoulement under the European Convention on Human Rights'*, 10 European Journal of Migration and Law (2008) 277–314.
1048 COM(2001) 510 final.
1049 ECJ 17 February 2009, *Elgafaji*, Case C-465/07, para. 28.

Article 15(b) and prohibited by Article 3 ECHR – torture, inhuman treatment and degrading treatment – are well-defined in the ECtHR's case law outside the context of *refoulement*. The special stigma of 'torture' attaches only to deliberate inhuman treatment causing very serious and cruel suffering. and may involve such reprehensible conduct as Palestinian hanging,[1050] the administration of electric shocks,[1051] and *falaka*, i.e. foot whipping.[1052] For conduct to amount to other forms of inhuman and degrading treatment proscribed by Article 3 ECHR, the ECtHR consistently holds that such treatment must attain 'a minimum level of severity'.[1053] Whether treatment attains this level depends on all facts and circumstances of the case, including the nature and context of the treatment in question, the manner and method of its execution, its duration, its physical or mental effects, and the personal circumstances of the victim.[1054]

In *refoulement* cases it will not always be possible to predict, precisely, what the treatment upon return will be. Often, therefore, the treatment to which an applicant may be subjected is not explicitly examined by the ECtHR. It merely stipulates, as a general principle, that an assessment needs to be made of the situation in the receiving country in the light of the requirements of Article 3 ECHR.[1055] If the ECtHR establishes that there is indeed a real risk of proscribed treatment without being able to identify what treatment exactly, it uses the shorthand 'ill-treatment' instead.[1056]

Even though harm must meet the threshold of a minimum level of severity, the ECtHR has accepted that quite divergent types of harm may fall within the scope of Article 3 ECHR. Apart from physical harm, the Court has confirmed, in the context of expulsion, that psychological harm[1057] – but also forms of socio-economic destitution or discrimination – can attract the expelling state's responsibility.[1058] Not all types of socio-economic harm can be brought within the ambit of Article 3, however. When an expellee complains about forms of maltreatment such as extreme poverty, a lack of medical care or dire humanitarian living conditions, it seems that the ECtHR distinguishes between two types of situations.

[1050] ECtHR 18 December 1996, *Aksoy v. Turkey*, No. 21987/93.
[1051] ECtHR 10 October 200, *Akkoc v. Turkey*, Nos. 22947/93 and 22948/93; ECtHR 2 November 2004, *Yaman v. Turkey*, No. 32446/96.
[1052] ECtHR 27 June 2000, *Salman v. Turkey*, No. 21986/93; ECtHR 4 April 2006, *Corsacov v. Moldova*, No. 18944/02.
[1053] ECtHR 18 January 1978, *Ireland v. The United Kingdom*, No. 5310/71, para. 162.
[1054] E.g. ECtHR 23 September 1998, *A. v. The United Kingdom*, No. 25599/94; ECtHR 10 July 2001, *Price v. The United Kingdom*, No. 33394/96.
[1055] ECtHR 28 February 2008, *Saadi v. Italy*, No. 37201/06, para. 126.
[1056] Eg ECtHR 5 September 2013, *K.A.B. v. Sweden*, No. 886/11, para. 97.
[1057] *Soering*, para 111, referring to 'the ever present and mounting anguish of awaiting execution of the death penalty.'
[1058] *M.S.S.*, para. 263.

If the deprivation is the result of deliberate actions or omissions of the authorities in the receiving state (which may also be non-state actors), such deprivation must be tested against the normal threshold of a minimum level severity. Thus, in the case of *M.S.S.*, the ECtHR accepted not only that Greece had violated Article 3 ECHR for failing to address the needs of an asylum seeker who had spent months living in a state of the most extreme poverty, unable to cater for his most basic needs; but also considered Belgium to have violated Article 3 for having transferred the asylum seeker, pursuant to the Dublin Regulation, to Greece, thereby knowingly exposing him to such treatment.[1059] Likewise, in *Sufi and Elmi*, the Court considered that the dire humanitarian conditions for internally displaced persons in southern and central Somalia, including in the refugee camps, were predominantly due to the direct and indirect actions of the parties to the conflict.[1060] Because the circumstances in the camps amounted to treatment reaching the threshold of Article 3 of the Convention, return there would violate Article 3 ECHR.

If, on the other hand, socio-economic hardship is predominantly attributable to a general situation of poverty or to the receiving state's lack of resources, the ECtHR only exceptionally accepts that expulsion is prohibited. In such cases, the ECtHR underlines that the Convention is essentially directed at the protection of civil and political rights, and that it does not fall on Contracting States to alleviate disparities in living conditions around the world.[1061] The Convention cannot, therefore, be construed as obliging States Parties to refrain from expulsions in order to provide free and unlimited socio-economic services to all aliens present on their territories.[1062] The ECtHR does, however, retain some flexibility in bringing such situations within its supervision. It considers that expulsion can be prohibited but only if 'the humanitarian grounds against removal are compelling'.[1063] In the case of *S.H.H. v. The United Kingdom*, the ECtHR applied this test to the expulsion by the United Kingdom of a disabled man (his lower right leg and penis had both been amputated as a consequence of a rocket attack) to Afghanistan. The Court found that the inadequacies in the care for persons with disabilities stemmed from a want of resources on the part of the Afghan government, and were not a result of the authorities' deliberate acts or omissions.[1064] Because the man had previously managed to support himself in Afghanistan, the

---

[1059] Ibid, para. 367.
[1060] *Sufi and Elmi*, para. 282.
[1061] *N. v. The United Kingdom*, para. 44; ECtHR 29 January 2013, *S.H.H. v. The United Kingdom*, No. 60367/10, para. 89.
[1062] Ibid.
[1063] Ibid, at paras. 43 and 92, respectively.
[1064] *S.H.H. v. The United Kingdom*, paras. 91–92.

Court did not consider the humanitarian grounds against his removal compelling.

The issue of socio-economic deprivation has evolved chiefly in cases concerning the return of seriously ill people. In *St. Kitts* (1997), the ECtHR had found that the expulsion of a convicted drug runner who was in the terminal stage of AIDS would entail 'a real risk of dying under most distressing circumstances and would thus amount to inhuman treatment'.[1065] The ECtHR found the humanitarian considerations against removal compelling, in view of the facts that the applicant was critically ill and close to death, that he could not be guaranteed any medical care in his home country, St. Kitts, and that he had no family or other social support. Even though many medical expulsion cases have, since that judgment, been brought before it, the ECtHR has never again found a violation of Article 3. The Grand Chamber of the Court clarified, in *N. v. The United Kingdom* (2008), that:

> Aliens who are subject to expulsion cannot in principle claim any entitlement to remain in the territory of a Contracting State in order to continue to benefit from medical, social or other forms of assistance and services provided by the expelling State. The fact that the applicant's circumstances, including his life expectancy, would be significantly reduced if he were to be removed from the Contracting State is not sufficient in itself to give rise to breach of Article 3. The decision to remove an alien who is suffering from a serious mental or physical illness to a country where the facilities for the treatment of that illness are inferior to those available in the Contracting State may raise an issue under Article 3, but only in a very exceptional case, where the humanitarian grounds against the removal are compelling.[1066]

It is, furthermore, doubtful whether, even if the threshold of compelling humanitarian grounds is met, suffering which flows from naturally occurring phenomena or illness can lead to eligibility for international protection under the Qualification Directive. This is because, as explained in the previous chapter (section 7.4.2), Article 6 of the Directive requires there to be an 'actor of persecution or serious harm'. It is difficult to identify a responsible 'actor' in the event of disaster or illness.

Article 15(c): serious and individual threat to a civilian's life or person by reason of indiscriminate violence in situations of international or internal armed conflict

The last category of harm is phrased in somewhat enigmatic terms. The language of Article 15(c) Qualification Directive differs from any known prohibition of

---

[1065] ECtHR 2 May 1997, *D. v. The United Kingdom (St. Kitts)*, No. 30240/96, para. 53.
[1066] *N. v. The United Kingdom*, para. 42.

refoulement applicable in the region of the European Union.[1067] It provoked considerable controversy in the immediate aftermath of adoption of the first phase Directive. Put bluntly, the question was whether this newly formulated ground for asylum enlivened an entitlement to protection for entire populations struck by (civil) war, thus vastly expanding the personal scope of the institution of asylum, as previously known in international law; or that it merely clarified and codified the ECtHR's case law that also in situations of general violence, a person must show individual features for being protected from expulsion.[1068] Those favouring the first approach emphasised that the words 'indiscriminate violence' necessarily articulated a risk of general applicability, whilst more cautious minds pointed out that the provision still required there to be an 'individual threat'.[1069]

The discussion ran in parallel with the progressive case law of the ECtHR on the relevance of a general situation of violence for establishing a real risk, including the *NA.* judgment of 2008, as discussed above. In the case of *Elgafaji*, the Court of Justice had occasion to address the debate. It was asked whether Article 15(c) was to be interpreted as offering protection only in situations which already fall within the scope of Article 15(b) – and thus within that of Article 3 ECHR.[1070] The Court of Justice held Article 15(c) to be a provision of which the content differed from that of Article 3 ECHR, that the interpretation of Article 15(c) must be carried out independently, and that Article 15(c) has its own field of application.[1071] In interpreting the meaning of Article 15(c) however, the Court employed language that closely resembled that of the ECtHR in its *NA.* judgment. It concluded that 'the existence of a serious and individual threat is not subject to the condition that the applicant adduce evidence that he is

---

[1067] Outside Europe, the extension of asylum to persons fleeing from general conflict did find a basis. According to the Convention Governing the Specific Aspects of Refugee Problems in Africa (OAU Convention), 10 September 1969, 1001 U.N.T.S. 45, Article 1(2): '[t]he term "refugee" shall also apply to every person who, owing to external aggression, occupation, foreign domination or events seriously disturbing public order in either part or the whole of his country of origin or nationality, is compelled to leave his place of habitual residence in order to seek refuge in another place outside his country of origin or nationality.' Also see the (non-binding) Cartagena Declaration on Refugees, Colloquium on the International Protection of Refugees in Central America, Mexico and Panama, 22 November 1984, para III(3): '[the definition or concept of a refugee includes] persons who have fled their country because their lives, safety or freedom have been threatened by generalized violence, foreign aggression, internal conflicts, massive violation of human rights or other circumstances which have seriously disturbed public order.'

[1068] For a discussion: J. McAdam, 'The European Union Qualification Directive: The Creation of a Subsidiary Protection Regime', 17 *International Journal of Refugee Law* (2005), 461 at 479–487; R. Piotrowicz and C. van Eck, 'Subsidiary Protection and Primary Rights', 53 *International and Comparative Law Quarterly* (2004), 107 at 132–136.

[1069] Ibid.

[1070] ECJ 17 February 2009, *Elgafaji*, Case C-465/07.

[1071] Ibid, paras. 28, 33, 36.

specifically targeted by reason of factors particular to his personal circumstances.'[1072] It further reasoned that:

> the existence of such a threat can exceptionally be considered to be established where the degree of indiscriminate violence characterising the armed conflict taking place reaches such a high level that substantial grounds are shown for believing that a civilian, returned to the relevant country would, solely on account of his presence on the territory of that country or region, face a real risk of being subject to that threat.[1073]

Hence, just as the ECtHR, the Court of Justice discarded the argument that the existence of a serious and individual threat presupposes that a person must always show that he or she is specifically targeted.

Even though the Court of Justice considered the scope of Article 15(c) to be different from Article 3 ECHR, its interpretation closely resembles the ECtHR's reasoning in *NA.*, and that of later Strasbourg case law. It remains difficult to identify, therefore, the circumstances under which Article 15(c) Qualification Directive may provide protection over and above Article 3 ECHR. Indeed, in *Sufi and Elmi*, the ECtHR noted that, although it was not competent to express any views on the scope of Article 15(c) of the Qualification Directive, Article 3 ECHR offers comparable protection to that afforded by Article 15(c) of the Qualification Directive, in view of the interpretation given to the latter provision by the Court of Justice in *Elgafaji*.[1074] In sum, Article 15(c) has not created a revolutionary new ground for asylum, but simply reflects the softening of the 'special distinguishing features' language within the ECtHR's case law – which in itself was quite revolutionary.

8.4. DIPLOMATIC ASSURANCES

Diplomatic assurances refer to an undertaking by the receiving state to the effect that the person concerned will be treated in accordance with human rights. Although diplomatic assurances may be relevant for refugee status determination as well,[1075] the legal regime on diplomatic assurances has chiefly developed in the context of expulsion and extradition before the ECtHR. This makes it appropriate to exclusively deal with it in this chapter. The Qualification Directive contains no specific provision on diplomatic assurances. It follows that the issue of diplomatic assurances plays a role primarily in determining whether someone

---

[1072] Ibid, para. 43.
[1073] Ibid.
[1074] *Sufi and Elmi*, para. 226.
[1075] UNHCR Note on Diplomatic Assurances and International Refugee Protection, Geneva, August 2006.

meets the general definition of eligibility for subsidiary protection of Article 2(f) of the Directive. Diplomatic assurances are not, in and of themselves, sufficient to remove a real risk of ill-treatment. It transpires from ECtHR's case law that, once diplomatic assurances are on the table, it must be determined whether they, in their practical application, will provide a sufficient guarantee so as to effectively remove the real risk of ill-treatment.[1076]

Reliance on diplomatic assurances has been a longstanding practice in extradition law, where they serve the purpose of enabling the requested state to extradite without acting in breach of its human rights obligations. Their use is common in death penalty cases, but they are also sought if the extraditing state has concerns about the fairness of judicial proceedings in the receiving state. In extradition cases, it is often clear what treatment the extradited person can expect to receive. It is often known which criminal charges are made and which sentence is sought. Consequently, it can be relatively straightforward to determine the value and effectiveness of the assurances. In *Soering*, for example, the ECtHR was not convinced by the assurances provided by the United States authorities. These consisted merely of an assurance from the prosecuting authorities that the United Kingdom government would be granted representation to the judge at the time of sentencing, through which the United Kingdom could indicate its wish that the death penalty should be neither imposed nor carried out. The Court considered that this did not significantly reduce the risk of a capital sentence being imposed or carried out.[1077] In two later extradition cases involving the United States as receiving party, the Court did attach decisive importance to the diplomatic assurances provided by the US authorities, which were seen to reduce the risk of proscribed ill-treatment to negligible proportions.[1078] In these cases, there had been affidavits sworn by the responsible American District Attorney that the prosecution would not seek the death penalty in respect of the applicants and that the United States courts would not be able to impose the death penalty of their own motion.

The ECtHR was also satisfied with diplomatic assurances in a few post-9/11 cases, where the question was whether the United States would not detain terrorist suspects in Guantánamo Bay – where, according to some authorities, a human being is considered to be without rights – or would put them before a military tribunal or would seek and impose the death penalty. In the cases of *Al-Moayad* and *Babar Ahmad*, the Court found that Diplomatic Notes from the United States, to the effect that the applicants would not transferred to Guantánamo Bay, effectively took this risk away. The notes were sufficiently

---

[1076] *Othman (Abu Qatada) v. The United Kingdom*, para. 188.
[1077] *Ibid*, para. 93.
[1078] ECtHR 3 July 2001, *Nivette v. France* (adm. dec.), No. 44190/98; ECtHR 16 October 2001, *Einhorn v. France* (adm. dec.), No. 71555/01.

precise, issued by the competent authorities, and there was no evidence that U.S. assurances were not respected in practice.[1079]

The assessment of the worth of diplomatic assurances may be more difficult in situations where a person is expelled or extradited to countries with a (systematically) doubtful human rights record. In several judgments involving assurances provided by Turkmenistan and Tunisia, the ECtHR noted that it was difficult to rely on assurances in view of general country reports providing a picture of systematic ill-treatment in prisons.[1080] The ECtHR considered on a general note that 'diplomatic assurances are not in themselves sufficient to ensure adequate protection against the risk of ill-treatment where reliable sources have reported practices resorted to or tolerated by the authorities which are manifestly contrary to the principles of the Convention.'[1081] It also confirmed that the fact that a receiving state has signed up to human rights Conventions is in itself no effective guarantee against ill-treatment.[1082]

When it comes to diplomatic assurances, *Othman* (2012) has become the leading case.[1083] In *Othman*, the ECtHR summarised its previous case law on the matter and formulated a two-step approach. First, it must be determined whether the general human rights situation in the receiving state excludes accepting assurances whatsoever.[1084] If that is not the case, the second step consists of an in depth examination of the quality of assurances and practices in the receiving state. The Court formulated no less than eleven 'factors' that are of relevance in making that examination. These are, *inter alia*, whether the assurances are specific or are general and vague; who has given the assurances, and whether that person can bind the receiving state; the length and strength of bilateral relations between the sending and receiving states; whether compliance with the assurances can be objectively verified through diplomatic or other monitoring mechanisms; and whether the applicant has previously been ill-treated in the receiving state.[1085]

[1079] ECtHR 20 February 2007, *Al-Moayad v. Germany*, No. 35865/03, paras. 67–68; ECtHR 6 July 2010, *Babar Ahmad a.o. v. The United Kingdom*, Nos. 24027/07, 11949/08 and 36742/08, para. 108.

[1080] ECtHR 23 October 2008, *Soldatenko v. Ukraine*, No. 2440/07; ECtHR 19 June 2008, *Ryabikin v. Russia*, No. 8320/04; ECtHR 28 February 2008, *Saadi v. Italy*, No. 37201/06; ECtHR 24 February 2009, *Ben Khemais v. Italy*, No. 246/07; ECtHR 24 March 2009, *O. v. Italy*, No. 37257/06; ECtHR 24 March 2009, *Abdelhedi v. Italy*, No. 2638/07; ECtHR 24 March 2009, *Ben Salah v. Italy*, No. 38128/06; ECtHR 24 March 2009, *Bouyahia v. Italy*, No. 46792/06; ECtHR 24 March 2009, *C.B.Z. v. Italy*, No. 44006/06; ECtHR 24 March 2009, *Darraji v. Italy*, No. 11549/05; ECtHR 24 March 2009, *Hamraoui v. Italy*, No. 16201/07; ECtHR 24 March 2009, *Soltana v. Italy*, No. 37336/06.

[1081] ECtHR 28 February 2008, *Saadi v. Italy*, No. 37201/06, para. 147; ECtHR 19 June 2008, *Ryabikin v. Russia*, No. 8320/04, para. 119.

[1082] *Saadi v Italy*, para. 147.

[1083] ECtHR 17 January 2012, *Othman (Abu Qatada) v. The United Kingdom*, No. 8139/09.

[1084] Ibid, para. 188.

[1085] Ibid, para. 189.

It should be noted that, because diplomatic assurances are often at issue in cases concerning persons who are deemed to constitute a danger to public order, such persons may well be excluded from subsidiary protection status, even if the assurances fail to remove the risk. As explained in the following section, the Qualification Directive excludes from subsidiary protection various categories of persons who may be deemed to be of questionable past or character, regardless of whether they are protected from expulsion by Article 3 ECHR.

8.5. CESSATION, EXCLUSION AND ENDING OF SUBSIDIARY PROTECTION

It was described in the previous chapter that the regime for denying and terminating refugee status in the meaning of the Qualification Directive by and large coincides with the cessation and exclusion clauses of the Refugee Convention.[1086] In turn, the EU legislature has aligned, albeit with some variations, the regime for denying and terminating subsidiary protection with the refugee regime.

The incorporation of the exclusion clauses into the subsidiary protection regime may seem surprising, in view of the absolute character of Article 3 ECHR and Article 19(2) of the EU Charter of Fundamental Rights. Even though Article 3 ECHR protects persons from expulsion, irrespective of their past or character, the EU legislature wished to reserve, as much as possible, the access to the subsidiary protection regime to *bona fide* asylum seekers. This is possible because persons protected against expulsion under the ECHR are not, merely on account of such protection, entitled to a resident status. In *Bonger v. The Netherlands*, the ECtHR considered, in respect of a complaint of an Ethiopian national who was refused a residence permit on the basis of Article 1F of the Refugee Convention, but who was not expelled because the Dutch authorities considered that his expulsion would violate Article 3 ECHR, that 'neither Article 3 nor any other provision of the Convention and its Protocols guarantees, as such, a right to a residence permit.'[1087] Persons who are excluded from subsidiary protection cannot invoke the rights of the Directive, yet may be able to invoke protection against expulsion by virtue of Article 3 ECHR or Article 19(2) of the Charter.

[1086] The chief difference being the facultative clause of denying refugee status to persons who can be considered to constitute a danger to the Member State (Article 14(4) Qualification Directive).

[1087] ECtHR 15 September 2005, *Bonger v. The Netherlands*, No. 10154/04.

8.5.1. CESSATION OF SUBSIDIARY PROTECTION

The only ground for cessation of subsidiary protection mentioned in the Qualification Directive is the 'ceased circumstances' clause: 'a third-country national or a stateless person shall cease to be eligible for subsidiary protection when the circumstances which led to the granting of subsidiary protection status have ceased to exist or have changed to such a degree that protection is no longer required' (Article 16(1)). Although the wording is slightly different from Article 1C(5) and (6) of the Refugee Convention (and Art. 11(1)(e) and (f) Qualification Directive), the effect is probably the same. The clause is subject to the same conditions as in the refugee regime, i.e. i) it must be established that the change of circumstances is significant and of non-temporary nature; and ii) it may not be applied in respect of persons who have suffered from atrocious forms of ill-treatment, and who, on account of psychological trauma or otherwise, should not be expected to repatriate – even if the conditions in the country of origin have fundamentally changed.[1088]

Although the ceased circumstances clause does not as such play a role in the case law of the ECtHR, that Court does verify, in examining the degree of risk of ill-treatment upon return, whether a regime change is of durable character and has taken away the root causes of serious human rights violations. In response to the democratic transition in Tunisia, for example, the ECtHR referred to the dismantling of the oppressive structures of the former regime and the putting into place of elements of a democratic system. This showed 'the determination of the Tunisian authorities to once and for all eradicate the culture of violence and impunity which prevailed during the former regime.'[1089]

The absence of the other cessation clauses (Art. 1C(1)-(4) Refugee Convention) in the Directive's subsidiary protection regime means that the conduct mentioned in those clauses is no self-standing ground for ending subsidiary protection. Those clauses refer to voluntary acts of the individual, as a consequence of which the individual must be presumed to have normalised the relationship with his country of origin or the acquisition of a new nationality. It is therefore possible to assume, for example, that, if a person who has been granted subsidiary protection voluntarily re-establishes himself in his country of origin, he does not necessarily forfeit his status as subsidiary protection beneficiary.

[1088] Article 16(1) and (2).
[1089] ECtHR 15 November 2011, *Al Hanchi v. Bosnia*, No. 48205/09.

8.5.2. EXCLUSION FROM SUBSIDIARY PROTECTION

Article 17 of the Qualification Directive incorporates the exclusion clause of Article 1F of the Refugee Convention into the EU subsidiary protection regime. Thus, a person with respect to whom there are serious reasons for considering that he has committed an international crime or a serious crime, or has been guilty of acts contrary to the purposes and principles of the United Nations, is excluded from being eligible for subsidiary protection. Contrary to the exclusion regime for refugees of Article 12 Qualification Directive, Article 17 does not include the exclusion clauses of Articles 1D and 1E Refugee Convention. It is, however, possible that the substance of Articles 1D and 1E Refugee Convention, which see, respectively, to persons receiving protection from other UN agencies than UNHCR, such as UNRWA, and persons who enjoy protection in another country equivalent to that as nationals of that other country, informs the establishment of a real risk in the meaning of Article 2(f) of the Directive.

On the other hand, the grounds for excluding persons from subsidiary protection are wider in three respects than those for refugees. Firstly, Article 17(1)(d) lists as an excluded category persons in respect of whom there are serious reasons for considering them to constitute a danger to the community or the security of the Member State. This category was not taken up in Article 1F, but, in somewhat more qualified terms, in Article 33(2) of the Refugee Convention, allowing for the expulsion of refugees if such grounds are present. In the Qualification Directive's refugee regime, the exclusion of this category is facultative (Article 14(4)), but in the subsidiary protection regime it is mandatory. Secondly, in formulating the exclusion ground of Article 1F(b) Refugee Convention, Article 17(1)(b) of the Directive omits the conditions that the serious crime is of a 'non-political' nature and that the crime has been committed outside the country of refuge prior to admission. Thirdly, Article 17(3) lists a facultative exclusion clause in respect of persons who have committed a crime prior to admission into the Member State which is punishable by imprisonment in the Member State, and if that person has left the country of origin solely to avoid criminal sanctions. If a Member State chooses to apply this clause, it must establish that the crime has actually been committed, since the provision does not refer to 'serious reasons for considering'. The effect of this clause is that a Member State may widen the scope of crimes which serve as basis for exclusion from subsidiary protection to any crime which is punishable by imprisonment in the Member State, provided asylum is sought 'solely in order to avoid sanctions'.

8.5.3. DENIAL AND TERMINATION OF SUBSIDIARY PROTECTION

If a person meets all the elements of the cessation clause or the exclusion clauses, subsidiary protection must be terminated or may not be granted (Art. 17(1) and 19(1) and (3)(a) Qualification Directive). A third ground for terminating subsidiary protection is if it transpires that the status was fraudulently obtained (Art. 19(3)(b)).[1090] The Directive holds, in Article 19, that, in these three situations, subsidiary protection status must be ended ('shall'). The only exception is the facultative exclusion clause of Article 17(3), i.e. persons who have committed any crime prior to admission in the Member State that is punishable by imprisonment in that Member State. Member States are not required to apply this exclusion clause, nor is it is a mandatory ground for denying or terminating subsidiary protection.

It must be remembered that after five years of residence, an international protection beneficiary becomes entitled to long-term resident status.[1091] The grounds for withdrawal of that status are no longer governed by the Qualification Directive, but by the Long-Term Residence Directive.[1092]

8.5.4. ABSOLUTE CHARACTER OF THE PROHIBITION OF REFOULEMENT

Exclusion from subsidiary protection raises issues in light of the absolute character of non-*refoulement* under human rights instruments, including Article 3 ECHR and Article 19(2) of the EU Charter. The absolute character of Article 3 is firmly established in the ECtHR's case law.[1093] Further, Article 3 ECHR is *notstandfest*: no derogation is permitted in time of war or other public emergency (Art. 15(2) ECHR). Whereas Article 1F of the Refugee Convention is meant to exclude persons who are 'undeserving' of protection, the European Court of Human Rights has consistently reasoned that the right protected by Article 3 ECHR is so fundamental that it applies to anyone who is within the jurisdiction of a Contracting State.

This is despite the fact that, in extradition and expulsion cases, the absolute nature of Article 3 is sometimes considered as problematic – most notably when it comes to the deportation of terrorist offenders or suspects or other persons deemed to constitute a danger to society. Especially after the events of 9/11, some Contracting States argued before the ECtHR that the guarantees afforded by

---

[1090] Article 19(3)(b).
[1091] See section 4.7.
[1092] Ibid.
[1093] ECtHR 1 June 2010, *Gäfgen v. Germany*, No. 22978/05, para. 87; ECtHR 6 April 2000, *Labita v. Italy*, No. 26772/95, para. 119.

Article 3 ECHR should not be absolute in cases where a state proposed to remove an individual from its territory who had been involved in terrorist activities. In face of the threat created by international terrorism, the risk of future ill-treatment should, in such cases, be balanced with national security considerations.[1094] Already in *Chahal*, however, concerning the expulsion of a Sikh separatist who was suspected of involvement in terrorist conspiracies, the Grand Chamber of the ECtHR had concluded that Article 3 is equally absolute in expulsion cases, and that (on this particular point, by 12 votes to 7) 'the activities of the individual in question, however undesirable or dangerous, cannot be a material consideration.'[1095]

Importantly, the ECtHR upheld this reasoning in all its post-9/11 case law – in relation not only to Article 3 but also Article 2 and the Sixth Protocol abolishing the death penalty. The absolute character of Article 3 was re-emphasised unanimously by the Court's Grand Chamber in *Saadi v. Italy*:

> The Court notes first of all that States face immense difficulties in modern times in protecting their communities from terrorist violence. It cannot therefore underestimate the scale of the danger of terrorism today and the threat it presents to the community. That must not, however, call into question the absolute nature of Article 3.
>
> Accordingly, the Court cannot accept the argument that a distinction must be drawn under Article 3 between treatment inflicted directly by a signatory State and treatment that might be inflicted by the authorities of another State, and that protection against this latter form of ill-treatment should be weighed against the interests of the community as a whole. Since protection against the treatment prohibited by Article 3 is absolute, that provision imposes an obligation not to extradite or expel any person who, in the receiving country, would run the real risk of being subjected to such treatment. As the Court has repeatedly held, there can be no derogation from that rule. It must therefore reaffirm the principle stated in the *Chahal* judgment that it is not possible to weigh the risk of ill-treatment against the reasons put forward for the expulsion in order to determine whether the responsibility of a State is engaged under Article 3, even where such treatment is inflicted by another State. In that connection, the conduct of the person concerned, however undesirable or dangerous, cannot be taken into account, with the consequence that the protection afforded by Article 3 is broader than that provided for in Articles 32 and 33 of the 1951 United Nations Convention relating to the Status of Refugees. (...)
>
> The Court considers that the argument based on the balancing of the risk of harm if the person is sent back against the dangerousness he or she represents to the community if not sent back is misconceived. The concepts of 'risk' and 'dangerousness' in this context do not lend themselves to a balancing test because they are notions that can only be assessed independently of each other. Either the

---

[1094] ECtHR 28 February 2008, *Saadi v. Italy*, No. 37201/06, para. 122.
[1095] *Chahal v. The United Kingdom*, para. 80.

evidence adduced before the Court reveals that there is a substantial risk if the person is sent back or it does not. (...)

With regard to the second branch of the United Kingdom Government's arguments, to the effect that where an applicant presents a threat to national security, stronger evidence must be adduced to prove that there is a risk of ill-treatment, the Court observes that such an approach is not compatible with the absolute nature of the protection afforded by Article 3 either. (...)

The Court further observes that similar arguments to those put forward by the third-party intervener in the present case have already been rejected in the *Chahal* judgment cited above. Even if, as the Italian and United Kingdom Governments asserted, the terrorist threat has increased since that time, that circumstance would not call into question the conclusions of the *Chahal* judgment concerning the consequences of the absolute nature of Article 3.[1096]

In an attempt to reconcile the wish to expel undesired persons with human rights considerations, a practice is emerging under which states increasingly try to procure diplomatic assurances, as discussed in section 8.4, above. In the case of *Othman*, for example, the United Kingdom, aware that Article 3 ECHR precluded the deportation of terrorist suspects to Jordan in view of reports indicating widespread torture and ill-treatment of persons involved in terrorism in Jordan, had concluded a Memorandum of Understanding with the Jordanian government which provided a range of assurances on the treatment of returned persons by Jordan.[1097] Although the ECtHR considered the quality of the assurances sufficient to take away the risk that Mr. Othman would be ill-treated, it nonetheless found that expulsion would be prohibited, because there remained a risk that evidence obtained by torture would be used against him in his trial before the Jordanian court.[1098] It was only after having sought fresh diplomatic assurances from Jordan, in the form of a mutual assistance treaty that included a number of fair trial guarantees, that Othman could finally be lawfully deported.[1099]

The gap in personal scope in respect of dangerous persons between both the refugee and subsidiary protection regime in the Qualification Directive, on the one hand, and the prohibition of *refoulement* in human rights law, on the other, means, concretely, that there are persons who may not be expelled but who are neither entitled to a resident status under Union law. A Member State may grant such a person a status in accordance with national law, may try to persuade a third state into accepting the person, may try to procure diplomatic assurances to obviate human rights concerns in the receiving state, or may simply abstain

---

[1096] ECtHR 28 February 2008, *Saadi v. Italy*, No. 37201/06, paras. 137–141.

[1097] ECtHR 11 January 2012, *Othman (Abu Qatada) v. The United Kingdom*, No. 8139/09.

[1098] See also section 8.4, above.

[1099] Treaty on Mutual Legal Assistance in Criminal Matters between the United Kingdom of Great Britain and Northern Ireland and the Hashemite Kingdom of Jordan, London, 24 March 2013.

from forcible removal in the hope that the person will voluntarily leave the country – and if he does not do so: accept a situation of illegal stay. Although the latter scenario is rather undesirable for the person in question but also for the state, the ECtHR has considered that a decision of exclusion with as consequence denial of a residence permit is not in itself 'degrading' in the meaning of Article 3 ECHR. It would seem that protection under Article 3 can come into play in such a situation only if it would result in such harrowing hardship that the threshold of a 'minimum level of severity' is met. Nor does a situation of illegal but tolerated stay easily come within the ambit of Article 8 ECHR. In respect of one such complaint, concerning a person who was excluded on the basis of Article 1F Refugee Convention but not deported by virtue of Article 3 ECHR, the ECtHR noted that neither Article 8 nor any other Convention provision guarantees a right to work or to earn a living.

8.6. CONTENT OF SUBSIDIARY PROTECTION

The European Convention does not contain a 'right to asylum', but merely prohibits exposure to ill-treatment by way of expulsion. The prohibition of *refoulement* does not bring with it an entitlement to a residence permit or rights relating to societal participation and protection. The ECHR thus allows for practices such as 'tolerated stay' or 'discretionary leave to remain', under which some categories of migrants are simply not forcibly expelled, but are neither granted a residence permit, which may further implicate restrictions in the sphere of access to the labour market and social security benefits. Accordingly, and contrary to the normative guidance provided by the Refugee Convention in respect of refugee status, there are no specific international rules setting forth what the content of subsidiary protection is – apart from the prohibition from *refoulement*. As a minimum, we can agree that a Member State must guarantee the basic rights and benefits that it must accord to anyone present in its territory, in accordance with general human rights standards such as those of the ECHR, the EU Charter of Fundamental Rights and the European Social Charter.[1100]

Possibly, the right to asylum laid down in Article 18 of the EU Charter of Fundamental Rights may provide further guidance on the contents of asylum for refugees as well as subsidiary protection beneficiaries, but the Charter also makes clear that it merely reaffirms the rights as they result from common constitutional traditions and international obligations common to the Member

---

[1100] Cf. *M.S.S. v. Belgium and Greece*, paras. 249–264; European Committee of Social Rights 20 October 2009, *Defence for Children International (DCI) v. The Netherlands*, No. 47/2008; European Committee of Social Rights 23 October 2012, *Defence for Children International (DCI) v. Belgium*, No. 69/2011.

States.[1101] A key achievement of the Qualification Directive of 2004 was that it extensively defined the content of subsidiary protection status. The Directive set forth that subsidiary protection status comprises a range of rights and benefits in the sphere of work, social welfare, healthcare, education, housing and documentation. It hence assured that beneficiaries were granted a formal status, allowing them to participate and integrate in society. The EU legislature opted, however, for granting a lower level of rights and benefits to subsidiary protection beneficiaries than to refugees. For example, whereas refugees were entitled to a residence permit valid for at least three years, beneficiaries of subsidiary protection were entitled to a residence permit valid for at least one year. This differentiation was seen to reflect the potentially more temporary nature of the latter category.[1102] For instance, persons fleeing from general violence – who may be difficult to define as refugee but may be entitled to subsidiary protection – will often not be in permanent need of protection.

The assumption that subsidiary protection is always or necessarily of a more temporary nature is, however, debatable.[1103] This gives rise to the question of whether distinctions in the content of protection are necessary and objectively justified. When proposing to recast the Qualification Directive, the European Commission therefore suggested, also with a view to simplifying procedures, equalising the rights of the two categories.[1104] The Council watered down some of these suggestions nonetheless, resulting in a Directive that still differentiates, in a limited number of respects, between refugee status and subsidiary protection status. Member States that employ this distinction must, according to Article 46(2) of the Procedures Directive, grant a right to appeal against a decision considering an application unfounded in relation to refugee status.

The Directive does not differentiate in respect of rights and benefits in the following spheres, of which the content was discussed in section 7.6:

- Family unity (Article 23)
- Access to employment (Article 26)
- Access to education (Article 27)
- Access to procedures for recognition of qualifications (Article 28)
- Healthcare (Article 30)
- Representation, guardianship and family unity of unaccompanied minors (Article 31)
- Access to accommodation (Article 32)
- Freedom of movement within the Member State (Article 33)

[1101] EU Charter of Fundamental Rights, Preamble.
[1102] COM(2001) 510 final, p. 7.
[1103] COM(2009) 551 final, p. 8; UNHCR, Response to the European Commission's Green Paper on the Future Common European Asylum System, September 2007.
[1104] COM(2009) 551 final, p. 8.

In respect of the following areas, the Directive does differentiate:

Residence permit (Article 24(2))

Subsidiary protection beneficiaries are entitled to a residence permit which must be valid for at least one year and renewable for at least two years – as opposed to the residence permit for refugees that must be valid for at least three years and renewable.

Travel document (Article 25(2))

Contrary to refugees, subsidiary protection beneficiaries are not entitled to a refugee travel document (often termed 'refugee passport') under Article 28 of the Refugee Convention and the Schedule to the Refugee Convention. They must, however, be granted another travel document enabling them to travel outside the Member State. Such a document will commonly be an alien's passport. The latter document will not have the words 'Convention of 28 July 1951' on its cover, is not necessarily valid in all states that have ratified the Refugee Convention, and does not make the holder immediately recognisable as in need of protection against removal to his home state.

Social welfare (Article 29(2))

Member States may reduce social welfare granted to subsidiary protection beneficiaries to 'core benefits'. But in respect of these core benefits, the level must be the same as that granted to nationals. The Directive does not define what belongs to the core of social welfare.

Access to integration facilities (Article 34)

Although subsidiary protection beneficiaries are on equal footing as refugees entitled to access to integration programmes, these programmes may be different, taking into account the specific needs of beneficiaries of subsidiary protection status.

FURTHER READING

J. McAdam, 'The European Union Qualification Directive: The Creation of a Subsidiary Protection Regime', 17 *International Journal of Refugee Law* (2005) 461–516.
J. McAdam, *Complementary Protection in International Refugee Law*, Oxford University Press (2007).

H. Battjes, *European Asylum Law And International Law*, Leiden/Boston: Martinus Nijhoff (2006).

M. Foster, *International refugee law and socio-economic rights: Refuge from deprivation*, Cambridge University Press (2007).

K. Hailbronner (ed.), *European Immigration Law*, Munich: C.H. Beck (2010).

H. Lambert, 'Protection Against Refoulement from Europe: Human Rights Law Comes to the Rescue', 48 *International and Comparative Law Quarterly* (1999) 515–544.

N. Mole and C. Meredith, *Asylum and the European Convention on Human Rights*, Strasbourg: Council of Europe Publishing (2011).

S. Peers and N. Rogers (eds.), *EU Immigration and Asylum Law: Text and Commentary*, Leiden/Boston: Martinus Nijhoff (2006).

R. Piotrowicz and C. van Eck, 'Subsidiary Protection and Primary Rights', 53 *International and Comparative Law Quarterly* (2004), 107–138.

K. Wouters, *International Legal Standards for the Protection from Refoulement*, Antwerp: Intersentia (2009).

PART IV

ENFORCEMENT AND PROCEDURAL PROTECTION

9. EXTERNAL BORDER CONTROLS, VISAS AND EXPULSION MEASURES

9.1. INTRODUCTION

9.1.1. GENERAL REMARKS

The first impression a traveller gets of a country is the style in which border control is exerted. Roughly, border control may show two completely different faces of a state: the cooperative, efficient and solution-oriented face of an open society, and the unsympathetic, bureaucratic and keep away face of a control state. Normally, reality is somewhere in between. To a certain extent, the more liberal face of Europe is reserved for EU citizens, and the more bureaucratic and harsh face, for third-country nationals. Border control is 'a multi-layer system aimed at facilitating legitimate travel and tackling illegal immigration'.[1105] It is for sure that few issues are so essential to immigration policies as border control. While a policy of completely open borders would not be inconceivable,[1106] such a policy would have the obvious disadvantage that the means are lacking to have command over who is entering or leaving the territory. Together with measures to enforce the removal of persons from the territory, measures to regulate entry to the territory are key instruments of any immigration policy.

Nowadays, these key instruments are very much Europeanised. Coordinated efforts controlling external borders have become a more and more common phenomenon, especially at those land and sea borders, which are hard to control. A good example of the intertwined European interests with border control was the 'Arab Spring' in Tunisia in 2011, leading to 25,000 undocumented immigrants coming by boats to the Italian island of Lampedusa. At the behest of Italy, the European agency, Frontex, began an operation ('Hermes'), intensifying border controls in the Mediterranean. Further, Italy proposed that the immigrants who had safely reached Lampedusa would be distributed amongst the Member States. Though this suggestion was turned down, the same effect was reached due to another aspect of Europeanisation

---

[1105]   Hague Programme, OJ C 53, 3.3.2005.
[1106]   See, for instance, J.H. Carens, 'Aliens and Citizens: The Case for Open Borders', 49 *The Review of Politics*, No. 2 (1987), pp. 251–273.

that was already established, namely the abolishment of internal border controls and the right to free circulation for holders of a residence permit. Eventually, Italy legalised the immigrants, thus enabling them to access the internal area of the EU.

This chapter provides an overview of EU legislation on measures of immigration control of third-country nationals.

It does not deal with Union law measures criminalising acts facilitating illegal entry, such as Articles 26 and 27 Schengen Implementing Convention and Directive 2002/90/EC, defining the facilitation of unauthorised entry, transit and residence.

9.1.2. STRUCTURE OF THE CHAPTER

In this chapter, legislation applicable to the various forms and instruments of immigration control is dealt with under general headings: entry, visas, short-term stay, expulsion, exclusion, detention, data storage, and operational cooperation. The subject matter is governed by a number of Regulations and one Directive. Many of these instruments are derived from the Schengen Implementing Convention of 1990 (SIC). The rules on border control and visas could originally be found in Articles 1–25 of the Schengen Implementing Convention. Most of these provisions have been replaced by EU measures.[1107] Thus, from the original part of the Schengen Implementing Convention on border control and visas, only Articles 1 (definitions), 18 (long-term visas), 19–22 (movement within the internal area) and 25,[1108] are still in force. Some of these Articles have been amended by way of a Regulation.[1109]

[1107] Since 16 March 2006, the movement of persons across borders is governed by an EU Regulation normally referred to as the 'Schengen Borders Code' (SBC). The Schengen Borders Code replaces Articles 2–8 SIC. A 'Visa Code' (Regulation (EC) 810/2009), replacing Articles 9–17 SIC entered into force on 5 October 2009, and became operational on 5 April 2010. Further, Articles 23 and 24 SIC have been replaced by Directive 2008/115/EC on returning illegally staying third-country nationals ('the Returns Directive'). The provisions on the Schengen Information System (Article 92–119, except 102 A) have been replaced by the SIS II regulation (Regulation (EC) 1987/2006 of 20 December 2007 on the establishment, operation and use of the second-generation Schengen Information System (SIS II), OJ L 381/4, 28 December 2006).

[1108] This provision contains an obligation for Member State issuing a residence permit to consult the Member State who entered an alert for the purpose of refusing entry in the Schengen Information System and *vice versa*.

[1109] See Regulation 265/2010, OJ 2010, L85/1.

9.2. BORDER CONTROLS

9.2.1. ABOLITION OF CONTROLS AT THE INTERNAL BORDERS

Internal borders may be crossed at any point without a border check on persons, irrespective of their nationality, being carried out. This is stated in Article 20 Schengen Borders Code. This means that the common territory of the Member States belonging to the 'Schengen Area' is freely accessible for anyone present on that soil. As the UK and Ireland do not take part in the Schengen Area and maintain their border controls, this is only true for the continental part of the EU. Further, the Schengen Area also comprises four countries outside the EU: Norway, Iceland, Switzerland and Liechtenstein. Three European microstates, Monaco, San Marino and Vatican, having no border controls with the surrounding Schengen countries, are *de facto* part of the Schengen Area as far as their accessibility is concerned. On the other hand, new Member States must first take necessary measures before they are allowed to abolish their border controls. Romania and Bulgaria, being Member States since 2007, were only allowed to fully join the Schengen *acquis* as of 1 January 2014. Cyprus and Croatia (which became a Member State in 2013) are still in the process of taking preparatory measures to become ready for 'Schengen'.

In the case of a serious threat to public policy or internal security, a Member State may exceptionally reintroduce border controls at its internal borders for a limited period described in Article 23 Schengen Borders Code. Further, according to Article 21 of this code, the abolition of internal border controls does not affect the exercise of police powers insofar as they do not have an effect equivalent to border checks; security checks on persons at ports and seaports; the possibility for a Member State to provide, by law, for an obligation to hold or carry papers and documents; and the obligation on third-country nationals to report their presence on the territory of any Member State. In the *Adil* case,[1110] the Court of Justice specified that border surveillance and the monitoring of foreign nationals by a Member State, to carry out checks in a geographic area 20 kilometres from the internal land border, with a view to establishing whether the persons stopped satisfy the requirements for lawful residence in that Member State, are compatible with Articles 20 and 21 of the Schengen Borders Code.

[1110] ECJ 19 July 2012, *Adil* Case C-278/12 PPU. See also ECJ 22 June 2010, *Melki and Abdeli*, Cases C-188/10 and C-189/10.

9.2.2. ENTRY: THE SCHENGEN BORDERS CODE

The Schengen Borders Code establishes rules governing the border control of persons crossing the external borders.[1111] Furthermore, it provides for the absence of border control of persons crossing the internal borders between the Member States. Thus, once a person has been granted entry into the common territories of the Schengen states, he is factually free to travel between the countries. Although the Regulation covers both movements of EU citizens and third-country nationals, most provisions focus on third-country nationals. Persons enjoying the EU right of free movement are subject to a minimum check at the borders, while third-country nationals are subject to a thorough check (Article 7). The travel documents of third country nationals are systematically stamped on entry and exit (Article 10(1)).

To a large extent, the Schengen Borders Code contains technical rules regarding, for instance, the opening hours of border crossing points, separate lanes for EU citizens and for non-EU citizens at airports, the stamping of travel documents, staff and resources for border control, and the temporary reintroduction of internal border controls. But this code also contains substantive provisions relating to the allowing or refusal of entry of individuals concerned and the procedural guarantees in the case of refusal of entry. These will be dealt with in the following two paragraphs.

9.2.3. ENTRY CONDITIONS UNDER THE SCHENGEN BORDERS CODE

This paragraph is not about entry conditions for *EU citizens* and other persons enjoying the EU right of free movement. For them, the requirements are laid down in the Citizens' Directive (see Chapter 2 of this book). Union citizens have the right to enter the territory of a Member State for a period of up to three months without any conditions or any formalities other than the requirement to hold a valid identity card or passport.[1112] The same applies to family members of EU citizens, but if they have the nationality of a third country, they may be subject to a visa requirement according to the Visa Requirement Regulation.[1113]

Entry conditions for *third-country nationals* who do not enjoy the EU right of free movement, are laid down in the Schengen Borders Code. According to

---

[1111] Article 1 Schengen Borders Code.
[1112] Articles 4, 5, 6 Citizens' Directive 2004/38.
[1113] Council Regulation (EC) No. 539/2001 of 15 March 2001 listing the third countries whose nationals must be in possession of visas when crossing the external borders and those whose nationals are exempt from that requirement, OJ L 81, 21 March 2001, p. 1. This Regulation is amended regularly.

Article 5(1) of this code, the entry conditions for third-country nationals, for stays not exceeding three months per six-month period, are the following:

(a) they are in possession of a valid travel document (normally: a passport) or documents authorising them to cross the border;
(b) they are in possession of a valid visa, if required, pursuant to the Visa Requirement Regulation, except where they hold a valid residence permit;
(c) they justify the purpose and conditions of the intended stay, and they have sufficient means of subsistence, both for the duration of the intended stay and for the return to their country of origin or transit to a third country into which they are certain to be admitted, or are in a position to acquire such means lawfully;
(d) they are not persons for whom an alert has been issued in the Schengen Information System for the purposes of refusing entry;
(e) they are not considered to be a threat to public policy, internal security, public health or international relations of any of the Member States, in particular where no alert has been issued in Member States' national databases for the purposes of refusing entry on the same grounds.

A third-country national who fails to meet one or more of the entry conditions must be refused entry to the territories of the Member States.[1114] However, the fourth paragraph of Article 5 provides for some derogations. An important derogation is Article 5(4)(c) Schengen Borders Code, according to which third-country nationals who do not fulfil one or more of the conditions laid down in paragraph 1 may be authorised by a Member State to enter its territory on humanitarian grounds, on grounds of national interest, or because of international obligations. In that case, the right to enter is limited to that state's territory, but in practice, access to the whole Schengen territory will be open, as there is no internal border control. Article 5(4)(c) of the code leaves room for national discretion by allowing entry on grounds of purely national considerations – humanitarian grounds or grounds of national interest.

Apart from the derogations of Article 5(4), another provision of the code, namely Article 13(1), restricts the application of the principle of refusing entry to those who do not meet all conditions, by stipulating that this principle shall be without prejudice to the application of special provisions concerning the right of asylum and to international protection. Special provisions on the right of asylum and to international protection are to be found in the Qualification Directive and in other legislation belonging to the Common European Asylum System (see Chapter 6). These provisions do not, however, explicitly mention a right of access to the territory, nor do they contain specific entry conditions for asylum

---

[1114] Article 13(1) Schengen Borders Code.

seekers. Although the practical meaning of the reference to the right of asylum and to international protection in the context of the Schengen Borders Code is therefore not entirely clear, the provision of Article 13(1) is important, because it acknowledges that asylum seekers who do not fulfil all the entry conditions may not simply be refused entry.

Further, according to Article 13(1), the principle of refusal is without prejudice to the issue of long-stay visas. It is understandable that the possession of a residence permit or a long-stay visa that entitles its holder to a longer period of stay makes it unnecessary to obtain an authorisation for a short period of stay.

9.3. VISAS

9.3.1. VISAS: SHORT-TERM AND LONG-TERM VISAS

EU visa requirements are not applicable to Union Citizens and citizens of associated third countries (the EEA countries of Norway and Iceland, and further, Switzerland and Liechtenstein) enjoying the right to free movement. Third-country nationals are subject to the Visa Requirement Regulation. Some categories of third-country nationals require a visa for crossing the external borders; others do not. If a third-country national is exempt from a visa requirement, he must apply for leave to enter at the border in accordance with the rules laid down in the Schengen Borders Code. The Visa Requirement Regulation enumerates the third countries whose nationals must be in possession of a visa when crossing the external borders, and those whose nationals are exempt from that requirement.[1115]

The Visa Requirement Regulation only refers to *short-stay* visas as defined in the Visa Code, that is, visas for transit through, or intended stays on, the territory of the Member States not exceeding 90 days in any 180-day period.[1116] The issuing of *long-stay visas* remains, in principle, allotted to national competence of the Member States. Article 18(1) Schengen Implementing Convention states that visas for stays exceeding three months shall be national visas issued by one of the Member States in accordance with its national law or Union law. Such visas shall be issued in a uniform format for visas set out in Regulation 1838/95 with a heading carrying the letter D. Whereas a long-term visa often anticipates the issuing of a residence permit in the host Member State, it should be borne in mind that Member States, when deciding on long-term visas, may be bound by Union legislation on legal immigration, for example, by

---

[1115] Council Regulation (EC) No. 539/2001.
[1116] See also ECJ 3 October 2006, *Nicolae Bot*, Case C-241/05.

the Family Reunification Directive,[1117] or the Student Directive.[1118] EU citizens do not need any visa for crossing the borders of the Member States.[1119]

According to Article 18 (2) Schengen Implementing Convention, long-stay visas shall have a period of validity no longer than one year. If a Member State allows an alien to stay for more than one year, the long-stay visa shall be replaced before the expiry of validity by a residence permit. Third-country nationals who hold valid residence permits issued by one of the Member States may, on the basis of that permit and a valid travel document, move freely for up to three months in any six-month period within the territories of the other Member States, provided that they fulfil the entry conditions in Article 5(1)(a),(c) and (e) Schengen Borders Code. If a Member State decides to grant a visa solely for its own territory, this is a national visa, according to Article 5(4) of the Schengen Borders Code. In the *Anafé* judgment, the Court of Justice said that a Member State which issues to a third-country national a re-entry visa – within the meaning of Article 5(4)(a) – cannot limit entry to the Schengen area solely to points of entry to its national territory.[1120]

9.3.2. VISAS: THE SCHENGEN VISA

There is a uniform European short-stay visa for all countries joining the Schengen *acquis*. The 'Schengen visa' was originally established in the Schengen Implementing Convention of 1990. More elaborate rules on the Schengen visa are presently laid down in the Visa Code. 'Visa' in the sense of this Regulation means an authorisation issued by a Member State with a view to:

(a) transit through or an intended stay in the territory of the Member States of a duration of no more than 90 days in any 180-day period; or
(b) transit through the international transit areas of airports of the Member States.

'Uniform visa' means a visa valid for the entire territory of the Member States; and a 'visa with limited territorial validity' is a visa valid for the territory of one or more Member States, but not all Member States. Further, there is an 'airport transit visa', meaning a visa valid for transit through the international transit areas of one or more airports of the Member States. Article 3 of the Visa Code sets out under which circumstances an airport visa may be required. A visa can be issued for more than one entry. According to Consideration 8 of the Preamble,

---

[1117] Directive 2003/86.
[1118] Directive 2004/114 on the admission of third-country nationals for the purposes of studies, pupil exchange, unremunerated training or voluntary service, OJ L 375, 23 December 2004.
[1119] Article 5 Citizens' Directive.
[1120] ECJ 14 June 2012, *Anafé*, Case C-606/10.

multiple-entry visas should be issued in order to lessen the administrative burden of Member States' consulates and to facilitate the smooth travelling for frequent or regular travellers, provided that the conditions are met. Applicants known to the consulate for their integrity and reliability should, as far as possible, benefit from a simplified procedure.

Normally, uniform visas are applied for at, and issued by, the diplomatic missions or consular posts of the Member States. According to Article 4(2) Visa Code, visas may also be issued at the external borders by the authorities responsible for checks on persons. Articles 5, 6 and 7 Visa Code establish which diplomatic missions or consular posts of which Member State are responsible for processing a visa application. Member States may cooperate in relation to the reception of visa applications in various forms, mentioned in Article 8 Visa Code.

9.3.3. CONDITIONS FOR OBTAINING A SCHENGEN VISA

The conditions for obtaining a uniform visa run parallel to the entry conditions of Article 5 Schengen Borders Code,[1121] but the visa conditions place great emphasis on the providing of evidence that the applicant is *bona fide* and sufficiently able to support himself. Articles 9–17 Visa Code lay down the rules and modalities for visa applications. Applicants for a visa must normally lodge an application no more than three months before the intended visit; they should normally appear in person when lodging an application, presenting an application form, a valid travel document, a photograph, allow the capturing of fingerprints, and pay the visa fee. Further, they must provide supporting documents proving the purpose of the journey; accommodation, or proof of sufficient means to cover accommodation costs; provide evidence of the possession of sufficient means of subsistence both for the duration of the stay and the return or transit; and information allowing to assess the applicant's intention to leave the territory of the Member States before the expiry of the visa for which an application is being submitted. Where applicable, they must produce proof of possession of adequate and valid travel insurance. Each of these requirements is elaborated in further provisions of the Visa Code.

In Article 32(1) Visa Code, the reasons for refusing a visa are laid down. A special provision is given in Article 35(6) on applications at the border. An application for a uniform visa cannot be refused on other grounds than those mentioned in the Visa Code.[1122]

[1121]   According to Article 18(4) Visa Code, the examination of the visa application shall ascertain whether the applicant fulfils the entry conditions set out in Article 5(1) Schengen Borders Code.

[1122]   ECJ 19 December 2013, *Koushkaki*, Case C-84/12.

A negative decision regarding a visa application or a visa already issued may be given in different variations: *refusal (Article 32), inadmissibility (Article 19), refusal of extension (Article 33), annulment (Article 34), revocation (Article 34), and refusal of a visa with limited territorial validity (Article 2(2)).*

The application may be *refused* on grounds mentioned in Article 32 Visa Code. The decision stating the precise reasons for the refusal shall be given by means of a standard form set out in Annex VI (Article 32(2) Visa Code). Applicants refused visa shall have the right to appeal (Article 32(3) Visa Code). Appeals shall be conducted against the Member State that has taken the final decision on the application and in accordance with national law.

Inadmissibility of the visa application is, according to Article 19 Visa Code, declared when the application has not been lodged within the period of three months before the start of the intended visit, when the application form does not contain the required items, when the biometric data of the applicant have not been collected, or when the visa fee has not been collected.

Annulment shall happen if it becomes evident that the conditions for issuing the visa were not met at the time of the issuing of that visa, in particular, if there are serious grounds to believe that the visa was fraudulently obtained (Article 34(1) Visa Code).

A visa shall be *revoked* where it becomes evident that the conditions for issuing the visa are no longer met (Article 34(2)). Failure of the visa holder to produce, at the border, one or more of the supporting documents referred to in Article 14(3), may not, however,automatically lead to a decision to annul or revoke the visa (Article 34(4)). Further, a visa *may* be revoked at the behest of the visa holder (Article 34(3)).

Visa holders whose visa has been annulled or revoked have the right to appeal, unless the visa was revoked at the request of the visa holder (Article 34(7) Visa Code). Obviously, a right to appeal is an essential tool for visa holders because it may lead to correcting wrong decisions. Under the Visa Code, appeal is possible against refusal, annulment and revocation of a visa. A remedy is not, or not explicitly, made available in cases of inadmissibility, the refusal of extension, and refusal of a territorially limited visa, but it may be contended that these are just variations of a refusal of a visa, against which appeal should be possible.

9.3.4. VISAS: THE LEGAL CHARACTER OF SHORT-TERM STAY

There is room for some discussion on the character of the rights of third-country nationals who meet the entry conditions of the Schengen Borders Code and who possess – if required – a valid uniform visa. Do they automatically have a right to enter the common territories and a right to stay there during the allowed period of short stay? Or, if the right is not automatic, what is it then? According to Article 30 Visa Code, the mere possession of a short-stay visa or a transit visa does not confer an automatic right of entry. Further, the Schengen Borders Code remains tacit over any right to enter when the requirements are fulfilled. Article 5 of the code enumerates the conditions, and Article 13 says that a person who does *not* fulfil all the entry conditions must normally be refused entry. But if there are no grounds to *refuse* entry, is the person concerned then entitled to *enter* the Schengen Area? The code does not say explicitly that a person who does meet all conditions has a claim to enter. In practice, the ultimate power to decide on a right to enter is laid in the hands of the border guards when a traveller passes the control post. However, there is no ground to assume that a border guard possesses any legal power to refuse entry once the conditions are met. From the systematic coherence of the relevant provisions it follows that there must be a right to enter for anyone who meets the conditions,[1123] but this right must, apparently, be confirmed by the border guard before it can be effected.

Once the external border is lawfully crossed, the third-country national has a right to move freely within the territories of the Schengen states throughout the period of validity of the visa or, when the person does not need a visa, for a maximum period of 90 days in any 180-day period. Logically, this must imply that persons have some sort of a right of legal residence during the short stay period. However, this type of lawful stay cannot be equated with a residence permit. The right to stay stems from Union law and is subject to its conditions. In the *Nicolae Bot* judgment,[1124] the Court of Justice indeed used the terminology of a 'right to stay'. This right is exhausted when the allowed maximum period of legal stay is consumed.

From the text of the Schengen Implementing Convention, it is not clear whether or not the right to short stay is made dependent on fulfilling further formalities after entry. According to Article 22(1), third-country nationals who have legally entered the territory of one of the Member States in the Schengen area shall be obliged to report, in accordance with the conditions laid down by each Schengen state, to the competent authorities of the Schengen state whose territory they enter. They may report either on entry or within three working days of entry, at the discretion of the Schengen state whose territory they enter. Often, this reporting duty is fulfilled by the hotel where a tourist is registering. Most tourists are not aware that they have to report, and where to do it.

Is the reporting obligation a constitutive condition for the creation or for the continuity of the right to stay? If it were a constitutive condition, a third-country

---

[1123] See, for a similar question, namely whether there is a right to obtain a visa if the conditions of the Visacode are met, ECJ 19 December 2013, *Koushkaki*, Case C-84/12.

[1124] ECJ 3 October 2006, *Nicolae Bot*, Case C-241/05, paras. 25, 27, 35. The findings of the Court have led to Regulation 610/2013 amending, amongst others, the Schengen Borders Code, The Schengen Implementing Convention, the Visa Code.

national who failed to report in time would be staying illegally in the country as of the last day of the period within which he had to report himself. If this were true, it would mean that a holder of a uniform visa who did not go to a hotel but stayed with friends and did not report himself to any authority would be staying illegally in the Schengen area, even if the term of validity of the visa had not yet expired. This proposition does not seem easily reconcilable with the system of explicit revocation or annulment of visas. If the third-country national, after legally entering the territory, no longer fulfils the conditions, his visa can be revoked, according to Article 34(2) Visa Code. This system entails that the visa must be considered to be valid until the moment of revocation. There are indications that this is also the opinion of the Court of Justice, at least when annulment is concerned. In the case of *Min Khoa Vo*, the Court of Justice said that the Visa Code obliges the Member States not to hinder the movement of visa holders unless the visas have been duly and properly annulled.[1125]

On the other hand, for third-country nationals who are not subject to a visa requirement, the right to short stay ends automatically if the conditions are no longer fulfilled. According to Article 23 Schengen Implementing Convention, third-country nationals who do not, or no longer, fulfil the short-stay conditions applicable within the territory of a Schengen state shall *normally* be required to leave the territories of the Member States immediately. According to Article 11(1) Schengen Borders Code, the authorities may presume that a third-country national does not, or no longer, fulfil(s) the conditions of duration of stay applicable within the Member State concerned if the travel document of a third-country national does not bear any stamp of the border guard.

9.4. RETURN AND REMOVAL

9.4.1. THE RETURNS DIRECTIVE

On 16 December 2008, the Directive on Common Standards and Procedures in Member States for Returning Illegally Staying Third-Country Nationals was adopted (Returns Directive).[1126] The final date on which this far-reaching

---

[1125] ECJ 10 April 2012, *Min Khoa Vo*, C-83/12 PPU, para. 45. However, if this obligation conflicts with another obligation under EU law, namely to prescribe and enforce effective, proportionate and dissuasive penalties against human smugglers, the Visa Code does not preclude national provisions under which assisting illegal immigration constitutes an offence subject to criminal penalties in cases where the persons smuggled, third-country nationals, hold visas which they obtained fraudulently by deceiving the competent authorities of the Member State of issue as to the true purpose of their journey, without prior annulment of those visas.

[1126] Directive 2008/115/EC of the European Parliament and of the Council on common standards and procedures in Member States for returning illegally staying third country nationals, OJ 2008 L 248/98.

Directive had to be transposed into the national law of the Member States was 24 December 2010. Since then, the Court of Justice has issued a number of judgments in which the Directive is interpreted.[1127] As its title suggests, the Returns Directive sets out common standards and procedures for returning illegally staying third-country nationals. Article 1 Returns Directive stipulates that standards and procedures on returns must be in accordance with fundamental rights as principles of Union law as well as international law, including refugee protection and human rights obligations.

The Returns Directive has introduced a set of instruments that were not unknown in themselves, but are systemised in a rather new way, obliging the Member States to make quite rigorous adaptations to their existing legislation. Of particular note is the central function of the 'return decision', without which no detention or entry ban may be issued, and the obligatory character of the entry ban can have a disciplining effect. Further, the European scale of the system is new. From now on it is not sufficient for the completion of the return if a person leaves the territory of a Member State – he must leave the whole territory of the EU before he can be said to have complied with his returning obligation. In case law and commentaries, the detention paragraphs have drawn most attention to date.

The Directive is without prejudice to more favourable provisions of multilateral and bilateral agreements concluded between the EU or one or more of the Member States on the one hand, and one or more third countries, on the other (Article 4(1)); and without prejudice to any provision which may be more favourable for the third-country national laid down in the EU *acquis* on immigration and asylum (Article 4(2)). Further, paragraph 3 of Article 4, holds that '[t]his Directive shall be without prejudice to the right of Member States to adopt or maintain provisions that are more favourable to persons to whom it applies provided that such provisions are compatible with this Directive.'

According to Article 2(3), the Returns Directive does not apply to persons enjoying the EU right of free movement.[1128] Further, Article 2(2) of the Directive states that Member States may decide not to apply the Returns Directive in two categories of cases: (a) third-country nationals who are subject to a refusal of entry under the Schengen Borders Code or who have been apprehended or intercepted in connection with the irregular crossing of the external borders, and who have not subsequently obtained authorisation to stay; and (b) third-country nationals who are subject to return as a criminal law sanction or as a consequence of a criminal law sanction according to national law, or who are

---

[1127] With the *Kadzoev* judgment, the Court was even earlier than December 2010, as Bulgaria had transposed the Directive already in 2009 (ECJ 30 November 2009, *Kadzoev,* Case C-357/09 PPU, para. 7).

[1128] See the definition in Article 2(5) Schengen Borders Code.

subject to extradition procedures. If the obligation to return flows from a decision of an administrative authority, this last exception is not applicable.[1129]

In general, the Returns Directive must be applied in accordance with the fundamental rights and principles recognised, in particular, by the Charter of Fundamental Rights (Recital 24). An important provision that guides the actions of Member States throughout implementing the Directive's provisions is Article 5. This Article obliges Member States, firstly, to take due account of the best interests of the child, family life and the state of health of the third-country national concerned; and, secondly, obliges Member States to respect the principle of non-*refoulement*.

9.4.2. RETURNS DIRECTIVE: WHAT IS NOT COVERED?

Before describing the Returns Directive in more detail, it is necessary to pay attention to what is not covered. Three important fields fall beyond the scope of the Directive. The Directive does (a) not affect Union citizens, and is (b) not applicable to asylum seekers. For these two categories the issue is, under which alternative legislative regime they fall. Further, (c) the Directive does not affect the competence of Member States to make criminal law. In several cases before the Court of Justice, the issue was raised as to the extent to which criminal law provisions drafted by Member States may, nevertheless, undermine the effectiveness of the Returns Directive.

9.4.2.1. *Union Citizens*

Firstly, the Directive is not applicable to Union citizens and citizens of associated third countries (the EEA countries, Norway and Iceland; and, further, Switzerland and Liechtenstein) enjoying the right to free movement. Nor is the Directive applicable to their family members, regardless of their nationality (Article 2(3)). As was shown above, these persons have a right to free access to the Member States and are only subject to a minimum check at the borders. The primary bearers of the right to free movement are free from any visa requirement. Their family members may be subject to a visa requirement if the state of their nationality is listed in the Visa Requirement Regulation, but they must, according to Article 5(2) Directive 2004/38, be facilitated in obtaining such a visa, free of charge and on the basis of an accelerated procedure.

As the coercive measures of the Returns Directive are not applicable to these categories of persons, the Member States can exert control only under their national legislation within the boundaries set by Directive 2004/38. However, the possibilities for control are rather limited, as the persons concerned have a

---

[1129] ECJ 28 April 2011, Case C-61/11 PPU *Hassen El Dridi*, para. 49.

powerful right to move and reside freely within the territory of the Member States.

Detention for the purpose of expelling a person enjoying the right to free movement will normally be a violation of Union law, as such a person is presumed to have a right not to be expelled. Detention orders may not be imposed on the sole basis of failure to present a valid identity card or passport. According to the *Oulane* judgment,[1130] the presentation of a valid identity card or passport for the purpose of proving that a person is a Union citizen is an administrative formality, the sole objective of which is to provide the national authorities with proof of the right that the person in question has directly, by virtue of his status. If the person concerned is able to provide unequivocal proof of his nationality by other means, the host Member State may not refuse to recognise his right of residence on the sole ground that he has not presented one of these documents.

Expulsion of a Union citizen is only legitimate if there is an actual threat of public policy, public security or public health in the strict sense of Articles 27, 28 and 29 of Directive 2004/38. This is also true if an expulsion order can, under the national legislation of a Member State, be issued as a penalty, or emerges as a legal consequence of a custodial penalty (Article 33 Directive 2004/38). If such an expulsion order, as set out in Article 33, is enforced more than two years after it was issued, the Member State shall check that the individual concerned is currently and genuinely a threat to public policy or public security, and shall assess whether there has been any material change in the circumstances since the expulsion order was issued.

Only if expulsion is allowed for reasons of public policy, public security or public health, may detention with a view to deportation be justified. The same goes for an entry ban, referred to in Directive 2004/38 as an 'exclusion order'. Exclusion orders are not defined in this Directive. They are referred to in Article 32 Directive 2004/38, but merely in respect of the right to ask for their termination. It is presumed by the Directive that such measures can be taken under national law of the Member State. However, they must be validly adopted in accordance with Union law,[1131] which, assumingly means that it must first be assessed that a threat of public policy (*etc.*), in the sense of Article 28 Directive 2004/38, exists. Article 32 Directive 2004/38 rules that persons excluded on grounds of public policy or public security may submit an application for lifting of the exclusion order after a reasonable period. What is considered a reasonable period will depend on the circumstances. In any event, such an application may be submitted after three years from the enforcement of the final exclusion order, by putting forward arguments to establish that there has been a material change in the circumstances that justified the decision ordering their exclusion. The

---

[1130] ECJ 17 February 2005, *Oulane*, Case C-215/03.
[1131] Article 32(1) Directive 2004/38.

Member State concerned shall reach a decision on this application within six months of its submission. The persons referred to in this provision shall have no right of entry to the territory of the Member State concerned while their application is being considered. However, they are not prevented from staying in another Member State, as an exclusion under national law of a Member State can only have national effect.

9.4.2.2. Asylum Seekers

Secondly, the Returns Directive is not applicable to asylum seekers, as they may not – by the mere fact of submitting an asylum application – be considered to be 'illegally staying' in the sense of Article 3. The Court of Justice concluded, in the *Kadzoev* judgment, para. 45, that the detention of an asylum seeker falls beyond the scope of the Returns Directive.[1132] In the judgment in *Arslan*,[1133] the Court specified that the Returns Directive does not apply to a third-country national who has applied for international protection under the Qualification Directive during the period from the submission of the application to the adoption of the decision at first instance on that application, or, as the case may be, until the outcome of any action brought against that decision is known.

Special rules of Union law governing the detention of asylum seekers can be found in the Reception Conditions Directive (see section 6.4 for a more detailed description).

9.4.2.3. Criminal Law Penalising Legal Stay

Thirdly, the Returns Directive does not, in principle, affect the freedom of Member States to make criminal laws. Nevertheless, there are important exceptions. Shortly after the implementing date of the Directive, the issue arose as to whether criminal legislation may be used to penalise the mere fact that persons are illegally staying in a Member State. Would that not undermine the system of the Returns Directive? In the *El Dridi* judgment, the Court of Justice held that Member States may not apply rules, even criminal rules, which are liable to jeopardise the achievement of the objectives pursued by the Returns Directive, and, therefore, deprive it of its effectiveness.[1134]

However, it turned out to be difficult to precisely demarcate to what extent illegal stay may be criminalised or not. In the *El Dridi* judgment, the Court of Justice found that the Directive precludes a Member State's legislation, which provides for a sentence of imprisonment to be imposed on an illegally staying third-country national on the sole ground that he remains, without valid

---

[1132] ECJ 30 November 2009, *Kadzoev*, Case C-357/09.
[1133] ECJ 30 May 2013, *Mehmet Arslan*, Case C-534/11, para. 49.
[1134] ECJ 28 April 2011, *Hassen El Dridi*, Case C-61/11 PPU, para. 55.

grounds, on the territory of that State, contrary to an order to leave within a given period. The Court underlined that the order in which the stages of the return procedure established by the Returns Directive are to take place corresponds to a gradation of measures to be taken in order to enforce a return decision, a gradation which goes from the measure which allows the person concerned the most liberty, namely granting a period for his voluntary departure; to measures which restrict that liberty the most, namely detention in a specialised facility; the principle of proportionality must be observed throughout those stages.[1135]

But in the same judgment, the Court considered that Member States are not precluded from adopting, with respect for the principles and the objective of the Returns Directive, provisions regulating the situation in which coercive measures have not resulted in the removal of a third-country national staying illegally on their territory.[1136] This was worked out in the *Achughbabian* judgment.[1137] The Court said that the Directive is not designed to harmonise, in their entirety, the national rules on the stay of foreign nationals. The Directive does not preclude the law of a Member State from classifying an illegal stay as an offence, and laying down penal sanctions to deter and prevent such an infringement of the national rules of residence.[1138] However, imprisonment on the basis of such a criminal law provision, is not permitted, as long as the 'return procedure' established by the Returns Directive has not been applied.

The reason the Court gives for its objections against criminal imprisonment during the return procedure is that it risks delaying the expulsion. It does not, according to the Court, 'contribute to the achievement of the removal which that procedure pursues, namely the physical transportation of the relevant individual out of the Member State concerned.'[1139] This is also true for other forms of deprivation of liberty, like home detention. In the *Sagor* judgment, the Court clarified that Member States must guarantee that enforcement of the deprivation of liberty on the basis of a national provision criminalising illegal stay 'must come to an end as soon as the physical transportation of the individual concerned out of that Member State is possible.'[1140]

The discussion referred to above is confined to imprisonment and other forms of deprivation of liberty. The Returns Directive does not preclude penalising illegal stays by third-country nationals by means of a fine that may be replaced by an expulsion order.

[1135] Paras. 41, 42.
[1136] Para. 60.
[1137] ECJ 6 December 2011, *Achughbabian*, Case C-329/11.
[1138] Para. 28.
[1139] *El Dridi*, para. 59; *Achughbabian*, para. 37; *Sagor*, para. 44.
[1140] ECJ 6 December 2012, *Sagor*, Case C-430/11, para. 47.

9.4.3. THE RETURN DECISION AS THE BASIS OF THE RETURNING PROCEDURE

'Illegal stay' is defined in the Directive as: the presence on the territory of a Member State of a third-country national who does not fulfil, or no longer fulfils, the conditions of entry, as set out in Article 5 of the Schengen Borders Code; or other conditions for entry, stay or residence in that Member State. This definition is slightly different from the definition of 'illegally staying third-country national' in the Employers' Sanctions Directive (see section 9.5, hereunder).

The Directive does not provide for a procedure assessing whether a person is illegally staying or not. According to the *Achughbabian* judgment, the Directive does not preclude a third-country national from being placed in detention with a view to determining whether or not his stay is lawful. The competent authorities must have a brief but reasonable time to identify the person under constraint and to research the information enabling it to be determined whether that person is an illegally staying third-country national.[1141] In para. 31, the Court considered:

> Determination of the name and nationality may prove difficult when the person concerned does not cooperate. Verification of the existence of an illegal stay may likewise prove complicated, particularly where the person concerned invokes the status of an asylum seeker or a refugee. That being so, the authorities are required, in order to prevent the objective of (the Returns Directive) (…) from being undermined, to act with diligence and take a position without delay on the legality or otherwise of the stay of the person concerned. Once it has been established that the stay is illegal, the said authorities must, pursuant to Article 6(1) of the said directive and without prejudice to exceptions laid down by the latter, adopt a return decision.

The term 'expulsion' is not used in the Directive. Instead, the concepts of 'return' and 'removal' are introduced. According to Article 3(3) 'return' means the process of going back, whether in voluntary compliance with an obligation to return or enforced, to one's country of origin, to a country of transit in accordance with EU or bilateral readmission agreements, or to another third country to which the third-country national concerned voluntarily decides to return, and in which he or she shall be accepted. As it was already noted above, the definition of 'return' implies that the person goes to a third country, and accordingly, that he leaves the territory of the EU.

A 'return decision' is an administrative or judicial decision stating or declaring the stay of a third-country national to be illegal and imposing or stating an obligation to return.[1142] 'Removal' is the enforcement of the obligation

---

[1141]   ECJ 6 December 2011, *Achughbabian*, Case C-329/11, paras. 29–31.
[1142]   Article 3(4).

to return, namely the physical transportation out of the country.[1143] Member States are allowed to adopt a combined administrative or judicial decision on the ending of legal stay, together with a return decision or a decision to removal or entry ban.[1144]

The key rule of the Returns Directive, laid down in Article 6(1), is that Member States *shall* issue a return decision to any third-country national staying illegally on their territory. But there are exceptions to this rule. First, when the third-country national has a right to stay in another Member State, he shall be required to go to that Member State. Second, when the third-country national is taken back by another Member State under bilateral agreements or arrangements existing at the date of entry into force of the Directive, it is the responsibility of the latter Member State to issue the return decision. Third, Member States may, at any moment, decide to grant an autonomous residence permit or other authorisation for compassionate, humanitarian or other reasons. And fourth, if a third-country national staying illegally in its territory is the subject of a pending procedure for renewing his residence permit or other permit offering the right to stay, a Member State must consider refraining from issuing a return decision until the pending procedure is finished.[1145]

Intrinsically, the most far reaching of those exceptions is the humanitarian clause of Article 6(4) Returns Directive. The discretion to grant a residence permit 'at any moment' is wide, and the grounds for legalising the stay of the third-country national ('or other reasons') are not limited in any sense. There are two moments in which this clause may play a role: the moment of deciding whether a return decision will be issued, and any further moment at which it can be opportune to decide whether the return decision should be withdrawn and replaced by a residence status. Consequently, when a Member State considers issuing a return decision, it must always, at the same time, consider whether there are reasons for granting a residence permit instead. Further, when a Member State has issued a return decision and eventually comes to the conclusion that neither voluntary return nor forced removal are realistic prospects, it should consider using the clause of Article 6(4) Returns Directive to legalise stay in order to terminate an unsolvable situation.

The return decision forms the basis of the returning procedure under the Directive. Only when such a decision has been taken, are further coercive measures, such as detention and issuing an entry ban, permitted.

[1143]   Article 3(5).
[1144]   Article 6(6).
[1145]   Article 6(2)–(5).

9.4.4. VOLUNTARY RETURN AND REMOVAL

As a rule, any return decision must allow for a period of voluntary departure.[1146] This period must range between 7 and 30 days, and may be extended if necessary, for example, in the case of children attending school.[1147] On the other hand, Member States may refrain from granting a period for voluntary return or grant a period shorter than 7 days if there is a risk of absconding, if an application for legal stay has been dismissed as manifestly unfounded or fraudulent, or if the person poses a risk to public security, public order or national security.[1148] During the period for voluntary return, obligations may be imposed aimed at avoiding the risk of absconding (regular reporting to the authorities, the depositing of money, the submission of documents or an obligation to stay in a certain place).[1149] The return decision may only be enforced after the period for voluntary departure has expired, unless, during that period, a risk of absconding arises.[1150] Where Member States use – as a last resort – coercive measures in order to carry out the removal, such measures must be proportionate, and must not exceed reasonable force. They must be implemented in accordance with fundamental rights, and with due respect for the dignity and physical integrity of the person concerned.[1151]

Member States must postpone removal when it would violate the principle of non-*refoulement*, or as long as the suspensive effect pending judicial or administrative appeal is granted. Further, Member States may postpone removal by taking into account specific circumstances of the individual. In that case, measures involving the regular reporting to the authorities, the depositing of money, the submission of documents, or an obligation to stay in a certain place, may be imposed on the individual.[1152] During the periods for which removal has been postponed, Member States shall provide the persons concerned with a written confirmation that the period for voluntary return has been extended, or that the return decision will temporarily not be enforced.[1153] Further, Member States must ensure that family unity with family members present in their territory is maintained; that emergency healthcare and essential treatment of illness are provided; that minors are granted access to the basic education system, subject to the length of their stay; and that special needs of vulnerable persons are taken into account.[1154]

[1146]   Article 7.
[1147]   Article 7(1) and (2).
[1148]   Article 7(4).
[1149]   Article 7(3).
[1150]   Article 8(2).
[1151]   Article 8(4).
[1152]   Article 9.
[1153]   Article 14(2).
[1154]   Article 14(1).

With regard to the return and removal of unaccompanied minors, the Directive requires additional guarantees. Before a return decision is made, assistance by appropriate bodies other than the authorities enforcing return shall be granted with due consideration, given to the best interests of the child. Before removal, the authorities of the Member State must satisfy themselves that the minor will be returned to a family member, a nominated guardian, or that there are adequate reception facilities in the country of return.[1155]

9.4.5. DETENTION

Detention may, according to the Returns Directive, only be applied in order to prepare return and/or carry out the removal process, if no other sufficient but less coercive measures can be applied in the concrete case, in particular, when there is a risk of absconding, or when the third-country national concerned avoids or hampers the preparation of return or the removal process. Moreover, any detention shall be for as short a period as possible, and only maintained as long as removal arrangements are in progress and executed with due diligence.[1156] Detention shall be maintained for as long a period as these conditions are fulfilled and it is necessary to ensure successful removal.[1157] When it appears that a reasonable prospect of removal no longer exists for legal or other considerations, or the other conditions are no longer fulfilled, detention ceases to be justified, and the person concerned must be released immediately.[1158] Each Member State must set a maximum period of detention, which may not exceed six months, and may be extended to 12 months in cases where, regardless of all reasonable efforts, the removal operation is likely to last longer owing to a lack of cooperation by the third-country national concerned or delays in obtaining the necessary documentation from third countries.[1159]

As the system of the Returns Directive is based on a maximum duration of detention for the purpose of removal, the question arose as to whether the Member States are allowed to detain illegally staying third-country nationals by criminalising illegal residence on their soil. The Court of Justice has dealt with this question in a number of judgments, discussed above in section 9.4.2.

In the *Kadzoev* judgment, the Court of Justice made clear that the provision on the maximum duration is hard law, and that the person concerned must be released immediately, even if he is not in the possession of valid documents, his conduct is aggressive, and he has no means of supporting himself and no

---

[1155] Article 10.
[1156] Article 15(1).
[1157] Article 15(5).
[1158] Article 15(4).
[1159] Article 15(5).

accommodation or means supplied by the Member State for that purpose. The possibility of detaining a person on grounds of public order and public safety cannot be based on the Returns Directive.[1160]

Compared to the ECtHR's application of Article 5(1)(f) ECHR (see also section 10.7), the Returns Directive provides important additional guarantees on the detention of aliens subject to deportation measures, in particular, the limitation of its duration and the requirement that detention may only be applied as a measure of last resort. According to the Court of Justice, detention ceases to be justified and the person concerned must be released immediately when it appears that, for legal or other considerations, a reasonable prospect of removal no longer exists, for instance, when it appears unlikely that the person concerned will be admitted to a third country.[1161] However, where the maximum duration has been reached, the question of whether there is a reasonable prospect of removal no longer arises.[1162] Regarding procedural guarantees and judicial review, the Directive lays down that detention must be ordered by administrative or judicial authorities, in writing, and with reasons being given in fact and in law.[1163] In the case of detention ordered by administrative authorities, Member States must:

- either provide for a speedy judicial review of the lawfulness of detention to be decided on as speedily as possible from the beginning of detention; or
- grant the third-country national concerned the right to take proceedings by which the lawfulness of detention shall be subject to a speedy judicial review to be decided on as speedily as possible from the launch of the relevant proceedings. In this case Member States must immediately inform the third-country national concerned about the possibility of submitting such an application.[1164]

The third-country national concerned must be released immediately if the detention is not lawful. In every case, detention must be reviewed at reasonable intervals of time, either on application by the third-country national concerned or *ex officio*. In the case of prolonged detention periods, reviews shall be subject to the supervision of a judicial authority.[1165]

[1160]   ECJ 30 November 2009, *Kadzoev*, Case C-357/09 PPU, paras. 70, 71.
[1161]   Ibid., paras. 63–67.
[1162]   Ibid., para. 60.
[1163]   Article 15(2).
[1164]   Ibid.
[1165]   Article 15(3).

9.4.6. DETENTION CONDITIONS UNDER THE RETURNS DIRECTIVE

According to Article 16(1) Returns Directive, detention shall be carried out, as a rule, in specialised detention facilities. Where a Member State cannot provide accommodation in a specialised detention facility and has to resort to prison accommodation, the third-country nationals under detention must be separated from ordinary prisoners.

Third-country nationals kept in detention shall be allowed – upon request – to establish, in 'due time', contact with legal representatives, family members and competent consular authorities.[1166] Particular attention shall be paid to the situation of vulnerable persons, and emergency healthcare and essential treatment of illness must be provided.[1167] Relevant and competent national, international and non-governmental organisations and bodies must have the possibility to visit detention facilities, to the extent that they are being used for detaining third-country nationals in accordance with the Returns Directive. Such visits may be subject to authorisation.[1168] Third-country nationals kept in detention shall be systematically provided with information that explains the rules applied in the facility and sets out their rights and obligations.[1169]

According to Article 17(1) of the Directive, unaccompanied minors and families with minors shall only be detained as a measure of last resort and for the shortest appropriate period of time. It is questionable what the added value of this provision is, since Article 15(1) already holds that any detention must be for as short a period as possible, and refers to detention as permissible only when less coercive measures do not suffice. Families detained pending removal must be provided with separate accommodation guaranteeing adequate privacy, and minors in detention must have the possibility to engage in leisure activities, including play and recreational activities appropriate to their age, and – depending on the length of their stay – access to education.[1170] Unaccompanied minors must, as far as possible, be provided with accommodation in institutions with personnel and facilities that take into account the needs of persons of their age. Further, the best interest of the child must be a primary consideration in the context of the detention of minors pending removal, which also follows from Article 5(a) RD.[1171]

[1166]   Article 16(2).
[1167]   Article 16(3).
[1168]   Article 16(4).
[1169]   Article 16(5).
[1170]   Article 17(2–3).
[1171]   Article 17(4–5).

9.4.7. DETENTION: UNFORESEEN SITUATIONS

In cases where an exceptionally large number of third-country nationals to be returned, places an unforeseen heavy burden on the capacity of the detention facilities of a member state or on its administrative or judicial staff, such a Member State may, according to Article 18 Returns Directive, as long as the exceptional situation persists, decide to allow for longer periods for judicial review and to take urgent measures in respect of the conditions of detention derogating from those set out in the Directive. However, when resorting to such exceptional measures, the Member State concerned must inform the European Commission. It is also required to inform the Commission as soon as the reasons for applying these exceptional measures have ceased to exist. The Member States are not allowed to derogate from their general obligation to take all appropriate measures, whether general or particular, to ensure the fulfilment of their obligations arising out of the Returns Directive.

9.5. EMPLOYERS' SANCTIONS

9.5.1. THE EMPLOYERS' SANCTIONS DIRECTIVE

This Directive is meant as a measure against illegal immigration and illegal employment. According to the Preamble, a key pull factor for illegal immigration into the EU is the possibility of obtaining work in the EU without the required legal status. Action against illegal immigration and illegal stay should therefore include measures to counter that pull factor. The centrepiece of such measures should be a general prohibition on the employment of third-country nationals who do not have the right to be resident in the EU, accompanied by sanctions against employers who infringe that prohibition.

The core provision of the Employers' Sanctions Directive 2009/52 is Article 1, containing an EU prohibition on the employment of illegally staying third-country nationals. To this effect, the Member States are obliged to prohibit the employment of illegally staying third-country nationals in national law (Article 3). Infringement of this national prohibition must be made subject to the sanctions and measures laid down in the Directive. The Union law prohibition on the employment of illegal third-country nationals is framed in general terms. Specific provisions as to the scope and the implementation of prohibition are formulated as instructions to the national legislature of the Member States with regard to the national prohibition. A Member State may decide not to apply the prohibition to illegally staying third-country nationals whose removal has been postponed and who are allowed to work in accordance with national law (Article 3(3)).

The Directive lays down minimum common standards on sanctions and measures to be applied in the Member States against employers who infringe the prohibition on the employment of illegal third-country nationals. As the Directive contains minimum norms, paragraph 4 of the Preamble stipulates that Member States should remain free to adopt or maintain stricter sanctions and measures and to impose stricter obligations on employers. The Directive also contains minimum provisions designed to be beneficial for the affected third-country nationals, particularly regarding a right to claim back payments (Article 6) and a right to lodge complaints against the employers (Article 13). According to Article 15 Employers' Sanctions Directive, Member States may adopt or maintain provisions that are more favourable to third-country nationals in relation to Articles 6 and 13, provided that such provisions are compatible with the Directive.

The definition of 'illegally staying third-country national' does not fully run parallel to the definition of 'illegal stay' in the Returns Directive (see section 9.4.3, above). According to Article 2(b) Employers' Sanctions Directive, 'illegally staying third-country national' means a third-country national present on the territory of a Member State, who does not fulfil, or no longer fulfils, the conditions for stay or residence in that Member State. Under Article 3(2) of the Returns Directive, illegal stay is the presence on the territory of a Member State, of a third-country national who does not fulfil, or no longer fulfils, the conditions of entry as set out in Article 5 of the Schengen Borders Code, or other conditions for entry, stay or residence in that Member State. The possible rationale behind this different formulation is that Returns Directive may be applied to removal, detention and entry bans of third-country nationals refused entry at the border, a situation in which it is hardly conceivable that the persons concerned will be employed.

According to Article 4 Employers' Sanctions Directive, Member States must oblige employers to require that a third-country national, before taking up the employment, holds and presents to the employer a valid residence permit or other authorisation for his or her stay. Secondly, employers must keep, for at least the duration of the employment, a copy or record of the residence permit or other authorisation for stay available for possible inspection by the competent authorities of the Member States. Thirdly, they must notify the competent authorities designated by Member States of the start of employment of third-country nationals within a period laid down by each Member State.[1172] The risk for employers that they may be held liable for accepting false documents is qualified in Article 4(3). Member States are to ensure that employers who have fulfilled their obligations set out in Article 4(1) shall not be held liable for an infringement of the

---

[1172] Member States may provide for a simplified procedure for notification where the employers are natural persons and the employment is for their private purposes. Member States may provide that notification is not required where the employee has been granted long-term residence status under Council Directive 2003/109.

prohibition, unless the employers knew that the document presented as a valid residence permit or another authorisation for stay was a forgery.

9.5.2. SANCTIONS

Sanctions against the employer will normally be administrative sanctions. Only in special cases does Article 9 oblige the Member States to ensure that infringement of the prohibition constitutes a criminal offence. In both cases the Directive requires effective, proportionate and dissuasive sanctions against the employer (Articles 5, 9). According to Article 5 Employers' Sanctions Directive, the administrative sanctions shall include: (a) financial sanctions which shall increase in amount according to the number of illegally employed third-country nationals; and (b) payments of the costs of return of illegally employed third-country nationals in those cases where return procedures are carried out. Member States may instead decide to reflect at least the average costs of return in the financial sanctions under point (a). Reduced financial sanctions may be provided for where the employer is a natural person who employs an illegally staying third-country national for his or her private purposes and where no particularly exploitative working conditions are involved (Article 5(3)). Article 9(1) of the Directive lists the circumstances under which intentionally committed infringement of the prohibition must constitute a criminal offence. These circumstances include the situations where the infringement is repeated, where the infringement is accompanied by particularly exploitative working conditions, and where the infringement relates to the illegal employment of a victim of human trafficking or a minor.

The Directive provides for an obligation of employers to make back payments to the employed workers (Article 6, dealt with below) and provides for a number of other measures of a dissuasive nature (Article 7):

(a) exclusion from entitlement to some or all public benefits, aid or subsidies, including EU funding managed by Member States, for up to five years;
(b) exclusion from participation in a public contract as defined in Directive 2004/18/EC on the coordination of procedures for the award of public works contracts, public supply contracts and public service contracts for up to five years;
(c) recovery of some or all public benefits, aid, or subsidies, including EU funding managed by Member States, granted to the employer for up to 12 months preceding the detection of illegal employment;
(d) temporary or permanent closure of the establishments that have been used to commit the infringement, or temporary or permanent withdrawal of a licence to conduct the business activity in question, if justified by the gravity of the infringement.

9.5.3. RIGHTS OF EMPLOYEES

Rights of employees are laid down in Articles 6 and 13. Notable, in this respect, is that illegally employed third-country nationals must be systematically and objectively informed about their rights under these two provisions before the enforcement of any return decision. Article 6 Employers' Sanctions Directive regulates obligations for employers to make back payments. In respect of *each* infringement of the prohibition, Member States must ensure that the employer is liable to pay:

(a) any outstanding remuneration to the illegally employed third-country national;
(b) an amount equal to any taxes and social security contributions that the employer would have paid had the third country national been legally employed;
(c) where appropriate, any cost arising from sending back payments to the country to which the third-country national has returned or has been returned.

In the calculation of the payments, an employment relationship of at least three months duration shall be presumed unless, among others, the employer or the employee can prove otherwise (Article 6(3) Employers' Sanctions Directive).

As regards procedural rights to obtain payments, Member States must ensure that illegally employed third-country nationals may introduce a claim, subject to a limitation period defined in national law, against their employer, and eventually enforce a judgment against the employer for any outstanding remuneration, including in cases in which they have returned. As an alternative, national legislation may also provide that the third-country national may call on the competent authority of the Member State to start procedures to recover outstanding remuneration without the need for them to introduce a claim in that case (Article 6(2)). Further, Member States must ensure that the necessary mechanisms are in place to ensure that illegally employed third-country nationals are able to receive any back payment of remuneration which is recovered as part of the claims, including in cases in which they have (been) returned (Article 6(4)).

Article 13 obliges Member States to provide for effective mechanisms through which third-country nationals in illegal employment may lodge complaints against their employers. Third parties that have a legitimate interest in ensuring compliance with this Directive may engage either on behalf of, or in support of, an illegally employed third-country national, with his or her approval, in any administrative or civil proceedings provided for with the objective of implementing this Directive. Providing assistance to third-country nationals to lodge complaints is not to be considered as facilitation of unauthorised residence under Council Directive 2002/90/EC defining the facilitation of unauthorised entry, transit and residence.

Notably, in situations where the infringement concerns exploitative working conditions or the illegal employment of minors, the Directive places an *obligation* on Member States to define in national law the circumstances under which the third-country national *may* be granted a residence permit of limited duration, linked to the duration of criminal proceedings (Article 13(4) Employers' Sanctions Directive). Reference is made here to the arrangements regarding third-country nationals who fall within the scope of Directive 2004/81 (victims of human trafficking, not dealt with in this book). Although the grant of a residence permit is not phrased in mandatory terms, the Member States are obliged to formulate conditions for considering whether to grant a permit. In respect of cases where residence permits of limited duration have been granted under Article 13(4), Member States must, according to Article 6(5), define under national law the conditions under which the duration of these permits may be extended until the third-country national has received any back payment of his or her remuneration recovered under Article 6(1).

The liability of legal persons – as defined under national law (Article 2(g) Employers' Sanctions Directive) – is regulated in Article 11. Member States must ensure that legal persons may be held liable for the criminal offence referred to in Article 9 where such an offence has been committed for their benefit by any person who has a leading position within the legal person. A legal person may be also be held liable where the lack of supervision or control by this person, has made possible the commission of the criminal offence for the benefit of that legal person by a person under its authority. Liability of a legal person shall not exclude criminal proceedings against natural persons who are perpetrators, inciters or accessories in the criminal offence. According to Article 12, Member States may decide that a list of employers, who are legal persons and who have been held liable for the criminal offence referred to in Article 9, is made public.

Article 8 Employers' Sanctions Directive provides rules in cases of subcontracting. Where the employer is a subcontractor, Member States must ensure that the contractor of which the employer is a direct subcontractor may, either in addition to, or in place of, the employer, be liable to pay the financial sanctions imposed under Article 5, and any back payments due under Article 6(1)(a) and (c) and Article 6(2) and (3). Additionally, Member States must ensure that the main contractor and any intermediate subcontractor, where they knew that the employing subcontractor employed illegally staying third-country nationals, may be liable to make these payments in addition to, or in place of, the employing subcontractor or the contractor of which the employer is a direct subcontractor. Contractors who have undertaken so-called 'due diligence' obligations, as defined by national law, are not liable to make these payments.

9.6. EXCLUSION

9.6.1. LISTING IN THE SIS AND ENTRY BAN

There is an essential, though undissolved relationship, between two instruments excluding a person from the territory of the Union: the SIS alert and the entry ban under the Returns Directive.

The *SIS alert* is a measure that was created in 1990 by the Schengen Implementing Convention. Nowadays, this measure is regulated in two interconnected sources of EU law. It is the SIS II Regulation that contains rules on the alert as such, and it is Article 5 of the Schengen Borders Code that contains the legal enforcement of an alert. Article 5 Schengen Borders Code holds that entry *shall* be refused to persons for whom an alert has been issued in the SIS for the purposes of refusing entry. There are, however, some exceptions to the obligation of Member States to refuse entry, which are described in section 9.2.3, above. The technical and data protection conditions on entering an alert are laid down in the SIS II Regulation 1987/2006.[1173] There is no clear maximum duration of validity of an alert. According to Article 29 SIS II Regulation, an alert is not kept any longer than necessary to achieve the purposes for which they were entered. Not later than after three years, the Member State entering the alert shall review the need to keep it. The conditions for entering an alert are laid down in Articles 21 and 24 SIS II Regulation (see the next section). The effect of a SIS alert is that a person is excluded from entering all Schengen states.

It is not clear how an *'entry ban'*, as defined in the Returns Directive, may relate to a SIS alert. The Returns Directive defines an entry ban as 'an administrative or judicial decision or act prohibiting entry into and stay in the territory of the Member States for a specified period, accompanying a return decision.'[1174] The entry ban may not, in principle, last for longer than 5 years. According to the Returns Directive, the length of the entry ban shall be determined with due regard to all relevant circumstances of the individual case, and shall not, in principle, exceed five years, except when the third-country national represents a serious threat to public policy, public security or to national security.[1175] The intended effect of the measure is exclusion from entry to 'the Member States'. As the Returns Directive does not regulate how this effect is to be realised, an entry ban will only be effective in practice if it is accompanied by a SIS alert. Recital 18 of the Returns Directive says that Member States should have rapid access to information on entry bans issued by other Member States in

---

[1173]   Regulation (EC) No 1987/2006 of 20 December 2006 on the establishment, operation and use of the second generation Schengen Information System (SIS II). The SIS II Regulation is replacing Articles 92–119 of the Schengen Implementing Convention.

[1174]   Article 3(6) Returns Directive.

[1175]   Article 11(2) Returns Directive.

accordance with the SIS II Regulation. Apparently, the SIS alert is meant to play a supportive role to the entry ban, but there are important inconsistencies in the way in which the two instruments are shaped in the Returns Directive and the SIS II Regulation respectively. This is further illustrated in the next section.

9.6.2. CONDITIONS FOR ENTERING AN ALERT IN THE SIS II AND FOR ISSUING AN ENTRY BAN UNDER THE RETURNS DIRECTIVE

According to Article 24 SIS II Regulation, data on third-country nationals in respect of whom an alert has been issued for the purposes of refusing entry or stay shall be entered on the basis of a national alert taken on the basis of an individual assessment. The SIS II Regulation distinguishes between alerts which must, and alerts which may, be entered into the SIS. An alert *must* be entered if a national alert is based on a threat to public policy or public security or to national security which the presence of the third-country national in question in the territory of a Member State may pose.[1176] The Regulation stipulates that this is in particular the case in situations of:

(a) a third-country national who has been convicted in a Member State of an offence carrying a penalty involving deprivation of liberty of at least one year;
(b) a third-country national in respect of whom there are serious grounds for believing that he has committed a serious criminal offence or in respect of whom there are clear indications of an intention to commit such an offence in the territory of a Member State.

An alert *may* be entered when the national alert is based on the fact that the third-country national has been subject to a measure involving expulsion, refusal of entry or removal which has not been rescinded or suspended, that includes, or is accompanied by, a prohibition on entry or, where applicable, a prohibition on residence, based on a failure to comply with national regulations on the entry or residence of third-country nationals.

Before issuing an alert, Member States must, according to Article 21 SIS II, determine whether the case is adequate, relevant and important enough to warrant entry of the alert in SIS II. As it emerges from these conditions, Member States must enter alerts in the SIS II on the basis of criminal convictions, serious suspicions and may enter alerts on the rather broadly formulated ground of failure to comply with national immigration rules.

[1176] Article 24(2) SIS II Regulation.

The last category in particular is relevant with regard to an entry ban under the Returns Directive. This Directive links the entry ban to a return decision, which shall normally be issued in case of illegal presence of a third-country national. Often such a person can be said to have failed to comply with national regulations on the entry or residence, as Article 24 SIS II formulates them.

Under the Returns Directive, return decisions must always be accompanied by an entry ban if no period for voluntary departure has been granted or if the obligation to return has not been complied with. In other cases return decisions *may* be accompanied by an entry ban.[1177] Though the Directive obliges the Member States to issue an entry ban in the above-mentioned situations, it softens this obligation by stating that Member States may refrain from issuing, withdrawing or suspending an entry ban in individual cases for humanitarian reasons.[1178] Further, Member States may withdraw or suspend an entry ban in individual cases or certain categories of cases for other – unspecified – reasons.[1179] Member States are obliged, moreover, to 'consider withdrawing or suspending an entry ban where a third country national who is the subject of an entry ban can demonstrate that he/she has left the territory of a Member State in full compliance with a return decision.'[1180] A final category to which a special regime applies are victims of trafficking in human beings who have been granted a residence permit pursuant to the Directive 2004/81/EC. They may not be made the subject of an entry ban unless no period for voluntary return has been granted and provided that the third-country national concerned does not represent a threat to public policy, public security or national security.[1181]

In the SIS II Regulation specific guarantees are formulated with regard to data protection requirements.[1182] Further, a special regime applies to alerts concerning third-country nationals who are beneficiaries of the right to free movement, normally because they are members of the family of an EU citizen utilising his or her right to free movement. According to Article 25 SIS II, an alert of such a person shall be in conformity with the rules adopted in implementation of Directive 2004/38. This provision can be said to codify the ECJ's judgment in the case *Commission v. Spain*.[1183] In that judgment, the Court of Justice considered that the specific public policy criteria applicable to the regime on the free movement of persons (presently laid down in Directive 2004/38) are violated when a Member State refuses entry into the Schengen Area to third-country nationals who are the spouses of Member State nationals, on the sole ground that they were persons for whom alerts were entered in the SIS

[1177] Article 11(1) Returns Directive.
[1178] Article 11(3), third paragraph, Returns Directive.
[1179] Article 11(3), fourth paragraph, Returns Directive.
[1180] Article 11(3), first paragraph, Returns Directive.
[1181] Article 11(3), second paragraph, Returns Directive.
[1182] See chapters V and VI of the SIS II Regulation in particular.
[1183] ECJ 21 January 2006, *Commission v. Spain*, Case C-503/03.

for the purpose of refusing them entry. The Court referred to its body of case law concerning the free movement of persons, and held that the Member State should first verify whether the presence of those persons constituted a genuine, present and sufficiently serious threat to one of the fundamental interests of society. Moreover, the Member State issuing the alert should make supplementary information available to the consulting state to enable it to gauge, in the specific case, the gravity of the threat that the person for whom an alert has been issued is likely to represent.[1184]

Two provisions of SIS II relate to appeal rights of individuals. According to Article 24(1), the decision to issue a *national* alert shall be taken on the basis of an individual assessment. Appeals against these decisions must be provided for in accordance with national legislation. Article 43 relates to remedies concerning alerts *entered into the SIS II*. Any person may bring an action before the courts or the authority competent under the law of any Member State to access, correct, delete or obtain information or to obtain compensation in connection with an alert relating to him. The Member States undertake mutually to enforce final decisions handed down by the courts or authorities referred to in paragraph 1, without prejudice to the provisions of Article 48 regarding liability of Member States.

Under Article 48 SIS II, each Member State shall be liable, in accordance with its national law, for any damage caused to a person through the use of N.SIS II. This also applies to damage caused by the Member State that issued the alert, where the latter entered factually inaccurate data or stored data unlawfully.

The picture emanating from combining the rules applying to those two measures leads to a number of inconsistencies, both regarding the coordination between the two and regarding the grounds for taking these measures, the proportionality standards, the duration and the termination.[1185]

9.7. DATA STORAGE

Systematic data gathering and data exchange of information concerning third-country nationals happens through the Schengen Information System (SIS II), the Visa Information System (VIS) and Eurodac. Mention should also be made of Directive 2004/83 of 29 April 2004 on the obligation of carriers to communicate passenger data.[1186] Furthermore, Member States are obliged to transmit a variety of data relating to third-country nationals to the European

---

[1184]   Ibid., especially paras. 44–59.
[1185]   See, for an extensive comment on this issue, Note on the coordination of the relationship between the Entry Ban and the SIS alert: an urgent need for legislative measures, of 8 February 2012, by the Meijers Committee, www.commissie-meijers.nl.
[1186]   OJ L 261, 6 August 2004.

Commission (Eurostat). According to Article 13(5) Schengen Borders Code, Member States 'shall collect statistics on the number of persons refused entry, the grounds for refusal, the nationality of the persons refused and the type of border (land, air or sea) at which they were refused entry.' These statistics must be transmitted to the European Commission, which is obliged to publish, every two years, a compilation of the statistics provided by the Member States. Regulation 862/2007 on Community statistics on migration and international protection obliges Member States to supply to the Commission a variety of statistics relating to international migration, international protection, the prevention of illegal entry and stay, residence permits and returns.[1187]

The provisions of the SIS II Regulation relating to alerts for the purpose of refusing entry and stay were already discussed above. Hereunder, we will focus mainly on the general functions of the SIS and the other immigration databases.

The *Schengen Information System* (SIS) was established under the Schengen Implementing Convention in 1990, and became operational in 1995. In 2004 and 2005, the use and utilities of the SIS were extended, by giving Europol, Eurojust and national law enforcement authorities access to SIS data. In 2006, an extended version, called SIS II, was adopted.[1188] New functions added to the second-generation SIS are the inclusion of biometric data, the addition of new categories of data, and the possibility of running searches on the basis of incomplete data. A further novelty of SIS II is that persons listed on the EU terrorist lists based on decisions by the Sanctions Committee of the UN Security Council can be included in the SIS (Article 26 SIS II).

SIS II contains alerts for the purpose of refusing entry or stay. Data on third-country nationals, in respect of whom an alert has been issued for the purposes of refusing entry or stay, must be entered on the basis of an individual assessment (Article 24(1) SIS II). SIS II is composed of:

(a) a central system ('Central SIS II') composed of a technical support function ('CS-SIS') containing a database, the 'SIS II database' and a uniform national interface ('NI-SIS');
(b) a national system (the 'N.SIS II') in each of the Member States, consisting of the national data systems which communicate with Central SIS II. An N.SIS II may contain a data file (a 'national copy'), containing a complete or partial copy of the SIS II database; and
(c) a communication infrastructure between CS-SIS and NI-SIS (the 'Communication Infrastructure') that provides an encrypted virtual

---

[1187] Articles 3–7 Regulation 862/2007.
[1188] Regulation 1987/2006, *OJ* L 381/4, 28.12.2006. See, for an extensive exposé, Evelien Brouwer, *Digital Borders and Real Rights: Effective Remedies for Third Country Nationals in the Schengen Information System*, Leiden/Boston: Martinus Nijhoff Publishers, 2009, Chapter 4.

network dedicated to SIS II data and the exchange of data between SIRENE Bureaux as referred to in Article 7(2).

SIS II data are entered, updated, deleted and searched *via* the various N.SIS II systems. Entering data into the SIS II for the purpose of refusing entry may be in conflict with obligations under EC law or international law. Although the new SIS II Regulation now expressly states in Article 25 that an alert concerning a third-country national who is a beneficiary of the right of free movement within the Community must be in conformity with the rules adopted in implementation of that Directive, it is less clear how the SIS relates to third-country nationals invoking community legislation on immigration and asylum. In the Preamble of SIS II, it is said that it is necessary to further consider harmonising the provisions on the grounds for issuing alerts concerning third-country nationals for the purpose of refusing entry or stay and to clarifying their use in the framework of asylum, immigration and return policies. According to Article 24(5) SIS II, the Commission is obliged to review the application of Article 24 three years after the date on which the SIS II Regulation will be declared applicable.[1189] On the basis of that review, the Commission must, using its right of initiative in accordance with the Treaty, make the necessary proposals to modify the provisions of this provision to achieve a greater level of harmonisation of the criteria for entering alerts.

The *Visa Information System (VIS)*[1190] concerns the exchange of data between Member States on short-stay visas and visa applications of third-country nationals. Data regarding citizens of more than a hundred countries who apply for a visa and who are covered by the Visa Requirement Regulation, will be stored in the system. The information stored includes biometrics (photographs, fingerprints) and written information in respect of the name, address, and occupation of the applicant, the date and place of application, and any decision of the responsible Member State to issue, refuse, annul, revoke or extend a visa. The purpose of the Visa Information System is to counter visa shopping (persons applying for a visa in more than one Member State), to facilitate the fight against fraud and checks at the external borders, and to assist in the identification of those not meeting the conditions for entry, stay or residence in the participating Member States.

In the data system of *Eurodac*, fingerprints of asylum seekers and illegal migrants are stored, for the purpose of checking whether the migrant has previously lodged an asylum application in another Member State (see, further, section 6.3.5).

[1189] See Article 55(2) SIS II. The Council will declare SIS II applicable once the system has been successfully tested. As of November 2008, the tests were still ongoing.

[1190] Council Decision 2004/512/EC of 8 June 2004 establishing the Visa Information System (VIS).

9.8. OPERATIONAL COOPERATION

Operational cooperation between Member States in the sphere of external border control is coordinated by Frontex (*Frontières extérieures*), the European Agency for the management of operational cooperation at the external borders of the EU Member States. This agency was established by a Regulation of 26 October 2004.[1191] The founding Regulation was later amended by Regulation (EC) No 863/2007, establishing a mechanism for the creation of Rapid Border Intervention Teams. It was last amended by Regulation (EU) No 1168/2011. The seat of the agency is Warsaw, Poland.

Frontex was established in lieu of a supranational corps of European border guards, and leaves primary responsibility for the control and the surveillance of external borders with the Member States. According to Recital 4 of Regulation 2007/2004, the agency 'facilitates the application of existing and future Union measures relating to the management of external borders by ensuring the coordination of Member States' actions in the implementation of those measures'. The Frontex Regulation contains a special provision on cooperation with the UK and Ireland, which do not take part in the Schengen *acquis*.[1192] Shortly before adoption of the Frontex Regulation, the United Kingdom had expressed the intention to participate in the Regulation, but this was refused by the Council on the ground that the UK did not take part in closely related parts of the Schengen *acquis*.[1193]

The main tasks of Frontex consist of coordinating operational cooperation between Member States in the field of the management of external borders; the setting up of European Border Guard Teams, assisting Member States with training of national border guards; carrying out risk analyses; following up on the development of relevant research; assisting Member States in circumstances requiring increased technical and operational assistance; and providing Member

---

[1191] Regulation (EC) 2007/2004, OJ L 349/1, 25 November 2004 (Frontex Regulation). According to Article 24 of this Regulation, the Agency took up its responsibilities from 1 May 2005.

[1192] Article 12.

[1193] After the Council's refusal to allow the UK to take part in the Frontex Regulation, the UK lodged an action for annulment of the Frontex Regulation with the ECJ. The ECJ dismissed the action by holding that the Council's refusal was in conformity with the relevant provisions of the Protocol integrating the Schengen *acquis* into the framework of the European Union ('the Schengen Protocol'), which was annexed to the EC Treaty by the Treaty of Amsterdam. According to this Protocol, the United Kingdom (and Ireland) can only take part in the adoption of new measures relating to the Schengen *acquis* if it also takes part in the area of the Schengen *acquis*, which forms the context of the measure. *United Kingdom v. Council*, ECJ 18 December 2007, Case C-77/05, paras. 56–71. On the same day, a similar judgment was delivered on the refusal to allow the UK to participate in Regulation 2252/2004 on biometric standards in passports; *United Kingdom v. Council*, ECJ 18 December 2007, Case C-137/05.

States with support in organising joint return operations.[1194] The Agency is a body of the Union and has legal personality.[1195]

Frontex acquired notoriety for setting up joint operations at the southern maritime borders of the EU, with a view to curb illegal migration by sea from Asia and Africa to Member States such as Greece, Italy, Spain and Malta. To that end, several Member States participated in operations of sea border control and the identification of migrants arriving at Europe's southern maritime borders. Under the revised Regulation, the primary instruments for such cooperation are European Border Guard Teams, which consist of border guards of the Member States.

The (legal) environment in which Frontex operates is sometimes contested. The frequent occurrence of boat tragedies, such as the Lampedusa shipwreck of 3 October 2013 and questionable 'control' practices such as the pushing back of irregular migrants, have raised widespread concerns about the relationship between maritime border controls and human rights.[1196] The European Court of Human Rights issued a landmark judgment in the case of *Hirsi v. Italy*, on the compatibility of Italy's so-called push back-policy with the prohibitions of *refoulement* and collective expulsion. The case did not concern operations coordinated by Frontex, but Italy's practice in 2009 of summarily returning migrants, who had been intercepted on the high seas, to Libya. The ECtHR underlined the importance of interviewing intercepted persons and allowing them the opportunity to express reasons for refraining from return. It also considered that effective remedies should be in place to enable migrants to obtain a thorough and rigorous assessment of their objections against return before the removal is enforced. Because the Italian operations did not provide such remedies, they were in violation of Articles 3 and 4 of Protocol 4 ECHR.[1197]

To make the work of Frontex and border controls in general more effective, a European Border Surveillance System (Eurosur) was established in 2013.[1198] The system's aim is to detect and prevent cross-border crime, to detect and prevent illegal border crossings and to contribute to saving the lives of migrants at sea. It provides a system that allows all national authorities with a responsibility for border surveillance (e.g. border guard, police, coast guard, navy) and Frontex, to coordinate their activities and to share information. The EUROSUR Regulation requires Member States and Frontex to fully comply with fundamental rights, in particular the prohibition of *refoulement* and the protection of personal data.

[1194] Article 2 Frontex Regulation.
[1195] Article 15.
[1196] European Union Agency for Fundamental Rights.
[1197] ECtHR 23 February 2012, *Hirsi Jamaa a.o. v. Italy*, No. 27765/09.
[1198] Regulation (EU) No. 1052/2013 of 22 October 2013.

FURTHER READING

S. Peers, E. Guild, J. Tomkin, *EU Immigration and Asylum Law (Text and Commentary) Vol. 1 Visas and Border Controls,* Leiden, Martinus Nijhoff (2012).

S. Peers, *EU Justice and Home Affairs Law* (3rd edition) Oxford University Press (2011).

K. Zwaan (ed.), *The Returns Directive, Central Themes, Problem Issues, and Implementation in selected Member States,* Nijmegen, Wolf Legal Publishers (2011).

E. Brouwer, *Digital Borders and Real Rights: Effective Remedies for Third-Country Nationals in the Schengen Information System,* Leiden/Boston: Martinus Nijhoff (2008).

M. den Heijer, *Europe and Extraterritorial Asylum,* Oxford, Hart Publishing (2012).

M. den Heijer, *'Reflections on Refoulement and Collective Expulsion in the Hirsi Case',* International Journal of Refugee Law (2013) Vol. 25(2), 265–290.

Roberta Mungiano, *'Frontex: towards a Common Policy on External Border Control',* EJML 2013, 359–385.

Sokol Dedja, *'Human Rights and EU Return Policy: the Case of EU-Albania Relations',* EJML 2012, 95–114.

Stephanie Grant, *'Recording and Identifying European Frontier deaths',* EJML 2011, 135–156

10. PROCEDURAL GUARANTEES FOR MIGRATING INDIVIDUALS

10.1. INTRODUCTION

In the preceding chapters, the emphasis was on the material rights and obligations of migrants in Europe. In this last chapter of the book, the procedural side will be shown. In practice there is often a huge gap between deserving and obtaining a right. Attorneys and judges know that most of their time and knowledge is occupied by procedural issues and that defining the involved material rights and obligations is often the easiest part. It would go beyond the character of this book to delve too deeply into procedural matters, which tend to be very technical. But it would definitely be wrong to fully ignore the procedural rules, as they are often the essence of the play. In this chapter, guarantees for effective and fair procedures are at the forefront.

In the EU Regulations and Directives on migration law, provisions on procedural remedies are often framed in summary terms and do not always extensively elaborate on the required procedural guarantees. For instance, in the Family Reunification Directive, the relevant Article 18 says not much more than that the individuals affected by a negative decision have 'the right to mount a legal challenge'. And in the SIS II Regulation, Article 43 mainly states that 'any person may bring an action under the law of any Member State'. Likewise, for EU citizens and their family members, the procedural guarantees are relatively succinctly formulated in Article 31 Directive 2004/38.

Sometimes provisions refer more explicitly to fundamental procedural guarantees, like Article 13 of the Returns Directive, stating that the third-country national concerned 'shall be afforded an effective remedy to appeal against or seek review of decisions related to return (…) before a competent judicial or administrative authority or a competent body composed of members who are impartial and who enjoy safeguards of independence'. Also, Article 46 Procedures Directive, dealing specifically with the procedural protection to be afforded to asylum seekers, secures an 'effective remedy before a court or tribunal'. Still, even these provisions leave much room for insecurity about the real level of procedural guarantees that is required.

Judicial review in European migration law is basically a matter for the national courts of the Member States. Abidance of European Union law by the Member States *vis-à-vis* individuals is guarded by the national judges, according to their national procedural legislation. However, national procedures must enable individuals to effectively invoke their rights under Union law. In this respect, the Court of Justice plays an important supervisory role. National judges may ask the Court of Justice, by means of preliminary questions, whether national procedural rules are compatible with applicable Union law. Sometimes, written EU legislation is available to help answer these questions, but often the Court must have recourse to unwritten law. Over time, the Court has thus developed jurisprudence on requirements for effective national procedures, formulated as general principles. The Court developed these – and other – general principles, based on provisions of the European Convention on Human Rights, but also on common traditions in the Member States. It is settled case law that the requirements flowing from the protection of fundamental rights are binding on Member States whenever they are required to apply EU law.[1199]

Therefore, it is important to know what guiding principles can be invoked when interpreting the procedural provisions in relevant Regulations and Directives.

10.2. THE CHARTER OF FUNDAMENTAL RIGHTS

10.2.1. THE CHARTER AND THE PRINCIPLES

The primary location of such principles is the Charter of Fundamental Rights of the European Union In section 1.7 of the first chapter of this book, the central place of the Charter in Union law was explained. As far as procedural protection is concerned, the Charter contains one pertinent provision, Article 47, laying down 'the right to an effective remedy and to a fair trial'.[1200] The provisions of the Charter contain the essence of the applicable principles. It is for the Court of Justice to explain the meaning of these provisions in concrete situations. Hereby the Court relies on its extensive case law on 'general principles of EU law' developed in the past decades, long before the Charter came into existence.

In determining the meaning and scope of the principles, the Court does not mechanically copy the case law of the European Court of Human Rights but follows his own path, as the Court of Justice has the specific task to explain EU law and the meaning of fundamental rights for the interpretation of specific EU

[1199] ECJ 1 March 2011, *Chartry*, Case C-457/09, para. 22; ECJ 12 November 2010, *Asparuhov Estov*, para. 13, and cited earlier case law.
[1200] Articles 48, 49 and 50 Charter contain specific guarantees for criminal proceedings, but these are not applicable to the field this book is dealing with.

law issues. The doctrine developed by the Court on general principles is now codified in Article 6(3) TEU:

> Fundamental rights, as guaranteed by the European Convention for the Protection of Human Rights and Fundamental Freedoms and as they result from the constitutional traditions common to the Member States, shall constitute general principles of the Union's law.

In the relationship between the Charter and the principles, the latter are the deeper source from which the Court draws its inspiration. The Court consistently considers the *written* principles laid down in the Charter as 'giving expression' to the *unwritten* principles developed by the Court. In the same way, Article 47 of the Charter gives expression to the 'principle of effective judicial protection'.[1201]

10.2.2. ARTICLE 47 OF THE CHARTER

Article 47 of the Charter states:

> Everyone whose rights and freedoms guaranteed by the law of the Union are violated has the right to an effective remedy before a tribunal in compliance with the conditions laid down in this Article.
>
> Everyone is entitled to a fair and public hearing within a reasonable time by an independent and impartial tribunal previously established by law. Everyone shall have the possibility of being advised, defended and represented.
>
> Legal aid shall be made available to those who lack sufficient resources in so far as such aid is necessary to ensure effective access to justice.

Article 47 of the Charter combines core elements of Articles 6(1)[1202] and 13[1203] of the European Convention of Human Rights. By formulating the procedural guarantees in one single Article, the Charter makes clear that no distinction is made in the level of protection afforded. This is an improvement compared to the approach of the ECHR, which was drafted in a time (1950) when administrative law, and more specifically, migration law, were still underdeveloped fields. The fundamental guarantees given in Article 6(1) ECHR concerning a fair and public

---

[1201] ECJ 1 March 2011 *Chartry*, Case C-457/09, para. 25; ECJ 28 July 2011, *Samba Diouf*, Case C-69/10, para. 49; ECJ 6 November 2012, *Otis*, Case C-199/11, para. 46.

[1202] Article 6(1) ECHR: 'In the determination of his civil rights and obligations or if any criminal charge against him, everyone is entitled to a fair and public hearing within a reasonable time by an independent and impartial tribunal established by law. (…).'

[1203] Article 13 ECHR: 'Everyone whose rights and freedoms as set forth in this Convention are violated shall have an effective remedy before a national authority notwithstanding that the violation has been committed by persons acting in an official capacity'.

hearing within a reasonable time before an independent and impartial tribunal established by law, are only formulated with respect to the determination of civil rights and obligations or of any criminal charge. In the *Maaouia* judgment[1204] the European Court of Human Rights made the decision to interpret Article 6 ECHR as not being applicable to 'decisions regarding the entry, stay and deportation of aliens'. As a consequence, in migration matters, the ECtHR since then concentrated on extensively interpreting the procedural guarantees offered by Article 13 ECHR securing an effective remedy for everyone whose rights and freedoms set forth in the ECHR are violated.

As the Charter does not divide the procedural protection over two provisions, the specific part of the ECtHR's case law dealing with such a division, is not relevant for the interpretation of the Charter. But for the rest, it is very fruitful to look at the extensive jurisprudence of the ECtHR on Articles 6 and 13 ECHR. Still, it must be kept in mind that ECHR jurisprudence is only of indirect importance for the explanation of the Charter. In cases within the scope of EU law, it is 'necessary to refer only to Article 47 Charter'.[1205]

Since Article 47 Charter became binding law, the Court of Justice has had some opportunity to give its opinion on the merits of this provision. In the *Otis* judgment,[1206] the Court shows how it connects the text of the provision with the broader doctrine of fair proceedings.

> The principle of effective judicial protection laid down in Article 47 of the Charter comprises various elements; in particular, the rights of the defence, the principle of equality of arms, the right to access to a tribunal and the right to be advised, defended and represented.[1207]
>
> With regard, in particular, to the right of access to a tribunal, it must be made clear that, for a 'tribunal' to be able to determine a dispute concerning rights and obligations arising under EU law in accordance with Article 47 of the Charter, it must have power to consider all questions of fact and law that are relevant to the case before it.[1208]
>
> The principle of equality of arms, which is the corollary of the concept of a fair hearing (…) implies that each party must be afforded a reasonable opportunity to present his case, including his evidence, under conditions that do not place him at a substantial disadvantage vis-à-vis his opponent.[1209]

In an extensive research on effective remedies in EU asylum procedures, Reneman has shown that Article 47 Charter applies to its full extent in all cases

---

[1204]   ECHR 5 October 2000, app. 39652/98, *Maaouia v. France*.
[1205]   ECJ 6 November 2012, *Otis*, Case C-199/11, para. 46.
[1206]   ECJ 6 November 2012, *Otis*, Case C-199/11.
[1207]   ECJ 6 November 2012, *Otis*, Case C-199/11, para. 48.
[1208]   ECJ 6 November 2012, *Otis*, Case C-199/11, para. 49.
[1209]   ECJ 6 November 2012, *Otis*, Case C-199/11, para. 71.

falling within the scope of EU law.[1210] In section 11.1.1 of the book, she concludes:

> In all fields of EU law, whether it is competition, EU sanctions, equal treatment or asylum, similar aspects of EU or national procedures raise questions as to their compatibility with EU procedural rights. In all kinds of procedure parties may claim that, for example, a lack of suspensive effect of the appeal, limitations of the right to be heard, evidentiary rules or a limited scope or intensity of judicial review undermines their right to an effective remedy and/or impedes the effective exercise of their rights granted under EU law. The EU Court's judgments regarding such claims are relevant not only for the specific procedure at issue, but for all procedures in which EU law is invoked. From this case law principles emerge which are applicable to all fields of EU law. This is how the EU Court's judgments in, for example, competition, EU sanction or equal treatment cases become relevant for the interpretation of the EU right to an effective remedy in asylum cases.

In this way, the Court of Justice secures a consistent body of procedural protection rules applicable to the whole field of Union law.

10.2.3. THE RIGHT TO GOOD ADMINISTRATION

With some exaggeration, it could be said that once a court is accessed against a wrongful act or omission of the administration, it is in principle too late. Normally, wrongful acts should be prevented by good administration. Often, specific guidelines for good administration can be found in the relevant Regulations and Directives governing EU migration law. For instance, Article 6 of the Schengen Borders Code rules that border guards shall, in the performance of their duties, fully respect human dignity, and that any measures taken in the performance of their duties shall be proportionate to the objectives pursued by such measures. According to Article 13(2) Schengen Borders Code, entry may only be refused by a substantiated decision stating the precise reasons for refusal. Further, Chapter II of the Asylum Procedures Directive is an example of specific guidelines for good administration.

The Charter of Fundamental Rights secures the right to good administration in Article 41. According to the text of that provision, the right applies to the institutions, bodies, offices and agencies of the Union. Further, as it is placed in Title V under the heading 'citizen's rights', it could be argued that the right be only destined for EU citizens. However, in the *M.M.* judgment of 2012, the Court of Justice simply stated that the provision is of general application, 'as follows from its very wording'.[1211]

[1210]   M. Reneman, *EU Asylum Procedures and the Right to an Effective Remedy*, Oxford: Hart, 2014.
[1211]   ECJ 22 November 2012, *M.M*, Case C-277/11, para. 84.

According to Article 41, every person has the right to have his or her affairs handled impartially, fairly, and within a reasonable time. This right includes, under Article 41(2):

a. The right of every person to be heard, before any individual measure which would affect him or her adversely is taken;
b. The right of every person to have access to his or her file, while respecting the legitimate interests of confidentiality and of professional and business secrecy;
c. The obligation of the administration to give reasons for its decisions.

Further, Article 41(3) provides for a right to reparation of damage. The right, given in Article 41(4), to write to the institutions in one of the languages of the Treaties, seems less suitable for analogous application to the relation between migrants and the Member States.

In the *M.M.* judgment, the Court of Justice has stated that the right to be heard in all proceedings is inherent in the general principle of EU that the rights of the defence must be observed. This right is now affirmed not only in Articles 47 and 48 of the Charter, but also in Article 41. The observance of this right is required in all proceedings that are liable to culminate in a measure adversely affecting a person, even where the applicable legislation does not expressly provide for such a procedural requirement.[1212] In paragraphs 87 and 88 of the *M.M.* judgment, the Court made the following principal considerations:

> The right to be heard guarantees every person the opportunity to make known his views effectively during an administrative procedure and before the adoption of any decision liable to affect his interests adversely (...).
> That right also requires the authorities to pay due attention to the observations submitted by the person concerned, examining carefully and impartially all the relevant aspects of the individual case and giving a detailed statement of reasons for their decision (...); the obligation to state reasons for a decision which a sufficiently specific and concrete to allow the person to understand why his application is being rejected is thus a corollary of the principle of respect for the rights of the defence.

The Court of Justice has thus left no doubt as to the general validity of the principles of good administration for all EU migration proceedings.

[1212]   ECJ 22 November 2012, *M.M*, Case C-277/11, paras. 81–86.

10.3. EFFECTIVE PROCEDURAL PROTECTION IN EU MIGRATION LAW

10.3.1. INTRODUCTION

As was already said in this chapter, the various Regulations and Directives governing EU migration law contain more or less extensive provisions on the procedural protection to be afforded, both in respect to good administration and in respect to judicial review. In the following sections, the main features of procedural protection in matters of entry, application for legal stay, return, expulsion, exclusion and detention, are catalogued. When appropriate, referral is made to relevant case law of the Court of Justice or the European Court of Human Rights.

Some procedural issues, specific to migration law, are always popping up in one or another form, due to the circumstance that a migrant may be subject to control measures of the receiving country. During the application or during appeal, the migrant is always in the position that his or her right to stay is still to be assessed or is denied and contested. In this insecure position, important standard questions relate to a right to have one's expulsion suspended or, if applicable, a right to be provisory allowed entry, and a right not to be detained or otherwise restricted in one's liberty.

10.3.2. UNION CITIZENS AND THIRD-COUNTRY NATIONALS

In the following sections, only the rules concerning third-country nationals shall be described. Here, some attention is given to the position of Union citizens. For Union citizens, there is far less EU legislation regulating procedural protection in migration cases. For them, the point of departure is, that they are free to enter and leave any Member State and that they have clear rights to reside in Member States other than their own. Member States are primarily expected to facilitate free movement. Only in serious cases of threat of public policy, public safety of public health, may Union citizens be limited in their freedom of movement. Many of he problems third-country nationals are coping with in cases of entry, application for stay, expulsion, or entry ban, do simply not exist, at least not to that extent, for Union citizens.

Chapter VI of the Citizens' Directive contains three Articles (27–29) delimiting the reasons of public policy (*etc.*) for which a Union citizen may be limited in his freedom. Articles 30 and 31 contain procedural protection rules. Article 32 and 33 guarantee that a removal measure is reconsidered after a reasonable period (see sections 2.2.5–2.2.8).

10.4. ENTRY PROCEDURES

10.4.1. INTRODUCTION

As long as a migrant does not effectively enter the receiving country, he is, as it were, the sole bearer of his migration problem. This especially so for a third-country national, having no presumed right to enter an EU Member State. A country, not wishing to receive a migrant, can, in principle, simply confine itself to just refusing entry in order to effectuate that he stays out. It is for the migrant to realise migration. This position may disadvantage the migrant with regard to the extent to which his right to good administration is recognised in practice.

10.4.2. VISA CODE

If a visa is required according to the Visa Requirement Regulation, the third-country national must comply with the conditions laid down in the Visa Code. However, even after obtaining a visa, he has no automatic right of entry (Article 30). Procedural guarantees regarding the application for visas in the Visa Code (Articles 9–17) are rather of a bureaucratic nature. They focus at regulating how the person concerned must adduce the relevant information proving that he or she complies with the conditions and what he must pay. Apart from the emphasis on human dignity, professional and respectful manners, high standards and good administrative methods in Recitals 6 and 7, there are no abundant guarantees of good administration or effective procedures *vis-à-vis* the applicant. On the other hand, the authorities have a range of possibilities to deny a visa. As described in section 9.3.3, above, the Visa Code knows five types of negative decisions: *refusal (Article 32), inadmissibility (Article 19), refusal of extension (Article 33), annulment (Article 34), revocation (Article 34), and refusal of a visa with limited territorial validity (Article 2(2))*. There is no explicit obligation to give reasons for decisions other than the refusal. According to Article 32(3) Visa Code, the refusal of the application and the reason for it must be communicated by means of a standard form. Only against the refusal, annulment and revocation the Visa Code provides for an explicit right to appeal (Article 32(3)). How the other types of denying a visa may be challenged remains undisclosed. As to the possibility to appeal against a refusal, the Visa Code contains no requirements regarding procedural guarantees: the Code merely says that the procedures falls under the national legislation of the Member State which took the final decision.

The Visa Code is quite unclear about the responsibility for the Member States to secure that their consulates handle the visa applications with the required care, the more so, as a Member State may make representation arrangements according to which the consulate of another Member State represents it with handling the applications. As yet, it has not been established to what extent Member States may also transfer the responsibility for good administration and effective judicial protection to other Member States.

In the judgment on the *Koushkaki* case, the Court said that the national authorities have a wide discretion in the examination of a request for a visa in so far as it concerns the conditions for the application of Articles 23(4), 32(1) and 35(6) Visa Code and the assessment of the relevant facts. However, those authorities must carry out an individual examination of the visa application which takes into account the general situation in the applicant's country of residence and the applicant's individual characteristics, *inter alia*, his family, social and economic situation, whether he may have previously stayed legally or illegally in one of the Member States and his ties in his country of residence and in the Member States.[1213]

In the case of *Min Khoa Vo*[1214] the Court of Justice said that the Visa Code obliges the Member States not to hinder the movement of visa holders, unless a visa has been duly and properly annulled. However, if this obligation may conflict with another obligation under EU law, namely to prescribe and enforce effective, proportionate dissuasive penalties against human smugglers. Prior annulment of visas is not necessary for the application of national criminal law punishing the persons assisting illegal immigration where these persons smuggled third-country nationals holding visas obtained fraudulently.

10.4.3. SCHENGEN BORDERS CODE

The Schengen Borders Code is better equipped than the Visa Code with respect to provisions securing good administration. According to Article 13(2), entry may only be refused by a substantiated decision stating the precise reasons for the refusal. The decision must be taken by an authority empowered by national law, and must take effect immediately. The substantiated decision stating the precise reasons for the refusal must be given by means of a standard form, filled in by the authority empowered by national law to refuse entry. The completed standard forms must be handed to the third-country national concerned, who acknowledges receipt of the decision to refuse entry by means of that form.

Persons refused entry under the Schengen Borders Code have the right to appeal, which must be conducted in accordance with national law. A written indication of contact points able to provide information on representatives competent to act on behalf of the third-country national in accordance with national law must be given to the third-country national. Lodging an appeal

---

1213 ECJ 19 December 2013, *Koushkaki*, C-84/12, para. 69.
1214 ECJ 10 April 2012, *Min Khoa Vo*, C-83/12 PPU, para. 45.

does not have suspensive effect on a decision to refuse entry. Without prejudice to any compensation granted in accordance with national law, the third-country national concerned is, where the appeal concludes that the decision to refuse entry was ill-founded, entitled to correction of the cancelled entry stamp, and any other cancellations or additions which have been made, by the Member State which refused entry.

In principle, the Court of Justice will have to apply the principles of effective judicial review and good administration recognised in Articles 41 and 47 Charter to visa applications and entry applications at the border.[1215] In that respect, EU law is potentially forceful. For instance, in the *Z.Z.* judgment, concerning a refusal to admit an EU citizen to the territory of the host Member State for reasons of public policy on the basis of secret information, the Court formulated some important considerations regarding the impact of Article 47 Charter, which were expressly linked to the applicable Citizens' Directive, but might arguably also be applied to cases of third-country nationals.[1216] The Court said that the fundamental right to an effective legal remedy would be infringed if a judicial decision were founded on facts and documents which the parties themselves, or one of them, have not had an opportunity to examine, and on which they have therefore been unable to state their views. But in exceptional cases, a national authority may oppose the precise and full disclosure to the person concerned of the grounds which constitute the basis of a decision taken under Article 27 Citizens' Directive, by invoking reasons of state security. In such a case, the court with jurisdiction in the Member State concerned must have at its disposal, and apply, techniques and rules of procedural law which accommodate, on the one hand, legitimate state security considerations regarding the nature and sources of the information taken into account in the adoption of such a decision, and, on the other hand, the need to ensure sufficient compliance with the person's procedural rights, such as the right to be heard and the adversarial principle. The competent national authority has the task of proving, in accordance with the national procedural rules, that state security would in fact be compromised by precise and full disclosure to the person concerned of the grounds which constitute the basis of a decision taken under Article 27 Citizens' Directive and of the related evidence. There is no presumption that the reasons invoked by a national authority exist and are valid.

In contrast, under the ECHR, topics of denial of entry are not likely to fall within the range of conceivable violations of the Convention, let alone that questions of good administration or effective access to courts come to the fore. Even if family life is at stake, the refusal of entry has only in exceptional cases been considered a violation of Article 8 ECHR by the Strasbourg Court.[1217] A

[1215] ECJ 22 November 2012, *M.M*, Case C-277/11.
[1216] ECJ 4 June 2013, *Z.Z.*, Case C-300/11.
[1217] Sen, Rodrigues da Silva.

rare example of relevant case law is the *Dalea* case.[1218] The ECtHR did consider the possibility that an interdiction to the Schengen area in the form of an alert in the Schengen Information System (SIS) could amount to an interference in the private life of a Romanian business man under Article 8 ECHR (at the time, Romanian citizens had no right to free movement within the EU yet). Mr. Dalea claimed that the SIS alert, issued by the French authorities, prevented him from travelling for private or professional purposes in a number of important countries. Thus, his professional activities were affected, while his business partners had difficulties understanding why he could not travel to the Schengen area. His private life was affected, as he had to cancel a medical operation in France. Mr. Dalea had the SIS alert challenged before the French *Conseil d'État*, which requested the competent French authorities to give the underlying reasons for issuing the alert. However, the requested information was not provided in more detail than that the alert was issued on request of the French Direction for the Surveillance of the Territory. Nevertheless, the *Conseil d'État* judged that the file justified the refusal to rectify the alert, without further indication as to what the reasons for the alert had been. The ECtHR, carefully formulating its considerations in hypothetical terms, said that, in as far as the SIS alert could be considered an interference in Mr. Dalea's private life, he had the right to guarantees against arbitrary measures based on reasons of national security. However, when it concerns entry to the territory, states have an important margin of discretion with regard to the guarantees they offer against arbitrary treatment. The Court emphasised that Mr. Dalea had been granted the possibility of judicial control of the measure imposed to him. Even if he never had the possibility of challenging the precise reason for the alert, he had been given all the other information in the file, and he was informed – in general terms – that the alert was based on considerations of the safety of the state, public order and public security. The ECtHR found that the lack of a possibility of having full access to the information was an interference that was justified by reasons of public safety. The complaint was declared manifestly ill-founded.

10.5. PROCEDURES APPLYING FOR LEGAL STAY

10.5.1. INTRODUCTION

Applying for legal stay often goes together with applying for permission to enter. Normally, third-country nationals are required to wait abroad while being allowed to enter. However, this is not the case in asylum cases, for which it is characteristic that the applicant arrives at the border or in the territory without

---

[1218]   ECtHR 21 December 2006, *Dalea*, nr. 964/07, admissibility decision.

due permission. This situational difference can explain the difference in harmonisation between voluntary and forced migration rules. As long as the migrant stays neatly outside the territory, no urgent need is apparently felt by the EU to coordinate relevant application procedures more than superficially. But if the migrant can invoke guarantees laid down in asylum law to apply for protection once he arrives in the territory of the Member States, there is an EU interest in coordinating the processing of the applications in the various Member States.

10.5.2. VOLUNTARY MIGRATION

In matters of voluntary migration, Member States are left considerable freedom to organise application procedures for third-country nationals. For instance, in the Family Reunification Directive, Member States may determine whether an application for entry and residence shall be submitted by the sponsor or by the family members (Article 5(1). Likewise, in issues of research or highly qualified work, Member States may decide whether the application must be made by the worker or by the employer (Article 10 Blue Card Directive, Article 14 Researchers Directive, Article 4(1) Single Application Directive).

As was said above, issues of entry and residence are closely connected in the area of voluntary immigration. Applications are often lodged from abroad. Article 5 Family Reunification Directive expressly states that an application shall be submitted and examined when the family members are residing outside the territory of the Member State in which he sponsor resides, though Member States may derogate from that rule in appropriate circumstances (see also articles 10(2) Blue Card Directive and 14(2) Researchers Directive). Whether a request for entry and residence must be made in the form of a visa or otherwise is left to the discretion of the Member States. As was shown in section 9.3.1, long-term visas are strictly national visas, not harmonised by Union law.

Article 5(4) Family Reunification Directive contains basic guidelines for good administration: the person who submitted the application must be given a written notification of the decision as soon as possible, and in any event, no later than nine months from the date on which the application was lodged. This term may be extended in exceptional circumstances linked to the complexity of the examination of he application. However, it is for the Member States to regulate in their national legislation what the consequences are of exceeding the term. Reasons shall be given for the decision rejecting the application. For admission of workers, Article 11 Blue Card Directive and Article 8 Single Application Directive contain similar rules. Less precise are the guidelines in Article 18 of the Students Directive and Article 15 Researchers Directive. The right to appeal is, in all cases, left to national legislation without further specifications as to procedural guarantees. It will be up to the Court of Justice to work this out. As yet, the Court of Justice has not make any judgment on application proceedings for third-country nationals in voluntary migration.

The European Court of Human Rights, in its turn, has, on some occasions, criticised the use of 'excessive formalism' barring access to the application procedure for family reunification. In *Rodrigues da Silva v. The Netherlands*,[1219] the ECtHR found that the Dutch authorities, by attaching paramount importance to the fact that the applicant resided illegally on the territory, indulged in excessive formalism. In a number of complaints against the Netherlands which were terminated before the Court came to a judgment because the applicants were given a residence permit during the procedure, the Court asked the Netherlands whether the position of the authorities, refusing a permit for the sole reason that the applicant should have applied for a visa from abroad prior to asking a residence permit, was excessively formalistic.[1220] In *G.R. v. The Netherlands*,[1221] the ECtHR characterised a disproportion between the administrative charge at issue and the actual income of the applicant's family, depriving the applicant of access to the competent administrative tribunal, as an extremely formalistic attitude of the Dutch authorities, which unjustifiably hindered the applicant's use of an otherwise effective domestic remedy. There had therefore been a violation of Article 13 of the Convention.

10.5.3. ASYLUM

In contrast to voluntary migration, the application procedures for asylum seekers are harmonised in great detail. The Dublin Regulation determines in which Member State an application must be lodged, and the Procedures Directive pretends to establish 'common procedures' for granting and withdrawing international protection. These instruments were already extensively discussed in Chapter 6. In the context of asylum applications, the Court of Justice has had the opportunity to show the importance of the principle of good administration and the right to be heard.

In *H.I.D. and B.A.*,[1222] the EU Court stressed, that the basic principles and guarantees[1223] for the processing of asylum applications, which apply to all forms of procedure, confer rights upon applicants for asylum without discrimination between applicants for asylum from a specific third country whose applications might be the subject of a prioritised examination procedure

---

[1219] ECtHR 31 January 2006, *Rodrigues da Silva and Hoogkamer v. The Netherlands*, No. 50435/99, para. 44.
[1220] ECtHR cases 7137/07; 31893/05; 8257/07; 40012/08; 39670/11.
[1221] ECtHR 10 January 2012, *G.R. v. The Netherlands*, No. 22251/07, para. 55.
[1222] ECJ 13 April 2012, *H.I.D. and B.A.*, Case C-175/11.
[1223] See Article 31 Procedures Directive 2013/32 (recast).

and nationals of other third countries whose applications are subject to the normal procedure. All applicants must enjoy a sufficient period of time within which to gather and present the necessary material in support of their application, thus allowing the determining authority to carry out a fair and comprehensive examination of those applications and to ensure that the applicants are not exposed to any dangers in their country of origin.

In the *M.M.* judgment[1224] the Court upheld the right to be heard in the case of a system having two separate procedures, one after the other, for examining applications for refugee status and applications for subsidiary protection respectively. It is for the national court to ensure observance, in each of those procedures, of the applicant's fundamental rights, and, more particularly, of the right to be heard in the sense that the applicant must be able to make known his views before the adoption of any decision that does not grant the protection requested. In such a system, the fact that the applicant has already been duly heard when his application for refugee status was examined does not mean that that procedural requirement may be dispensed with in the procedure relating to the application for subsidiary protection.

In the *Samba Diouf* judgment,[1225] the Court of Justice confirmed that the principle of effective judicial protection is a general principle of EU law to which expression is now given by Article 47 of the Charter of Fundamental Rights of the European Union. The Court had to determine whether the fact that there is no appeal against the decision to examine the application for asylum under an accelerated procedure denies the applicant for asylum his right to an effective remedy. It said that the Procedures Directive and the principle of effective judicial protection do not preclude national rules under which no separate action may be brought against the decision of the competent national authority to deal with an application for asylum under an accelerated procedure, provided that the reasons which led that authority to examine the merits of the application under such a procedure can in fact be subject to judicial review in the action which may be brought against the final decision rejecting the application.

Prior to these judgments of the Court of Justice, the European Court of Human Rights had already formed extensive case law on Article 13 ECHR. In cases of expulsion potentially resulting in treatment contrary to Article 3 ECHR in the receiving country, the Court has underlined the importance of the possibility of independent and thorough review of the expulsion order, particularly regarding the consequences of expulsion. In asylum cases before the ECtHR the emphasis is seldom on the expulsion as such. Usually, the question is, whether the expellee should have been protected against *refoulement* by more careful assessment of his material asylum claim by the

---

[1224] ECJ 22 November 2012, *M.M.*, Case C-277/11.
[1225] ECJ 28 July 2011, *Samba Diouf*, Case C-69/10, paras. 48, 49.

administrative or judicial authorities. In the case of *Chahal*, the ECtHR considered that:

> In such cases, given the irreversible nature of the harm that might occur if the risk of ill-treatment materialised and the importance the Court attaches to Article 3, the notion of an effective remedy under Article 13 requires independent scrutiny of the claim that there exist substantial grounds for fearing a real risk of treatment contrary to Article 3. This scrutiny must be carried out without regard to what the person may have done to warrant expulsion or to any perceived threat to the national security of the expelling State.[1226]

In the case of *Jabari v. Turkey*, where no serious investigation of the asylum claim took place, the Court required an 'independent and rigorous scrutiny of a claim that there exist substantial grounds for fearing a real risk of treatment contrary to Article 3'.[1227] In a more recent case, of *Abdolkani and Karimnia v. Turkey*,[1228] the Court was struck by the fact that both the administrative and judicial authorities in Turkey remained totally passive regarding the applicant's serious allegations of a risk of ill-treatment if returned to Iraq or Iran. The lack of any response by the national authorities regarding the applicants' allegations amounted to a lack of the 'rigorous scrutiny' that is required by Article 13 of the Convention.

Given their potential irreversible nature, a vital issue in cases of expulsion is whether the appeal has suspensive effect. This is particularly important when there is a risk that deportation would expose a person to a treatment prohibited by Article 3 ECHR. Here, Article 13 provides a clear standard. In the *Čonka* judgment,[1229] the Court said that 'the notion of an effective remedy may prevent the execution of measures that are contrary to the Convention and whose effects are potentially irreversible (…). Consequently, it is inconsistent with Article 13 for such measures to be executed before the national authorities have examined whether they are compatible with the Convention.' In the case of *Gebremedhin v. France*[1230] the Court considered that for a remedy to be effective in a situation involving *refoulement*, it must have automatic suspensive effect. This may either mean that the appeal itself suspends the execution of expulsion or that there is a possibility for a request for interim measures during the handling of which the individual may not be expelled.[1231] Access to legal assistance was deemed relevant by the ECtHR in paras. 114 and 115 of the *Abdolkani and Karimnia* judgment.

[1226]   ECtHR 15 November 1996, *Chahal v. United Kingdom*, No. 22414/93, para. 131.

[1227]   ECtHR 11 July 2000, *Jabari v. Turkey*, No. 40035/98, paras. 49–50.

[1228]   ECtHR 1March 2010, *Abdolkani and Karimnia v. Turkey*, No. 30471/08, para. 113.

[1229]   ECtHR 5 February 2002, *Čonka v. Belgium*, No. 51564/99, paras. 61, 62, 63.

[1230]   ECtHR 26 April 2007, *Gebremedhin [Gaberamadhien] v. France*, No. 25389/05, para. 66.

[1231]   See also ECtHR 11 December 2008, *Muminov v. Russia*, No. 42502/06, para. 102.

10.6. EXPULSION PROCEDURES

10.6.1. INTRODUCTION

In the phenomenon of expulsion, the whole complex of the migration problem culminates. It is the decisive stage of the discussion of whether a person is allowed residence or not. When it comes to expulsion, the question of whether one is entitled to any form of legal stay has normally already been decided on. Still, the threat of removal is not seldom countered by a claim that expulsion would violate a prohibition of *refoulement* or a right to family life. In essence, the migrant thus intends to avert the threat of expulsion by going back to the initial stage of the migration procedure, that is, the application. But once this stage is definitely passed, and if the migrant is not returning voluntarily, removal boils down to a merely practical problem that is often complicated by lack of travel documents and a non-cooperative attitude of both the migrant and the authorities of countries of destination. Forced removal is an intrusive measure, which may not be carried out arbitrarily or regardless of the personal situation of the expellee.

The significance of the Returns Directive for good administration and effective remedies is considerable. By establishing common standards and procedures regarding the treatment of third-country nationals who have no legal stay in a Member State, a binding framework is brought about, obliging the Member States to carry out removal using the least coercive measures possible. The Directive contains provisions on the procedural safeguard of a written and substantiated decision (Article 12). With regard to the remedies to be afforded, Article 13(1) requires the usual guarantee of an effective remedy before a competent judicial or administrative authority 'or a competent body composed of members who are impartial and who enjoy safeguards of independence' (which are precisely the essential guarantees characteristic for judges). Further, Article 13(2) contains a special paragraph about temporarily suspending the enforcement of decisions related to return. On detention, the Directive gives even more specific guarantees in Article 15(2)(3). However, the broader importance of the Directive is that it pays due attention to principle of proportionality, the needs of vulnerable persons, family members, children and securing medical care (Articles 4(4), 5, 8(4), 9, 10, 14, 16, 17).

Under the Returns Directive, removal can take place only after a return decision has been issued, that is, after it has been duly established that the person concerned has no right to legal stay. Before forced removal can take place, a period for voluntary return must be granted. Member States are *obliged* to postpone removal when it would violate the principle of non-*refoulement* or for as long as suspensory effect is granted (Article 9(1) Returns Directive). Further, Member States are *allowed* to postpone removal for an appropriate period taking into account the specific circumstances of the individual case, taking into account the physical state or mental capacity of the person, and technical reasons such as a lack of transport capacity or failure of the removal due to lack of identification (Article 9(2)). During the period of postponement of removal, Member States shall, as far as possible, ensure that family unity with family members present in the territory is maintained, that emergency healthcare and essential treatment of illness are provided, that minors are granted access to the basic education system subject to the length of their stay, and that special needs of vulnerable persons are take into account (Article 14(1) Returns Directive). Member States shall provide a written confirmation that the return decision will temporarily not be enforced (Article 14(2) Returns Directive).

Special guarantees are given with regard to unaccompanied minors. Before a return decision of unaccompanied minors takes place, assistance by appropriate bodies other than the authorities enforcing return shall be granted, with due consideration of the best interests of the child (Article 10(1) Returns Directive). Before removing an unaccompanied minor, the authorities should be satisfied that he or she will be returned to a member of his or her family, a nominated guardian or adequate reception facilities in the state of return (Article 10(2)).

The Returns Directive leaves discretion to the Member States as to the way in which the common standards and procedures are implemented. But, as is stated in Article 1, the common standards and procedures of the Directive must be applied in accordance with fundamental rights as general principles of Union law as well as international law, including refugee protection and human rights obligations.

It is up to the national courts to control the correct application in individual cases. While the Court of Justice may be important for clarifying the meaning and content of the guarantees laid down in the Returns Directive on request of the national courts, it has no jurisdiction to consider individual complaints. At the moment of writing, the Court of Justice had not yet given opinions on procedural protection regarding removal under the Returns Directive, but the European Court of Human Rights has long since played an important role in expulsion cases. Hereunder, some important judgments of the ECtHR on expulsion will be discussed.

10.6.2. GOOD ADMINISTRATION ON EXPULSION UNDER THE ECHR

The European Court of Human Rights has developed a doctrine of 'the quality of law' which is of particular importance to the prevention and redress of arbitrary decision-making. This doctrine is based on a requirement which is common to several provisions of the Convention, including Article 8 ECHR and Article 2 Fourth Protocol, under which an interference or restriction must be *in accordance with law*. This requirement has different levels of application. First of all, it must be investigated whether the disputed measure has any basis in domestic law at all. Second, if there is a domestic legal basis, its quality must meet a certain standard regarding accessibility and foreseeability.

In the *Al Nashif* judgment the Court elaborated on the element of foreseeability, stating that 'a rule's effects are "foreseeable" if it is formulated with sufficient precision to enable any individual – if need be with appropriate advice – to regulate his conduct'.[1232] In addition, there must be safeguards to ensure that discretion left to the executive is exercised in accordance with the law and without abuse, even where national security is at stake.[1233] In general, the 'law' must provide the necessary safeguards against *arbitrariness*. In the case of *Al Nashif*, who was lifted from his bed and instantaneously expelled, without the authorities following any form of adversarial procedure, without giving any reasons, and without any possibility for appeal to an independent authority, the Court found a violation of Article 8 ECHR, because 'deportation was ordered pursuant to a legal regime that does not provide the necessary safeguards against arbitrariness'.[1234] In general, in order to avoid arbitrariness, it is necessary that an *individual assessment* of the relevant circumstances and interests takes place.

The mere fact that a person is staying illegally in the country does not, in itself, provide sufficient ground for assuming that expulsion is not arbitrary. In the *Liu v. Russia* judgment, the Court considered that a deportation procedure following a decision that a person's presence is unlawful must also provide for sufficient safeguards against arbitrariness. Because the deportation had been ordered according to a procedure not allowing for any form of independent review or adversarial proceedings, the Court found that 'the legal provisions on the basis of which the first applicant's deportation was ordered did not provide for the adequate degree of protection against arbitrary interference'.[1235] In *C.G. and others v. Bulgaria* the Court summarised its jurisprudence on the requirement of 'in accordance with law' as follows:

> The Court has consistently held that the first of these requirements does not merely dictate that the interference should have a basis in domestic law, but also relates to the quality of that law, requiring it to be compatible with the rule of law. The phrase thus implies that domestic law must be accessible and foreseeable, in the sense of being sufficiently clear in its terms to give individuals an adequate indication as to the circumstances in which and the conditions on which the authorities are entitled to resort to measures affecting their rights under the Convention. The law must moreover afford a degree of legal protection against arbitrary interference by the authorities. In matters affecting fundamental rights it would be contrary to the rule

---

1232   ECtHR 2 June 2002, *Al Nashif v. Bulgaria*, No. 50963/99, para. 119.
1233   Ibid, paras. 121–123.
1234   Ibid, para. 128.
1235   ECtHR 6 December 2007, *Liu v. Russia*, No. 42086/05, para. 68.

of law for a legal discretion granted to the executive to be expressed in terms of unfettered power. Consequently, the law must indicate the scope of any such discretion conferred on the competent authorities and the manner of its exercise with sufficient clarity, so as to give the individual adequate protection against arbitrary interference (…).[1236]

Further, a general standard requiring an individual assessment of whether expulsion is justified is implied in Article 4 Fourth Protocol ECHR, prohibiting *collective expulsion*. Collective expulsion, within the meaning of Article 4 of Protocol No. 4, is to be understood as any measure compelling aliens, as a group, to leave a country, except where such a measure is taken on the basis of a reasonable and objective examination of the particular case of each individual member of the group.[1237] According to the ECtHR, the prohibition of collective expulsion entails that an expulsion must be made 'on the basis of a reasonable and objective examination of the particular case of each individual'.[1238] This implies that there must be a genuine individual assessment of the circumstances of each person whose expulsion is ordered. In the *Čonka v. Belgium judgment*, a family of Slovakian nationals of Roma origin, whose asylum applications had been rejected, were detained and served deportation orders to enforce an order to leave the territory. The Court noted that the only reference to the personal circumstances of the applicants was to the fact that their stay in Belgium had exceeded three months:[1239]

> In particular, the document made no reference to their application for asylum or to the decisions of 3 March and 18 June 1999. Admittedly, those decisions had also been accompanied by an order to leave the territory, but by itself, that order did not permit the applicants' arrest. The applicants' arrest was therefore ordered for the first time in a decision of 29 September 1999 on a legal basis unrelated to their requests for asylum, but nonetheless sufficient to entail the implementation of the impugned measures. In those circumstances and in view of the large number of persons of the same origin who suffered the same fate as the applicants, the Court considers that the procedure followed does not enable it to eliminate all doubt that the expulsion might have been collective.
>
> That doubt is reinforced by a series of factors: firstly, prior to the applicants' deportation, the political authorities concerned had announced that there would be operations of that kind and given instructions to the relevant authority for their implementation (…); secondly, all the aliens concerned had been required to attend the police station at the same time; thirdly, the orders served on them requiring them

---

1236   ECtHR 24 April 2008, *C.G. and others v. Bulgaria*, No. 1365/07, paras. 39, 40.
1237   ECtHR 23 February 1999, *Andric v. Sweden*, No. 45917/99.
1238   ECtHR 23 February 1999, *Juric v. Sweden*, No. 45924/99; ECtHR 23 February 1999, *Andric v. Sweden*, No. 45917/99; ECtHR 5 February 2002, *Çonka v. Belgium*, No. 51564/99, para. 59; ECtHR 16 June 2005, *Berisha and Haljiti v. Macedonia*, No. 8670/03; ECtHR 20 September 2007, *Sultani v. France*, No. 45223/05, para. 81.
1239   ECtHR 5 February 2002, *Čonka v. Belgium*, No. 51564/99, paras. 61, 62, 63.

to leave the territory and for their arrest were couched in identical terms; fourthly, it was very difficult for the aliens to contact a lawyer; lastly, the asylum procedure had not been completed.

In short, at no stage in the period between the service of the notice on the aliens to attend the police station and their expulsion did the procedure afford sufficient guarantees demonstrating that the personal circumstances of each of those concerned had been genuinely and individually taken into account.

The requirements of an individual assessment and of the quality of law are not only important in the stage of the making of a decision or the preparation of a measure. They remain important in the stage of appeal against such decisions or measures.

The impact of the above-mentioned case law of the ECtHR for good administration under the Returns Directive may seem obsolete, as the primary requirements formulated by the ECtHR to prevent arbitrary decision-making are properly laid down in the Directive. Still, this jurisprudence underlines that the requirements of the Returns Directive must be taken seriously. The cases of Čonka and Al Nashif were against states that were then (Belgium), or are now (Bulgaria), members of the EU.

10.6.3. JUDICIAL REVIEW OF EXPULSION UNDER THE ECHR

The 'quality of law' doctrine has also emerged as a source of minimum standards for judicial review, apart from the standards given in Articles 6 and 13 ECHR. Here we see that Article 8 ECHR, which appears at first sight to be only pertinent to family life and privacy, has developed into a provision of much wider impact. In some judgments, the Court attached similar consequences to the 'quality of law' aspect of Article 8 as with regard to the effective remedy requirement of Article 13. In the case of *C.G. and others v. Bulgaria* [1240] the following standard passage in the Court's reasoning, developed since the *Al Nashif* judgment, [1241] can be found:

(...) even where national security is at stake, the concepts of lawfulness and the rule of law in a democratic society require that deportation measures affecting fundamental human rights be subject to some form of adversarial proceedings before an independent authority or a court competent to effectively scrutinise the reasons for them and review the relevant evidence, if need be with appropriate procedural limitations on the use of classified information. The individual must be able to challenge the executive's assertion that national security is at stake. While the

---

[1240]   ECtHR 24 April 2008, *C.G. and others v. Bulgaria*, No. 1365/07, para. 40.
[1241]   ECtHR 2 June 2002, *Al Nashif v. Bulgaria*, No. 50963/99.

executive's assessment of what poses a threat to national security will naturally be of significant weight, the independent authority or court must be able to react in cases where the invocation of this concept has no reasonable basis in the facts or reveals an interpretation of 'national security' that is unlawful or contrary to common sense and arbitrary (…).

A formal possibility of judicial review is not sufficient. In the *C.G.* case, the Court considered, in the light of Article 8, that the applicant did not enjoy the minimum degree of protection against arbitrariness on the part of the authorities, despite having the formal possibility of seeking judicial review of the decision to expel him. The case concerned expulsion for reasons of national security. The Court found that the Bulgarian legal framework did not provide the minimum guarantees required under Article 8 of the Convention:

> In particular, Bulgarian law does not contain sufficient safeguards to ensure that the authorities deploying special means of surveillance faithfully reproduce the original data in the written record (…), and does not lay down proper procedures for preserving the integrity of such data (…). Moreover, in the instant case, the file contains no information making it possible to verify whether the secret surveillance measures against the first applicant were lawfully ordered and executed, nor was this aspect of the matter considered by the courts in the judicial review proceedings.

10.7. DETENTION PROCEDURES

Under the Returns Directive, detention for the purpose of removal is tied to a set of restrictive conditions, as described in sections 9.4.5–9.4.7 above. Unless other sufficient but less coercive measures can be applied effectively in a specific case, Member States may only keep in detention a third-country national who is the subject of return procedures under the Directive, in order to prepare the return and/or carry out the removal process, in particular when there is a risk of absconding or the third-country national concerned avoids or hampers the preparation of return or the removal process (Article 15(1) Returns Directive).

The Returns Directive contains fairly precise instructions for good administration. Detention shall be ordered by administrative or judicial authorities, in writing, with reasons being given in fact and in law. When the detention has been ordered by administrative authorities, Member States shall either provide for a speedy judicial review of the lawfulness of detention to be decided as speedily as possible from the beginning of detention, or grant the third-country national concerned the right to take proceedings, by means of which the lawfulness of detention shall be subject to a speedy judicial review to be decided on as speedily as possible after the launch of the relevant proceedings. In such case, the Member State shall immediately inform the third-country national concerned about the possibility of taking such proceedings. In every case, detention shall be reviewed at reasonable intervals of time, either by application of the individual or *ex officio* (Article 15(3)).

The third-country national shall be released immediately if the detention is not lawful (Article 15(2) Returns Directive). Paragraph 4 of Article 15 specifies that detention is no longer justified when it appears that a reasonable prospect if removal no longer exists. The maximum period of detention is 6 months, which may be extended with another 12 months if, regardless of all reasonable efforts, the removal operation is likely to last longer owing to lack of cooperation of the individual or delays in obtaining the necessary documentation form third countries (Article 15(5)(6)). The Returns Directive must be implemented in accordance with the Charter, in particular with Article 6 securing the right to liberty and safety of the person (see Article 1 and Recital 24 of the Directive).

For detained asylum seekers, Article 9 of the Reception Conditions Directive prescribes a speedy judicial review of the lawfulness of detention to be conducted *ex officio* and/or at the request of the applicant. Where, as a result of the judicial review, detention is held to be unlawful, the applicant concerned shall be released immediately. Detention shall be reviewed by a judicial authority at reasonable intervals of time, *ex officio* and/or at the request of the applicant concerned, in particular whenever it is of a prolonged duration, relevant circumstances arise or new information becomes available, which may affect the lawfulness of detention. In cases of a judicial review of the detention order, Member States shall ensure that applicants have access to free legal assistance and representation, as described in Article 9 of the Directive.

The guarantees offered by these EU Directives are more detailed, and go, in some aspects, further than those afforded by the ECHR. In comparison to the Reception Conditions Directive, the Human Rights Court is rather reticent and casuistic in its interpretation of the guarantees offered by Article 5 ECHR to immigrants. The Grand Chamber of the ECtHR saw, in the *Saadi v. UK* judgment,[1242] no need for a full assessment of all relevant circumstances in order to determine whether detention of aliens under Article 5(1)(f) ECHR is necessary and proportionate.[1243] However, if children are involved, a full necessity test of detention is required by the Human Rights Court. In the judgment on *Mayeka and Mitunga v. Belgium* the Court found that detention of a five-year old girl violated Article 8 ECHR.[1244] And in the judgments on *Rahimi*,[1245] and *Popov*,[1246] the Court again required a last resort test for detention of children. Thus, the ECtHR is more restrained in protecting the right to personal liberty of migrants

---

[1242] ECtHR 29 January 2008, *Saadi v. United Kingdom*, No. 13229/03.
[1243] *Ibid*, paras. 70–71.
[1244] ECtHR 12 October 2006, *Mayeka and Mitunga v. Belgium*, No. 13178/03.
[1245] ECtHR 5 April 2011, *Rahimi v. Greece*, No. 8687/08.
[1246] ECtHr 19 January 2012, *Popov v. France*, No. 39472/07 and 39474/07.

than Article 15(1) Returns Directive, which requires that detention should be the last resort.

The detention of aliens may also be considered under Article 3 ECHR, when conditions of detention are so detrimental as to amount to inhuman or degrading treatment. In the case of *Riad and Indiab v. Belgium*, the Court found that holding two asylum seekers of Palestinian nationality for more than 10 days in detention in the transit zone of Brussels airport, in which there was no external area for walking or taking physical exercise, no arrangement for food and drinks, and no radio or television to ensure contact with the outside world, so as to cause them considerable mental suffering, was in violation of Article 3 ECHR.[1247] Accordingly, it transpires that detention conditions are relevant both under Article 3 and Article 5(1)(f) ECHR. Under Article 3 ECHR, conditions of detention may not amount to inhuman or degrading treatment; while under Article 5(1)(f) ECHR, detention conditions are one factor in determining whether detention should be branded as arbitrary. In the case of *Saadi v. United Kingdom*, the Court considered that to avoid being branded as arbitrary under Article 5(1)(f), the place and conditions of detention should be appropriate, and found it of particular importance that the detention facility for asylum seekers where the applicant had been detained 'was specifically adapted to hold asylum seekers and that various facilities, for recreation, religious observance, medical care and, importantly, legal assistance, were provided'.[1248]

The position of a detainee is precarious as he is dependent on the authorities for almost everything. Therefore, it is important that Article 5(2) ECHR prescribes that everyone who is arrested shall be informed promptly, in a language which he understands, of the reasons for his arrest and of any charge against him. In the *Saadi v. United Kingdom* judgment, the Court found that a delay of 76 hours in providing reasons for detention was not compatible with the requirement of the provision that such reasons should be given 'promptly'.[1249]

It is also of vital importance that the person who is detained has timely contact with a lawyer, who can represent him in the outer world and who can preserve his rights and his legal interests. Article 5 does not provide for a right to legal assistance. Article 6(3)(c) ECHR does, but this provision is not, according to the *Maaouia* judgment,[1250] applicable to situations of expulsion. Analogous to Article 8 ECHR however, the 'quality of law' has come to the fore under Article 5(1) ECHR as an important doctrine limiting the discretionary powers of authorities in ordering and maintaining detention of migrants. In *Amuur v. France*, a family of Somali asylum seekers had been held at the transit zone of Paris-Orly airport for 20 days, without being able to rely on existing French

---

[1247] ECtHR 24 January 2008, *Riad and Idiab v. Belgium*, Nos. 29787/03 and 29810/03.
[1248] ECtHR 29 January 2008, *Saadi v. United Kingdom*, No. 13229/03, paras. 74, 78.
[1249] *Ibid*, para. 84.
[1250] ECtHR 5 October 2000, *Maaouia v. France*, No. 39652/98, para. 40.

legislation regarding detention, because the French legislation did not apply to the holding of aliens in an international zone. The Court held that:

> Where the 'lawfulness' of detention is in issue, including the question whether 'a procedure prescribed by law' has been followed, the Convention refers essentially to national law and lays down the obligation to conform to the substantive and procedural rules of national law, but it requires in addition that any deprivation of liberty should be in keeping with the purpose of Article 5, namely to protect the individual from arbitrariness (...). In order to ascertain whether a deprivation of liberty has complied with the principle of compatibility with domestic law, it therefore falls to the Court to assess not only the legislation in force in the field under consideration, but also the quality of the other legal rules applicable to the persons concerned. Quality in this sense implies that where a national law authorises deprivation of liberty – especially in respect of a foreign asylum seeker – it must be sufficiently accessible and precise, in order to avoid all risk of arbitrariness.[1251]

The Court concluded that because no rules were applicable to the detention of the asylum seekers, regarding, *inter alia*, limits as regards the length of time of detention; legal, humanitarian and social assistance; or procedures and time-limits for access to such assistance, Article 5(1) had been violated.[1252] Similar standards apply to persons who are detained with a view to being expelled or extradited.[1253]

10.8. ENTRY BAN AND SIS-ALERT

There is a close functional relationship between an *entry ban* under the Returns Directive and an *alert on refusal of entry* under the SIS II Regulation. An entry ban cannot have its intended effect of barring entry to the territories of the Member States (Article 3 point 6 Returns Directive) without being accompanied by an alert in the Schengen Information System. An entry ban alone does not result in the person concerned not being allowed to enter other Member States. Article 13 Schengen Borders Code prescribes only in case of an alert that entry must be refused at the external borders. One would thus expect that EU law would provide for a strict coordination of the application of the two connected measures, for instance, ensuring that the termination or suspension of the one would automatically entail the termination or suspension of the other. However, there is no trace of such coordination, nor any indication that the EU legislature has been aware of the problem.

As a consequence of this lacuna, there are no EU rules of good administration concerning the coordinated application of entry bans and SIS alerts. Worse, the

---

[1251] ECtHR 25 June 1996, *Amuur v. France*, No. 19776/92, para. 50.
[1252] *Ibid*, para. 53.
[1253] ECtHR 11 December 2008, *Muminov v. Russia*, No. 42502/06, para. 122.

provisions on good administration and remedies in the two instruments differ and sometimes contradict each other. The Returns Directive provides some guarantees of good administration with regard to entry ban decisions. Entry ban decisions must be issued in writing and give reasons in fact and in law, as well as information on available legal remedies. The information on reasons in fact may be limited where national law allows for the right of information to be restricted, in particular in order to safeguard national security, defence, public security, and the prevention, investigation, detection and prosecution of criminal offences.[1254] The SIS II Regulation, for its part, obliges Member States in Article 42 to inform the third-country national in writing of the alert in accordance with the Data Protection Directive 95/46/EC, enclosing with it a copy of the national decision (the entry ban?) giving rise to the alert. There is no obligation to provide information concerning remedies, let alone that the person concerned is warned that he should lodge a separate appeal against the alert.

Member States must, under the Returns Directive, provide, upon request, a written or oral translation of the main elements of decisions related to return, including information on the available legal remedies in a language the third-country national understands or may reasonably be supposed to understand.[1255]

The remedies against an entry ban and a SIS alert are differently shaped. According to Article 13 Returns Directive, third-country nationals must have an effective remedy to appeal against, or seek review of, decisions related to return before a competent judicial or administrative authority or a competent body composed of members who are impartial and who enjoy safeguards of independence. This authority or body shall have the power to review decisions related to return, including the possibility of temporarily suspending its enforcement, unless temporary suspension is already applicable under national legislation. The third-country national concerned must have the possibility to obtain legal advice, representation, and, where necessary, linguistic assistance.[1256] The SIS II Regulation is partly less elaborate, as it does not specify on procedural guarantees, but partly offers an essentially wider protection. According to Article 43 SIS II Regulation, any person may bring an action before the courts or the authority competent under the law of any Member State to access, correct, delete or obtain information, or to obtain compensation in connection with an alert relating to him. The provision is framed in data

---

[1254] Article 12(1) RD.

[1255] Article 12(2) RD. However, the RD allows for an exception on this translation obligation with regard to persons who have illegally entered the territory of a Member State and who have not subsequently obtained an authorisation or a right to stay in that Member State. In this case decisions related to return shall be given by means of a standard form, as set out under national legislation, which must be accompanied by 'generalised information sheets' in at least five of the languages which are most frequently used or understood by illegal migrants entering the Member State concerned (Article 12(3) RD).

[1256] Article 13(1)–(3) RD.

protection terms and does not explicitly state that the proportionality of the measure may be challenged.

In contrast to the Returns Directive, the SIS II Regulation establishes an inter-state judicial competence, which is, however, drafted in rather summary wording. The action may be brought in 'any Member State'. According to Article 43(2), the Member States undertake mutually to enforce final decisions handed down by courts or authorities of 'any Member State'. Article 48 SIS II states that each Member State shall be liable for any damage caused to a person through the use of the Information System. This shall also apply to damage caused by the Member State that issued the alert, where the latter entered factually inaccurate data or stored data unlawfully. If the Member State against which an action is brought is not he Member State issuing the alert, the latter shall be required to reimburse, on request, the sums paid out as compensation, unless the use of the data by the Member State requesting reimbursement infringes the SIS II regulation.

Thus, a person with regard to whom an entry bans and an alert are issued, must launch two appeals, one being confined to the courts of the Member State issuing the entry ban and the other being possible in 'any Member State'. It goes without saying that normal people will not be aware of these complications. Only with the help of a specialised lawyer may one be able to make use of the available remedies. Under the Returns Directive, Member States are obliged to ensure that necessary legal assistance and/or representation is granted, if so requested, free of charge, in accordance with relevant national legislation or rules regarding legal aid.

The Court of Justice has not yet adjudicated on these matters. Under the ECHR, issues of entry bans or exclusion have been dealt with in relation to Article 8. In section 10.4.3, the disappointing *Dalea* decision of the ECtHR was already discussed. From the Court's case law on Article 8 ECHR, it has become clear that an exclusion order must be proportionate in the light of all interests involved. We refer to section 5.9. for a general overview. Although in that chapter the discussion was primarily about the justification of expulsion measures, in balancing the relevant interests the Court also took into consideration the duration of the exclusion order and what the effects of an exclusion order would be on a person's private or family life. In some cases the Court found an exclusion order permissible only if its duration was limited in time.[1257]

[1257] For cases in which the unlimited duration of an exclusion order was considered as a factor supporting the conclusion that it was disproportionate, see ECtHR 13 February 2001, *Ezzouhdi v. France*, No. 47160/99, para. 35; ECtHR 17 April 2003, *Yilmaz v. Germany*, No. 52853/99, paras. 48–49; and ECtHR 22 April 2004, *Radovanovic v. Austria*, No. 42703/98, para. 37. For cases in which the limited duration of an exclusion order was considered as a factor in favour of its proportionality, see ECtHR 10 July 2003, *Benhebba v. France*, No. 53441/99, para. 37; ECtHR 13 January 2000, *Jankov v. Germany* (adm. dec.), No. 35112/97; and ECtHR 18 October 2006, *Üner v. The Netherlands*, No. 46410/99, para. 65. In ECtHR

10.9. FINAL REMARKS

The impact of Articles 41 and 47 of the Charter on EU migration procedures has yet to evolve, but the Court of Justice has already made clear that both provisions are fully applicable and that they must be interpreted in line with the general principles of the Union's law identified by the Court in its earlier jurisprudence. In this manner, a consistent and all-encompassing system of good administration and effective judicial protection can be shaped for everybody within the scope of application of Union law.

In contrast, the European Court of Human Rights has shown reluctance to secure for immigrants the same level of procedural protection as is offered to the nationals of a Member State. Apparently, the entry, stay and expulsion of aliens are conceived as matters so central to a state's sovereignty that states must also be granted substantial – but not unfettered – discretionary power in enforcing their immigration legislation. The most appropriate provision guaranteeing fair and impartial judicial supervision, Article 6 ECHR, has been interpreted as not being applicable to cases of entry, stay and deportation of aliens. Likewise, while detention is normally considered arbitrary if it is not necessary or proportionate to the aim pursued, for example, because other less severe measures can suffice to achieve the stated aim, this principle does not apply to aliens' detention in general. On the other hand, the ECtHR has also extended the scope of procedural standards implied in provisions that do not explicitly deal with such protection, like Articles 3 and 8 ECHR.

Thus, the standards of the Charter tend to be higher than those of the ECHR, which was the basis of the Charter. Possibly, the ECtHR will be encouraged by the attitude of the Court of Justice to overcome its hesitation in securing an appropriate and consistent level of procedural protection to non-nationals.

FURTHER READING

A.M. Reneman, *EU Asylum Procedures and the Right to an Effective Remedy*, Oxford, Hart Publishing.

Dana Baldinger: *Rigorous Scrutiny versus Marginal Review. Standards on judicial scrutiny and evidence in international and European asylum law*, Wolf Legal Publishers (2013).

Christoph-David Munding, *Das Grundrecht auf effektiven Rechtsschutz im Rechtssystem der Europäischen Union*, Berlin, Duncker & Humblot, (2010).

---

31 July 2008, *Omoregie a.o. v. Norway*, No. 265/07, para. 67, the Court found it of relevance that the entry ban for five years allowed for the possibility of an application for re-entry after two years.

A.M. Reneman, 'Access to an Effective Remedy before a Court or Tribunal in Asylum Cases', in E. Guild and Paul Minderhoud (eds.), The First Decade of EU Migration and Asylum Law, Leiden/Boston: Martinus Nijhoff Publishers 2011, 401–436.

A.M. Reneman, 'An EU Right to Interim Protection during Appeal Proceedings in Asylum Cases?', EJML 2010, 407–434.

LIST OF CASES

INTERNATIONAL CASE LAW

(FORMER) PERMANENT COURT OF INTERNATIONAL JUSTICE

PCIJ, *Jurisdiction of the Courts of Danzig (Pecuniary Claims of Danzig Railway Officials who have Passed into the Polish Service, against the Polish Railways Administration)* (Advisory Opinion), 3 March 1928, Series B – No. 15, pp. 17–18.

INTERNATIONAL COURT OF JUSTICE

ICJ, *Colombian-Peruvian asylum case, Judgment*, 20 November 1950, ICJ Reports 1950, p. 266 at p. 274.

ICJ, *Nottebohm Case (Liechtenstein v. Guatemala)* (judgment), 6 April 1955, ICJ Reports 1955, p. 23.

ICJ, *Reparation for Injuries Suffered in the Service of the United Nations* (Advisory Opinion), 11 April 1949, ICJ Reports 1949, p. 178.

ICJ, *Territorial Dispute (Libyun Aruh Jamuhiriyu v. Chad)* (judgment), 3 February 1994, ICJ Reports 1994, p. 23, §45.

EUROPEAN COURT OF HUMAN RIGHTS

ECtHR, *A. v. The United Kingdom*, 23 September 1998, No. 25599/94.

ECtHR, *A.A. v. UK*, 20 September 2011, No. 8000/08.

ECtHR, *A.B. v. Sweden*, 31 August 2004, No. 24697/04.

ECtHR, *Abdelhedi v. Italy*, 24 March 2009, No. 2638/07.

ECtHR, *Abdolkhani and Karimnia v. Turkey*, 22 September 2009, No. 30471/08.

ECtHR, *Abdulaziz, Cabales and Balkandali v. United Kingdom*, 28 May 1985, Nos. 9214/80, 9473/81, 9474/81.

ECtHR, *Adam v. Germany* (Dec.), 4 October 2001, No. 43359/98.

ECtHR, *Ahmut v. The Netherlands*, 28 November 1996, No. 21702/93.

ECtHR, *Akkoc v. Turkey*, 10 October 200, Nos. 22947/93 and 22948/93.

ECtHR, *Aksoy v. Turkey*, 18 December 1996, No. 21987/93.

ECtHR, *Al Hanchi v. Bosnia*, 15 November 2011, No. 48205/09.

ECtHR, *Al-Jedda v. UK*, 7 July 2011, No. 27021/08.

ECtHR, *Al-Moayad v. Germany*, 20 February 2007, No. 35865/03.

ECtHR, *Al Nashif v. Bulgaria*, 21 June 2002, No. 50964/99.

ECtHR, *Al-Saadoon and Mufdhi v. UK*, 2 March 2010, No. 61498/08.

ECtHR, *Al-Skeini v. UK*, 7 July 2011, No. 55721/07.

ECtHR, *Ammari v. Sweden*, 22 October 2002, No. 60959/00.

ECtHR, *Amrollahi v. Denmark*, 11 July 2002, No. 56811/00.

ECtHR, *Amuur v. France*, 25 June 1996, No. 19776/92.

ECtHR, *Anam v. the United Kingdom*, 7 June 2011, No. 21783/08.

ECtHR, *Andrejeva v. Latvia*, 18 February 2009, No. 55707/00.

ECtHR, *Andrey Sheabashov v. Latvia*, 22 May 1999 (Dec.), No. 50065/99.

ECtHR, *Andric v. Sweden*, 23 February 1999, No. 45917/99.

ECtHR, *Antwi v. Norway*, 14 February 2012, No. 26940/10.

ECtHR, *Avetissov v. Sweden*, 5 March 2002, No. 71427/01.

ECtHR, *B. v. Sweden*, 26 October 2004, Appl. No. 16578/03.

ECtHR, *Babar Ahmad a.o. v. The United Kingdom*, 6 July 2010, Nos. 24027/07, 11949/08 and 36742/08.

ECtHR, *Bader and Kanbor v. Sweden*, 8 November 2005, No. 13284/04.

ECtHR, *Baghli v. France*, 30 November 1999, No. 34374/97.

ECtHR, *Bah v. the UK*, 27 September 2011, No. 56328/07.

ECtHR, *Bahaddar v. The Netherlands*, 19 February 1998, No. 25894/94.

ECtHR, *Beldjoudi v. France*, 26 March 1992, No. 12083.

ECtHR, *Bello v. Sweden*, 17 January 2006, No. 32213/04.

ECtHR, *Benhebba v. France*, 10 July 2003, No. 53441/99.

ECtHR, *Ben Khemais v. Italy*, 24 February 2009, No. 246/07.

ECtHR, *Ben Salah v. Italy*, 24 March 2009, No. 38128/06.

ECtHR, *Berisha and Haljiti v. Macedonia*, 16 June 2005, No. 8670/03.

ECtHR, *Berrehab v. The Netherlands*, 21 June 1988, No. 10730/84.

ECtHR, *Biao v. Denmark*, 25 March 2014, No. 38590/10.

ECtHR, *Bonger v. The Netherlands*, 15 September 2005, No. 10154/04.

ECtHR, *Bouchelkia v. France*, 29 January 1997, No. 23078/93.

ECtHR, *Boughanemi v. France*, 24 April 1996, No. 22070/93.

ECtHR, *Boujlifa v. France*, 21 October 1997, No. 25404/94.

ECtHR, *Boultif v. Switzerland*, 2 August 2001, No. 54273/00.

ECtHR, Bousarra v. France, 23 September 2010, No. 25672/07.

ECtHR, *Bouyahia v. Italy*, 24 March 2009, No. 46792/06.

ECtHR, *C. v. Belgium*, 7 August 1996, No. 21794/93.

ECtHR, *C.B.Z. v. Italy*, 24 March 2009, No. 44006/06.

ECtHR, *C.G. and others v. Bulgaria*, 24 April 2008, No. 1365/07.

ECtHR, *Chair and J.B. v. Germany*, 6 December 2007, No. 69735/01.

ECtHR, *Chahal v. the United Kingdom*, 15 November 1996, No. 22414/93.

ECtHR, *Chandra v. The Netherlands*, 13 May 2003, No. 53102/99.

ECtHR, *Ciliz v. The Netherlands*, 11 July 2000, No. 29192/95.

ECtHR, *Collins and Akaziebie v. Sweden*, 8 March 2007, No. 23944/05.

ECtHR, *Čonka v Belgium*, 5 February 2002, No. 51564/99.

ECtHR, *Corsacov v. Moldova*, 4 April 2006, No. 18944/02.

ECtHR, *Cossey*, 27 September 1990, No. 10843/84.

ECtHR, *Cruz Varas and others v. Sweden*, 20 March 1991, No. 15576/89.

ECtHR, *D. v. The United Kingdom (St. Kitts)*, 2 May 1997, No. 30240/96.

ECtHR, *Dalea*, 21 December 2006, (Dec.) No. 964/07.

ECtHR, *Dalia v. France*, 19 February 1998, No. 26102/95.

ECtHR, *Darraji v. Italy*, 24 March 2009, No. 11549/05.

ECtHR, *D. H. and others v. the Czech Republic*, 13 November 2007, No. 57325/00.

ECtHR, *Drozd and Janousek v. France and Spain*, 26 June 1992, No. 12747/87.

ECtHR, *Dudgeon*, 22 October 1981, No. 7525/76.

ECtHR, *Ebrahim v. The Netherlands*, 18 March 2003, No. 59186/00.

ECtHR, *Einhorn v. France*, 16 October 2001, No. 71555/01.

ECtHR, *El Boujaïdi v. France*, 26 September 1997, No. 25613/94.

ECtHR, *El-Masri v. the Former Yugoslav Republic of Macedonia*, 13 December 2012, No. 39630/09.

ECtHR, *Ezzouhdi v. France*, 13 February 2001, No. 47160/99.

ECtHR, *F. v. The United Kingdom*, 22 June 2004, No. 17341/03.

ECtHR, *F.H. v. Sweden*, 20 January 2009, No. 32621/06.

ECtHR, *F.N. v. Sweden*, 18 December 2012, No. 28774/09.

ECtHR, *Gäfgen v. Germany*, 1 June 2010, No. 22978/05.

ECtHR, *Gaygusuz v. Austria*, 16 September 1996, No. 17371/90.

ECtHR, *Gebremedhin [Gaberamadhien] v. France*, 26 April 2007, No. 25389/05.

ECtHR, *Gomes v. Sweden*, 7 February 2006, Appl. No. 34566/04.

ECtHR, *G.R. v. The Netherlands*, 10 January 2012, No. 22251/07.

ECtHR, *Gül v. Switzerland*, 19 February 1996, No. 23218/94.

ECtHR, *H. and B. v. The United Kingdom*, Nos. 70073/10 and 44539/11).

ECtHR, *Hamraoui v. Italy*, 24 March 2009, No. 16201/07.

ECtHR, *Haydarie a.o. v. The Netherlands*, 20 October 2005, No. 8876/04.

ECtHR, *Hendrin Ali Said and Aras Ali Said v. Hungary*, 23 October 2012, No. 13457/11.

ECtHR, *Hilal v. the United Kingdom*, 6 March 2001, No. 45276/99.

ECtHR, *Hirsi v. Italy*, 23 February 2012, No. 27765/09.

ECtHR, *Hirsi Jamaa a.o. v. Italy,* 23 February 2012, No. 27765/09.

ECtHR, *H.L.R. v. France*, 29 April 1997, No. 24573/94.

ECtHR, *H.N. v. Sweden*, 15 May 2012, No. 30720/09.

ECtHR, *Hode & Abdi v. United Kingdom*, 6 November 2012, No. 22341/09.

ECtHR, *I. v. Sweden*, 5 September 2013, No. 61204/09.

ECtHR, *I.I.N. v. The Netherlands*, 9 December 2004, No. 2035/04.

ECtHR, *İletmiş v. Turkey*, 6 December 2005, No. 29871/96.

ECtHR, *I.K. v. Austria*, 28 March 2003, No. 2964/12.

ECtHR, *I.M. v. The Netherlands*, 25 March 2003, No. 41226/98.

ECtHR, *I.M. v. France*, 2 February 2012, No. 9152/09.

ECtHR, *Ireland v. The United Kingdom*, 18 January 1978, No. 5310/71.

ECtHR, *Jabari v. Turkey*, 11 July 2000, No. 40035/98.

ECtHR, *Jankov v. Germany* (Dec.), 13 January 2000, No. 35112/97.

ECtHR, *Javanmardi and Ahmadi v. Sweden*, 19 March 2002, No. 65538/01.

ECtHR, *Javeed*, 3 July 2001 (Dec), No. 47390/99.

ECtHR, *Jerry Olajide Sarumi v. UK*, 26 January 1999 (Dec.), No. 43279/98.

ECtHR, *J.H. v. the United Kingdom*, 20 December 2011, No. 48839/09.

ECtHR, *Juric v. Sweden*, 23 February 1999, No. 45924/99.

ECtHR, *K.A.B. v. Sweden,* 5 September 2013, No. 886/11.

ECtHR, *Kaya v. Germany*, 28 June 2007, No. 31753/02.

ECtHR, *Keegan v. Ireland*, 26 May 1994, No. 16969/90.

ECtHR, *Khodzhayev v Russia*, 12 May 2010, No. 52466/08).

ECtHR, *Kilic v. Denmark* (Dec.), 22 January 2007, No. 20277/05.

ECtHR, *Kiyutin v. Russia*, 10 March 2011, No. 2700/10.

ECtHR, *Konstantinov v. The Netherlands*, 25 April 2007, No. 16351/03.

ECtHR, *Koua Poirrez v. France*, 30 September 2003, No. 40892/98.

ECtHR, *Kroon v. The Netherlands*, 27 October 1994, No. 18535/91.

ECtHR, *K.R.S. v. the United Kingdom* (Dec.), 2 December 2008, No. 32733/08.

ECtHR, *Kwakye-Nti and Dufi e v. the Netherlands*, 7 November 2000, No. 31519/96.

ECtHR, *Labita v. Italy*, 6 April 2000, No. 26772/95.

ECtHR, *Liu and Liu v. Russia*, 6 December 2007, No. 42086/05.

ECtHR, *Lokpo and Touré v. Hungary*, 20 September 2011, No. 10816/10.

ECtHR, *Lupsa v. Romania*, 8 June 2006, No. 10337/04.

ECtHR, *Maaouia v. France*, 5 October 2000, No. 39652/98.

ECtHR, *Mamatkulov and Askarov v. Turkey*, 6 February 2003, Nos. 46827/99 and 46951/99.

ECtHR, *Mamatkulov v. Turkey*, 4 February 2005, Nos. 46827/99 and 46951/99.

ECtHR, *Marckx*, 13 June 1979, No. 6833/74.

ECtHR, *Maslov v. Austria* (Chamber), 22 March 2007, No. 1638/03.

ECtHR, *Maslov v. Austria* (Grand Chamber), 23 June 2008, No. 1638/03.

ECtHR, *Mayeka and Mitunga v. Belgium*, 12 October 2006, No. 13178/03.

ECtHR, *Mehemi v. France*, 13 July 1995, No. 19465/92.

ECtHR, *Mehemi v. France*, 26 September 1997, No. 25017/94.

ECtHR, *Mehemi v. France*, 10 April 2003, No. 53470/99.

ECtHR, *Modinos*, 22 April 1993, No. 15070/89.

ECtHR, *Mohammed Hussein and Others v. the Netherlands and Italy* (Dec.), 2 April 2013, No. 27725/10.

ECtHR, *Mohammed v. Austria*, 6 June 2013, No. 2283/12.

ECtHR, *Mokrani v. France*, 15 July 2003, No. 52206/99.

ECtHR, *Moustaquim v. Belgium*, 18 February 1991, No. 12313/86.

ECtHR, *M.S.S. v. Belgium and Greece*, 21 Jan. 2011, No. 30696/09.

ECtHR, *Muminov v. Russia*, 11 December 2008, No. 42502/06.

ECtHR, *Müslim v. Turkey*, 26 April 2005, No. 53566/99.

ECtHR, *M.Y.H. a.o. v. Sweden*, 27 June 2013, No. 50859/10.

ECtHR, *N. v. Finland*, 26 July 2005, No. 28885/02.

ECtHR, *N. v. Sweden*, 20 July 2010, No. 23505/09.

ECtHR, *NA. v. The United Kingdom*, 17 July 2008, No. 25904/07.

ECtHR, *Nagula v. Estonia* (Dec.), 25 October 2005, No. 39203/02.

ECtHR, *Nasimi v. Sweden*, 16 March 2004, No. 38865/02.

ECtHR, *Nasri v. France*, 13 July 1995, No. 19465/92.

ECtHR, *Nduwayezu v. Sweden*, 8 December 2009.

ECtHR, *Niedzwiecki v. Germany*, 25 October 2005, No. 58453/00.

ECtHR, *Nivette v. France* (Dec.), 3 July 2001, No. 44190/98.

ECtHR, *Norris*, 26 October 1988, No. 10581/83.

ECtHR, *Nunez v. Norway*, 28 June 2011, No. 55597/09.

ECtHR, *O. v. Italy*, 24 March 2009, No. 37257/06.

ECtHR, *Olsson v. Sweden* (No. 2), 27 November 1992, No. 13441/87.

ECtHR, *Omojudi v. UK*, 24 November 2009, No. 1820/08.

ECtHR, *Omoregie a.o. v. Norway,* 31 July 2008, No. 265/07.

ECtHR, *Onur v. United Kingdom,* 17 February 2009, No. 27319/07.

ECtHR, *Othman (Abu Qatada) v. The United Kingdom,* 17 January 2012, No. 8139/09.

ECtHR, *Ould Barar v. Sweden,* 19 January 1999, No. 42367/98.

ECtHR, *Popov v. France,* 19 January 2012, No. 39472/07 and 39474/07.

ECtHR, *Price v. The United Kingdom,* 10 July 2001, No. 33394/96.

ECtHR, *Radovanovic v. Austria,* 22 April 2004, No. 42703/98.

ECtHR, *Rahimi v. Greece,* 5 April 2011, No. 8687/08.

ECtHR, *Razaghi v. Sweden,* 11 March 2003, No. 64599/01.

ECtHR, *R.C. v. Sweden,* 9 March 2010, No. 41827/07.

ECtHR, *Rees,* 17 October 1986, No. 9532/81.

ECtHR, *Riad and Idiab v. Belgium,* 24 January 2008, Nos. 29787/03 and 29810/03.

ECtHR, *R.J. v. Sweden,* 19 September 2013, No. 10466/11.

ECtHR, *Rodrigues da Silva and Hoogkamer v. The Netherlands,* 31 January 2006, No. 50435/99.

ECtHR, *Rustamov v Russia,* 3 July 2012, No. 11209/10.

ECtHR, *Ryabikin v. Russia,* 19 June 2008, No. 8320/04.

ECtHR, *S.A. v. Sweden,* 27 June 2013, No. 66523/10.

ECtHR, *Saadi v. Italy,* 28 February 2008, No. 37201/06.

ECtHR, *Saadi v. United Kingdom,* 29 January 2008, No. 13229/03.

ECtHR, *Said v. The Netherlands,* 5 July 2005, No. 2345/02.

ECtHR, *Salah Sheekh v. The Netherlands,* 11 January 2007, No. 1948/04.

ECtHR, *Salkic and Others v. Sweden,* 29 June 2004, No. 7702/04.

ECtHR, *Salman v. Turkey,* 27 June 2000, No. 21986/93.

ECtHR, *Samsonnikov v. Estonia,* 3 July 2012, No. 521788/10.

ECtHR, *Schalk and Kopf v. Austria,* 24 June 2010, No. 30141/04.

ECtHR, *Schober v. Austria,* 9 November 1999, No. 34891/97.

ECtHR, *Şen v. The Netherlands,* 21 December 2001, No. 31465/96.

ECtHR, *S.F. v. Sweden,* 15 May 2012, No. 52077/10.

ECtHR, *Shamayev and Others v. Georgia and Russia,* 12 April 2005, No. 36378/02.

ECtHR, *S.H.H. v. The United Kingdom,* 29 January 2013, No. 60367/10.

ECtHR, *Sidikovy v Russia,* 20 June 2013, No. 73455/11.

ECtHR, *Sinnarajah v. Switzerland,* 11 May 1999, No. 45187/99.

ECtHR, *Slivenko a.o. v. Latvia* (Grand Chamber), 9 October 2003, No. 48321/99.

ECtHR, *S.M. v. Sweden,* 10 February 2009, No. 47683/08.

ECtHR, *Soering v. The United Kingdom,* 7 July 1989, No. 14038/88.

ECtHR, *Soldatenko v. Ukraine,* 23 October 2008, No. 2440/07.

ECtHR, *Soltana v. Italy,* 24 March 2009, No. 37336/06.

ECtHR, *S.R. v. Sweden,* 23 April 2002, No. 62806/00.

ECtHR, *Streletz, Kessler and Krenz v. Germany,* 22 March 2001, Nos. 34044/96, 35532/97 and 44801/98.

ECtHR, *Sufi and Elmi v. The United Kingdom,* 28 June 2011, Nos. 8319/07 and 11449/07.

ECtHR, *Sultani v. France,* 20 September 2007, No. 45223/05.

ECtHR, *Suso Musa v Malta,* 23 July 2013, No. 42337/12.

ECtHR, *Tekdemir v. The Netherlands,* 1 October 2002, No. 49823/99.

ECtHR, *T.I. v. United Kingdom* (Dec.), 7 March 2000, No. 43844/98.

ECtHR, *Tomic v. The United Kingdom,* 14 October 2003, No. 17837/03.

ECtHR, *Tuquabo-Tekle a.o. v. The Netherlands*, 1 December 2005, No. 60665/00.
ECtHR, *Udeh v. Switzerland*, 16 April 2013, No. 12020/09.
ECtHR, *Üner v. The Netherlands*, 18 October 2006, No. 46410/99 (Grand Chamber).
ECtHR, *Vilvarajah and Others v. The United Kingdom*, 30 October 1991, Nos. 13163 to
    -65/87 and 13447 to -8/87.
ECtHR, *Yakubov v Russia*, 8 November 2011, No. 7265/10.
ECtHR, *Yaman v. Turkey*, 2 November 2004, No. 32446/96.
ECtHR, *Yildiz v. Austria*, 31 October 2002, No. 37295/97.
ECtHR, *Yilmaz v. Germany*, 17 April 2003, No. 52853/99.
ECtHR, *Z. and T. v. UK*, 28 February 2006 (Dec), No. 27034/05.
ECtHR, *Zokhidov v Russia*, 5 February 2013, No. 67286/10.
ECtHR, *Zubeyde v. Norway*, 28 February 2002, No. 51600/99.

(FORMER) EUROPEAN COMMISSION OF HUMAN RIGHTS

EComHR, *C.B. v. Germany*, 11 January 1994, No. 22012/93.
EComHR, *I.B. v. Federal Republic of Germany*, 24 May 1974, No. 6242/73,.
EComHR, *Maikoe and Baboelal v. The Netherlands*, 30 November 1994, No. 22791/93.
EComHR, *X. v Belgium*, 29 May 1961, No. 984/61.
EComHR, *X v Federal Republic of Germany*, 26 March 1963, No. 1802/62.
EComHR, *X v. Federal Republic of Germany*, 19 July 1968, No. 3110/67.

EUROPEAN COURT OF JUSTICE

ECJ, *Abatay and Sahin*, 21 October 2003, Joint Cases C-317/01 and C-369/01.
ECJ, *Abdulla*, 2 March 2010, Cases C-175/08, C-176/08, C-178/08 and C-179/08.
ECJ, *Achughbabian*, 6 December 2011, Case C-329/11.
ECJ, *Adil*, 19 July 2012, Case C-278/12 PPU.
ECJ, *Åkerberg Fransson*, 26 February 2013 (Grand chamber), Case C-617/10.
ECJ, *Akman*, 19 November 1998, Case C-210/97.
ECJ, *Akrich*, 23 September 2003, Case C-60/00.
ECJ, *Aladzhov*, 17 November 2011, Case C-434/10.
ECJ, *Alarape and Tijani*, 8 May 2013, Case C-529/11.
ECJ, *Altun,* 18 December 2008, Case C-337/07.
ECJ, *Anafé*, 14 June 2012, Case C-606/10.
ECJ, *Antonissen*, 26 February 1991, Case C-292/89.
ECJ, *Arslan*, 30 May 2013, Case C-534/11.
ECJ, *Asparuhov Estov*, 12 November 2010.
ECJ, *Ayallti v. Germany*, C-513/12.
ECJ, *Aydinli*, 7 July 2005, Case C-373/03.
ECJ, *B and D*, 9 November 2010, Cases C-57/09 and C-101/09.
ECJ, *Barkoci and Malik*, 27 September 2001, Case C-257/99.
ECJ, *Baumbast and R.*, 17 September 2002, Case C-413/99.
ECJ, *Bekleyen*, 21 January 2010, C-462/08.

ECJ, *Bibi Mohammed Imran v. the Netherlands*, 10 June 2011, Case-155/11 PPU.

ECJ, *Bidar*, 15 March 2005, Case C-209/03.

ECJ, *Birden*, 26 November 1998, C-1/97.

ECJ, *Bolbol*, 17 June 2010, Case C-31/09.

ECJ, *Bond van Adverteerders*, 26 April 1988, Case 352/85.

ECJ, *Bonsignore*, 26 February 1975, Case 67/74.

ECJ, *Bozkurt*, 6 June 1995, Case C-434/93.

ECJ, *Brey*, 19 September 2013, Case C-140/12.

ECJ, *Broede*, 12 December 1996, Case C-3/95.

ECJ, *Boucherau*, 27 October 1977, Case 30/77.

ECJ, *Calfa*, 19 January 1999, Case C-348/96.

ECJ, *Carpenter*, 11 July 2002, Case C-60/00.

ECJ, *Cetinkaya*, 11 November 2004, Case C-467/02.

ECJ, *Chakroun*, 4 March 2010, Case C-578/08.

ECJ, *Chartry*, 1 March 2011, Case C-457/09.

ECJ, *Chen*, 19 October 2004, Case C-200/02.

ECJ, *Cimade and GISTI*, 27 September 2012, Case C-179/11.

ECJ, *Collins*, 23 March 2004, Case C-138/02.

ECJ, *Commission v. Belgium*, 26 May 1982, Case 149/79.

ECJ, *Commission v. France*, 26 February 1991, Case C-154/89.

ECJ, *Commission v. Spain*, 21 January 2006, Case C-503/03.

ECJ, *Commission v. the Netherlands*, 26 April 2012, Case C-508/10.

ECJ, *Commission v. the Netherlands*, 29 April 2010, Case C-92/07.

ECJ, *Commission v. Austria*, 4 October 2012, Case C-75/11.

ECJ, *Costa Enel*, 15 July 1964, Case 6/64, ECR 1964, 585.

ECJ, *Cowan*, 2 February 1989, Case 186/87.

ECJ, *Demir*, 7 November 2013, Case C-225/12.

ECJ, *Demirel*, 30 September 1987, Case 12/86.

ECJ, *Demirkan*, 24 September 2013, Case C-221/11.

ECJ, *Dereci and others,* 15 November 2011, Case C-265/11.

ECJ, *Derin*, 18 July 2007, Case C-325/05.

ECJ, *Doğan*, 7 July 2005, Case C-383/03.

ECJ, *Dogan,* 10 July 2014, Case C-138/13.

ECJ, *Dörr and Ünal*, 2 June 2005, Case C-126/03.

ECJ, *Dülger*, 19 July 2012, Case C-451/11.

ECJ, *Eind*, 11 December 2007, Case C-291/05.

ECJ, *Elgafaji*, 17 February 2009, Case C-465/07.

ECJ, *Ergat*, 16 March 2000, Case C-329/97.

ECJ, *Eroğlu*, 5 October 1994, Case C-355/93.

ECJ, *Ertanir*, 30 September 1997, Case C-98/96.

ECJ, *Fahmi*, 20 March 201, Case C-33/99.

ECJ, *Förster*, 18 November 2008, Case C-158/07.

ECJ, *Garcia Avello*, 2 October 2003, Case C-148/02.

ECJ, *Gaydarov*, 17 November 2011, Case C-430/10.

ECJ, *Gebhard*, 30 November 1995, Case C-55/94.

ECJ, *Genc*, 4 February 2010, Case C-14/09.

ECJ, *Grzelczyk*, 20 September 2001, Case C-184/99.

ECJ, *Gülbahce*, 8 November 2012, Case C-268/11.

ECJ, *Günaydin*, 30 September 1997, Case C-36/96.

ECJ, *Güzeli*, 26 October 2006, Case C-4/05.

ECJ, *Halaf*, 30 May 2013, Case C-528/11.

ECJ, *Hassen El Dridi*, 28 April 2011, Case C-61/11 PPU.

ECJ, *H.I.D.*, 6 May 2008, Case C-175/11.

ECJ, *H.I.D. and B.A.*, 13 April 2012, Case C-175/11.

ECJ, *Iida v. Germany*, 8 November 2012, C-40/11.

ECJ, *Jia*, 9 January 2007, Case C-1/05.

ECJ, *Jipa*, 10 July 2008, Case C-33/07.

ECJ, *Josemans*, 16 December 2010, C-137/09.

ECJ, *K. v Bundesasylamt*, 6 November 2012, Case C-245/11.

ECJ, *Kadiman*, 17 April 1997, Case C-135/95.

ECJ, *Kadzoev*, 30 November 2009, Case C-357/09.

ECJ, *Kamberaj*, 24 April 2012, Case C-571/10.

ECJ, *Kastrati*, 3 May 2012, C-620/10.

ECJ, *Kaur*, 20 February 2001, Case C-192/99.

ECJ, *Kahveci and Inan,* 29 March 2012, Cases C-7/10 and C-9/10.

ECJ, *Kempf,* 3 June 1986, Case 139/85.

ECJ, *Kol*, 5 July 1997, Case C-285/95.

ECJ, *Koushkaki*, 19 December 2013, Case C-84/12.

ECJ, *Kurz*, 19 November 2002, Case C-188/00.

ECJ, *Kuş*, 16 December 1992, Case C-237/91.

ECJ, *Kziber,* 31 January 1991, Case C-18/90.

ECJ, *Lawrie-Blum*, 3 July 1986, Case 66/85.

ECJ, *Levin*, 23 March 1982, Case C-53/81.

ECJ, *Luisi and Carbone*, 31 January 1984, Joined Cases 286/82 and 26/83.

ECJ, *MA and Others*, 6 June 2013, Case C-648/11.

ECJ, *Mangat Singh*, 15 May 2012, Case C-502/10.

ECJ, *Martínez Sala*, 12 May 1998, Case C-85/96.

ECJ, *Melki and Abdeli*, 22 June 2010, Cases C-188/10 and C-189/10.

ECJ, *Mesbah*, 11 November 1999, Case C-179/98.

ECJ, *Metin Bozkurt*, 22 December 2012, Case C-303/08.

ECJ, *Metock*, 25 July 2008, Case 127/08.

ECJ, *Micheletti and Others*, 7 July 1992, Case C-369/90.

ECJ, *Min Khoa Vo*, 10 April 2012, C-83/12 PPU.

ECJ, *M.G.*, 16 January 2014, Case 400/12.

ECJ, *M. M. v Minister for Justice, Equality and Law Reform, Ireland and Attorney General*, 22 November 2012, Case C-277/11.

ECJ, *Morson and Jhanjan*, 27 October 1982, Cases 35/82 and 36/82.

ECJ, *MRAX*, 25 July 2002, Case C-459/99.

ECJ, *Nazli*, 10 February 2000, Case C-340/97.

ECJ, *Nicolae Bot*, 3 October 2006, Case C-241/05.

ECJ, *N.S. and M.E.*, 21 December 2011, Joined Cases C-411/10 and C-493/10.

ECJ, *O. and B.*, 12 March 2014, Case C-456/12.

ECJ, *O, S and L,* 6 December 2012, Case C-356/22.

ECJ, *Onuekwere,* 16 January 2014, Case C-378/12.

ECJ, *Otis,* 6 November 2012, Case C-199/11.

ECJ, *Oulane,* 17 February 2005, Case C-215/03.

ECJ, *Panayotova,* 16 November 2004, Case C-327/02.

ECJ, *Parliament v. Council,* 7 July 1992, Case C-295/90.

ECJ, *Parliament v. Council,* 27 June 2006, Case C-540/03.

ECJ, *Parliament v. Council,* 6 May 2008, C-133/06.

ECJ, *Pehlivan,* 16 June 2011, Case C-484/10.

ECJ, *Petrosian,* 29 January 2009, Case C-19/08.

ECJ, *P.I.,* 22 May 2012, Case C-348/09.

ECJ, *Pieck,* 3 July 1980, Case C-157/79.

ECJ, *Rahman,* 5 September 2012, Case- C-83/11.

ECJ, *Raulin,* 26 February 1992, Case C-357/89.

ECJ, *Reed,* 17 April 1986, Case 59/85.

ECJ, *Reyes,* 16 January 2014, Case C-423/12.

ECJ, *Reyners,* 21 June 1974, Case 2/74.

ECJ, *Rottmann,* 2 March 2010, Case C-135/08.

ECJ, *Royer,* 8 April 1976, Case 48/75.

ECJ, *Ruiz Zambrano,* 8 March 2011, Case C-34/09.

ECJ, *S. and G.,* 12 March 2014, Case C-457/12.

ECJ, *Saciri,* 27 February 2014, Case C-79/13.

ECJ, *Sagor,* 6 December 2012, Case C-430/11.

ECJ, *Sagulo and others,* 14 July 1977, Case 8/77.

ECJ, *Sahin,* 17 September 2009, Case C-242/06.

ECJ, *Salahadin,* 2 March 2010, Cases C-175/08, C-176/08, C-178/08 and C-179/08.

ECJ, *Samba Diouf,* 28 July 2011, Case C-69/10.

ECJ, *Savas,* 11 September 2000, Case C-37/98.

ECJ, *Sedef,* 10 January 2006, Case C-230/03.

ECJ, *Sevince,* 20 September 1990, Case C-192/89.

ECJ, *Sotgiu,* 12 February 1974, Case 152/73.

ECJ, *Soysal,* 19 February 2009, Case C-228/06.

ECJ, *Surinder Singh,* 7 July 1992, Case C-370/90.

ECJ, *Tetik,* 23 January 1997, Case C-171/95.

ECJ, *Toprak and Oguz,* 9 December 2010, Case C-303/08.

ECJ, *Torun,* 16 February 2006, Case C-502/04.

ECJ, *Trojani,* 7 September 2004, Case C-456/02.

ECJ, *Tsakouridis,* 27 November 2010, Case C-145/09.

ECJ, *Tum and Dari,* 20 September 2007, Case C-16/05.

ECJ, *Tural Oguz,* 21 July 2011, Case C-186/10.

ECJ, *Unal.* 29 September 2011, Case C-187/10.

ECJ, *United Kingdom v. Council,* December 2007, Case C-77/05.

ECJ, *Van Binsbergen,* 3 December 1974, Case 33/74.

ECJ, *Vander Elst,* 9 August 1994, Case C-43/93.

ECJ, *Van Duyn,* 4 December 1974, Case 41/74.

ECJ, *Van Gend & Loos,* 5 February 1963, Case 26/62 ECR 1963, 1.

ECJ, *Vatsouras and Koupatantze*, 4 June 2009, Cases C-22/08 and C-23/08.
ECJ, *X, Y and Z*, 7 November 2013, Cases C-199/12, C-200/12, and C-201/12.
ECJ, *Y and Z*, 5 September 2012, Cases C-71/11 and C-99/11.
ECJ, *Z.Z.*, 4 June 2013, Case C-300/11.
ECJ, *Zhu and Chen*, 19 October 2004, Case C-200/02.
ECJ, *Ziebell*, 18 December 2012, Case C-371/08.

NATIONAL CASE LAW

NETHERLANDS

Afdeling bestuursrechtspraak Raad van State, 19 March 1996, No. R.02.91.2947 *Rechtspraak Vreemdelingenrecht* 1996, 95.

UNITED KINGDOM

House of Lords, *Regina v. Secretary of State for the Home Department*, 3 November 2005, [2005] UKHL 66.

House of Lords, *R (on the application of Quila and another) (FC) (Respondents) v Secretary of State for the Home Department (Appellant)*; and *R (on the application of Bibi and another) (FC) (Respondents) v Secretary of State for the Home Department (Appellant)*, [2011] UKSC 45 (12 October 2011).

UNITED STATES OF AMERICA

U.S. Supreme Court, *Nishimura Ekiu v. United States et al.*, 18 January 1892, 142 U.S. 651, p. 142.

UNITED NATIONS TREATY BODIES DOCUMENTS

HUMAN RIGHTS COMMITTEE, GENERAL COMMENTS

HRC, *General Comment No. 17: Rights of the Child*, 1989.
HRC, *General Comment No. 27*, 2 November 1999, UN Doc. CCPR/C/21/Rev.1/Add.9.
HRC, *General Comment No. 31 (2004)*, CCPR/C/21/Rev.1/Add.13.

HUMAN RIGHTS COMMITTEE, JURISPRUDENCE

HRC, *Vidal Martins v. Uruguay*, Communication No. 57/1979, 23 March 1982.
HRC, *Kindler v Canada*, 30 July 1993, CCPR/C/48/D/470/1991.

INDEX

ABOUT THE AUTHORS

Pieter Boeles is Emeritus Professor of Immigration Law at the University of Leiden and was Chairman of the Institute of Immigration Law until October 2009. Presently, he works as Visiting Professor at VU University Amsterdam. He is a member of the Dutch Advisory Committee on Aliens' Affairs and a member of the Meijers Committee (Standing Committee of Experts on International Immigration, Refugee and Criminal law).

Maarten den Heijer is Assistant Professor of International Law at the Amsterdam Center for International Law. His PhD thesis, Europe and Extraterritorial Asylum, defended at the University of Leiden, was published in 2012 by Hart Publishing, Oxford and Portland. He is vice-chairman of the Meijers Committee, member of the editorial board of *European Human Rights Cases* (EHRC) and member of the editorial board of the *Netherlands Yearbook of International Law*. He is also a member of the board of the Foundation for Refugee Students UAF.

Gerrie Lodder holds a master's degree in law and political science. She is a Senior Researcher and Lecturer at the Leiden Institute of Immigration Law and a member of the Editorial Board of the Commentary on European Migration Law.

Kees Wouters is a Senior Refugee Law Advisor at the Division of International Protection of UNHCR in Geneva. In the past Kees Wouters has worked as a researcher and lecturer at the Institute of Immigration Law at the University of Leiden Law, where he obtained his doctoral (PhD) degree with his thesis on International Legal Standards for the Protection from Refoulement (Intersentia, 2009). He was also a member of the sub-Committee on Asylum and Refugee Law of the Meijers Committee and has worked for various non-governmental organisations in the Netherlands, such as Amnesty International and the Dutch Council for Refugees. He has also worked in Asia as a staff member and lecturer at the Office of Human Rights Studies and Social Development of Mahidol University in Thailand (2000–2004) and as a lawyer for the Centre on Housing Rights and Evictions (COHRE).

IUS COMMUNITATIS SERIES

Published titles within the series:

1. STEFAN GRUNDMANN, *European Company Law. Organization, Finance and Capital Markets*, 2nd edition, Cambridge-Antwerp-Portland, Intersentia, 2011
   ISBN 978-1-78068-019-4
2. ANDRÉ KLIP, *European Criminal Law. An Integrative Approach*, 2nd edition, Cambridge-Antwerp-Portland, Intersentia, 2012
   ISBN 978-1-78068-001-9
3. PIETER BOELES, MAARTEN DEN HEIJER, GERRIE LODDER and KEES WOUTERS, *European Migration Law*, Cambridge-Antwerp-Portland, Intersentia, 2014
   ISBN 978-1-78068-155-9
4. KARL RIESENHUBER, *European Employment Law. A Systematic Exposition*, Cambridge-Antwerp-Portland, Intersentia, 2012
   ISBN 978-1-78068-080-4
5. NORBERT REICH, HANS-W. MICKLITZ, PETER ROTT and KLAUS TONNER, *European Consumer Law*, 2nd edition, Cambridge-Antwerp-Portland, Intersentia, 2014
   ISBN 978-1-78068-086-6